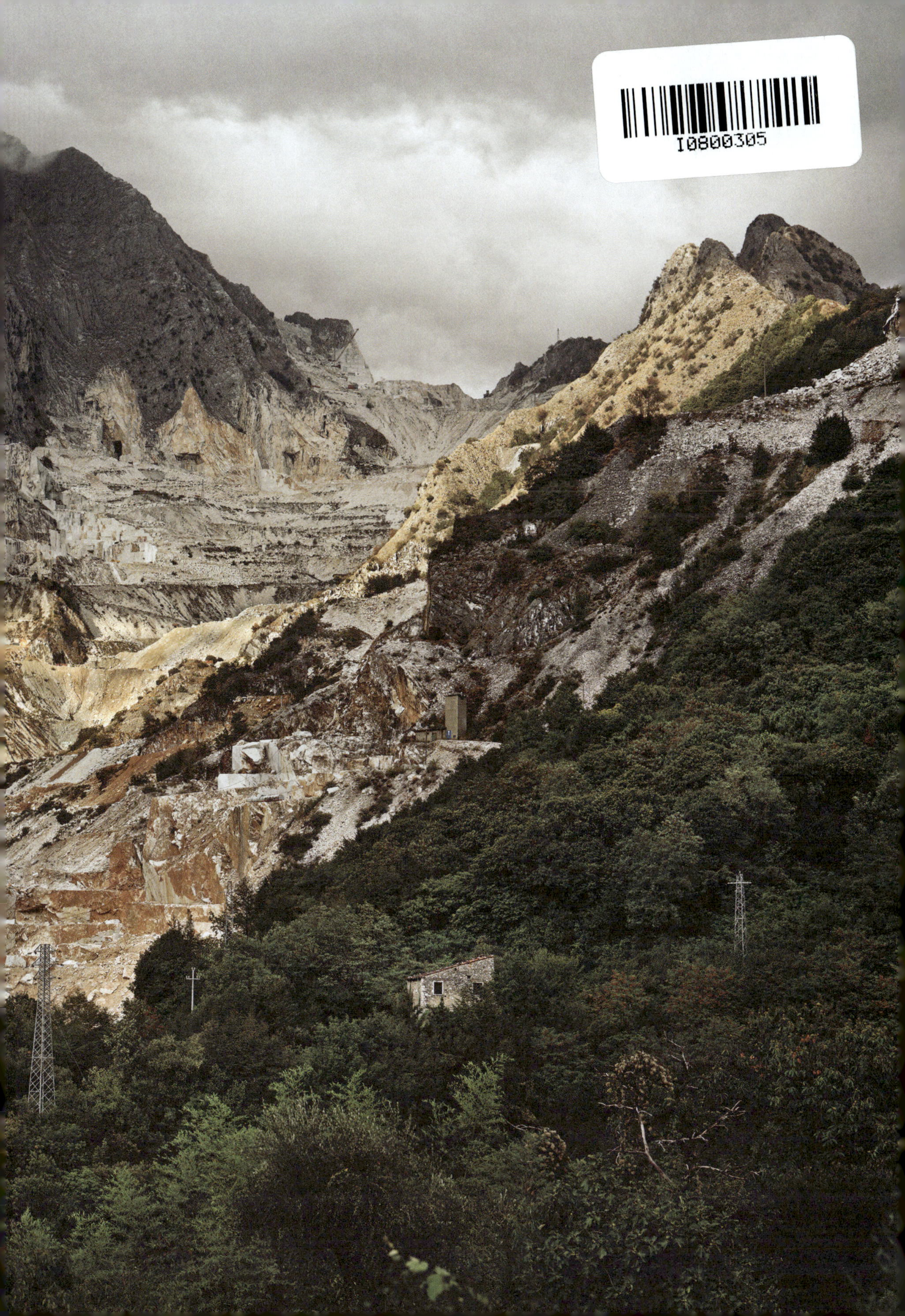

Edward Burtynsky

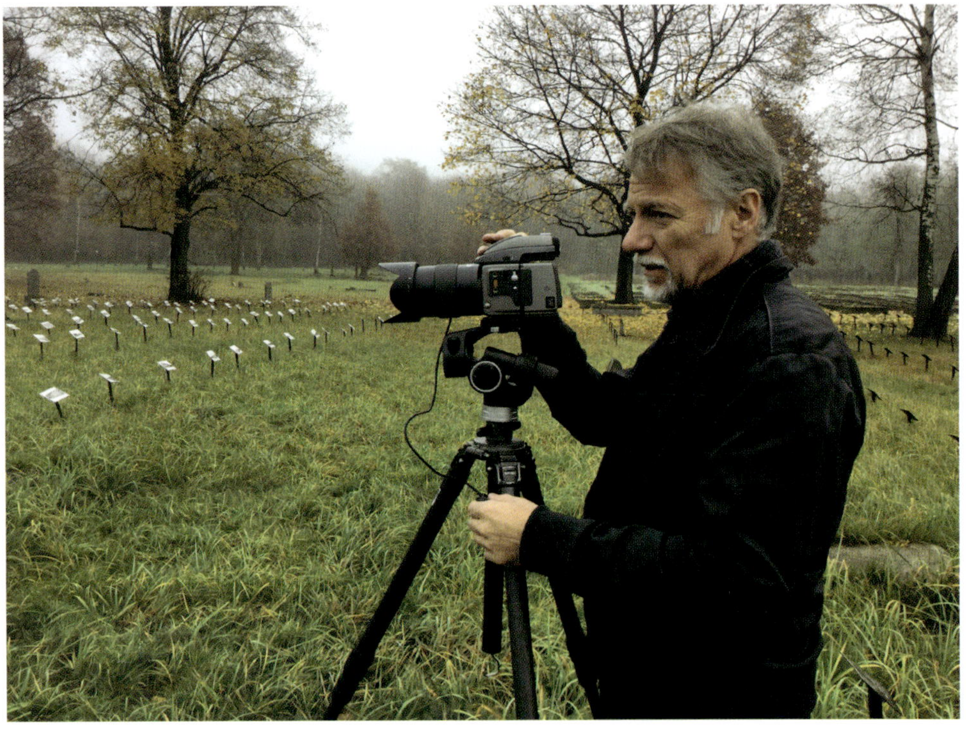

Edward Burtynsky, Lodz, Poland, 2014. Photograph by Tomasz Frydel

Edward Burtynsky

The Biography

JAMES KING

SUTHERLAND HOUSE

TORONTO, 2026

Sutherland House
416 Moore Ave., Suite 304
Toronto, ON M4G 1C9

First edition, May 2026

If you are interested in inviting one of our authors to a live event or media appearance, please contact sarah@sutherlandhousebooks.com and visit our website at sutherlandhousebooks.com for more information.

We acknowledge the support of the Government of Canada.

Manufactured in Turkey
Cover designed by Lena Yang
Book composed by Karl Hunt

Library and Archives Canada Cataloguing in Publication
Title: Edward Burtynsky : the biography / James King.
Names: King, James, 1942- author
Description: Includes bibliographical references and index.
Identifiers: Canadiana (print) 20260118281 | Canadiana (ebook) 2026011829X | ISBN 9781997701132 (hardcover) | ISBN 9781997701149 (EPUB)
Subjects: LCSH: Burtynsky, Edward, 1955- | LCSH: Photographers—Canada—Biography. | LCSH: Photography, Industrial. | LCGFT: Biographies.
Classification: LCC TR140.B87 K56 2026 | DDC 770.92—dc23

ISBN 978-1-997701-13-2
eBook 978-1-997701-14-9

CONTENTS

INTRODUCTION

This book is an exploration of the life and art of Canadian photographer Edward Burtynsky, one of the most important contemporary artists dedicated to investigating large-scale human incursions into the surface of the earth, to dealing with climate change, and to demonstrating the proliferation of toxins that threaten the very existence of civilization. This narrative–focused on the aesthetic means that Burtynsky has utilised to frame those issues–describes in detail the unfolding of his artistry.

Through a long and varied career, Burtynsky has charted the ways in which humankind is systematically destroying the biodiversity of our planet and, by extension, itself, and has devoted most of his creative life to this endeavour. One of the major thrusts of this book is about Burtynsky's crusade–through his photographs–to display the earth's destruction. In vivid, visually compelling ways, he shows a world in crisis. Put another way, his work emphasizes how various forms of extraction have endangered its survival. By inclination, he is an explorer who investigates how humanity is at odds with nature, but he realizes that many forms of extraction have been–and remain necessary–for existence. Burtynsky's work both probes and encapsulates that paradox.

A book about Burtynsky becomes an "issue" one centred on global warming, climate change, and globalization. Although Burtynsky has been accused of making sublime images out of destruction, in reality he has highlighted the devastations wrought by late-stage capitalism. As he continues to work, his reputation continues to grow exponentially and is buttressed by the large number of exhibitions of his work held every year in all parts of the world.

This book's narrative begins with Burtynsky as a child and then a young man, engaged with nature, who then earned his stripes by working in two fields that were destined to become subjects of his art: gold mining and automotive manufacturing. It then traces his formative years while attending Ryerson Polytechnic Institute (now Toronto Metropolitan University). Burtynsky's early black-and-white photographs from that period reveal a fascination with landscape.

He began photographing "pristine" landscapes, but soon came to the conclusion that he was one hundred years too late; documenting the pristine, to him, felt more like a mere form of nostalgia. Then he realized that he could show how landscape had been significantly altered in the "pursuit of progress." That became his major theme, and the obsession that underscores all his work.

In sticking to this resolve, he has focused on making dramatically seductive images of the devastation our era has imposed on the earth. In so doing, he has consistently made art that transcends his own experience–and that of his audience. In the process, his life has become, in many ways, an adventure story about exploring the perils facing humanity.

He is ruthlessly methodical: "In a lot of my work, I'll return to my subject four, maybe five, times. When I take pictures the first time, I'll just walk through and respond to whatever impulse tells me might be a good shot. I let what I see form its own composition in the landscape–and then I'll come back and do whatever I can to make that shot work."[1]

He also has strong opinions about how his images should be interpreted:

> I'm trying to create images where you first get taken in by the whole image and the largeness of the place that's being described, and then you reread the image and pick apart the small details that tell the story. There's a second narrative within the piece that you can use to understand the scale of a piece. But it is the first impression of the image that makes you come to it and makes you want to look at it. This is a fundamental thing that I always try to do in my work. Because if somebody doesn't stop to look, they miss the whole point.[2]

Most of Burtynsky's images are landscapes. That photographic genre in North America has a rich, complex history beginning with the work of Carleton Watkins, Darius and Tabitha Kinsey, William Henry Jackson, and Eadweard Muybridge. They were followed early in the 1930s by the pristine, deep focus images of members of the f/64 group such as Ansel Adams and Edward Weston. Later in the 1930s, there was serious questioning about what landscape photography had become–there is the less idealized work of Margaret Bourke-White, Walker Evans, and Frederick Sommer, for example. In the 1970s, Robert Adams and Lewis Baltz produced images of landscapes overcome by man's voracity.

Burtynsky's work, from 1980 onward, can be linked to artist-photographers with similar interests, such as Richard Misrach, David T. Hanson, David Maisel, and, especially, Emmet Gowin. All have produced ecologically based work demonstrating the various ways in which the well-being of the planet has been transgressed. As such, Burtynsky's art is devoted to some of the most defining concerns of our time, and he is not alone in employing photography to show the ravages our planet has suffered. More recently, concerns about the Anthropocene have led many other photographers into producing images expressing those apprehensions. In what ways, then, does the work of Burtynsky stand apart from what has become an increasingly crowded arena?

First, Burtynsky's entire career has been focused on showing how the precarious interactions between humanity and nature are evidenced in landscape. Two, he is a storyteller who photographs in sequences that can be read as narratives. Third, Burtynsky's propensity to reveal the abstractions produced in nature–both unspoiled and despoiled–has a wide variety of manifestations. Fourth, unlike some of his competitors, he goes out of his way to show unspoiled landscapes. Fifth, he frames his images in startling, often visceral, ways that not only capture the essence of what is shown but also force the viewer to see the natural world differently.[3] Sixth, he thinks in vertical rather than linear terms. His propensity is to examine issues in depth before connecting them in straight lines.

Put another way, Burtynsky's approach allows him to see into the possibilities of an image in a way that transforms it into art. He is a patient angler, who waits for his prey to come to him.

Burtynsky–the artist as photographer–infuses art-historical references into his images. His knowledge is extensive, extending to Caspar David Friedrich and J. M. W. Turner and to movements such as Cubism and Fauvism. He is especially drawn to Abstract Expressionists such as Jackson Pollock; for Burtynsky, that movement "flattened space" and in the process created an "alloverness" that treated the whole surface democratically with no central focus or figure.[4] When he composes his images, Burtynsky often allows his familiarity with the history of art to guide him. This methodology distinguishes him from most contemporary photographers.

His work is punctuated by extremely precise framing, detail, and texture–he is also skilful at capturing the essence of a landscape at the instant it fully reveals itself. Another reason Burtynsky is successful is that he retains the eye of a black-and-white photographer. When he moved to colour, he recalled, "[I] brought a lot of my black and white sensibility to the new work. I tried to find landscapes that literally looked like black and white images in the real world with small bits of muted colour coming through."[5] As he told a journalist in 2012, "I like the tones of browns and gray–I love more neutral tones."[6] He has also pointed out that because "we perceive the world in colour, it seems naturally more familiar. I believe my work in colour functions in such a way as to make the familiar seem unfamiliar."[7] That paradox encapsulates his entire career.

By design, Burtynsky's images are monumental. Their large sizes impart a sense of grandeur; their attention to detail is exacting; in many images, repeated inspection reveals a wealth of small details. Moreover, these enormous flat surfaces are like picture windows that invite the viewer to enter the worlds created.

As with many of his confreres, as mentioned earlier, Burtynsky has been accused of making photographs that focus on what has been called the toxic sublime. In other words, he makes stunning photographs displaying how ravaged the earth has been rendered by man-made intrusions. Such images are only awe-inspiring, some observers claim, because their points of view are so removed from the reality of the dreary landscapes they inhabit.

That may be true, but such images work in a complicated way. The viewer may be astonished by a new, daring point of view but close inspection reveals degradation. In this two-part process, Burtynsky allows his audience to experience a heightened aesthetic emotion and then forces that audience to confront the reality of what has been perceived as beautiful.

On this point, Burtynsky has been crystal clear. In the Western tradition, artists have always had the license to make images of horror and destruction. Writers are allowed to tell stories about the sorrows and horrors of the human condition. "There seems [to] be a perception that if a photograph is made visually appealing through composition, light, texture, etc., but if it depicts a human tragedy or negative consequence, then some unwritten and undefined moral transgression has occurred."[8]

The gruelling physical journeys Burtynsky undertakes demonstrate his relentless quest to tell the truth about the ecological perils facing humanity. In essence, this book offers an intimate account of the artist's engagement with both the natural world and the unnatural world. The narrative travels to many places, including various parts of Canada and the United States, Mexico, China, Germany, Spain, Italy, India, Bangladesh, Australia, Russia,

Chile, Malaysia, Indonesia, and Africa, including Nigeria, Kenya, Botswana, Namibia, Madagascar, South Africa, and Ethiopia.

One aspect of his life is emphasized in this book: he is a skilled entrepreneur who has carefully crafted his reputation, and this part of his story has many interesting twists and turns. Overall, however, this is the story of a person who has had a relatively tranquil domestic life and who, in his dealings with others, is consistently considerate, affable, and empathic. But Edward Burtynsky's inner creative life remains that of a man on fire. He is relentless in pursuing a lead and seeing where he can take it.

Burtynsky, it should be emphasized, sees himself as–like all of us–complicit in the escalating ecological devastation captured in his images. According to Baudelaire, photography was destined to become the vehicle that would show the *reality* of nature. Burtynsky has fulfilled that claim.

The reality that Burtynsky captures is one not apparent to most of us. His photographs shock because he allows his viewers to see the world in astounding new ways through his penetrating eyes. That world may be beautiful, but the nature of that beauty is often terrifying.

1 A BOY AND A CAMERA

One of Edward Burtynsky's earliest memories is of exploring his environs with a camera. "As a kid, my favourite place was an abandoned factory. It had enormous old windows and was full of machinery. I would go in there at different times of day and photograph. But that was just me with a camera, doing what I liked to do."[1] Not satisfied with one view, he would take a series of shots, since no single image could encompass what his eye could see and what the camera was able to capture. From the beginning, this was "a contemplative approach. You find your way to the image slowly. I think because I was introduced to painting when I was a kid, I looked upon the ground glass the same way that you might look at a blank canvas–a space to be filled. The beauty of it was that it was filled so quickly and with such exquisite detail."[2]

ORIGINS

The story of Edward Burtynsky's life begins in Soviet-controlled Ukraine, where his parents, Petro (Peter) Buratynsky and Marussia (Mary) Mishlov, were from. Peter was born in Kosiv, a town in the southwestern Ukrainian region of Hutsulshchyna, up among the Carpathian mountains, in 1918; Mary was born on July 6, 1924, in a village in Kyiv Oblast in north-central Ukraine. (Edward changed the spelling of his surname to Burtynsky in 1996.)

In reflecting on his origins, Burtynsky wrote: "I was begot by a father & mother who were born and raised in villages in Ukraine; [they lived] 'off the land.' My father was a shepherd in the Carpathian mountains and he would tell me stories of singly going on three months grazing with a flock of sheep, of incredible mountains and lush valleys." The son added: "He consciously pursued artistic inclinations."[3] Not much else is known about Peter's early life.

More information is available about Mary's childhood and adolescence. She was the fourth child of a farming family. In 1929, when she was five years old, Stalin imposed collectivism in Soviet-controlled Ukraine, a movement that forced labourers to relinquish their lands to collective farms. This disruption led to a steep drop in production and many uprisings. Mary's life and that of her family were disrupted by the Holodomor–the Great Starvation–when she was nine years old. To maintain the export of wheat in exchange for foreign currency, the people of Ukraine were prevented from using the wheat they had harvested.

She remembered: "There was nothing to eat. The Russians came and took everything from the house and then they searched the house looking for anything else they could seize."[4] Her father once outsmarted the authorities by arranging bags of wheat as if they were a bed and then placing his children on top of the contraband so that the bags were concealed. When his wife became ill, he was able to provide her with wine and vermouth he had secreted away.

Neighbours became treacherous. One day, Mary was picking weeds for the family cow when a female neighbour approached and asked Mary to come with her: "I have better grass. You can pick it." The girl was tempted to take up the apparently kind offer. Just then, her father arrived home and summoned her. As Mary soon learned, that had been a lucky escape.[5]

Her mother later warned Mary to go nowhere near that woman's place, which operated as a guest house. Her daughter–a very beautiful girl of twelve–lived there with her mother and was a friend of Mary's, and so Mary might have been enticed to visit her. Only later were maternal fears proved correct as when visitors entered that house, they never came out. To avoid starvation, both mother and daughter systematically killed their guests and pickled their corpses in barrels in the basement.

When Mary was twelve years old, in 1936, her mother died and her father remarried. Then, it was rumoured he was on a list of those to be eliminated. He fled, leaving the children in the care of their stepmother. She recalled: "My mother was very young when she died. She was only thirty-seven years old . . . That was tough. When my father left that night, the next morning I had to go to school. I stayed in during recess. I could now cry. I went in a corner. I remained there and cried. I don't have a mother. No father. That's my life." And she had, she told herself, to "get used to that."[6]

Five years later, in June 1941, Germany invaded Ukraine. Later that month, Nazi troops arrived in Mary's village and, by December, virtually all of Ukraine was under enemy control. The retreating Soviets adopted a scorched-earth policy: flooding mines, destroying crops, and disabling industrial plants. Ukraine was ravaged by two opposing forces that saw the territory as a pawn to be used in any way they chose.

Mary vividly remembered the Germans arriving by the hundreds on motorbikes. The raiders took everything they could: eggs were stolen and chickens slaughtered. The inhabitants of the village were once again reduced to starvation.

Having reached the age of seventeen in 1941, Mary became one of the *ostarbeiters* (Eastern workers); these were young men and women who were sent west to work on farms and in factories to support the German war effort. One day, she was whisked away in a car and then packed onto a crowded train that stopped in Poland, where she and her fellow passengers took showers and were disinfected. Then the train continued on to Germany, where they were housed in a school. The morning after their arrival, the entire group was assembled and placed on offer to farmers. Mary was selected by a sugar beet grower in Lomitz who needed only one worker. She remained with him and his wife for three years–she even had a room to herself. In the town near the farm, she met Katya, who came from the same village as her, and formed a close friendship.

When Germany surrendered in 1945, the Soviets wanted displaced Ukrainians to return home, but Mary refused to do so. As a result, she lived as a displaced person in a refugee camp–rooming in an abandoned army barracks–near Hanover for five years. There, she met and married a Polish-Jewish comedian named Walter Lasinski with whom she had a daughter, Khrystyna (Krys), who was born in 1949.

That same year, to forge a new life, Lasinski immigrated to Kapuskasing in northern Ontario, where workers were needed to work in the bush for the Ministry of Lands, Forests, and Mines. These workers were allowed to immigrate to Canada on the condition that they stayed for at least a year. (During the First World War, many Ukrainians had been placed there in internment camps and so Kapuskasing had many Ukrainian-speaking inhabitants.) After six months in Canada, Walter applied for Mary and Krys to join him. So, in 1950, mother and child travelled by ship to Halifax, and then by train to Montreal and Kapuskasing.

Not long after they arrived, the relationship between Mary and Walter crumbled, mainly because of his drinking and womanizing. At this point, Walter disappeared. Mary subsequently met and fell in love with Peter Buratynsky, who had made his way to northern Ontario to Kapuskasing, after spending time in refugee camps in Germany. Like Walter, he too had come to northern Ontario on the understanding he would work on a government-regulated one-year term as a Land and Forests surveyor. He stayed employed in Kapuskasing for four years.

Just as little is known about his childhood and early manhood, Peter's life during the Second World War is a blank. Mary was certain he was never an *ostabeiter* and claimed he never told her about his activities from 1941 to 1945. A piece of shrapnel remained embedded in his back and there was a now-lost photograph of him in a military uniform. If he had been in the Resistance, he would not have required a uniform; also, he would probably have told of his exploits. There is the possibility that he was one of the quarter of a million Ukrainians who, in some capacity, collaborated with the Germans to fight the Russians by joining the Ukrainian Auxiliary Police, the Ukrainian National Army, the SS Galicia, or a similar group. Such activity would obviously not have been readily shared in post-war Canada.

Mary and Peter decided that they would, in secret, leave Kapuskasing and make their way to Winnipeg, where there was a substantial Ukrainian community. To reach Winnipeg, Mary, Peter, and Krys travelled by car to Sault Ste. Marie, but discovered upon arrival there that there was no road (at that time) to take them to Manitoba. They would have to go through the States to reach Winnipeg, and they did not possess passports or documents that would allow them entry at the American border. At that time, the only other way to get to Winnipeg was along Highway 11, which went back through Kapuskasing. Not wanting to be spotted there, Mary and Krys stayed at a motel in Sault Ste. Marie and Peter returned briefly to work in Kapuskasing. Then, attracted to the idea of settling in southern Ontario's Golden Horseshoe, the couple decided to head to the village of Jordan, where Katya, Mary's friend, lived on a farm.[7]

ST. CATHARINES

After a brief stay with Katya, the small family moved in 1952 to nearby St. Catharines, where Peter obtained work on the General Motors line as a welder in the original McKinnon factory, which had been transformed that year into a gigantic malleable and grey foundry. Peter had not wanted to work on the line, but he could not obtain a clerical post and so he took a job he rightly felt was far beneath his abilities. As his son recalled, "It was a good job–like winning the lottery . . . He could afford a house, my mother didn't have to work . . . but he was artistically inclined, and never able to pursue that."[8]

Peter bought a piece of land on Dorothy Street and, with the help of friends, built a one-storey house there. He rented the upstairs as an apartment, and the Buratynsky family occupied the downstairs. There, Ola Anna (Ollie) was born in 1953.

Next door to the house on Dorothy Street, Peter began constructing a bungalow; he then sold the first house, and the family had to move to its garage because the bungalow was not yet ready. There, Edward Taras was

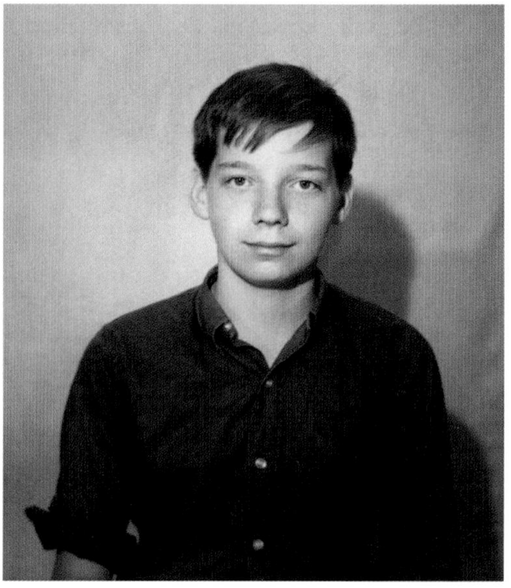

Edward Burtynsky, c. 1964

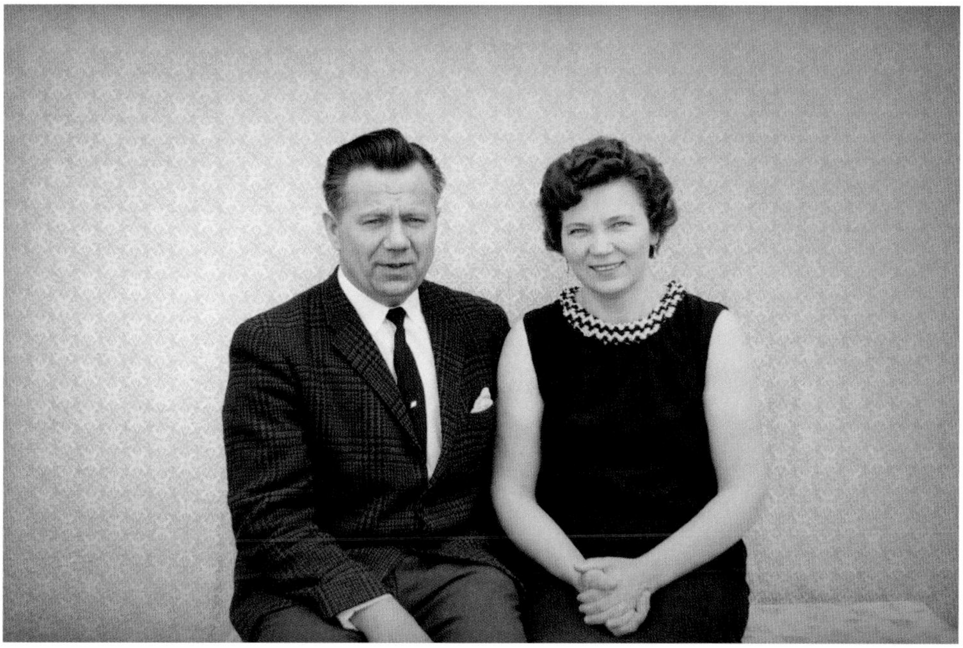

Mary and Peter Buratynsky, c. 1965

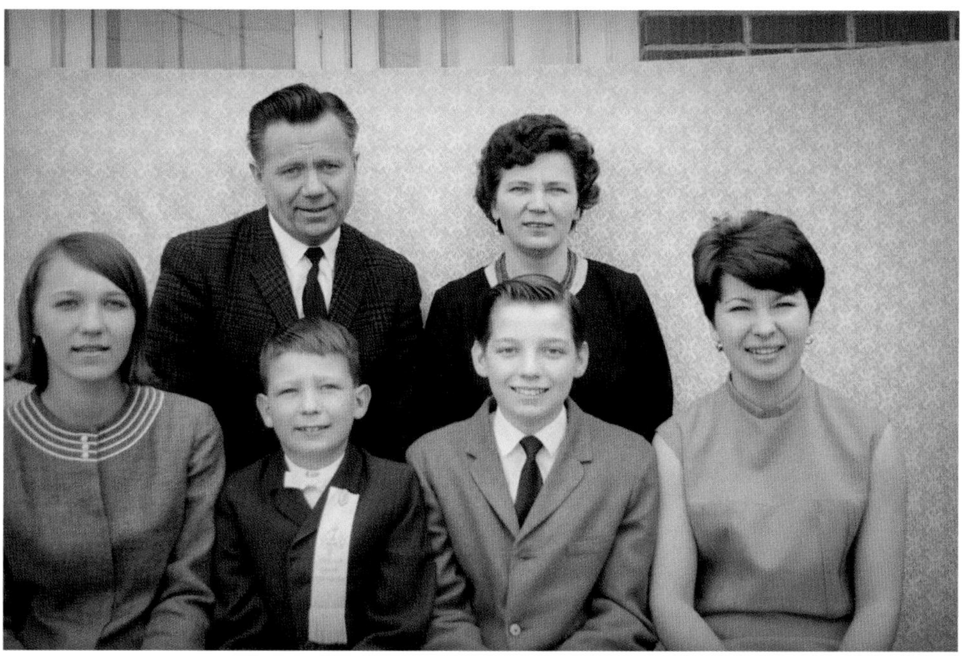

Ollie, Michael, Edward, and Krys Buratynsky with Mary and Peter, c. 1960

born on February 22, 1955. Peter gave his son that middle name in honour of Taras Shevchenko (1814-1861), the Ukrainian poet and nationalist. Ollie remembered her tiny brother in his crib constantly dropping his soother to the floor. To their considerable annoyance, she and Krys constantly had to retrieve it.[9]

Michael–the couple's third child–was born when the family had moved to the bungalow, but then the family moved again shortly afterward, to Spruce Street. "When I was a kid," Burtynsky remembered, "our house backed up on the Queen Elizabeth Highway, which was once the route of the Welland Canal. I used to imagine what it would be like to have ships from all around the world passing by."[10] He would cycle there and "trade fruit for trinkets and cigarettes with the sailors. I remember being overwhelmed by the scale of the ships."[11]

St. Catharines may have been labelled the "Garden City," but its economy and culture were dominated by General Motors. "At the age of seven," Burtynsky reminisced, "I saw engines being cast and steering knuckles being stamped out of red-hot ingots held with tongs by men in silver suits on massive forge presses that shook the ground and could be heard halfway across the city. Once I knew what was behind those bland brick walls that contained the factory, I would forever understand that place differently than before I entered." He added: "I think that early experience sent me on a lifelong pursuit to quench my curiosity and to see and record what lay beyond [other] barb wire fences and brick walls."[12]

FATHER AND SON

As a boy, Edward was dreamy. He was jolted when he entered kindergarten at Queen Mary School because he spoke mainly Ukrainian–it took him a while to become comfortable in English. In all, he was an indifferent student, he recalled. If a subject intrigued him, he could do exceptional work. Otherwise, he struggled academically.

At home, Edward was a different child in large part because Peter, although a strict disciplinarian, encouraged his son to explore his creative side. His father, the son reminisced, remained "part of [a] whole kind of creative culture where everybody did woodworking or painting." (His hometown of Kosiv is famed for the elaborately coloured ceramics and tiles produced there.)

While in Kapuskasing, Peter enrolled in a mail-order art school in Washington, D.C. His surviving drawings demonstrate considerable talent. His son recalled: "Probably out of all the Ukrainian men in St. Catharines, he was the most creative. He drew all the original plans for the hall of the Ukrainian Youth Association. And then he constructed and decorated the stage sets for the plays and all the theatricals performed there. I would be brought in to help him make these stage sets."[13] The Buratynsky family were active members of the St. Catharines Ukrainian community and attended the Ukrainian Catholic Church, where Edward was an altar boy.

At home, father and son frequently sat side by side, each painting on a canvas. "I was seven years old when I discovered my love of making art," Burtynsky remembered. "I loved the tubes of oil paint and the smell of linseed oil and the names of their colours: burnt umber, chromium blue, cadmium red."[14] He admired the paintings by Peter on the walls of the living room. "There was one above the piano, of the famous Ukrainian poet, Taras Shevchenko, playing an instrument known as a bandura. I remember that one kind of resonated with me; it was always central in the living room."[15]

At his father's instigation, Edward became aware of the landscape of Ontario. "From the time I was very young my father would take me with him on trips to Kapuskasing and Cochrane–godforsaken places. I sat in cars and watched this endless country go by . . . I camped and I canoed. I would paddle and look at the shoreline I knew had not been affected by man, a seemingly endless expanse that marched onward with this feeling of eternity and immutability."[16]

His first experience of transcendent natural beauty was when he biked the fifteen kilometres from St. Catharines to Niagara Falls: "[I]t was always

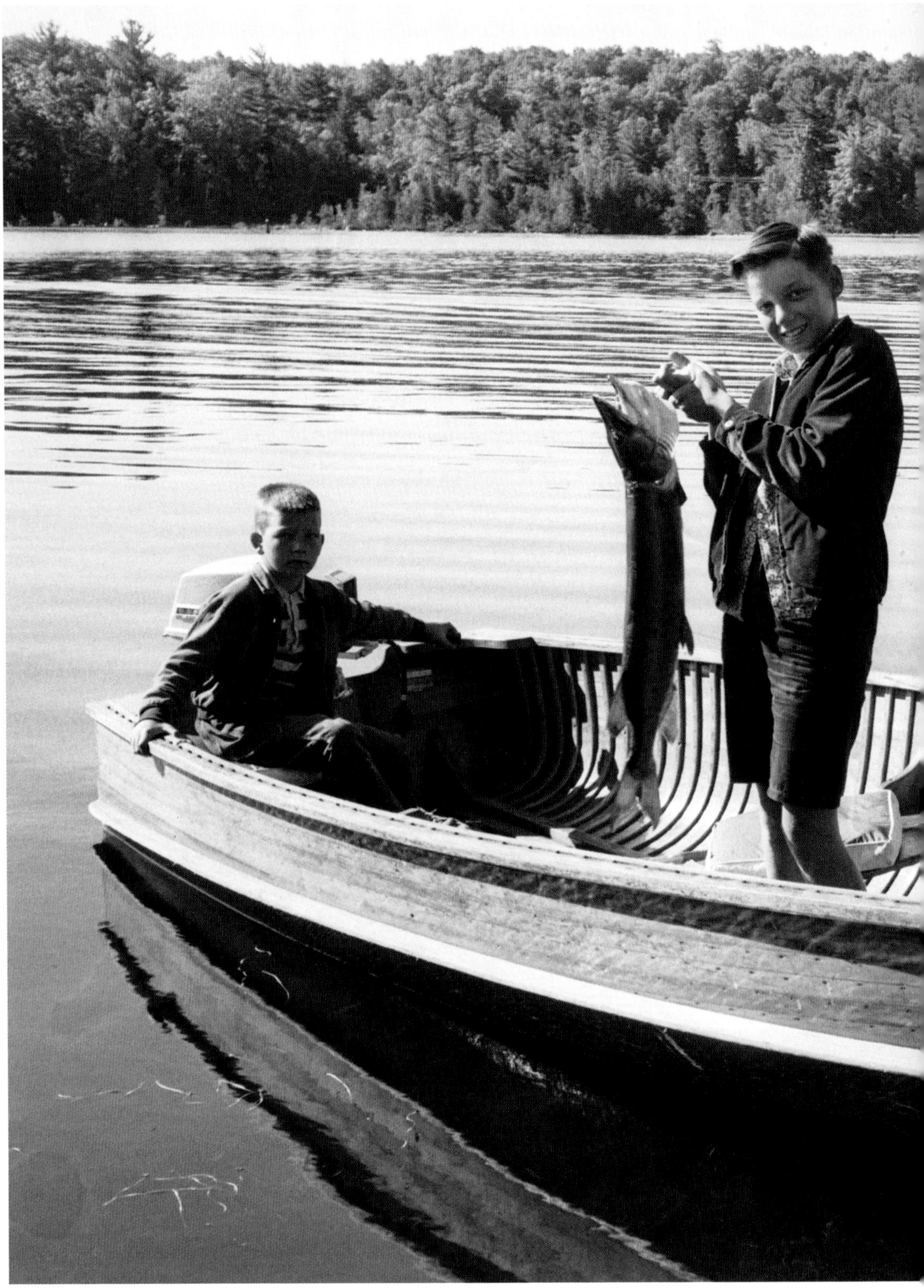

Michael and Edward Buratynsky, c. 1967

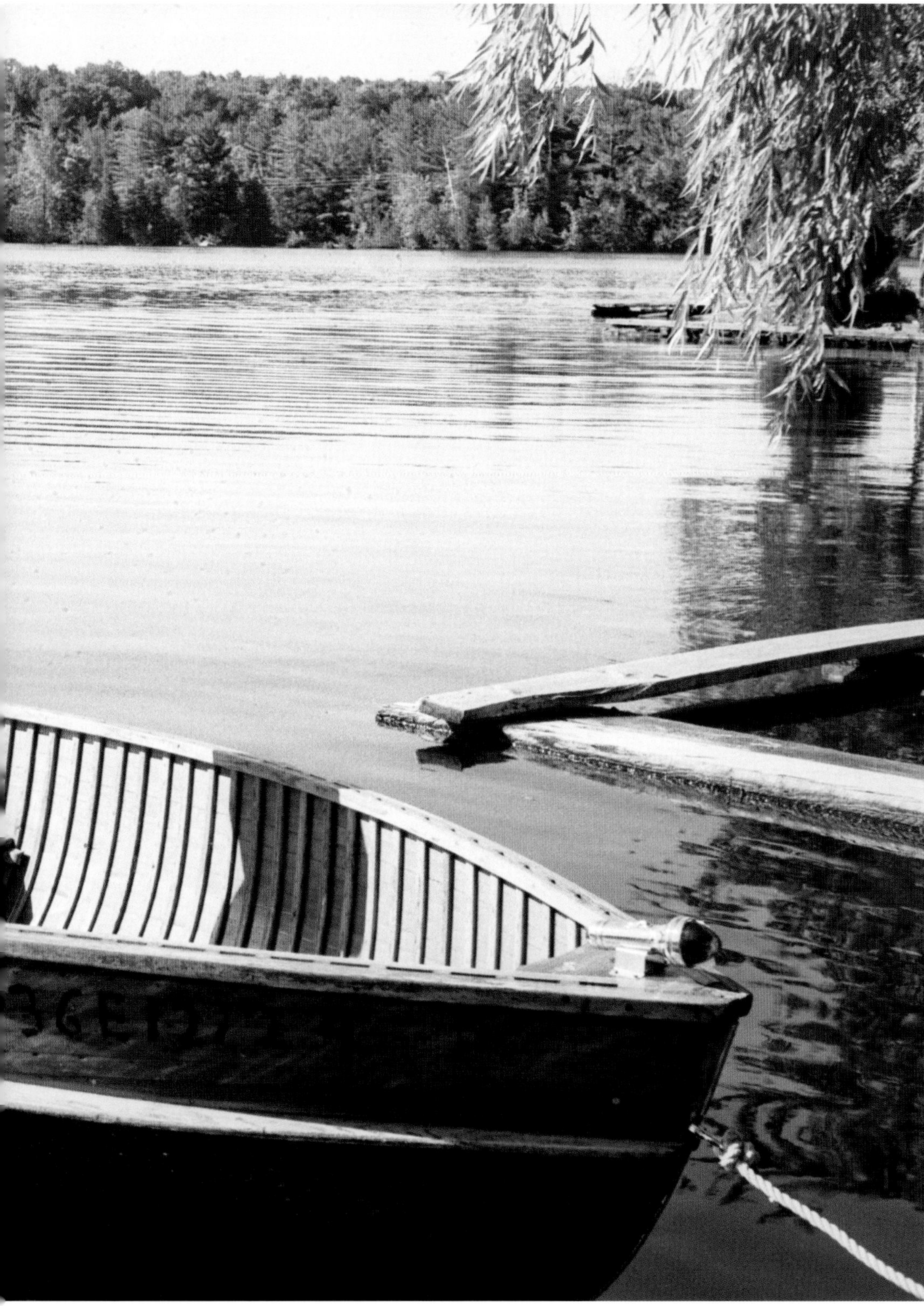

a crazy, sublime experience to be standing at the top of the escarpment, seeing the scale of that landscape and contemplating the incredible volume of water forever cascading over the edge. I once found a rather treacherous footpath that led down to the Whirlpool Rapids, where one could watch the mesmerizing undulations of fifteen-foot standing waves."[17]

The son idolized his father: "[I] remember the photographs of him in our family album, dressed as though he were about to go on safari–looking down [at] the barrel of a pistol–carrying a canoe. He had great stories of the Canadian North also. He talked about the amazing fishing that he had experienced in virgin lakes–the time he hooked a sturgeon, and it towed him about the lake in his canoe–[about] building docks and surveying land. It was ugly work–blackflies, mosquitoes, bloodsuckers, bitter winters and soggy slushy springs."[18]

Peter introduced Edward to photography:

> One day, he saw an ad in the *St. Catharines Standard*, and we went to see a widow who had a darkroom full of equipment. I guess when her husband died everything to do with his hobby had been shoved into this room. We spoke to her, and she said, "Take the whole thing for twenty-five dollars." I guess she realized it would have a good home.
>
> There were three 35mm cameras, a bulk loader and cassettes, an enlarger and how-to manuals. It wasn't high-end stuff, but it was everything I needed.
>
> In the basement we set up boards on the oil tanks feeding the furnace drums to hold the trays. Then we built a little bench next to the furnace for the enlarger. Dad wasn't very good at English, so it was up to me to read the manuals and figure it all out. And that is where I learned how to develop film and print black and white.[19]
>
> The first few times, a neighbourhood friend a few years older than me helped me figure it all out. Then [my father] realized that I was doing well and backed away. I wasn't in competition with him in the darkroom–that became my space. Every once in a while, he would do

> a family portrait and I'd process and print it. It was interesting as well because I think this eventually fed into my whole entrepreneurial side, because he said, "Look, I'm not going to buy you new chemistry, and I'm not going to buy you film."[20]
>
> I remember the first roll of film I took. It was wintertime and I wanted to shoot a roll of film to practice processing it, so I took an entire 36-exposure roll of my dog, Tippy. He was jumping around in the snow outside, and then I processed the film and made a contact, so there were 36 similar pictures of him. I picked one out and printed an enlargement it. That was [my] first 8-by-10 print. So, I had just made that picture earlier in the day and all of a sudden, it's emerging in a tray in the orange light of a safelight. To me it was like magic–I was mesmerized.[21]

This roll has disappeared, but there is another one–made at about the same time–in which Tippy appears in the last image. The other shots are experimental, wherein the young photographer investigated how light acts upon objects such as lamps and clocks that he had built in woodshop class.

At the age of eleven, Edward displayed precocious entrepreneurial ambitions when he started up a business taking photos of children at the Ukrainian Youth Centre and then offering them for sale. The photos, each given a catalogue number, were inserted into a photo album. Then Edward would canvass sales from parents, who were invited to look at the selection. He invited Ollie to join him on a commission basis. If she sold a photo for 50 cents, she would receive a lowly 10 cents in commission because, he told her, he had to purchase the chemistry and the paper, and develop the pictures.[22]

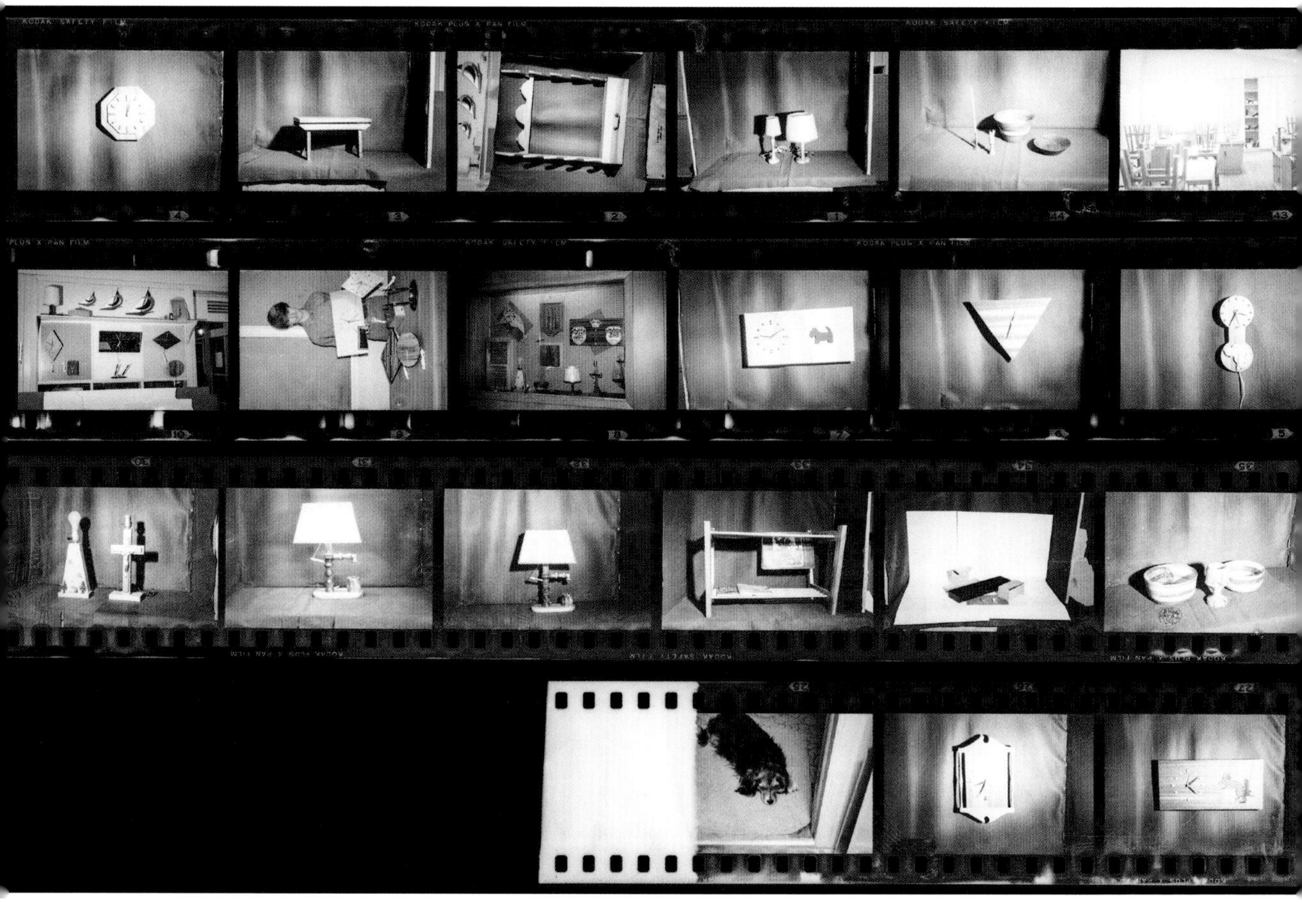

Early Edward Burtynsky contact sheet, c. 1966–67

When Edward reached adolescence, his relationship with his father changed radically–and, in fact, completely deteriorated. Edward, the teenager, as is natural, had become withdrawn and insubordinate while, at the very same time, Peter developed cancer and had a kidney removed. "And so we started having more and more conflict. We really were not getting along. I was trying to stay away from him as much as possible."

The boy remained outwardly lackadaisical. "I was one of those kids who, you'd say, 'Go sweep the garage,' and half an hour later I'd be following ants. I'm sure my dad looked at me and [felt] I was . . . 'hopeless'–and he kind of made me feel that way. He got really short-tempered, probably resentful about what had happened [to him as a result of his illness] . . . So I butted heads with him in a bad way. At one point, he said, 'You're not going to amount to anything. I'm going to work on your brother,'" Edward remembered. "There is nothing more motivating than [when] someone who is important to you says you can't achieve something. It's one of those motivators where you say, 'Fuck you–just watch me.'"[23]

Around that time, Edward–who had been an ardent Catholic–experienced a loss of faith: "I was having a hard time at home with my father, and I wanted something that I could experience that had more meaning to me." But he could not get his "head around limbo"–the belief that unbaptized babies were trapped for eternity at the edge of Hell. "So at that age, I began to search for meaning in a new way. I began to look closely at Nature and it resonated with me was that I was part of Nature, that we all had evolved from Nature. . . . Nature became my key to understanding my place in the world." The boy also became convinced that there was no life after death: "And so I thought, there is one life after death and that's being an artist. Then I became convinced that I would become an artist, someone who left marks after death."[24]

Just as he had warned, Peter, dissatisfied with everything Edward did, began to favour Michael, who had not reached adolescence. The thirteen-year-old Edward thought about running away but, two years later, he recalled: "I'm fifteen and that's when he passes away. But I remember in the last year he was out of commission almost six months . . . He was in the hospital. He was not home very much. I remember him coming home a bit and then going back in."[25]

In his last years, Peter became certain that his cancer had developed because of the toxic pneumatic oils (PCBs) used on the welding line at General Motors. He took his anger out on his family, and became violent and physically abusive. Edward summed up his father's tragic situation: "He worked there for fifteen years and did not enjoy his lot in life at all. He acquired a bitter streak, and all of the family were scared of him and his ruthless temper."[26] He added:

> I remember when he was in the hospital just before he died. He asked to see me. And he knew he was going to die. When I looked at him, I couldn't recognize him because he was ninety-five pounds. He was like skin and bones. And his voice was very weak. He said, "Look, I'm not going to be here much longer. You're going to be the oldest male in the family, so you're taking over." It kind of made me feel guilty–but it was a relief. I took more responsibility for the family and assumed direction for my life.[27]

In December 1979, at the age of twenty-five, Edward recalled the paradoxical position in which he had been placed as he wrote in one of his notebooks: "I was ten years old and all I wanted to be was a fisherman. My father felt that I should raise my expectations and become someone who is respected. I was punished a lot for disrespect . . . I was in constant fear of his presence. It seems that his eyes had entrance everywhere, and he waited for my imperfections and then pounced on them. I guess he saw it as a survival training course. My father wanted me to be an artist. He must have felt that artists were respected by people. I'd like to believe that my father took pride in making something out of nothing."[28]

The boy's interest in the magic of photography may have been inspired by his "very artistically inclined" father, but this fascination became a double-edged sword.[29] His father had great expectations for his son–he wanted him to become the artist he had not become–but, at the same time, he informed the child that he would never achieve any such expectations. In his teenage years and into his twenties, his relationship with his father haunted Edward. As he wrote in 1979: "I have no heroes. I fear success. I desire acceptance and dread rejection."[30]

GRIT

When Peter died, Mary, having faced much trauma in her early life, remained stalwart. Her husband had not worked at GM long enough for her to collect a pension large enough to raise a family, but his life insurance paid off the mortgage. At that point, she had only $300 in the bank.

One of the first things Mary did was to take driving lessons. She also obtained work at the Lightning Fastener Company, which employed more than five hundred people making five million zippers annually. While at Lightning, Mary also worked nights at Silverwood Dairy as a cleaner. Some nights Edward would accompany her and perform tasks such as emptying wastebaskets and sweeping and mopping floors. One bonus was getting an ice cream sandwich or a Creamsicle from the freezer. Orange Creamsicles were his favourite. When Lightning closed in 1982, Mary cleaned houses, did domestic chores, or house-sat for people while they were on vacation.

She remained fiercely independent and refused to take money from her children. Edward had always been close to his mother and, at this time, he took strength from her strength. That relationship would endure throughout his whole life–"more than she knows," he once confessed to his diary.[31] Like his mother, he sized up situations quickly and then took all means necessary to reach his goals. Determined to overcome any setback, he developed a practical turn of mind.

He had marketed his photographs at the age of eleven. Two years later, he began finding more ways to earn money and was inventive in finding employment–he had no interest in having a poor-paying paper route, like some of his friends. For a while, he sold bingo cards at a hall, but one money-making scheme was particularly ingenious. The mother of one of his friends had been a Fuller Brush saleswoman and had kept the company's brochure, which Edward looked at one day. He wondered who bought this stuff, and she informed him that it was an excellent and very saleable product. If a salesperson put in an order of over $100, the commission was $20. If they sold over $200, they got $80. Impressed by the opportunity offered, he took the catalogue and started to go door to door, assuring homeowners he was acting in place of his mother, who was ill. "I can take your order on her behalf," he would tell would-be customers. The ploy worked. Whenever he needed money, he would sell $200 in merchandise and be $80 richer. His first major purchase was a Raleigh ten-speed bicycle for $90.

At fifteen, he sometimes hung out with friends in the family garage, but he kept busy finding other ways of earning money. He operated a popcorn machine at a racetrack, helped collect the takings from pinball machines and overhauled them when they broke, and repaired jammed pin machines in bowling alleys. A year later, he obtained his driver's license.

Although he envisioned himself as "a horse putting blinders on and looking in one direction," he had no idea where he was heading by the time he graduated from St. Catharines Collegiate in 1972, where his courses had included mechanical drafting and isometric drawing.

"St. Catharines," he recalled, "was a blue-collar town and the real jobs were in the skilled trades. Tool and die making was at the top of the food chain. I did try to become a tool and die maker but there just wasn't any apprenticeships, so I went into printing. I wasn't really happy with it: it was just a grind job, pushing papers through a press."[32]

There were other jobs. After he graduated, he worked at Hayes Dana, which built frames for large trucks. Edward was involved in feeding the large form presses. He was seventeen, and his older co-workers were seasoned in moving things along on an assembly line. He was not adept and sometimes got behind. Then it was "hell on earth, but it paid well."[33] For two weeks of work he received $1,200 and bought a used Datsun for a thousand. He acquired a canoe with his second paycheck. When he was laid off after seven months, he found work on the assembly line at the Ford plant in Oakville.

Shortly afterward, a friend sold him on the idea of joining him in Red Lake Gold Mine in Balmertown, up in northern Ontario near the border with

Manitoba. Edward's first job underground at the mine was as a trammer: when ore came down a chute, he dumped broken rock onto tramcars and then delivered it to the shaft. A bit later, he obtained better-paying work as a stoper's helper, which involved going into the upper stopes of the gold face and then drilling and blasting the gold out of the ore veins. He also worked briefly at a mine in Ear Falls.

"You go down," he recalled, "like, two-thirds of a mile into the earth, and then walk along these drifts for another thousand feet, climb up, and you are somewhere in the middle of fucking rock."[34] And, he remembered, what he saw: "in a flash when the rock face was laid bare were strata and seams imbedded with the lineage of the earth. The Stone Age, the Bronze Age, the Iron Age, timelessly preserved."[35]

He remained at Red Lake for about four or five months before returning to St. Catharines. At loose ends, uncertain of his future, he remembered his early fascination with cameras: "I decided to take some night school courses in photography."[36]

(1974–1982)

2 LEARNING HOW TO LOOK

NIAGARA COLLEGE

As a boy of eleven, Burtynsky had been entranced by the allure of photography. That interest had been pushed aside by the ongoing conflicts with his father and his death. The youngster found diverse ways to earn money but later, as a young man, he searched without success for a way to make a living. In the midst of that struggle, he decided to revisit his childhood fascination with photography by enrolling in a night course at Niagara College. Over the next eight years, what began as a casual interest blossomed into an obsession.

"The teacher," he recalled, "was Archie Hood. He gave us interesting things to do, and he showed us slides of accomplished work. That made me think and let me know there was a bigger world of photography out there."[1]

The decision to take Hood's course was not completely serendipitous. The young man needed a change of direction:

> A great deal of the motivating forces behind me were my first experiences as a labourer. I had done quite a few humiliating jobs. They were jobs that neglected my intellect and my pride . . . and left me with one reason for persisting, and that I was doing it for money. I have a strong drive in me to be successful–in society success is often misinterpreted as acquiring materialistic gains. That illusion was shattered in my first year of work after buying a car and outfitting myself with possessions that were valued in my peer group. I realized I was no better off than before. In fact, I felt a definite regression in my intellect.[2]

Hood's assignments were focused on a topic that fascinated the young man: the environment. "We would go outdoors," the instructor recalled, "and we would photograph different things on an ecological basis. My assignments were done in this way because it was an easy way of making people understand and be available, having subjects available to photograph. We went outdoors and everything was done outdoors in those days."

In these classes, Burtynsky's earlier interest in landscape was revived. From childhood he been fascinated by the natural world, and by the geography of Canada in particular. Hood reminded his student that:

> Successful works of art are ones that people stop at and so if I wanted to see what was working, watch and see where people stop in a gallery show and then try to understand what it is about that image that captures the collective imagination. I followed his advice and began to search for work that spoke to me and my ideas about landscape as well as images that had the potential to stop people and get them thinking about where and what this place is, who made it and for what purpose.[3]

"When students went above and beyond the call of duty," Hood recalled, "I would support them and try to inspire them." With exceptional students, he recommended they pursue their talents. "At that particular time, Ryerson [now Toronto Metropolitan University] was the best around, and I suggested to him that if he was truly interested in the craft, then he should try to get the best education possible."[4] That recommendation put Burtynsky on notice. Perhaps he should become a photographer? "I enrolled in 1976," he said, "that's where I was really ignited."[5]

Just before leaving St. Catharines to move to Toronto, Burtynsky was employed briefly at GM, removing the carcinogenic oils from the machines and floor on the assembly line where Peter had worked. Many of his father's peers had also developed cancer, and so efforts were being made to remove the PCBs, which were the obvious cause. "The men were just dropping like flies, which was weird because I was going in there removing it and spraying things contaminated with skull and crossbones . . . all the guys sitting around claim[ed] there's no problem. I'm putting on creams to protect myself and the workers call[ed] me sissy. They told me, 'We've used to this stuff. It's no problem.'"

When GM offered him a management position and the prospect of steady employment, he was indifferent. "My mother kept saying, 'You got a great job, you can have a house.'" Despite her plea, he said, "I knew in my heart I wanted to be an artist."[6]

RYERSON

From the time of its invention in 1822, photography had been treated as an ugly duckling by the art establishment. It was seen as a threat, a mechanical approach that could replicate reality that had no artistic merit but could possibly supplant fine art. The irony was that early photographers took turns trying to make their images look like paintings. In this battle of seeming opposites, the true potential of photography as a unique art form was often overlooked.

In 1948, the Ryerson Institute of Technology was established as a training school for veterans of the Second World War.

> Admission and instruction at the school were handled by military officers with skills in the field and were strictly focused on establishing successful commercial careers. After the school became Ryerson Polytechnical Institute in 1964, it continued to offer, as it had since 1953, a three-year diploma in photography with a small motion picture component. [As] an advanced trade school, it emphasized practical skills for its first two decades before its identity was challenged by a revolution in the Seventies in photographic thought.[7]

The head of the photography programme, Reginald Soames, had been a liaison officer with the Canadian Armed Forces during the war and, before that, had been a commercial photographer in New York in the 1930s. Soames's department had a military feel: the predominately male students were required to wear jackets and ties, and were referred to by their surnames. In 1967, Soames had asked entering students why they had chosen to enroll. When one replied, "I want to be an artist using photography as my medium," Soames had curtly responded, "Well, then you've come to the wrong place."[8]

The situation outside of Ryerson, however, was changing. In 1967, Jean Sutherland Boggs, the director of the National Gallery of Canada, began adding photographs to the gallery's collection. The work of Canadian photographers as varied as Suzy Lake, Arnaud Maggs, and Yousuf Karsh was gaining international recognition. Public galleries were exhibiting photography, and artist-run centres were popping up across the country and offering alternatives to established exhibition spaces. The Still Photography Division of the National Film Board (NFB) expanded its output and began a travelling exhibition programme.

The first English-language film of Italian director Michelangelo Antonioni, *Blow-Up*, was released in 1966. An intellectual thriller with a fashion photographer as a protagonist, the film was responsible for expanding perceptions of photography in popular culture. After *Blow-Up*, Canadian artist and photographer Arnaud Maggs claimed, "It was quite cool to be a photographer at that moment in time." Indeed, the marketplace was adjusting accordingly: illustration fell out of fashion with art directors and advertisers who now favoured photography in its place. Photography, consequently, became more lucrative.[9]

By 1976, when Burtynsky arrived at Ryerson, however, the divide between faculty who focused on teaching technical skills and those who espoused photography as an art form remained. He sensed correctly, however, that the situation at Ryerson was also changing. The new faculty at Ryerson imparted a radical new energy to the established programme and injected "photography as art" into the curriculum. Students at Ryerson were put into direct contact with cutting-edge approaches to photography through their teachers: Dave Heath had studied with Eugene Smith, the doyen of street photography; and Don Dickinson had studied with Minor White, who introduced elements of abstraction into his work.

As well, in 1967, a group of Canadians and Americans who had studied at the Rochester Institute of Technology (RIT) had joined the faculty at Ryerson. RIT had strong connections with the George Eastman House in its home city. As part of its mission, Eastman House, founded in 1949 and devoted exclusively to photography, opened its doors to talks and lectures by advanced photographers such as Frederick Sommer and Emmet Gowin. Exhibitions there featured the work of earlier greats such as Ansel Adams, Edward Weston, and Imogen Cunningham. Through contacts with Eastman House, many celebrated photographers were invited to deliver the Kodak Lectures at Ryerson.

For Burtynsky, the move from St. Catharines to Toronto was daunting. For the first time, he saw homeless men on the streets "sleeping and sitting on benches . . . it was a reminder to me that if I didn't get it right, then it was a possibility I could end up like that."[10] He did not have a safety net–self-reliance became key to his existence.

The size of the city was overwhelming: "I remember the first time I came to Toronto alone. I found myself looking up at skyscrapers . . . I was bowled over by the scale at which we operate, the kinds of things we can create. For things to be on this scale, I thought, there has to be something equally monumental in the landscape where we have taken all this material from."[11] He framed his thoughts in another way in an interview with the Canadian Broadcasting Corporation (CBC): "I had worked in industry and I started to put the yin and the yang together that, to create these towers, there was an equal or greater act of extraction. I started to understand that, in our whole existence, the act of destruction is greater than the act of creation."[12]

Once settled in Toronto, Burtynsky led a very active social life and quickly made friends with his fellow students, like Marcus Schubert and Paul Lowry, although he was unusually quiet in classes and seminars.

In 1976, as Burtynsky observed first-hand, the concept of photography as art had gained a substantial toehold at Ryerson. Burtynsky remembered,

> In my first year, I had a teacher named Rob Gooblar [who had studied at the Rhode Island School of Design]. I recall on one occasion I went into the studio and he was sitting on a white box with a light suspended above him. He was very theatrical. He took a seashell and put the light behind it, to show how its complex inner structure was revealed. For about an hour he talked about the seashell–its geometry, its translucence, what kinds of images it conjured up, the relationship it had to the sea, what kind of animal inhabited it–the myriad ways in which one can consider this simple object.[13]

Gooblar was responding to Edward Weston's investigations of the innumerable complexities of seashells. As a teacher, Gooblar made his students aware of Weston's daring experiments in capturing the inner lives of objects. He "was teaching us the multi-faceted aspects of composition–that it is never a straight reading, it is never as simple as it first presents

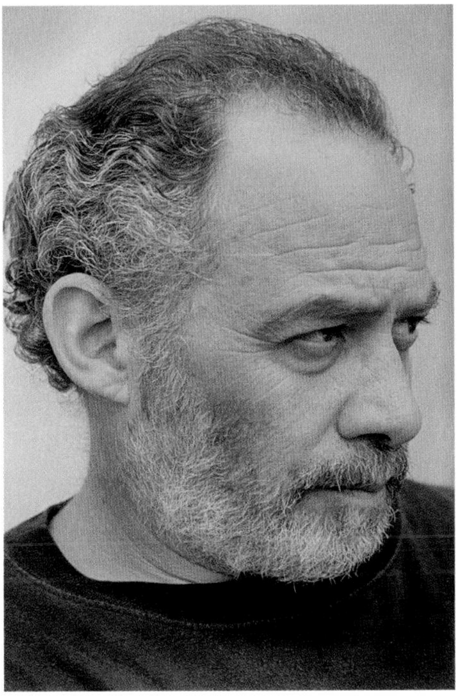

Edward Burtynsky, *Robert Gooblar*, 1978

itself . . . and he was teaching us the concepts of visual language. How do we transform objects? How do we give them symbolic meaning?"[14] Similar in his approach to Gooblar was Don Dickinson, who developed Ryerson's first course in the history of photography.[15]

In that first year, Burtynsky's imagination was fired up when Gooblar told his class: "Go out and make a set of images that speak to the idea of the evidence of man."[16] This assignment was not unlike the tasks Archie Hood had set for him, and it meshed with Burtynsky's own preoccupations about man's relationship to landscape. He responded by taking photographs of the Welland Canal. "The idea really resonated with me because I was able to step out of myself–as if an alien landed here and looked at the landscape for the first time. I had to say, 'Okay, I know all about this, but how am I going to look at the world with fresh eyes.' . . . Starting off with the Welland Canal made me think about what happens when man has finished with something, then walks away." And the immediate thing that came to

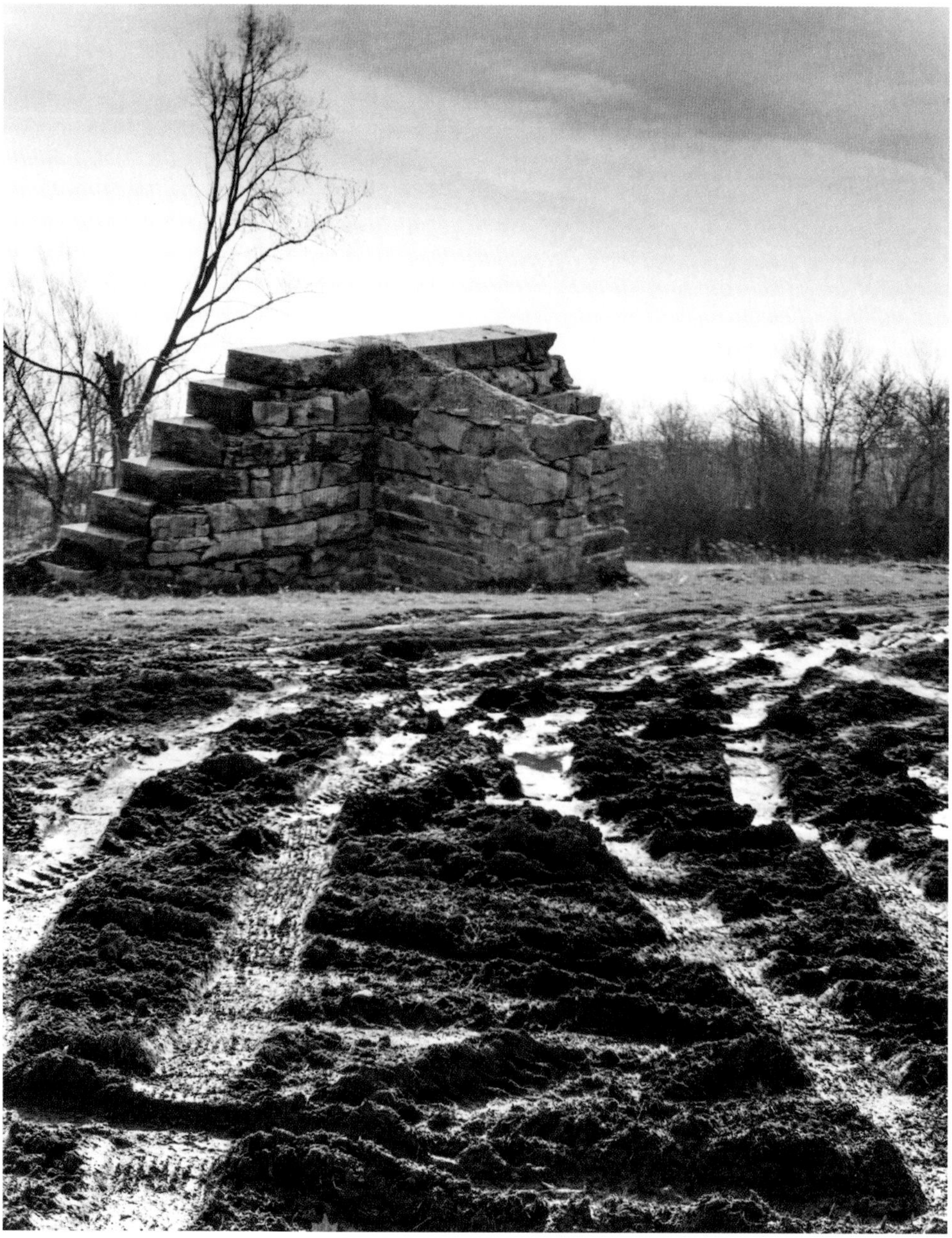

Edward Burtynsky, *Welland Canal*, c. 1966

mind, he recalled, "were the things that are left behind, the things that are forsaken, like ruins–there's evidence of some life that occurred there."[17]

Six years later, he said in reflection,

> I must say that this assignment has never left me. The way I see it is that any straight, perfect edge (not including the horizon line) found in nature can be construed as being associated with mankind. The word "evidence" then became my driving force to search for things that were on the edge of being disguised as natural, and yet they have the stamp of man to them. I have a fascination with the word "decay" though decay is rather an awful label . . . Thus my venture in pursuit of ruins began.[18]

Phil Bergeron was another influential instructor. His teaching style, Burtynsky remembered, "showed a deep understanding of art history and all forms of art [and] was delivered with intelligence wit and humour."[19]

Marta Braun's lectures on art history also opened a world that had been previously closed to him. Caspar David Friedrich's mystically inspired landscapes showed him that an artist's inner subjectivity can infuse renditions of nature. "I was exposed to Caspar David Friedrich in 1976. What I realized was that nature was somehow segregated from the human condition. The Romantics actually invented nature, and in part because they saw the industrial revolution coming. They realized nature was threatened by this evolution and so they reinvented nature."[20] He was similarly inspired by Turner's landscapes and waterscapes, especially the way the English artist blended the representational with elements of abstraction. When he looked at them, he knew what it was like to be "diminished by the forces of nature and be inspired by awe and fear simultaneously."[21]

When Braun discussed the innovations of the Abstract Expressionists–especially those of Jackson Pollock–Burtynsky began to see how portrayals of nature could be nuanced with abstraction. His notebooks from 1978 to 1982 are replete with references that indicate Braun had inspired him to explore all kinds of art beyond the classroom. That nudge later became

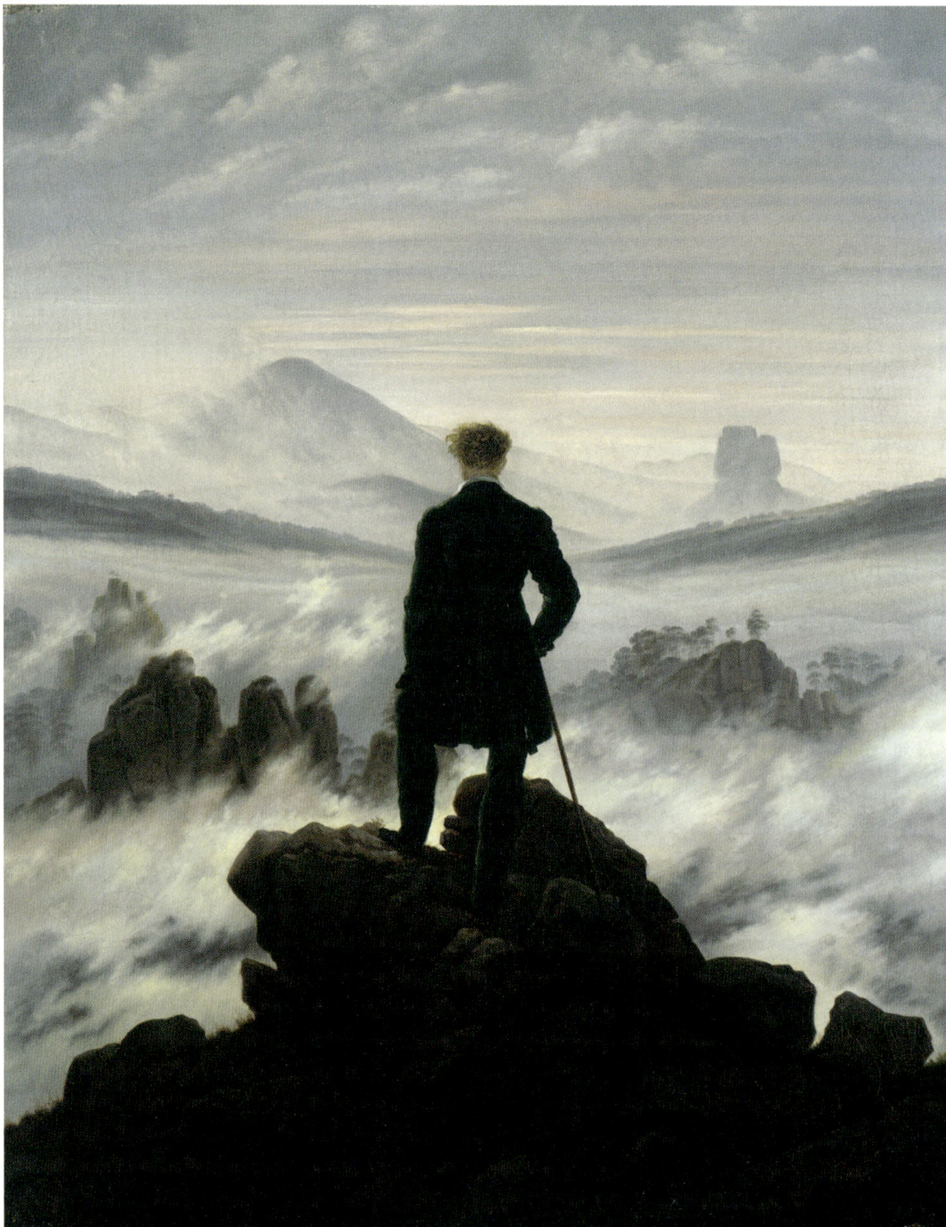

Caspar David Friedrich, *Wanderer above a Sea of Fog*, oil on canvas, c. 1817. Hamburg Kunsthalle

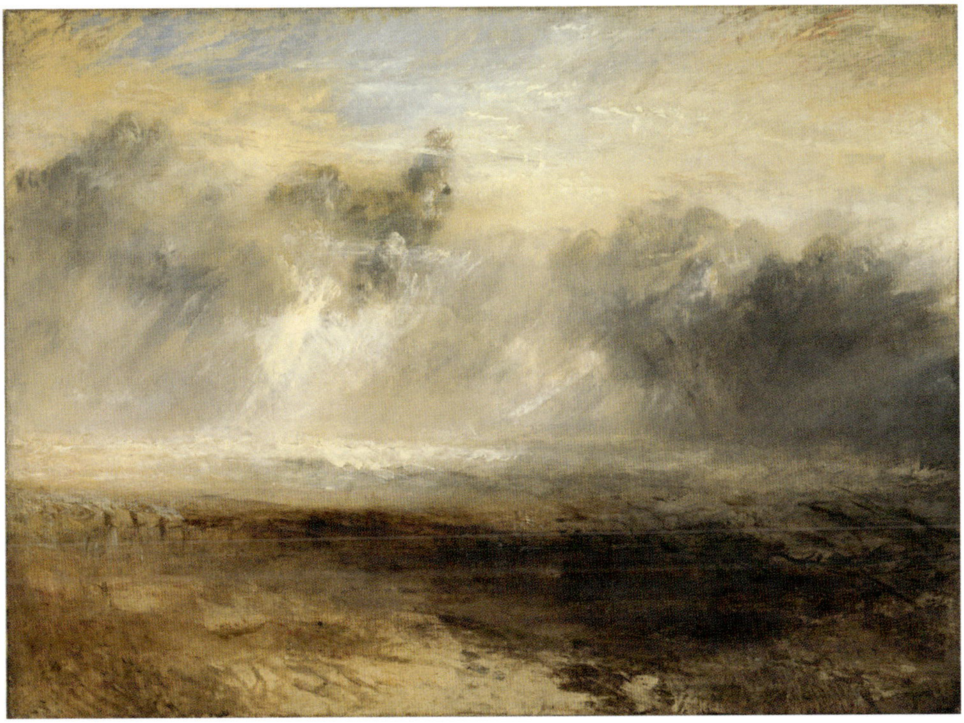

Joseph Mallord William Turner, *Breakers on a Flat Beach*, oil on canvas, c. 1817. Tate Gallery

a constant in his praxis because he often framed shots informed by the artists he admired. This propensity is one of the distinguishing hallmarks of his practice.

Bob Scott and Murray Pomerance gave a course that made Burtynsky and his fellow students more aware of how culture operates in society. Marcus Schubert recalled that this course was basically about "developments in media; their effects on society." The two teachers emphasized concepts laid out in the book *Frame Analysis* by Irving Goffman, an approach that examined how certain images, metaphors, and stereotypes operated in society. Burtynsky later said, "So, their job was to basically make us aware of the various constructs that we create to navigate the world in order to be persuasive. And so, it was kind of a back door to how to make better images."[22]

Burtynsky's instructors each assisted him in several ways, and he cited three in particular: "Robert Gooblar for instilling me with a delicate sense of appreciation for what I see. Don Dickinson for turning my head at a critical moment in my development. Murray Pomerance for grinding my face into contemporary mythology and iconography."[23] Of them, Gooblar was the one who took a personal interest in the young man: "He gave me a toy Spider-Man camera as a gift. It used to take 126 film and had one of those cubes with four flashes that turned as you cocked the camera. He inspired me to go on when no one was paying attention to my work."[24]

Burtynsky rebelled against one of the new approaches to art photography. "At the urging of another instructor [Dave Heath] I tried my hand at street photography, but it was a disaster. I would shoot and shoot with a Leica M3 and at the end of the day I had absolutely no idea if any picture

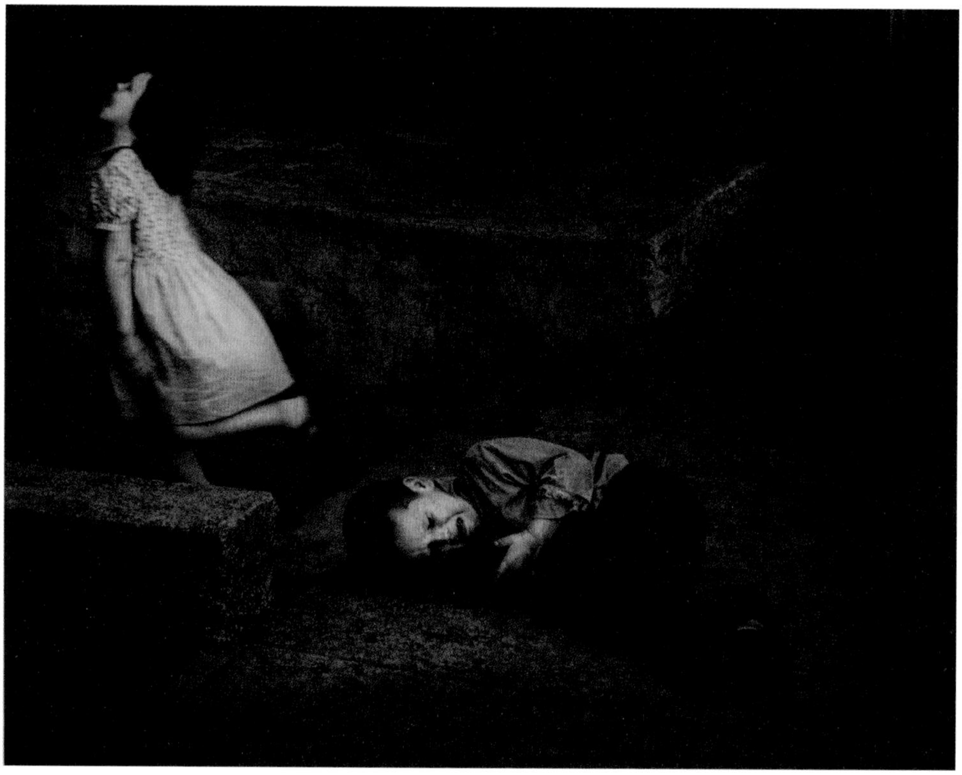

Dave Heath, *Vengeful Sister, Chicago*, 1956. Boston Museum of Fine Art

I took was worth anything at all. I would look at the contact sheets and be totally confused. I couldn't find myself in there. It wasn't how I saw photographically."[25]

Although he rejected the street photography of Garry Winogrand and Robert Frank, Burtynsky was impressed when, during his first year at Ryerson, he heard Winogrand lecture on how "an image succeeded when form and content were on an equal footing–one did not dominate the other. In photography if you go too far one way it becomes reportage, too far the other way it just becomes a formalist exercise."[26] Winogrand also told the young student: "I make photographs to see what the world looks like as a photograph."[27] On a field trip to Niagara Falls, Burtynsky observed Winogrand in action and how "he never raised the viewfinder of the camera to his eye to compose his shots impressed me . . . [he was] responding to how the world unfolds, and trusting that some of the many pictures he took would resolve as compositions." When Burtynsky asked him what made a good photograph, Winogrand promptly replied: "A great photograph wrestles both form and content into unity. If each aspect presents equally, you have a great image. . . . Walk the middle, and that's where you'll find the art."[28] In his subsequent career, Burtynsky would seek that middle and, like Winogrand, he remained fascinated by what the world looks like as a photograph.

Burtynsky's early student work shows an indebtedness to the finely crafted work of Edward Weston and Minor White, in which a simple object is transformed through emphasizing texture by prolonged exposure time, by concentrating on the placement of the light source, and by isolating an object from its normal sphere of existence. Moreover, the young photographer's skillfully arranged industrial photographs betray a knowledge of what Charles Sheeler had done in the 1930s.

In sorting out his thoughts on the path he wanted to pursue in his profession, Burtynsky compared the landscape photography of Ansel Adams to the documentary street photography of Robert Frank: "Adams comes from a traditional sensibility, viewing the natural landscape as a

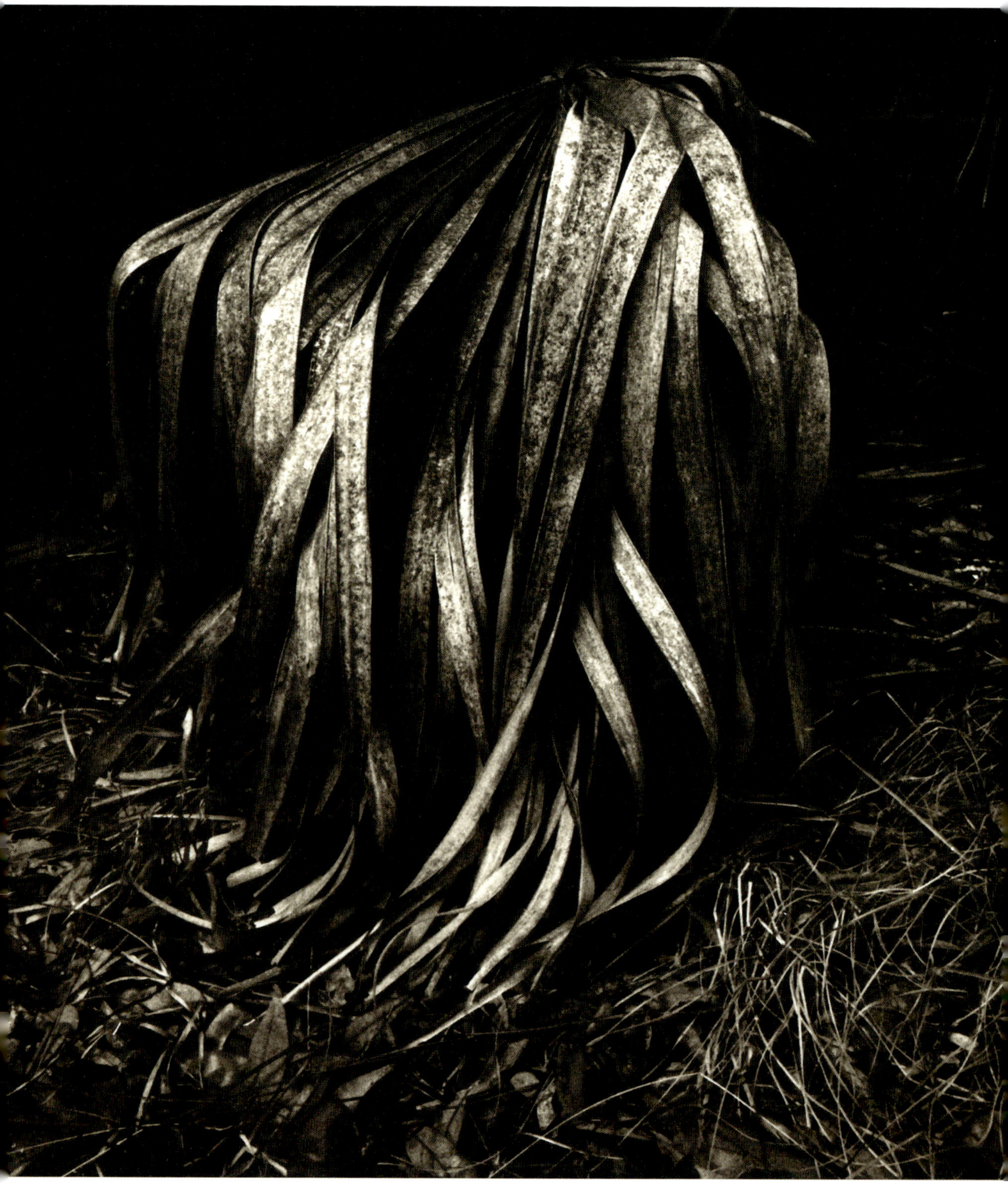

Edward Burtynsky, *Palms*, c. 1976

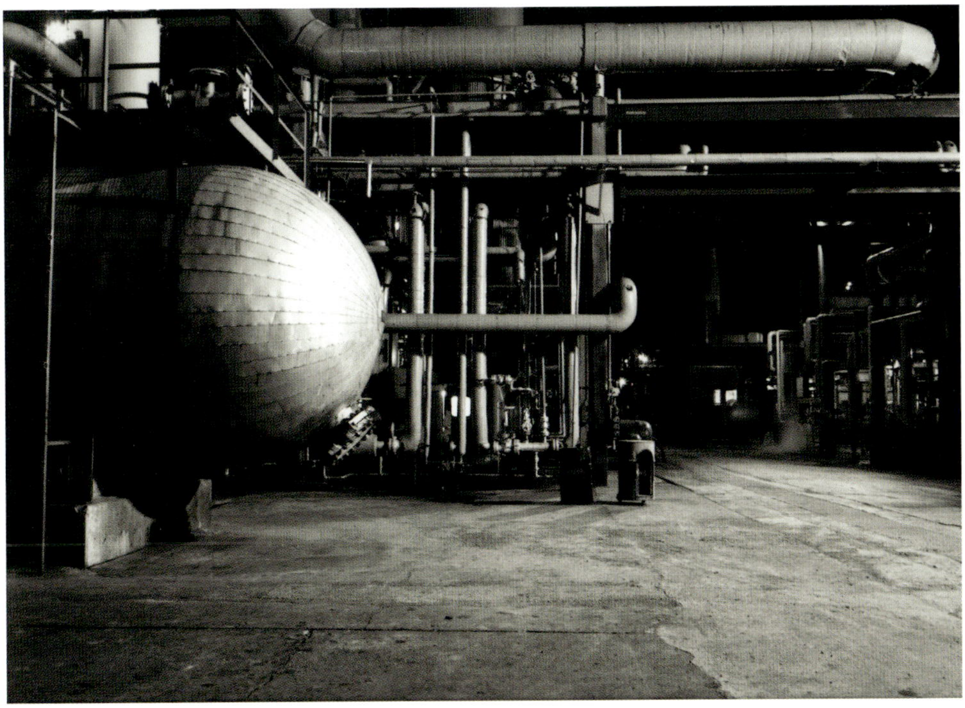

Edward Burtynsky, *Factory Interior*, c. 1978–79

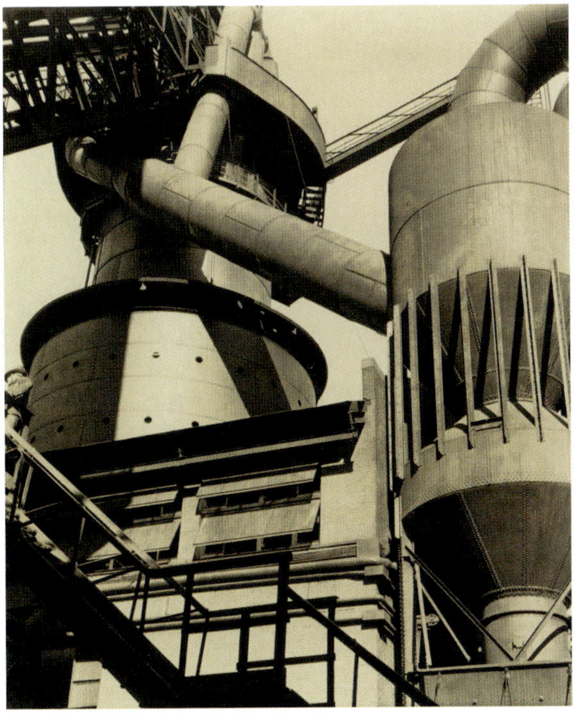

Charles Sheeler, *Criss-Crossed Conveyors, River Rouge Plant, Ford Motor Company*, 1927. Museum of Modern Art, New York

mystical phenomenon. . . . [An image by him] stands on its own needing little support to understand the subject of his photograph." Then he made an important distinction: "With Adams one can easily forget the photographer and consider the surface of the print only, whereas with Frank one cannot escape the presence of the photographer."[29] He felt that Adams's photographs had a transcendent quality that allowed viewers to immerse themselves in them, whereas the self-reflexivity of Frank was theatrical and therefore distracting.

An overriding preoccupation with perception haunted Burtynsky. He ruthlessly questioned himself: *what am I putting in the frame?* The photographer who assisted him in answering this question was Paul Caponigro, the American photographer known for his mystically infused landscapes and still lifes. At the time, he wrote, "I feel that he creates these wonderful & splendid little worlds by putting a frame onto it in just the right way. He is very succinct in this idea & in his frame all is eliminated except that which speaks." However, he was also aware of how his work deviated from Caponigro: "Where Paul tries to show us a metaphor for his experience in a particular environment, my concern is to show a metaphor that is not a result of experience but something that is set apart from the normal path of experience. I look for the obscure & maybe even surreal in

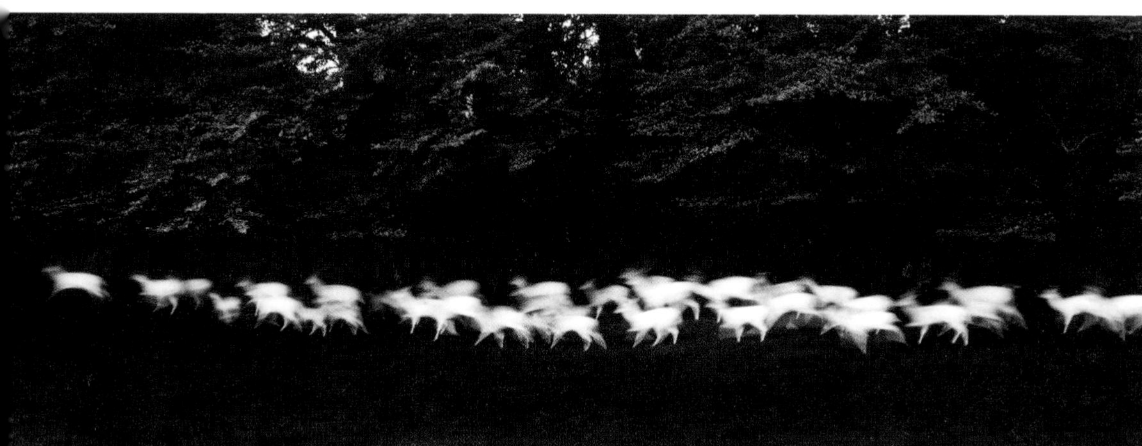

Paul Caponigro, *Running White Deer*, 1967. Los Angeles County Museum of Art

nature. . . . I look for unique subject matter. I look for things that are not associated in the normal realm of experience."[30] Burtynsky also wanted "to achieve a succinctness in isolating that which is harmonious with my idea. To isolate what is most powerful in my subject matter. I want to create charged objects."[31]

The heart of the Ryerson program was made up of weekly, three-hour "crits," in which students displayed their work for appraisal by their teachers and classmates. Heath was relentless in asking students what they had attempted to accomplish and then pointing out how they had failed. In essence, he was telling them–often in an abrasive manner–how they had failed to conjoin form and content. He insisted that a photographer's intent in composition had to match the resulting photograph.[32]

The classes Burtynsky took in his second year at Ryerson were crucial in his career as a photographer. At that time, he began using view cameras

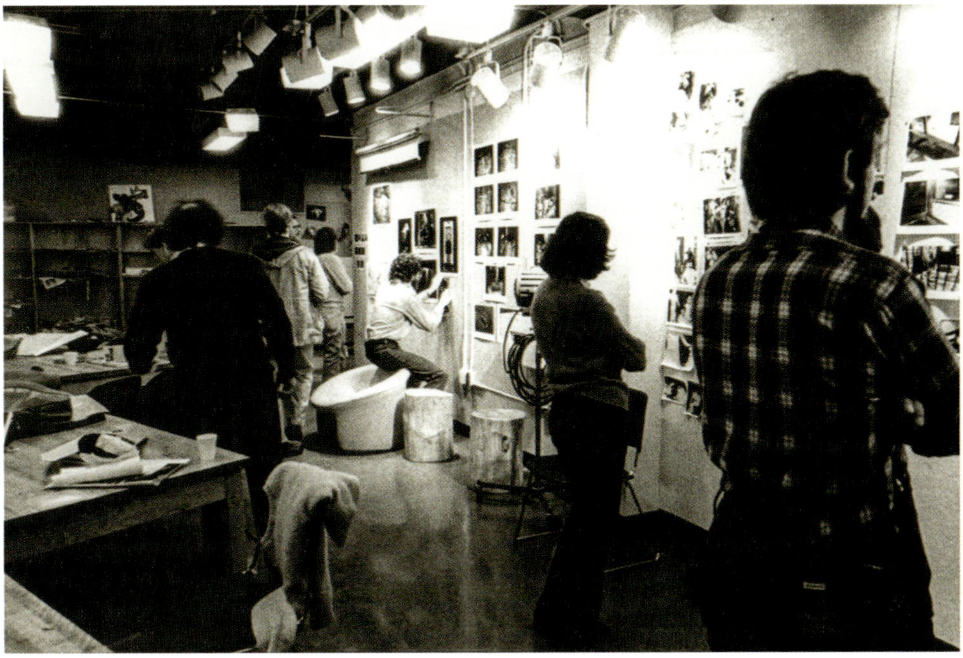

Edward Burtynsky, Crit Session at Ryerson, c. 1978. Photograph by Matthew Plexman

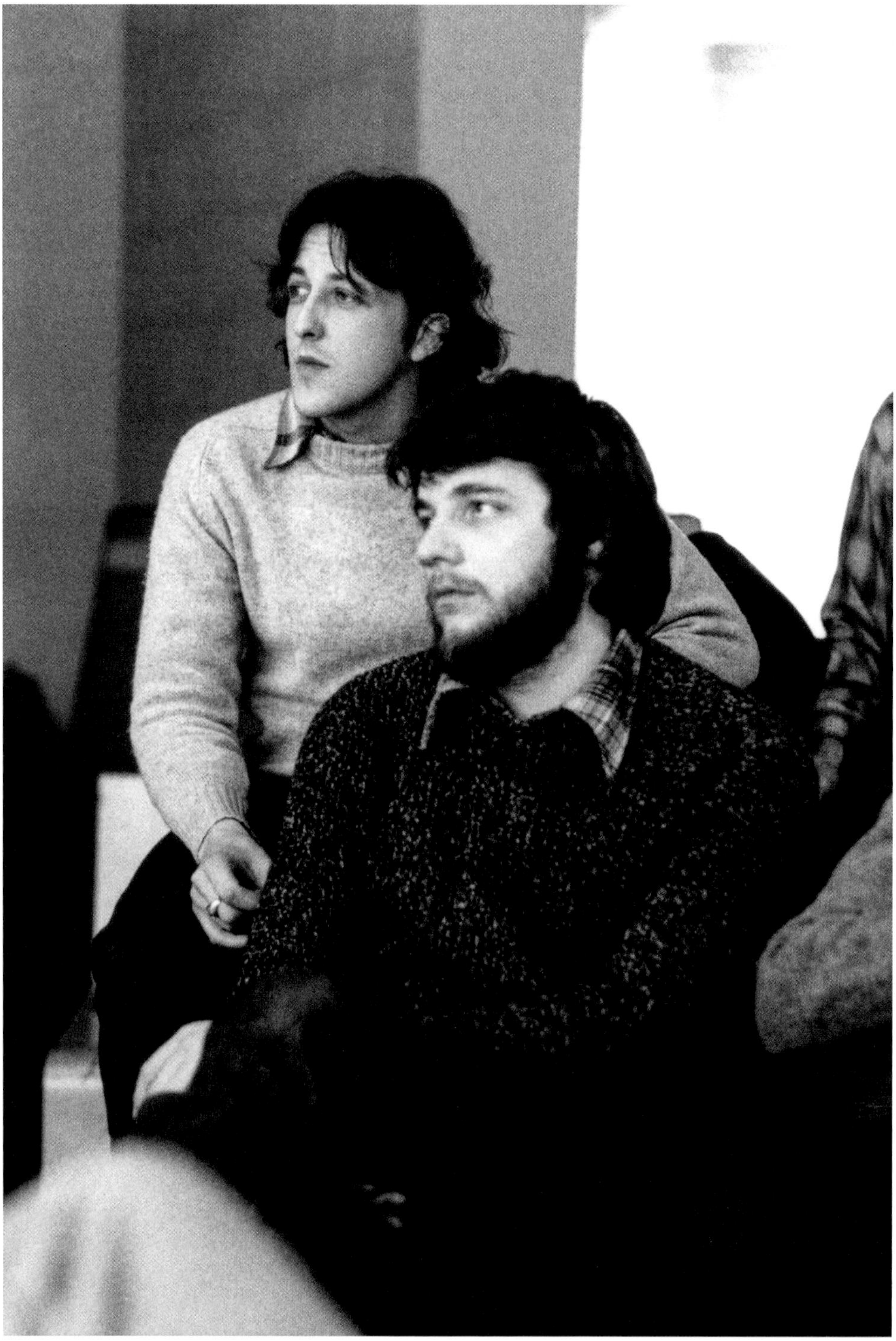

Marcus Schubert and Edward Burtynsky during crit session, c. 1978. Photograph by Matthew Plexman

and ventured into using colour. From the age of eleven, he had worked almost exclusively in black and white. Consequently, he was aware of the various shades of black, grey, and white in taking photographs and he wanted to incorporate that sensibility into his use of colour. Up to that time, colour had been restricted to fashion and commercial photography. He looked intently at the work of photographers like Eliot Porter, Stephen Shore, William Eggleston, and Joel Meyerowitz, who were among the first to use colour in art photography.

For Burtynsky, colour became an essential ingredient in his tool kit. While he understood the alluring provenance of black-and-white photography, and especially appreciated the tonal grades it could achieve, colour had its own attractions. One reason for choosing to work in colour was that most canvases in the Western tradition were created in a full range of hues, and he wanted his work to appeal to those who collected fine art rather than those who collected only photographs. (Later, he would, for similar reasons, make his photographs extremely large.) He was also drawn to the immediacy of colour, and how it heightens the sensations of the viewer. Black-and-white photography could be extremely sensuous, but colour was even more so.

At the same time, he became partial to "that really super high resolution, the great tonal variations that large format cameras provided."[33] He realized that no industrial landscapes paired the view camera with colour. He began to wonder if he should explore that possibility.

THEORY VERSUS PRACTICE

After his Datsun died, Burtynsky purchased a Volvo station wagon, which allowed him to carry lots of equipment in its cargo area. He had become zealous in searching for subject matter that would allow him to put theory into practice.

In the spring of 1978, he, Marcus Schubert, and Paul Lowry drove in Schubert's Pinto station wagon to Jekyll Island, off the coast of North

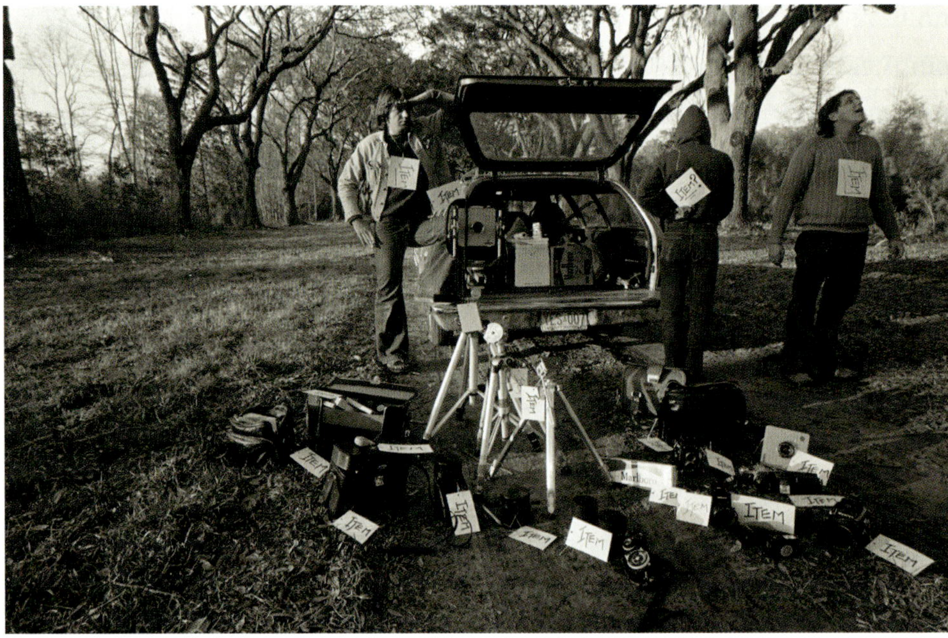

The car here is a Pinto owned by Marcus Schubert, c. 1978. This photograph was taken on the trip to Georgia with Paul Lowry (back to camera). Burtynsky is on the left; Schubert on the right

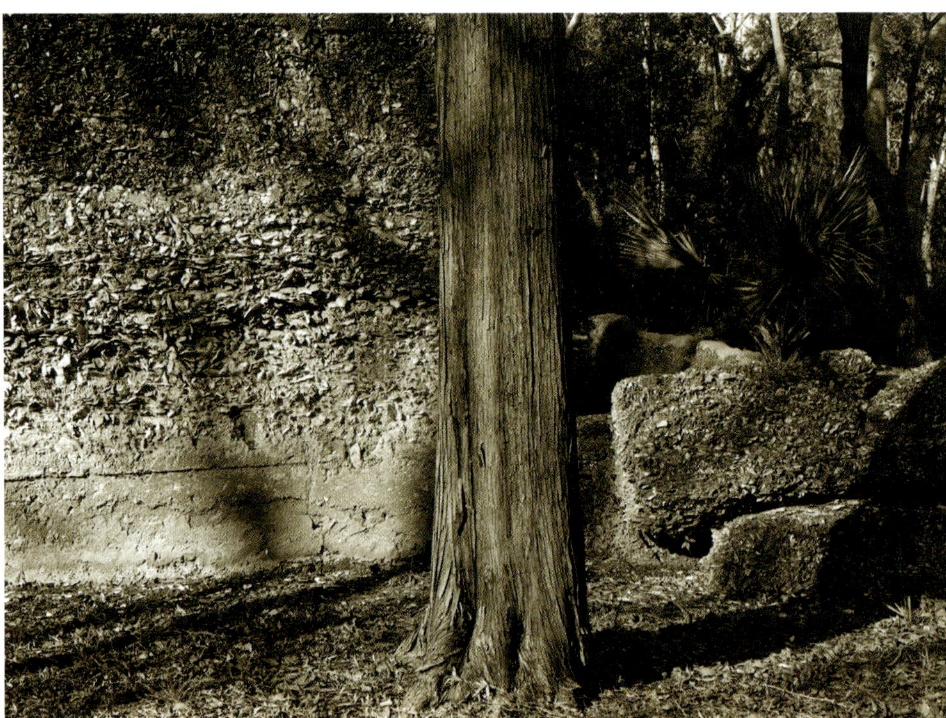

Edward Burtynsky, *Wormsloe*, 1978

Carolina, and to Wormsloe, Georgia. In both places, they were looking at tabby ruins (eighteenth-century plantation houses, constructed using limestone, sand, and shell, that had fallen into disrepair). Burtynsky's focus was on pieces of architecture that had disintegrated and were in the process of being reduced to rubble. Put another way, he was looking at buildings that had become ruins.

The following year, early in the spring, Burtynsky and Schubert drove to South Carolina in search of exotic landscapes, especially those overrun by kudzu. Also known as Japanese or Chinese arrowroot, this invasive plant covers everything in its path. Kudzu often looks beautiful, depending on the structures it envelops, but it suffocates everything it covers.

Schubert took some images of kudzu but, for Burtynsky, the trip was a non-starter: none of the few shots he took still exist. The most exciting part of this foray occurred when he and Schubert were arrested by the U.S. military for taking photos on restricted roadside property. The two Canadians were escorted by multi-vehicle convoy to a military camp, interrogated, and then sent on their way with a strict warning to be careful where they photographed.

Later that year, Burtynsky set out by himself in his Volvo. He scoured the White Mountains in New Hampshire and the Blue Ridge Parkway and Shenandoah Parkway in Virginia. In Centralia, a town in northern Pennsylvania, he came across a coal mining fire that had been burning underground since 1962.

"This was a world where no human can live, hotter than the planet Mercury," the investigative reporter David DeKok observed. "Its atmosphere [is] as poisonous as Saturn's. At the heart of the fire, temperatures easily exceeded 540 degrees Celsius. Lethal clouds of carbon monoxide and other gasses swirled through the rock chambers."[34] The residents of Centralia told the young photographer that, if he was so inclined, he could wander around. "And they told me . . . you could see [where] heat and smoke were coming off [people's lawns], as it's kind of scorching the earth as it's moving underground."[35]

From Centralia, Burtynsky drove ten miles to Frackville. "I remember I stopped, and got out, and stood beside the car. I was surrounded by hills of coal slag. White birch trees were growing up through the black mounds, and ponds were full of lime green water . . . Slowly I turned 360 degrees, and in that entire horizon there was nothing virgin. It totally destabilized me. I thought, is this Earth? I had never seen anything transformed on this scale . . . There was a very surreal quality to that space." He told himself: "This is what I have to do."[36] At that time, he recalled, "I took some photographs of it, and didn't think much of them, and they kind of sat as

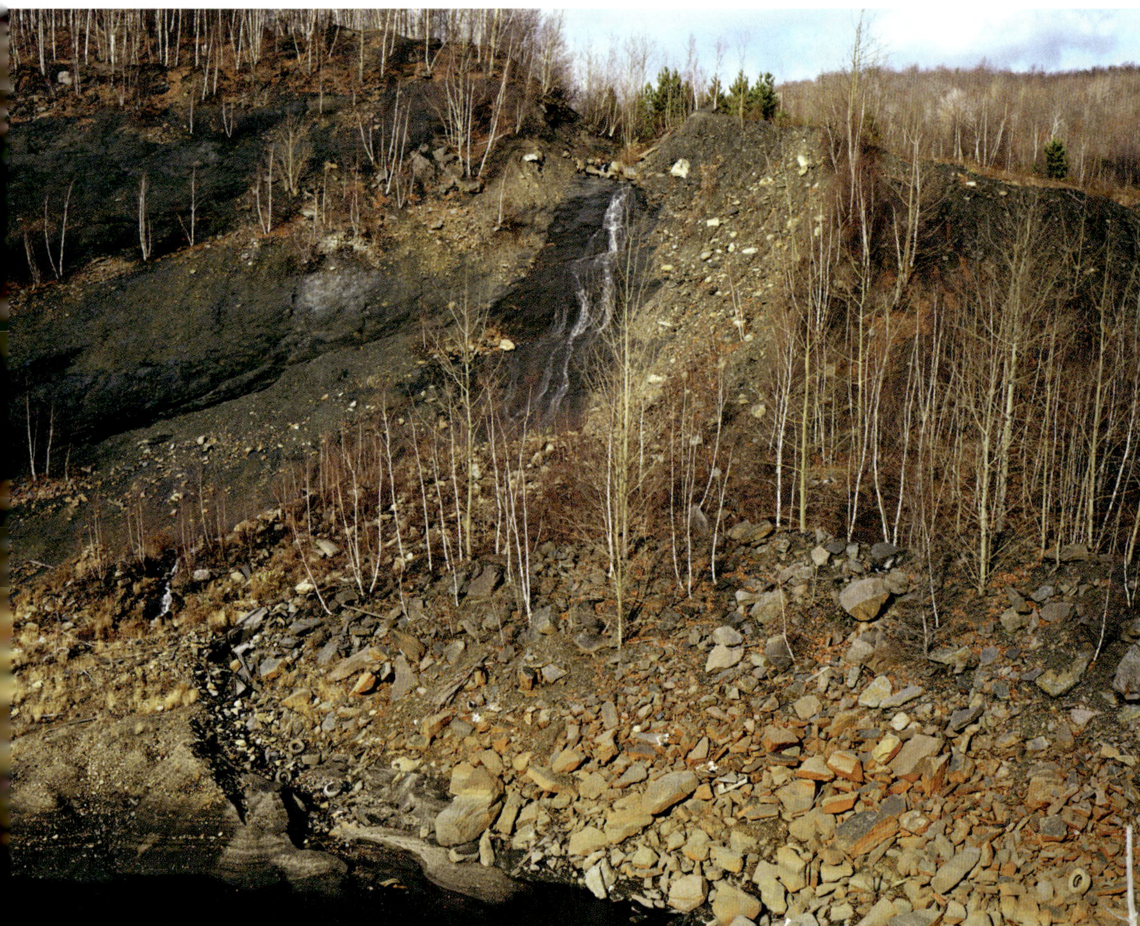

Edward Burtynsky, *Frackville*, 1978

contact sheets for about a year."[37] He needed time to take in exactly what had happened to him.

On his trip, Burtynsky had come into touch with the kind of images he wanted to create, but he remained unsure how to achieve that goal. There was a further complication: while in Ottawa at the National Gallery, he had come across an old photo of a quarry by August Sander. That image–"a vast pit presented from a confusing vantage point suggesting that the world had been tilted on its side"–encouraged him to explore the tension between realism and abstraction.[38] Burtynsky had stared at the photograph "for

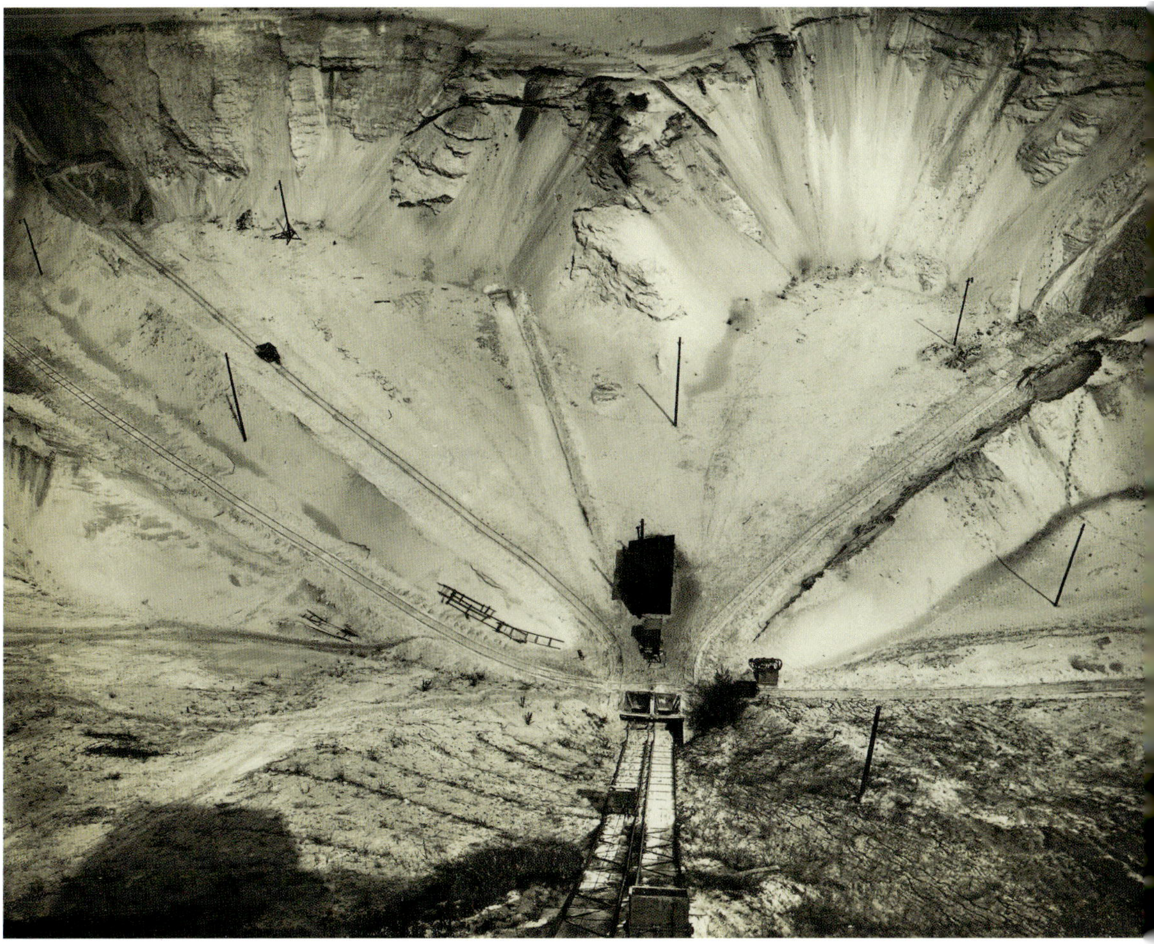

August Sander, *Quartz Quarry and Construction Site, near Cologne*, c. 1932. J. Paul Getty Museum

over a minute before I could begin to figure out what I was looking at, and a minute is like an eternity to just comprehend what you're seeing. It was exciting." Kirsten Hoving has commented that "Sander's photograph showed Burtynsky how an unusual perspective could make a scarred landscape both visually disturbing and [compellingly] beautiful."[39] In 1982, however, he had not yet figured out how he would merge the "disturbing" and the "beautiful."

HIATUS

After three years at Ryerson, Burtynsky dropped out of school. "There were 2 reasons for this," he recalled. "Reason One was that I had lost my thread as to what I wanted to pursue. I wanted to do large format landscape and my teachers at the time thought I was heading in the wrong direction" by not taking up street photography.

> I [had] sort of lost my path and I needed the time to figure out where to go. The second reason was I was already $15,000 in debt at the end of the third year and I didn't want to go to $20K to do my fourth.
>
> I took a couple of years off and worked in the corporate sector. First, I got a job in IBM's photography department, doing plates for government cheques in Ottawa. After about a year, I was hired by the Ontario Hospitals Association. The OHA distributes information about new legislation and developments to its member hospitals. They sent me to hospitals with writers to shoot the photos for the stories they'd be covering in their newsletters.

He was given an empty space and the funds to build a darkroom and acquire equipment. "Suddenly, I was making connections in the industry. It took me a year and a half to build the department, but that experience was a training ground for starting my own photo lab down the line."[40]

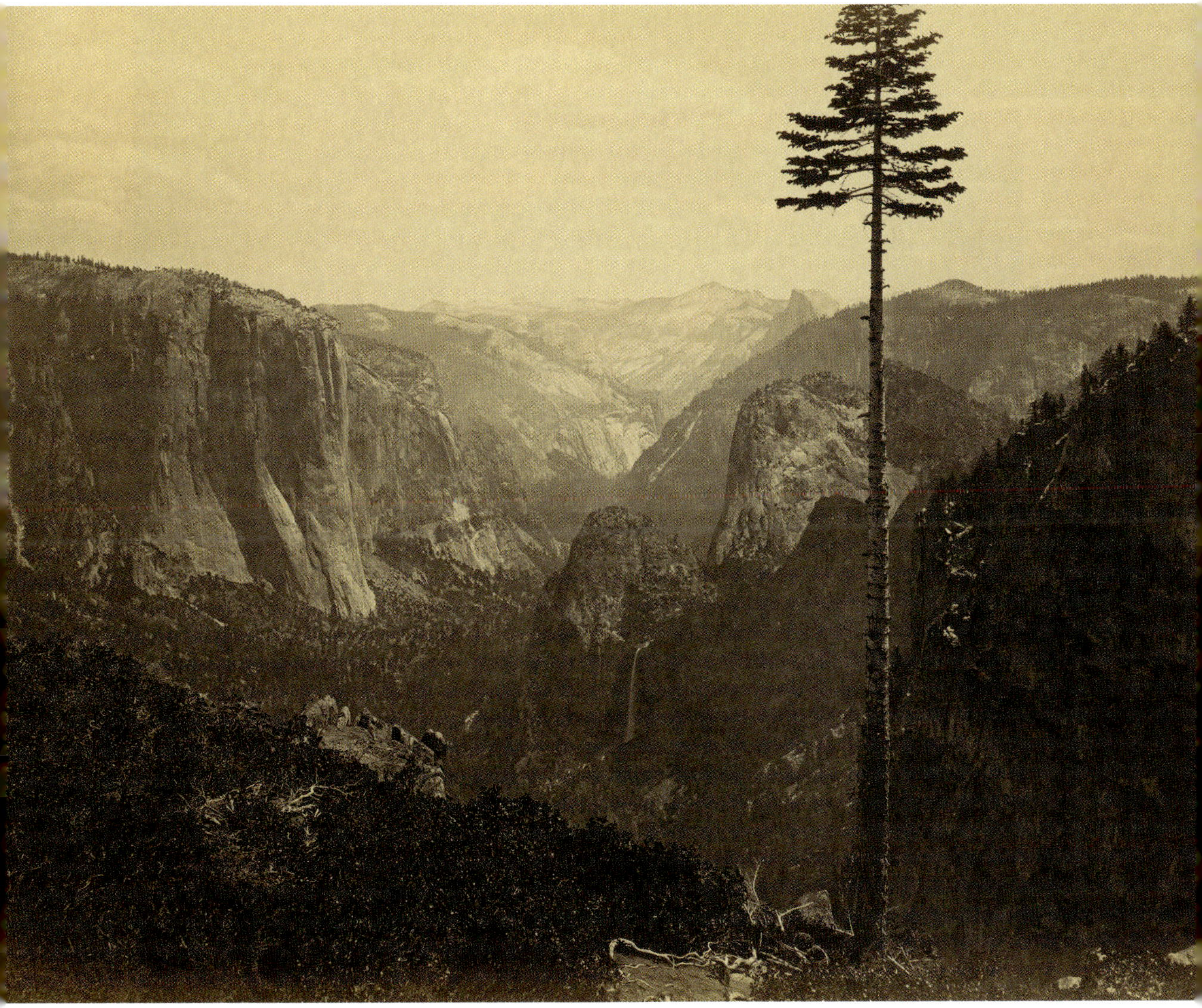

Carleton Watkins, *Sentinel Rock, Yosemite Valley,* c. 1872. The Metropolitan Museum of Art

Early in 1980, he drove to New York City to look at all kinds of art. He had another startling revelation at the Metropolitan Museum of Art when seeing the prints of the American photographer Carleton Watkins. "They were remarkable, with an aliveness in the images. . . . I was just starting to shoot large format in the landscape and what really impressed me was what Watkins, and other photographers of the nineteenth century, went through to get their shots. . . . What they went through was phenomenal: they were part chemists and part pioneers . . . [Those prints] were stunning. I have rarely seen prints that excited me as much as those landscapes."[41]

Back in Ontario, Burtynsky photographed dense brush. When he photographed *Grasses, Bruce Peninsula*, he had another eureka moment:

> In the spring of '81, on a shooting trip to the Bruce Peninsula, I was exploring cottage country lifestyle. I wanted to visualize how people create personal environments while trying to get closer to nature. One morning while driving around I noticed a patch of fresh new grass emerging along the roadside. I pulled over and set up my 4x5 looking for a composition. I found something unexpected, different from other work I was doing. While looking at those grasses, I felt the shot could benefit from a hint of extra brightness. This would be one

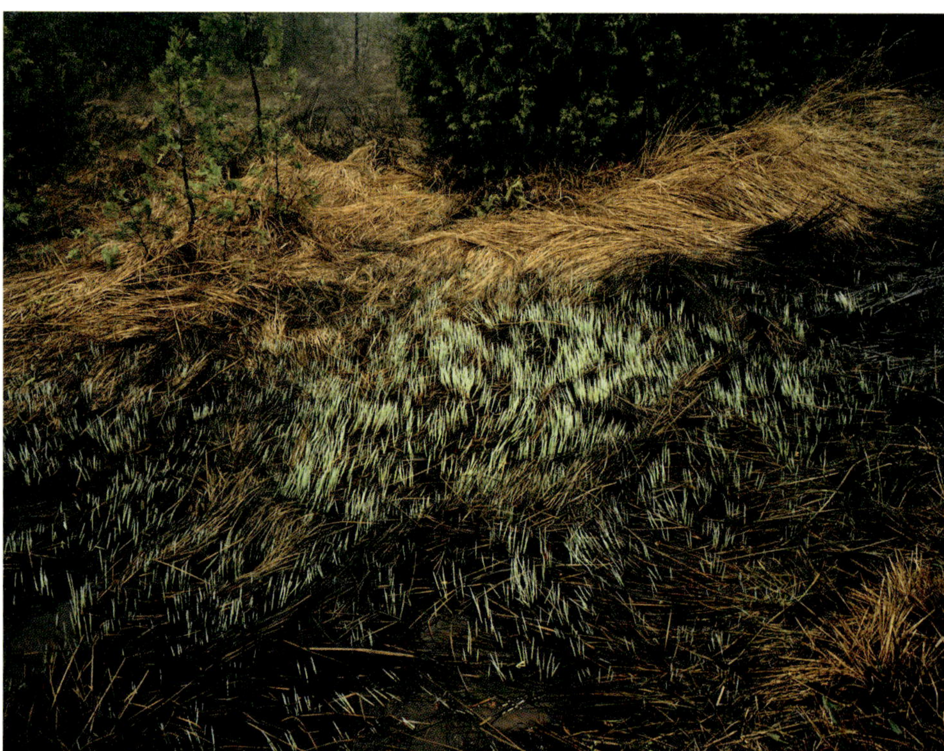

Edward Burtynsky, *Grasses, Bruce Peninsula*, 1981

> of the earliest times I would use a strobe light in the landscape . . . I took one shot with and another without fill light. The one with flash was by far the better version, where subtle green colours in the grass were highlighted, and came forward luminescent with an uncanny presence.
>
> This image became the most profound of the trip. It affected my thinking about edge-to-edge visual information, texture, abstraction, abundance of detail and flattening out the image plane. In a way, this photograph marks the birth of my understanding about colour in the landscape. Making the image had opened a way of seeing that reminded me of mid-20th century abstract expressionist painting, a period in art that I loved and felt inspired by.
>
> I enlarged *Grasses* as a 20 × 24 inch print in my darkroom and pinned it up. Back then, when I believed I had a good image I would do that; I'd pin it up and spend a long time looking at it, thinking about it, and referring to it for all the aspects that were intriguing to me. I was creating a foundation. This led to my current working process, using images that I feel are successful and building on the clues they offer. What reveals itself informs me. I learn from the work, using the strongest elements as new departure points for improvement and variation. I think of the *Grasses* image as a genesis for the work that was to come.[42]

That image became pivotal in Burtynsky's career:

> It was the first opportunity to do some images for myself . . . I'm not sure why I chose the Bruce Peninsula, but I did, and I wasn't actually in pursuit of images like *Grasses*. I was looking at cottage country in dormancy–a place where we humans bond with nature and find respite from the pressures of urban life. I took a lot of those photos, but I also saw the potential in the texture, tone, and colour of the matted snow free landscapes. I shot *Grasses* and then did a few more. . . . When I

> started printing the work, I preferred the pure landscapes . . . I then went on building on that theme of wild trees & brush.[43]

On the same day he took *Grasses*, another image he took struck his fancy. He felt *Landscape #4* possessed "greater centrality [than *Grasses*] with a clump of lighter reeds in the center foreground and a more gestural 'Pollock' wildness to the dogwood branches."[44] Since childhood, Burtynsky had fished, camped, and trekked in such settings–such experiences were the lifeblood of his entrancement with nature. In *Landscape Study #12*, the sliver of landscape at the top, the shack in the middle, and the fence at the bottom are contrasted to the white space that fills most of the composition. In this early image, he skillfully blended the figurative and the abstract.

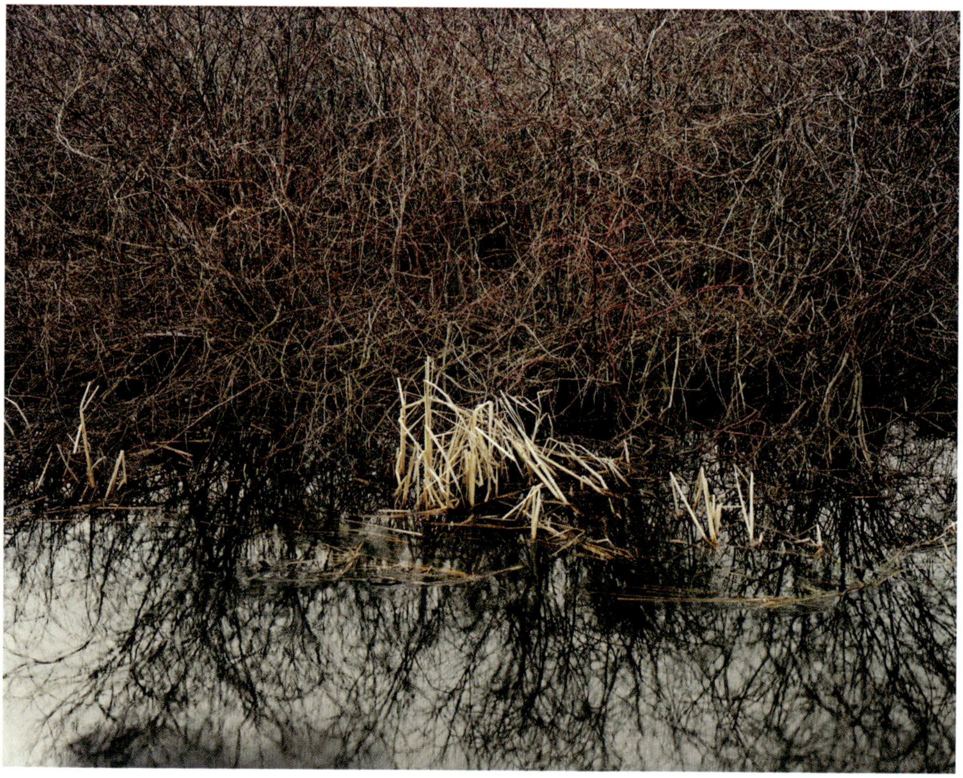

Edward Burtynsky, *Landscape #4*, 1981

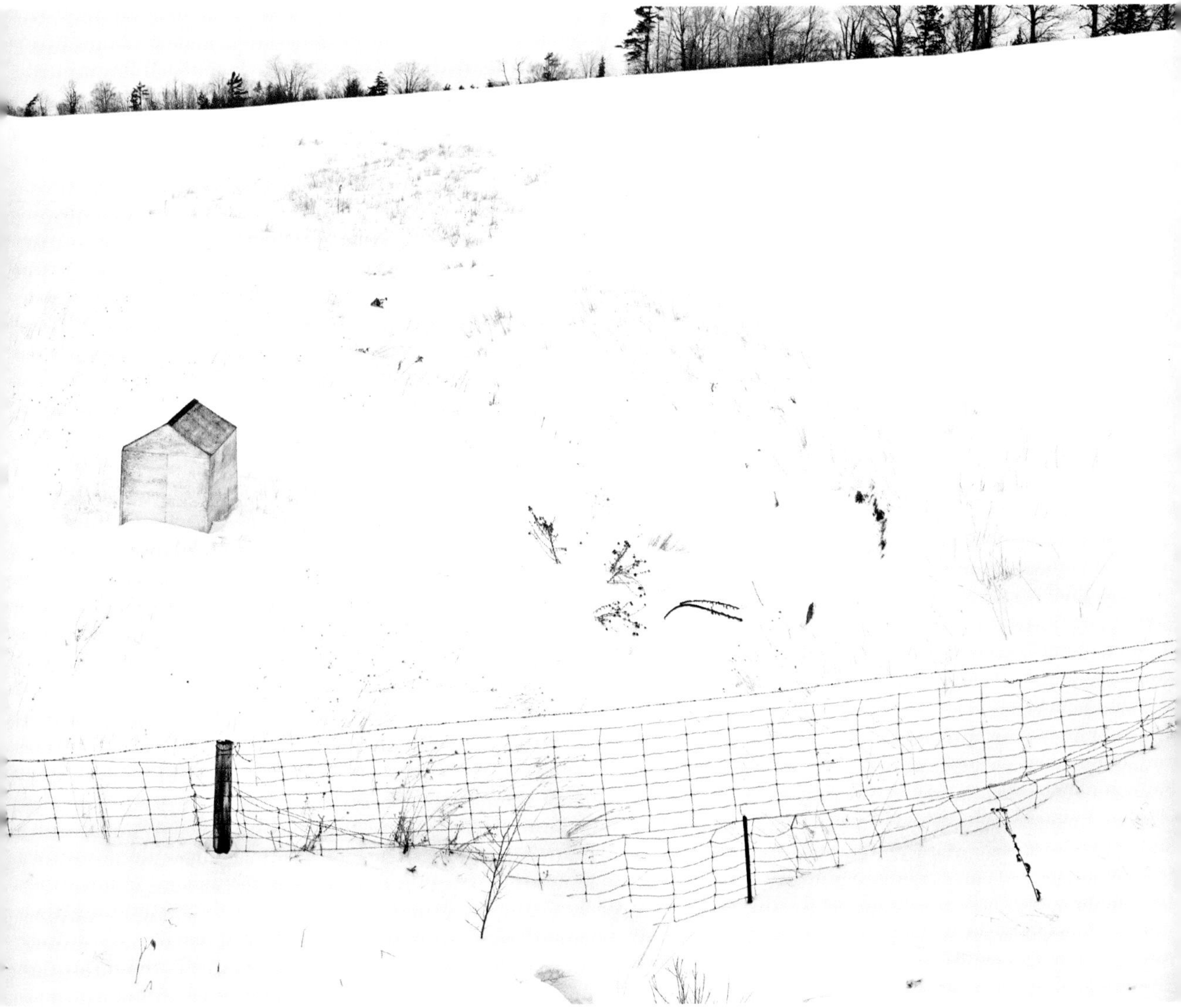

Edward Burtynsky, *Landscape Study #12*, 1981. This image was originally titled *White Snow (North of Kleinburg)*

Burtynsky returned to Ryerson for the 1981-1982 school year to finish his degree. That year, he submitted a proposal for a major project: "I will be using the 4 × 5 camera and colour film. The work I will do will revolve around landscape. I will be looking at both rural and urban environments. I will take an open-minded approach to my subject matter and focus on what is dramatic in it. The elements that presently interest me in my photographs are forms which I find contain energy. What I hope to achieve this year is to become precise in identifying subject matter that contains this energy and to isolate only the elements that contribute to it." He added: "The form my final presentation will take is to produce a group of about 20 photographs that I will present in the Ryerson Gallery."[45]

That exhibition was *Landscapes and Greenhouses*. The photographs for it were taken in various parts of Ontario during his road trips searching for subject matter: the Don Valley, Leamington, the Holland Marsh, the University of Toronto campus, and Stoney Creek.

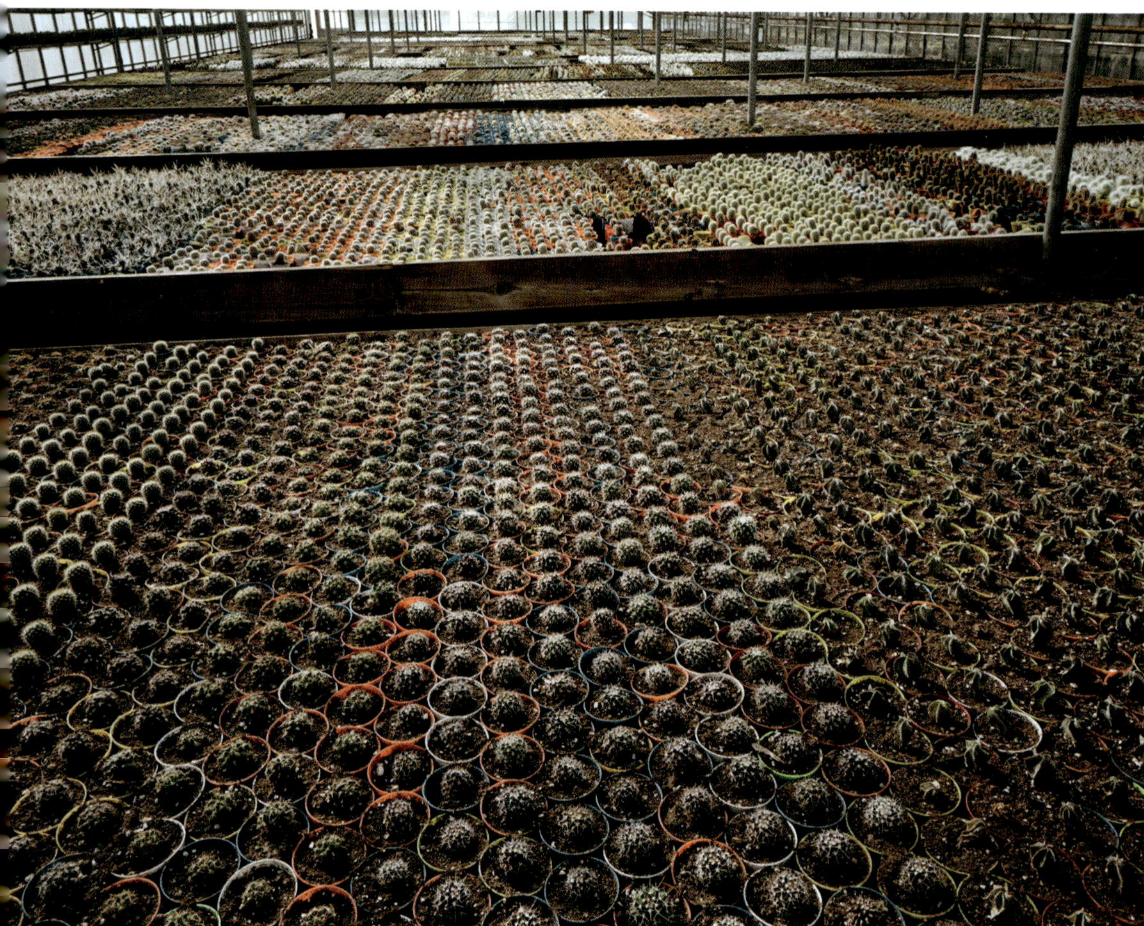

Edward Burtynsky, *Greenhouse*, c. 1982

For Burtynsky, "There had to be an overall organization of flow and gesture in a pristine environment." That winter, he found himself "at odds with the landscape and thus I had a hard time motivating myself to photograph it. In contemplating the problem. I arrived at the concept of photographing greenhouses as landscapes. As I began to photograph these womb-like environments, my interest in them grew."[46] The link for the photographer was between the natural world and glass buildings made to assist–and enhance–nature.

At a garage sale in Toronto, Ed met Jeannie Baxter, also a Ryerson student. Jeannie was from Hamilton, and the youngest child of Wilson Balfour Baxter, a widow and descendant of the Southam newspaper clan. In 1980, Ed and Jeannie moved in together; they married five years later. (The couple had two daughters–Meghan, born in 1994, and Katya, born in 1998. Burtynsky and Baxter divorced in 2007; in 2019, Burtynsky married Julia Johnston.)

Early in the 1980s, Burtynsky was selling prints for seventy-five dollars. Jeannie told him he was crazy to charge so much. She recalled: "He was questioning what he was doing. He could see it was a hard way to make a living." Since it was difficult to get colour prints developed at a reasonable cost, Burtynsky set up a darkroom in the basement of the house they rented.

During his two years at Niagara College and four at Ryerson, Burtynsky had become proficient in all the technical aspects of making photographs, but he had also immersed himself in all aspects of photographic history, especially landscapes. Watkins's images of Yosemite Valley moved him, as did later ones of the same subject by Ansel Adams. For him, both men showed pristine, majestic beauty. The problem for Burtynsky was that he had become certain that nature no longer existed in the same way–if it had ever had.[47]

Despite some uncertainties, he realized, "a significant change has occurred in my relationship to my work. I am now confident in this endeavour and feel that what I am doing is indeed a worthy occupation to devote myself to."[48] During his Ryerson years, he had fretted that this was not the case but, in March 1982, those doubts had vanished. At Frackville, he had witnessed man's desecration of the natural world; on the Bruce Peninsula, he had encountered unspoiled nature. These were the two extremes to which his career would be devoted.

(1982–1985)

3 TRAVELS WITH A VOLVO

Burtynsky travelled more widely and for longer periods of time after graduating from Ryerson. On long trips, his Volvo became his home away from home. He stockpiled his gear in it, and the car often served as a bedroom: "I'd pull up into a parking lot and find a spot near a building."[1] He also recalled the beginning of his 1983 trip: "I remember starting up my Volvo and pulling out by myself on a four-month long adventure. My car, camera and film, money for gas, and all of North America that could be accessed by road. Nothing since has ever held that excitement, that sense of pure adventure and discovery–and absolute freedom."[2] In April 1985, he wrote that he felt "traveling alone promotes a strong sense of purpose in me as well as a confidence in my own ideas. I feel that I am able to harness the muses and direct them to the scenes that hold meaning for me (as well as others)."[3]

Earlier in the same year, he had gone as far as Denver, Colorado. The following year, with the assistance of a Canada Council for the Arts

Short-Term grant, he returned to Colorado and made his way to Zabriskie Point in Death Valley, California, Arches National Park, Capitol Reef in Utah, and Mount St. Helens in Washington. He also photographed at the Griffith Iron Ore Mine in Ontario and was in Sudbury, Ontario, and Roanoke, West Virginia. He and Jeannie also flew on vacation to Paris that May. The following year, 1985, was a whirlwind: in six weeks, he was in upper state New York; British Columbia (Skihist Provincial Park, Fraser River, Thompson, River, Hope, Spences Bridge, and Sparwood); Butte, Montana; Alberta; Bingham Mines, Utah; and Inco in Sudbury. He was casting a wide net on the lookout for what he referred to as "tangled landscapes," which he attempted to see through the lens of Abstract Expressionism.

Burtynsky's imagination was not fully focused in these years, although he wanted to concentrate on the interactions between man and nature. He ended up dividing his work into two areas of concentration: "industries that process nature (fish factories, mining, logging, taxidermy) & splendid nature herself. In this work I am to shed light upon the interface between man & nature. I'm interested in exploitation (not necessarily in a negative sense). Obviously man must appropriate land & kill for food in order to survive. My position is that although this is true, man's methods have alienated him from his environment, and he must be careful with his treatment of it. I also find beauty in the wasteland."[4]

More specifically, he became fixated on showing how human beings alter or interfere with the natural world. In reflecting on these issues, he further split his subject matter from 1983 to 1985 into groupings: taxidermy, packing plants, homesteads, mines, and railcuts. "I had [another] category I called my asides, as in Shakespeare. This other material didn't quite fit into the normal plot, but it was interesting. So, I would shoot it because maybe somewhere in the future I'd figure it out. I decided to follow my instincts. So, I picked that habit up along the way."[5]

Throughout his career, Burtynsky has worked in series. When a videographer once asked him why photographers such as he worked in sequences, he replied, "I've never questioned that way of working–in fact–it is how I make sense of the subject. Early in my career (1982-ish) I saw what I was doing as having a mental set of drawers and in each drawer, I would add images as I came across them." Such an approach "worked for me and it structured my work rather than making it a random walk through the world."[6]

TAXIDERMY

Taxidermy was a subject that intrigued Burtynsky and Marcus Schubert, and both took photographs of assorted examples. Burtynsky's interest began in 1982 when driving on his way to the Bruce Peninsula near Georgian Bay. While looking for a mine, he stopped at a taxidermist's studio to ask directions. The photographer, as the art historian Martha Langford later said, "found himself in a face-to-face encounter with a half-reconstructed bear. The shop, like all the others he would discover, was dirty and cluttered. The disorganization and density of information intrigued him." In inspecting these images, Langford pointed out: "Huge denatured trophies are absurdly contrasted with the tools and materials of immortalization."[7]

A successful taxidermist, it can be claimed, brings a dead animal back to life: the appearance of the animal is preserved, even while its innards have been replaced by stuffing attached to its skeleton or to polyfoam forms. Taxidermy also can be said to go against nature because it does not allow a dead animal to pass away; instead, it is transformed into a new guise–a form of art. Throughout his career, Burtynsky would examine how man, in a multiplicity of perverse ways, interferes with nature and, in this way, taxidermy falls under his purview. He realized that such contradictions drew "power into my images . . . [like] 'the tranquil look of a deer in a messy ugly taxidermy shop.'" In taxidermy, he recalled, "we moved from hunting for survival and protein to hunting for affirmation of the male ego."[8]

The celebrated nineteenth-century American taxidermist William Temple Hornaday had travelled as a young man to places such as India, Ceylon, and Sarawak to collect specimens, and saw no contradiction between collecting specimens in those locations and then displaying the results at the United States National Museum. Later, appalled at how bison had been decimated in the American West, he became a fierce conservationist who did not want animals killed so they could serve as trophies. Hornaday's sentiments were identical to Burtynsky's.

Burtynsky's taxidermy images–taken in places as diverse as Hundred Mile House, British Columbia, and Denver, Colorado–have an uneasy edge

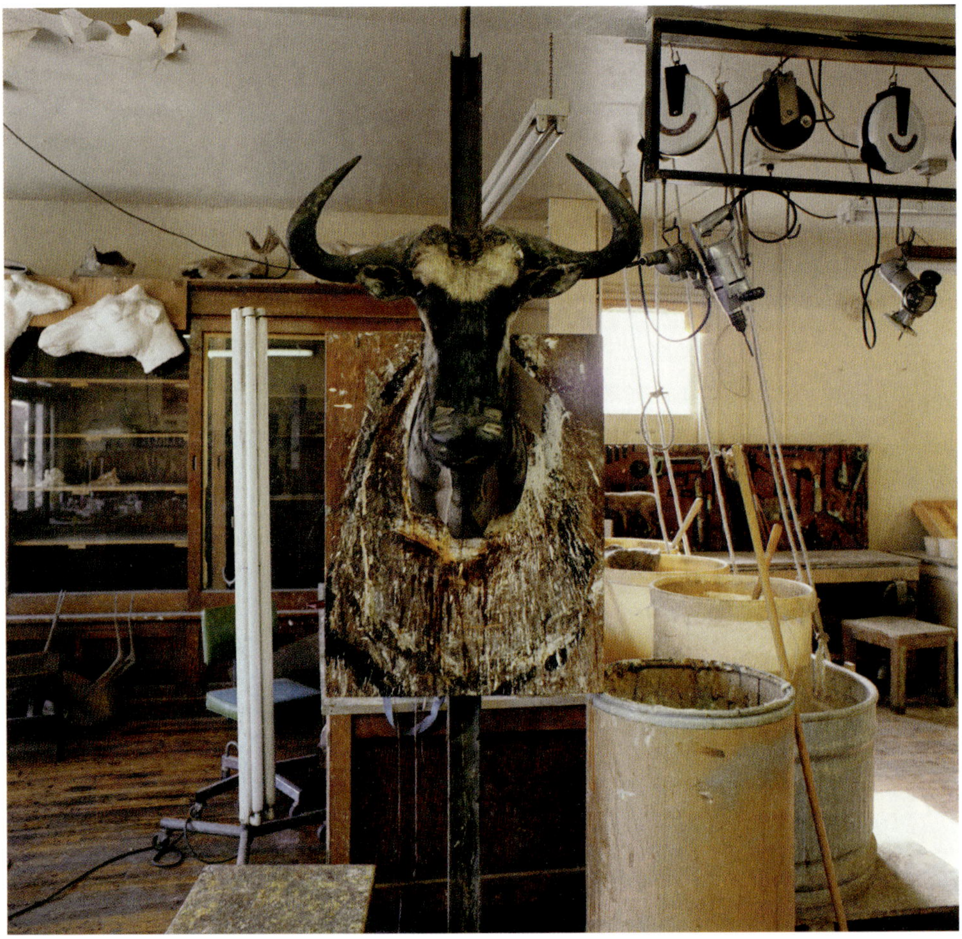

Edward Burtynsky, *Wildebeest*, 1982

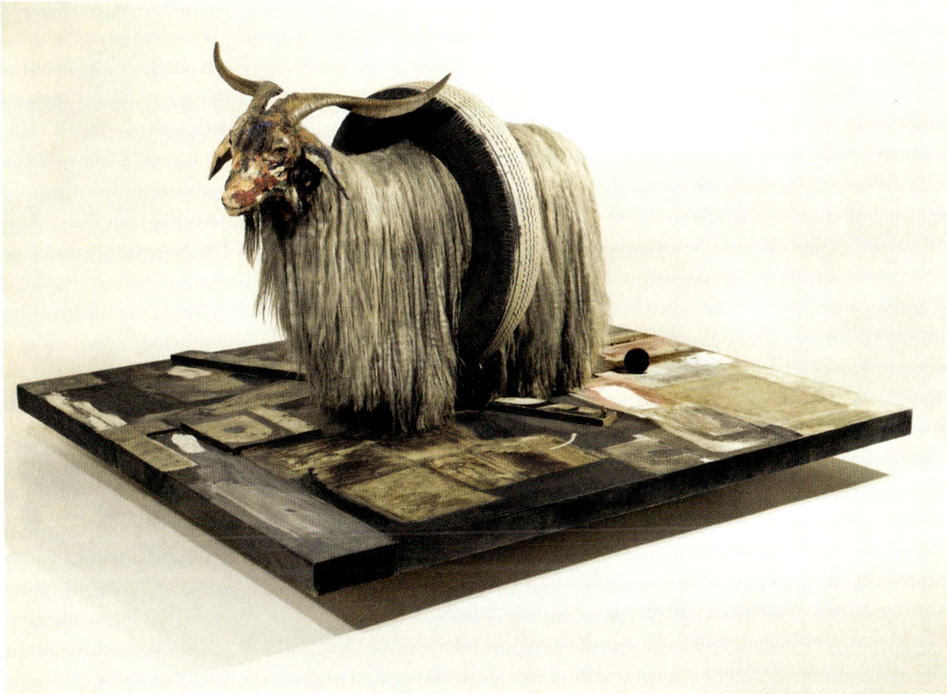

Robert Rauschenberg, *Monogram*, combine, 1955–59. Moderna Museet, Stockholm

to them. The trophies on the wall in *The Filing Cabinet* contrast sharply with the interior of the office; some of the animals stare at the viewer, and the birds are caught in flight. In another photograph, the animal parts look like remnants from a slaughterhouse. *Wildebeest* is reminiscent of Robert Rauschenberg's combine, *Monogram* (1955-1959)–and just as disquieting.

Burtynsky told a friend about a day in Colorado in 1982. He was "idly poking about in a Denver, Colorado, bookstore. He was pretty much fresh out of photo school and like many young photographers with artistic ambitions he was trying to feel his way toward a subject that could become his life's work . . . To become yet another photographer of pristine landscapes seemed about as exciting as returning to his summer jobs as a miner's assistant or clean-up man in an auto-plant. The closest he [got] to nature photography on that Colorado trip was making pictures of stuffed animals."[9]

PACKING PLANTS

The packing plant images are deliberately off-putting in a way similar to the ones in *Taxidermy*. This series–done in 1982 and 1983–concentrates on displaying how produce and animals are dealt with in an industrialized society. In *The Ketchup Plant*, the contrast between the line of bright-red ketchup bottles zig-zagging across the image and the grey stainless-steel interior of the factory suggests that something natural (tomatoes) has been jammed into bottles in an aberrant way.

There is also an uneasy silence in the *Chicken Packing Plant*, taken on Toronto's Spadina Avenue, where the corpses of animals knocked off the conveyor belt are strewn; the tools hanging at the left add an additional air of menace. Burtynsky was worried that this set of photographs might be a failure. He was harsh in passing judgment on himself: "I have very clear ideas about what I'm after but when I frame them, I'm not sure if it's saying anything."[10]

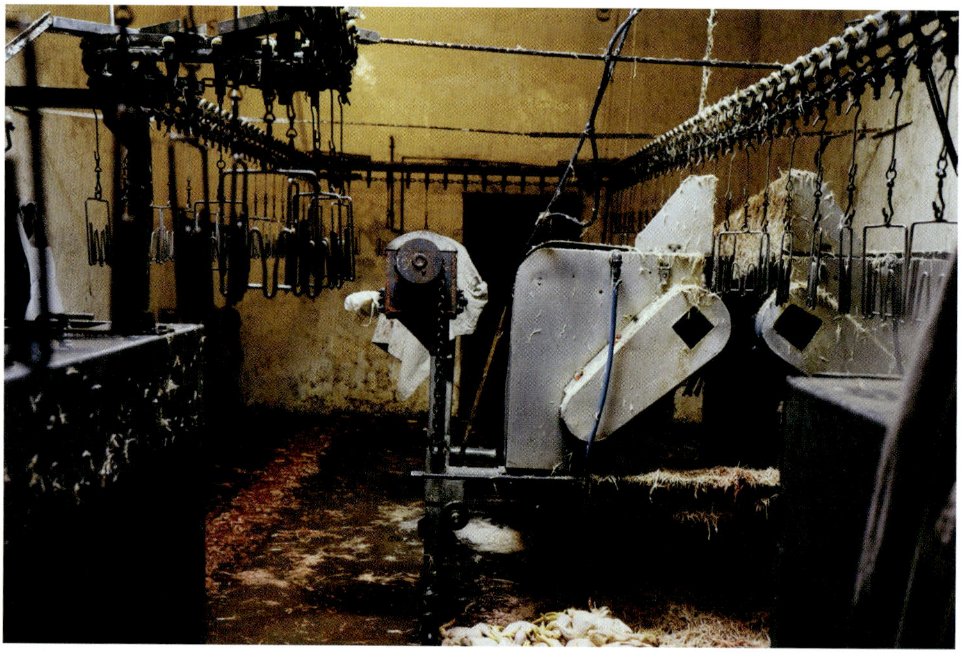

Edward Burtynsky, *Chicken Packing Plant*, c. 1982–83

Taken together, the taxidermy and packing plant images depict a society at odds with how to deal with nature, especially animals. An animal can become a work of art, a trophy that can induce nostalgia (as in preserving a dead pet) or triumph (a hunting trophy). Or animals can be callously butchered to be consumed.[11]

HOMESTEADS

From 1983 to 1985, Burtynsky created four series of images (forty-four in total) that he grouped under the umbrella title *Breaking Ground*: *Homesteads* (thirteen), *Mines* (fourteen), *Inco Landscapes* (two), and *Railcuts* (fifteen). The choice of the word "breaking" is significant because each series reveals a different way of breaching the landscape.

In zeroing in on *homesteads*, Burtynsky was following in the tradition of the eight photographers whose work was shown at Eastman House in Rochester, New York, from October 1975 to February 1976 in the exhibition entitled *New Topographics: Portraits of a Man-Altered Landscape*. Many of the images display landscape scenery encroached upon by motels, suburban houses, parking lots, and the like. Earlier photographers, like Margaret Bourke-White and Walker Evans, had shown less than idealized landscapes, but the new topographers were more direct in demonstrating how man was imposing himself on landscape–and despoiling it.

Burtynsky's *Homesteads* images are like those of three contributors to the landmark exhibition–Joe Deal, Lewis Baltz, and in particular, Robert Adams–although Burtynsky shoots from a higher vantage point than they did. Of the 168 items shown at the Rochester exhibition, only 8 by Stephen Shore were in colour. Moreover, as Burtynsky was aware, books with colour illustrations such as Eliot Porter's in *In Wilderness Is the Preservation of the World* (1962) featured highly idealized images.[12] In his series, Burtynsky used the techniques of the new topographers and, in his use of colour, repudiated Porter's presentation of romanticized landscapes at the same time.

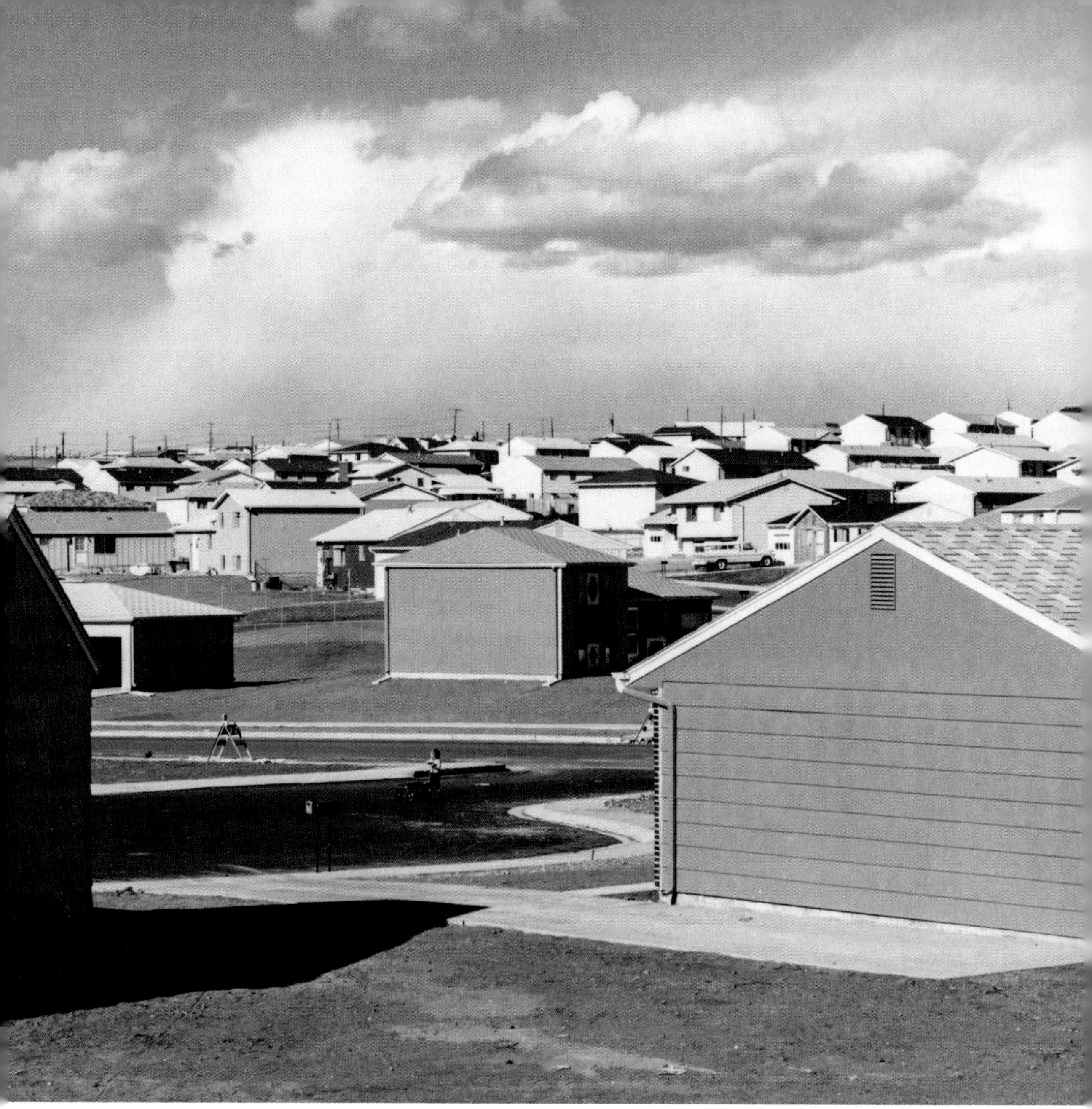

Robert Adams, *Colorado Springs, Colorado*, 1970. The Museum of Modern Art

Burtynsky's employment of colour in his homesteads gives intrusions into landscape a tender poignancy. In *Homesteads #32*, the seemingly pastoral landscape is hemmed in gently on both sides by water, but the horses grazing in the field are fenced and the rail line weaves through the left side, parallel to the dirt road. Technology has made the horses redundant.

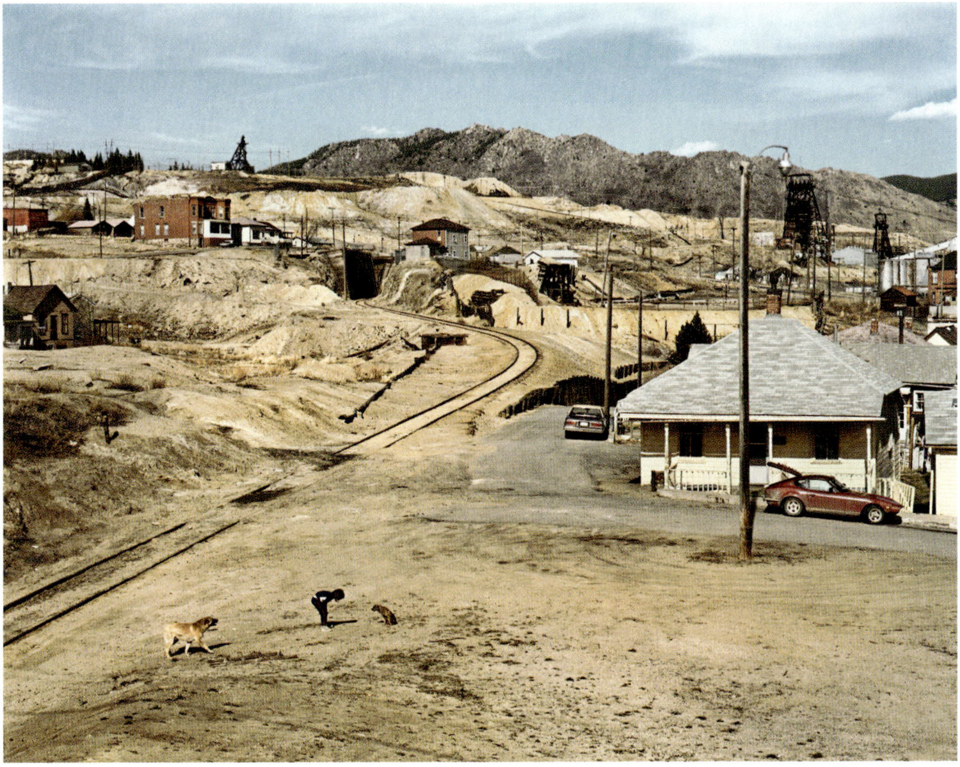

Edward Burtynsky, *Homesteads #29*, Walkerville, Montana, 1985

A boy playing with his dogs at the bottom of *Homesteads #29* is the focus but behind him is the entrance to a mine. The sand-coloured terrain is barely relieved by the grey mountains and blue sky in the background. Burtynsky recorded how he obtained this picture on May 5, 1985: "I photographed Raymond who lived in one of the houses I had framed up. So, I got him to play in a blank area of the image. He willingly obliged me . . . Raymond was a neat kid. He's something like me in that he's not bashful when he wants to know something."[13]

Reflecting years later on this image, Burtynsky added more details:

> On this particular trip I ended up going to Butte, Montana (a town that back then had a population of about 25,000) to see the Anaconda Copper Mine. The mine had been shut down the year prior to my arrival, and

when I visited there were only about 6 people left working there. The town was in a freefall; nearly 6,000 people were out of work and the town was devastated socially and economically. People were desperate. But what revealed itself to me during my visit–what I captured with this picture–was a glimmer of resilience in the community. In this bleak environment, where the mine had gone through and left barren patches here and piles of refuse there, this young boy still found a world of his own with his dogs. He seemed blissfully unaware of the devastatingly transformed industrial landscape left behind. There was this moment, and with it an understanding that life goes on, that humans will adapt, and these environments become normal for the people who live there, for worse or for better.[14]

MINES

Burtynsky's epiphany at Frackville had been a moment of both clarity and sadness: "I want to do the mined landscape."[15] In 1981, Burtynsky had put the Frackville images aside. He was not sure what to do with the insights that had overwhelmed him. It was not until 1983 and 1984 that he was ready to tackle mines as a subject.

The first digging at the Kennecott Copper Mine in Bingham Canyon, Salt Lake County, Utah–one of the largest open-pit copper mines in the world–took place in 1906. At first glance, some of Burtynsky's images of this place look like photographs of amphitheatres from Greece and Rome. At second glance, the viewer realizes that these enormous structures have been constructed by the constant blasting to extract copper.[16]

The image of the abandoned mine shaft at Crean Hill, near Sudbury, can be read in a similar way. The contrast between the textures of the rock formation and its reflection appears tranquil. On closer inspection, the striations on the surface of the rocks and the metal netting holding the surface together add tension to the image–this is subjugated landscape.

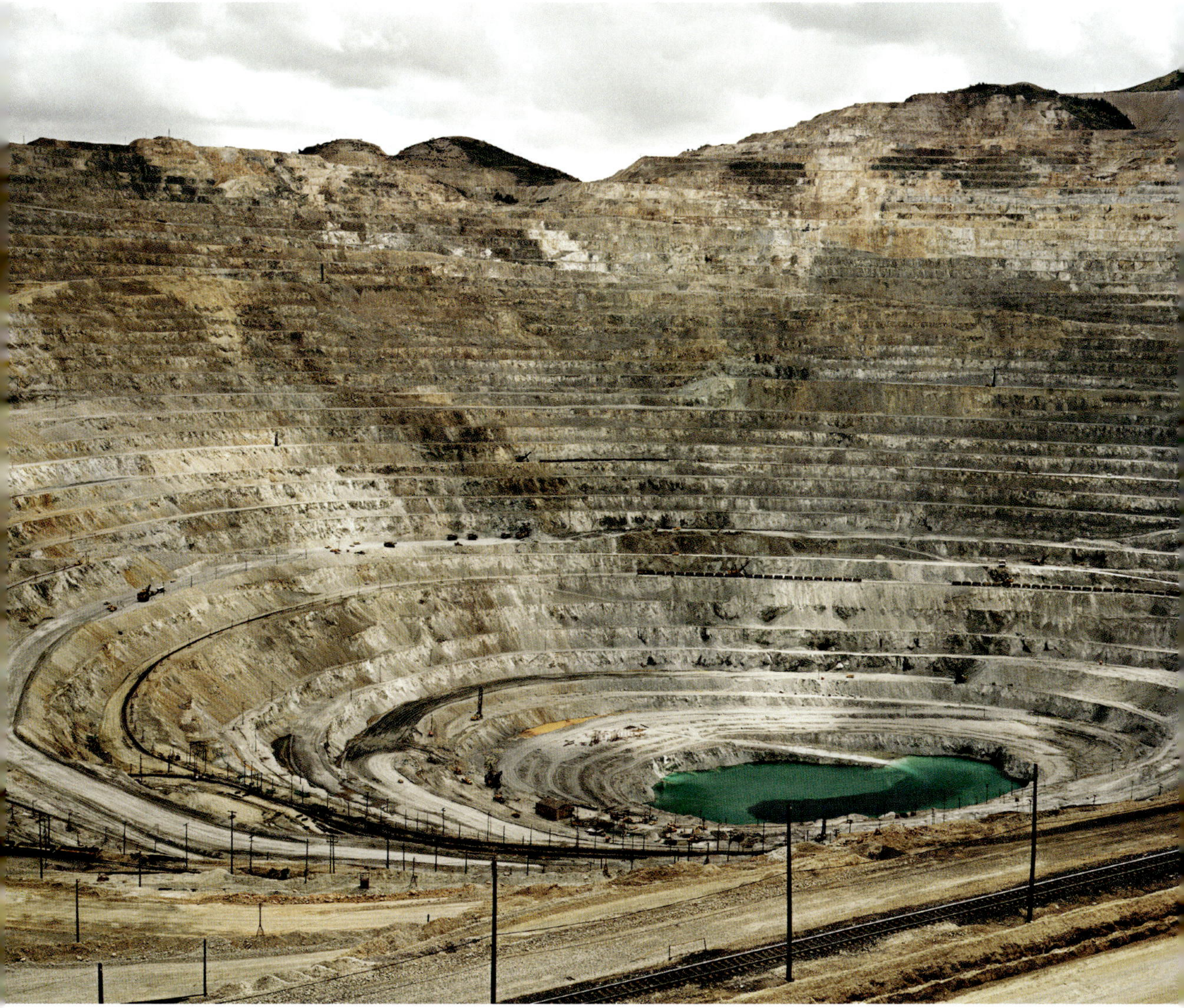

Edward Burtynsky, *Mines #22*, Kennecott Copper Mine, Bingham Valley, Utah, 1983

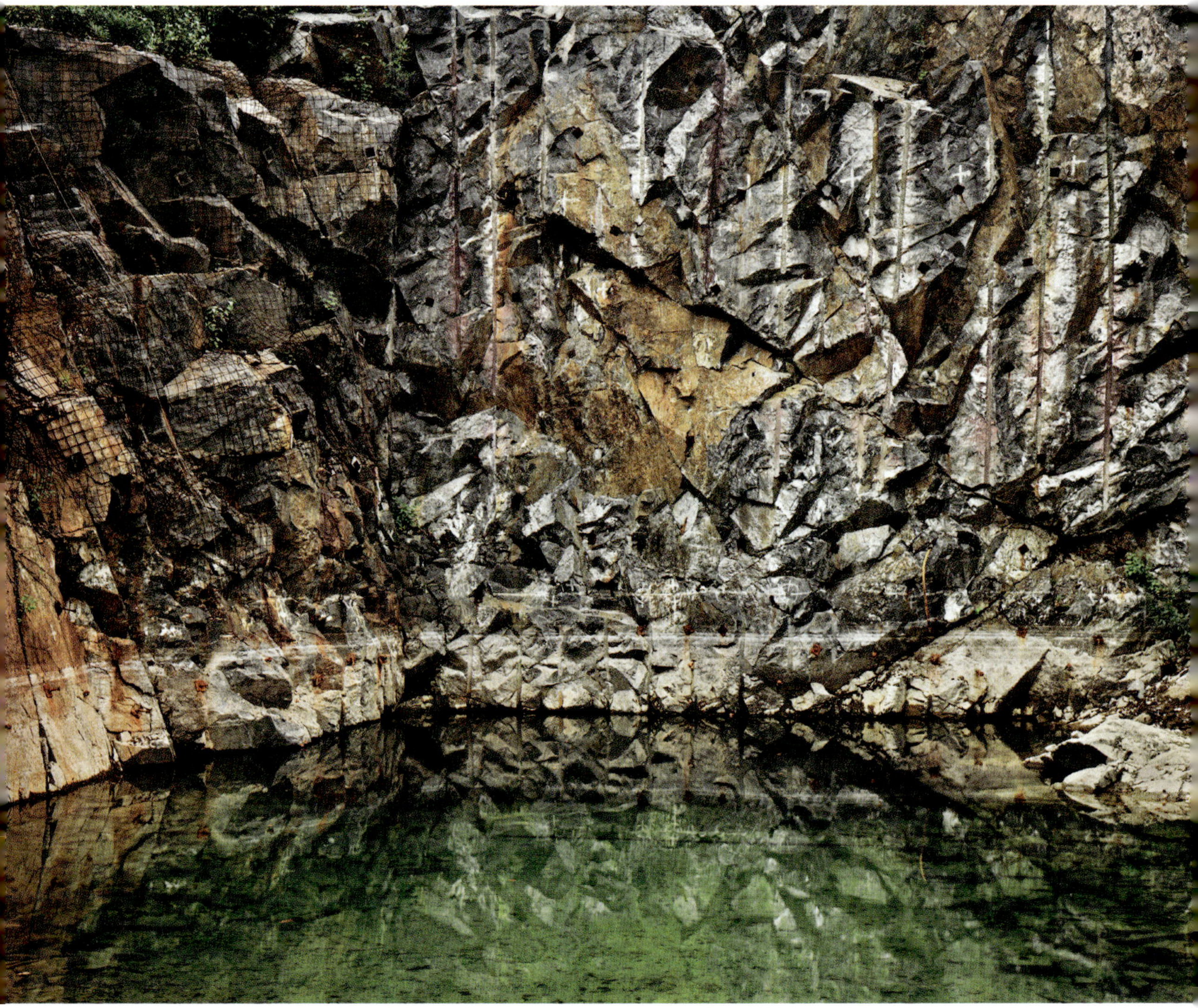

Edward Burtynsky, *Mines #13*, Inco Abandoned Mine Shaft, Sudbury, Ontario, 1984

These two images are among the earliest manifestations in Burtynsky's canon of the "industrial sublime." The Kennecott Mine appears to be a splendid piece of architecture; the one at Crean Hill, picturesque. This is not so. What appears to be attractive must be re-evaluated. Such images are key to understanding Burtynsky's work: their beauty is seductive, but the viewer must ponder the meaning of that beauty.

The disparity between man and nature is captured chillingly in *Mines #43, Berkeley Pit, Anaconda Copper Mine* where the "architecture" of a mine is contrasted to that of the town at the right. An image such as *Mines #14, Anaconda Copper Mine* is more straightforward in showing how mines disrupt the landscape, and displays a restrained palette of colours–a characteristic of Burtynsky's work. His claim that he brought a black-and-white sensibility to colour can be further seen in *Mines #19, Westar Open Pit*

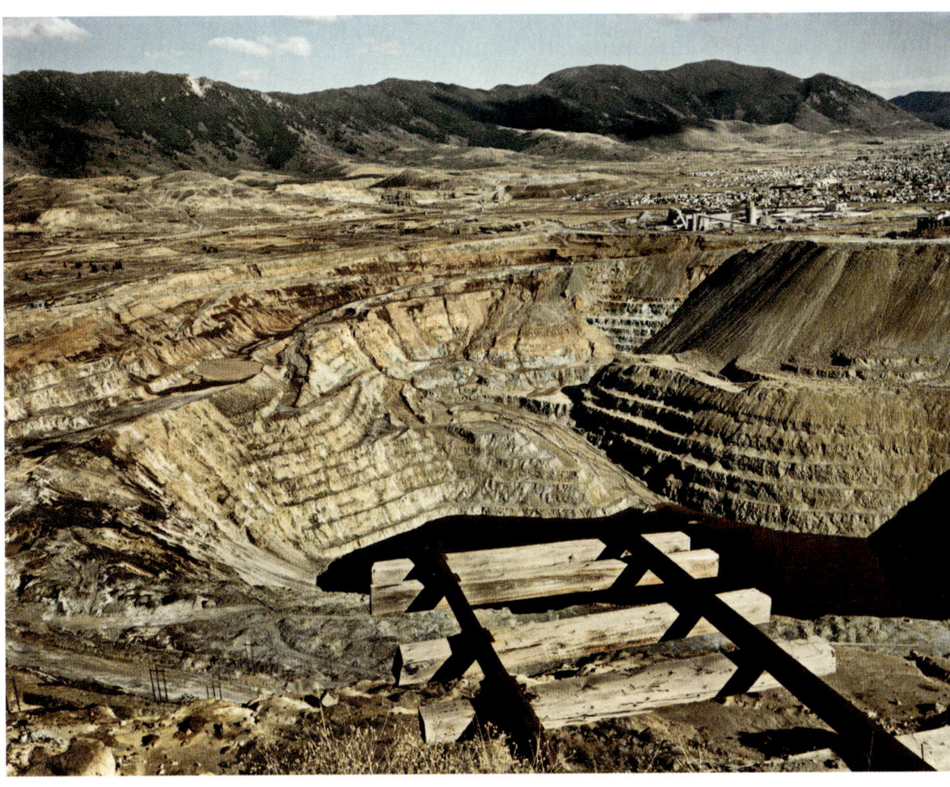

Edward Burtynsky, *Mines #43*, Berkeley Pit, Anaconda Copper Mine, Butte, Montana, 1985

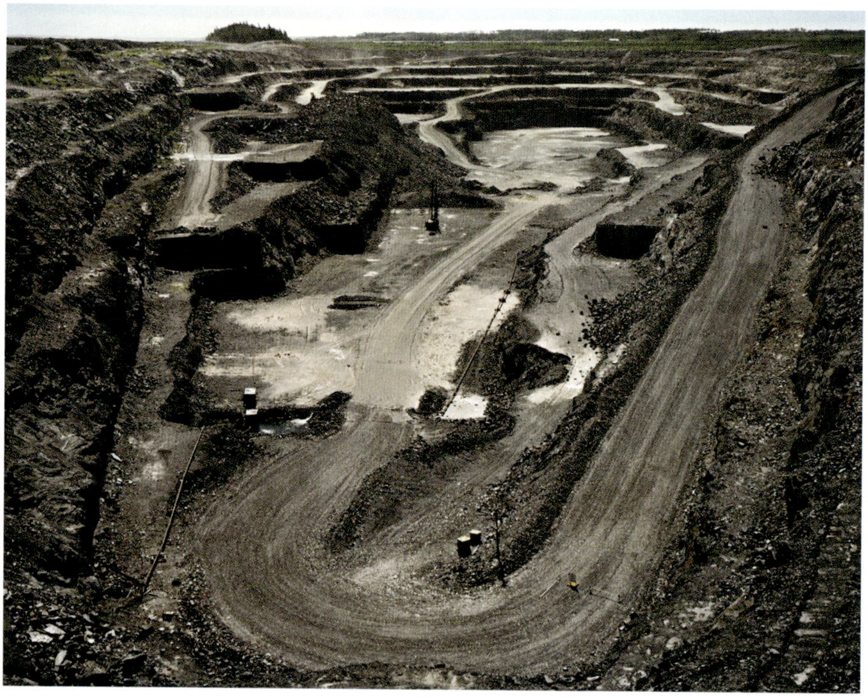

Edward Burtynsky, *Griffith Iron Ore Mine #1*, Township of Ear Falls, Ontario, 1983

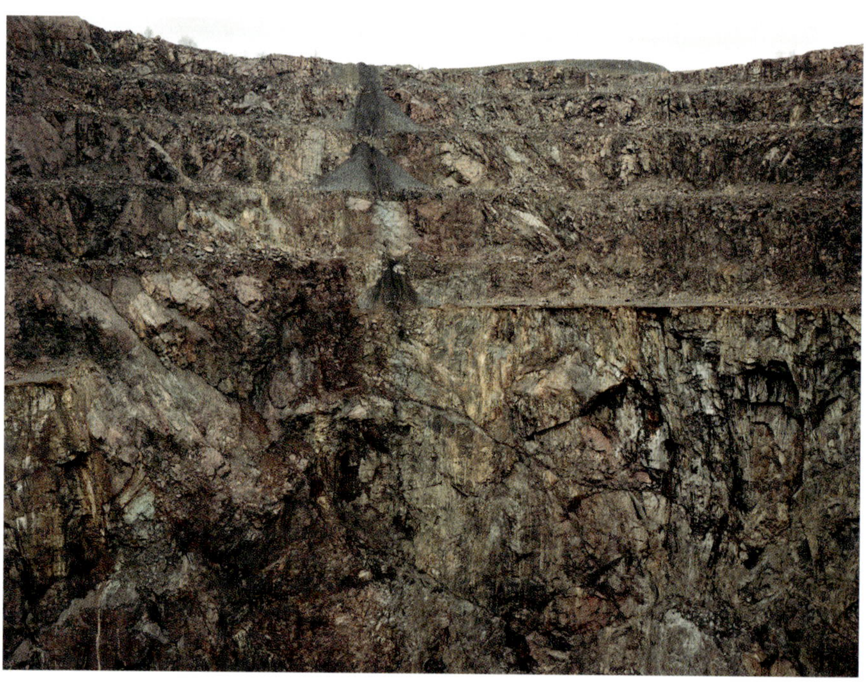

Edward Burtynsky, *Incoland #16*, 1984

Mine and, especially, in an image not in the *Breaking Ground* series, *Griffith Iron Ore Mine #1*.

Two images in the *Breaking Ground* portfolio were taken on land belonging to Inco in Sudbury, Ontario. In *Incoland #16*, the texture of the scarred rock is captured; by placing the four triangle-shaped pieces at the top of the image, Burtynsky made a subtle contrast between the four horizontal layers and the rock below it.

Three years later, in 1987, Inco, the world's largest producer of nickel, commissioned Burtynsky to take photographs of its Thompson Lake mines in Manitoba to use for public relations. There are twenty-eight contact

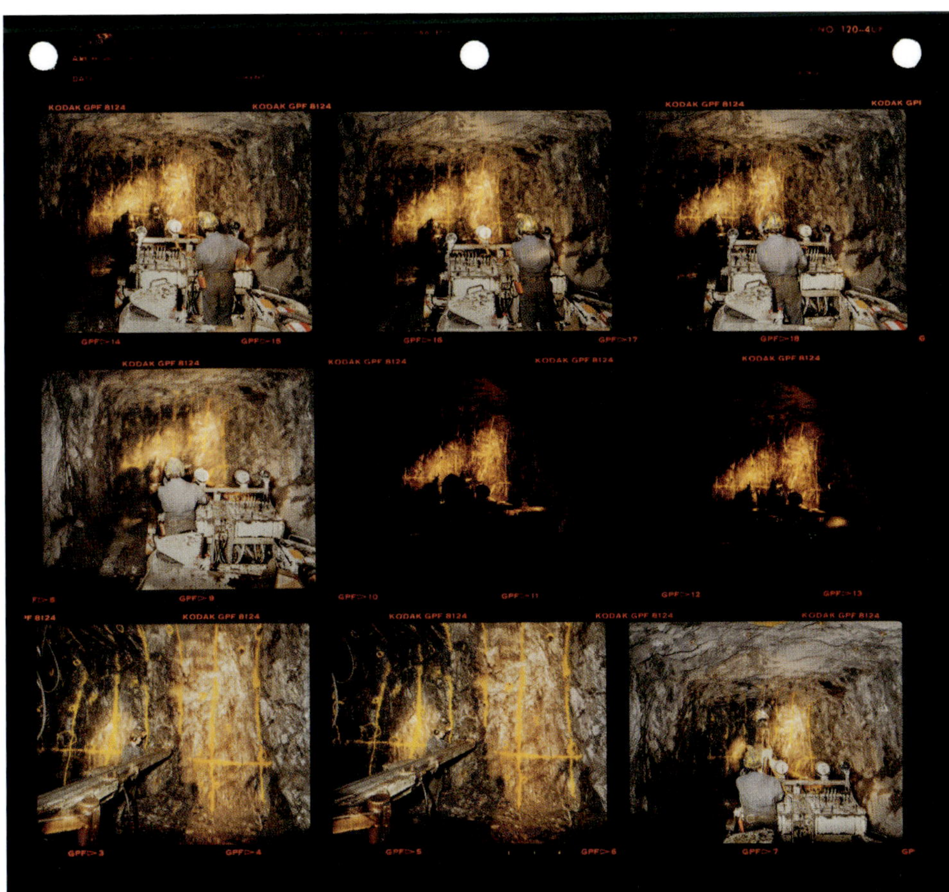

Edward Burtynsky, *Inco Commission* contact sheet 24, 1987

sheets. The images on some resemble those taken at the Kennecott Copper Mine, but others tell a different story. The underground shots on sheet twenty-four depict a hellish terrain in which the bright lights needed to see the walls of the mine create an eerie gold reflection.

RAILCUTS

Most of the railcut images were taken by Burtynsky in 1985. The railcuts themselves were made between 1881 and 1885 by some of the seventeen thousand Chinese men who came to Canada to work on the 250-mile western section of the Canadian Pacific Railway in British Columbia contracted by Andrew Onderdonk. The Chinese were badly paid and often worked in extremely dangerous conditions; approximately seven hundred were killed in work-related accidents.

The railway may have been a nationalist effort to unite Canada, but its construction was carried out using racist tactics. Burtynsky's images do not comment directly on the historical incidents behind the construction of the CPR, but they silently commemorate the Chinese who fulfilled the imperialist ambitions of people such as Onderdonk, who saved himself from bankruptcy by paying his workers one dollar a day out of which they had to pay for food and gear.

As in *Railcuts #5*, a number of these images–many taken from the other side of a canyon–show the thin line of cuts crossing between the rugged rock face above and below them. "This project is on track," Burtynsky wrote on April 22, 1985, because "of how it fits the compositional pattern I'm placing upon it. I allow about ¼ of the frame below the track & ¾ above. I find this allows for a sense of the scale as well as a format to contain those incredible rock faces."[17]

These compositions resemble the zip paintings by the Abstract Expressionist Barnett Newman, wherein a thin line is surrounded on either side by large blocks of colour. In such paintings, tension is created by

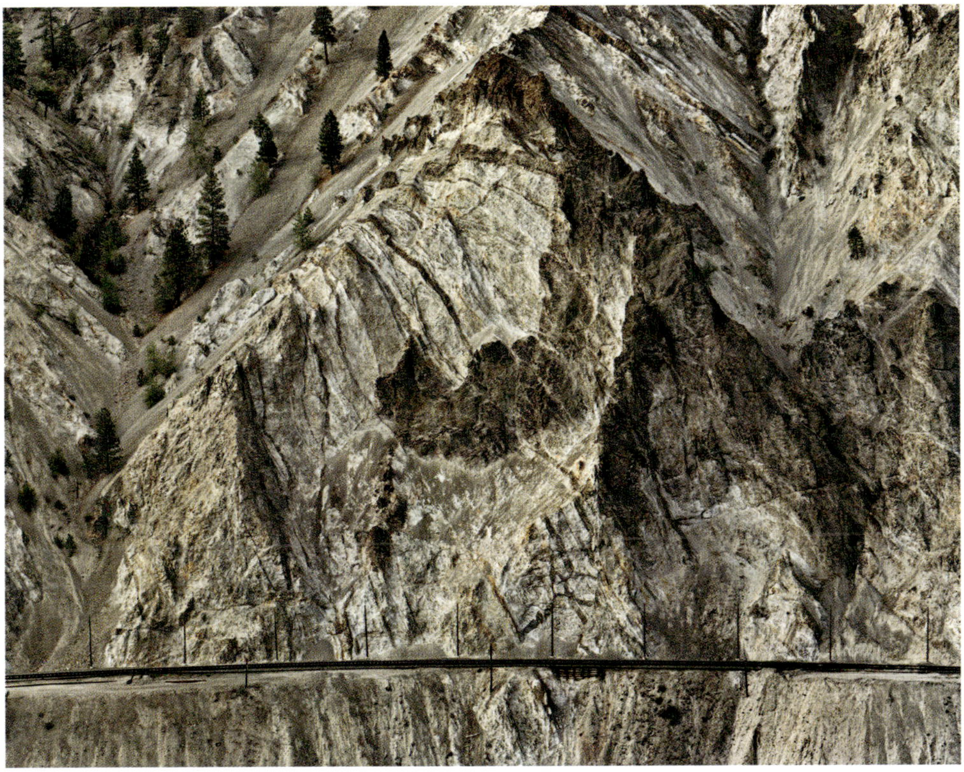

Edward Burtynsky, *Railcuts #5*, C.N. Track, Thompson River, British Columbia, 1985

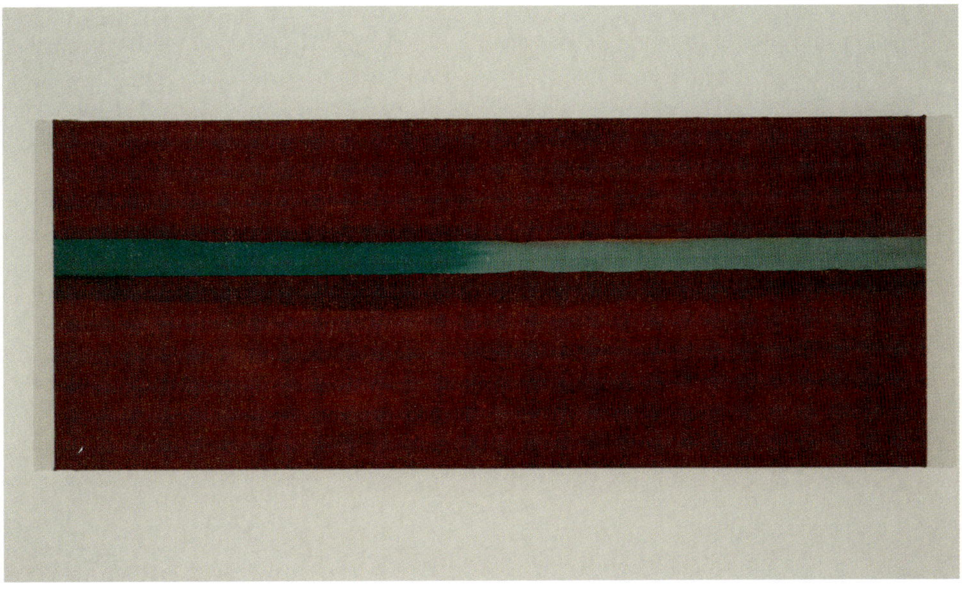

Barnett Newman, *Horizon Light*, oil on canvas, 1949. Sheldon Museum of Art

opposing forces. Burtynsky does something very similar in his photographs. The viewer's attention is focused on the narrow cuts while, at the very same time, the rock face above the cuts looks as if it could crush those lines at any moment. A different strategy is used in *Railcuts #14*, which shows a rickety ladder that would have taken the workers down to the surface they were to cut. Even getting to work spots was perilous.

Lori Pauli has pointed out, "Even in his choice of a title for this series, Burtynsky informs us that his photographs do not share an aesthetic agenda with earlier images of the railway such as Carlton Watkins' *Cape Horn Near Celilo* (1867). The title *Railcuts* evokes a sense of direct physical

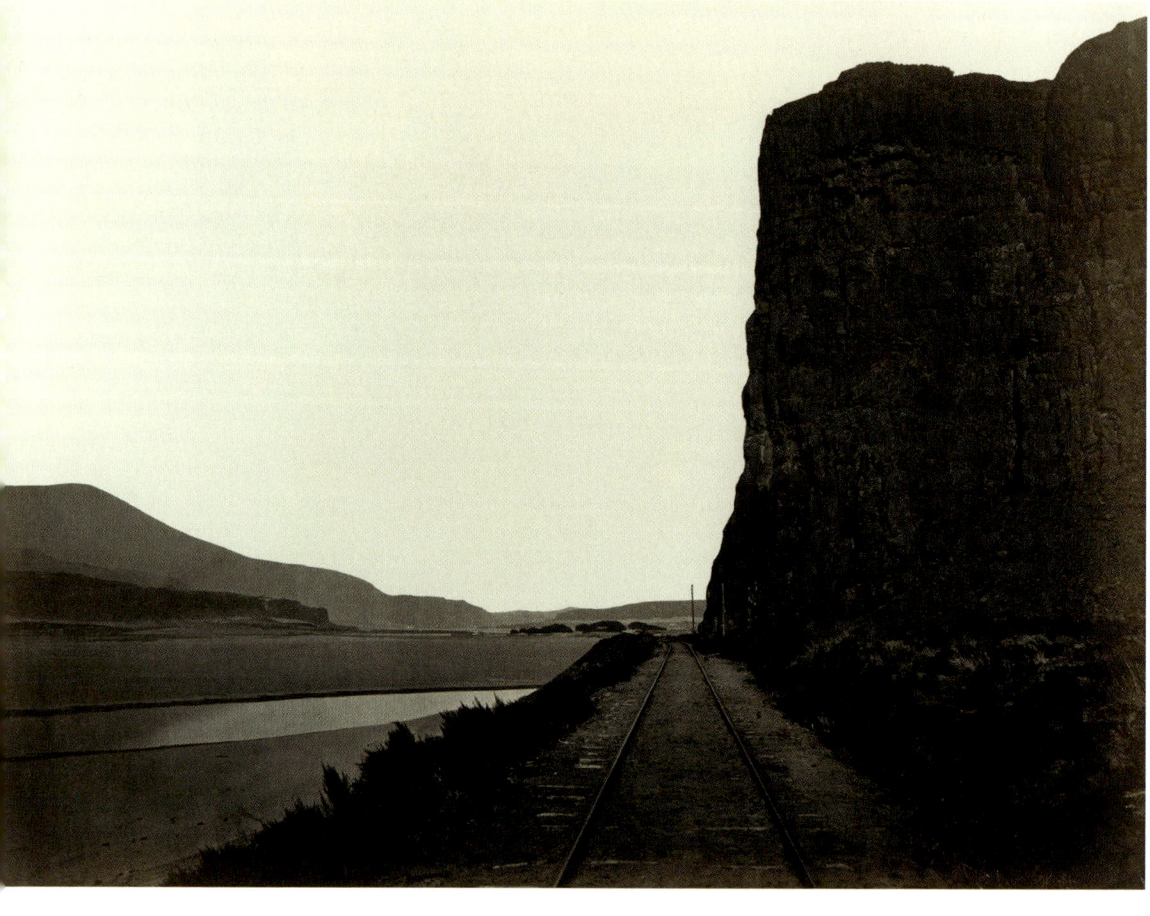

Carlton Watkins, *Cape Horn near Celilo*, Oregon, 1867. The Metropolitan Museum of Art

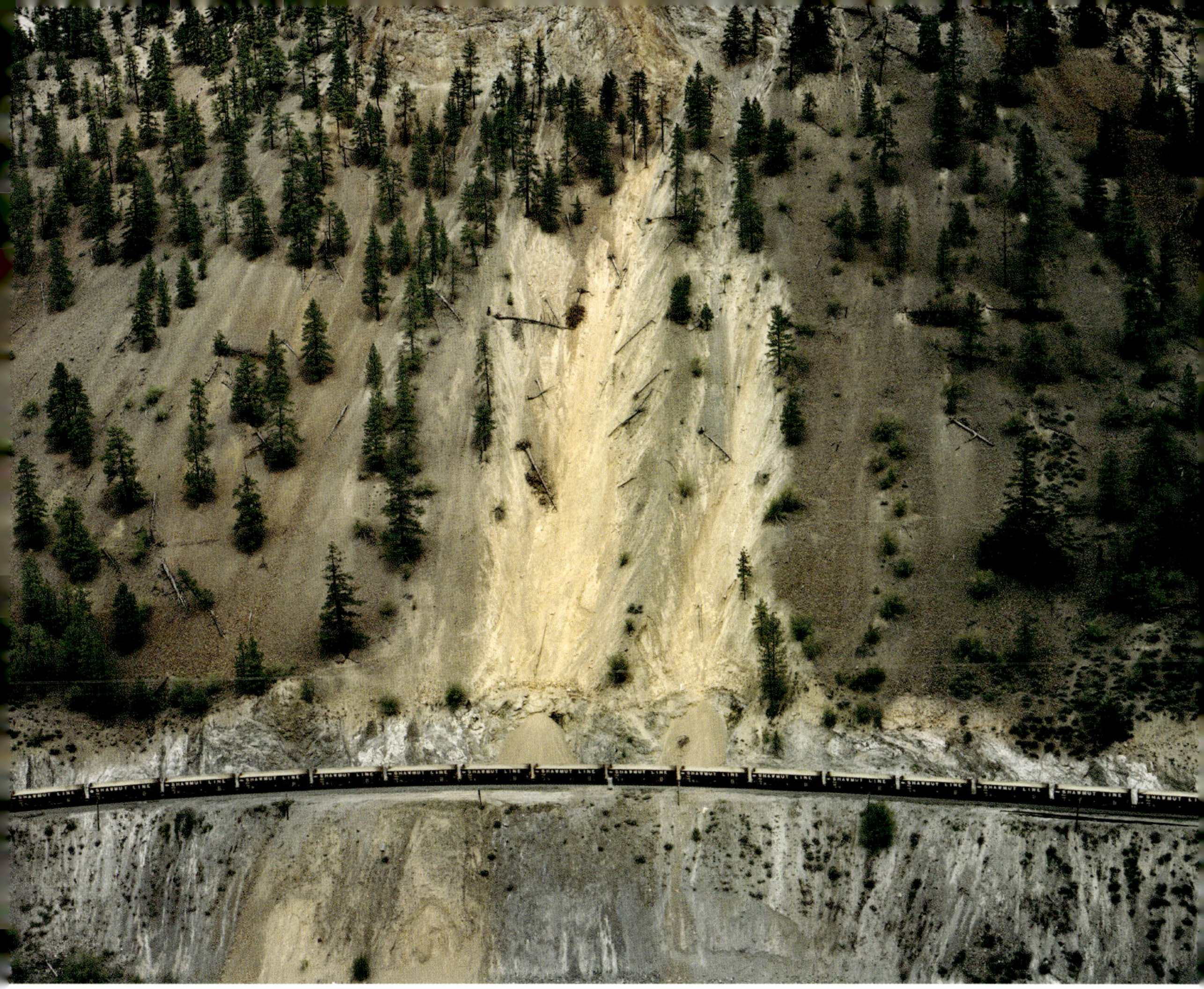

Railcuts #1, C.N. Track, Sikhist Provincial Park, British Columbia, 1985

contact with the land. Blasted rock-faces fill most of the frames in these images, and the tightly cropped views of the railway line seen head-on are strangely airless and even claustrophobic." For her, the photographs in this series "look like monochromatic colour-field paintings in soft brown, sand and white."[18]

For Burtynsky, *Railcuts #1* remained the key image in this series: "As it turned out, serendipitously, this train having arrived at that exact moment became a perfect metaphor for the scale of taking from nature. With the landscape matching the cargo, it appeared that the very mountain itself was filling up the train."[19] He had waited two days to get that shot.

MOUNT ST. HELENS

Burtynsky's images from 1983 of Mount St. Helens in Washington State are examples of one of his "asides." Three years before Burtynsky visited the site, the volcano erupted–the deadliest such event in the United States. Fifteen miles of railway, 185 miles of highway, 47 bridges, and 200 homes were destroyed; 57 people were killed. A debris avalanche, triggered by an earthquake, had caused a lateral eruption that considerably reduced the mountain's summit, leaving a one-mile-wide, horseshoe-shaped crater.

This celebrated disaster attracted the attention of several photographers, including Emmet Gowin and Frank Gohlke, both of whom took aerial photographs at the site. Gowin emphasized texture in his images and Gohlke the structure of the crater. David Maisel visited the St. Helens region the

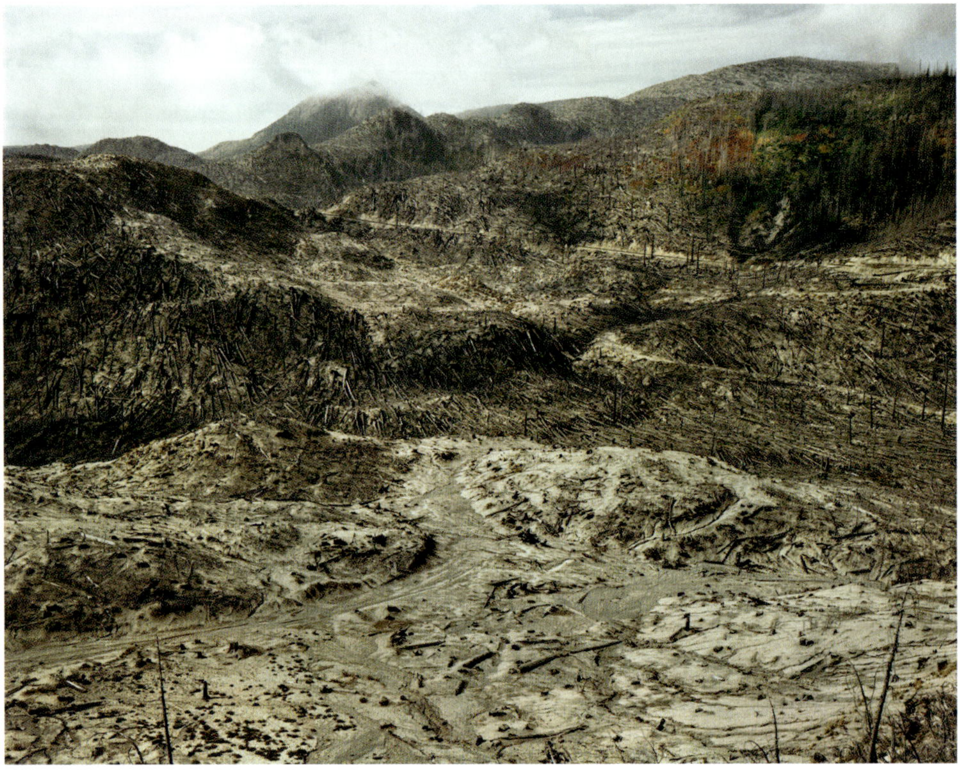

Edward Burtynsky, *Mount St. Helens Blowdown*, 1986

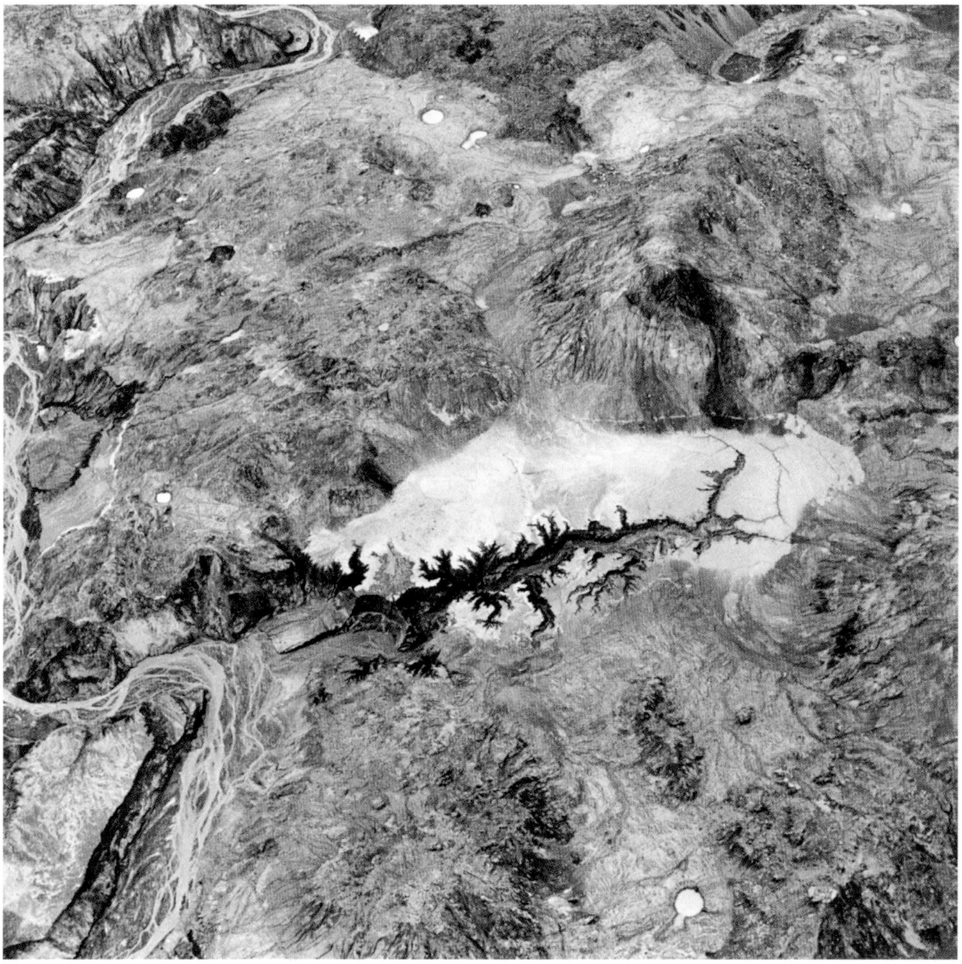

Emmet Gowin, *Toutle River Valley, Mount St. Helens*, 1981–82. Courtesy of Emmet Gowin

same year as Burtynsky, where Maisel took both aerial and ground images there. In contrast, Burtynsky, from a considerable distance, emphasized devastation by organizing his image into three parts: the ravaged, bleached landscape in the foreground; the desolate, brownish one in the middle; and the pale grey summit of the mountain in the background.

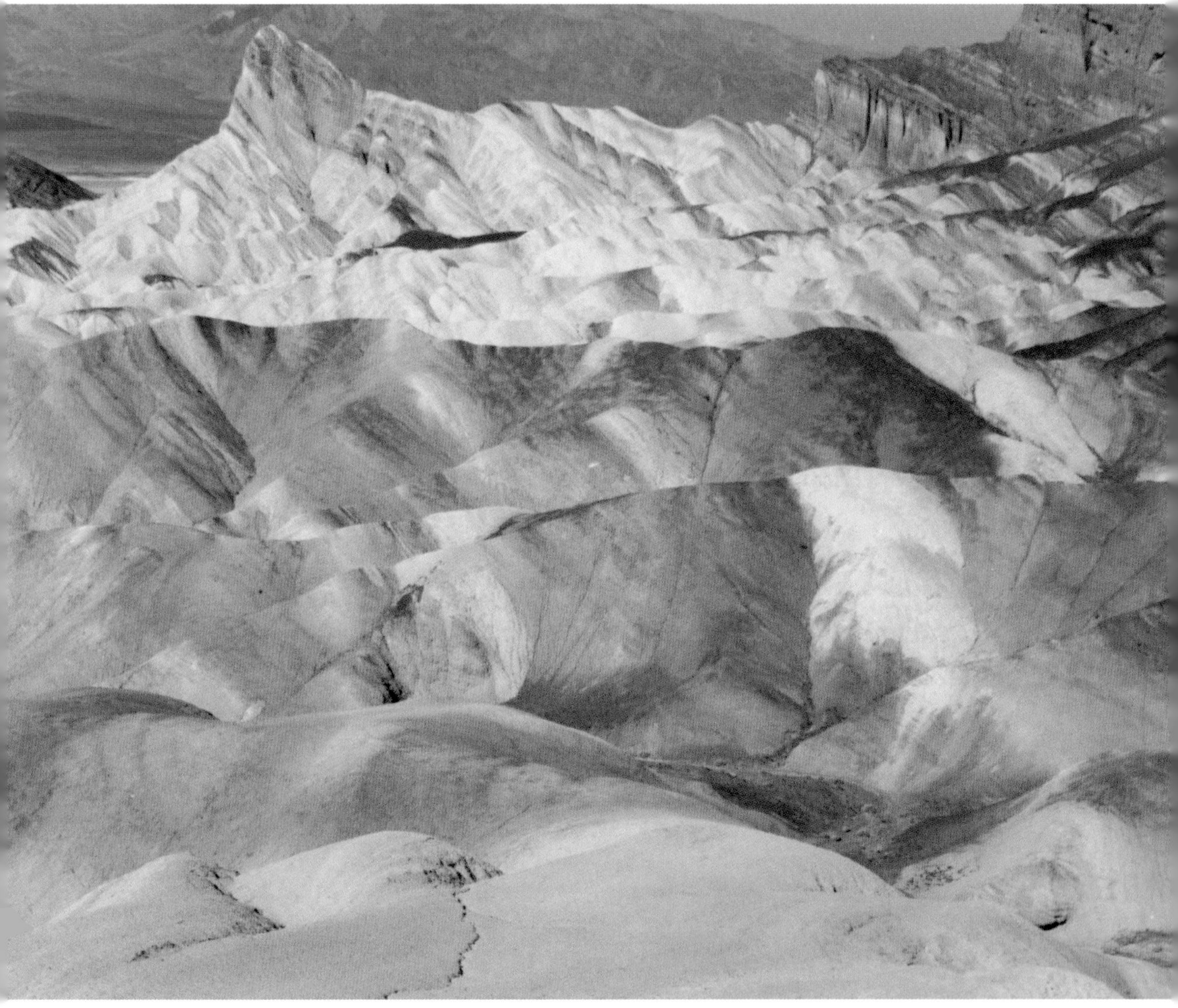

Edward Burtynsky, *Zabriskie Point*, 1983

THE DESERT

On October 3, 1983, Burtynsky wrote in his diary, “In the past two days I have been photographing the desert for the first time. It is quite a sight to behold. Some people don’t see beauty in the desert. I don’t understand.” But he found using colour in this setting difficult: “So much rust. I’ve been close to giving in to black and white several times.” He was very unsure about what he had shot at Capitol Reef (“The reason being that I had to work awfully hard to find [good shots]”) and questioned himself (“Am I looking for something that isn’t there?”)[20] His intricacy in capturing the desert is perhaps best seen in *Zabriskie Point, Death Valley, California.*

Burtynsky realized that the kind of landscape images he wanted to make posed considerable problems: “The kind of beauty I look for in nature does not occur that often. If I were looking for postcards, my film stock would now be depleted. These images are plentiful.”[21] The kind of images he wanted to make were rarefied.

He remained overly self-critical. On May 12, 1985, he had serious reservations about the *Homesteads* series. To him, these images seemed “anti-climactic to my mining work. I just fell into it, and it had spectacular qualities built right in. But this recent work has no such element . . . Where is the photographer in this work & what is he trying to say? The truth is that at this point I can only say that my eye & my intuition has drawn me to it & I’m not one to argue with those forces.”[22] For Burtynsky, his intuition led him in many directions. He learned to accept that it sometimes led him astray.

THE PIONEERS

In contemplating what he had achieved early in his career, Burtynsky was mindful of how he had during his time at Ryerson been influenced by “the early pioneers . . . [who] affected me in their directness and honesty”:

Robert Adamson, David Octavius Hill, Carlton Watkins, Darius and Tabitha Kinsey, and Francis Firth. He added others to his pantheon: Paul Caponigro "for his mind, his mood, Edward Weston, Robert Adams, and Minor White for the potentials in the thing itself, Paul Strand, and Walker Evans for a sense of the importance of document. Frederick Sommer for his intellectual constructions with the medium, and Emmet Gowin."[23] This compilation, although made in a spirit of humility, hints at the heights he hoped to achieve in his profession.

During a brief stay in France in 1984, there was a pivotal moment when Burtynsky realized that an artist had to pursue his own path, no matter the consequences. Entranced by his visit to the *art brut* Le Palais Idéal in Hauterives, a whimsical castle of grottoes created by postman Ferdinand Cheval, he reflected: "I felt his whimsy & his childlike joy in creating this palace out of mud & stones, and I knew he would enjoy having others partake of his creation, as I have. And that little palace has given him immortality. He must have had a healthy ego to carry out that project."[24]

Burtynsky understood he had put together a wide range of highly accomplished work–attracting attention to it, he found, could be a daunting task. His own ego would be severely challenged.

On May 1, 1985, he confided his aspirations and anxieties to his diary: "What value does what I am doing have . . . & am I fulfilling an obligation to make the most of my talents & potentials? I think that's all anyone can expect from an individual. . . . I make it a point to show as many people as I can my work. I can anticipate their response & I'm seldom wrong. In a way it tells me where the people are at. Most like photography & almost all are impressed by my work. It's a good feeling to know that. Now all I have to do is convince them to buy my work, to support future endeavours. That is the ultimate challenge and I'm not sure that it is worth the effort . . . I suppose I'm looking for someone who will say so."[25]

(1985–1990)

4 80 SPADINA AVENUE

Attracting attention in the highly competitive field of photography was for Burtynsky one step forward, two steps backward. His first exhibition after the Ryerson one was a joint show in May 1984 with Marcus Schubert, called *In the Keeping Room*, and was held at the New Image Gallery, a locale that often showed the work of Ryerson graduates in the west Toronto neighbourhood known as The Junction. The images on display by both men were, as the title hints, of taxidermy, although some landscapes called *Prescribed Burns* and a suite of anatomical studies by Schubert were also part of the exhibition, which ran for about three weeks. After its Toronto debut, the show opened for two months in January 1985 at the Presentation House Gallery in Vancouver. *Earthworks*, Burtynsky's first solo exhibition, was held in 1984 at Toronto's Moment in Time Gallery and the following year at the Kitchener-Waterloo Art Gallery.

From 1982 to 1986, Burtynsky sold or placed on consignment fewer than a hundred prints. In 1982, he sold a copy of the 1981 experimental landscape *White Snow (North of Kleinburg)* (renamed *Landscape Study #12*) for $30 and presented Rob Gooblar with a copy[1] (see p. 49). Further sales in 1982 amounted to $125. The following year, he took in $750; that sum included two copies of *White Snow* that sold for $175 and $125, respectively. (He also received a Canada Council for the Arts grant.) The following year the tally markedly improved: $12,000–the purchasers were the National Film Board and the Art Bank. In 1985, sales were down to $6,500.[2]

About this time, he also prepared a typewritten list of twenty-five prints (limitation of twenty-five each) for sale from images made between 1981 and 1984. They were available in two sizes (16 × 20 and 20 × 24 inches). Framed, they were priced at $225 and $275, respectively. For more information, would-be purchasers could telephone Burtynsky in Toronto or Wilson Baxter, Jeannie's mother, in Hamilton.

TORONTO IMAGE WORKS

Burtynsky, the boy, had been a risk taker: he had demonstrated considerable grit in raising money through an assortment of jobs. In 1985, his back was against the wall. He had managed to drum up limited showings at galleries, but he was not earning enough money from selling his photographs to support himself. Determined to find a way to finance his career, he decided to shake things up. He realized he did not "want to live a freelance, erratic lifestyle. I wanted something that was reliable, something that could allow me an ongoing stream of income."[3] An escape route presented itself. He had learned a great deal at the Ontario Hospitals Association about creating a photo lab and decided to establish one on his own.

In the early 1980s, there was no space in Toronto where photographers could print their work, especially in colour. As Jeannie Baxter recalled, her husband "set up" drum printing [a wet chemical developing process] in the basement of the house they were renting on Springmount Avenue. "So, we had a pretty rough basement and he had to get plastic and coat all the ceilings and floors; he also had this cocoon room, which is where he worked on drums. And he did that for six months. And he had really inconsistent results and he was banging his head against the wall. Plus, he was going nuts because he was working in the basement all day, every day."[4]

In Buffalo, the photographer Jorge Campos had launched a darkroom rental facility where photographers could print their own work.[5] Burtynsky began escaping his cramped darkroom and driving to Buffalo; he also had friends who travelled there. Jeannie recalled,

> And he thought, "I can do [the same]." So, he started Image Works [at 80 Spadina Avenue] and starting Image Works wasn't easy because he had nothing. . . . And when he went to the bank, it wanted everything: collateral, firstborn male, the whole nine yards. Ed approached some investors . . . Anyway, he started it up.[6]
>
> We got all our friends together. It was like, *take out your frustrations, let's knock down the walls*. Ed was really good at talking people into stuff because of his enthusiasm. He was keen and he was young, and he had nothing. So, you know, people were pretty turned on by that whole concept of someone having a vision. And so, he conceived of the idea, and it started off fairly small. We had two thousand square feet and the dark rooms and a studio, and he was the only person along with another production person.

For Burtynsky, there were some advantages: "[I]t gave me the chance to experience new products just as they were coming on the market." Once again, he felt like the eleven-year-old boy who had found photography magical. "[I] wasn't worried about how much things cost or whether I was wasting material. Suddenly, I was a kid again."[7]

Morden Yolles, the celebrated structural engineer, restaurateur, and dedicated photographer, was an early client. In a discussion about the formation of Toronto Image Works, he said, "I was getting interested in printing in colour and I couldn't do that in my basement. And I talked about this with Ed, and I think it was through that meeting he started talking about the need for a facility where people could go and print in colour."[8] Yolles also made suggestions to the contractors about the layout of Image Works; he and Wolfgang Schubert, Marcus's father, were the principal investors of the first (of two) stock offerings.

The business plan emphasized the wide range of working spaces to be available: "12 darkrooms . . . [and other] print-finishing areas"; there would be an "extensive array of services including paper and chemicals for sale, custom printing, slide duplicating, processing of 8 × 10 contact sheets, and C-41 processing. User memberships could be purchased and there would be "a Gallery exhibiting not only works created on the premises but works with outstanding photographic merit as well."[9]

Located in a space at 80 Spadina Avenue, which had been leased in August 1985, Toronto Image Works opened its doors in January 1986, and became a meeting place where photographers met and assisted each other. Slowly, a customer base was achieved and a community established. Ed and Jeannie even considered installing an espresso bar. Sometimes, there would be as many as twenty people hanging around and, when the space became foggy, Burtynsky reluctantly banned smoking.

He had smoked his first cigarette at the age of eight and had become a heavy smoker. Afraid that the stress of running Image Works might lead to five packs a day, he joined Smoke Enders, quit, and never looked back. Dedicated smokers would congregate on the fire escape of the rear of the building. Jeannie recalled: "We had all sorts of different people who hung around. We had regular customers who would even sleep on the couch and, you know, spend almost a whole evening at Image Works. And at some point, when the business wasn't so great, we talked jokingly about turning the dark rooms into brothels and making some *real* money."[10]

Burtynsky was operating the machines; he was running film; he was printing. Some days he would do all-nighters and then continue right through to the next day: forty hours, forty-eight hours straight. Jeannie said,

> Well, at first customers didn't come. I was working in advertising at the time, and I would be here, and we had crazy hours. We were open from like eight in the morning till midnight. What were we thinking? We would stand there at the counter waiting for people and nothing. I mean, a few people came out of interest, but then Ed had this really good idea of offering free nights of printing. And there's nothing like a freebie to get people to come and check you out . . . people started coming and the word spread that it was very reasonable. And then he had cheap deals at the outset, and it started to go, but it was . . . a hard slog for many years. So, we kind of dropped out of the picture with friends and family for about ten years. And we worked like maniacs. And I joined full time after a couple of years. But before that, I would work my advertising job and then work nights at the counter. We knew every place you could have dinner after eleven p.m., every place. And it was slim pickings in those days . . . And then it started to go but it took a long time for us to make any money. It just was really hard going. Anything you made you reinvested back into the business.[11]

For Burtynsky, Image Works "was kind of my ballast. I was making some money on grants. I was making some money on sales. But the first two years, I didn't even take a salary. There were no funds left over every month for me to take a salary."[12] The idea that Image Works could provide financial security was fast disappearing.

Bad turned to worse when the economic crisis struck early in the 1990s. At the same time, Spadina Avenue was ripped up to put in a light rail transit line. This made Image Works inaccessible to customers, especially commercial firms. "Patrons wanting to drop off their films could not do so." At that juncture, Burtynsky recalled, "set up this courier service to go to their studios to pick up the film to bring it to me. That was costing me a lot of money. I was in survival mode." Difficulties with rental properties compounded a fraught situation. Burtynsky and Baxter owned several, and suddenly they could no longer ask for sufficient rent to pay the mortgages. He informed his landlord at Image Works: "If I pay you, I'm going to lose my business. Can you delay for a year? And he did. And then I went to Kodak and made the same arrangement with them."[13]

There was one positive side to the turmoil. Anticipating that the start-up of Image Works would eat up a considerable amount of time, Burtynsky, before the launch, had spent six weeks in 1985 travelling to various spots in Canada and the United States, taking photographs that he could print in his just-about-to-be-opened establishment.

RAPHAEL BERNSTEIN AND BANKS

Early in 1986, the investment banker, philanthropist, and collector Raphael Bernstein decided on a project he wanted to pursue. "Since I was in the investment business, I dealt with a lot of banks," Bernstein recollected,

> and I always wondered why banks looked the way they did. Whether they were old buildings or new buildings, they always seemed to have a very specific identity. Of course, if you're going to hire a distinguished architect and pay a lot of money for a building, you've got to have deep pockets. And back in those days, that's where the deep pockets were. So, I thought it would be interesting to investigate the history of banking buildings both in Canada and in the United States. So, I discussed this project with the Museum of Fine Arts in Houston, where I was a trustee, and after extensive conversations, they seemed to warm up to the idea.

Bernstein wanted to create a book on bank architecture based on *Court House: A Photographic Document* that had been published by Horizon Press in New York in 1978. Although edited by the British architect Richard Pare, the Canadian architect and philanthropist Phyllis Lambert was a full partner in this endeavour. A group of photographers from across America were commissioned to photograph courthouses and then the results were published.

The financier travelled to Ottawa, where he asked curators at the National Gallery of Canada and the National Film Board for names of photographers who could do large-format architectural photography in colour. Bernstein recalled: "And a couple of people pointed [Burtynsky] in my direction."[14] He also remembered that "Burtynsky's name just sort of rang a bell with me. . . . And it was the name Toronto Image Works. I identified with Ed Burtynsky because I thought that if somebody could run a business and be a promising photographer at the same time, perhaps there was some special talent that could be helpful to us. And so, I volunteered to go to Toronto Image Works and to meet Mr. Burtynsky. I did not tell him why I was coming. I just dropped in for a little chat with him."[15]

"And so, he comes back from Ottawa," Burtynsky reminisced, "bumps into me at the studio, and wants to see my architectural stuff. It so happens I had some because I was trying to do camera for hire. He looks at my portfolio of some commissions and says, 'I'm thinking of doing something similar to what's called the Courthouse Project.'"[16] Bernstein recalled: "He showed me some of his work that was on the wall . . . it became rather evident to me that here was indeed a special sort of a fellow who promised to go a long way and why shouldn't we help him?"

"Would you be interested?" Bernstein asked. "You're a young guy. You've done some work in this area. And I like that you have a mind attuned to business. Your management has to work. Everything has to work for it to succeed. Would you be interested in doing this project?"[17]

When Burtynsky agreed to go ahead, Bernstein asked: "Would you like to come to New York? I'll fly you. I'll pay for your ticket to come to New York and meet with me and the curators."[18] (Susan Wagg, the Montreal architectural historian, chose the buildings and Anne Tucker, the photography curator at the Houston Museum of Fine Arts, the photographers.)

That meeting was a great success, as Burtynsky recalled: "He flies me down, puts me up at the Carlyle Hotel. And he takes me into this room, and he starts to explain to me that what they want me to do is be the negotiator for the deal for all the photographers. So, they gave me all the parameters of what they wanted and all that. So, then I set the conditions, the day rates, the copyright ideas and everything. So, I gave them all my ideas, like right then and there, about what I thought would be fair. I wrote them all down. They took it all down. To my surprise, that was what we got written up and every photographer accepted it. So, it was just like that it became the deal for everyone."[19]

As Bernstein recalled,

> One of the first things that Ed did was the old headquarters of the Canadian Imperial Bank of Commerce in Toronto. He chose the ceiling of the bank. That location had some big problems because the lighting inside the bank had all kinds of magical colours due to the stained-glass windows. Ed explained to me later that he had gone to someone in the bank–a member of the echelon–and told him that he needed to get into the bank when it was dark and when there was nobody working. He would like to bring in his own lighting. And could he please get special permission to do that? Well, he lived up to the advance impressions that I had of him because he did get permission to do exactly that and made an absolutely stunning picture that we chose to use for the cover of the catalog, which we called *Money Matters: A Critical Look at Bank Architecture.*
>
> And it was such a stellar job and under such unusual circumstances, that Ed ultimately got chosen to do all the difficult buildings in the project. I remember he climbed up on a neighboring skyscraper in Minneapolis to get the Federal Reserve Bank there, and he did the same thing in Dallas and Houston. His activity for us was not only beautiful but very productive in terms of getting the show put together. He also volunteered to use Toronto Image Works on a very satisfactory basis

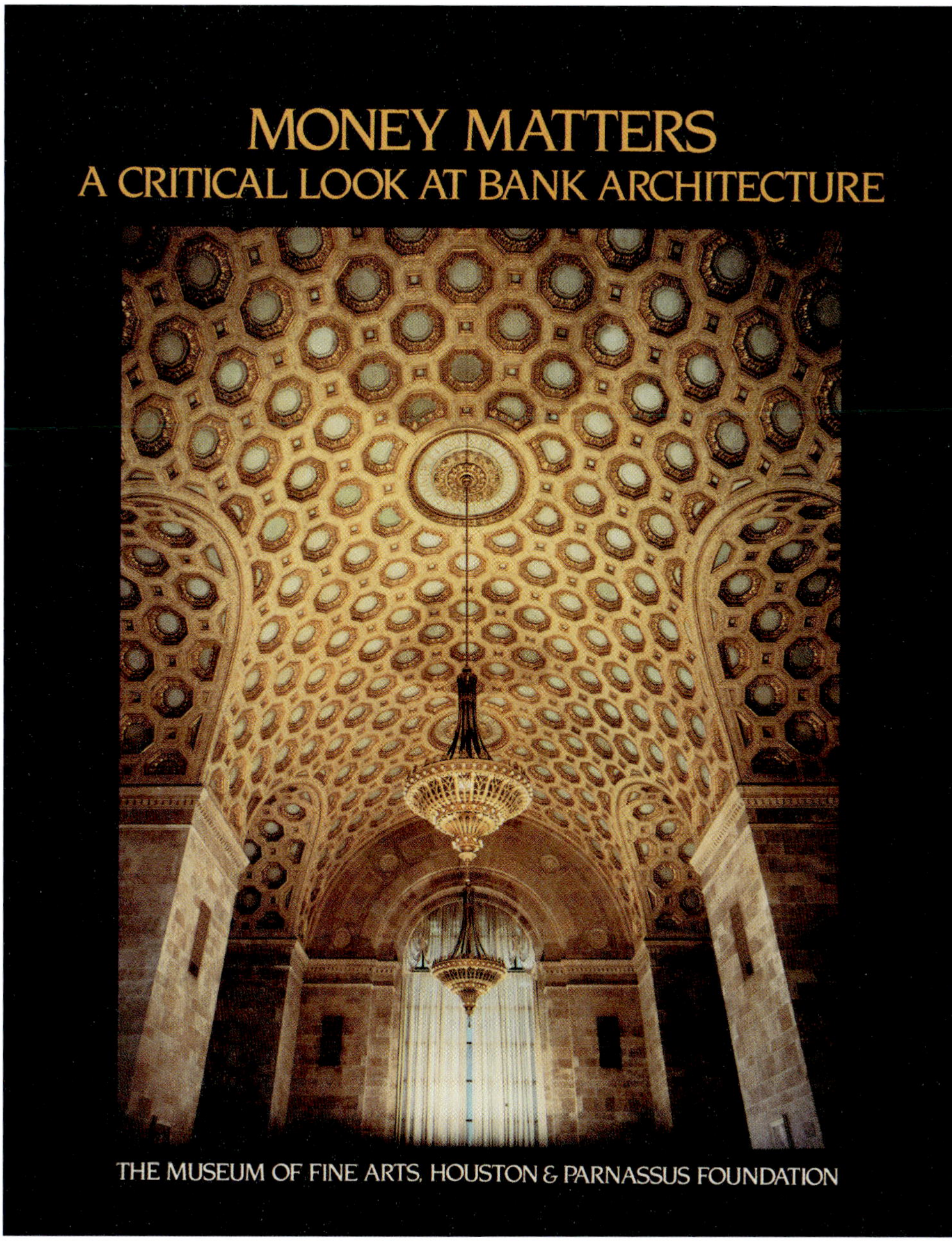

Dust jacket, *Money Matters*, 1990

> to help print photographs that were done by other photographers in the project.[20]

Bernstein placed great confidence in Burtynsky not only because of his artistry but because he was a problem-solver: "Some of the photographers that we picked needed babysitters. It was like changing diapers."[21] Many of the photographers were far more seasoned than Burtynsky–and so he was astounded at the authority given him. The exhibition opened in Houston and then travelled to Washington, Montreal, Chicago, and Vancouver before finally reaching the Royal Ontario Museum in Toronto.

The *Money Matters* exhibition was reviewed by Abigail Foerstner in the *Chicago Tribune* on April 5, 1991: "Architects' brick-and-mortar interpretations of banks as symbols of security and authority have scattered classical facades and steel-framed monoliths across North America for two centuries. Unleash upon this cultural pastiche 11 artists commissioned to photograph 56 bank buildings in the U.S. and Canada, and you have 'Money Matters: A Critical Look at Bank Architecture,' on exhibit through July 28 at the Chicago Historical Society." For her, Burtynsky's photograph of the ten-year-old Republic Bank Center (now the NCNB Center), Houston, was impressive:

> [His] surreal colour skyline of Houston suggests a futuristic city that is beautiful and powerful but unapproachable. A maze of streets and parking lots in the foreground of the picture seemingly blocks the way to a dreamlike empire of skyscrapers where sunlight is reflected in gold and bronze.
>
> In general] the photographs underscore a major theme of the exhibition in exploring the roles banks convey through their architecture. But the interpretive freedom granted the 11 photographers gives the exhibit its visual and historic strength. It covers nine periods of architecture, including Greek Revival, Victorian, Art Deco, and postmodern bank buildings.[22]

When the exhibition eventually reached the ROM, Burtynsky was outraged by the poor presentation there, especially as Bernstein had offered to underwrite the cost of staging it well. Burtynsky told the Toronto curators: "You could have advertised it. You could have done all kinds of stuff. You didn't. That's a lost opportunity."[23]

Reflecting on his contributions to *Money Matters* and its overall success, Burtynsky realized that this project had offered him a welcome change in direction: "I went from large, deep holes to tall buildings. I wanted to see if I could carry over the stylistic and conceptual approaches [I] developed while photographing mines . . . to buildings."

He had become, as he claimed, "the darling of the project."[24] In her essay in *Money Matters*, "Where One Stands and When One Stands There," Anne Tucker agreed:

> Assigning Edward Burtynsky to photograph skyscrapers involved . . . an intuitive leap. [He] had not previously photographed tall buildings. Rather he documented railcuts and open-pit mining excavations. . . . In both series, he surveys vast, man-altered landscapes, reducing their chaotic complexity to coherent, visual images. Coping with the gigantic scale of this industrial architecture created by miners and railroad engineers prepared [him] to approach towering skylines of 1970s boom towns such as Toronto, Houston, and Minneapolis.

Tucker also noted how Burtynsky "sought locations from which the bank was the apex of a pyramid, with the city falling away from its sides. He wanted it to appear rooted, as if its mass had grown out of the city." Commenting on the photographer's penchant for photographing near sunrise or sundown so the colour densities blended, she analyzed the image of the Republic Bank Centre: "the warm, yellow-crimson light of sunrise . . . heightens the colour of the bank's red granite exterior, bathing its neighbors in the same hue. Thus, the building's colour, as well as its height, signifies its dominant presence."[25]

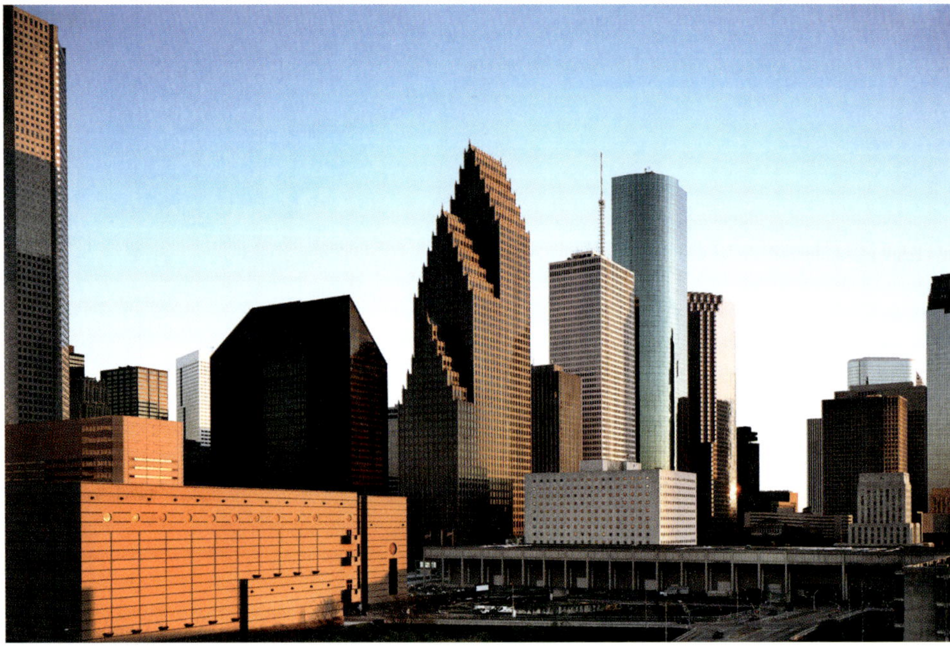

Edward Burtynsky, *Republic Bank Centre*, 1986

Overall, *Money Matters* was a smashing success. Bernstein reflected, "So that's how I first encountered Ed, and that was the project that put him on the walls of quite a few museums, both in Canada and in the U.S."[26]

In December 1986, just as the *Money Matters* project was under way, Bernstein purchased thirteen prints from Burtynsky for $3,900. That same month, the financier persuaded the Larry Miller Gallery in New York City to give the photographer a show (*Mines and Railcuts*); twenty-two works were sent there on consignment. In 1988, the Art Gallery of Houston bought copies of all twenty-two of Burtynsky's bank photographs. Bernstein also enthusiastically promoted Burtynsky among his friends and business colleagues.

When he met the photographer, Bernstein beheld a young entrepreneur very much in his own mould. Image Works "was taking all his energy, but his soul wanted to be an artist. And I think it took someone with some outside perspective to let him do both."[27] Soon afterward, when Burtynsky was again crestfallen and struggling to find new directions, the older man, in a fatherly way, offered further support.

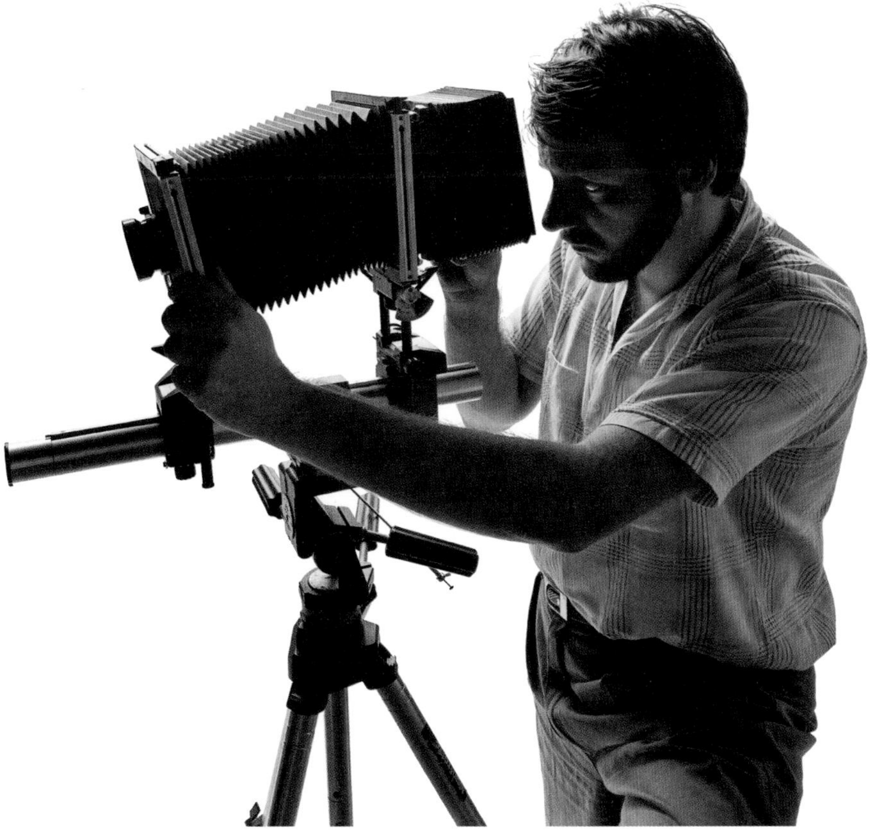

Edward Burtynsky, c. 1988. Photographer unknown.

(1988–1993)

5 IN PURSUIT OF RUINS

The *Money Matters* project had offered Burtynsky some relief from the tribulations of running Toronto Image Works. The publication in 1990 of the related exhibition catalogue gave him his first taste of how important book publications could be in fostering his career. He had also formed a strong bond with Raphael Bernstein.

Further good news was his first major exhibition organized by the Canadian Museum of Contemporary Photography: *Breaking Ground* opened at the Art Gallery of Hamilton in April 1988 and then circulated across Canada. His images of railcuts, open pit mines, and homesteads were on display to a much larger audience than ever before.

In her commentary written for the catalogue, Martha Langford astutely observed:

> Of the railcuts, mines, and homesteads, Burtynsky has spoken through his photographs in a rich, descriptive visual language. In 1988, it may be disconcerting to be drawn still to a beauty seemingly driven by expansionism; to be seduced, in effect, by the colonization of 19th century values. What is clarified in us by Burtynsky is a timeless fascination with those values and their monuments; a fascination with photogenic corruption; a fascination with photogenic tenacity; a fascination with pure photographic expression.[1]

Despite some breakthroughs, Burtynsky was still saddled with running Image Works and dealing with the myriad financial headaches that came with it. The business was also eating up his time–he was not free to explore new subjects.

NICHOLAS METIVIER

The bleakness in which Burtynsky was stuck was relieved by a glimmer of hope. Carol Tannenbaum, an avid collector of photography together with her husband Howard, volunteered to act as Burtynsky's agent. Although she did not have gallery space in Toronto, Tannenbaum specialized in marketing works by her artists to corporate clients at their offices. At an event held by Tannenbaum, Nicholas Metivier, a director of the Mira Godard Gallery, dropped in. He said that he "walked into a meeting room and there were these photographs of railcuts. And I went to Carol. I was very taken with them, not because it was photography. I didn't care. What I cared about and what fascinated me was the approach to this subject that the artist had taken and the quality of the work itself. And the abstraction in the work. That's good consistent work. I'd like to see more of it."[2] Tannenbaum handed him a copy of the *Breaking Ground* catalogue. Then she phoned Burtynsky to tell him of Metivier's reaction to the railcuts images and to suggest that he get in touch with him immediately. Burtynsky hesitated: "I was really busy. I was sleeping only five or six hours a night. I was losing money, and I was letting people go . . . I delayed getting in touch with him for two months. And finally, I said to myself, I should look him up."[3]

When they did meet, Metivier told Burtynsky that he was in the process of persuading Mira Godard to add photographs to their inventory. This was not an easy task, but Godard told Metivier that she might, under the right circumstances, be open to the idea.

DOUG CLARK

Bernstein and Metivier inspired Burtynsky to stick to his guns in pursuing his career as an artist-photographer. While Bernstein was the patron who opened a number of doors for his protégé, and Metivier provided launchpads that introduced Burtynsky's work to collectors eager to buy his work, it was Doug Clark who provided much needed moral support.

Clark, a photographer and photography curator, moved from Edmonton to Toronto at the age of thirty-six in 1986. As Burtynsky recalled:

> Doug arrived at my lab with his usual energetic personality and immediately brought his print production to my lab. My first impression of him was that he was not of the mild mannered, soft-spoken prevailing character of my fellow Canadians–myself included. He seemed to have the character of a boisterous American, something not everyone back then appreciated. Personally, I found it charming and could always tell when Doug came in. No matter where I was, his explosive laughter would suddenly erupt–about something clever or funny a staff member or customer had said–resounding throughout all corners of the lab.[4]

Burtynsky had never been shy about making the most of any opportunity that came his way, and constantly looked at various ways to advance his career. Inwardly, however, he remained deeply apprehensive. When he and Clark became friends, Burtynsky voiced those doubts to him. In response, his friend told him, "I would say you're on a good track, you're doing something, you've already been doing it for ten years. And people like it. Your work is steeped in the history of photography, it's steeped in modernism. Just keep making it, just create a universe so big that nobody's going to be able to ignore it."

There was one issue on which Clark held a strong opinion. He instructed his friend that "if you're going to get anywhere in the world, you've got to be a good speaker." He "pushed" Burtynsky into his first big speaking gig at the Ryerson Lecture series. Burtynsky, mindful he was following in the footsteps of some of the world's most celebrated contemporary photographers, was "nervous as hell."[5] That event was such a resounding success, however, that from that point on he rarely ever experienced stage fright.

ROCK OF AGES

Commissions were still hard to come by. In 1991, for example, Burtynsky was one of six photographers invited to contribute to *Mosaica: Photographic Explorations,* a book of days published by the Ukrainian Resource and Development Centre in Edmonton to celebrate the centenary of Ukrainian settlement in Canada. Four photographs by him were published.

Burtynsky remained despondent about his future. Whenever Bernstein was in Toronto, he would call in at Image Works. At one meeting, the photographer informed Bernstein: "If it doesn't work out in five years, and I can't make a go of it and keep doing my work, I'm going to have to give up being an artist and I'm just going to have to run this lab."[6]

Bernstein countered: "That would be not only unfortunate for you–it would also be unfortunate for the world if you did that."

"I'm just being eaten alive I can't find room to breathe," Burtynsky responded.

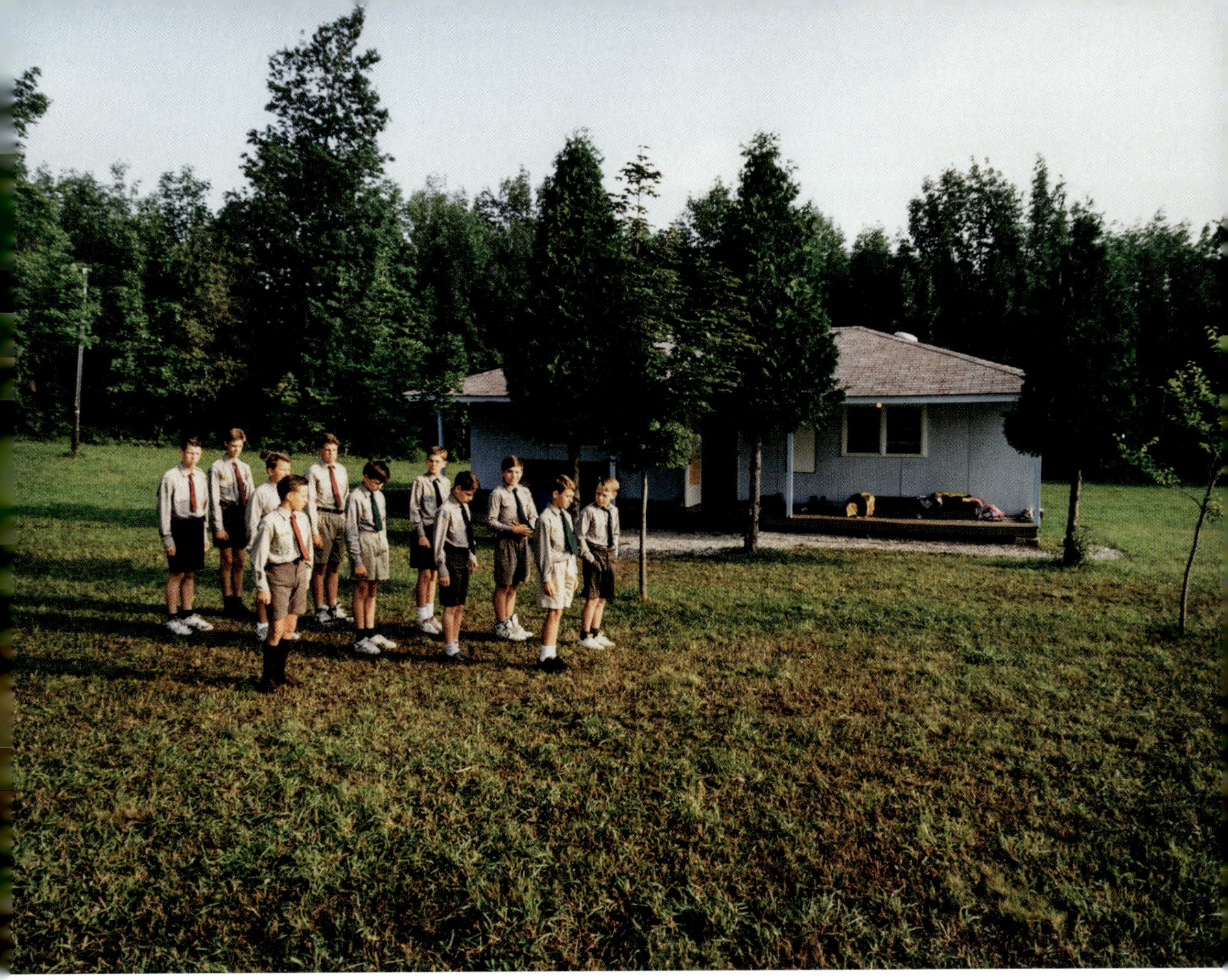

Edward Burtynsky, *Ukrainian Summer Camp #2*, 1991

"If you were going to do something right now, what would it be?"[7]

Put on the spot, Burtynsky fessed up: "I've always been interested in quarries. I have never seen one. I've seen mines, but I've never seen a stone quarry. I imagine in a stone quarry, blocks are taken out of a pit one block at a time. Those structural walls–they'd be like inverted architectonic walls. Almost like inverted architecture because they're moving a block at a time. . . . That's an image in my head. I've never seen one. But I think it would be fascinating to explore."[8] Burtynsky had photographed some mines as if they were abandoned amphitheatres; and so, he imagined, quarries might offer similar opportunities.

The fascination with quarries had been specifically generated by the work he had done on *Money Matters*: "I remember looking at buildings made of stone, and thinking, there has to be an interesting landscape somewhere out there because the stones had to have been taken out of the quarry one block at a time. I had never seen a dimensional quarry, but I envisioned an inverted cubed architecture on the side of a hill."[9] This was the first time, Burtynsky recalled, one of his series starting "purely with an idea."[10]

Bernstein obviously understood the link between banks and quarries and told Burtynsky, "I think that's a great idea. Okay, here's the deal. Go out and make a series, and I will buy ten of them from you. I don't know [how they'll turn out], but I'm going to buy ten. At least you'll get your expenses back, and we'll see if anyone else likes those pictures."[11]

Burtynsky travelled to a few quarries in Ontario and Quebec, but he found them unsuitable: they were neither large nor grand and did not excite his eye. "When I was in a quarry somewhere in Quebec on the border of Ontario and Quebec, I was saying to myself, *Oh, they're really small. I want big quarries*." When he described the situation to Bernstein, his friend told him he also had been researching quarries: "If you need big quarries, go to Barre, Vermont. Just get there, you'll find them."[12] That night, Burtynsky drove five and a half hours to Vermont. "The next morning, I wake up in Barre and then I start trying to figure out how to get into the quarries."[13]

All the quarries were operated by the Rock of Ages Corporation, which gave him permission to photograph. Burtynsky also made a point of gaining the trust of the guards at each site. He had a portfolio of some of his mining pictures, in which he was wearing a safety hat and steel-toed boots. He told the guards that he had worked as a miner and had photographed them but had recently become fascinated with quarries. "Then they'd look at the pictures of all the mines that I had done, and they'd let me in. They had become curious about what I would do."[14] After his first visit to Barre, Burtynsky took five additional trips to Vermont to explore more quarries–granite and marble, active and abandoned–in Barre, Rutland, Proctor, Danby, and Rochester.[15]

Still buried under the strain of running Image Works and dogged by fallout from the recession, he needed to make the best possible images: "I would find the right location and then light up a hash spliff just enough to shift my perception and dial down the noise in my head yet not altering enough that I would be unsafe standing on edges of the quarries on broken and unstable rocks. Worked like a dream and interestingly the images from these shoots were the ones that Nick Metivier saw and gave me my first commercial show in Toronto. The sales from those shows in the early '90s . . . are what I needed to stave off bankruptcy. Those images restarted my career without question."[16]

The *Stone Quarries* exhibition at the Mira Godard Gallery in 1992 was a resounding success. About fifteen of the large prints (40 × 50) were snapped up at $2,000 each. Within a year or so, forty to fifty more were sold. "All of a sudden," Burtynsky recalled, "corporations, banks and accounting offices and individuals loved them. This success allowed me to cover my losses. I could keep things going. I could breathe again."[17]

In *Canadian Art,* Robert Stacey observed that Burtynsky had "aimed his lens down into a cubic vortex that suggests both a post-Dantean inferno and a building site in Babel." Looking at these images,

> . . . it eventually dawns on one that, although signs of human interaction are all around us, there are almost no people there. Even when it is plain from the working equipment and johnny's-on-the spot that the quarry is still being operated, the overwhelming impression is one of desertion. This effect is increased by the rich palette of corrosion and mineral stains (rusts and blacks, greens and purples, taupes and oranges) that paint the ghostly pale walls and floors and dye the water at the bottom of abandoned pits and tailing ponds an opaque, milky green. These strangely beautiful effects not only mark the passage of time but signify the slow poisoning of the Earth. The irony of this beauty-in-ugliness is no less chilling for occurring to us as an afterthought.[18]

Stacey was one of the first critics to talk of "beauty-in-ugliness" in gazing at Burtynsky's images, and he made the valid point that responding to them is a two-step process.

CARRARA

Eager to capitalize on the success of the Vermont images, Burtynsky told Jeannie, "I think there's these other quarries. If I can go for three weeks, there's these quarries in Carrara [in Italy] that I think would be a great compliment to what I've done in Vermont." When Nicholas Metivier asked for the rationale behind this project, Burtynsky replied, "because I want to marvel at even more marble. The Carrara marble quarries are white, and I want to photograph white."[19]

Burtynsky knew nothing about setting up an international shoot, and he did not speak Italian. He asked other photographers for information and learned from a fashion photographer client of Image Works about Industria Studio in Milan. He approached them: "Do you know of someone who could help me scout? Who could get me into the Carrara marble quarries? Who could speak English and act as my interpreter?" His contact in Milan provided him with a name immediately: "I have the perfect guy for you."[20]

As a teenager Silvio Repetto had explored photography in company with his father. While a student at the faculty of architecture at the University of Florence, he decided to become a photographer and moved to Milan to study at IED (Istituto Europeo di Design). He graduated in 1991, and then worked as an assistant at Industria Studio.

When Burtynsky phoned Repetto, he informed him: "I want to hire you. I want you to take me around Carrara."[21] Repetto agreed immediately. Before he arrived in Italy, Burtynsky was under the impression he could approach one company–as in Vermont–and then gain access to all the sites. He said,

> It wasn't like that at all. There's three mountains, probably like 80 companies. All little, little companies. So, I get there, and I realized that my concept of how this was going to work was all wrong. But Silvio is an interesting guy. He thinks on his feet.

> So basically, these sites were all small. We would drive up to these quarries. I'd park. And while Silvio is chatting in Italian, I'd walk around scouting the whole thing out because it's usually just a small area. And then I'd go up to him and say, "Yay or nay."

If Burtynsky said yay, Silvio would continue negotiating. "And we went to quarry after quarry. I think I got turned down once. That was my first international shoot. And when I realized I could do this, I said, 'Okay, now the world is my subject.'"[22] He felt rejuvenated.

For the critic Jonathan Bordo, the Carrara photographs resemble paintings. "Some of the Carrara photographs make the quarry appear as a smooth white surface, so flat that one looks horizontally at the surface as much as one would look down on it." He also noted that Burtynsky pays "homage to the art of the Renaissance with a number of photographs that invoke the illusion of deep pictorial space–a quality invented by Renaissance artists."[23]

On February 24, 1994, the *Toronto Star*'s art critic Christopher Hume, just before the opening of Burtynsky's second exhibition at Mira Godard that included fifteen large photographs of the Carrara quarries, perceptively described how "[t]hese great pits, gouged out of the earth's surface during the course of decades, centuries, even millennia, are monuments to man's dominion over nature. They are also metaphors. The granite and marble that comes from these sites are a source of strength and beauty, but the quarries themselves are a symbol of man's vast destructive capacities."

Hume perfectly understood what Burtynsky was attempting:

> Though Burtynsky uses colour, his pictures could not be called colourful. Rock, after all, tends to look dull and grey from a distance. What makes stone visually fascinating are the infinitely varied patterns of its surfaces. More than anything except scale, Burtynsky's photos are informed by his profound appreciation for surface and texture. Quarries introduce a further layer of visual interest in the contrast

> between the natural formations and the rigid geometry imposed on them by industrious extractors. Here are whole mountains carved up, chunk by chunk, block and block, until nothing remains but rubble and empty space.[24]

Some years afterward, Burtynsky wanted to do a trade with the Rock of Ages executives–a print for some granite slabs: "I met with them, and I brought ten of my favourite pictures of the quarries. Most of them were of abandoned sections of the quarries. So, I rolled them all out–and they were big, 40 by 50 inch prints–and the whole board was there. And they were totally silent." After an uncomfortable, pregnant pause, Burtynsky asked: "What do you guys think?"

> Someone–I think it was the director of the quarry–finally said: "Why would anybody want one of these?" I'd never really had it put to me that way. I said something like, "Well, because they're interesting pictures and they talk about our taking a resource from the land. It's about that accumulated taking" . . . And he replied, "These just aren't interesting for us . . . These are sorry sights for us, because these are places where we can't get any more stone out of the ground, and we have to go somewhere else. They're the end of the line for us."[25]

A compromise was reached when the company's board suggested that Burtynsky photograph their "latest stuff with the best quality ore using the most up-to-date equipment. So I photographed it with an 8 × 10 camera and ended up making a big mural for them for a trade show."[26]

NEGATIVE SPACES

The quarries are man-made ruins but, unlike sites such as Chichen Itza, Angkor Wat, or Machu Picchu, they are not places where individuals once lived. Their architecture is never a building up but always a tearing down. Burtynsky pointed out that "in architectural appearance they are articulated in negative rather than positive space. This can best be seen in the *Rock of Ages* series, where the channeling and blasting-out of the blocks of stone have created imitation cliff-palaces, like faux Mesa Verdes, uninhabitable habitats-complete with ladders reaching from ledge to ledge."[27]

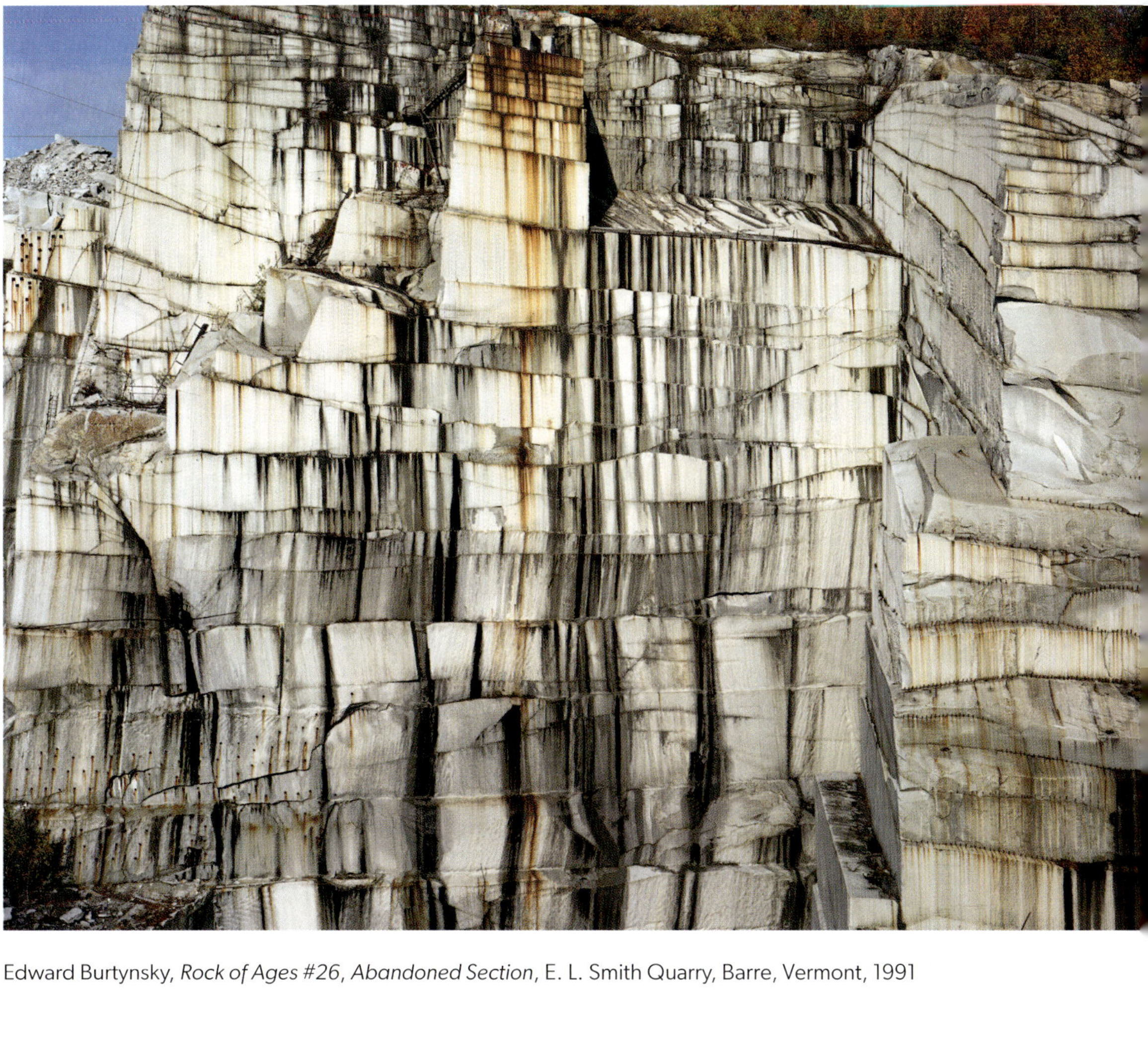

Edward Burtynsky, *Rock of Ages #26*, *Abandoned Section*, E. L. Smith Quarry, Barre, Vermont, 1991

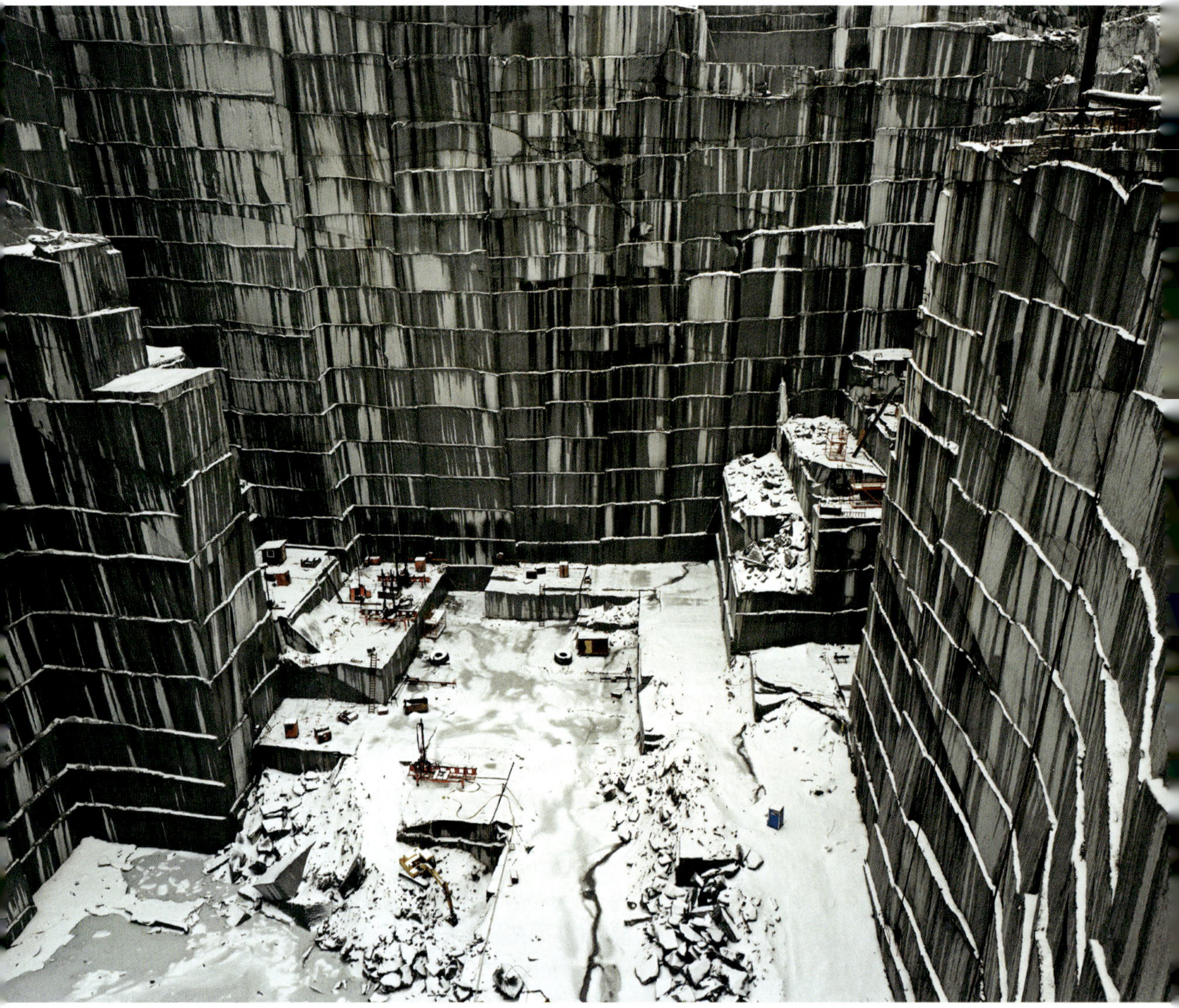

Edward Burtynsky, *Rock of Ages #15*, Active Section, E. L. Smith Quarry, Barre, Vermont, 1992

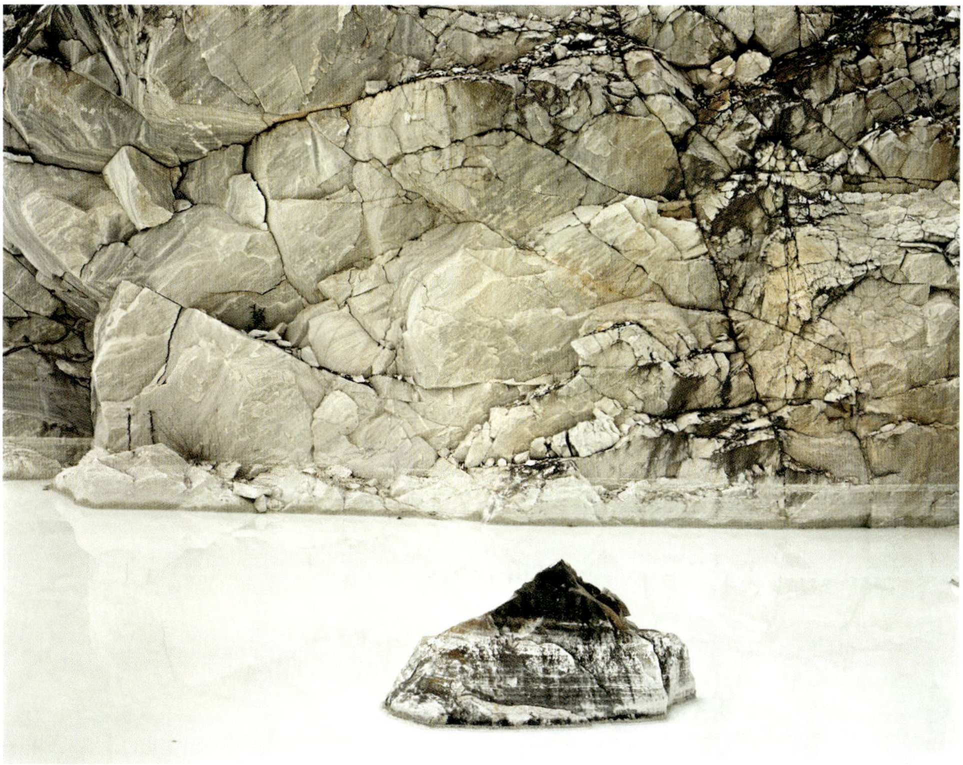

Edward Burtynsky, *OMYA #51*, Calcium Carbonate Waste Area, Proctor, Vermont, 1991

The E. L. Smith Quarry in Barre yielded the finest images from the *Vermont* series. Its white walls in the Abandoned Section demonstrate how much had been removed from the facing; in the Active Section, its spectacular depth and architectural remains can be seen. *Calcium Carbonate Waste Area*–despite its formidable title–inserts a gentle tranquility into the *Vermont* series. The stone fragment looks like a small sculpture residing peacefully in a Zen garden.

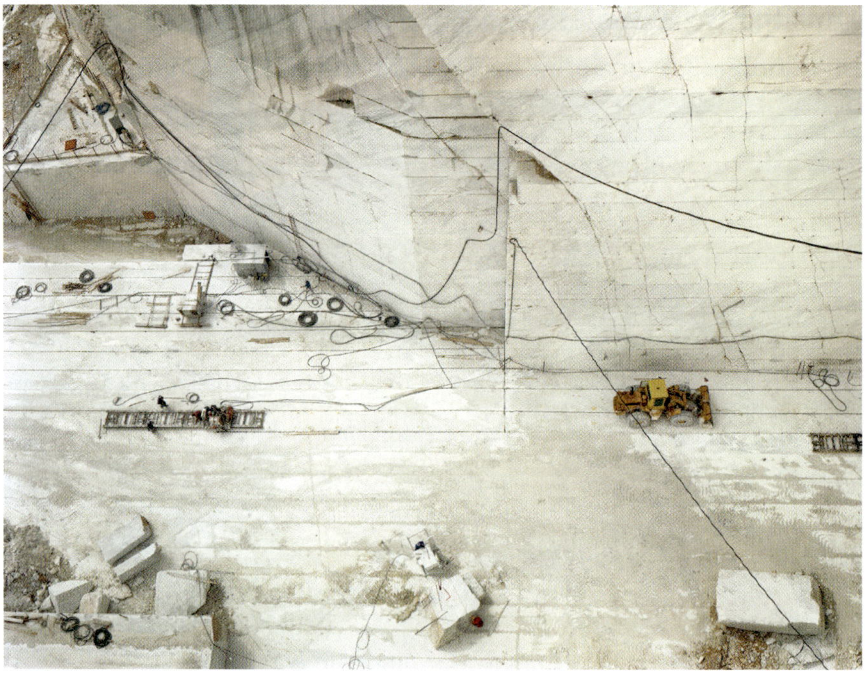

Edward Burtynsky, *Carrara Marble Quarries #24* and *#25*, 1993

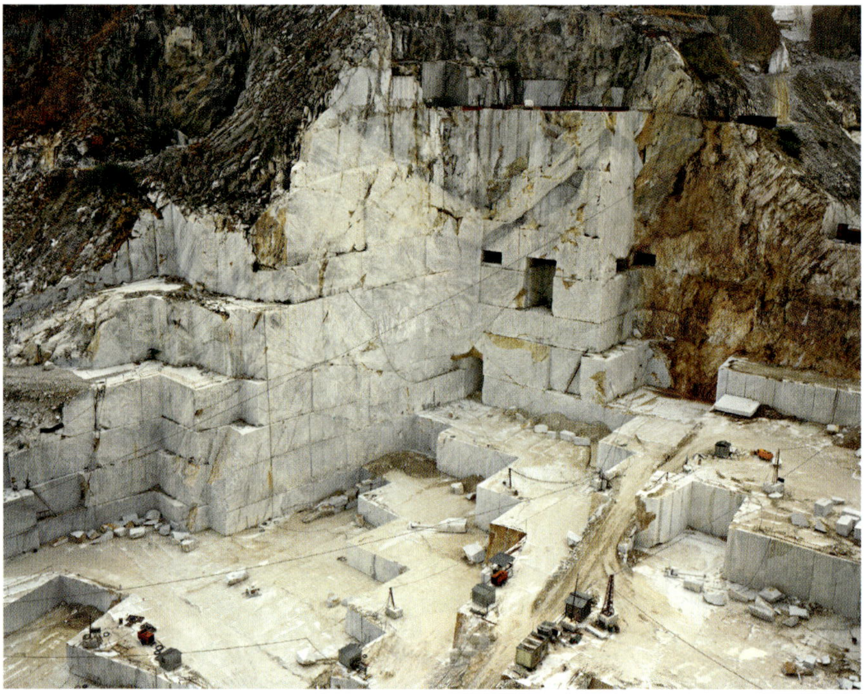

Edward Burtynsky, *Carrara Marble Quarries #4*, 1993

There was not as much white at Carrara as Burtynsky had hoped, although white predominates in *Carrara Marble Quarries #24* and #25. The architectural remains in *Carrara #4* resemble the site of an ancient ruin. Triangular and square shapes in *Carrara #21* form a compelling abstract pattern. In addition to looking at the quarries in isolation, some of the images in this sequence, such as *Carrara #24*, emphasize the quarry's place within its landscape.

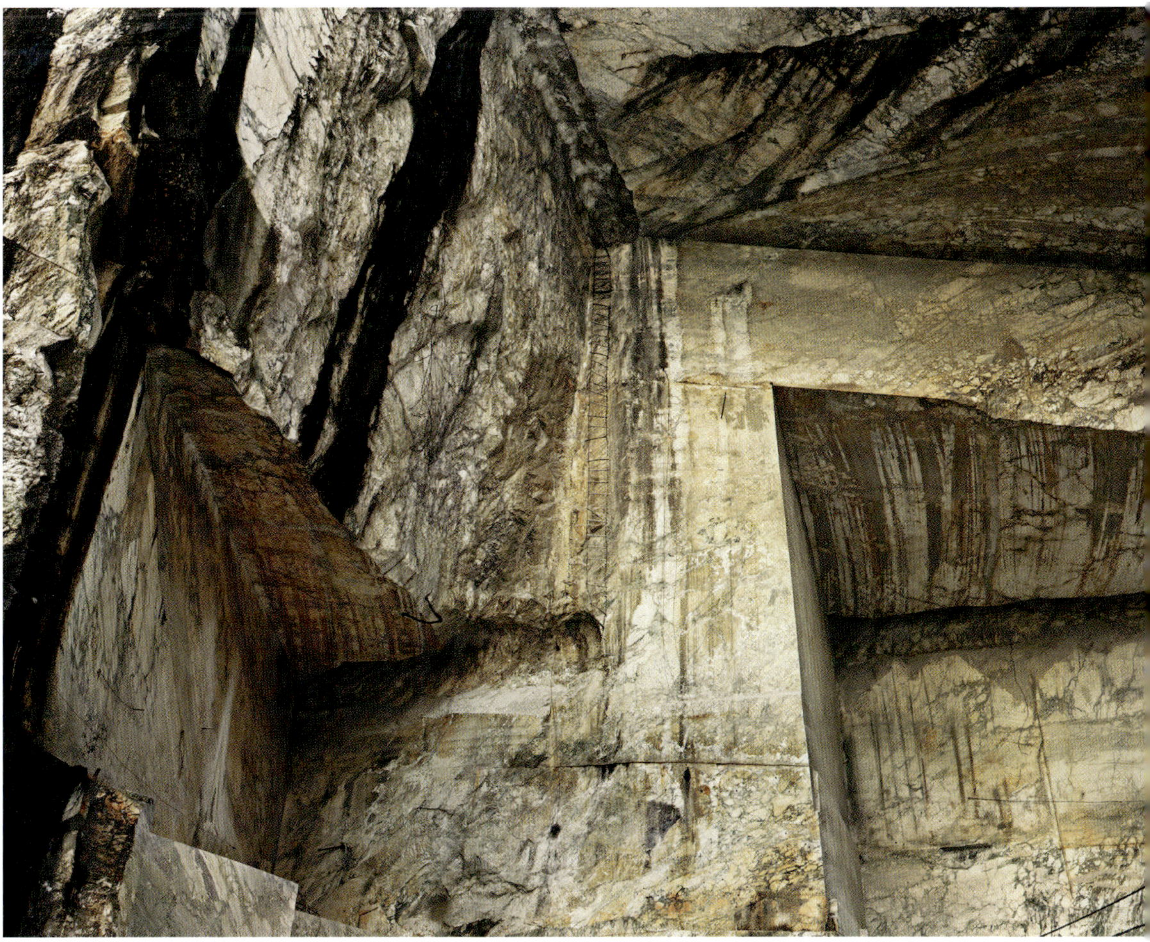

Edward Burtynsky, *Carrara Marble Quarries #21*, 1993

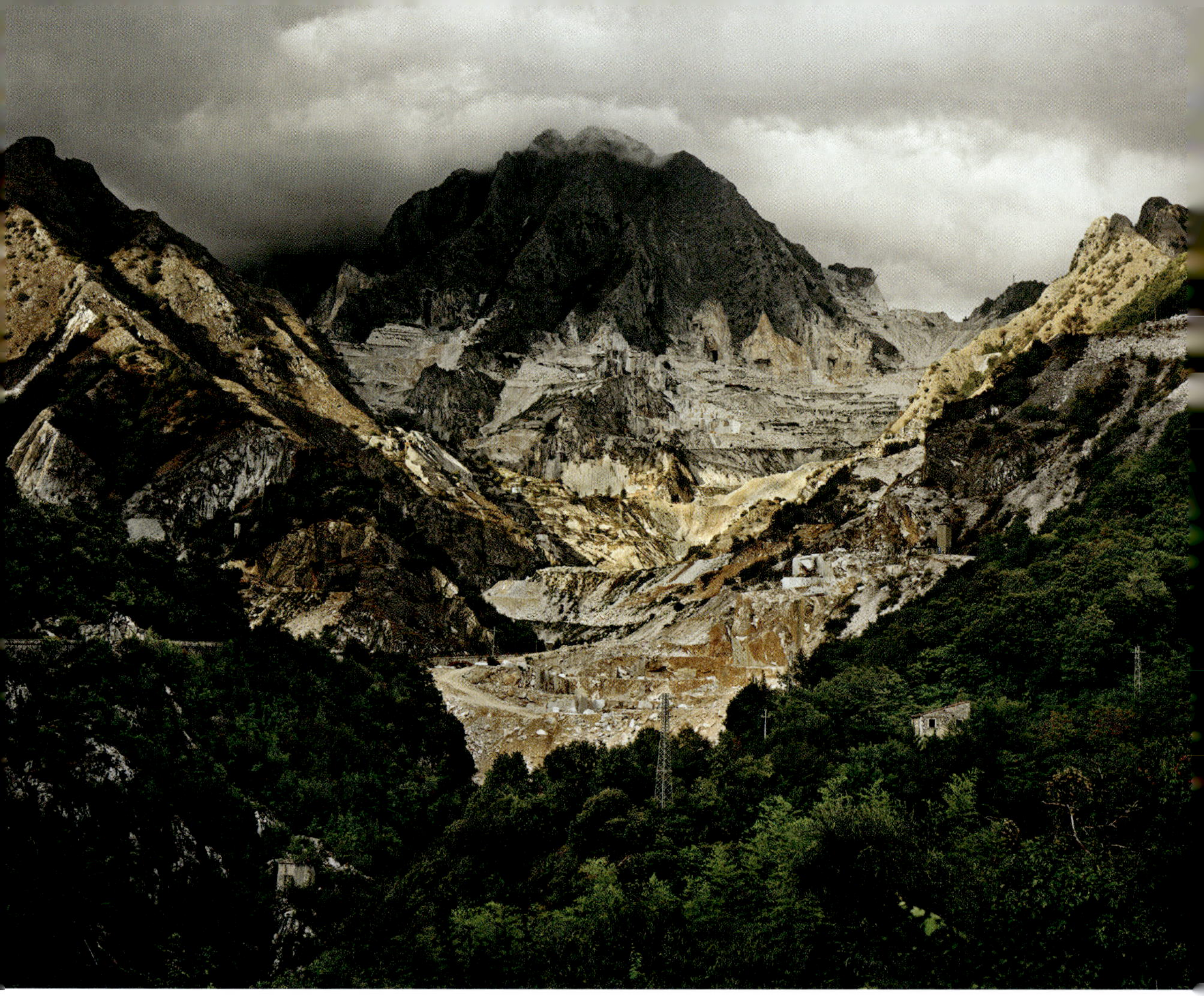

Edward Burtynsky, *Carrara Marble Quarries #20*, 1993

The magazine *Dwell*'s take on these images emphasized the link between architecture and ruins:

> For his *Quarries* series, Burtynsky turns his attention to the negative architecture of dimensional quarries. To many, these images serve as gaping testaments to the magnitude of our environmental impact on the earth, but they also reveal a sympathy between man and nature, a visual dialogue between imposed and naturally occurring strata. "There are many things the rock face can tell us about ourselves," says Burtynsky. "[It is imprinted with] our methodologies, our desires, our needs. It's an interesting metaphor for how technology seems larger

> than life, larger than our own lives." In this way, Burtynsky relays a vast system of actions and reactions–of human imprint, both positive and negative–through a keen and focused lens.[28]

A ruin is a relic–something left behind. Some early habitations are venerated because they are reminders of the past, especially of the achievements of vanished civilizations. They are tangible proofs of accomplishment. The ruins in Vermont and Carrara are dissimilar. Portions of these sites may resemble ancient sites, but the likenesses are superficial. They are extractions that destroy the integrity of the natural world. No one ever inhabited them. Having examined "monuments," Burtynsky next focused his attention on another kind of remnant–residual landscapes.

(1994–1999)

6 EARTHLY REMAINS

From 1991 to 1993, Burtynsky concentrated on monumental quarry sites. Then he changed course by examining three apparently dissimilar topics that would become *Tailings* (1995–1996), *Urban Mines* (1997), and *Tire Piles* (1999). The task he set himself was to make these new subjects as compelling and dramatic as the two previous series, and he recalled the commitment he had made to himself at Frackville: "This is what I have to do."[1] He would revisit not only his earlier interest in mines and the damage they wreaked on the environment but also extend his reach to two other examples of man-made devastation.

He was no longer chained to his desk. Problems in running Image Works had not vanished but, buoyed up by the success of the sales of the quarry images, he was able to take extended trips to Sudbury and Elliot Lake in northern Ontario, to nearby Hamilton, Ontario, and even further afield to Westley, California.

SUDBURY AND ELLIOT LAKE

The images of mines in *Breaking Ground* were an integral part of that project. It is not surprising then that the first topic on Burtynsky's new agenda was the Inco site in Sudbury. From 1984 on, he had been intrigued by the innate possibilities offered by that locale. Tailings are the waste stream left after a mineral is extracted from a mine; tailings ponds are dam facilities for the safe storage of tailings–they allow water to separate from the tailings. This interaction (oxidization) can create eerie colour combinations.

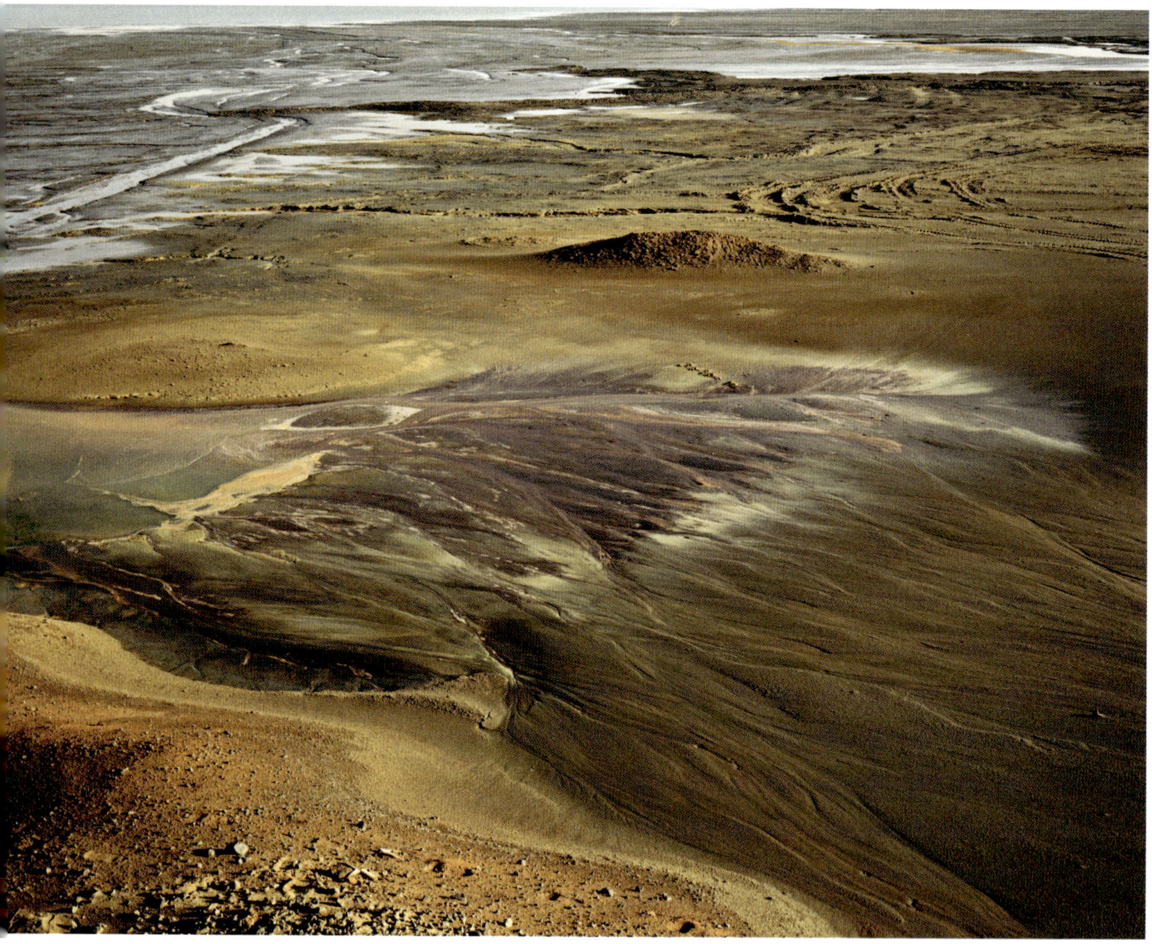

Edward Burtynsky, *Mines #15,* Inco Tailings Pond, Sudbury, Ontario, 1985

In 1985, Burtynsky had taken a photograph that showed the workings of a tailings pond: the dull purple, grey, and green sludge is juxtaposed against the brighter browns and yellows that confine it. The result is an abstract where two colour fields are in vivid contrast.

A decade later, in 1995 and 1996, he investigated the tailings themselves. In the new images he took at Sudbury, there are no pacific interactions. The intense red and orangy, lava-like tailings invade the black and already devastated landscape. Christopher Youngs observed that "there is a Fauvist beauty in a red river flowing over an ocher landscape . . . [on] closer inspection . . . [it] suggests the River Styx in Dante's *Inferno*."[2] The nickel tailings images are not in any way heightened, Burtynsky pointed out: "That colour orange is a result of the fact that in the mining process they don't remove the iron from the ore . . . they don't bother taking out the iron because it's not profitable enough to remove it. The iron oxide gets flooded into the tailings as waste–what you're looking at [are] basically rivers of rust."[3]

The geologist Harry Knight accompanied Burtynsky on one of his forays into the scorched landscape known as the Sudbury Basin, an enormous prehistoric impact site near Sudbury that measures 17 × 37 miles wide.

> When the meteor hit millions of years ago it fractured the earth's crust, allowing mantle magma to flow up along the edges of the crater. Tectonic torque has stretched the original site into an oval. For more than a century, this oval has been a motherlode of ore-bearing rock for the mines that dot the area. When mining–for nickel, for copper, for gold, and for other precious things–first started, extracting the ore was catch-as-catch can. Men would go into the woods, fell the trees, and drag the trunks back to make vast wooden cribs near the mines. Then they would pile the rock that had been brought up from below onto the cribs and set them on fire, burning the sulphur off in billowing black dark clouds that blew over the land. The rock around Sudbury owes its colour to those burn offs. Sulphuric acid rained down and etched it

> black. In places where winter ice has splintered the rock, or where it has been blasted away for roads and new suburban homes, you can see the original rock, and it is pink.[4]

In Burtynsky's photos, the lava inflicts itself on the black rock landscape.

As mentioned earlier, the reds and oranges in nickel tailings are caused by the oxidation of the iron that is left behind in the process of separating nickel and other metals from the ore. In contrast, uranium tailings, which are radioactive, have the consistency and colour of fine sand.[5] The muted browns and yellows of the Elliot Lake tailings transform the landscape into a desolate, lifeless wasteland. The dead trees standing among the ruins resemble a desolate battlefield in which there are no survivors. Christopher Youngs aptly observes, "The image of [this] uranium mine suggests the devastating aftermath of a nuclear storm choking nature."[6]

"By the time I arrived in Elliot Lake while on my tailings project," Burtynsky recalled, "more than half of the original uranium mines and tailings management areas in the region were no longer in operation . . . decommissioning of the remaining uranium mines at Elliot Lake had already begun in 1992, and would continue on for a decade, leaving yet another community in financial and environmental devastation . . . a torrential rain had caused a tailings breach, flowing much of that quartzite and other waste material from the extraction process out into the landscape, suffocating the trees and other flora in its path."[7]

The two sets of tailings images are mirror opposites. The nickel tailings show destruction in the making whereas the uranium ones display the results of such devastation. The Sudbury images are of the present–those of Elliot Lake, the past. Other antonyms come to mind: active versus passive; burning and burnt. In such landscapes, Angelika Paget has observed, "The perpetual push-and-pull between beautiful form and edgy subject matter is never resolved and purposefully left hanging in the air."[8]

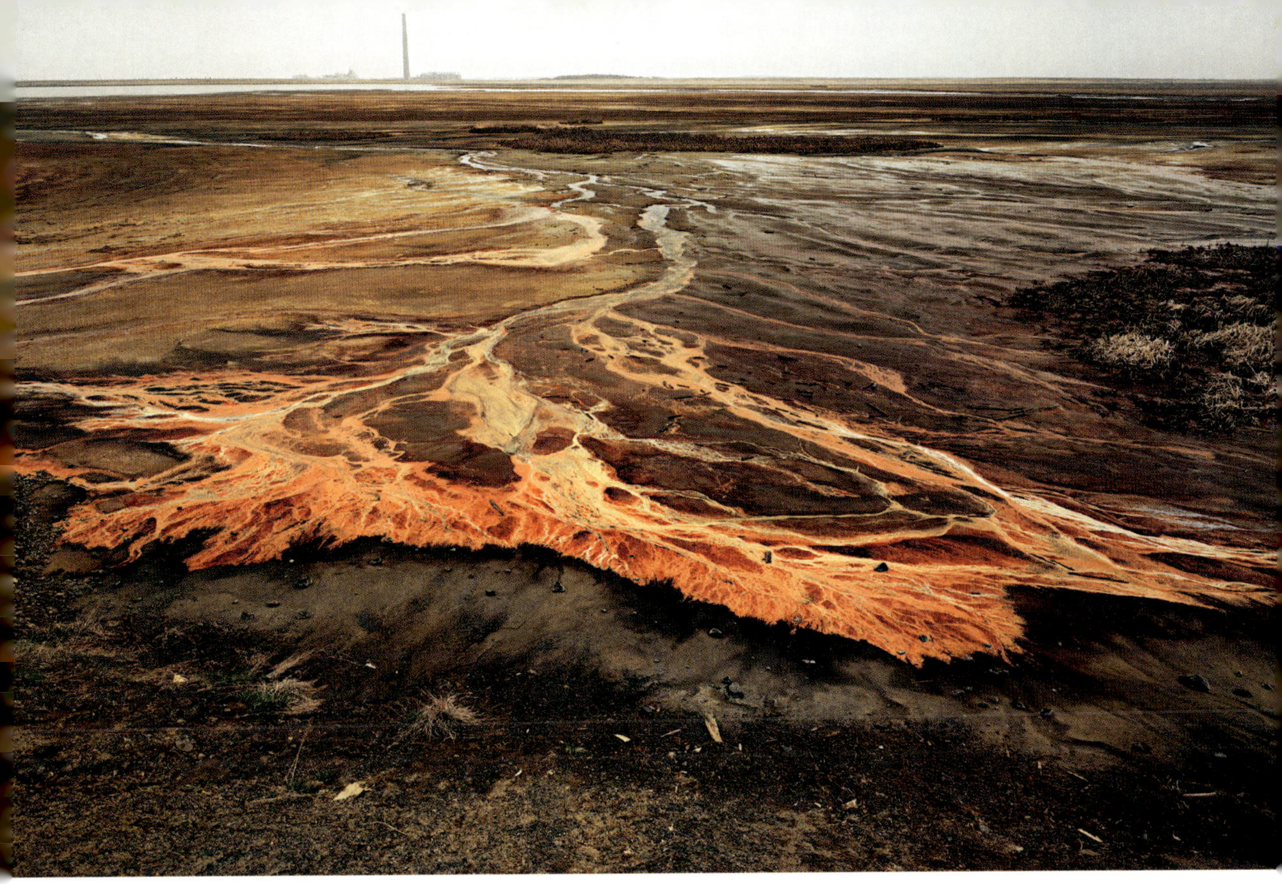

Edward Burtynsky, *Nickel Tailings #32*, Sudbury, Ontario, 1996

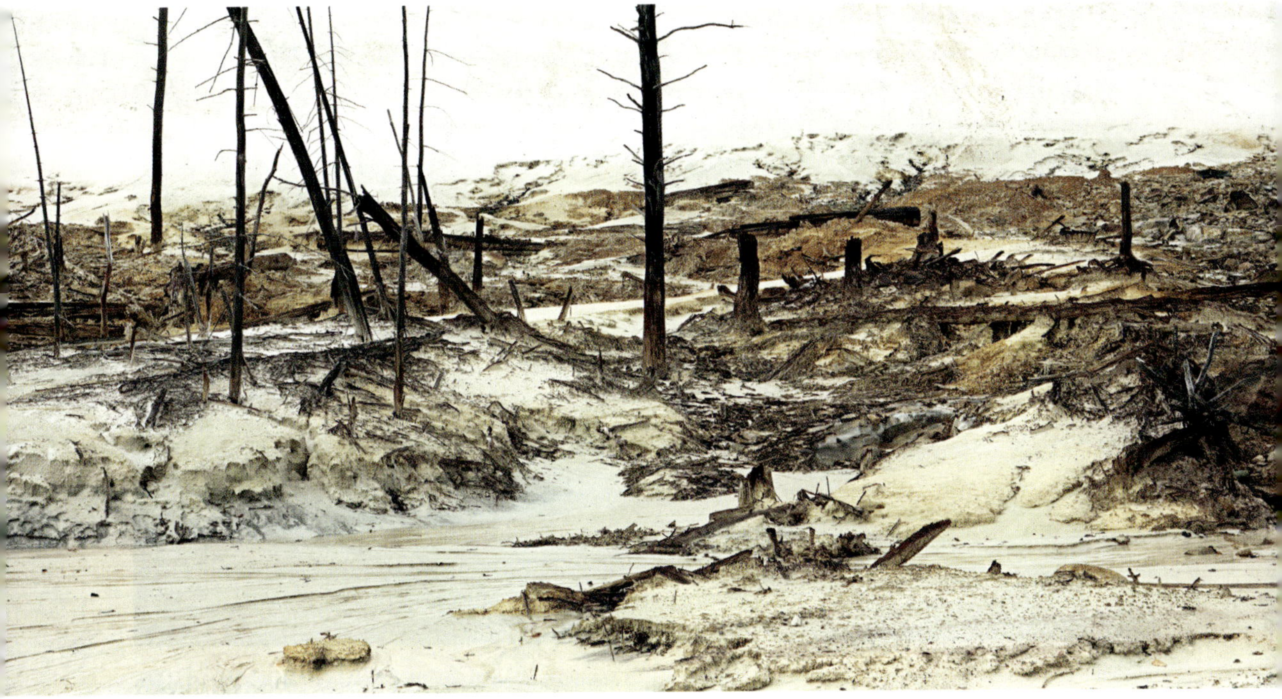

Edward Burtynsky, *Uranium Tailings #7*, Elliot Lake, Ontario, 1995

URBAN MINES

In November 1997, Burtynsky announced a new direction in his career, as the Halifax *Daily News* reported:

> My next series will be about densified metal. The big collecting yards where old cars and other waste materials are crushed into those huge tubes. I'm fascinated by these places where all the metal pools up on the outskirts of cities before it is re-entered into the consumer cycle. I wanted to build a branch off the main core of my work and not locate it strictly within the realm of landscape. I wanted to find the next place. I considered that here is primary mining–we go to the land, and we blast, and we take ore–that is the initial extraction. And then there is the relatively modern phenomenon of recycling–the source for the secondary level of extraction. This is the "urban mine." I felt it had a natural conceptual connection to everything I had done.[9]

In a *Globe and Mail* article published May 5, 1998, Dan Falk commented on this change: "As with his earlier work, Burtynsky has managed to find hidden forms, patterns, and colours in places where most of us wouldn't think of pulling over–in this case, the industrial plants of southern Ontario. . . . Some see Burtynsky's images as a critique of man's brutalization of the natural world; others might view it as a sympathetic bow to industry, creating beauty from ugliness. 'I don't know if you'd say a pile of squished tin cans is beautiful, but it's compelling,' Burtynsky said."

The photographer added: "I'm always looking for what makes an interesting photograph." But that search sometimes, he realized, created problems. He envisioned his images as a "survey of some of the things I see within society. The difficulty is, am I trying to estheticize the devastation or depletion? And quite frankly, it's not an easy question to answer."[10]

Recycling was an approach to "reclaim high value material that already existed in the recycling stream; rather than harvesting from the earth again

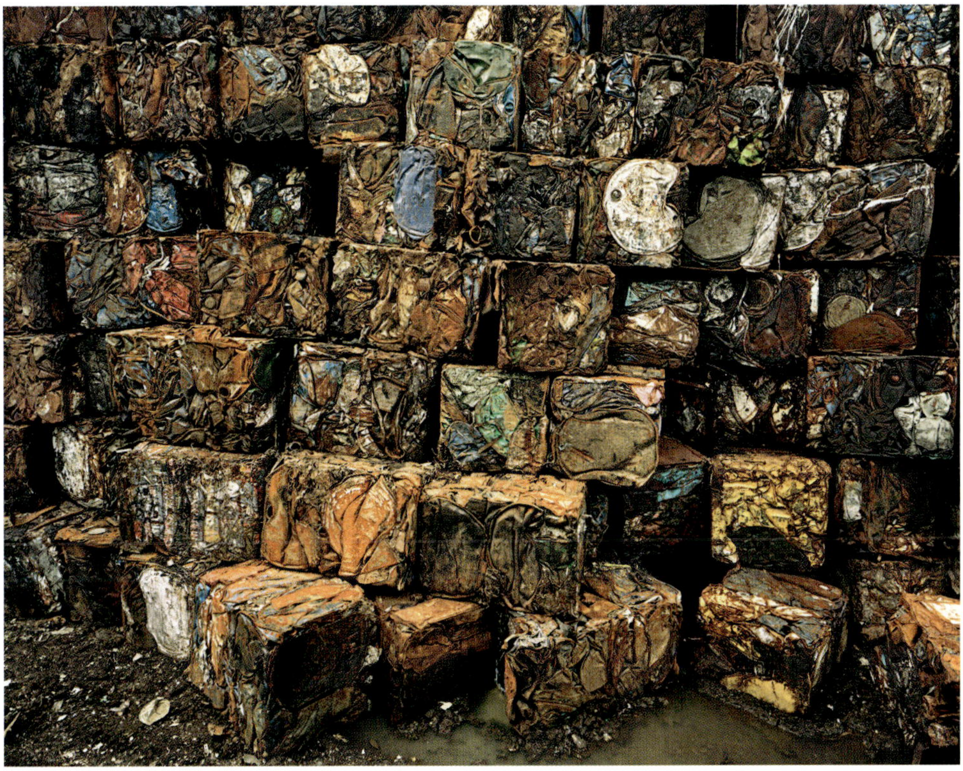

Edward Burtynsky, *Densified Oil Drums #4*, Hamilton, Ontario, 1997

and again." In his search for a suitable locale, he came across twenty-five acres of e-waste that the Waxman family, scrap merchants in Hamilton, had accumulated. The Waxmans "believed that there would soon be a way to process, sort, and repurpose those materials with technology, so they were buying it cheaply and storing it until a technique was developed to help convert it into usable materials. It made so much sense, with all the high-quality coppers and other precious metals in these products."[11]

Most of the photographs taken in Hamilton do not show the horizon and, as a result, have a claustrophobic, confined feel to them. At the time, they were not images that even seasoned photography collectors were comfortable with but some are the purest abstractions Burtynsky had yet attempted, and are reminiscent of the colour arrangements in Jasper Johns's *Alphabet* (1959). They also share some affinities with the colour

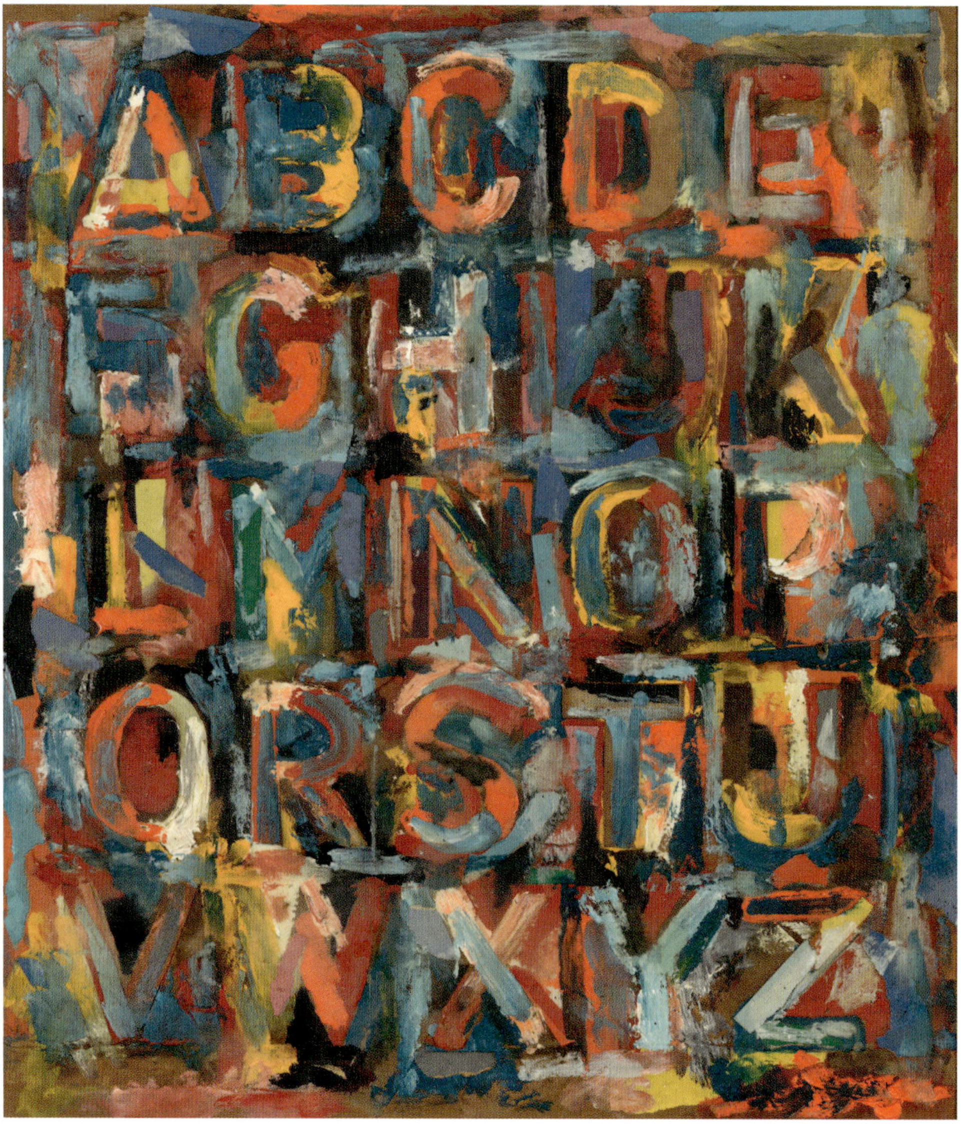

Jasper Johns, *Alphabet*, paper on hardboard, 1959. The Art Institute of Chicago

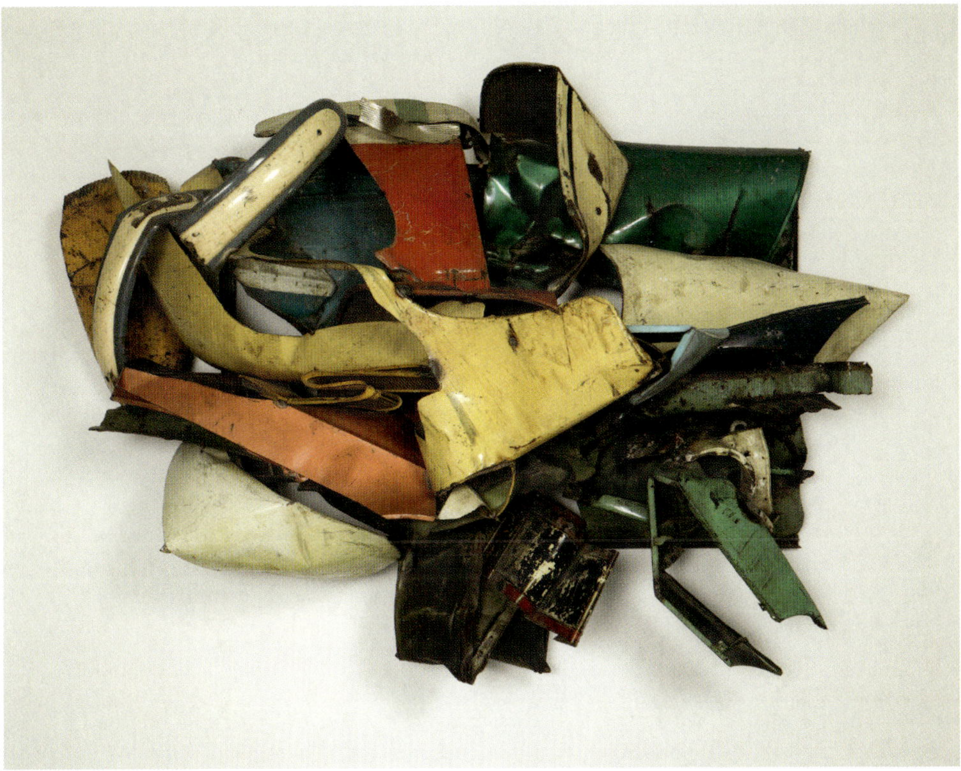

John Chamberlain, *Dolores James*, welded and painted steel, 1962. Guggenheim Museum

box arrangements of Paul Klee and can also be compared to the American sculptor John Chamberlain's assemblage pieces of scrap metal.[12] Some of the images of densified oil drums resemble the drip and splashing canvases of Jean-Paul Riopelle.

After Burtynsky photographed the site, the city of Hamilton forced the Waxmans to get rid of the materials. Since no technology was available to process it, and it could not be burnt, their collection was placed in containers and shipped to China.

OXFORD TIRE PILE

"I often look for the largest example of something–the largest mine, the largest quarry, the most active area. Massive operations result in the greatest and most complex transformations. The Oxford Tire Pile gave me a veritable canyon of 30 million tires to work with."

Since the mid-1950s, Ed Filbin, an entrepreneur in northern California, had been paid "tipping fees" by various automotive shops to truck away used tires, known as "baldies." Filbin stored everything he collected at his tire-disposal site, which consisted of forty acres of dry grassland near Highway 5 and the town of Westley, at the foot of the Diablo Range. Most locals had never visited the place–"they're up there somewhere," one observed. They had no interest in "Mount Goodyear."[13]

Like the Waxmans, Filbin was waiting for someone to come up with a recycling program for his collection. Meanwhile, residents wondered what would happen if the site ever caught fire, which some felt was only a matter of time. One local commentator wrote,

> This man-made landscape, of hills and high mountains of tires, visualizes the often-forgotten afterlife of commercial production . . . What seems to be a graveyard of tires marks in fact only the penultimate stage in the life cycle of the oil product. They spend several years in this "temporary storage," as they await an energy intensive recycling process and subsequent environmental cleanup. A special concern in managing such tire piles is fire control. Tire fires are extremely difficult to extinguish, and even after being extinguished externally may continue to burn inside, undergoing slow-burning pyrolysis for over decades. Such fires release copious amounts of carbon monoxide, lead, and arsenic.[14]

In the June 28, 1993, issue of *The New Yorker*, John McPhee interviewed Filbin, who cursed "the dirty rotten bureaucrats" who were harassing him about safety.[15] Four years later, Filbin sold his pile to Oxford Tire Recycling, which had a plan: "Tires don't decompose. They just sit. That's why most landfills won't accept them. No matter how far down you bury them, they always rise to the top as the other garbage rots. So, the idea was to take all those tires and burn them to make electricity."[16] That plan faltered when Oxford filed for bankruptcy.

Burtynsky, intrigued by McPhee's article, visited and photographed the site in June 1999. "While I was there," he recalled,

> I learned of another tire pile about 30 km away that was in a quarry. But this pile had caught fire and had been burning consistently for nearly

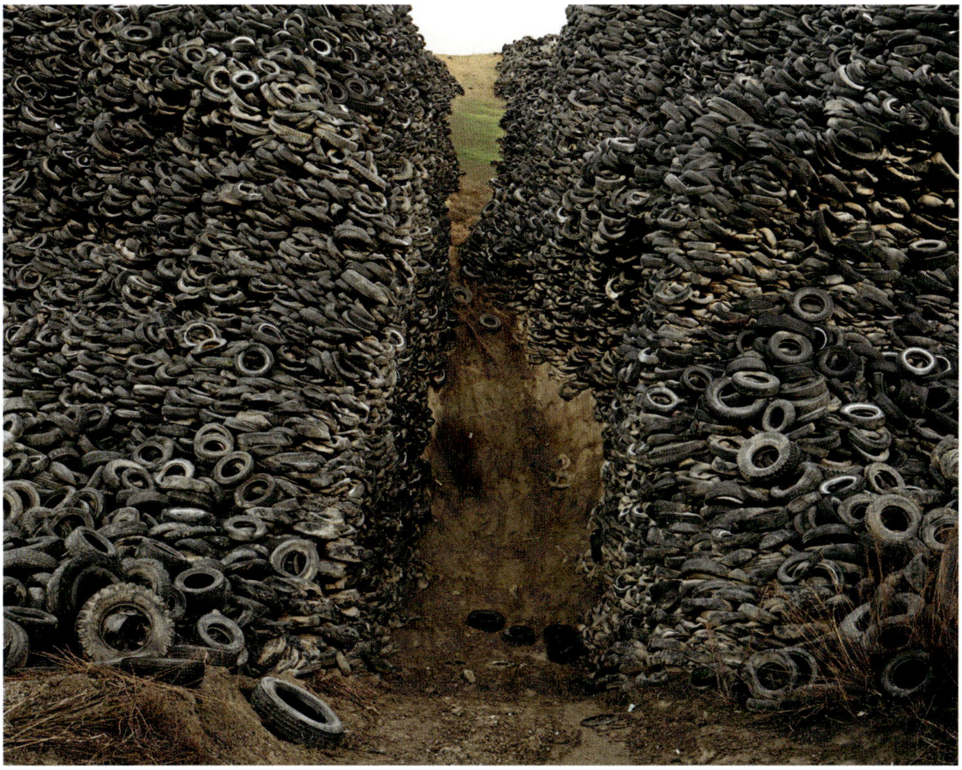

Edward Burtynsky, *Oxford Tire Pile #6,* Westley, California, 1999

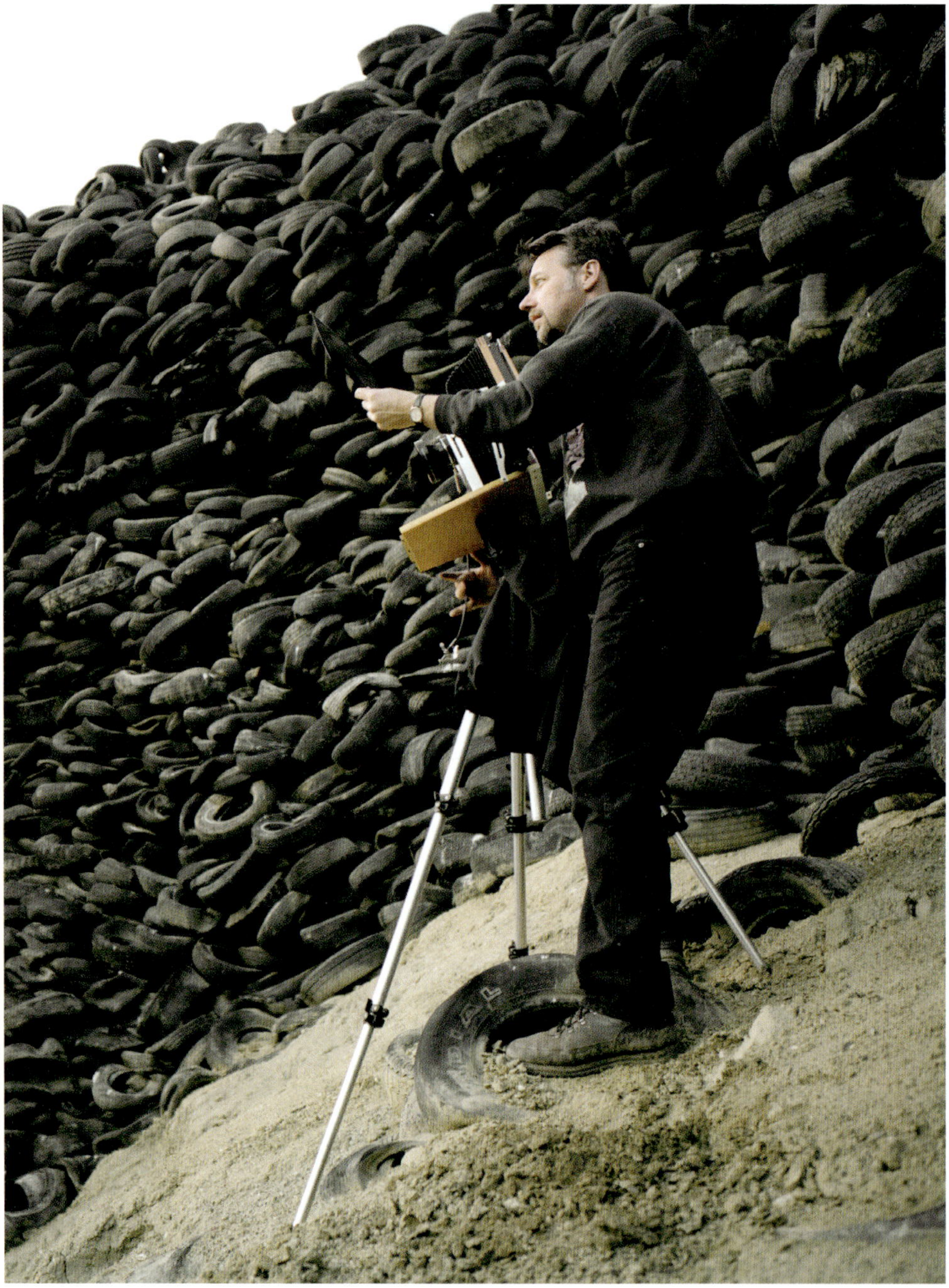

Edward Burtynsky at Westley, California, 1999. Photograph by Angela Curry

> two years at that point. Intrigued by the image this evoked, we set out with all my equipment to go and take a look. It was an apocalyptic scene, and we could only stay for about 20 minutes because of the splitting headaches and wheezing lungs brought on by the smoke and tire fumes . . . It took another four days to complete the tire pile project and then just a few months later in a turn of devastating luck (made worse by the complex circumstances of this industry), the Oxford tire pile was struck by lightning. 3,000 ft of smoke billowed into the air, with flames reaching, at peak, approx. 2,500 ft high. The blaze was reported at around 2000° and while workers on-site attempted to quell the fire with the plant's fire-suppression system, they were unsuccessful, and the pile burned for over 30 days. Toxins from the fire threatened local air quality and groundwater supplies, and reports suggest the tires melted into over 200K gallons of molten oil.[17]

Urban Mines and *Oxford Tire Pile* are more directly indebted to Abstract Expressionism than any of Burtynsky's previous photographs. Before, he had consistently framed his images by referencing abstraction; in these series, he made abstractions.

BORROMINI

In 1999–an especially busy year for Burtynsky–he travelled to Rome to photograph the architecture of Francesco Borromini (1599-1667). The photographer worked side by side with the scholar Joseph Connors to "evoke the illusionistic play of perspective, light and space in the creations of a master of Baroque architecture."[18] This venture was linked to Burtynsky's accomplishments in the *Money Matters* project: Raphael Bernstein's Parnassus Foundation funded this shoot, yet another instance of his abiding interest in advancing Burtynsky's career.

The interiors in these new images are filled with bright light and eschew the idea of stolidity that was so key to the corresponding ones of banks. The monochrome colour values in these photographs add to the airiness and delicacy of these images, so vastly different from Burtynsky's other work.

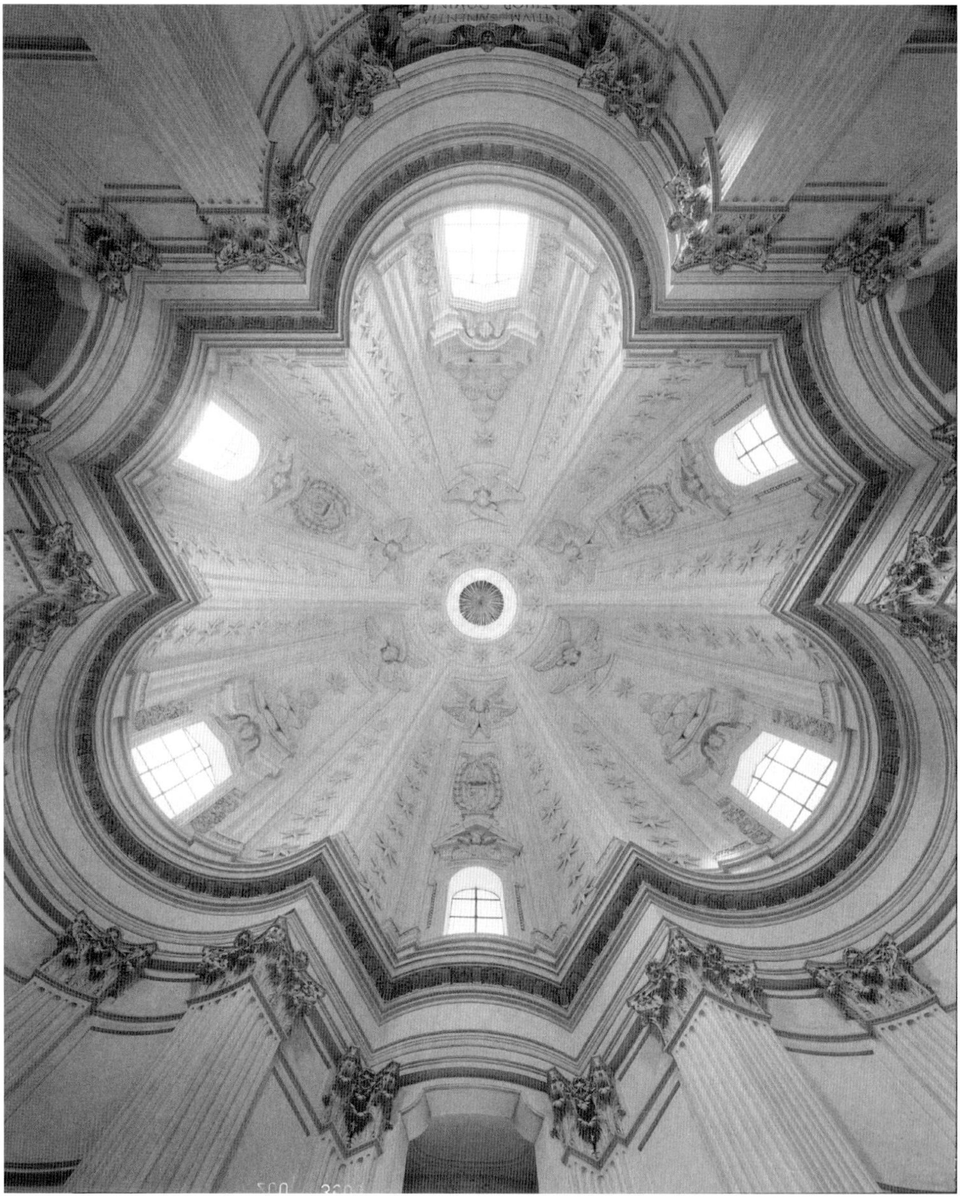

Edward Burtynsky, *Borromini #2*, Sant'Ivo alla Sapienza, Rome, 1999

He concentrated on seemingly small details to give the viewer a sense of how something apparently trivial can be worth looking at. The nave of Borromini's Sant'Ivo alla Sapienza, for example, is a six-pointed star: three are clover-like, the others concavely clipped. Burtynsky underscored this dichotomy by emphasizing the different sizes of the windows in his images. He had added a new string to his bow.

RESIDUAL LANDSCAPES

By 1999, Burtynsky had become a well-known photographer. *Tailings* was shown at the Mira Godard Gallery in 1996, as was *Urban Mines* in 1999.

To keep the momentum going, Burtynsky realized he had to promote himself. One way of doing so was through the creation of a substantial publication history. If a photographer becomes well-known and is hitting his target goal in sales, he wants to keep going forward. Books are extremely useful for that purpose, Burtynsky became convinced, because they provide the full context of an artist's work and demonstrate evidence of a substantial body of work. In that spirit, Burtynsky contacted the Toronto photographer and collector Michael Torosian, who had launched the Lumiere Press in 1986. Torosian's books, composed in lead, hand-printed and hand-bound, are "devoted exclusively to photography, and each book aspires in its concept, graphic design, and bookmaking craftsmanship to be the manifestation of its artistic content."[19] The company's first book was *Edward Weston: Dedicated to Simplicity*. In subsequent years, Torosian published books featuring Dave Heath, Paul Strand, and Lewis Hine, among others.

Starting early in the 1990s, Burtynsky and Torosian met annually, at Burtynsky's initiative, for lunch or dinner. These conversations centred on whether Torosian would publish a book about Burtynsky's work. Torosian was reluctant to go ahead unless there was support from a gallery–he wanted some sort of infrastructure in place to market the book. The dealer

Mira Godard was approached, but she was apathetic about this venture. (However, as discussed earlier, she would later change her mind about Burtynsky at the insistence of Nicholas Metivier.) Despite Torosian's reluctance, Burtynsky wanted to go ahead: "So," Torosian recalled, "he wrote me a check and we started work on the project."

Torosian visited Toronto Image Works and chose twenty-four images for the colour insert: five each from *Rock of Ages* and *Carrara*; three from *Urban Mines*; two each from *Railcuts, Oxford Tire Pile*, and *Nickel Tailings*; and one each from the *Kennecott Copper Mine, Westar Open Pit Mine, Inco Cave-in Pit, Inco Mine Shaft*, and *Uranium Tailings* series. The frontispiece was an additional photograph from *Rock of Ages*. In addition to this selection of images, there was a brief introduction by Torosian, along with a synthesis of two interviews he had conducted with Burtynsky on February 29 and May 4, 2000. *Residual Landscapes: Studies of Industrial Transfiguration*, published by Lumiere Press in 2001, was exactly what Burtynsky had hoped for: a published retrospective glance at his career to date.

But before its publication, he was searching for a new project–a challenge that would expand and extend his horizons. What that project would be, however, evaded him.

(2000–2001)

7 MONSTERS ON THE SHORE

INDIA AND BANGLADESH

The *Tire Pile* series had been inspired in part by John McPhee's article in *The New Yorker* in 1993; some years later, on the CBC Radio program *Ideas*, Burtynsky heard that, following the *Exxon Valdez* oil spill in 1989, it had been determined that single-hull vessels such as the *Valdez*, were unsound–a double-hull would have prevented the catastrophe. This finding led insurance companies from 2004 to insure only double-hulled vessels and now these huge, single-hulled ships had become dinosaurs, soon to be made extinct. Scrapping a tanker was a lengthy process; however, as they had to be dismantled by hand for recycling. Most of this type of work was done at Alang, in India, and Chittagong, in Bangladesh.

Fascinated by what he heard on the *Ideas* program, Burtynsky began researching the topic and came upon William Langewiesche's article "The

Shipbreakers," published in the August 2000 issue of *The Atlantic Monthly*. Langewiesche began his indictment of what he witnessed in Alang, a town in Gujarat, on the coast of the Arabian Sea: "on a six-mile stretch of oily, smoky beach, 40,000 men work to tear apart half of the world's discarded ships, each one a sump of toxic waste. Environmentalists in the West are outraged. The shipbreakers, of course, want to be left alone and maybe they should be."[1] The accompanying photos by Claudio Cambon (taken at Chittagong) and Dilip Mehta (taken at Alang) astounded Burtynsky: "The scenes reminded me of settings for a post-apocalyptic science-fiction tale."[2] He contacted Mehta, who told him, "You may be safer apprehended by the local thugs [at Alang] rather than the local police. At least the thugs could be bought out for money, but God knows what the cops would want from you."[3] Despite the warning, Burtynsky was inclined to go ahead.

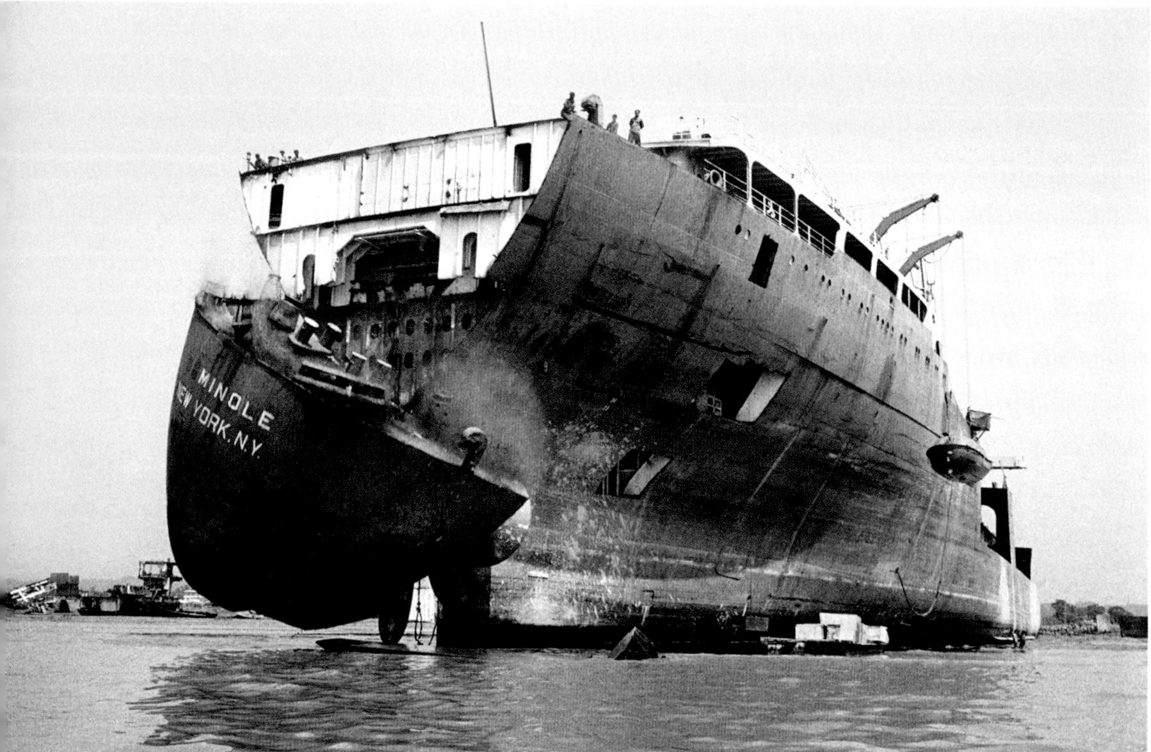

Claudio Cambon, *The Felling of the Fantail*, 1989. Courtesy of Claudio Cambon

Then more information became available. Greenpeace had led protests in Mumbai against the scrapping in Alang, pointing out that industrial countries did not have the right to ship toxic waste to developing nations and, moreover, that the waste was extremely carcinogenic. Burtynsky eventually decided not to go to India, but remained intrigued by Chittagong, in Bangladesh. There, in 1965, a cyclone had driven a twenty-thousand-ton ship on to a beach in Bangladesh. The event inaugurated a local industry of stripping ships for scrap.

Three years after the *Valdez* catastrophe, the distribution of single-hulled ships around the world for deconstruction began in earnest. Global Marketing Systems in Maryland was the company that arranged the final resting places for the vessels as it purchased distressed and surplus ships, reflagged them, and sent them off to various beaches on the Indian subcontinent.[4]

The Brazilian photographer Sebastião Salgado travelled to Bangladesh in 1993 and, as Langewische pointed out, "captured unforgettable images of gaunt laborers and broken ships."[5] Salgado's luminous black-and-white photographs show the vessels being taken apart, but he also emphasized the workers, trapped in a toxic wasteland. Burtynsky made himself familiar with those images, which he much admired. Undaunted, he became convinced that he could provide a different take on this ecological nightmare. He wondered if this was the opportunity he had been searching for.

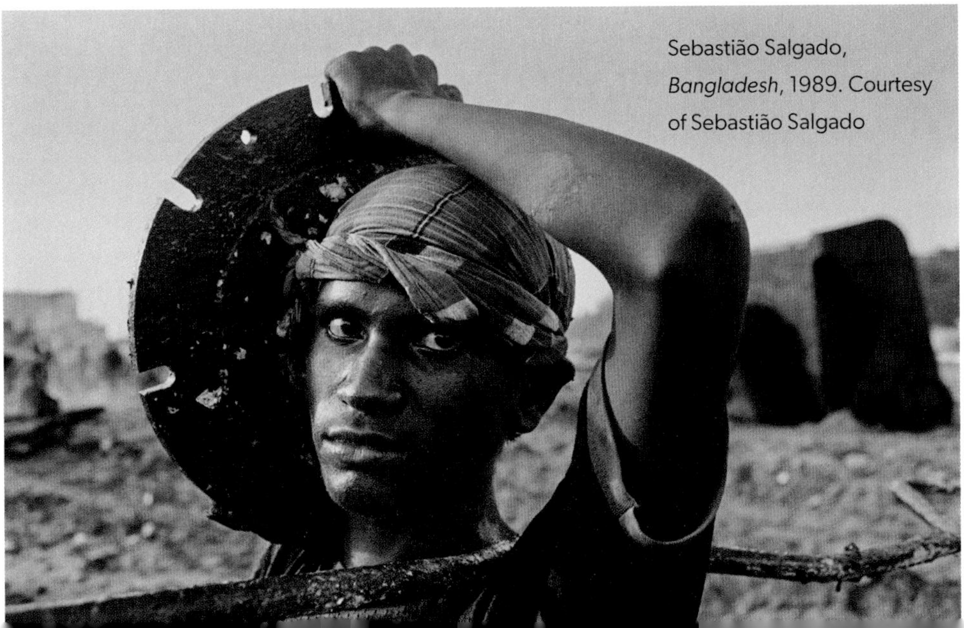

Sebastião Salgado, *Bangladesh*, 1989. Courtesy of Sebastião Salgado

Travelling to India and Bangladesh was an entirely new sort of undertaking for Burtynsky. How would he go about doing this? He soon found a way through Jim Panou, who had graduated from Ryerson in 1983–one year behind Burtynsky. Panou had a studio on the third floor above Image Works and used it on a regular basis, and he knew Burtynsky casually.

In 1998, Panou had visited Rajasthan and had seen the marble quarry at Makrana. One day, he bumped into Burtynsky on the stairs and said, "Ed, I've got a quarry for you in India that you should take a look at." Intrigued, Burtynsky responded, "When can we go? Can we investigate shipbreaking in India?"[6]

Before they left Canada on November 7, Panou researched shipbreaking sites and confirmed that access to Alang was, indeed, impossible. In any event, the ships there were squeezed tightly together on the beach, whereas the ones in Bangladesh, where Salgado and Cambon had worked, were spread across a much wider area. Panou also contacted an expatriate Canadian named David Buckley, who had lived in Chittagong for twenty-five years and ran Bangladesh Ecotours, to obtain up-to-date information about the shipbreaking yard. Buckley travelled to the site, sussed it out, and sent images to Panou so that he and Burtynsky had a good idea of what the site looked like in 2000.

Panou and Burtynsky hatched a plan. They would fly to Delhi and, from there, drive to Rajasthan to shoot at the Makrana quarry. After working there, they would head back to Delhi, fly to Dhaka from Kolkata, and then make their way to Chittagong, where Buckley would meet them. From there they drove each day of their stay to the Sitakunda coastal strip, where the world's second-largest shipbreaking yard was. Burtynsky joked about the travelling costs he had to assume: "My ticket to Bangladesh cost less than my overweight fees for my cameras and paraphernalia."[7]

Since he had first-hand knowledge of India, Panou suggested to Burtynsky that they play good cop, bad cop. As the bad cop, Panou would manage their itinerary and step in if any local tried to take advantage of them.

MAKRANA

The metaphoric rock at Makrana, in the Nagaur region of Rajasthan, exists in a single, enormous deposit; eight hundred mines (many illegal), employing forty-thousand labourers, operate in the area. Some sites focus on the kind

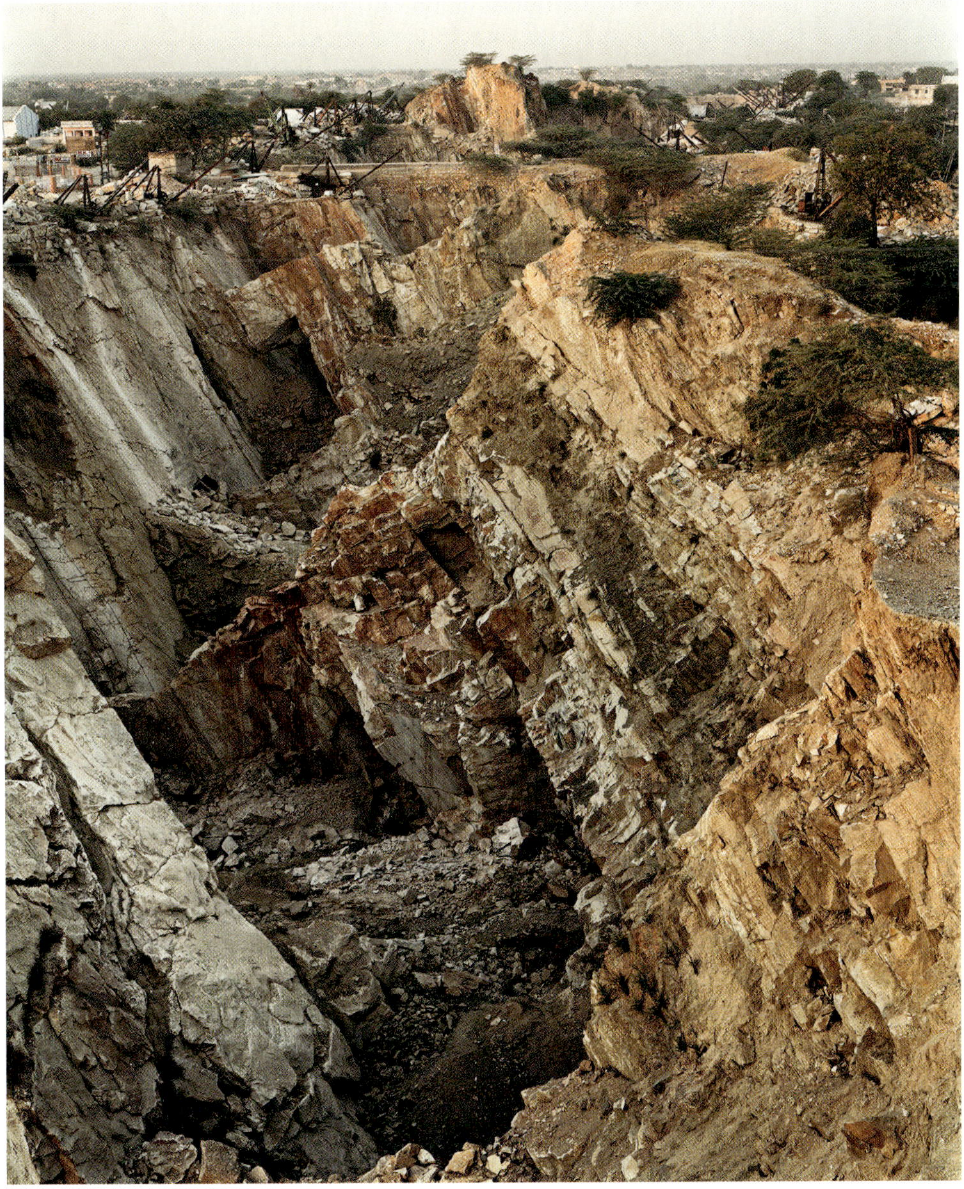

Edward Burtynsky, *Makrana Quarries #2*, Rajasthan, India, 2000

of white ivory that was used for the Taj Mahal and the Victoria Memorial in Kolkata, while others specialize in albeta (white with dark patterning) and varieties of pink, brown, and grey. There are a vast number of factories that cut and process marble.

Extraction there is done at a terrible human cost. The workers are mainly Dalits, members of the lowest caste, who are not provided with safety shoes, hard hats, or even masks to protect them from the heavy dust. Locals refer to these sites as the "Pits of Death."

The photos Burtynsky took at Makrana are very different from those in the *Rock of Ages* and *Carrara* series. In the Makrana photos, he emphasized views of deep cavities that lead the viewer's eye down to the marble and, in the process, accentuate the difficulties in locating the buried treasure. He also stressed its rich brown colours and stayed away from architectural elements. These new images underscore the brutal terrain of the Makrana quarries and provide a counterpoint to the relative tranquillity of the two earlier series.

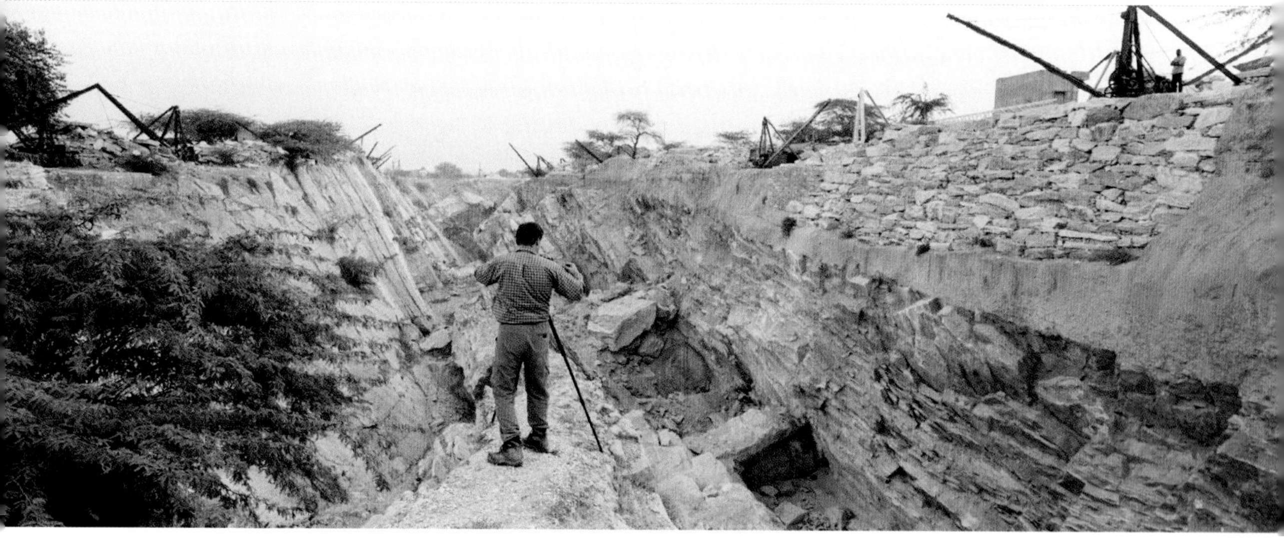

Burtynsky photographing at Makrana, 2000. Photograph by Jim Panou

SAMBHAR SALT LAKE

After shooting at Makrana for several days, Burtynsky and Panou took a break to explore the surrounding area. They visited the Sambhar Salt Lake, the largest saline lake in India, located in the Jaipur district of Rajasthan, approximately seventy kilometres from Makrana. Celebrated in the ancient epic the *Mahabharata*, the lake has long been a site of importance; in the nineteenth century, remnants of ancient terracotta figurines were discovered in the lake. Sambhar Salt Lake is also a Ramsar (recognized wetland of international importance) site because scores of flamingoes and other water birds migrate there from northern Asia and Siberia.

Most of the inhabitants of the thirty-eight villages surrounding the lake harvest salt from it. Extracting salt is a poor-paying, dangerous occupation. Many of the workers dig wells in the salt evaporation ponds to draw the briny groundwater to the surface, then wait for the water to evaporate and the white salt crystals to form. The labourers, constantly exposed to a relentless sun, face a host of dangers: their feet absorb the salt and can become septic; they inhale salt particles that can lead to high blood pressure and hypertension; they can become blind due to the intense reflections of the sun on water. In addition, the extraction of groundwater has made it virtually impossible for farmers in nearby regions to grow crops; there are all sorts of unauthorised borewells; and the ecology of the lake been affected, leading to a decrease in the flamingo population because the algae they feed on has been severely depleted.

Because his stay was short, Burtynsky added only seven photographs of the Sambhar region to his portfolio. Only one records the salt workers themselves; the other six show rooms that have been completely invaded by salt, and are eerie, ghostly spaces. In their focus on tactile white surfaces, these photographs resemble the abstracts of Robert Ryman.

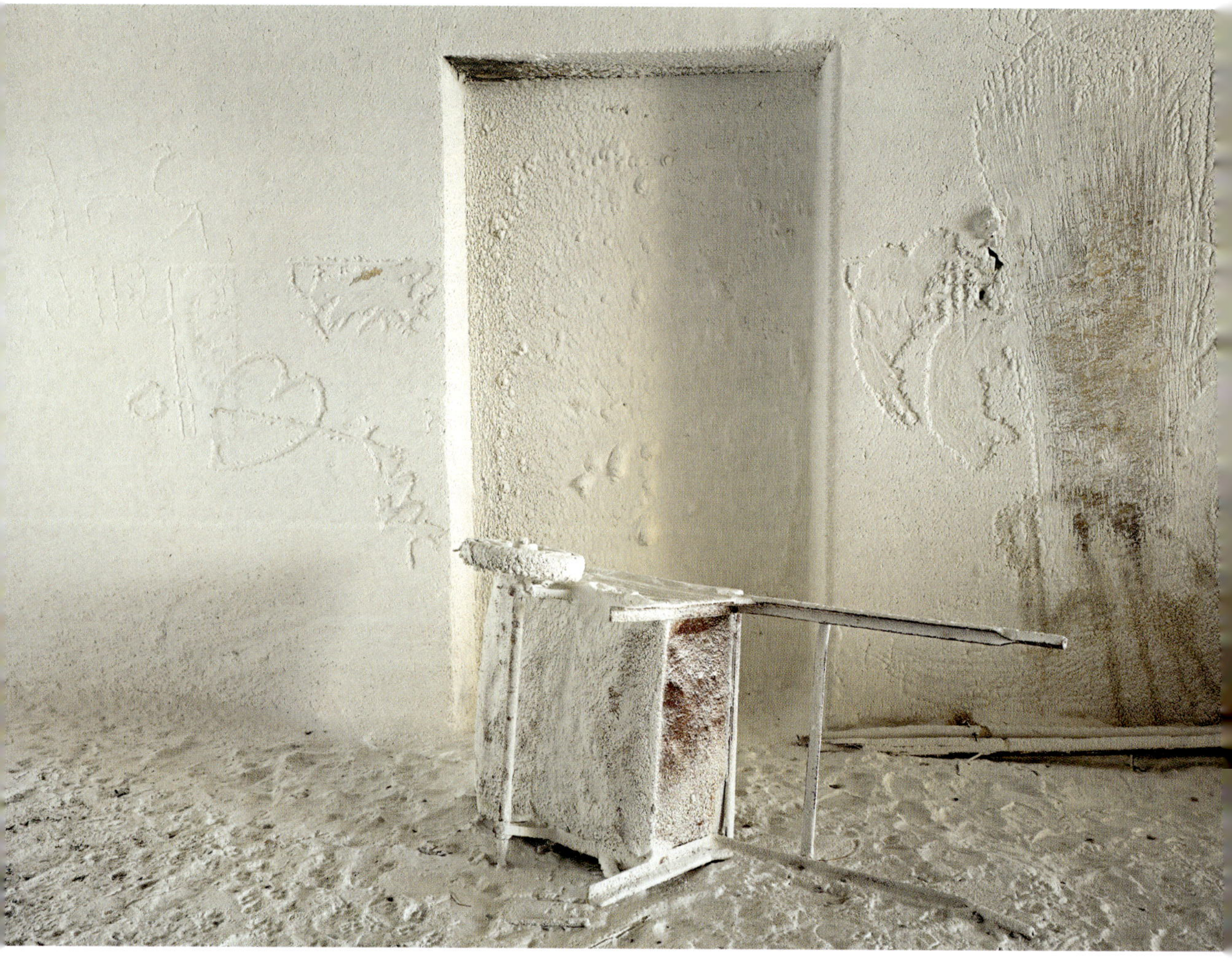

Edward Burtynsky, *Saltworks #5*, Sambhar Salt Flats, Rajasthan, India, 2000

Robert Ryman, *Surface Veil I*, oil and blue chalk on canvas, 1970. Guggenheim Museum

SHIPBREAKING

Burtynsky arose at 4 a.m. on his first full day near Chittagong, on the southeastern side of the Bay of Bengal. He was on site two hours later at sunrise after walking to the beach at Sitakunda: "Nothing in my life," he recalled, "could have prepared me for what I was about to see and experience. . . . I felt like I had been transported back 150 years to the days of the [I]ndustrial [R]evolution, the world Charles Dickens describes in *Hard Times*. I found myself wandering awestruck through a landscape littered with rusting colossi that loomed silently over scores of workers."[8] He had reached his much-sought destination.

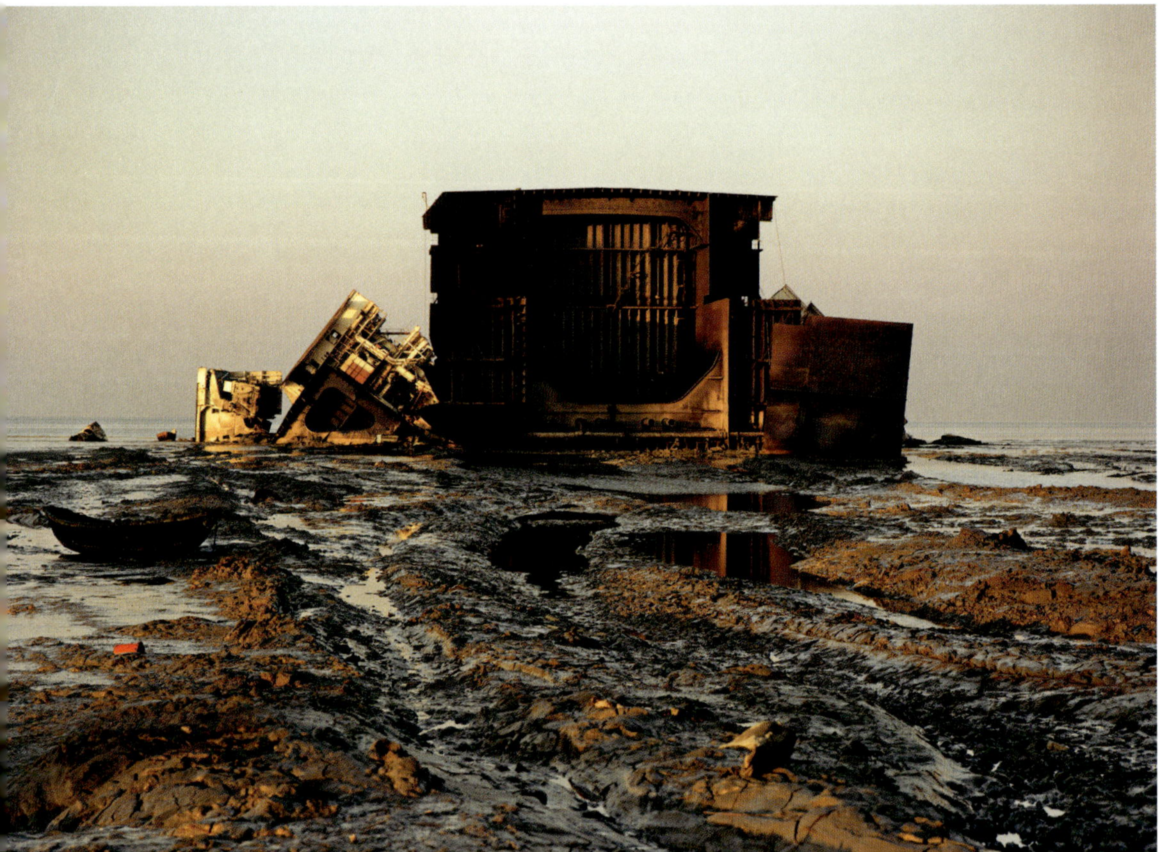

Edward Burtynsky, *Shipbreaking #1*, Chittagong, Bangladesh, 2000

He described the first photo he took: ‘I stopped in front of a partially broken ship to set up my camera. The massive enigmatic presence of this object imposed itself so completely upon the landscape that it took my breath away. I made my first exposure, *Shipbreaking #1*.”

One family owned the entire beach and leased out plots to about forty companies. Since the water near the beach was shallow, the ships would beach at different levels depending on how deep their keels were. On that forlorn beach, gazing at the vessels in various stages of being taken apart, Burtynsky's eye was enlivened. In the past, he had often seen his compositions through the lens of abstract expressionism, but these grisly forms are monumental pieces in the vein of the sculptor Richard Serra, an artist whose work he had long esteemed. Specifically, they resembled Serra's copper-coloured configurations such as *Snake* (1997) and the various *Torqued Ellipses* (1996–1999).[9] Glancing at an "upturned piece of engine-room housing," Burtynsky joked, "You know, if I was Richard Serra, I'd just pick this whole piece up and land it at MoMA."[10]

"Certain scenes that unfolded during that time continue to haunt me," he recalled. "Rounding a corner one day, we found ourselves smothered by dust. Realizing that it was a cloud of asbestos, we held our breath and ran. Another morning, we came upon two smouldering piles of ash. Inquiring, we were told that they were the remains of two workers who had met their demise the day before, each cut in half by a snapped winch-cable."

The horrors Burtynsky witnessed weighed heavily upon him, and he tried to capture those feelings. But it was an approach that was a two-edged sword: "One can look at these images as making political statements about the environment, but they also celebrate the achievements of engineering or the wonders of geology."[11] The scrap metal, he knew, was also Bangladesh's only source of iron, steel, and brass.

What exactly am I doing? he asked himself. He came to the conclusion that "I'm not using my art to browbeat corporations for the rack and ruin of our landscape. I'm trying [to cut] a slice out of the chaos and give [it] visual coherence so that the viewer can decide."[12]

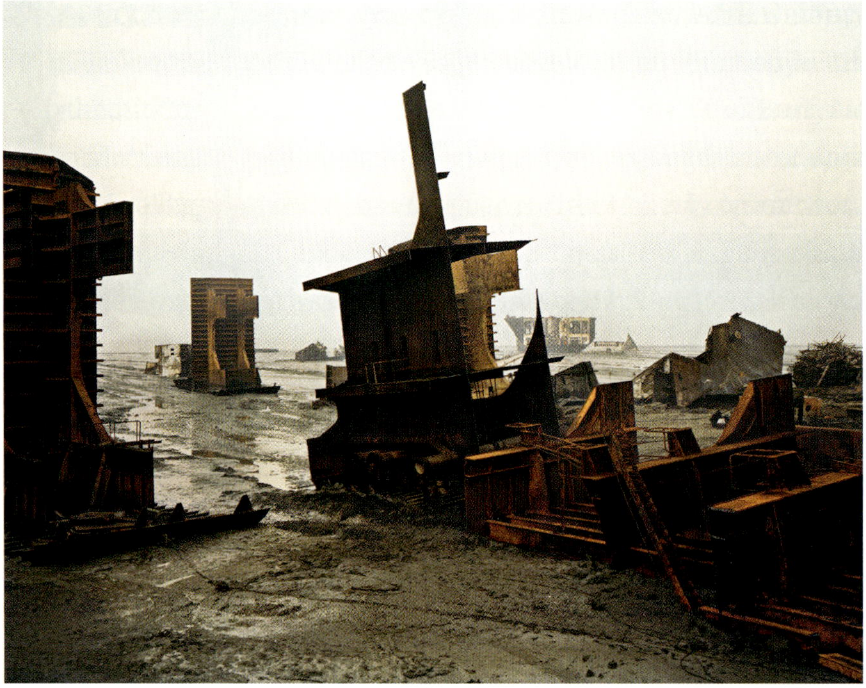

Edward Burtynsky, *Shipbreaking #10*, Chittagong, Bangladesh, 2000

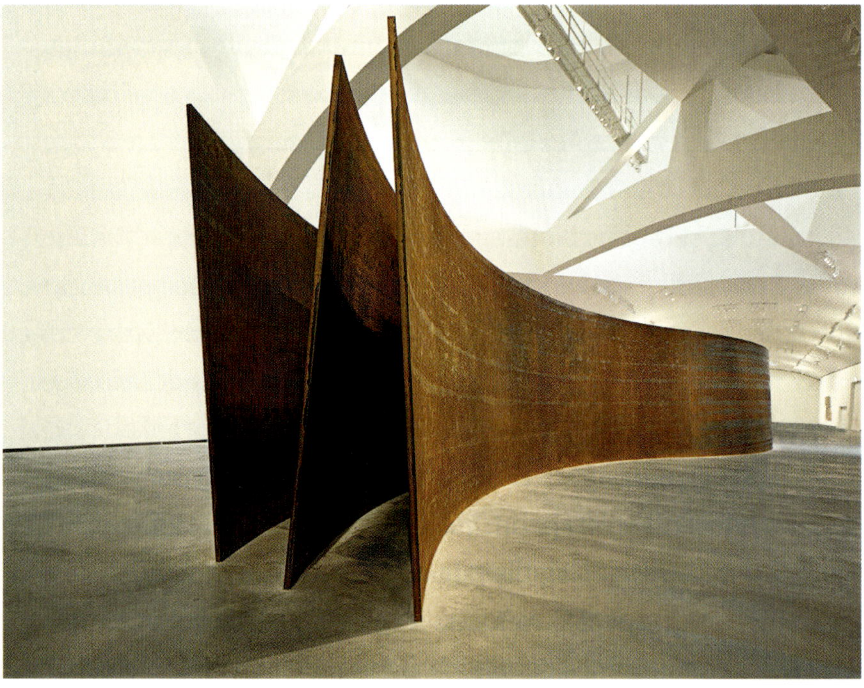

Richard Serra, *Snake*, three units of weathering steel, 1994–97. Guggenheim, Bilbao

The shoot on the beach at Sitakunda lasted about two weeks. It went smoothly for a week or so, but the place was so hot and sunny that Burtynsky could only shoot at first and last light. Then he came down with strep throat, became bedridden, and had to stay out of action for four days.

The twenty-four images from 2000 emphasize the size of the vessels, as huge, hideous sculptures that exist in a sinister twilight. There is a great deal of contrast–with the assistance of Agfa film–between the water on shore and the murky waters in which the various pieces are stranded. The reddish-brown surfaces of these ships must have reminded Burtynsky of the burnt orange colours in the Sudbury tailings.

Back in Canada, Burtynsky was pleased with the images he had made in Bangladesh and wanted to return there to explore the subject further. Panou, however, had other projects on the go and was not available. When he eventually returned to Sitakunda a year later, Burtynsky was accompanied instead by Noah Richler, who was doing an article on him for *Saturday Night*, and Jeff Powis, a documentary filmmaker.

Richler's vivid account of what he witnessed is a fitting accompaniment to Burtynsky's photographs:

> The long lines of boys and men–barefoot, knee-deep in the silver-grey mud–stretches out toward the hollow back end of a junked freighter half-a-mile out on the tidal flats. Leaning forward, chanting to keep in step, they are hauling a length of five-inch steel cable from a winch platform on the beach, the whole line swaying to one side when the weight of the cable on their shoulders becomes too much. They have come here from all over Bangladesh to work in the twenty-odd shipwreckers' yards strung along the shoreline a few miles of Chittagong. They bring in the decommissioned ships that lie grounded off the coast, cut them into scrap, and load them, piece by heavy piece, by hand and, on their backs, onto trucks that will carry the scrap to the salvage shops and

> "re-rolling" mills of Chittagong. It's filthy but necessary work in the shipping industry, and it's a boon to the country that has no iron ore and little industry of its own.

He also wrote, "Out on the mud, the massive, gaping stern of the junked freighter is silent, but terrifying. It looks like a temple, like a god, like a monster with cavernous, wide-open jaws, dwarfing the workers around it." And in the midst of this grisly scene was Burtynsky: "On the shore, there is man in clean clothes, so out of place he could be Victorian. He's a photographer . . . standing behind a large eight-by-ten view camera mounted on a tripod he's set on a flat over-turned section of the ship's hull."

Burtynsky pointed out to Richler that his set-ups could consume a lot of time: "Sometimes you can move ten steps forward, or ten steps back, and the image just isn't there. But at some point it clicks in your mind."[13] When necessary, he used telephoto lenses to compress the foreground: "It's in the middle ground that you experience the sweep of the landscape."[14]

During this trip, Burtynsky added forty-five images to his repertoire. Thirty roughly correspond to the first series. Another seven show workers away from the beach, storerooms, and assortments of scrap, reminiscent of *Urban Mines*; and eight display new buildings being constructed from rebars repurposed from the ships being torn apart.

Burtynsky's second set of images are of the wrecked ships in daylight–the twilight ambience has vanished. More emphatically than before, the new photographs emphasized the lives of the workers and the dangerous environment in which they laboured: the proximity to asbestos and hydrocarbons, the danger of being killed by falling metal parts, the possibility of being blinded by torch cutting. (So jarred was he by what he had witnessed, Burtynsky pledged the revenue of the sales of the first few images toward the purchase of safety equipment, such as goggles and breathing masks, for distribution to these workers.) By adjusting his approach during the 2001 trip, he looked more intently at the surfaces of the ship breaking enterprise and created a variety of abstractions.

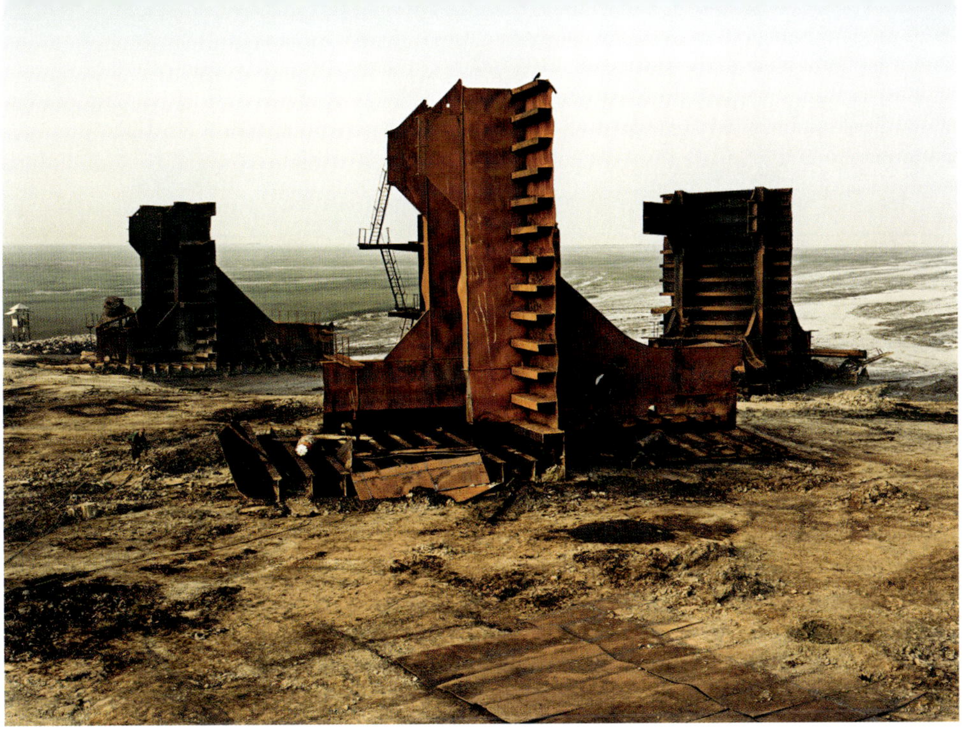

Edward Burtynsky, *Shipbreaking #27,* Chittagong, Bangladesh, 2001

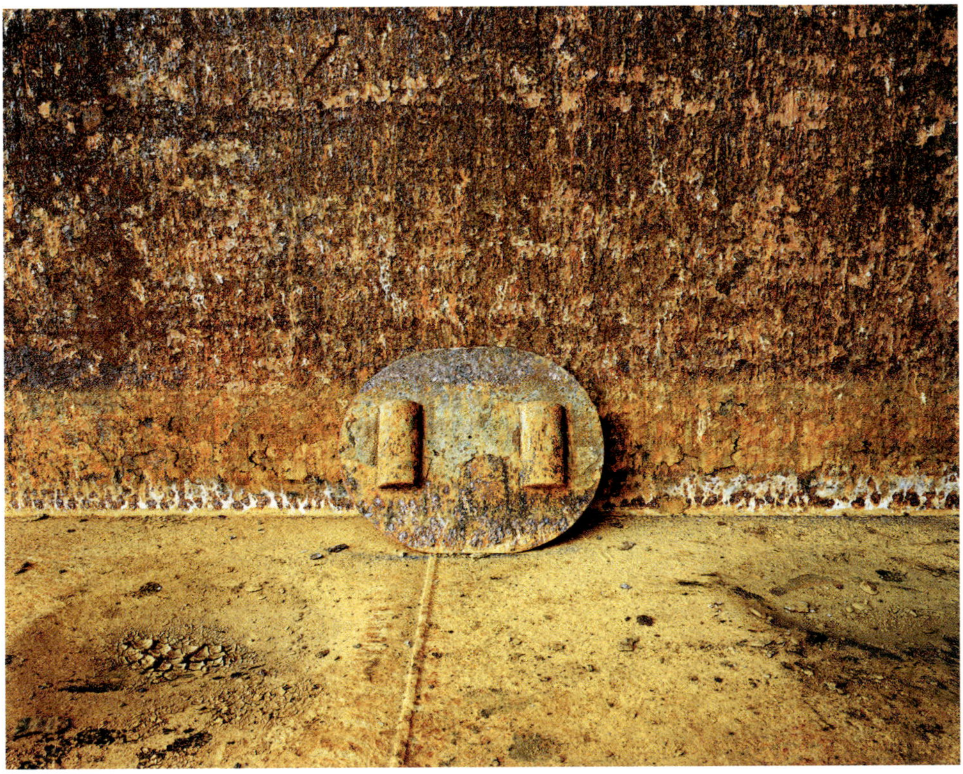

Edward Burtynsky, *Shipbreaking #45*, Chittagong, Bangladesh, 2001

In the end, Burtynsky created two complementary narratives. The first portrays shipbreaking in monumental, epic terms. The second captures the site in a quieter, more domestic mode.

In his review of the *Shipbreaking* exhibition at the Mira Godard Gallery in the April 25, 2001 issue of the *National Post*, John Bentley Mays described the photographer as an artist both "painterly and picturesque" and as a storyteller: "He creates tableaux, each narrating a different episode in the unfolding interaction of men, machine, environment. He puts name and face to the place." Mays understood fully that Burtynsky had made overwhelmingly beautiful images of disaster: "We are . . . on the Bay of Bengal, nearly 100 vessels have been hewn and hacked to pieces by local workers since 1980 . . . Burtynsky trapped the radiance raking across the beach and striking the rusted, wrecked remnants of ships, making them appear to glow like hot coals. Titanic ship-fragments scattered like sculptures on the mud flats in the glowing dawn mist . . . [Burtynsky's] fastidiously composed images of such things read like frames from a Hollywood movie, as lit by J. M. W. Turner, with atmospheric touches by Constable."[15]

Margaret Loke, in the *New York Times*, emphasized the abstract expressionist elements in these images:

> You wouldn't think that ships being broken up at the water's edge for scrap metal would have any saving aesthetic grace, but the Canadian photographer Edward Burtynsky would prove you wrong. In Chittagong, Bangladesh, he found the rusting carcasses of ships looking like grittily vibrant, brutalist sculptures. Mr. Burtynsky has a keen eye for theatrical form and colour, as well as a superb command of the large-format camera's capacity to record detail. And his imposing colour prints, most 40 by 50 inches, offer a vicarious sense of what he saw and felt: the monumental scale of the found art, the unexpected wonder of it all. The frontal *Shipbreaking # 38, Chittagong, Bangladesh* (2001), for instance, is an expressionist abstraction in dark brown and reddish orange.

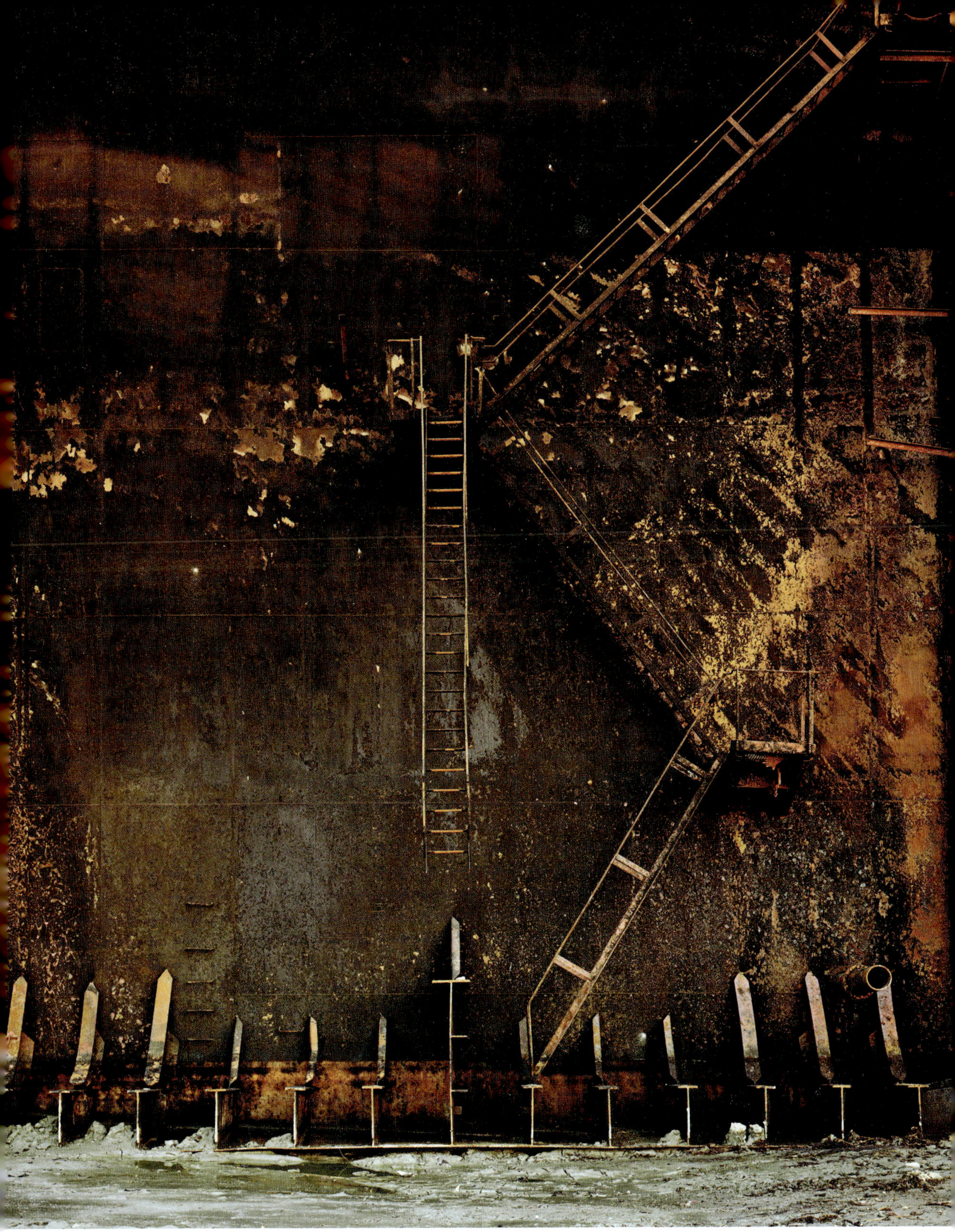

Edward Burtynsky, *Shipbreaking #38*, Chittagong, Bangladesh, 2001

> Delicate lines of vertical and zigzagging metal ladders in the middle of this "canvas" serve as subtle reminders that this was once a ship.[16]

The 2000 *Shipbreaking* project was the breakthrough Burtynsky had sought. As Nicholas Metivier pointed out, "What happened was that we had created enormous momentum and an eager market. People went absolutely nuts for those photographs."[17]

POSTSCRIPT

The shipbreaking images had a new iteration in 2010. Like many large-format photographers at the time, Burtynsky used Polaroid Type 55 positive/negative film when working. Twenty seconds after exposure, the 4 × 5 black-and-white images provide a guide to the photographer in determining exposure, sharpness, and alignment in composing his colour images. Two hundred such images were placed in a clearing bath, washed, dried, and kept by Burtynsky. Many of the colour prints that make up the *Shipbreaking* series originated in this way.

"Several years later," he recalled, "I asked an assistant to find [the Polaroids] and make a set of contact photos. To my horror, the news came back that all my sheets had stuck together, resulting in a single block of fused negatives. It seems that the relative humidity of the negatives while in Bangladesh was quite high, and over time they adhered to one another. However, they did come apart with a nasty sound, the emulsion tearing off and leaving parts of itself on adjacent sheets. I separated each one, putting them in archival sleeves and stored them again while I digested the loss. These were the physical relics of a pivotal moment in my life, and I didn't want to let them go."[18]

Somewhat later, he returned to them and made contact prints. "The distressed negatives, when printed, echoed the look of an earlier period of photography, when emulsions were more fragile."[19] He thought of these

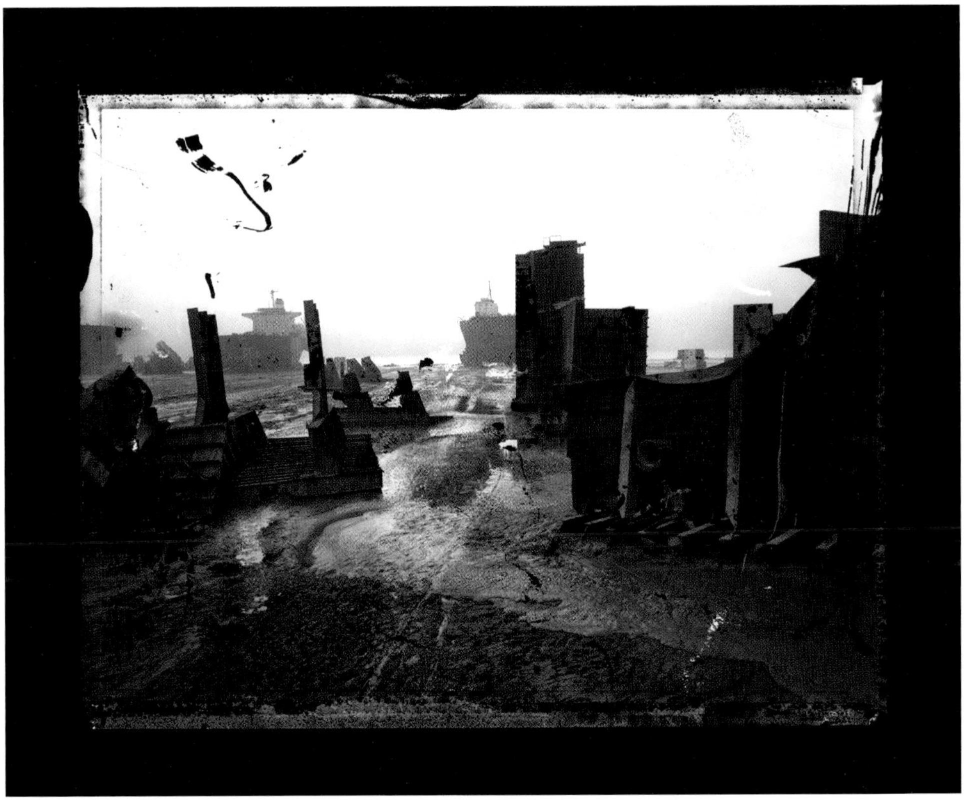

Edward Burtynsky, *Shipbreaking #13*, Field Proof, Chittagong, Bangladesh, 2000

ghostly images as *pentimento*: visible traces of underpainting on a canvas.

Burtynsky is a colour photographer who possesses the sensibility of a black-and-white one. The ten images in *Pentimento* (2010), all from 2000, underscore this and can be usefully compared to Salgado's earlier black-and-white images taken in Bangladesh in their intensity.[20] Drained of colour, the *Pentimento* images are stark, perhaps even more discomforting than their colour versions. The ships shown in the *Shipbreaking* series are in various states of disintegration and so the preservation of distressed images of them makes a fitting conclusion to this chapter in Burtynsky's career.

8 EFFICIENT MACHINES

MACHINE ART

Even as Burtynsky was travelling to India and Bangladesh, his imagination was pulling him in yet another direction.

He retained a fascination with industrial apparatus: transformers, oil refineries, and container ports. During his Ryerson days, he had photographed industrial sites and, in a sense, he was returning to base. All three of his new subjects of interest were conduits. Transformer stations translate the electrical energy they receive from distribution grids at several thousand volts (medium voltage) and adapt it to the low voltage needed for domestic use. A petroleum refinery is a process plant where crude oil is converted into gasoline and other consumer products. Huge truck-size intermodal containers transport all kinds of consumer goods over the world in giant ships.

There are only three transformer images–one is an overview of a site and the other two, shot at ground level, are abstractions where all sorts of vertical and horizontal grids interact with each other. The colours, an assortment of browns and silvers, also play off each other–as do the shadows.

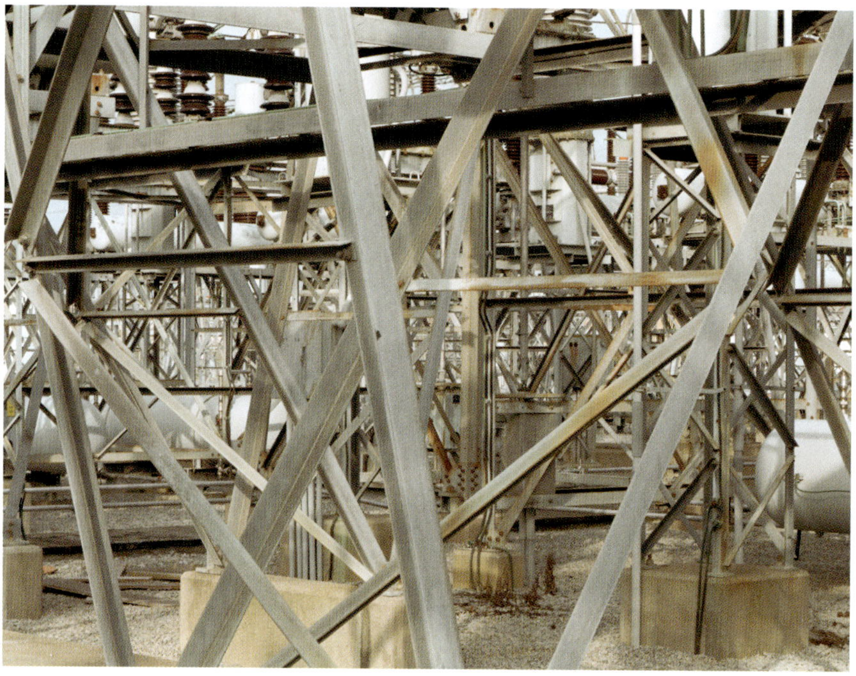

Edward Burtynsky, *Transformer Station #1*, 2000

The same observation is true of some of the new refinery images made in Oakville, Ontario, which he had photographed in 1978. In the new images, there is a division established between those images that emphasize highly polished surfaces and those that are older, out of the way, and have a matte finish. "A refinery," Burtynsky muses, "is clearly an architectural space but strangely inverted. Typically, a structure contains a machine, but because the refinery builds up a lot of heat and expresses gasses, the internal workings of the machine are on the outside." He adds: "I don't think when they build a refinery there is an overall vision of how

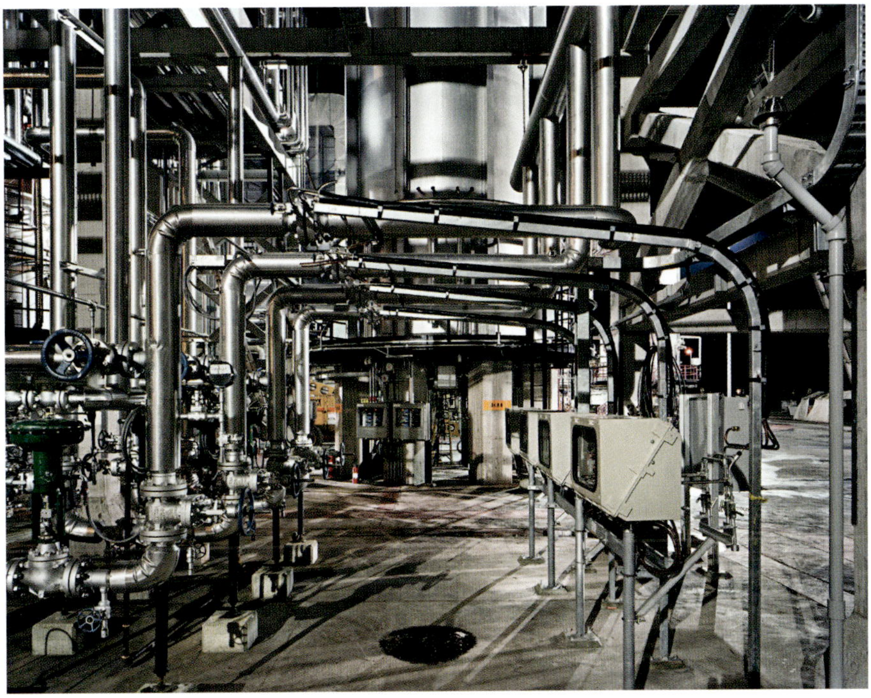

Edward Burtynsky, *Oil Refineries #8*, Oakville, Ontario, 1999

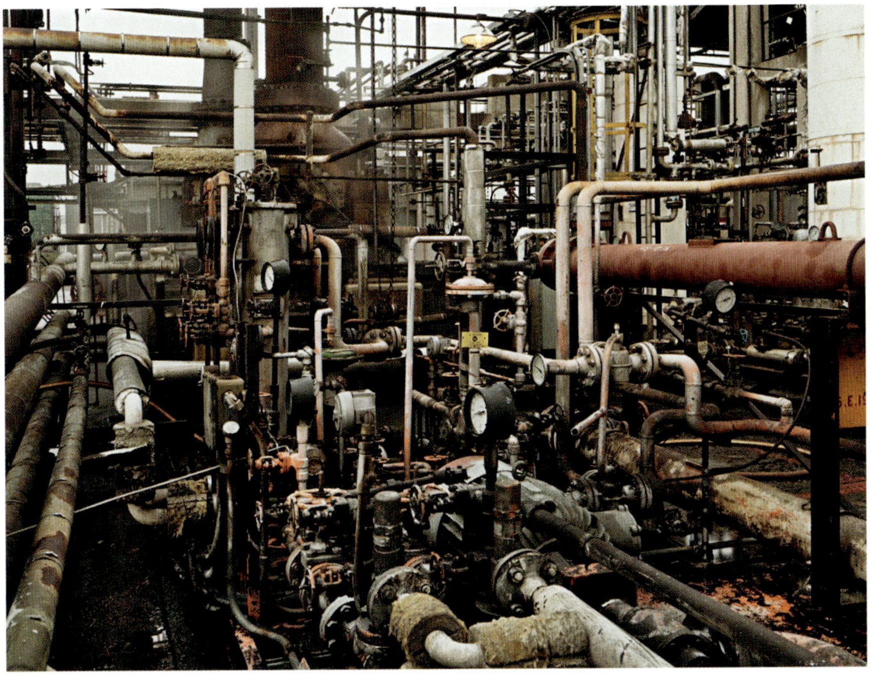

Edward Burtynsky, *Oil Refineries #9*, Oakville, Ontario, 1999

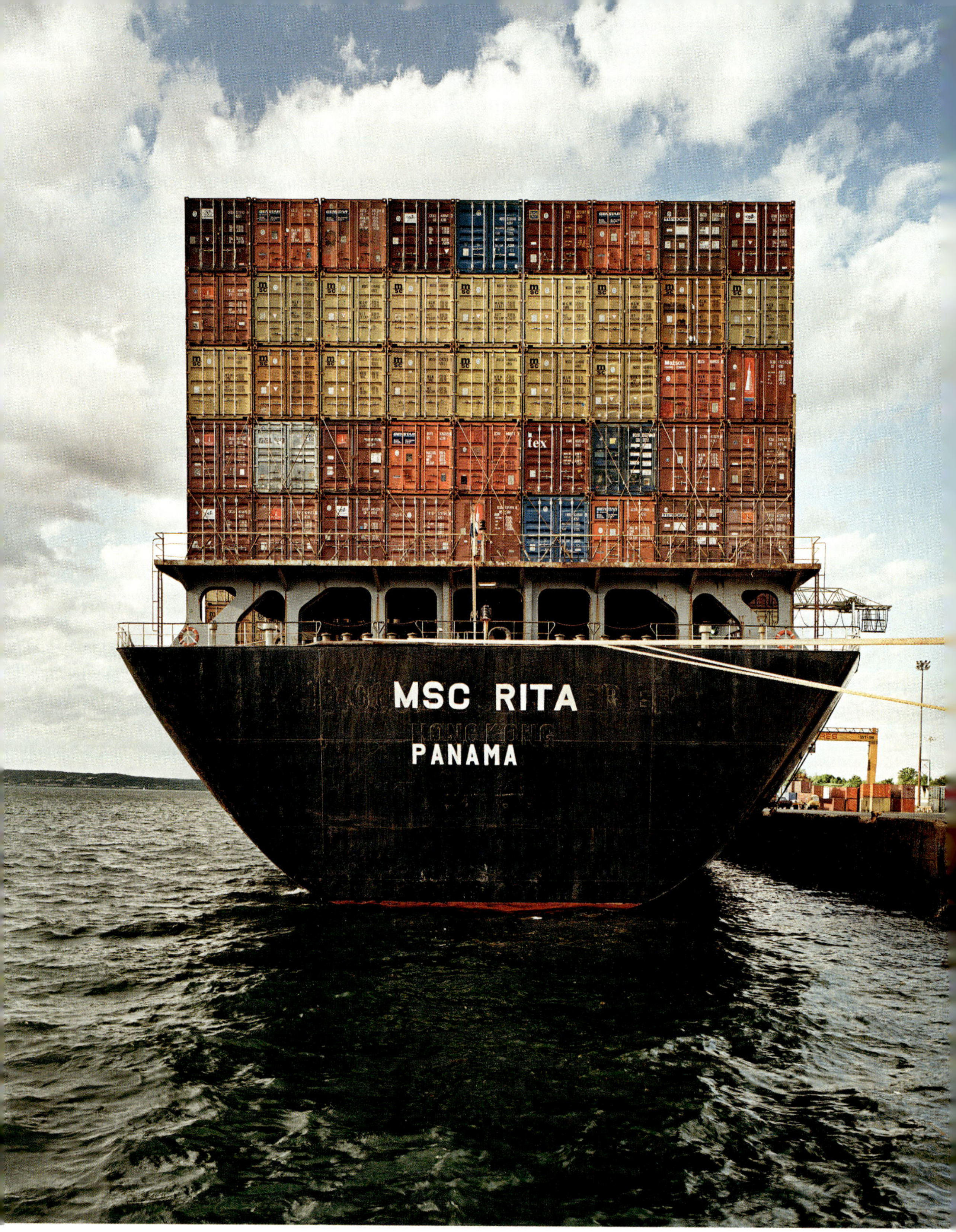

Edward Burtynsky, *Container Ports #17*, Ceres Port, Halifax, Nova Scotia, 2001

it's going to be constructed. They simply want to find the most efficient machine that does the task and with that premise the structure unfolds. It was interesting to me to work toward finding a way to visually reconcile that complexity."[1]

In this sequence, Burtynsky emphasized how newer sections of pipe are connected to older, rusted counterparts. The contrast is a glaring one. Images that display a shiny surface are reminiscent of Charles Sheeler (see p. 35) and suggest the power and magnificence of industry, but some are of badly worn pipes. Clint Roenisch has argued that Burtynsky "positively exalts the baroque splendour of these complex systems" and presents "the mesmerizing array of pipes in a seductive, corporeal manner."[2] This is true, but Burtynsky showed the other side of the coin in contrasting images. In this way, the "magnificence" of the pipes is called into question.

Abstraction can also be seen in the container images he took, and especially in the juxtaposition of strong primary colours against each other in a manner reminiscent of some images in *Urban Mines* (see p. 115). Since what is inside the containers is not visible, there is a sense of mystery–a curious sense of absence. As Burtynsky has reflected:

> We are surrounded by all kinds of consumer goods, and yet we are profoundly detached from the sources of these things. Our lifestyles are made possible by industries all around the world, but we take them for granted, as a background to our existence. I feel that by showing those places that are normally outside our experience, but very much a part of our everyday lives, I can add to our understanding of who we are and what we are doing.[3]

THE STUDIO

Following the success of the *Shipbreaking* series, Burtynsky was freed from the day-to-day running of Toronto Image Works as Jeannie took over the role. He had come to realize that he should put an infrastructure in place that would assist him in marketing, promoting, and exhibiting his work. In 2002, Burtynsky created a new section at his headquarters on Spadina Avenue. The Studio became a separate entity from Image Works: its function was to promote Burtynsky's own photographic work. He hired assistants to handle sales, to assist in the printing of his work, and in essence to help him promote his brand. As Raphael Bernstein had perceived years earlier, Burtynsky the artist was linked to Burtynsky the entrepreneur. A succession of assistants proved inadequate, however, until efficient, reliable Karen Machtinger came along, who survived at first working in a space the size of a broom closet. To this day, she remains the Studio's overseer.

Another addition was Marcus Schubert. Burtynsky and Schubert had remained close friends since their Ryerson days, and when Ed and Jeannie were living on Springmount Avenue, Marcus lived next door. The three often dined together and talked photography. Over many late-night discussions, while the Toronto lab was still in the ideation stage, Schubert had suggested the name "Image Works," which husband and wife then expanded to "Toronto Image Works." The thinking then was that the lab might expand to other Canadian cities and could be named by location.

After graduating from Ryerson, Schubert travelled widely throughout Europe and North America to explore his passion in photographing landscapes and *art brut* ("outsider") architecture with his 8 × 10 view camera. When he settled back in Toronto, he freelanced fabricating large-scale seasonal displays for Hazelton Lanes and taught ferro cement and wire sculpture courses–an expertise he had acquired as a result of his fascination and experience with *art brut*. In 2000, Schubert curated a large *Outsider* exhibition in Baltimore, *Treasures of the Soul*, for the American Visionary Art Museum. When those jobs faded in the autumn of 2002, he asked both Ed and Jeannie if there might be work for him at Toronto Image Works. Coincidentally, Burtynsky's first book, *Manufactured Landscapes*, was to go to press soon and had not yet been sequenced. Ed said to Marcus, "Do you have a minute?" Drawing on their shared aesthetic sensibilities, they sequenced the entire book that afternoon.

From then on, Schubert became the second member of the Studio, after Karen Machtinger, in what Burtynsky describes as a "small but mighty" hand-picked team. Schubert became the manager of publications and studio curator, along with being a sounding board, someone who offers frank, informed opinions, works on the development of projects, and assists in the editing of images. As new projects are brought to the viewing wall in the office, he marks up large work prints, making initial colour corrections. He helps prepare special project proposals, creates layouts, and oversees the installation of major exhibitions. Over the years, Burtynsky has recruited others to join Machtinger (who is now the director of studio operations and gallery operations) and Schubert (now director of publications, exhibitions and special projects) in the Studio. As of 2025, these include project coordinator Jim Panou, archivist and production manager Paul Sergeant, media and communications manager Alanna Smith, director of finance Connie Hitzeroth, and chief colour technician Dan Ebert.

Burtynsky's wife, Julia Johnston, is, as her husband often puts it, "the glue that holds it all together." His practice in the last decade has been considerably strengthened by her encouragement, support, and considerable acumen. She played a crucial role in developing the *Anthropocene* and *Africa* projects and in organizing the Saatchi exhibition. In the past decade, her organizational skills and savviness have made her husband's accomplishments more widely known.

RETROSPECTIVES

In 1985, the Kitchener-Waterloo Art Gallery had hosted one of Burtynsky's first solo exhibitions. To celebrate that event, he donated over fifty photographs to the gallery in 2001. The following year, the gallery commemorated the gift with an exhibition: *Works from Two Decades 1981–2001: A Gift to the Collection.* The exhibition was accompanied by a catalogue prepared by curator Clint Roenisch, who worked closely with Burtynsky in organizing the exhibition and prepared a detailed essay for the catalogue, titled "Dust Postponed: The Machinations of Man in the Work of Edward Burtynsky." This substantial exhibition catalogue is forty-nine pages long, with eight full-page colour photos and fifty-two black-and-white thumbnails of the entries.

The exhibition began with some images from *Shipbreaking* and then moved back in time to photos of Makrana, oil refineries, tire piles, urban landscapes, nickel tailings, Carrara, Rock of Ages, railcuts, homesteads, open nickel mines, greenhouses, taxidermy, and factory interiors. The unusual arrangement allowed the viewer to see the artist's recent work and then to move backward to his origins as a colour photographer.

Roenisch's essay precisely delineated the ambiguities in the works on show: "As an indictment of large-scale ecological misdeeds, they are unconvincing, and that is their strength. As works of art shot through with formal beauty the images brook few arguments. As a testament to the transient nature of all things, they are unwavering. What is troubling is the sheer visual weight of so much constant transformation and decline."[4]

The exhibition *Works from Two Decades* took place a year after Burtynsky's book with Lumiere Press, *Residual Landscapes*. While *Works from Two Decades* may be more comprehensive than *Residual Landscapes*, the latter contains Michael Torosian's key interview with the photographer. Both publications were important stepping stones in encapsulating Burtynsky's accomplishments.

A third major exhibition and publication soon followed with *Manufactured Landscapes*, a National Gallery of Canada retrospective that opened in

Ottawa in January 2003, and subsequently travelled to the Art Gallery of Ontario and the Brooklyn Museum of Art. The catalogue contains sixty-four full-page images, divided as follows: five from *Railcuts*; eleven from *Mines and Tailings*; fifteen from *Quarries*; twelve from *Urban Mines*, including *Tire Piles*; ten from *Oil Fields* and *Refineries*; and eleven from *Shipbreaking*. Unlike the Kitchener-Waterloo exhibition, homesteads, greenhouses, taxidermy, and factory interiors were omitted. The catalogue followed Torosian's lead in including the pivotal interview with Burtynsky, which was updated to include the *Shipbreaking* images. (Torosian interviewed Burtynsky a second time.)

For Lori Pauli, the curator, "there [was] something uncannily beautiful and breathtaking in the very expansiveness of these images–it is as if the vastness of their perspective somehow opens onto the larger view of things." In "Seeing the Big Picture," she offered the crucial point: "By making photographs as large as paintings, Burtynsky found the elusive harmony between content and harmony he had long been seeking."[5]

Kenneth Baker, in his essay "Form Versus Portent: Edward Burtynsky's Endangered Landscapes," inquired if Burtynsky was "an apologist for the industrial order and its new face, globalization? Is he a documentarian, a pictorial epicure, an ironist? Burtynsky's refusal to stand fast in any of these positions, explains the improbable emotional authority of his art."[6] Yet, in answer to his own questions, Baker asserted that Burtynsky "trusts his art to work upon us, and us to respond appropriately, without being told what that might mean."[7]

In "Edward Burtynsky: Traditions and Affinities," Mark Haworth-Booth related Burtynsky's "formulation" of the sublime to Edmund Burke's celebrated definition: "Whatever is fitted in any sort to excite the idea of pain and danger; that is to say, whatever is in any way terrible, or is conversant about terrible subjects, or operates in a manner analogous to terror, is a source of the *sublime*; that is to say, whatever it is productive of the strongest emotion, which the mind is capable of feeling."[8] The analogy is appropriate because Burtynsky inculcates a sense of the "terrible" in his various projects. Haworth-Booth also points out Burtynsky's strong affinity with Frederick Sommer, who photographed both gold mines and junkyards.

For Burtynsky, the retrospective was a major breakthrough. He joked with Christopher Waters of the *St. Catherines Standard*, saying, "You don't get a lot of retrospectives. You tend to get one in the middle of you career and, if you are lucky, you get one before you die. This is one when I am still alive and able to string a couple of sentences together."[9]

The retrospective, along with three substantial publications in 2001, 2002, and 2003, celebrated the photographer's achievements. Inspired by his two forays into the Indian subcontinent, Burtynsky next turned his attention to China. First, he explored the destruction wreaked by the Three Gorges Dam and then, in a much broader project, China's emergence as a manufacturing powerhouse–the world centre of globalization.

(2002–2005)

9 THE GREAT WALLS OF CHINA

VESTIGES

The Three Gorges Dam project first appeared on drawing boards around 1919, but plans for its construction were not approved until the National People's Congress did so in 1992. On paper, the dam promised significant benefits: it would generate an enormous amount of electricity, increase shipping capacity on the Yangtze, and reduce flooding downstream. A significant number of scientists were opposed to the project: the dam would sit on a seismic fault; ancestral towns and villages would be submerged and 1.3 million inhabitants would have to be resettled; major landslides could occur; the ecology of the area would be eradicated. When the odds were weighed, the Chinese government decided to go ahead with the project on the basis that more benefits would accrue than deficits.

A decade after construction began on the Three Gorges Dam, Burtynsky decided to investigate this work-in-progress. He wanted to inspect displacement–the destruction of buildings so that they would not interfere with the operations of the new waterway. What does such a major undertaking involve and what is the human cost?

Burtynsky, filmmaker Jeff Powis, and photographer and writer Lucas Lackner flew to Shanghai in the autumn of 2002; at their hotel, they met up with Noah Weinzweig, a camera operator and film producer who had lived in China for seven years and spoke fluent Mandarin. Weinzweig was to be the group's guide, translator, and photographic assistant. Like Jim Panou in 2000, Weinzweig was Burtynsky's local "fixer"–someone who had spent time researching a project in advance and then did everything on site to anticipate and fulfill the photographer's needs.[1] From Shanghai, the four flew almost one thousand miles west to Yichang, the closest access point to the dam.

As Lackner recalled, on a typical day, "we'd pile into a hired van with any driver willing to spend the day transporting us to the most graphic scenes of devastation. We hired porters, wandered about, set up, broke down, and scrambled for suitable images and perfect light. We initially travelled upriver [on the Yangtze] through a series of towns: Guizhou, Wushan, Fengjie, Yungang, and Wanzhou. The most effective river transportation came in the form of ageing Russian hydrofoils that ferried us and assorted locals and their belongings at high speeds through the Yangtze's treacherous waters." Each time they disembarked, the group employed porters to carry their assortment of bags and equipment cases. Then, the four had to "negotiate steep hillsides, and then hail taxies to either the newly built cities or to the rubble landscapes of the old ones. We clambered over the vestiges of cities and towns in what seemed like a post-apocalyptic wasteland." Each town was being rebuilt further away from the future reservoir and the old one was being destroyed. The group came upon neighbourhoods being demolished by workmen with sledgehammers. They saw families struggling to make do in deteriorating conditions. They smelled toxins emanating from cement factories. They struggled to breathe.

After Wanzhou, the four returned to the dam for their one-day "authorized" shoot. "Those spaces and views were simply breathtaking, colossal and otherworldly." They also witnessed the enormous pride of everyone working on the site. Before leaving the area, the group headed back upstream to Mingshan and Fuling, "clambering, shooting and once again absorbing the enormous changes." During their two-and-a-half weeks in China, "they had witnessed a chapter in the epic metamorphosis of a culture and its landscape."[2]

Burtynsky desperately wanted to take an image that would encapsulate the flattening of the cities in the Three Gorges area. At Wanzhou, he waited patiently for two days because a local informed him that a large wall was wobbling. "I asked him, 'How long would it take before it fell?' I set my camera up and waited half a day. The wall did not tumble. The next morning, I set up my camera and waited. Five hours went by before the wall crashed to the ground."[3]

One of Burtynsky and Weinzweig's expeditions almost landed them in jail as Burtynsky was photographing workers he saw working at an e-waste business. The police stopped them and "warned us that if we got caught again, we'd be thrown out of the country." Burtynsky moved quickly: "There was only one road out of town too, so I'd taken this image as quickly as possible, got back in the car and headed out. To our surprise and shock, a local informant jumped into our car while we were on the phone with the police and told them we were taking pictures of illegal activity. I was sure this was the end of my days shooting in China, but, through some fast talking, Noah convinced the police to let us go using some unrelated paperwork from Beijing stating we had permission. In all our adventures in China, that was the closest we came to getting into serious trouble."[4]

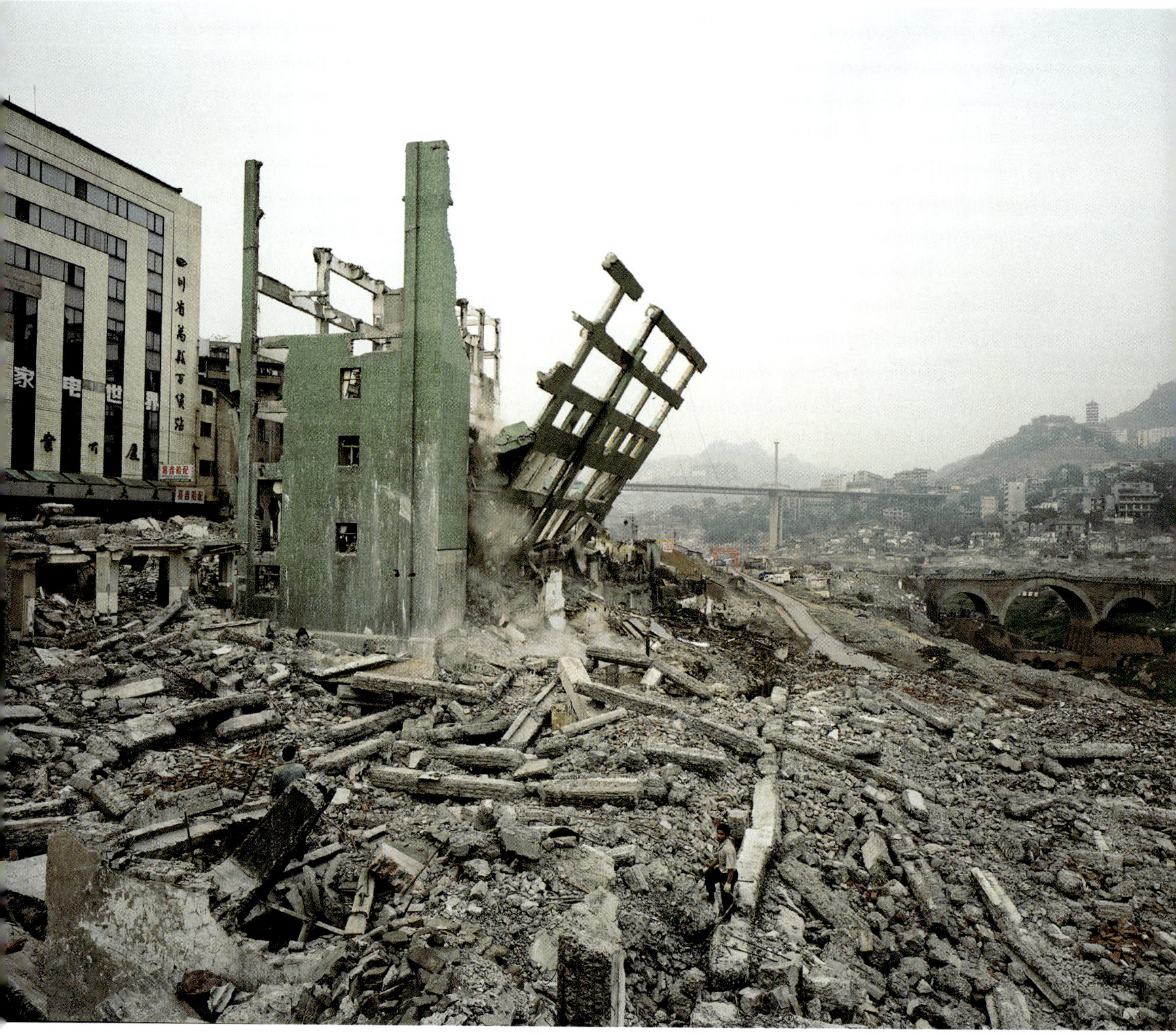

Edward Burtynsky, *Wan Zhou #4*, Three Gorge Dam Project, Yangtze River, China, 2002

Although some of Burtynsky's images show the dam in the process of being built, they concentrate on the wreckage imposed on the terrain. The photos are images of disintegration–they do not make an overt political or moral point. Is the tearing down progress or regression? The viewer is left to decide. Whatever judgment is reached, the shots remain plaintive images of destruction, loss, and destabilization. Burtynsky's narrative is about the tragedy of being forced to leave one's home and find a new one.

The portfolio *Before the Flood* contains forty images (thirty-eight taken in 2002, two in 2005): ten in Fengjie, fourteen in Wushan, nine in Wanzhou, and seven at the site where the dam was being built. One of the most remarkable aspects of these photographs is how, by design, many look monochromatic. This allows a synchronicity to be established between form and content: the reduction of everything to rubble is reflected

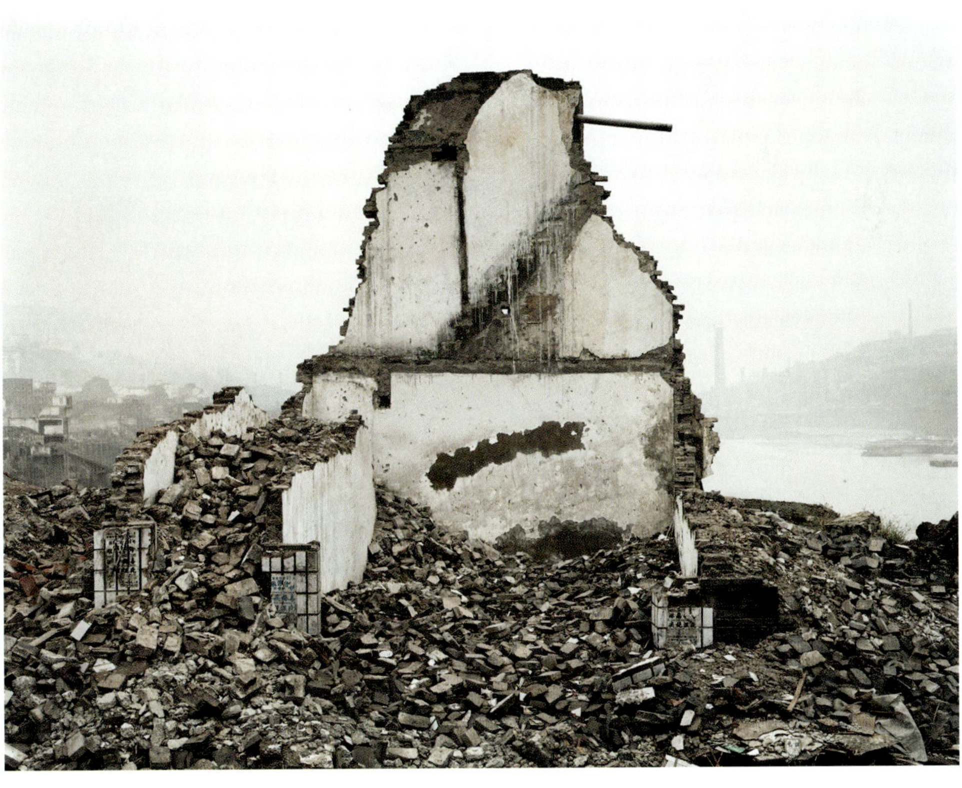

Edward Burtynsky, *Wan Zhou #10*, Three Gorge Dam Project, Yangtze River, China, 2002

in the avoidance of primary colours. For Burtynsky, the towns of Fengjie and Wanzhou were netherworlds. In one of the images from Wanzhou, the obliterated walls create a giant sculpture in grey and white rising from the rubble. Only the dark blue worn by the workers provides a modicum of colour. When bright colours are present, they are overpowered by the dingy colours of the landscape surrounding them. The fire in *Feng Jie #10* is startling because its energy is juxtaposed against the dull-coloured wreckage surrounding it. A similar fire burns at the side of the road in *Feng Jie #5*, as a man and a donkey take their leave–abandoning the old world and warily entering the new.

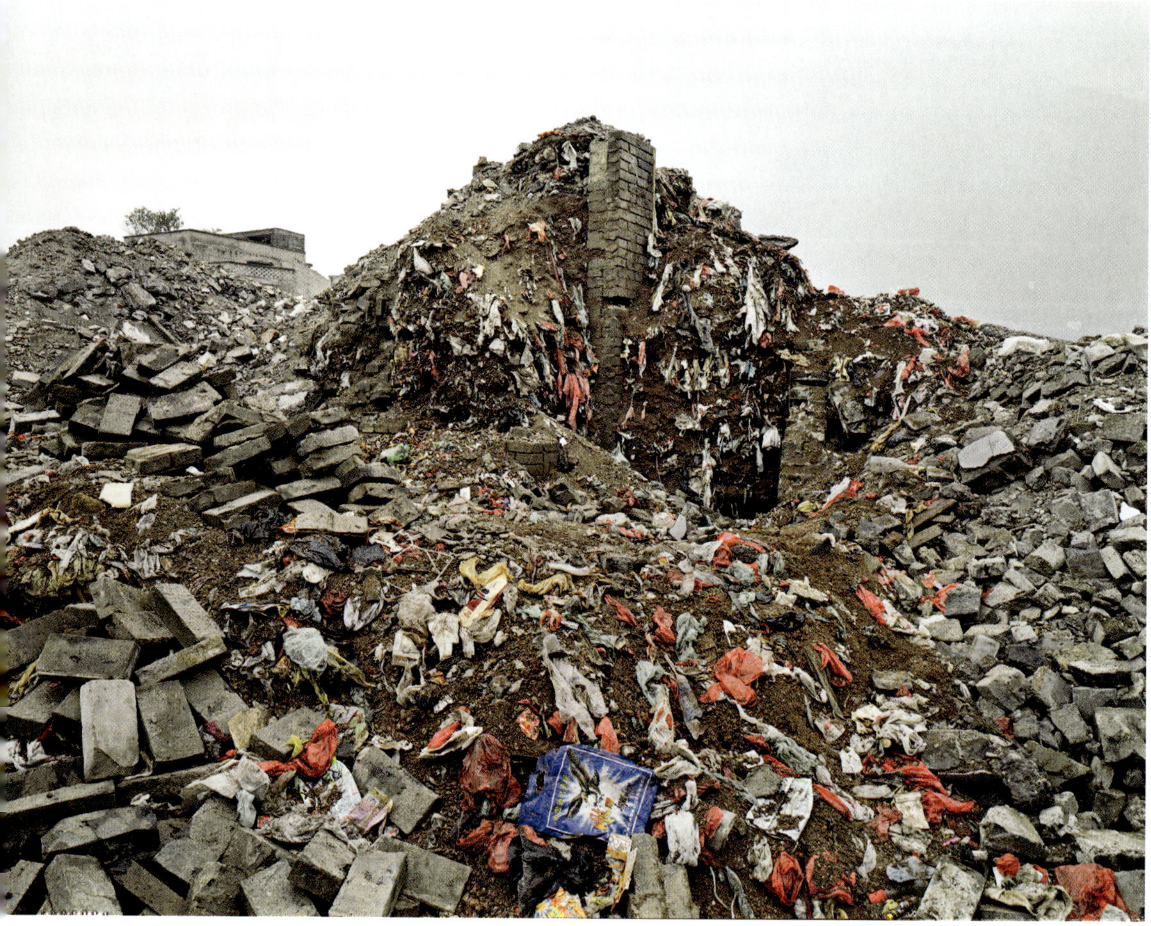

Edward Burtynsky, *Wushan #10,* Three Gorge Dam Project, Yangtze River, China, 2002

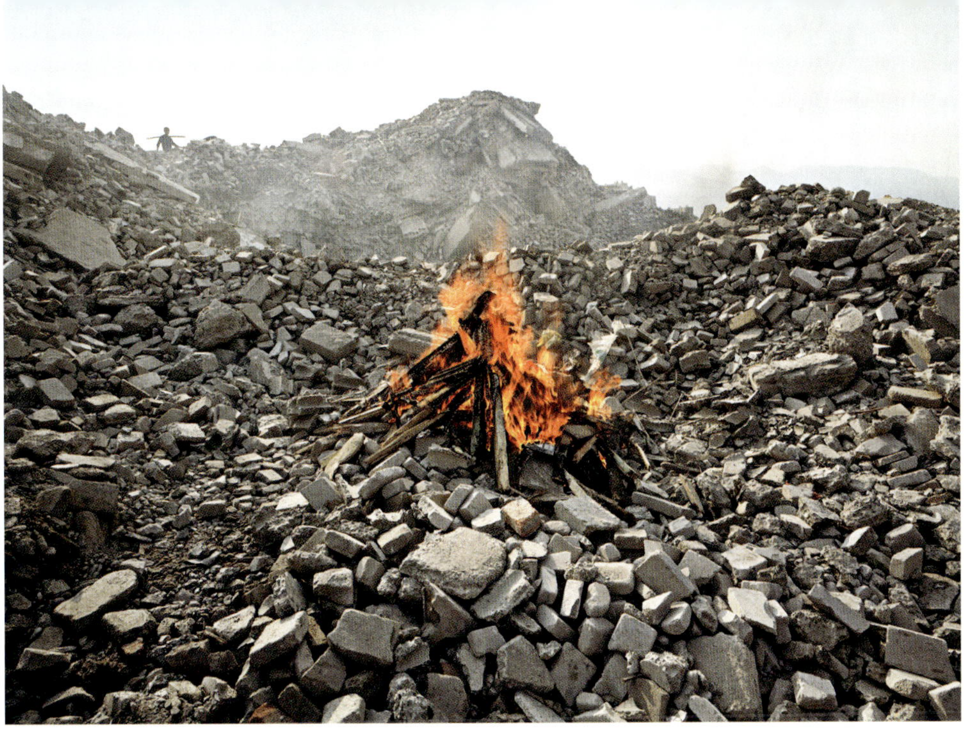

Edward Burtynsky, *Feng Jie #10*, Three Gorge Dam Project, Yangtze River, China, 2002

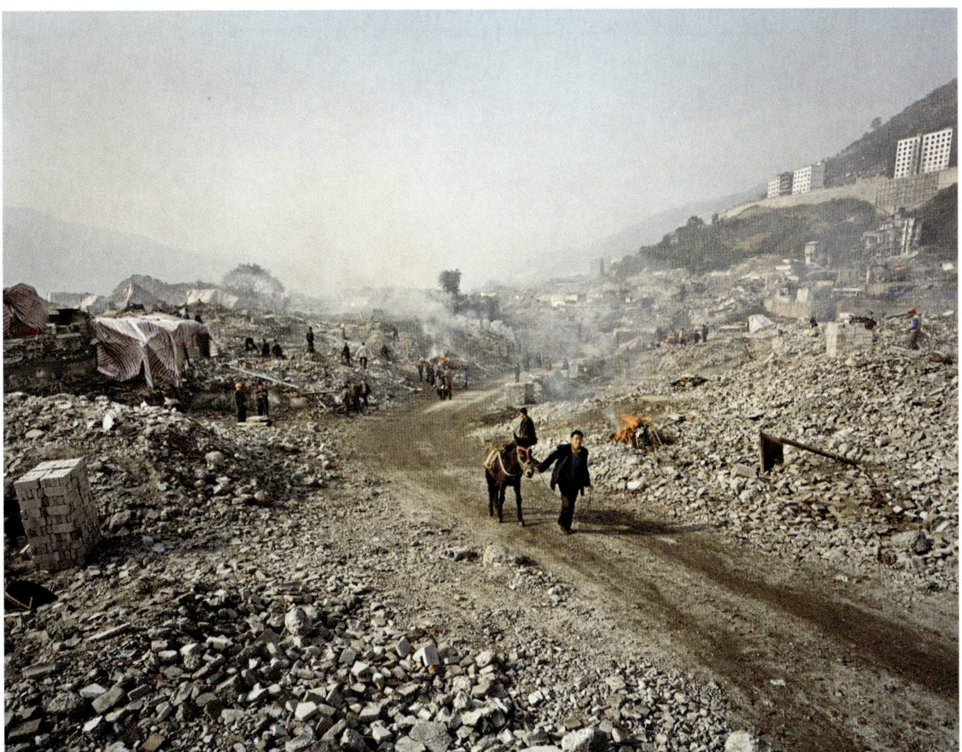

Edward Burtynsky, *Feng Jie #5*, Three Gorge Dam Project, Yangtze River, China, 2002

Some views of the dam follow this limited colour scheme as well. *Dam #4* is an unusual turn for Burtynsky because this view of the construction of the dam is in black and white. The lack of colour values emphasizes the austere, other worldly grandeur of the project at the very same time as it distances the viewer from it.

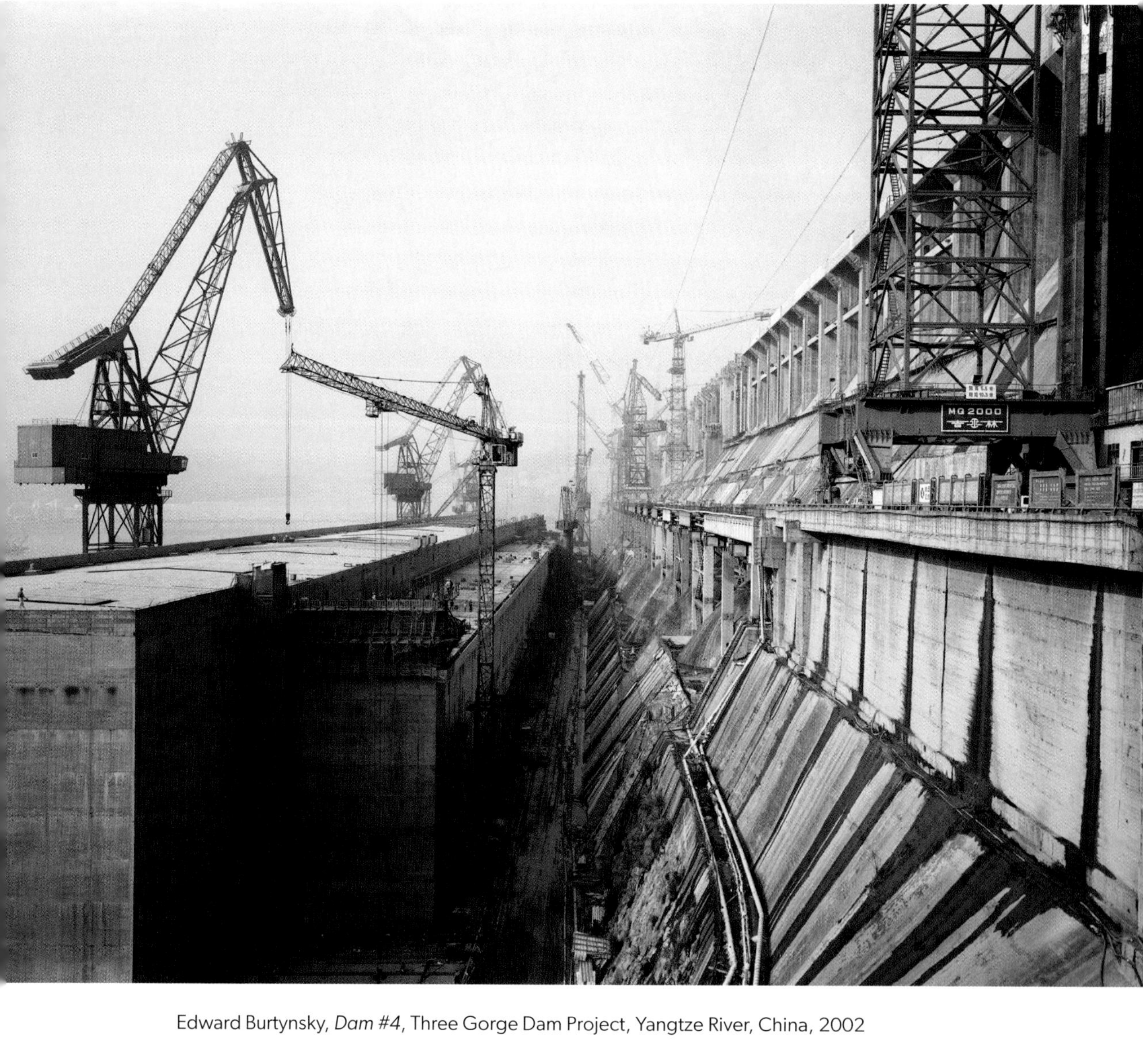

Edward Burtynsky, *Dam #4*, Three Gorge Dam Project, Yangtze River, China, 2002

"REFLECTING POOLS"

The construction of the Three Gorges Dam was a giant piece in the puzzle of "modernizing" China. Having depicted the "wreckage" that the dam's construction had created, Burtynsky returned there in 2004 and 2005 to look at another crucial aspect of the modernization of that country: China as a manufacturing powerhouse. He had touched on this issue in his shipping container series, as the contents concealed in many of those containers had originated in China. By focusing on manufacturing, Burtynsky would examine the interiors of many of those containers. And he wanted to tackle some other issues in the transformation of China: urban renewal; "ship making," rather than "shipbreaking"; the proliferation of "urban mines"; and the steel industry. He also wanted to examine another quarry.

This new China project began differently than the previous foray had. Burtynsky was travelling to China to take photographs; again, Noah Weinzweig was his fixer. And, as described earlier, Burtynsky had made a list of the subjects he wanted to investigate. The difference was that, this time, he was accompanied by a film crew that would make moving pictures of him making still images. The film would focus on the new China project, but it would also provide a portrait of Burtynsky the photographer. As envisioned by the director Jennifer Baichwal, the film would show Burtynsky at work but, at the same time, allow her to incorporate her own take on contemporary China.

Jeff Powis had taken about a hundred hours of footage in Bangladesh and China on previous trips documenting the shipbreaking and the Three Gorges projects, but his material did not gell in a way that satisfied Burtynsky. At that point, the photographer approached the producer Daniel Iron to ask if he could find someone suitable to make a documentary about his forthcoming trip to China. Iron immediately thought of Baichwal and her spouse cinematographer, Nicholas de Pencier of Mercury Films.

Burtynsky was enthusiastic about working with the couple because he had seen and been impressed by their film *The True Meaning of Pictures: Shelby Lee Adams' Appalachia* (2002), a documentary about the controversial American photographer. Meanwhile, Baichwal had looked at Powis's footage from the previous trip and determined that it could be a starting point, but that she would create a different type of film than Powis had envisioned.

She decided to "make a film that extended the meaning of the photographs into the time-based medium of film." And when she met with Burtynsky, she was forthright: "Ed, I'm not interested in a biography. [I] don't care that you came from St. Catharines and worked on the line at GM. I know all of that is important for your work, right? But what I'm interested in is doing an intelligent extension of the meaning of your work into film. Specifically, I want you to be an author, not a subject."[5]

Nick de Pencier was not free to travel with his wife to China, so Baichwal engaged the cinematographer Peter Mettler, who had been a student at Ryerson at the same time as Burtynsky. De Pencier became the film's producer.

As an "extension of the meaning" of Burtynsky's work, the documentary *Manufactured Landscapes* became a blend of two overlapping but different media and, in the process, a complex and intricate layering of moving and still images.

The film opens dramatically with an eight-minute tracking shot on a dolly that moves down the three-quarters of a mile that is the length of the floor of the massive EUPA megafactory in the southern Chinese city of Zhangzhou. The site calls itself the Factory of the World (its products included Black & Decker coffee makers and George Foreman Grills). The depiction of the length of the workspace and the vast assembly of workers in it create a visually spectacular tour de force. The footage then shifts to workers assembling outside for Burtynsky to photograph.

In taking this image, Burtynsky encountered unexpected obstacles:

> I wanted to get all 22,000 workers outside and organized in a way so that from a high vantage point their bodies would spell out "Factory of the World"–the words on a big sign that led into the factory. I had an idea to get 5,000 of the group in black t-shirts and the rest of them wearing their yellow uniforms. The only reason we didn't do it was because we couldn't get the timing right. With that realization, I looked instead at their regular daily processes and as I watched teams of workers come outside for a debrief with their foremen. I asked the factory owners if it was possible [that they remove the trucks] from the road and cover up some of the waste materials that were outside the buildings that would've appeared distracting. They agreed to do it and organized all the workers to come out on the same day and time. I got a forklift with a box to lift and position me to the vantage point I needed.

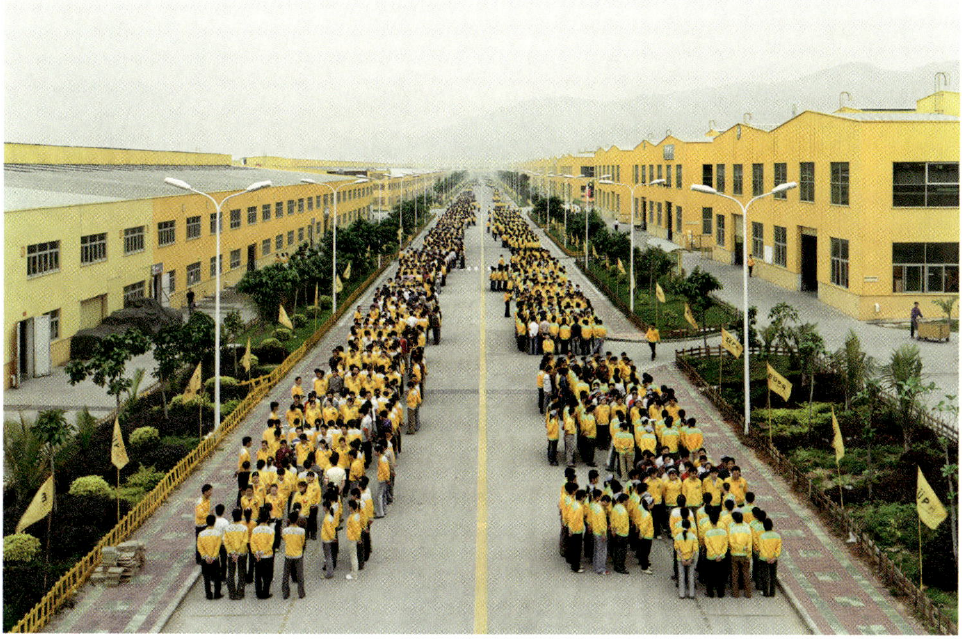

Edward Burtynsky, *Manufacturing #18*, Cankun Factory, Zhangzhou, China, 2005

Rarely does Burtynsky stage-manage, but "in this case I wanted to really showcase that unequivocally China was becoming the manufacturing leader of the world."[6]

Both the tracking shot and the group photograph are synecdoches representing the vast size of the Chinese workforce. "My images just show the baby toe of the elephant," Burtynsky observed.[7] Then, after these two sequences, he speaks about the emotional journey his work has taken him on. He describes his epiphany at Frackville; images of Sudbury, Elliot Lake, Rock of Ages, and Carrara, among other places, appear on screen; the film camera explores these images, in the process establishing a montage blending the two media.

Then, the film reverts to a shot of a factory floor where women are engaged in painstaking, repetitive work; their patient, careworn faces are revealed in close-ups. Then the action shifts to scavengers harvesting e-waste–at that point, images from the *Urban Mines* series appear (the point being made that the waste in Canada has been shipped to China). Then, abruptly, the film transitions to black-and-white footage shot by Powis at the Three Gorges, where rummagers there are shown hard at work shifting through e-waste.

Another assembly line of women at another factory, Sentai Electrical, then comes into view while a voice-over by a company representative reads a prepared script about the company's noble aims. The footage segues to a ship-building yard, where Burtynsky is setting up; he observes that globalization has led to the construction of enormous vessels to transport the goods manufactured in China. In a fine turn of irony, the footage shifts to shipbreaking in Bangladesh taken by Powis.

In a segment at Tianjin Steel, Burtynsky, Baichwal, and Weinzweig are informed by a bureaucrat that they cannot film there. The place is too dirty, the official says, and the pictures would be ugly as a result. Weinzweig assures her that Burtynsky will, despite the unsightliness of the site, make beautiful pictures of it. She and some other officials tentatively agree to let Burtynsky photograph, and then inspect some of his Polaroid negatives.

Only one image made at Tianjin Steel survives,[8] but those taken at Bao Steel are startling–virtually black and white–images. Years later, Burtynsky recalled, the visit to Bao had surprising consequences: "Curiously, several years after the release of the China book, somebody illegally took one of the images out of the book and turned it into a poster and launched an anti-Bao Steel campaign. And while this campaign had nothing to do with me, and the artwork was used without my consent, the company has since never let photographers or cinematographers back there."[9]

The documentary returns to the photographs made at the Three Gorges Dam and to footage–in colour, and black and white–taken there by Powis. The film then transitions to a huge diorama in Shanghai, where a guide rhapsodizes about the renewal of the city.

The documentary then spotlights a woman–a real estate agent–proudly showcasing her enormous, newly built house and garden to the camera crew. According to her, Shanghai has rightfully become a place for the young and therefore, she implies, she had the perfect right to build her home on appropriated land. In contrast, the city's old quarters are visited–obviously to be "displaced"–torn down–to make way for the "new" city.

"When I first went to Shanghai," Burtynsky reminisced, "I said, 'My god, this is capitalism on steroids. It's totally pumped up and it's going a hundred miles an hour.'" He also realized that in Shanghai, and all the other places he visited, that "as long as I was on subjects they felt were representing China as a forward-thinking, progressive country, and as long as we didn't touch on any human-rights issues or mingle with unhappy natives, the government was pretty open to us capturing that aspect of China's manufacturing might within the new world order."[10]

Taking photographs in Shanghai proved challenging when Burtynsky and Weinzweig were stopped by the police for shooting in an unauthorized neighbourhood. Weinzweig became anxious when the officers ordered them to take all their equipment to the police station.

He confessed to Burtynsky: "I'm getting a little nervous." Afterward, he reflected:

> Ed doesn't speak Chinese, so he's bored and, while we're waiting, he starts looking at his camera and he discovers some function he never knew about. This got him excited beyond belief. He's like, "Look, Noah, this is fantastic!" Meanwhile, the cops are figuring out what to do with us. I said, "Ed, can we talk about this later?"[11]

What Burtynsky and Baichwal achieved in the documentary was to create parallel narratives that each play to their individual strengths. Baichwal's footage shows people working on huge assembly lines, sorters going through recycling piles, ships being built, and neighbourhoods about to be demolished. As she promised, Baichwal ultimately provided cinematic equivalents–extensions–to Burtynsky's photographs. His take on China and, by extension, his commitment to investigating man's disregard for the natural world, is the focus of the film. In that sense, he is the film's author and not merely its subject.

Burtynsky's work in China also marked a major shift in how he envisioned his practice as a photographer. In his earlier work, he had concentrated on looking for patterns in what he has labelled a "compressed abstract expressionist" style. In China, more conscious of recording what he witnessed as evidence of political and social change, he became more aware of another strand: documentary photography. He phrases it this way: "There are two kinds of stylistic things that you'll find throughout my work. And some books have more of it and some have less of it . . . I bounce between them."[12]

Writing for *The Huffington Post* in July 2007, Bruno Giussani highlighted the film's many accomplishments:

> If you are planning (you should) to go see Jennifer Baichwal's documentary *Manufactured Landscapes* . . . make sure you get there in time, for nothing describes the scale and essence of today's globalized industry more tellingly than the opening scene: a tracking shot of the floor

> of a boundless Chinese factory, row after row after row of disciplined workers and efficient repetition that Stanley Kubrick could have filmed. *Manufactured Landscapes* is based on the work of photographer Ed Burtynsky, whose camera has captured stunning images of man-transformed landscapes around the world. Burtynsky is not much interested in micro: his focus is on vastness, on the scale of the environmental scars and transformations brought forth by industry, energy production and transportation. The documentary is a hybrid: it's a meditation that makes very little use of words, leaving it to images and situational sounds and noises to tell the story, and at the same time a convincing illustration of the monstrosity of today's global trade . . . [Burtynsky] extracts beautiful, sometimes poetic images from outrageous alterations and destructions of the environment. He calls himself an artist–not a reporter–and refrains from judging what he photographs or from politicizing it, wanting . . . to "make people think harder about our planet's future" without suggesting to them a direction.[13]

A short piece in *Flash* commented more succinctly to how the film was constructed, saying that Burtynsky's "images are all the more unbelievable for being real and director Jennifer Baichwal has produced a documentary which, in an unhurried and reflective manner, doesn't expose its subject so much as put you in its place for 90 minutes."[14]

Manufacturing Landscapes–the film–concentrates on industrial settings, recycling, shipyards, and urban renewal. In the ninety-six images taken in China in 2004 and 2005, however, Burtynsky also extended to subjects not treated in the documentary: abandoned factories, steel mills, and quarries.

The photographs devoted to manufacturing stress the gigantic scale on which these factories operate–as such, they are markedly different from the *Packing Plant* images of 1983. The images from China are jaw-dropping because of the vastness of scale that confronts the viewer.

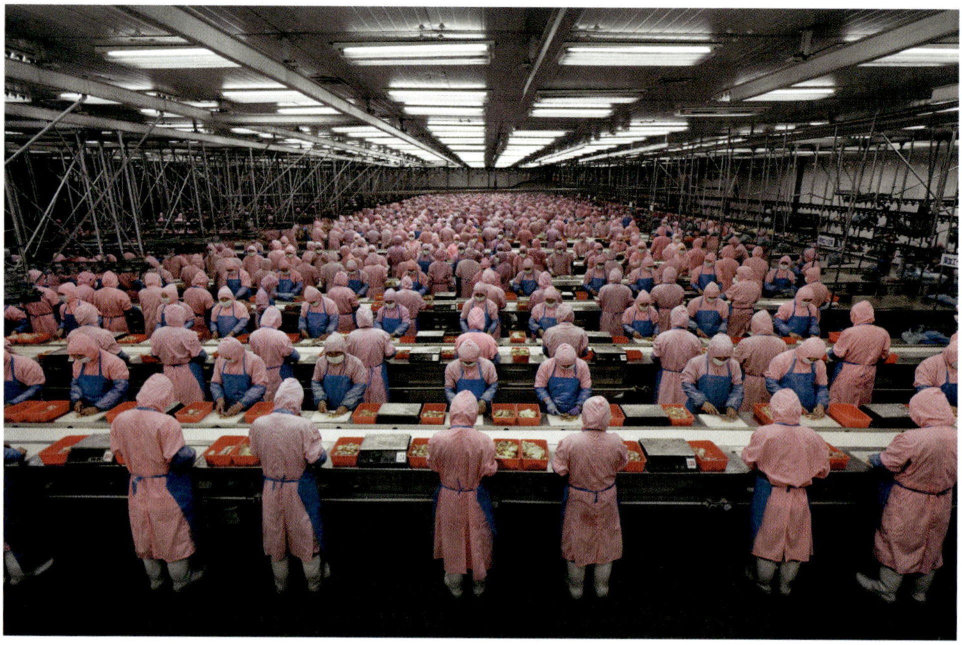

Edward Burtynsky, *Manufacturing #17*, Deda Chicken Processing Plant, Dehui City, Jilin Province, China, 2005

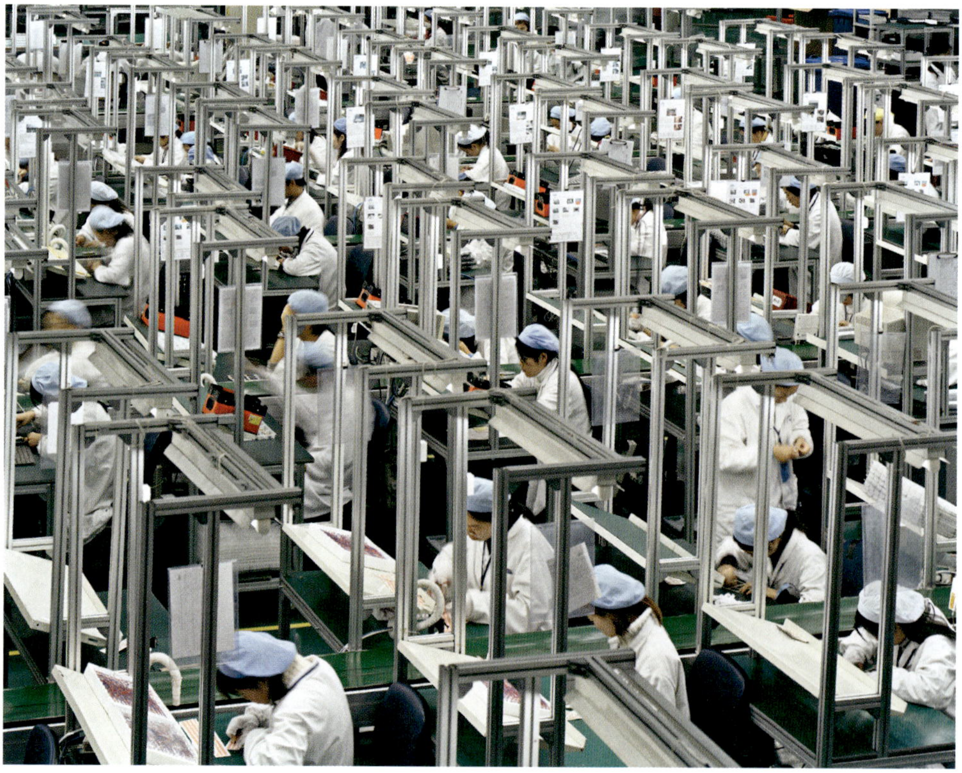

Edward Burtynsky, *Manufacturing #16*, Bird Mobile, Ningbo, Zhejiang Province, China, 2005

The twenty recycling images from China, in the same way, are reminiscent of a past series, *Urban Mines*, as the site documented there is much vaster than the one in Hamilton, Ontario (see p. 115). "Essentially," Burtynsky recalled, "I followed the e-waste to China."[15]

The bright colours from 1997 reappear, but the new images encompass larger areas of waste. The sheer detail in *China Recycling #10* overpowers the viewer's eyes and the interplay between grey and golden tones in *China Recycling #18* creates a strong abstract image reminiscent of Jackson Pollock's shattered particles and subdued colours in *Autumn Rhythm (Number 30)*.

Shipbreaking and shipbuilding should be polar opposites, but the new images are redolent of the older ones. The russet, copper colours reappear, and the ships under construction look like land-locked monsters reminiscent

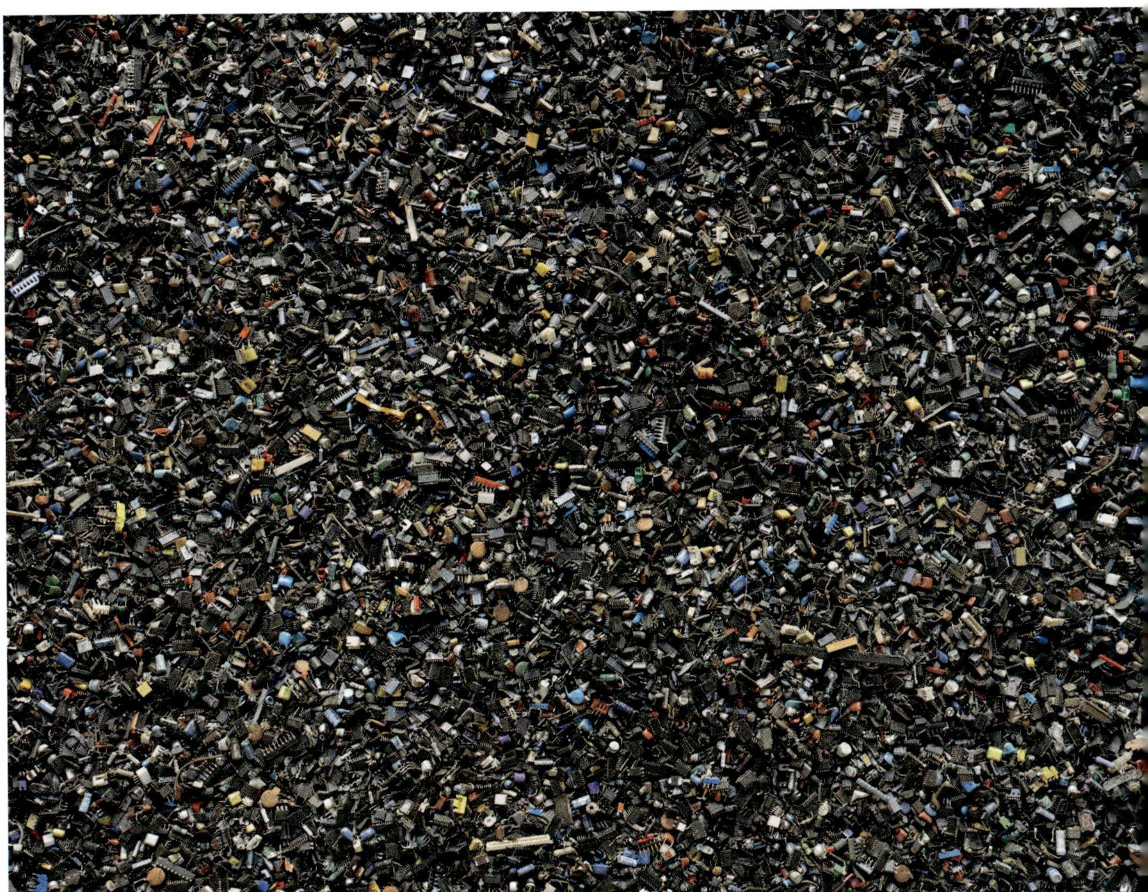

Edward Burtynsky, *China Recycling #10*, Guiyu, Guangdong Province, China, 2004

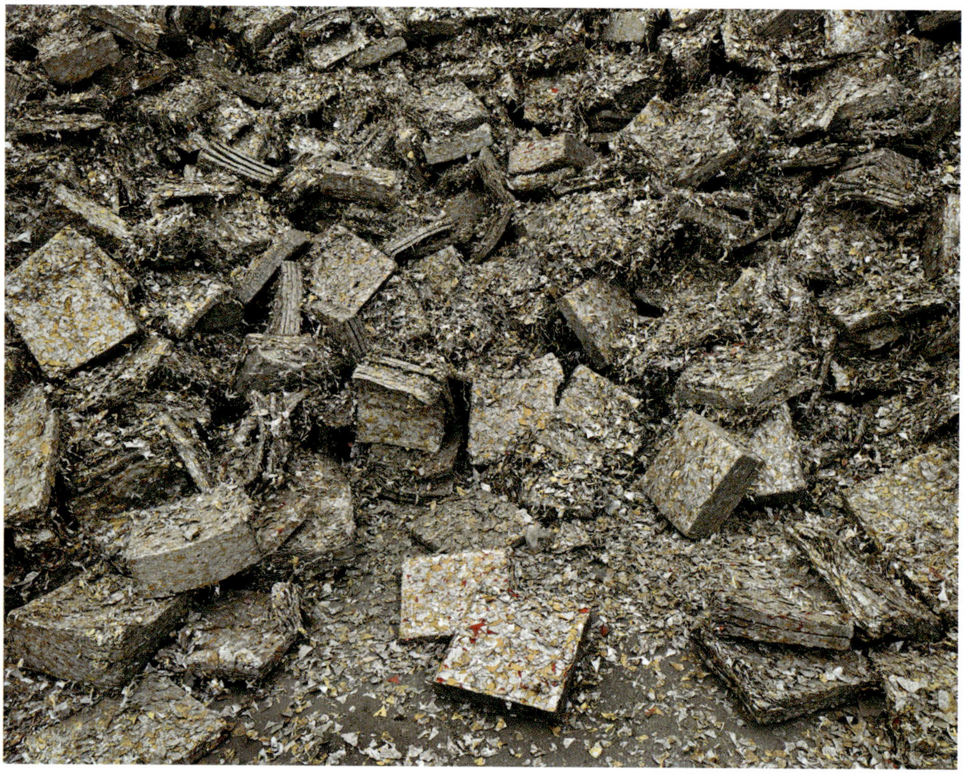

Edward Burtynsky, *China Recycling #18*, Cankun Aluminum, Xiamen City, Fujan Province, China, 2005

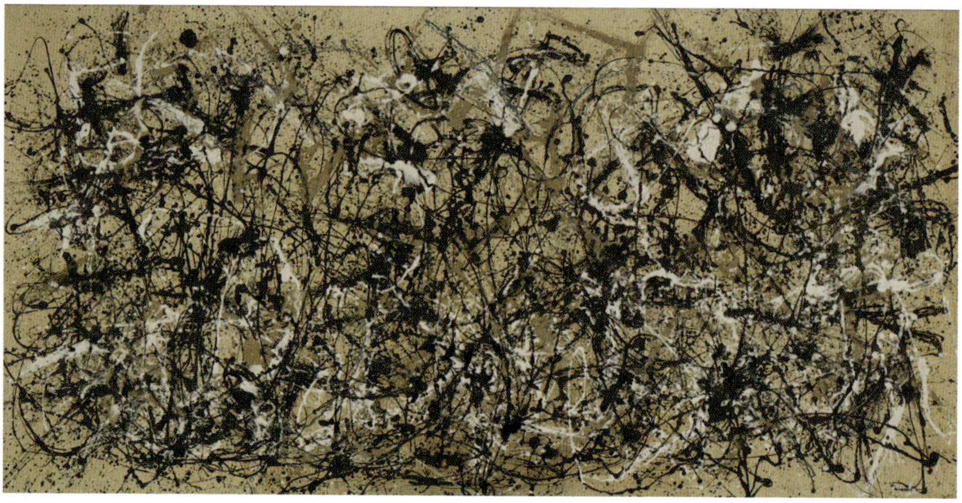

Jackson Pollock, *Autumn River (Number 30)*, drip painting, 1950. The Metropolitan Museum of Art

Edward Burtynsky, *Shipyard #4*, Qili Port, Zhejiang Province, China, 2004

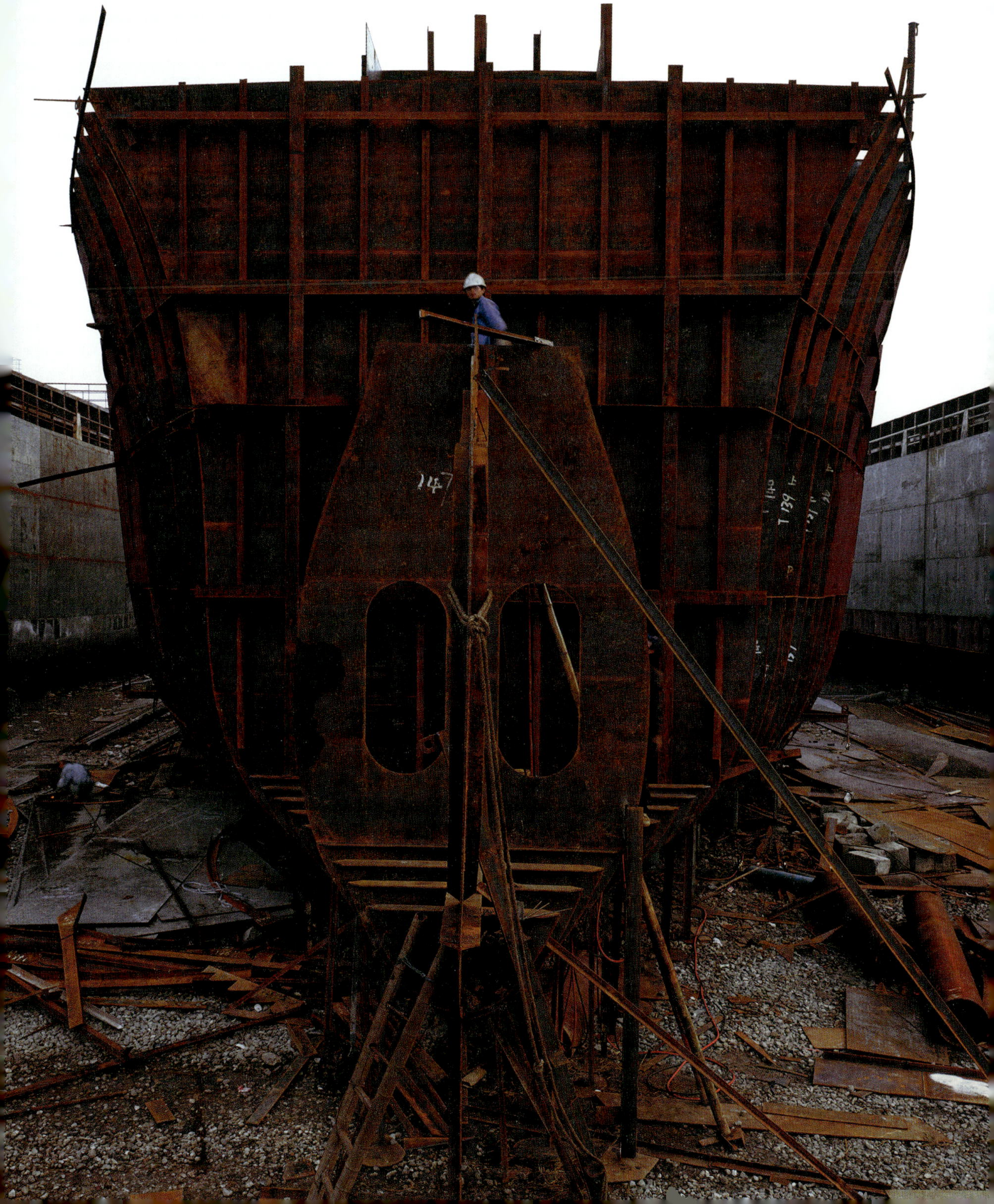

of their water-logged cousins in Bangladesh. The rusty mahogany colours in *Shipyard #4* are also reminiscent of those from Bangladesh; after all, the constructing and deconstructing of monster vessels is all part of globalization.

In *Manufactured Landscapes*, a note of bleak irony pervades the sequence in which the real estate agent puts her home on display. That tone is absent from Burtynsky's twelve images of urban renewal highlighting the discrepancy between old and new Shanghai.

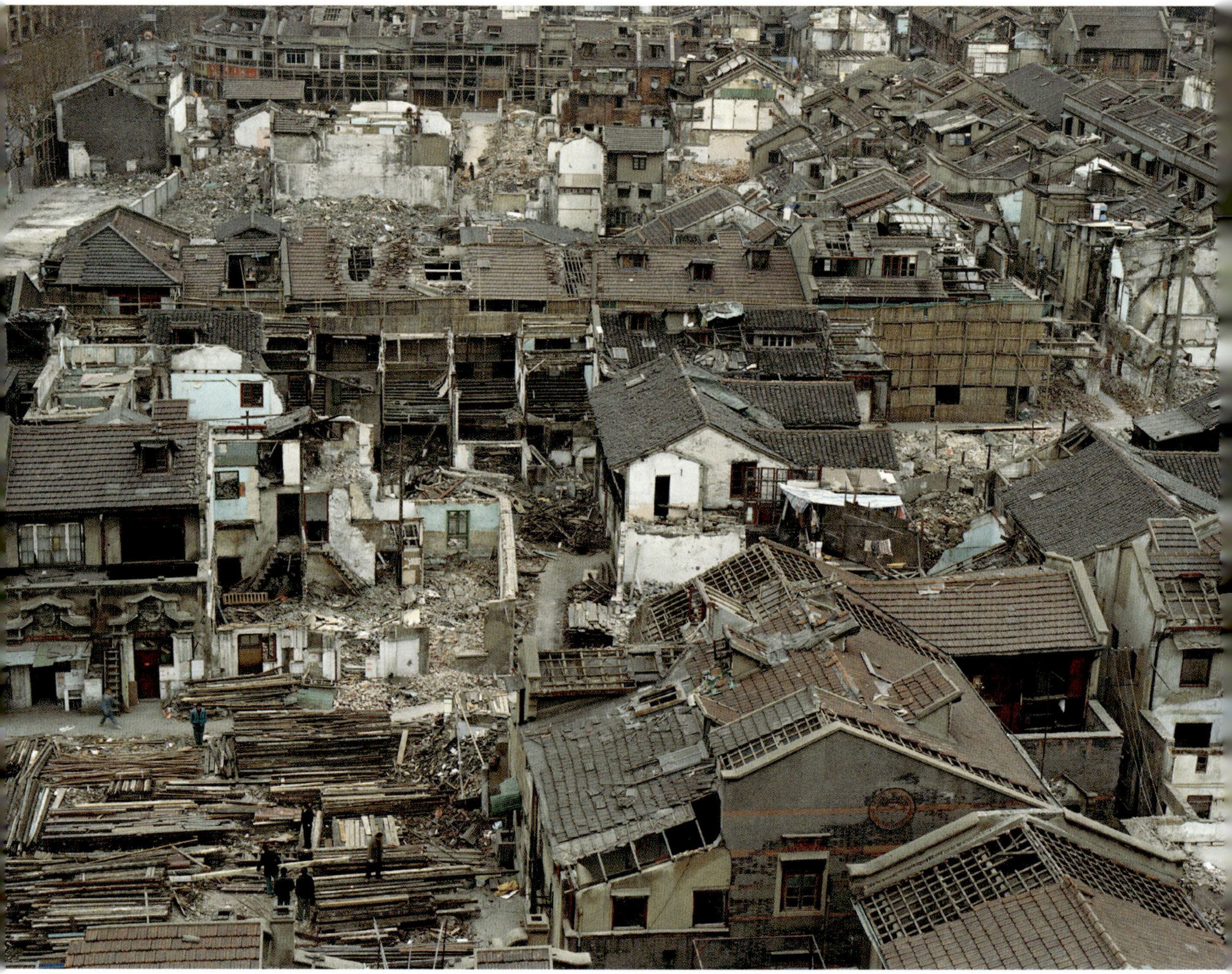

Edward Burtynsky, *Urban Renewal #4*, Hongkou District, Shanghai, China, 2004

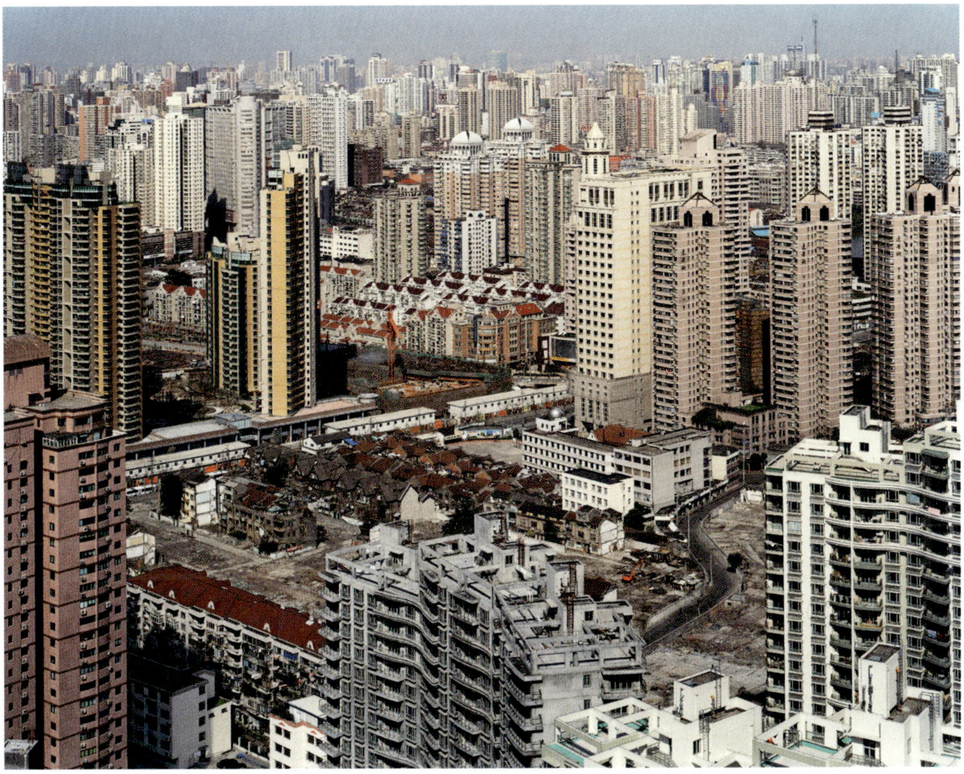

Edward Burtynsky, *Urban Renewal #5*, City Overview from Top of Military Hospital, Shanghai, China, 2004

The juxtaposition of the remains of the shabby, torn-apart home and the modern building behind it in *Urban Renewal #11*, *Hold Out #1* encapsulates part of Burtynsky's narrative. *Urban Renewal #9, Medium Density Suburb* was, for him, an unusual image–a sort of sub-story. "Normally, I wouldn't have gone for it. No one would ever buy this image, right? This image is an example of the quirky way I look at the world." Burtynsky passed by a vendor a number of times at this site and then photographed his wares: "This [unseen] guy has been left with wares nobody is interested in. He is scraping by, just trying to survive. He has been swallowed up."[16]

A pervading sense of loss can also be felt in the ten *Old Industry* images. As Burtynsky explains, the city of Shenyang "in the northeast Teixi district was China's industrial backbone and home to the most densely focused

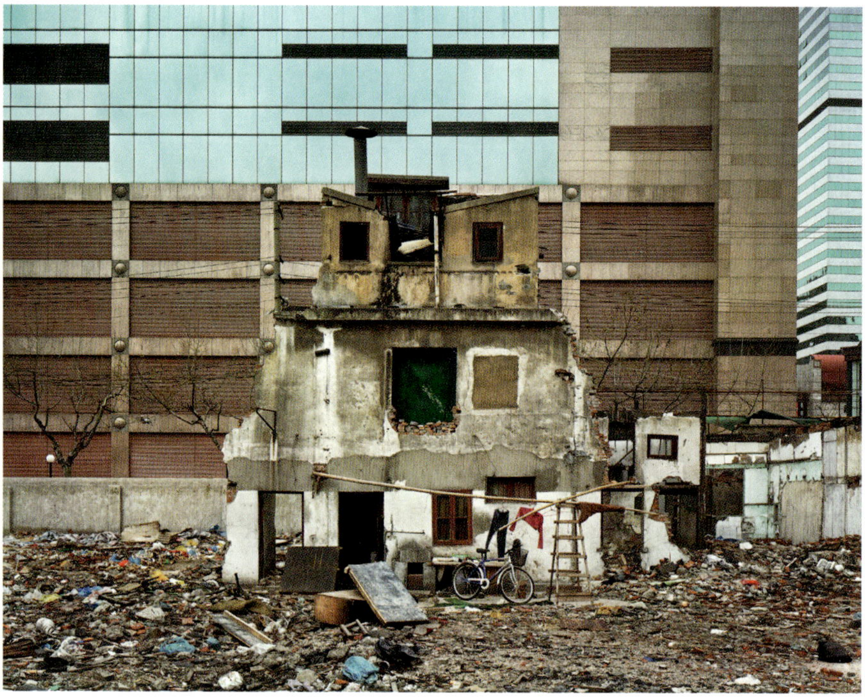

Edward Burtynsky, *Urban Renewal #11*, Shanghai, China, 2004

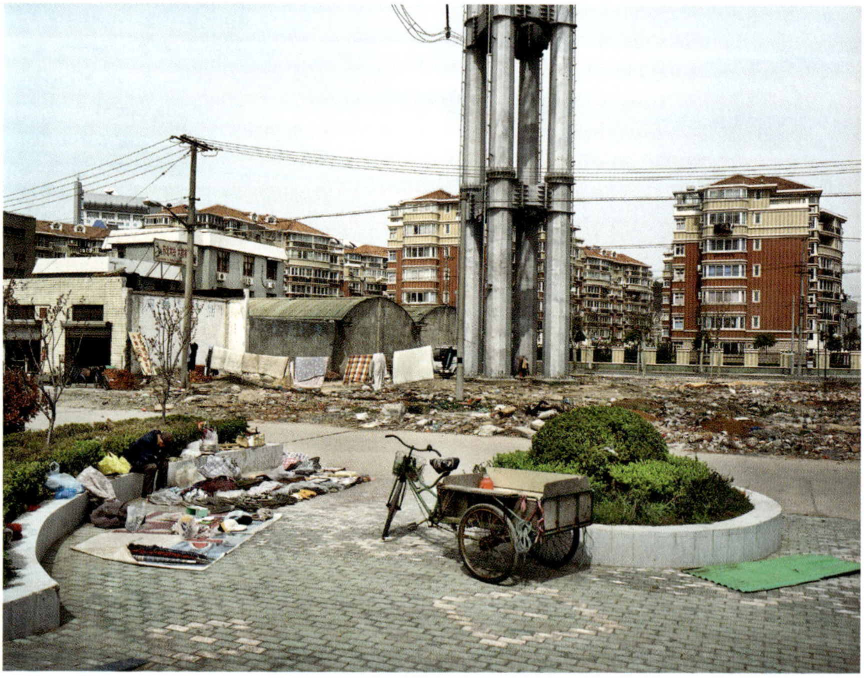

Edward Burtynsky, *Urban Renewal #9*, Medium Density Suburb, Shanghai, China, 2004

concentration of heavy industry until very recently. . . . Since the mid-1990s, 35 to 40 million workers in China's state-owned enterprises have lost their jobs to economic restructuring. . . . Property once used by these immense factories is now being designated as residential and commercial, spurring a real estate frenzy."[17]

These factories in Shenyang, once occupied by huge numbers of workers as in the manufacturing images, were now empty and about to demolished. The absence of the workers in this set of images conveys a sense of loss and abandonment.

As Azu Nwagbogu has astutely observed, "When the pyramids of Ancient Egypt were built in the pre-industrial era, they were isolated monuments to the power of a single autocrat. The Bao Steel pyramid, by contrast, is the

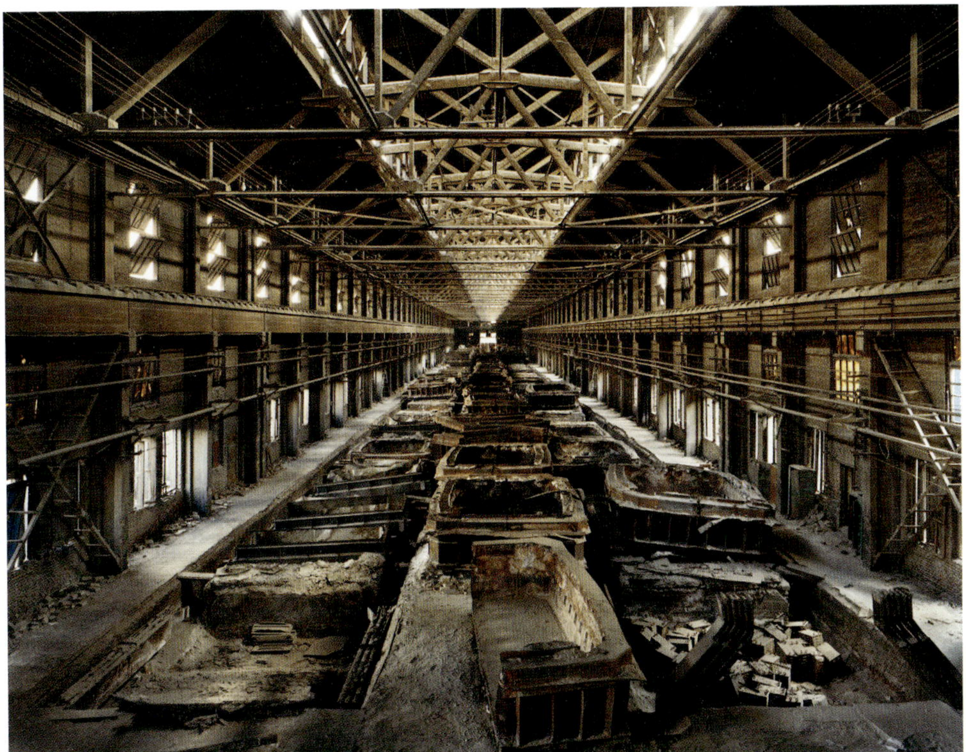

Edward Burtynsky, *Old Factories #9*, Fushun Aluminum Smelter, Fushun City, Liaoning Province, China, 2005

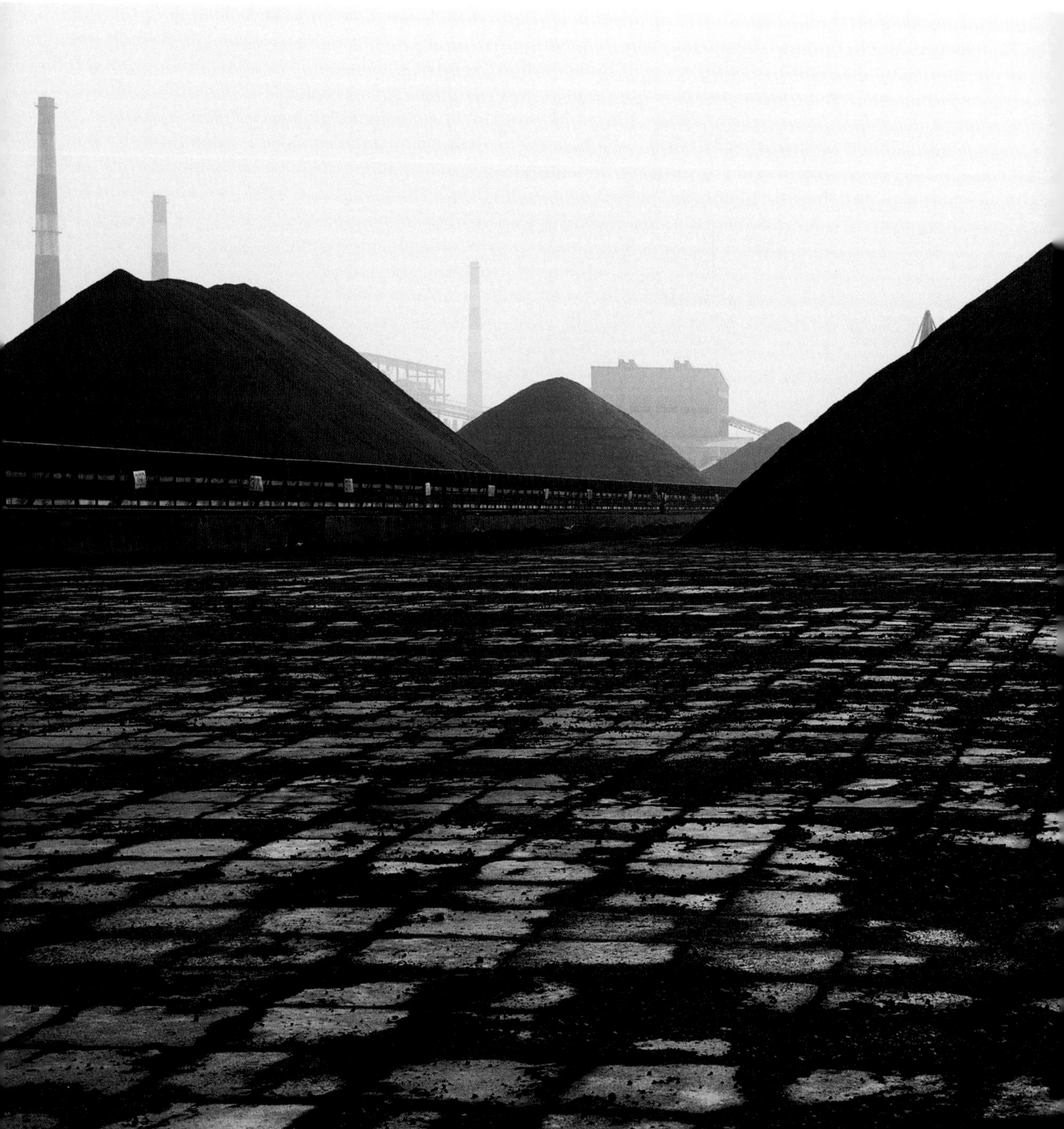

Edward Burtynsky, *Bao Steel #8*, Shanghai, China, 2005

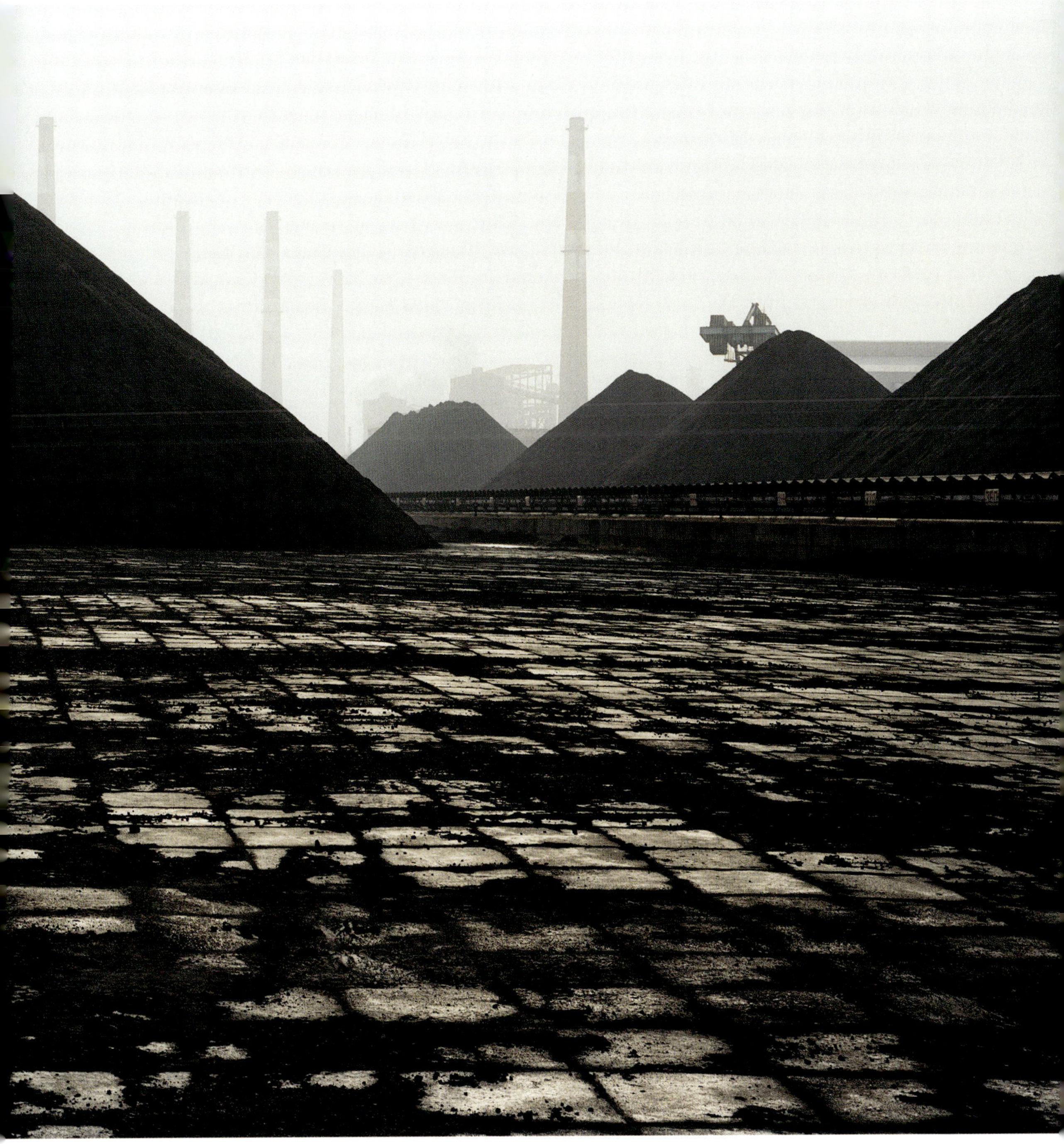

visual embodiment of the aggregate power of Chinese industries, for which the coal has been accumulated."[18]

There are about one hundred granite quarries at Xiamen. In the ten images he photographed there, Burtynsky emphasized the quarry exteriors, displayed a room in which the granite is sorted, and showed a space where artisans are carving granite into huge sculptures for export. One image of the workers, dwarfed by the surrounding walls, is a skilful composition in monochromatic values.

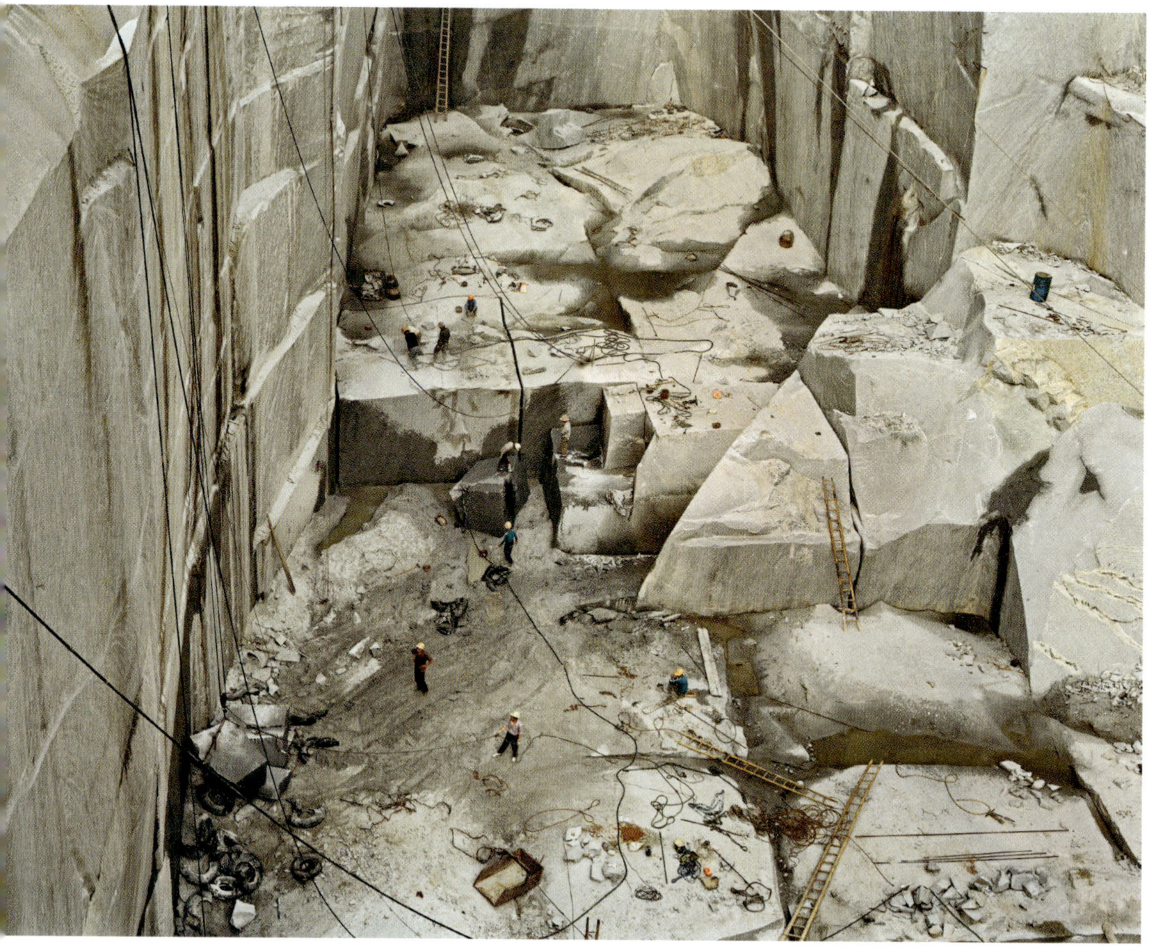

Edward Burtynsky, *China Quarries #3*, Xiamen Province, China, 2004

In the images Burtynsky made in China in 2002, 2004, and 2005, he discovered new subjects and new ways of reimagining previous ones. The vitality of China as the world's leading manufacturer is captured in his images of factory workers; those of urban renewal call into question what "renewal" means. The evidence he presents suggests that China has chosen mass eradication in the name of modernization–the same observation holds true for the earlier *Before the Flood* series. The massive heaps of coal photographed at Bao Steel are the sublime of the sinister. The old factories are disappearing–only to be replaced by scores of other, larger ones.

Burtynsky provided a new twist on the theme of recycling by returning to the subject matter of *Urban Mines*. But the problems inherent in recycling had escalated because of the amount of scrap dumped in China. Shipbuilding may be the opposite of shipbreaking, but the new vessels will carry consumer goods from China and then convey waste materials back to China.

The two China projects portray a country on a meteoric rise, but they question the cost. A plenitude of consumer goods means that many of those products will eventually return to China to be recycled. Both the scrapyards and the quarries release masses of carcinogens; in China, modernization often means wholesale destruction.

Burtynsky's images do not provide answers to troubling questions. "These images," he reflected, "are meant as metaphors [of] the dilemma of our modern existence. They search for a dialogue between attraction and repulsion, seduction and fear. We are drawn by desire–a chance at a good living–yet we are consciously or unconsciously aware that the world is suffering for our success. For me, images function as reflecting pools of our times."[19]

In 2003, Burtynsky, in cooperation with some of his dealers, published a small catalogue of *Before the Flood* images in Toronto. A year later, Gerhard Steidl released a substantially larger selection in what became a best-selling book, which is divided into seven parts: Three Gorges Dam, Steel and Coal, Old Industry, Shipyards, Recycling, Manufacturing, and Urban Renewal.

This was Burtynsky's first book with the renowned German publisher, and would lead to other collaborations. To him, these large, superbly printed books remain important milestones in his career because they are permanent repositories of his work, available to a wide public.[20]

Burtynsky has retained strong convictions about the prints themselves, however, particularly about their sizes:

> No matter what, I want to photograph the subject where it has found its greatest expression. The ideal way to then experience the work is in the large format and in the large prints. With a 4 × 5 ft. print, you can stand in front of it, drop into it, put your face six inches away and see the detail or stand back and get a sense of the whole. Ideally that is the way my work is best seen although you can get the essence of it through a book or the web. The real thing is that in such a print you [can have] an [out of body] "body experience," one that makes us wonder, makes us contemplate and meditate on the world we are creating. Photography is one of the few ways you can achieve that effect.[21]

10 BLACK GOLD

In the documentary *Manufacturing Landscapes*, Burtynsky had emphasized his interest in oil and how it occupied a significant space in everyone's life. Humankind had become overly dependent on fossil fuel but, in the process, oil had contaminated and poisoned the globe–this topic, he hinted in the film, would be his next focus. As he recalled, in the 1990s, "The car that I drove cross-country began to represent not only freedom, but also something much more conflicted. I began to think about oil itself: as both the source of energy that makes everything possible, and as a source of dread, for its ongoing endangerment of our habitat."[1]

In fact, Burtynsky had been intrigued by the countless metamorphoses of fossil fuel well before the two China projects, and had taken many images of this phenomenon. In 1997, he had photographed densified oil drums and scrap auto engines as part of the *Urban Mines* series; oil refineries in New Brunswick and Ontario and worn-out tires in California in 1999; shipbreaking in Bangladesh in 2000-1; and oil fields in Cold Lake, Alberta, in 2001. During the years devoted to China, he had pursued several related projects. Among them were images of sprawling highways in Los Angeles and New Jersey (2003), oil refineries in Texas (2004), and the Nanpu Bridge Interchange in Shanghai (2004).

Although the previous images document "oil" in a variety of ways, Burtynsky felt the narrative he wanted to tell was far from complete. Starting in 2006, he expanded his inventory of oil-themed images considerably: Auto Wreckers, Sikorsky, Tucson, 2006; State Oil Company of the Republic of Azerbaijan Oil Fields (SOCAR), Azerbaijan, 2006; Alberta Oil Sands, Fort McMurray, 2007; Highway 5, Los Angeles, 2009; Industrial Park, North Las Vegas, 2007; Bonneville, Utah, 2008; Birmingham, 2009; South Dakota, 2008; Breezewood, Pennsylvania, 2008; Detroit, 2008.

All of the previous images were taken using analog equipment. It wasn't until 2006 that Burtynsky first used digital when shooting the grey military jets at the Aerospace Maintenance and Regeneration Center (AMARC) in Tucson (see p. 195). This change freed him from worries about having his negatives ruined when going through security checks at airports. It also allowed him the freedom to make more shots.

In making these supplementary oil images, he was adding to his story and buttressing it. In the process, what would become *Oil* became a three-part narrative: *Extraction and Refinement*, *Transportation and Motor Culture*, and *The End of Oil*. There is also an appendix titled *Detroit Motor City*.

Extraction and Refinement consists of the earlier *Oil Refinery* images from St. John, New Brunswick, and Oakville, Ontario, but they are augmented by photographs of an oil refinery in Houston, Texas; oil fields in Cold Lake, Alberta, and around Bakersfield, Belridge, McKittrick, and Taft, California; and the Alberta oil sands. Once again, Burtynsky used helicopters at Bakersfield, Houston, and at a Volkswagen logistics yard.

The two new oil refinery images taken in Houston provide overhead views in which white storage tanks dot the picture. Those of the oil field at Cold Lake are reminiscent of the oil refinery images from 1999 that emphasized such places as being "cathedrals of pipes and valves" set in a "glimmering futuristic city."[2] At Cold Lake, the oil-containing glistening pipes zig-zag across a meadow bordered by trees. The man-made intrusion here may look benign, but any break in the line would be catastrophic to the survival of that landscape. In this image, abstract shapes and the natural world *seem* to be in harmony.[3]

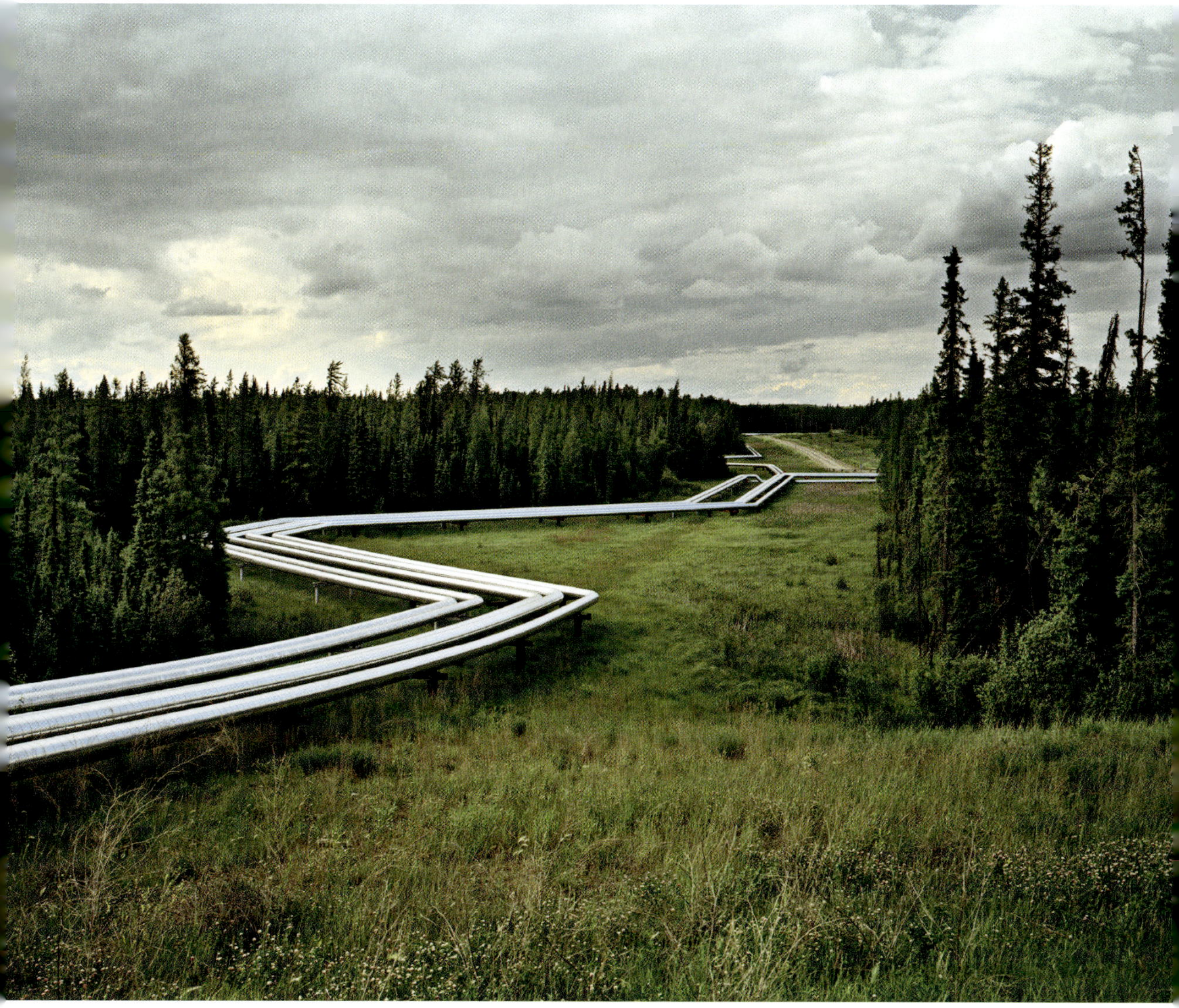

Edward Burtynsky, *Oil Fields #22*, Cold Lake Production Project, Cold Lake, Alberta, 2001

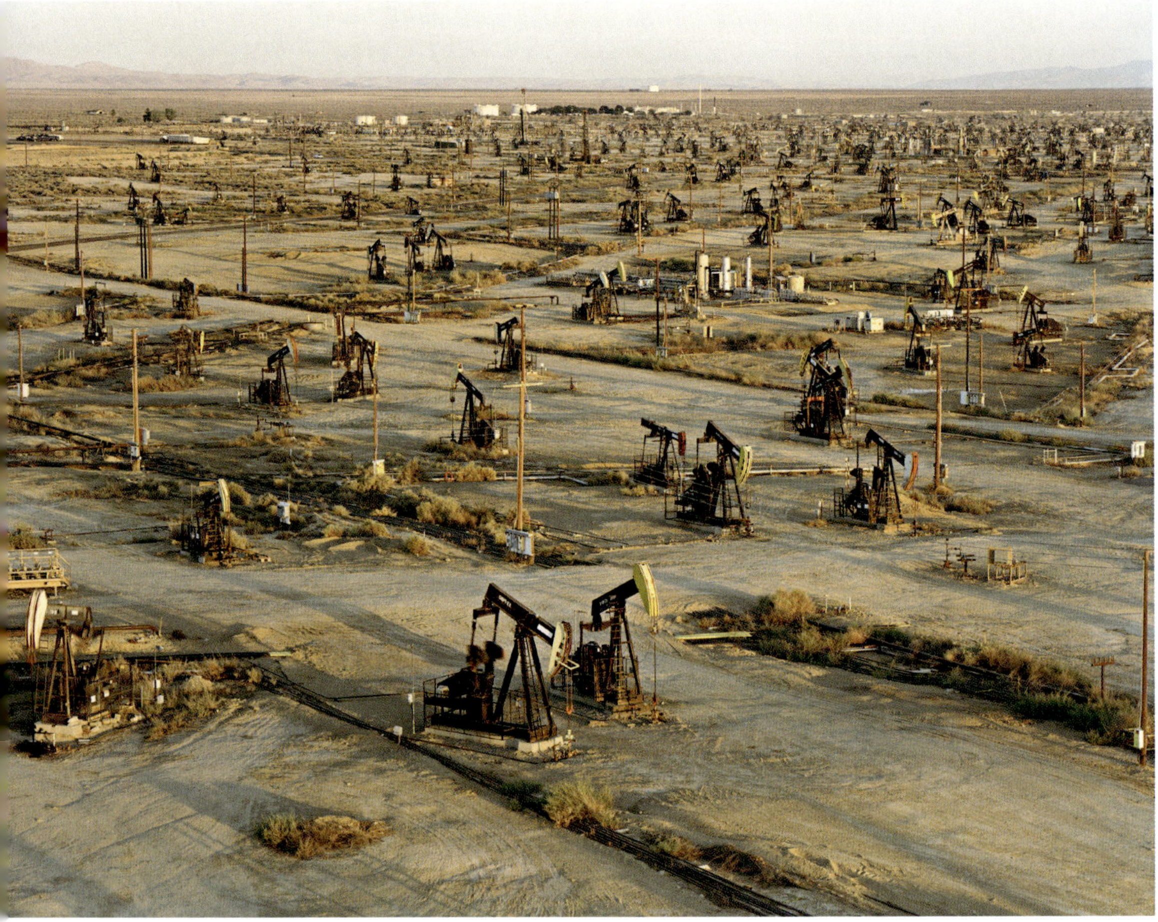

Edward Burtynsky, *Oil Fields #19a and 19b*, California, 2003

A darker narrative emerges in the images of California oil fields, in which large stretches of dry, parched land are penetrated by oil rigs that resemble monster insects seeking sustenance. Such images are reminiscent of the Elliot Lake photos of uranium tailings. In the earlier photographs, thin, shrivelled, dead trees stand in a scorched, dark-brown land; in the new photographs, robust machines burrow into the soil resembling giant mosquitoes drawing blood as the pump jacks suck oil from below the earth's surface. The view in *Oil Fields #27* may distance the viewer from the on-the-ground drilling, but it still vividly demonstrates how the landscape has been devastated by the quest for oil.

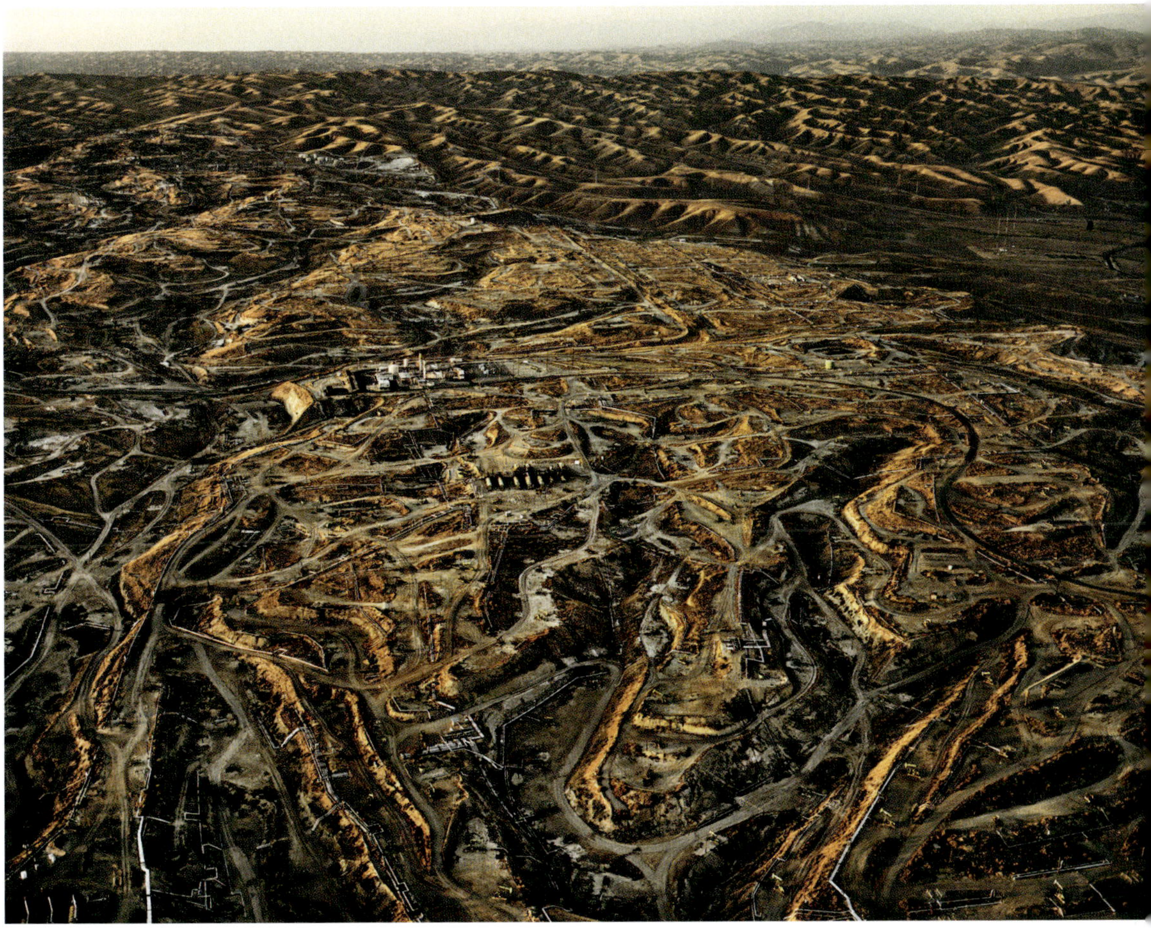

Edward Burtynsky, *Oil Fields #27*, Bakersfield, California, 2004

Burtynsky has sometimes been accused of aestheticizing ecological disasters, but no such charge can be levied at his images of the Athabasca oil sands at Fort McMurray in northern Alberta. Six years earlier, in 2001, he had attempted to gain access to the two oldest sites near Fort McMurray, operated by Syncrude and Suncor, but could only shoot what he could see from public roads.[4] Six years later, on a commission from *The Globe and Mail*, he took a different approach: "Some of these images were taken from a helicopter with the camera on a gyro, which helps stabilise rough motion. It was October, so it was very cold. We'd go up for two hours and then I'd have to sit in a hot tub and thaw for about an hour before we could go up again."[5] This approach was necessary, he recalled, because the authorities "wouldn't let me on the ground but when I rented a helicopter and shot from the air, it was a 'eureka moment.' I realized that was the way to show it. From the ground it would not look like much, but from the air you could tell the [real] story."[6] He had found a way to capture the scale of these operations.

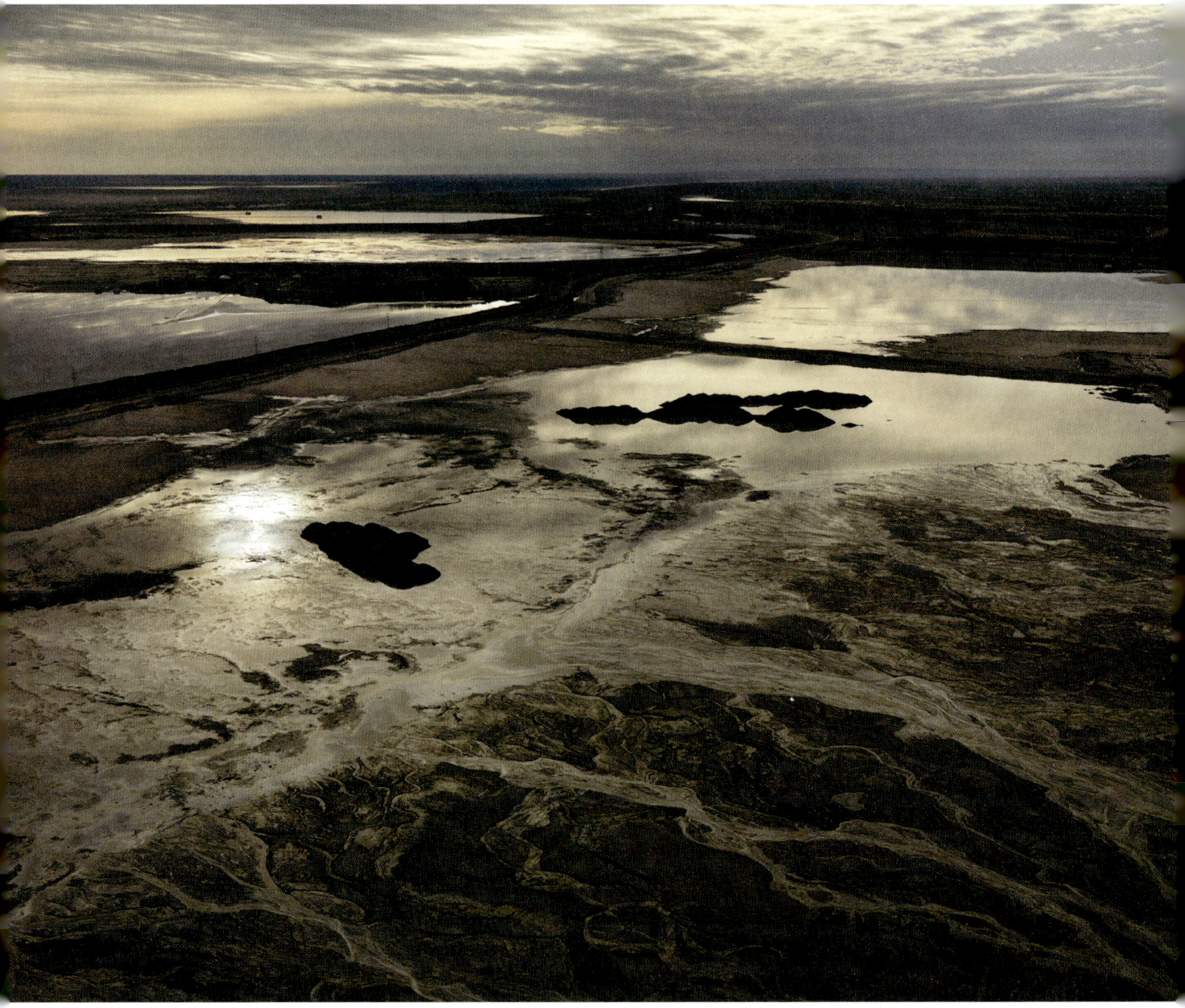

Edward Burtynsky, *Alberta Oil Sands #10*, Fort McMurray, Alberta, 2005

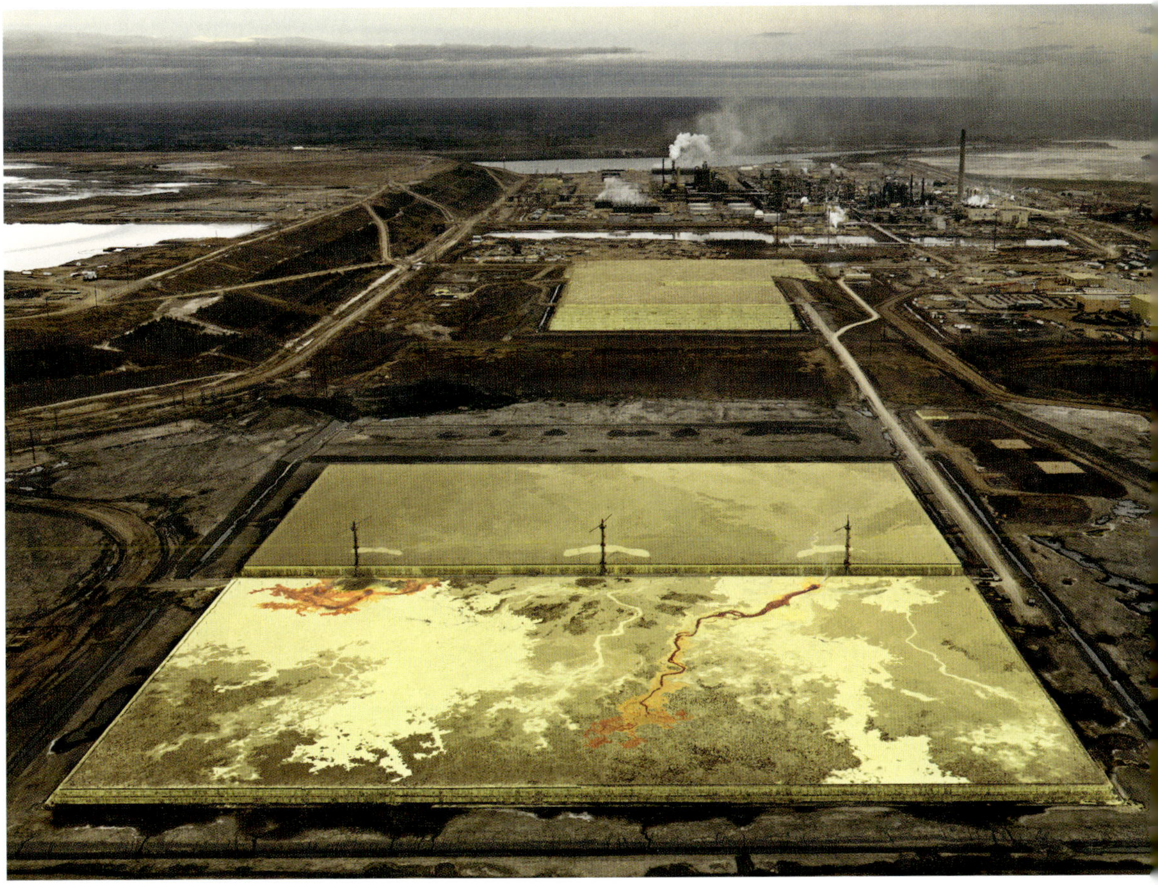

Edward Burtynsky, *Alberta Oil Sands #6*, Fort McMurray, Alberta, 2007

The oil sands contain a mixture of sand, clay, and water soaked with bitumen, a viscous form of petroleum, located beneath the surface and extending for 54,000 square miles. The heavy oil at Fort McMurray, which contain an estimated two trillion barrels, is much harder to extract than the crude at Cold Lake and extracting it has resulted in an ecocide–a catastrophic mutilation to the environment. *Alberta Oil Sands #10* is a grim, terrifying landscape of desecration. In the background of *Alberta Oil Sands #6*, smoke billows from the factories as they break down the bitumen, but the middle and foreground areas show yellowish, brownish rectangles of debris–the result of the burning off of sulphuric acid. The one nearest to the viewer is an ungainly abstract composition.

It was at this point in his career when Burtynsky realized "that views from ground level could not show the enormous scale of activity. I had to get up high, into the air, to see it from a bird's-eye perspective. Determined by the specifics of each location, I would find a way to make the most telling viewpoints . . . This pulling away from the earth has allowed me to see our world in ways once unavailable to artists."[7]

The first "pulling away" was in 2003, when he used a helicopter to film the cloverleaf where Highways 110 and 5 intersect in Los Angeles: "I wanted to look not only at the most intense highways and interchanges in the world, but also the fact that Los Angeles was a city built for the car. It had perfected the idea of urban sprawl . . . For this picture I went to Los Angeles and drove around and tried to find buildings to tell the story of this freeway from any vantage point on the ground. This photograph marked

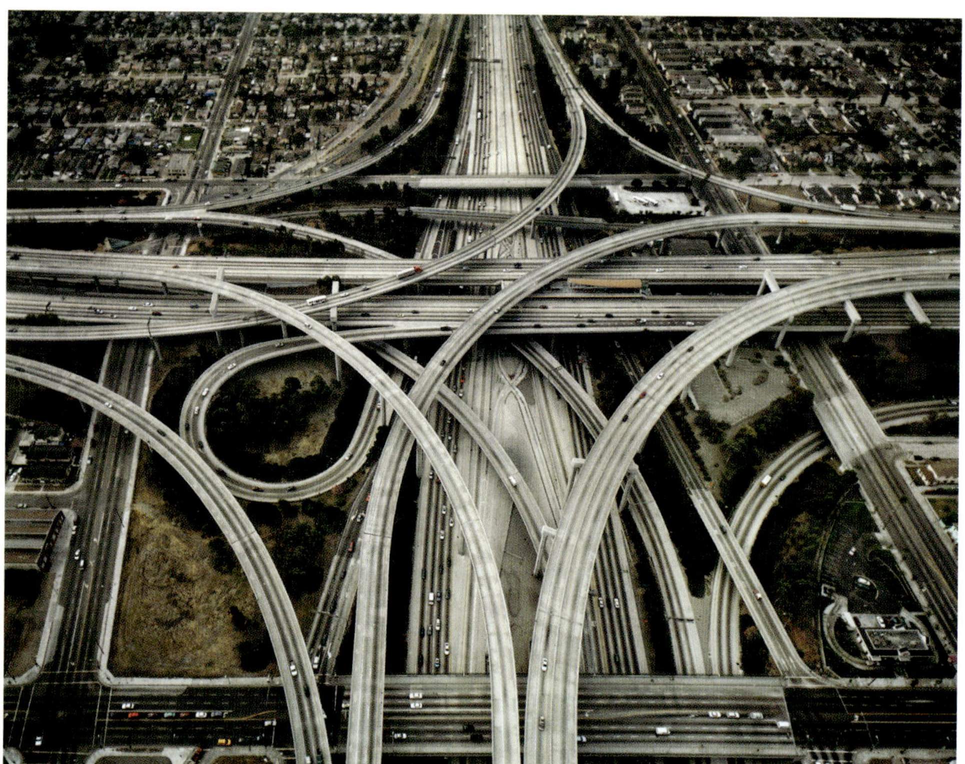

Edward Burtynsky, *Highway #1*, Intersection 105 & 100, Los Angeles, 2003

a breakthrough moment when I realized I couldn't take the pictures I wanted and the only thing that would get me that vantage point would be a helicopter, so I made the leap and rented one for the first time."[8]

This perspective would become more firmly ingrained in his practice. Burtynsky later employed, he recalled, "man-lifts, small fixed-wing aircraft, helicopters (both remote and piloted) and a specially fifty-foot pneumatic mast with camera mount and fibre-optic remote."[9] On one occasion, he used a balloon: it failed immediately as the photographer had no control over its direction.[10]

A crucial part of the oil project centred on cars. For Burtynsky, "The automobile is the main basis for our modern industrial world, giving us a certain freedom and changing our world dramatically. The automobile was made possible because of the invention of the internal combustion engine and its utilization of both oil and gasoline."

For Burtynsky, "motor culture" can be witnessed in the intertwining points of convergence on highways and huge lots packed with new cars fresh off the assembly line. More specifically, he recalled, "I began to [places]where vast communities come together with vehicles as the main attraction."[11] Some of these sites were where "road hogs" assembled to participate in and watch stock car races. The groups that Burtynsky photographed in Utah, South Dakota, and Iowa were rebels disassociated from American mainstream society; they were outsiders to the American dream, persons who considered themselves abandoned by their government. For them, the Wild West still existed.

He also visited one of the largest NASCAR races at the Talladega Superspeedway in Alabama, with 180,000 spectators: "It's a crazy thing with all these people coming together to watch cars go round in a circle at high speeds. Such races have been photographed many times, but I am interested in tying it in with the body of work I have done as an expression of the scale of motor culture, where everybody is rallying around the machine."[12]

The photographer and essayist Michael Mitchell, who accompanied Burtynsky, recalled: "We're in Sturgis [South Dakota] so Burtynsky can take photographs . . . he'll shoot the chaotic mass-individualism of mainstream America . . . By the time the Sturgis 2008 Rally is finished, 436 bikers will end up jailed, 370 will end up in emergency rooms and three will die. The estimated 415,00 bikers will leave 543 tons of garbage when they roar out of town."[13]

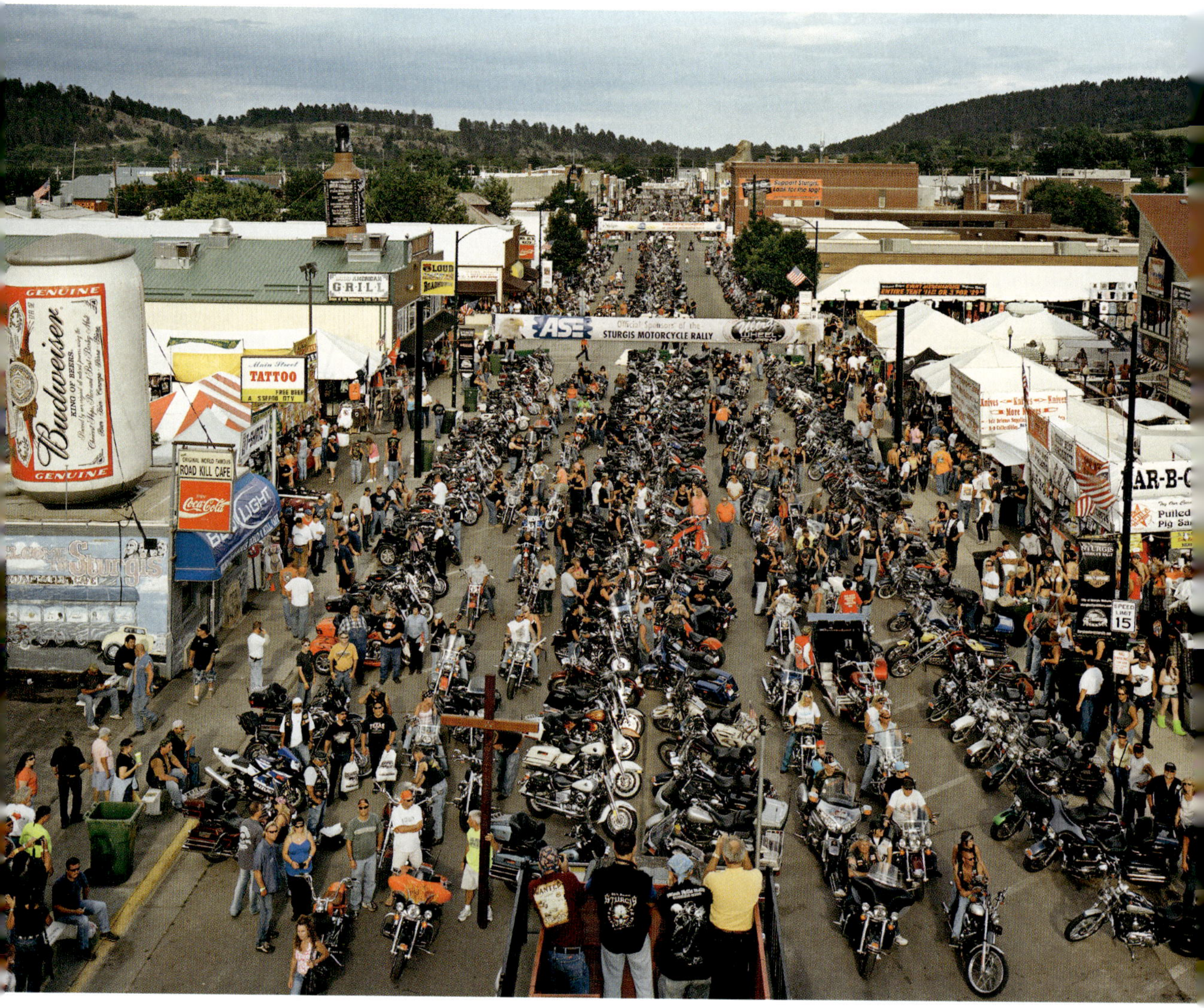

Edward Burtynsky, *Downtown Sturgis*, South Dakota, 2008

Mitchell also recalled that Burtynsky wanted to take a companion photograph to that of the workers assembled at the industrial park in Zhangzhou: "He'll shoot the main street of this small South Dakota city. Instead of the uniformed orderliness of the Chinese industrial worker, he'll show the chaotic mass individualism of mainstream America."[14] The critic and novelist Geoff Dyer was contemptuous of the result: "In China Burtynsky organized a photograph of yellow-jacketed workers arranged in deep perspectival recession along a street lined with yellow factories in Zhangzhou. It was such a striking and successful picture that Burtynsky decided to try something similar with a bunch of bikers in downtown Sturgis . . . with this image Burtynsky has formed his own tribute band. The result seems to me entirely without merit or purpose except insofar as it is yet another gig on the world tour called Oil."[15]

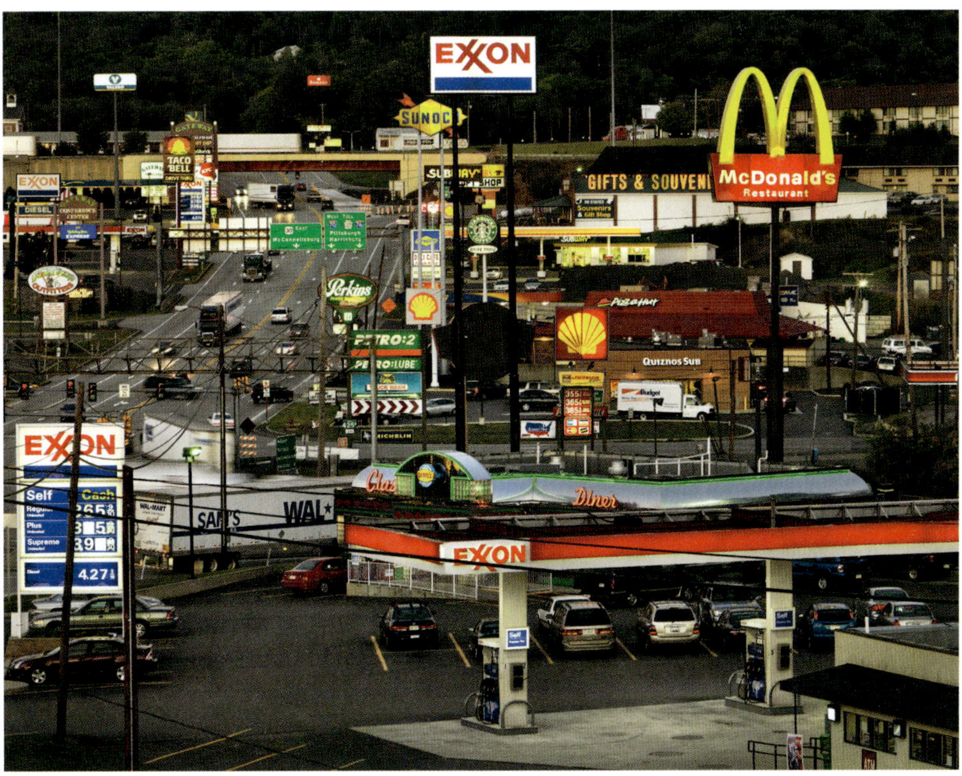

Edward Burtynsky, *Breezewood*, Pennsylvania, 2008

What Dyer overlooked was that Burtynsky, in those two images, was delineating the difference between disciplined Chinese and rowdy Americans. China is in the process of repurposing itself whereas the Americans in the desert have lost all sense of purpose. If Dyer found such images brassy, Gary Michael Dault understood that any vulgarity in all such images was intentional: "And there's a suitably congested jungle of gas stations in Breezewood, Pennsylvania, with Exxon, Sunoco and Shell signs competing for attention like placards at a political convention."[16] This image brings to mind Ed Ruscha's *Twentysix Gasoline Stations* (1963)–the photographs he made on the highway between Los Angeles and Oklahoma City. Those elegantly framed and stately iconic images elevated the stations to the status of high art; forty-five years later, Burtynsky captured the chaos in a maze of competing signage.

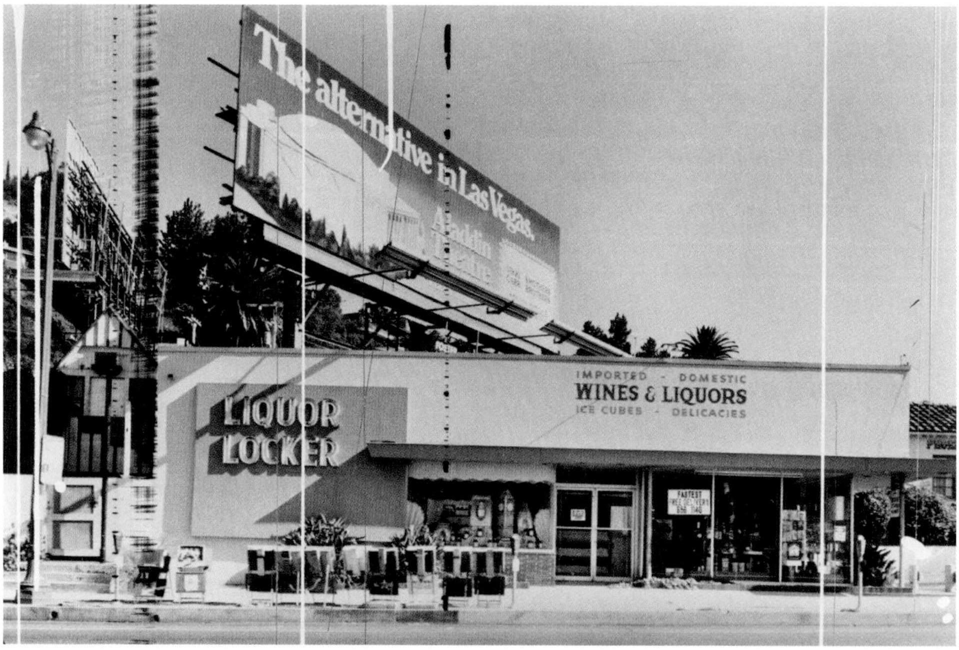

Ed Ruscha, *Liquor Locker* (from the *Sunset Strip Portfolio*), 1976, Tate Gallery. Courtesy of Ed Ruscha

In his *Shipbreaking* series, the photographer had showed one aspect of the end of oil, in the way broken ships remain full of carcinogen-filled petroleum, asbestos, and toxic marine paint. To that series, along with *Urban Mines* and the *Oxford Tire Pile*, he added three more subjects: the graveyards of airplanes and helicopters, a graveyard for wrecked automobiles, and the SOCAR Oil Fields in Baku, Azerbaijan.

Since 1965, more than four thousand military aircraft have been parked at AMARC, known as "The Graveyard," at Davis-Monthan Air Force Base in Tucson, Arizona. The Graveyard has even become a popular touring spot, with buses taking visitors around the huge site. In Burtynsky's images, the planes resemble enormous stranded birds, forever deprived of flight. Some stand at comfortable distances from each other and have been groomed for show; others, much of their hardware stripped, have no room to breathe.

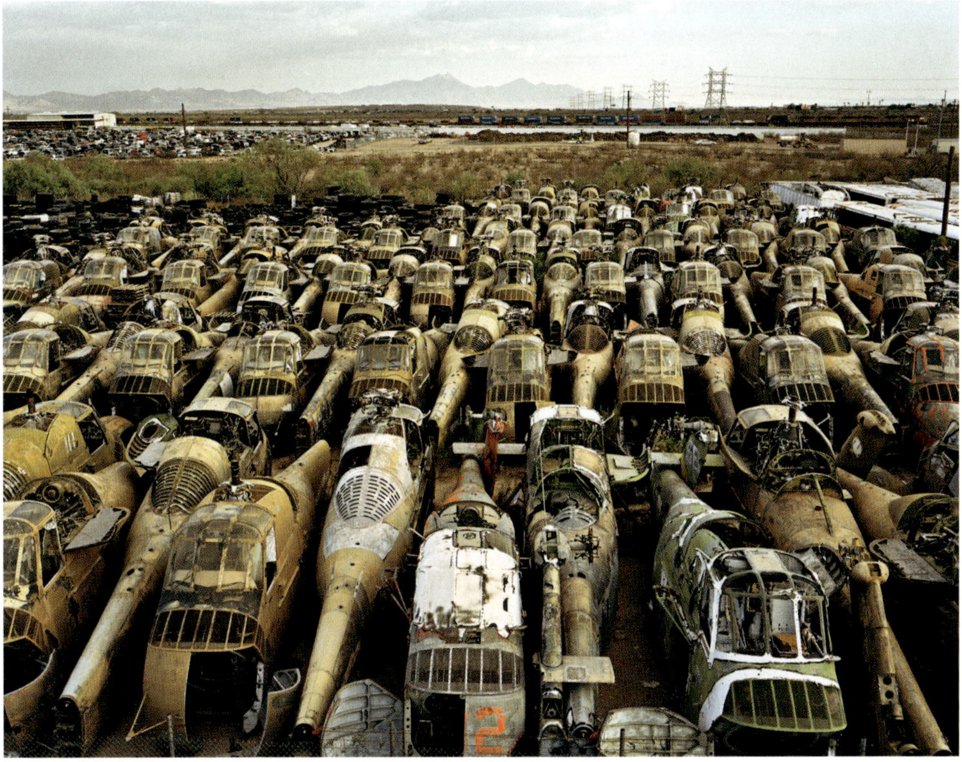

Edward Burtynsky, *Sikorsky Helicopter Scrap Yard*, Tucson, Arizona, 2006

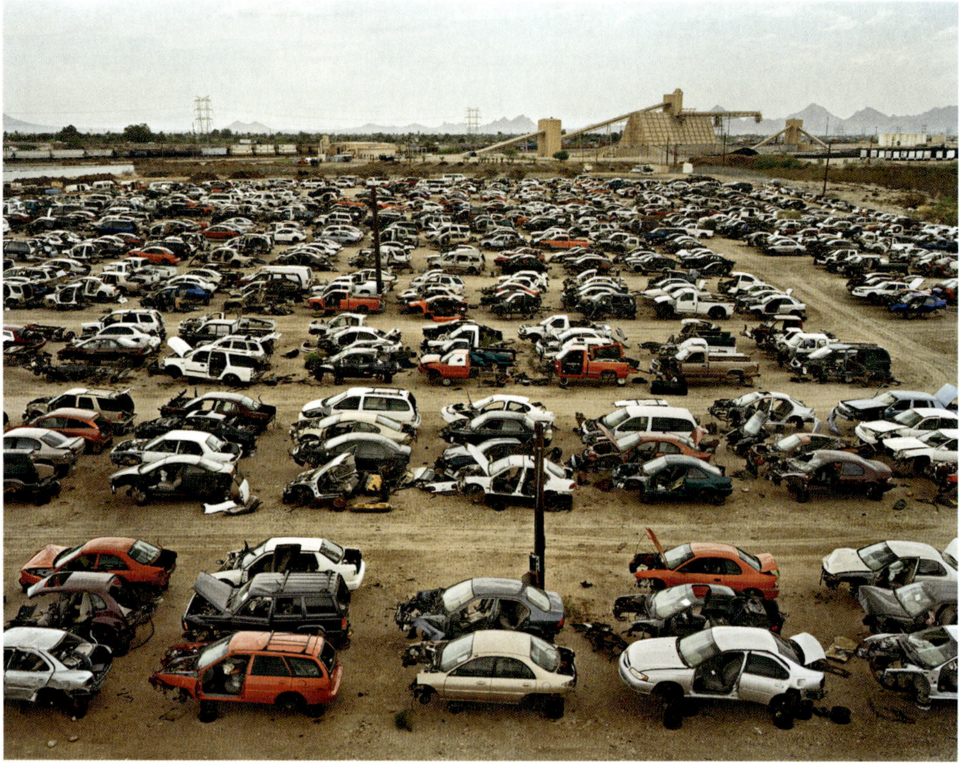

Edward Burtynsky, *Auto Wreckers #1*, Tucson, Arizona, 2006

There is also a special resting place for jet engines. Derelict cars have also been pillaged. In Tucson, they patiently sit side by side, awaiting further dismemberment.

Adding more oil fields to his collection was essential. For two years, Burtynsky tried to obtain permission to shoot at the Ghawar oil field in Saudi Arabia, but was turned away; he then decided to try his chances at another spot. Much of the petroleum industry in Azerbaijan is under the control of the State Oil Company of the Republic of Azerbaijan (SOCAR), and is centred in the city of Baku. There, Burtynsky visited a desolate spot that had become unproductive and, thus, abandoned. The earlier diptych *Oil Fields #19a and b* can be seen as a before shot and *SOCAR Oil Fields #1a and b* an after shot, where the spindly, ungainly apparatus sits on dry soil awash with black petroleum waste.

The Appendix is a fitting conclusion to the *Oil* project. In *Detroit–Motor City*, Burtynsky visited the design studio of the Ford Model T at the Ford Piquette Avenue Plant, which was built in 1904 and in use until 1910. There, in a manner reminiscent of his *Old Factories* series, he photographed the abandoned plant. For him, the plant was a chilling reminder of the past–of the GM factory where his father had worked and which, years later, he had cleansed of carcinogens.

Two years later, when he photographed the General Motors and Dana plants in St. Catharines, he had similar reflections. "[S]eeing the shuttered Dana plant and the withering of other manufacturing plants here was a

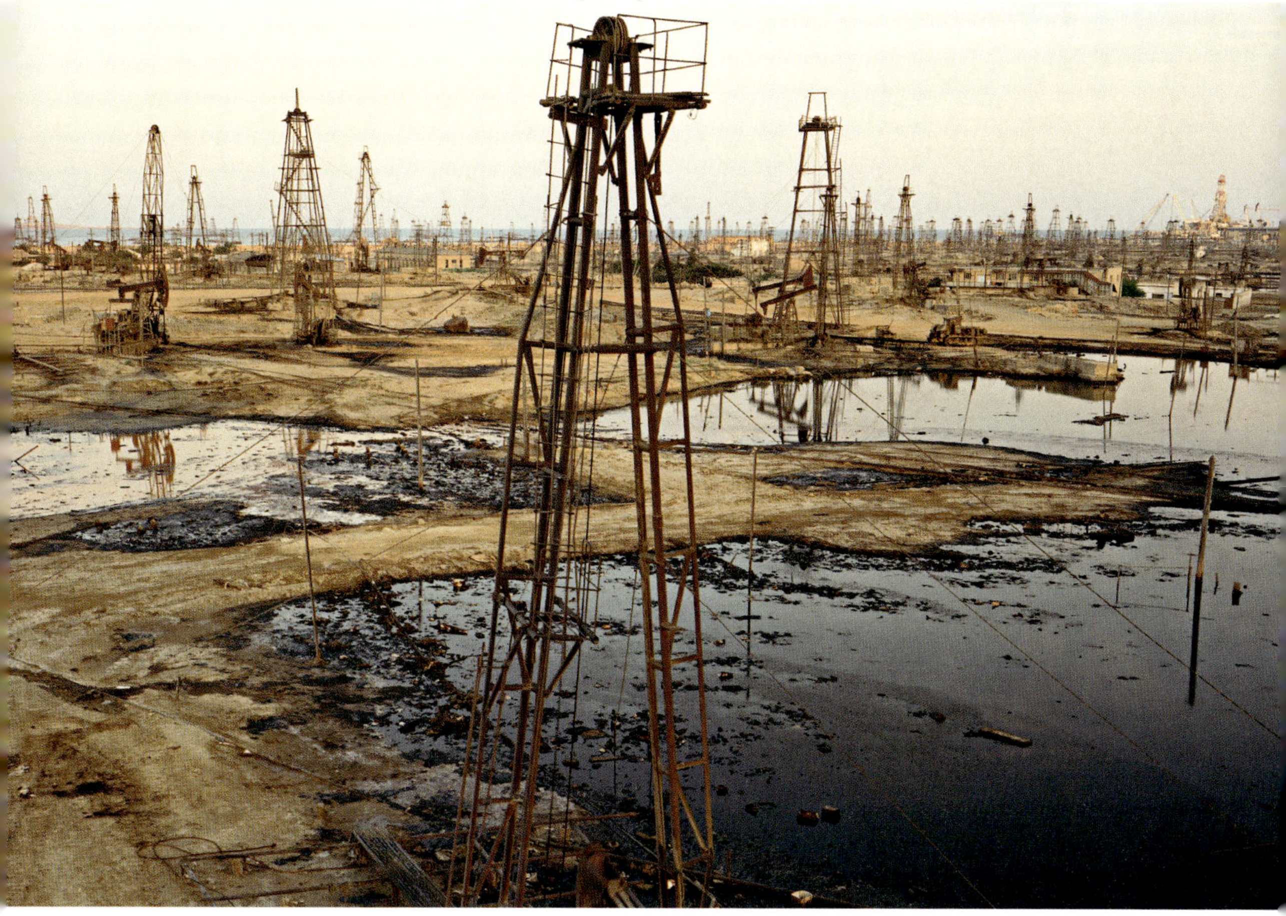

Edward Burtynsky, *SOCAR Oil Fields #1a and 1b*, Baku, Azerbaijan, 2006

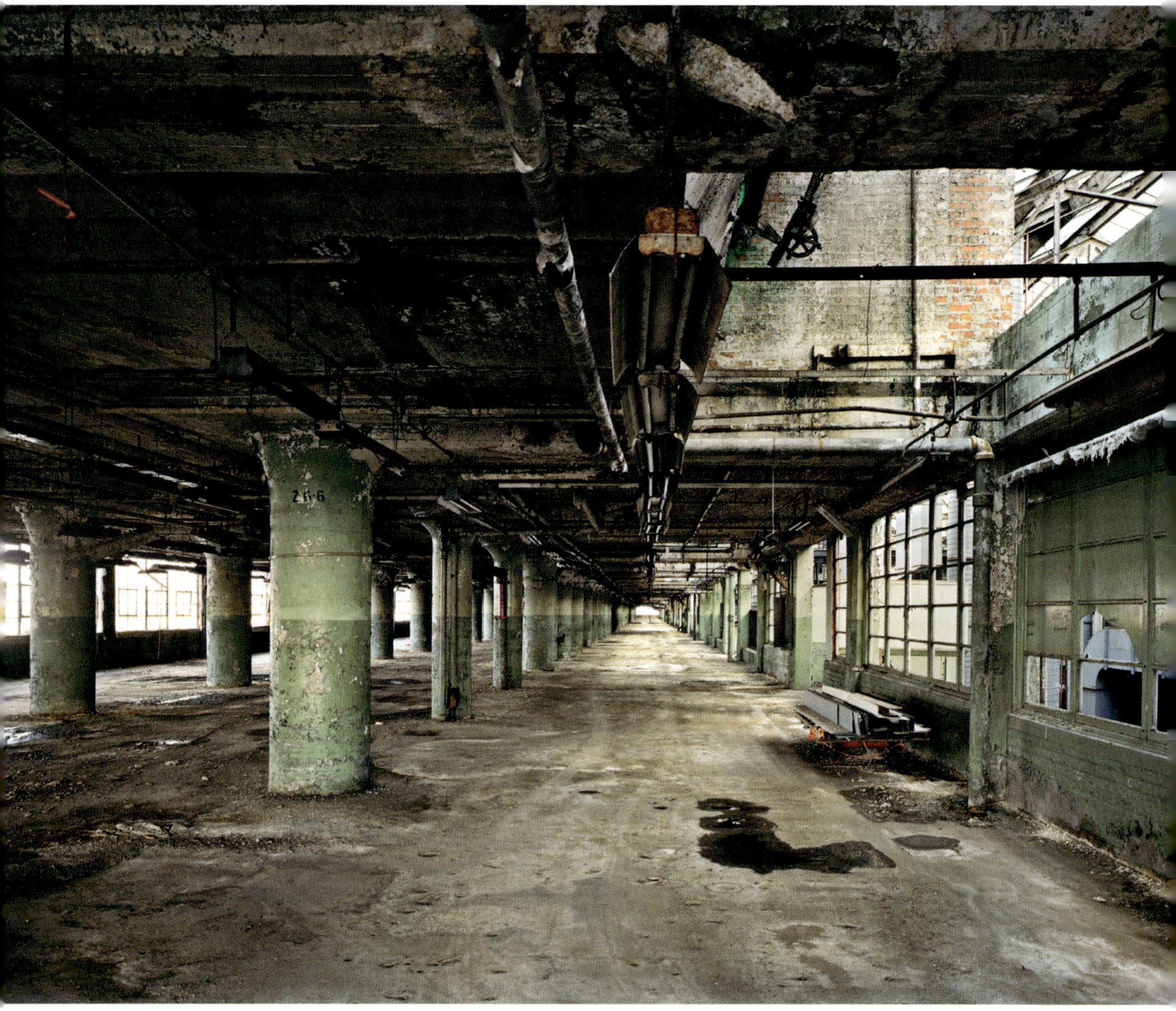

Edward Burtynsky, *Detroit #2*, 2008

bittersweet experience and a sobering reminder of the transformation that's gone on in industry, much of which has moved half a world away to China. The fact that the Dana plant was closed, and all the equipment was gone [made me sad] at not having a chance to see the actual machines that I worked on. I don't know where they went or who bought them, but it was a kind of melancholy moment that it's just gone quiet."[17]

In 2009, *The Art Daily* pointed out that Burtynsky was not:

> Concerned with acquiring a full view of all the oil fields. What he lays bare is not only the phenomenon of oil, but also a simple economic pattern that has enormous consequences–the extraction of a raw material, the consumption of it, and the waste that it leaves behind. As a photographer he shows us its intrinsic and aesthetic qualities through the composition, the distance that he adopts with respect to his subject (often from a high vantage point) and the strong balance with which he manages to unite conceptual with visual ideas . . . The strategy of Edward Burtynsky is simple: follow the oil. In this pursuit, his classically inspired, precise and detailed visual language is overwhelmingly effective. But the awe-inspiring quality of his photographs lies mainly in the suggestion of scale–both within the images and in the worldwide scope of his project.[18]

When the exhibition *Edward Burtynsky: Oil* opened at the Corcoran Gallery in Washington, D.C., in October of 2009, curator Paul Roth revealed that "[a] couple of years ago, we did a travelling Ansel Adams exhibition. So we wanted to focus on Adams as an environmentalist and invited a photographer who does landscape photography with an environmental slant to talk about their work in the context of Adams' work." On that occasion, Burtynsky mentioned he was putting together a portfolio on oil and was invited to show it at the Corcoran.

Roth spoke of Burtynsky's achievements and then added: "[T]hese aren't straightforward landscapes. His images have a strange mysterious sense about them, and I think at their best they provoke people to wonder what happened to the places he photographed."[19] This "mysterious sense" is encapsulated in a narrative that chronicles the continuing dependence on fossil fuel and the myriad ways in which it is destroying the planet. The oil project told its story in diverse ways and, in the process, provided a compelling story of exploitation, destruction, and waste.

(2006–2010)

11 POETIC EVIDENCE

Burtynsky's career had taken off in the ways he had hoped. In 2003, Nicholas Metivier left the Mira Godard Gallery to open his own, and Burtynsky followed him; his final show at Mira Godard was *Before the Flood* in 2003. Metivier exhibited four of Burtynsky's projects in quick succession: *Asian Quarries* in 2004, *Burtynsky China* in 2005, *Iberian Quarries* in 2007, and *Oil* in 2009.

Many accolades had come the photographer's way, including the Roloff Beny Photography Book Award in 2003 for *Before the Flood*, a TED Prize in 2005, being made an Officer of the Order of Canada in 2006, and being given honorary degrees from Queen's, Ryerson, and the Montserrat College of Art in 2007. Together with Jennifer Baichwal, he received the Rogers Best Documentary Film Award for *Manufacturing Landscapes* in 2006.[1]

In temperament, Burtynsky has always remained restless. Although aware of his accomplishments, he persevered in his exploration of the ravages imposed by man on nature. From 2006 to 2010, he added four series of images to his portfolio. Although he challenged himself to keep up with his competitors in both environmental and colour photography, he was, as he put it, "driven by my own need to tell and expand the story" to which he had dedicated his life. "How else," he asked himself, "can I add other ideas to the ones I've been building all these years?"[2]

IBERIA

Amid other projects, Burtynsky determined in 2006 to complete a series that he had worked on since 1991: quarries. To do so, he travelled to Borba, Pardais, and Bencatel in Portugal and Andalucia and Alicante in Spain. The Portuguese quarries are renowned for varieties of pink marble such as Rosa Aurora ("Pink Dawn"), Borba Pink, and Estremoz Pink.

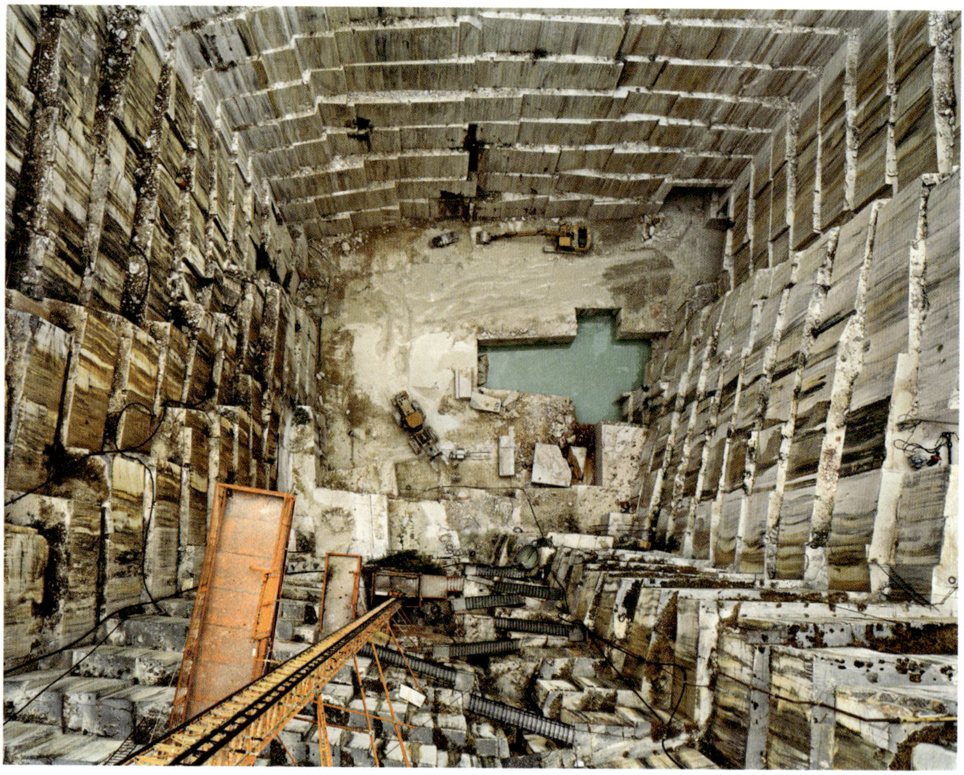

Edward Burtynsky, *Iberia Quarries #8*, Cochicho Co., Pardais, Portugal, 2006

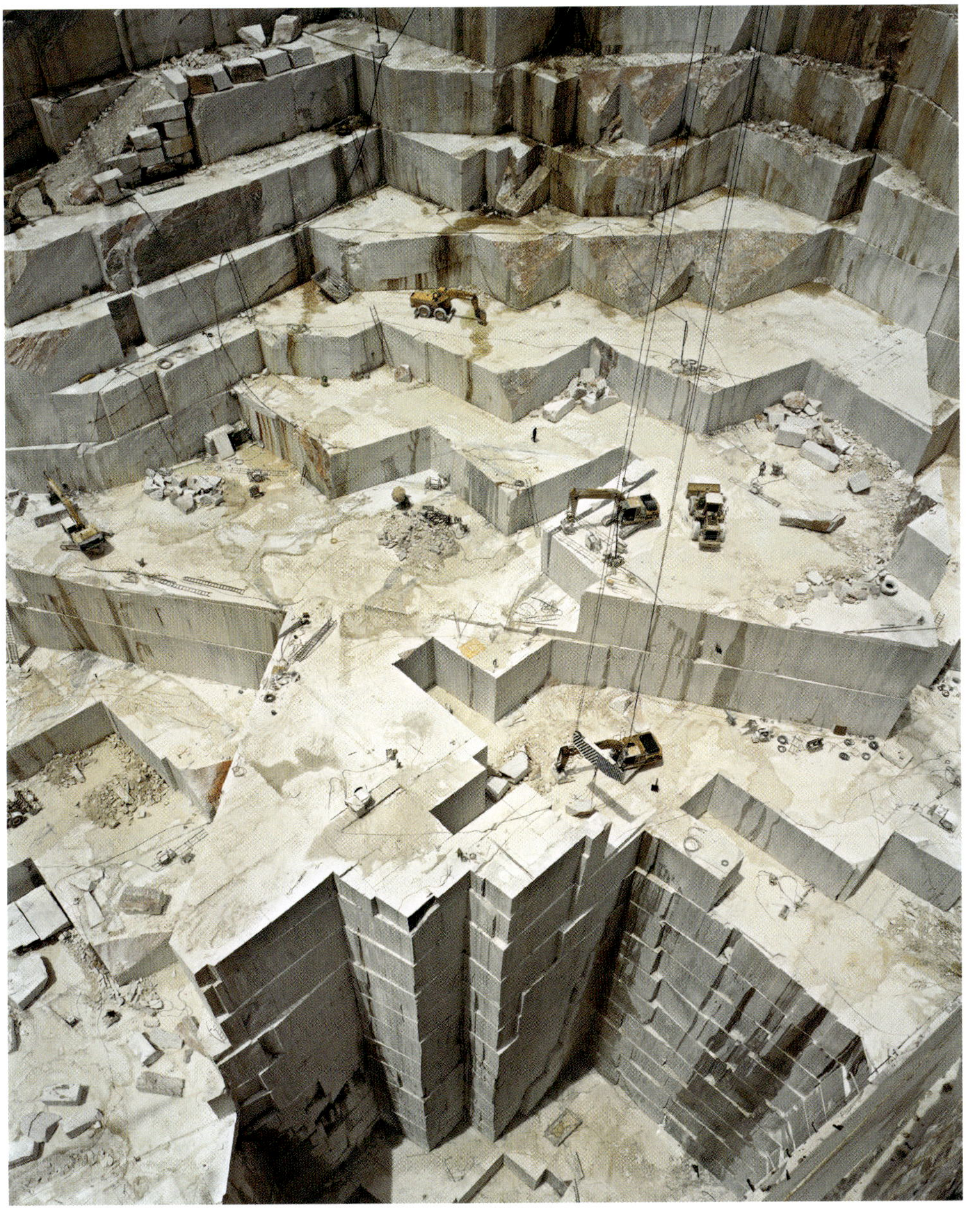

Edward Burtynsky, *Iberia Quarries #3*, Chochicho Co., Pardais, Portugal, 2006

Despite the success of his early images, he had not encountered a site that was the equal to the photograph by August Sander (see p. 43) he had seen years before at the National Gallery of Canada. At Pardais, he found what he was looking for in *Iberia Quarries #8*. Further architectural elements can be spotted in the skyscraper-like formations in the foreground of *Iberia Quarries #3*, and an altar-like formation (the pink clearly showing) can be observed in the centre of *Iberia Quarries #2*. As Michael Mitchell observed, the quarries in Portugal represented "the culmination and conclusion of a fifteen-year search for his dream image of an architecture turned inside out and upside down."[3]

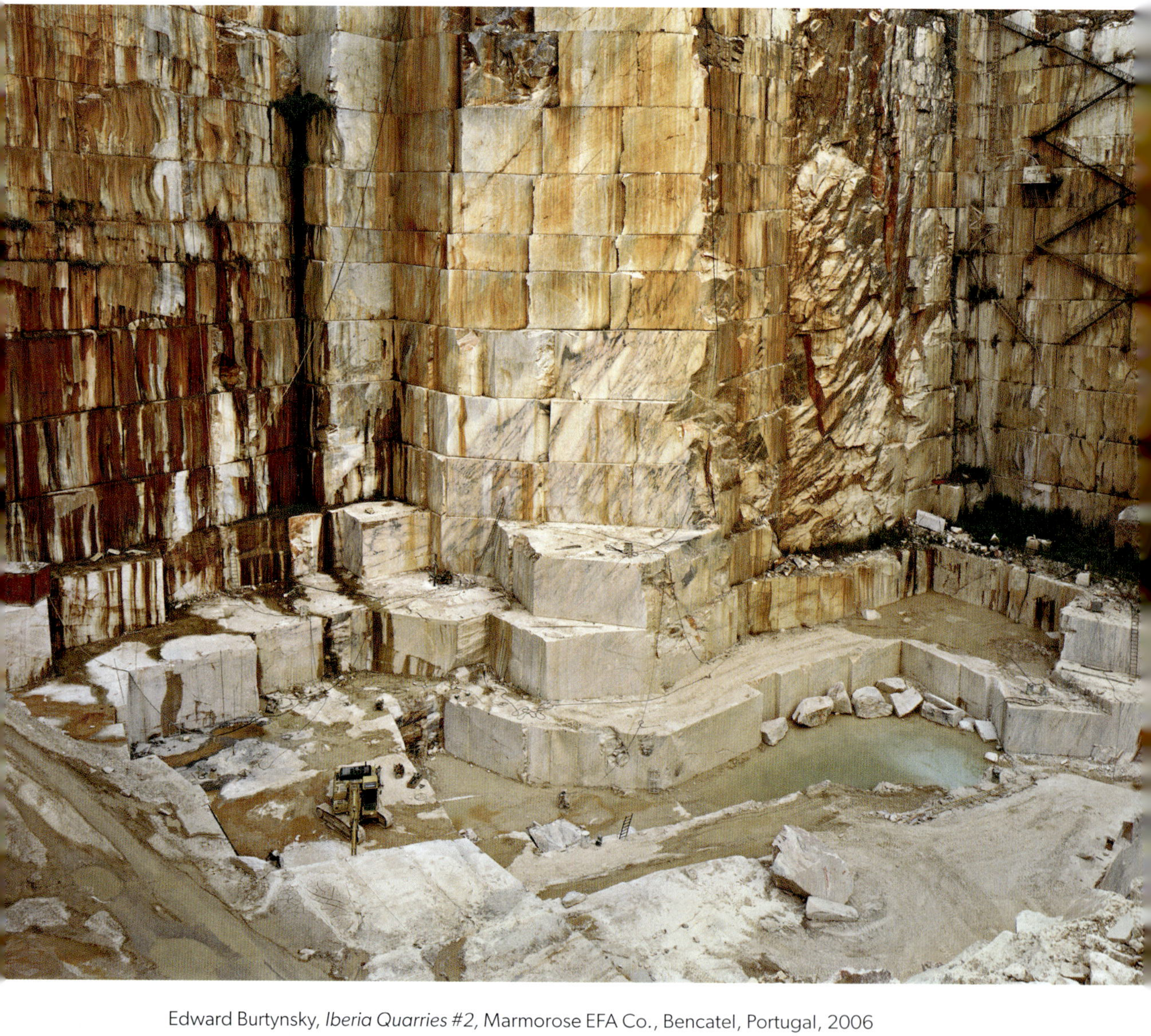

Edward Burtynsky, *Iberia Quarries #2*, Marmorose EFA Co., Bencatel, Portugal, 2006

The five series of quarries are an investigation into one form of man-made architecture that exists because people have made incursions into rock to provide building materials, as for the kind of bank architecture he had previously investigated.

After the *Quarries* series concluded, Burtynsky reflected that his "sense of architecture [was] conceived of as unintentional in practical terms, but as having high imperative in an imaginary world–a negative of architecture, shaped by the process of large-scale extraction, not erection. The key word for me in this is process. I am drawn to photographing large spaces in transition, spaces that evolve, changing from day to day as the direct result of human intervention. I find in those spaces a wealth of aesthetic material."[4] Burtynsky added: "[O]ur presence is dwarfed by the spaces we've created. It's an interesting metaphor for how technology seems larger than life, larger than our own lives."[5] For him, that was the industrial sublime.

After further deliberation, Burtynsky came to this conviction: "Photographing dimensional stone quarries was a deliberate act of going out to try to find something in the world that would match the kinds of forms I held in my imagination but had never seen in real life–the idea of inverted skyscrapers."[6]

RENOVATIONS

In 2007 and 2008, Burtynsky tackled two earth-bound projects when he was commissioned to document major renovations made at the Art Gallery of Ontario (AGO) in Toronto and the Art Gallery of Alberta (AGA) in Edmonton.[7]

The AGO was originally a stone Beaux-Arts building completed in 1918. Various renovations had been made over the years, but a two-storey structure grafted onto the front of the building at its Dundas Street entrance in the 1990s was unsightly. The Toronto-born architect Frank Gehry was invited to make the building more accessible, but his real mission was to transform the entire building into a vibrant, inviting, and contemporary space. Among his revisions, he created a glass façade that swells one storey at the front and a spiralling wood staircase that rises from the main floor and connects to the contemporary galleries. The Gallery Italia, a long, narrow sculpture corridor on the second floor, sits behind the glass façade.

In Edmonton, Randall Stout, a Gehry protégé, created an 85,000-square-foot, five-level building with steel and zinc on the outside and a stainless-steel ribbon running through the interior and exterior. That building's most remarkable feature is the four-storey atrium, which features an enormous sculpture.

Both projects–attempts to invigorate old spaces with new energy–were declarations that museums were not resting spots for art but zones in which art becomes a vital, living entity. Burtynsky was celebrated for showing

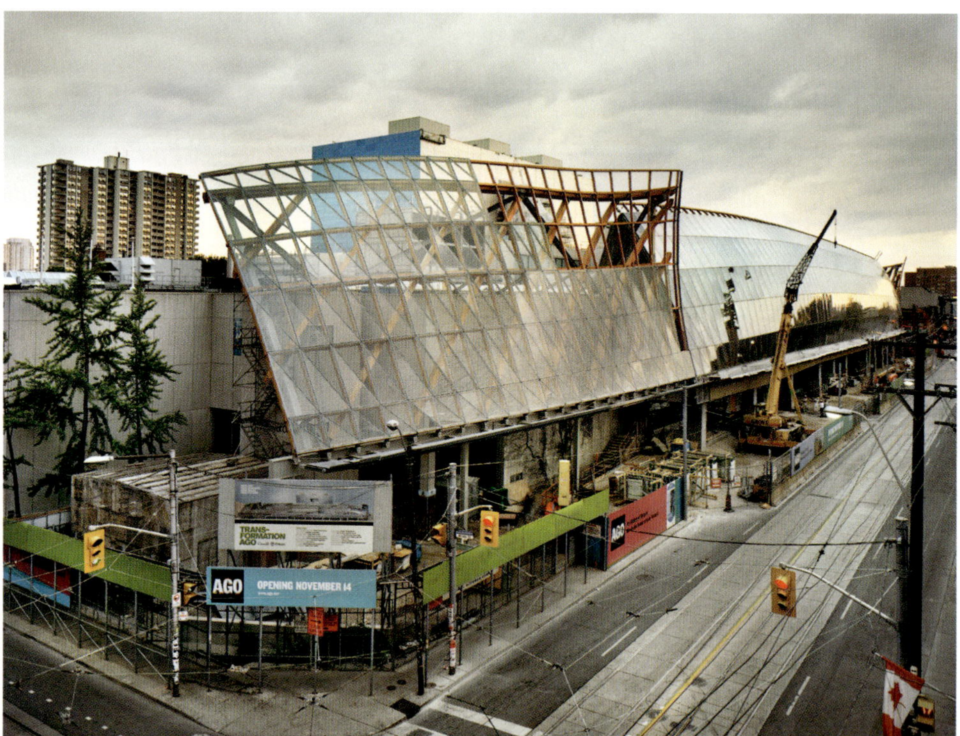

Edward Burtynsky, *Dundas Street Façade #2*, Art Gallery of Ontario, 2008

landscapes that had been ravaged, and these commissions allowed him to photograph places that were being restored.

The photographs taken in Toronto emphasize Gehry's innovations in rethinking the AGO's exterior and interior. The Edmonton photographs are dissimilar in that the building's gigantic post-modern, wave-like exterior is shown under construction, but emphasis is given to demonstrating how the building rose from the earth. Burtynsky also accentuates richly textured, abstract patterns and glistening steel abstractions reminiscent of his earlier *Oil Refinery* images. Reflecting on these two projects, he accurately pointed out, "Looking at and photographing extraordinary works of architecture is a passion of mine."[8]

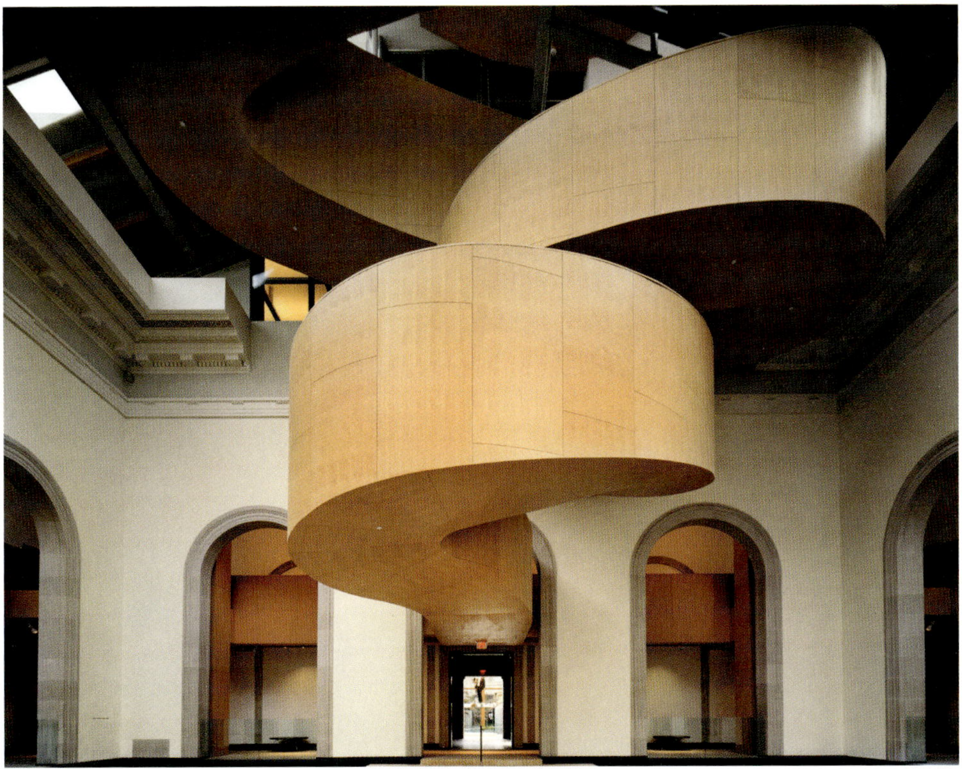

Edward Burtynsky, *Allan Slaight and Emmanuelle Gattuso Staircase*, Art Gallery of Ontario, 2008

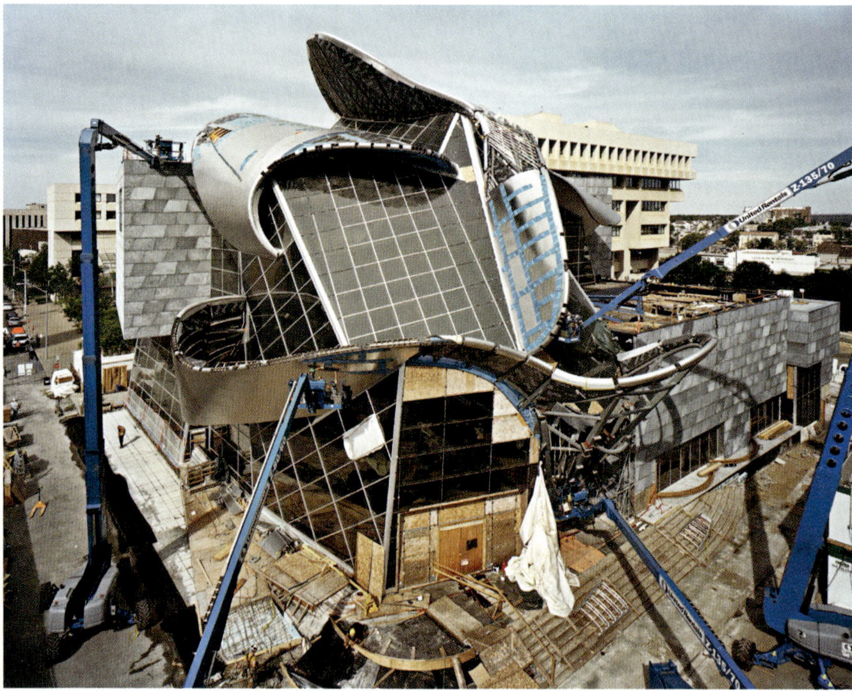

Edward Burtynsky, *Stainless Steel Installation: Looking North East,* Art Gallery of Alberta, 2009

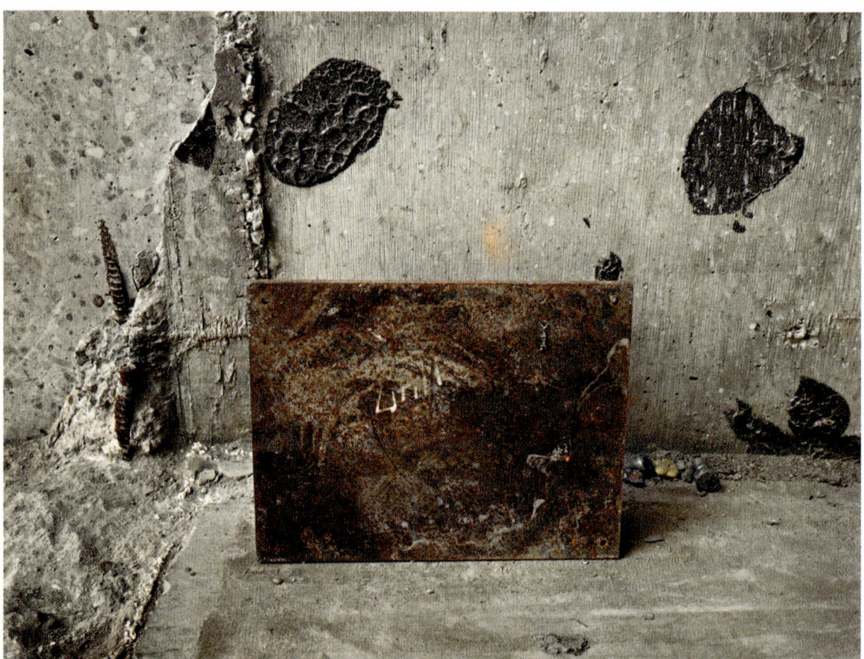

Edward Burtynsky, *Metal Plate Against Existing Building Wall,* Art Gallery of Alberta, 2009

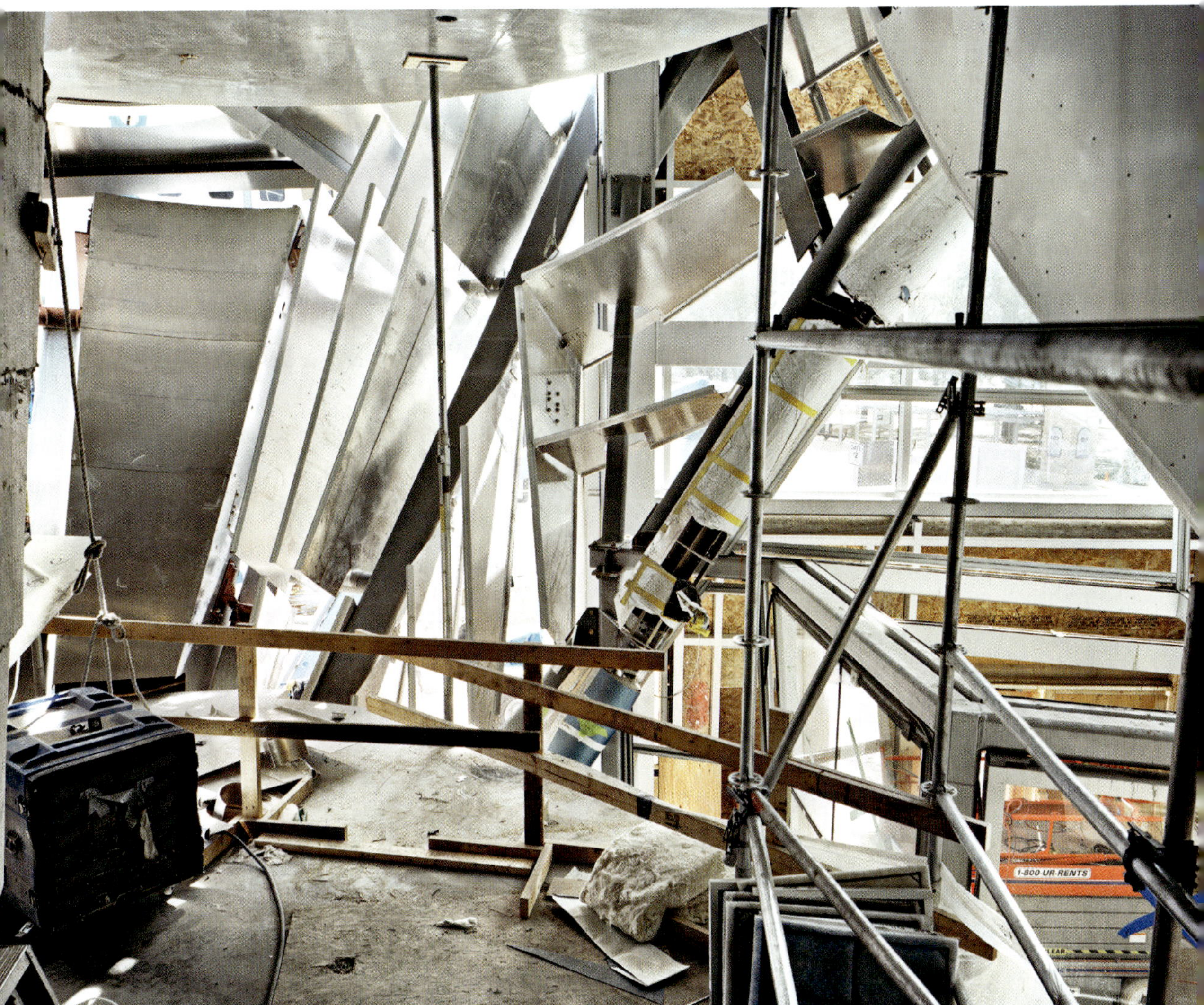

Edward Burtynsky, *Grand Stair: Between First and Second Floors*, Art Gallery of Alberta, 2009

MINESCAPES

In 2007, the year after the Iberia quarry shoot, Burtynsky had the opportunity to explore another form of deep space inserted by man into the earth, and to return to another favourite subject: mines. Previously, Burtynsky had held back from making statements that could be interpreted as being political. At this point in his career, however, he did not change direction as much as he inflected it. He still believed that his images should speak for themselves, but he was no longer as averse to speaking about their implications. Writing in 2009, he said,

> If the human experience can be considered a manifestation of dreams and desires, mines can be thought of as the source for the raw materials of that existence. On one level of understanding, the mineral rich ore is manufactured into the objects of collective desire: the automobiles we drive, televisions we watch, jets that fly us around the globe, houses that provide us with shelter and comfort, and an endless stream of gadgets and goods. If gold, silver, and diamonds are the valuables we bestow upon each other, to honour great citizens and profess our love, then are the great voids we leave in that residual landscape a lasting testament to these ambitions? The imagery I derive from these landscapes therefore becomes symbolic. What this civilization leaves in the wake of its progress may be opened and emptied earth, but in performing these incursions we also participate in the unwitting creation of gigantic monuments of our way of life.[9]

These reflections were triggered by his response to a project commissioned by the Australian biannual photography festival, FotoFreo 2008, to make images of mines in the western part of that continent. The *Silver Lakes* images from that shoot was the first all-digital images Burtynsky did.

On that trip, Joseph Hartman was Burtynsky's assistant. On one of their first days on site, Hartman later said, he forgot to take along a piece of equipment vital to that day's shooting. When the mistake was discovered, Burtynsky shrugged his shoulders, did what he could that day, and then suggested they head back to their hotel. He did not upbraid Hartman.[10]

The terrain of Western Australia is suffused with deep, reddish ochres, and this colourway dominates most of the photographs in the series. As in Portugal, Burtynsky found dramatic incursions into the surface of the

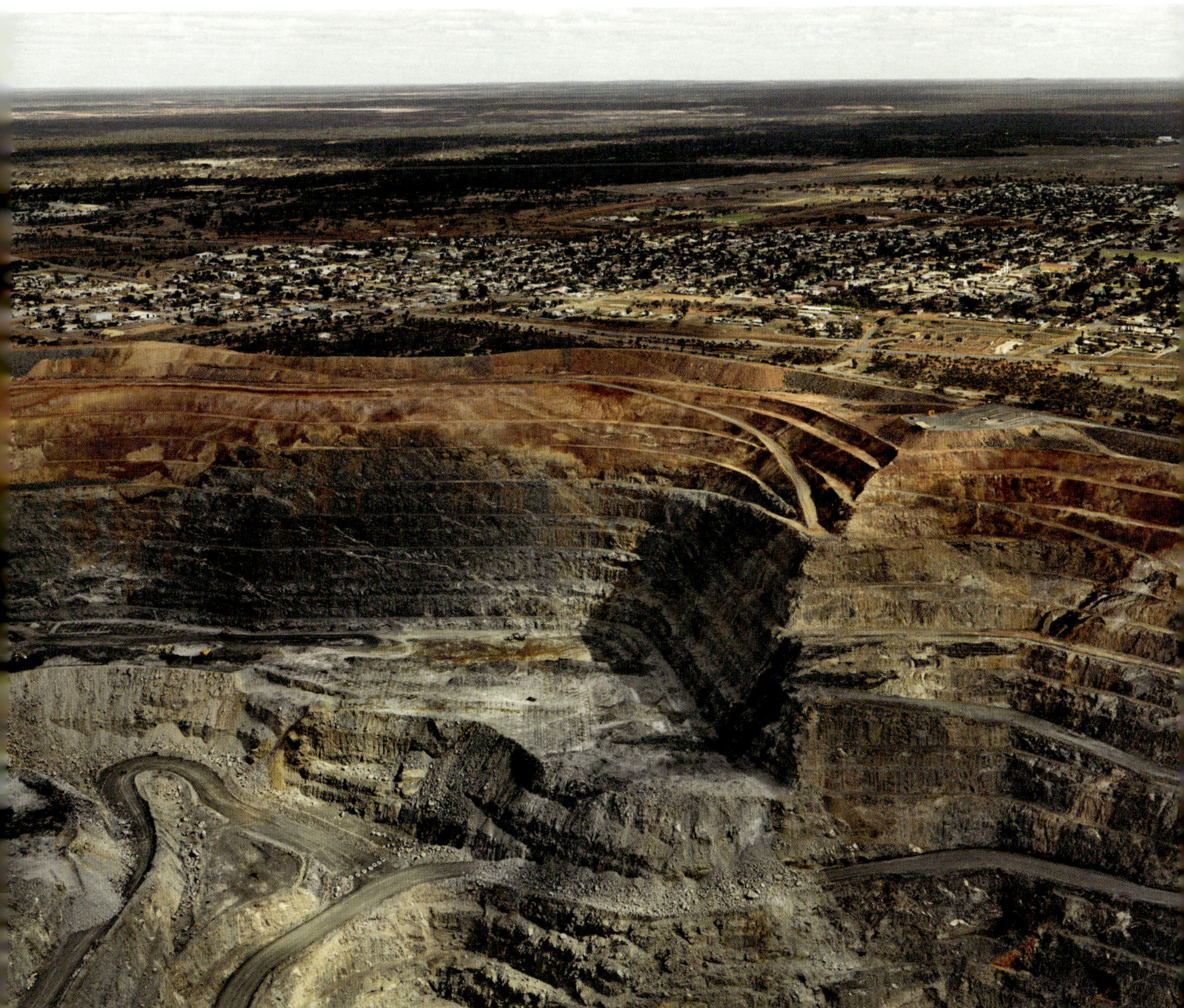

Edward Burtynsky, *Super Pit #4*, Kalgoolie, Western Australia, 2007

earth in the Super Pit at Kalgoorlie, Australia's largest gold mine. The contrast between the pit and the adjoining town in *Super Pit #4* is startling but becomes frightening when it becomes obvious the town has been eaten up by the mine–and that more disintegration is likely to follow. The depth of the mine is captured in *Super Pit #1*, where the carved-out paths move downward: a descent reminiscent of Dante navigating circles of Hell in his *Inferno*. The overhead shots of Lake Lefroy are among Burtynsky's finest abstracts as is *Tailings #1*.

The mines at *Silver Lake Operations #15* at Lake Lefroy, which are located on salt flats, appealed to Burtynsky "because that's where you get

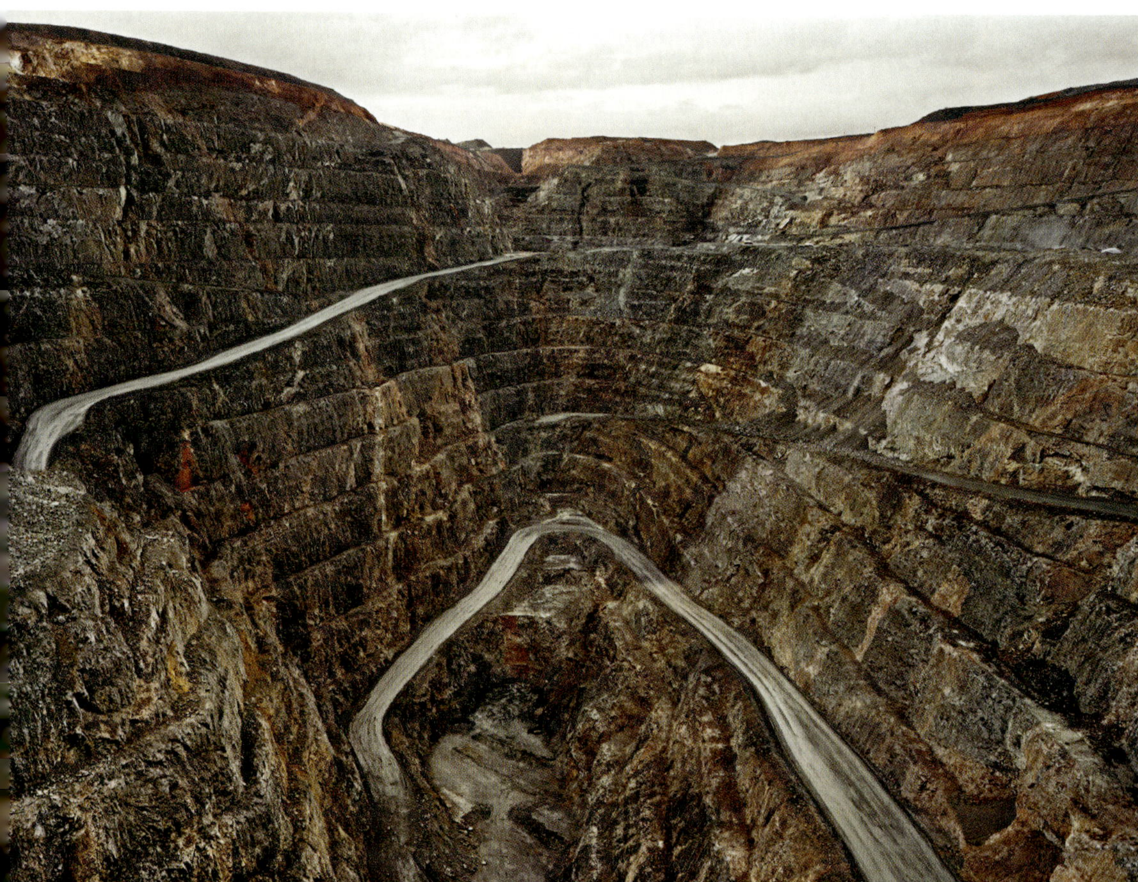

Edward Burtynsky, *Super Pit #1*, Kalgoorlie, Western Australia, 2007

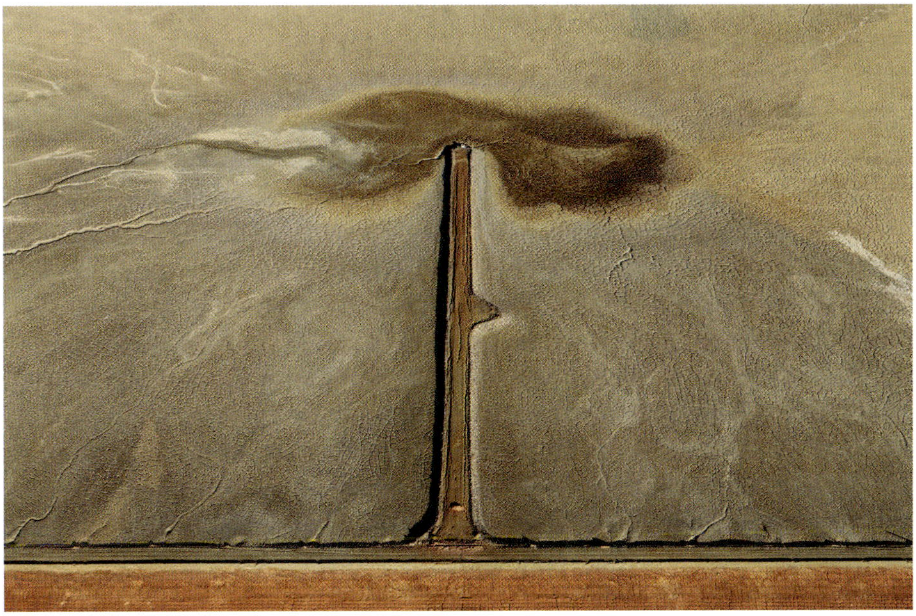

Edward Burtynsky, *Tailings #1*, Kalgoorlie, Western Australia, 2007

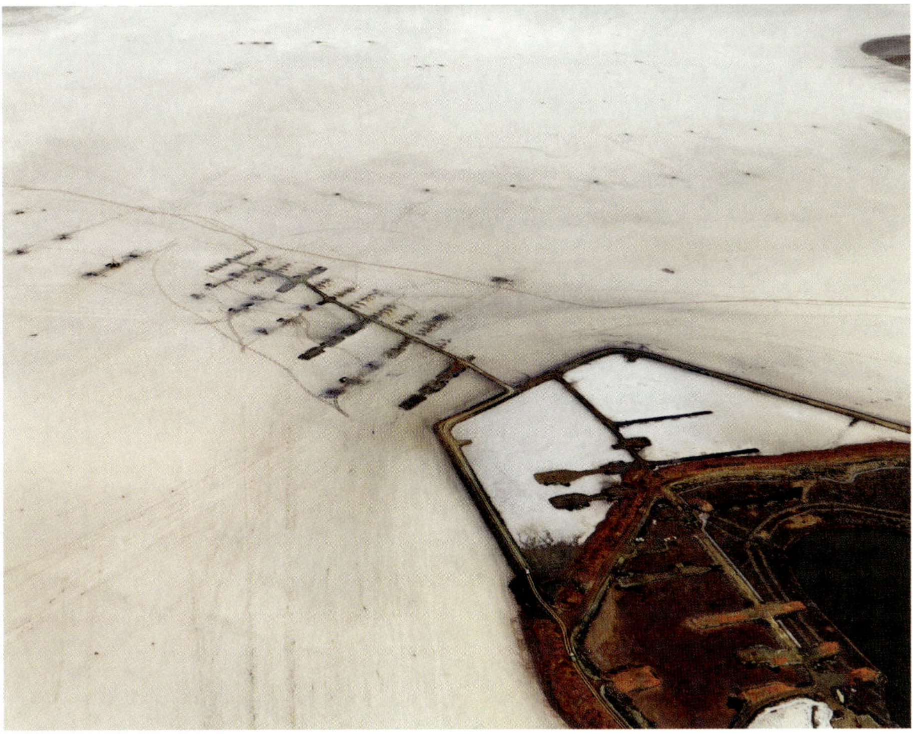

Edward Burtynsky, *Silver Lake Operations #15*, Lake Lefroy, Western Australia, 2007

this surreal-looking surface. I'd photographed mines for many years at this point, but what I wanted to do differently here was to shoot them from a helicopter with the door off."[11] He was lucky that day: fresh water "was sitting on the salt flats: the water was subtly reflecting the cloud activity on the salt flats. Their colour and texture through the moisture made the surface feel like an encaustic painting."[12]

The journalist Victoria Laurie recalled: "Burtynsky stood on the rim of deep mining pits, pointing his large format camera down towards the black and red tiered terraces lining the pit. Then he took low-level helicopter flights, his camera attached to a gyroscope to reduce movement in the air. He hovered over pink and white salt lakes crisscrossed with mining tracks; he passed vivid orange earth heaps that rose up in inverse proportion to the depth of open-cut operations beside them. 'The harsh light of Australia's high noon is hard to deal with because it throws shadows, but it was unusually cloudy and rain had cleared dust from the air the day before,' Burtynsky recalls. 'It was great luck and I thought, "I can't believe what I'm looking at."'"

Laurie also recognized the connection between this assignment of Burtynsky's and his earlier ones: "Burtynsky appears to eliminate human beings from his photographs. And then you realise their hand is everywhere in the pictures: they carved the marble cliffs in an Italian quarry into geometric blocks, they scattered iron junk across a [Bangladeshi] beach, they blasted gaping holes in Western Australia's remote northwest landscape."[13]

For Australians, Philip Goldswain argued, the *Minescapes* photographs provided "a lens through which we might consider the landscape and cities of Western Australia and the interdependent relationship between these two very different constructed environments. Many of these are transitory landscapes, destined for future refinement and reorganization. The wealth generated by the sale of these commodities has resulted in the transformation of Perth; ambitious urban infrastructure projects have redefined the length of the suburban metropolis as well as locating new cultural and sporting buildings in the centre of the city. These changes have recast the space of the city, shifting it from its previous preboom state."[14] The devastation of the land created new wealth, but at what price? That was the question Burtynsky was asking.

Burtynsky's friend, Michael Mitchell, observed: "What is at first glance a scarred landscape becomes poetic evidence of resources spent, nature transformed, as well as realized–or failed–hopes and dreams. The aerial images of the Silver Lake Operations at Lake Lefroy, and of the pits and tailings at Kalgoorlie are among the most handsome images Burtynsky has ever made. They combine a kind of mapping with a keenly felt experience of all the hard rock grit, dust and labour transforming these arid lands."[15]

For Burtynsky, a minescape is also a *mindscape*. These images invite the viewer to meditate on the nature of these extractions and to experience the scale of disruption they create.

SKYWARDS

Burtynsky had used planes and helicopters previously, but airborne photography became an even more integral part of his work during this period:

> During the twenty years since I first photographed the Sudbury mines, I have contemplated how to bring a new dimension to that body of work. Within the scope of my artistic practice, visual abstraction is something I often think about and venture to explore. When the world takes on a surreal dream-like appearance I stop, I look, and am compelled to make those pictures in those moments. Using the helicopter as a tool–a lofty tripod–I found that the strange, dizzying perspective on the landscape provided the new element I was after. The rare bird's-eye vantage provides for a view that incorporates the grand scale of what human intervention on our planet quite literally looks like with my desire to transcend that reality and create a work of art.[16]

He aspires to make images of what most people might think ordinary into something extraordinary.

That "new dimension" of the bird's-eye view became second nature to him, but he understood many other photographers had preceded him. The aerial mapping of enemy territory employed throughout the First World War was key to that military struggle, but the original functions of such images did not prevent the inclusion of sequential aerial views of a bombardment in progress from the Museum of Modern Art's first survey of the medium's history in 1937. Margaret Bourke-White filmed factories from the air in the mid-1930s. Later, in the United States, William Garnett did the same when he photographed housing developments and landscapes. In Canada, George Hunter, a pilot, made aerial colour images of industrial sites.[17]

At the time he had photographed Mount St. Helens (see p. 72), Burtynsky had not been aware that Emmet Gowin, Frank Gohlke, and David Maisel had taken aerial photographs there. Later, he would have learned of other aerial projects: David T. Hanson's images taken between 1982 and 1985 at Colstrip, Montana, and his 1985–1986 series *Waste Land*; David Maisel's *Black Maps* (1985), *The Forest* (1986), *The Mining Project* (1989), *The Lake Project* (2001-2002), and *Terminal Mirage* (2003-2005); and Emmet Gowin's *Nevada Test Site* images (1996).

Gowin had given a master class at Ryerson while Burtynsky was a student there, and his influence on Burtynsky had been a constant in the younger man's practice. Starting in the mid-1980s, Gowin had practised aerial photography in many other locations beyond the Nevada Test Site, such as Arizona, New Mexico, California, and the Czech Republic, among other places. In 2002, a selection of these photographs was published in *Changing the Earth: Aerial Photographs*. Echoes of Gowin's practice can be seen in Burtynsky's first aerial images by comparing, for instance, Gowin's *Pivot Irrigation near the One Hundred Circle Farm and the McNary Dam on the Columbia Dam on the Columbia River, Washington* (1991) and Burtynsky's 2012 *Pivot Irrigation #39*.

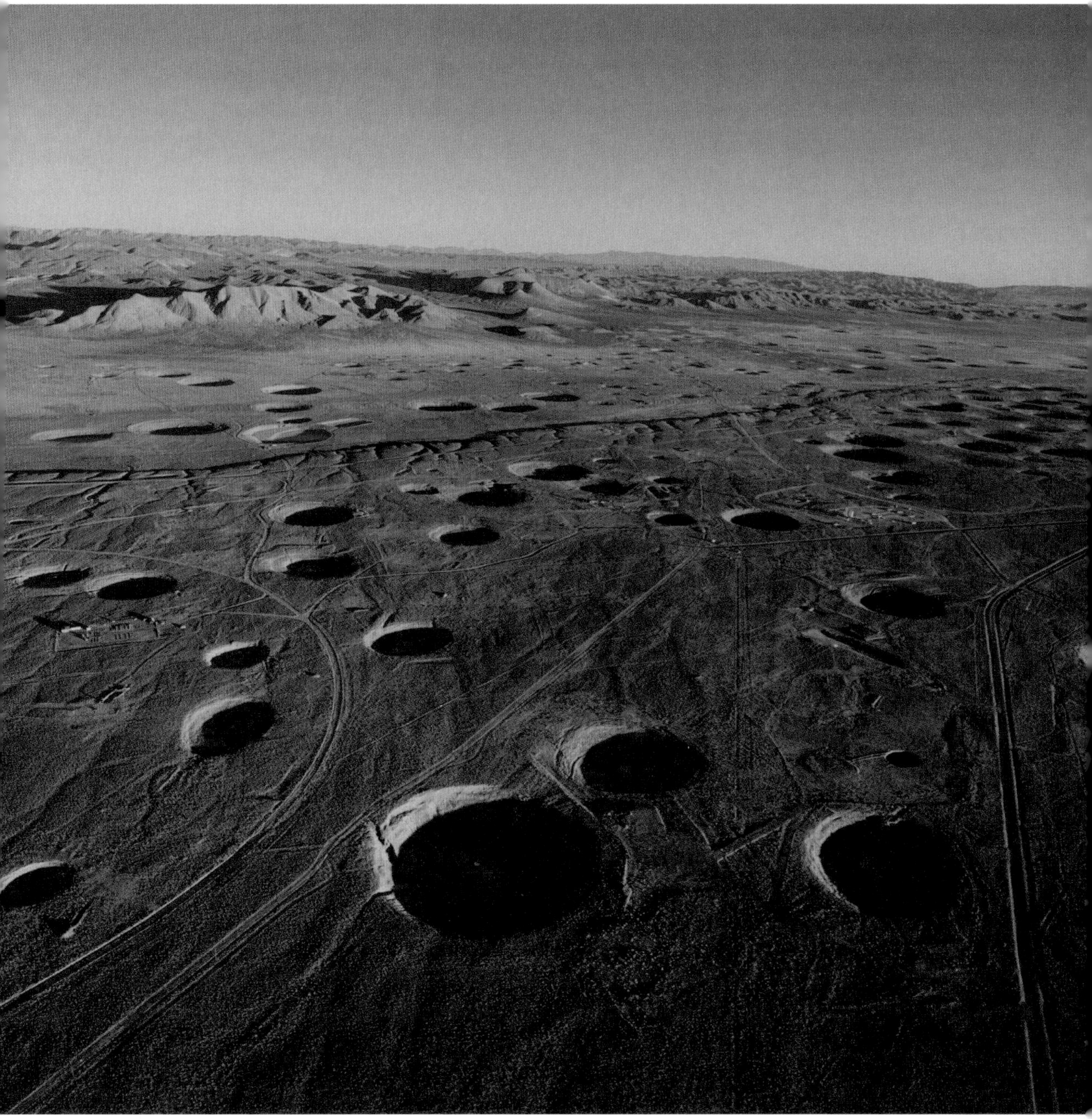

Emmet Gowin, *Subsidence Craters, Looking Southeast from Area B, Yucca Flat*, Nevada Test Site, 1996. Courtesy of Emmet Gowin

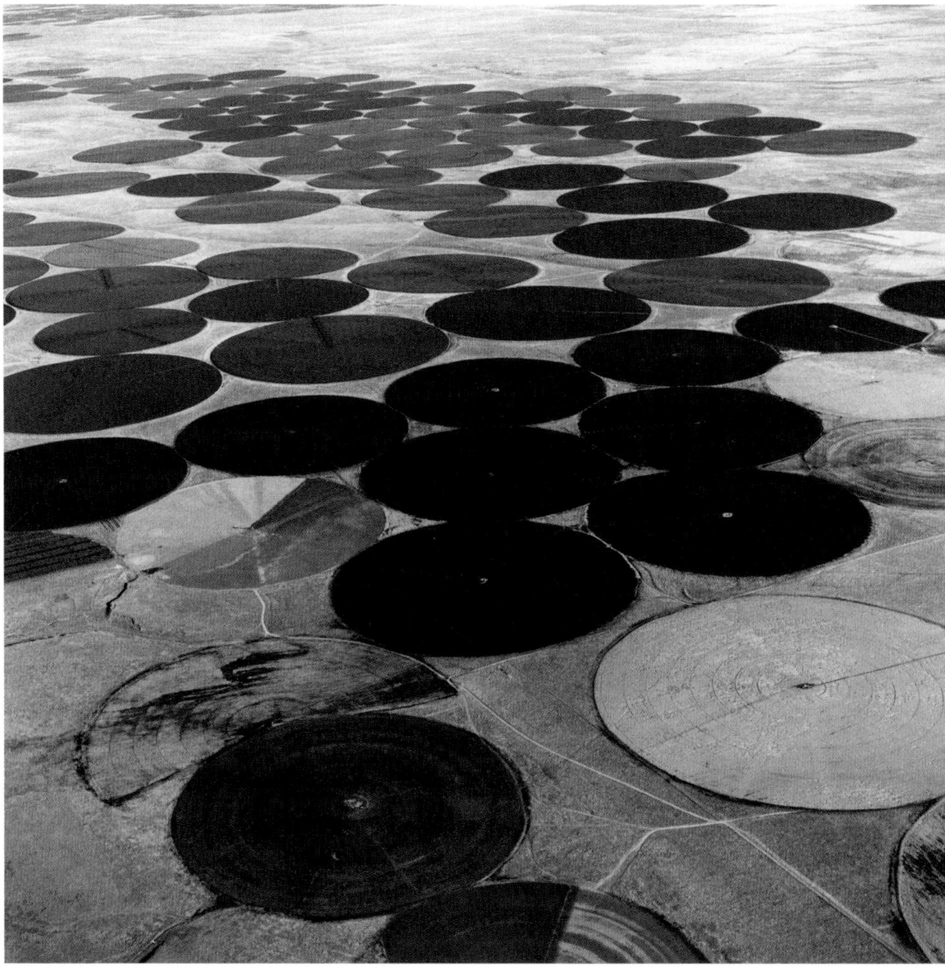

Emmet Gowin, *Large Circle Complex near the Columbia River*, Lincoln County, Washington, 1991. Courtesy of Emmet Gowin

The aerial photographer is dependent on technical assistance of a high order, especially when shooting from a helicopter. In such situations, Burtynsky recalled, "I have a fixed lens. When I see the possibility of an intriguing composition, I say to the pilot, 'go to this side.' Or, 'go down lower.' Or, 'crab backwards.' Or, 'go up a little higher.' As a result, I'm using the helicopter as a kind of floating point to say, 'OK. Freeze. Hold there as much as you can and then I'll shoot.'"[18]

Burtynsky was mindful that aerial photographs tend to look alike—photographing from the air creates "abstracted" images that are very different from normal modes of landscape representation. In making the decision to add this means to his tool box, he realized that his work would be compared to other aerial photographers. He felt the risk worth taking, because of his belief in the power of his own eye and because he often needed to be airborne to capture the essence of what he was photographing. In his practice, he still mixed a wide selection of viewing points.

COLOUR

Burtynsky knew he was one among many photographers incorporating aerial views in his work. He was also aware that the trend toward large-sized colour photographs was opening another competitive strand. Andreas Gursky and other members of the Düsseldor School in Germany and Jeff Wall in Canada followed such a trajectory. The critic Michael Fried has argued:

> One of the most important developments in the so-called visual arts of the past twenty-plus years has been the emergence of large-scale, tableau-sized photographs that by virtue of their size demand to be hung on gallery walls in the manner of easel paintings, and in other respects as well aspire to what might loosely be called the rhetorical, or beholder-addressing, significance of paintings while at the same time declaring their artifactual as photographs.[19]

Gursky's photography is rooted in the work of Bernd and Hilla Becher, who began photographing industrial structures in Germany such as blast furnaces, pitheads, silos, gas tanks, and water towers in the 1960s. Their images are in black and white, shot against a neutral sky, and printed on grids of between four and thirty images. They described these arrangements as "typologies" and referred to the buildings they photographed as "anonymous sculptures."[20] Their work deliberately challenged the gap between fine art and documentary photography. For them, their images were records of what existed and made links between similar pieces of architecture. Their photographs gained attention among the avant-garde.

Gursky perceived the images of the Bechers as minimalist and socially relevant. To emulate them, but to make his own mark, he printed his colour images in large sizes and focused on subjects he deemed socially relevant–some focus on consumerism as in *99 Cent* (1999), his view of the interior of a Los Angeles bargain store. He has never been hesitant to use digital technology to eradicate extraneous details. Like Burtynsky, many of his images gesture in the direction of abstraction.

Although Wall is a socially conscious photographer, he is not a minimalist. He began making large-scale colour photographs in 1978 in the form of back-lit transparencies. One of his most celebrated images is *Picture for Women* (1979), which shows the artist in his studio taking a snapshot of a woman; the photographer intended this as an update to Manet's *Un bar aux Folies Bergêre* (1882). As in this instance, Wall is a cerebral artist who infuses his images with conceits and tropes that often require his audience to possess a considerable artistic vocabulary.

Nicholas Metivier has pointed out that, in the work of Wall, Gursky, and the other Düsseldorf photographers, "there was a rejection of beauty and style, but Burtynsky flew in the face of that. His work has always been beautiful because of the quality of the print itself, which is why the photographs are so effective on a bigger scale."[21]

"When one looks at my images," Burtynsky has observed, "you don't need a text beside them, [because] the communication is all encoded in the image. To me that is the power of what an image can be. What I saw happening in a lot of post-modern work was that you needed to have the text, you needed to know the concepts before the work could make any sense. Separated from the text such work could not support itself. You had to be educated in the visual arts, the movements, and other things, to understand. I didn't want to go down that road. I wanted to feel the work could contain all the ideas."[22]

(2009–2016)

12 THE SHAPE OF WATER

"I began to think about water as a subject for my work in 2007, while . . . photographing gold mines in Australia . . . water took on a new meaning for me [when] I realized [it], unlike oil, is not optional. Without it we perish," Burtynsky observed.[1] Like *Manufactured Landscapes* and *China*, this new subject eventually led to a documentary (*Watermark*) and a substantial collection of images (*Water*).

The *Water* project–and many of those to follow–were done with Jim Panou's assistance. After their trip to Bangladesh in 2000, Panou had worked briefly in the Studio, adjusting colour values in the *China* series. After 2007, he often put his own work on hold to accompany his friend. His role remains as a "fixer," someone who negotiates access permissions with local officials, hires pilots, and generally makes sure everything clicks into place during a shoot.[2] Panou also searches Google Earth to find spots that might make suitable subject matter. Marcus Schubert recalled that

"Jim finds the actual spots and hires the helicopters with a flight plan with all the stops along the way. Every day and hour is accounted for. So, he prepares the call sheets for every shoot. He finds out what the topography looks like, what the colours are like, what the local industries are."[3] Panou himself sums up his role as being tied to "Ed's brain as far as image making is concerned." His task is also intuitive: "All I need to do is put suggestions in front of him to think them through." He thought water would be an excellent project and told Burtynsky so.[4]

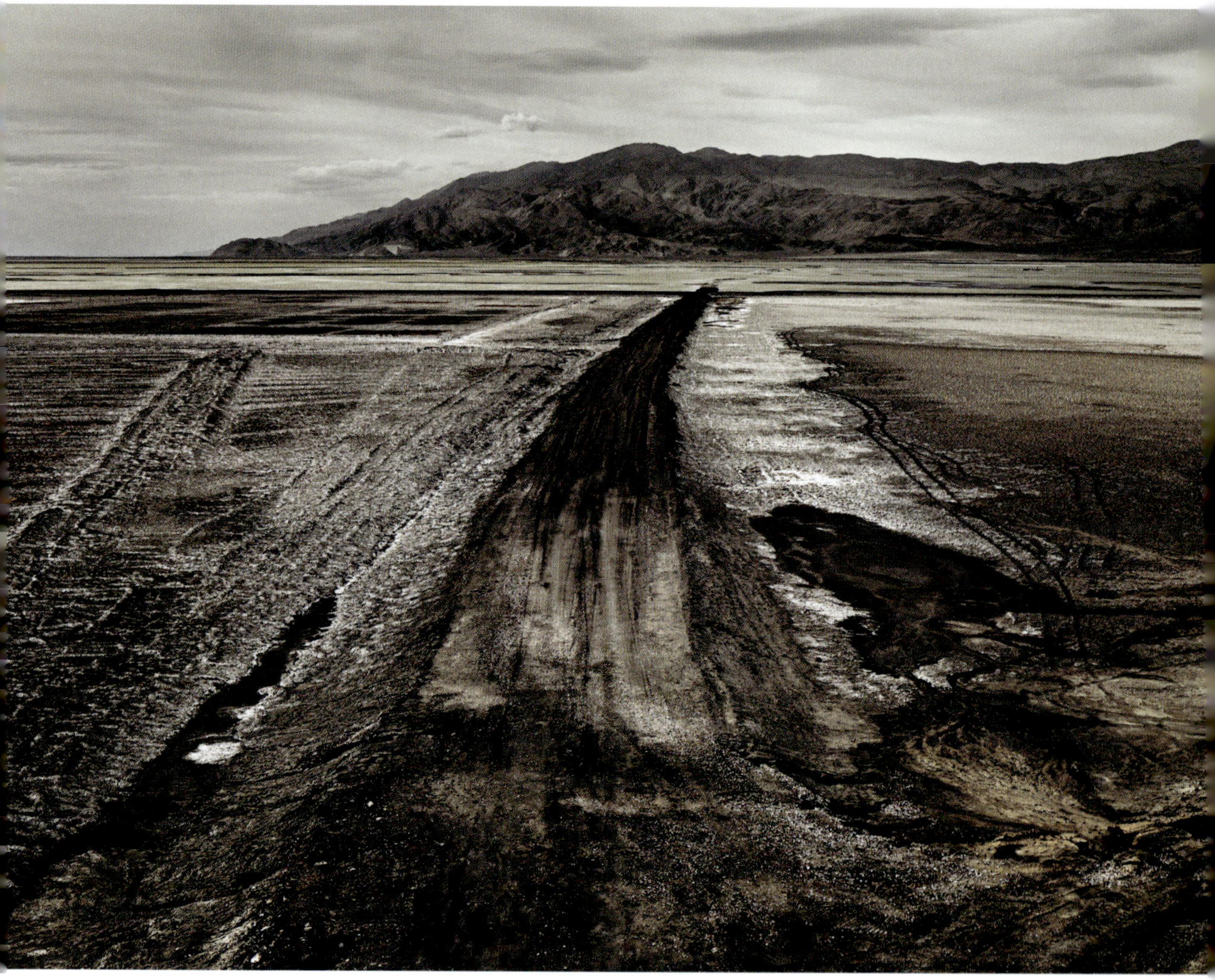

Edward Burtynsky, *Owens Lake #1*, California, 2009

By serendipity, soon after deciding about water as a subject, Burtynsky received an invitation from *National Geographic* to contribute to a single-themed issue on that subject and to focus on California. He visited Owens Lake, a site from where water had been diverted to service Los Angeles in 1913. "It became literally a dust bowl," he recalled. "It used to be agricultural land, so a lot of fertilizers and pesticides were embedded in the soil. And a lot of selenium . . . It was a bowl, so the storms would come in and lift the sand on to towns like Lone Pine. It featured some of the worst, most toxic dust storms in America."[5]

Burtynsky decided to use California as a test case for his new project. "Here," he was aware, "was a population of 38 million people. A small percentage of the water is from the state itself [but] the largest percentage of it is brought in from the seven surrounding states. It's kind of a negotiated landscape in terms of a lot of California's deserts. . . . That really helped me start to get my head around a project as vast as water."

He did eight weeks of shooting in California during the spring and summer of 2009. "Then," he recalled, "they released the article in 2010. I was well on my way. I was going past California into other things. Using that as my base, I built on the idea, eventually getting to the book."[6]

This new topic allowed him to explore further his fascination with aerial photography, although such expeditions could be risky. He told one journalist of hovering over frozen cliffs in Mount Edziza Provincial Park and, belatedly, it occurred to him this approach might be dangerous. "Are we safe?" he asked himself: "There were some moments when I was sitting up in the mountains in B.C. and the chopper was being bounced around like a ping-pong ball," he recalled. To get the perfect shot, Burtynsky would sit with the helicopter door wide open, while fierce winds buffeted the small aircraft.

He told the same journalist: "You're getting pitched all over the place, and it's 10 below zero, so you're freezing at the same time," he says. "There's always a lot of trust." Burtynsky has conceded that he has spent a lot of time hovering in tiny aircraft at four hundred feet above the ground–not exactly the safest practice. At that height, "If your engine goes, you don't have a chance to recover; you're going down and smashing," he said matter-of-factly.[7]

Despite the obvious risks, he felt his choices had been correct. "I thought about ways that I could build a body of work around the idea of water. Unlike my *Oil* and *China* projects, with *Water* I had no preconceived notions about what the images in such a project might look like. I trusted that my intuition would lead me to the pictures."

AN ACTIVIST ALARM

Watermark (2012), the second collaboration between Burtynsky and Baichwal, is structured differently from *Manufactured Landscapes*. In the earlier film, where Burtynsky's career was highlighted, the footage accompanied the photographer to various sites in China, and a sharply focused interplay was established between film footage and still photography. *Manufactured Landscapes* the film and *China* the book are companion pieces. In contrast, *Watermark* operates as a series of wide-ranging explorations emphasizing ironic juxtaposition. *Water* is organized into six distinct sections (Distress, Control, Agriculture, Aquaculture, Waterfront, Source). In the process, *Watermark* the film and *Water* the book became complementary–not companion–pieces.

Jennifer Baichwal understood how the two projects differed from each other: "I think some of the same oscillations in the editing room where the structure was being written echoed the process in *Manufactured Landscapes*, which initially had lots of expository information, but we realized that took away from [the fact] that the film is about an interesting artist [who] doesn't choose subjects that don't resonate with layers of meaning and information underneath." She also pointed out that, "at the back of the book, it is all explained. There are some interesting notes that let you contextualize."[8] The filmmaker does not have such an advantage.

De Pencier provided a description of how tasks were assigned: "A lot of times we would divide up. Ed would be looking at that more comprehensive view and vantage point, and often would be directing the remote-control helicopter, let's say, which we shared between his Hasselblad for stills and our video cameras. At the same time, Jennifer and I would go and find the more human narratives, the interviews, the moments of being, on a smaller level."[9]

In the film, Burtynsky speaks about the importance of water, how it is taken for granted as a resource, and how it is misused. His remarks are supplemented by brief interviews with those whose lives have been ruined by the misappropriation of water (Inocencia González Sainz and Polly Hankins) and by a Tahltan linguist (Oscar Dennis) who rhapsodizes about the restorative powers of water.

Watermark begins with a contrast between footage of the annual Xiaolangdi Dam silt release on the Yellow River in China and the parched, cracked earth of the Colorado River Delta in Mexico. The juxtaposition of the waves crashing violently at Xiaolangdi and the ghostly silence on the Colorado River Delta is startling. Further striking contrasts ensue: a sequence underscoring the excessive amounts of water used in a tannery segues to the pristine Stikine Watershed in Northern British Columbia; a dire warning by a scientist about global warming transitions to the Bellagio fountains in Las Vegas. The film displays the largest dustbowl in the United States at Owens Lake and then travels to Yunnan, China, where the diligent sharing of water has maintained the rice beds. In India, pilgrims throng to the enormous Kumbh Mela celebration to be rid of sins and spiritually renewed by bathing in water. Immediately after that sequence, surfers at Huntington Beach, California, and a prestige waterside housing project at Discovery Bay, California, are shown. The film ends with a leisurely cruise down the Stikine River that allows the viewer to witness primeval, unspoiled nature.

Watermark's reliance on juxtapositions led to disparate critical responses In the *Georgia Straight*, Janet Smith liked the way the "imagery speaks for itself, making chilling use of a soundtrack that underscores every scene with a sinister industrial rumble. White tannery toxins seeping into Bangladeshi rivers where parents bathe their children; towering dam projects that reduce red-helmeted Chinese workers to specks against concrete; giant rods of ancient ice being extracted from the Greenland crust: Baichwal manages to make these disparate scenes flow into a single, poetic river that is unfortunately headed in one hugely ominous direction."[10]

Many reviewers, however, echoed Nick Schager's notice in *The Onion:*

> An activist alarm is sounded via entrancing imagery–both moving and still–underscored by occasional narration and dialogue. It's an approach that, on a purely aesthetic level, can be hypnotic, as Baichwal and Burtynsky's visuals have an alternate beauty and terror that speaks to their core subject, the perilous relationship between man and his water supply. Unfortunately, while the documentary's points are clear, its desire to articulate them primarily through contrasts neuters some of its persuasiveness. There's a thinness to *Watermark*'s contentions about the potential perils of water misuse, due in large part to the filmmakers' disinterest in dispensing much contextual information about the various vistas they present.[11]

Although critical of the film's basic approach, Kenji Fujishima in *Slant* was sensitive of what the film had attempted to do and how it did it: "By keeping explanatory talking-heads interviews to a minimum, the filmmakers put their trust in the audience to draw their own conclusions based on what they present to us; they're less interested in offering concrete solutions to the world's water-shortage problem than in simply evoking troubling questions of whether we're ensuring our destruction as a species with the amount of water we use every day."[12]

Such notices did not consider fully that the filmmakers' objective was to provide an encyclopedic treatment of its vast subject because water as an abstract concept is alien to most people. The film offered its audience the opportunity to think globally and, in this way, to reflect on the use and misuse of a substance that is, like oil, finite.

"POETIC AND ABSTRACT"

In *Watermark*, Burtynsky examines the proofs of *Water* (2013) and is seen in conversation with his publisher. Some images in the book are of places not shown in the film: these include the Gulf of Mexico, the city of Benares (Varanasi) in India, the Alberta oil sands, the Salt River Pima-Maricopa Indian Reservation in Arizona, and, in Spain, the Almería peninsula and Monegros.

Water is prefaced by "Gulph of Mexico." The Information Section (fourteen pages) contains descriptive, one-page essays on the twenty-eight locales of which photographs were taken. There are essays by Wade Davis ("Water Notes") and Russell Lord ("Into the Deep"). In the Preface, Burtynsky states, "this project encompasses some of the most poetic and abstract work of my career."[13]

Watching a film and looking at images in a book are diverse experiences. This observation is particularly true in the case of *Watermark* and *Water*. The book is a portfolio of 113 images split into six sections. As with *China*, the divides alert the reader to what each segment contains but the subject of each image is not indicated–although the reader, as Baichwal observed, can easily turn to the image index at the back of the book to obtain this information.[14]

Some images were taken between 2007 and 2009, and seven in 2013. Most are from 2010 to 2012, however, and many of them were made when Burtynsky was travelling with Baichwal and de Pencier. The introductory image is an overhead shot of a pristine waterscape at Georgian Bay. That image is followed by seven photographs taken during the first six weeks after the 2010 Deepwater Horizon disaster off the coast of Louisiana in the Gulf of Mexico.

Distress is readily evident in the images of depleted Owens Lake, the Salton Sea, and the Alberta oil sands, but the seven images of the Colorado River Delta are even more poignant in that they show a parched, desolate riverbed. The word *Control* is used ironically in the next sequence, because the stepwells have become dysfunctional. While the Xiluodu Dam on the upper Yangtze is another attempt on the part of the Chinese to control water, the water exploding at Xiaolangdi showcases the power of water–a power man defies at his own risk. At pivot irrigation farms in Texas, machines with one-mile- and half-mile-diameter spans soak agricultural land that would otherwise be unusable. This water comes at a tremendous price–the draining of the Ogallala Aquifer. Dryland farming, as practiced in Spain at Monegros, is a form of agriculture that does not deplete the soil.

The rice terraces at Yunnan shown in Aquaculture have existed for centuries and a balance has been achieved in maintaining water through the rainy seasons and the harvesting of rice in the dry seasons. Water as an essential part of worship is the focus of Waterfront. The Ganges may be heavily polluted, but worshipers receive spiritual sustenance by bathing in it. The desire to live close to water is also documented in this section, but it leads in some instances to overcrowding and an encroachment on the natural world.

In the final section, there are two Sources. In Iceland, the heavy, persistent winds have led to *rofabards*, sand incursions. The blue twisting and turning in these images document the destruction of rivers of glacial runoff. The Sacred Headwaters, a subalpine drainage basin in British Columbia, is a territory belonging to ten First Nation groups and the source of three salmon rivers. It is so rich in natural resources (coal and coalbed methane) that various "development" projects have been planned–but ultimately rejected. Burtynsky's images of this place celebrate its untouched natural beauty.

Burtynsky was correct to claim that *Water* contained his most abstract work up to that point in his career. The photographs he took of the Gulf oil spill, the Colorado River Delta, stepwells, pivot irrigation, dry farming at Monegros, rice terraces, and Iceland move in this direction, but each is markedly different. Moreover, each of these sequences is infused with lyricism–with the photographer's desire to capture their essence in an intense, subjective way.

The Deepwater Horizon was an offshore oil rig, owned and operated by Transocean drilling for British Petroleum (BP), located sixty-six kilometres off the coast of Louisiana in the Gulf of Mexico. On April 20, 2010, the Deepwater Horizon exploded, creating the largest marine oil spill on record. Two days later, the rig sank.

The rig was situated 1,522 metres above the seabed and was drilling a well that was planned to go 5,486 metres deep into the rock below the seabed. When the cement core being poured fractured, oil travelled up the rig's platform; the explosion killed eleven workers and discharged oil into the Gulf at the rate of more than 60,000 barrels a day. The petroleum slick, which extended more than 149,000 square kilometres, reached the shores of Louisiana a month later and contaminated its marshes, estuaries, and wildlife. In all, an estimated 1,770 kilometres of coastline was damaged.

Fumbling steps were taken to remove the oil. Controlled fire burns sent up plumes of smoke. When this tactic did not work, planes dropped between 23,000 to 25,000 gallons a day of the highly toxic chemical Corexit on the contaminated water. This procedure was supposed to mix with oil and disperse it. When the Corexit hit the water, it produced huge streaks of bright red that contrasted with the blue of the ocean.

Soon after Jim Panou alerted Burtynsky to the oil spill, the two of them were on their way to Louisiana. Filming the spill by plane was complicated because BP controlled access not only to the airspace but the height at which planes could fly. When Burtynsky and Panou first arrived, all flying time had been booked but another environmental photographer, Daniel Beltrá, ceded one of his spots to them.

At first, BP attempted to control the optics of the ecological disaster by insisting that planes fly above it at about 25,000 feet. Then they changed the height restriction to 3,000 feet. From that vantage point, Burtynsky was able to take photos out of a helicopter. Beltrá's images captured the startling contrast between red and blue, whereas there was not as great a concentration of the interaction of the chemical with the water at the times Burtynsky was working.

On this shoot, Burtynsky framed his images in a manner markedly reminiscent of Abstract Expressionism. In *Oil Spill #9*, when the ultramarine and bright blue converge; the gesture can be seen in the patch of ultramarine

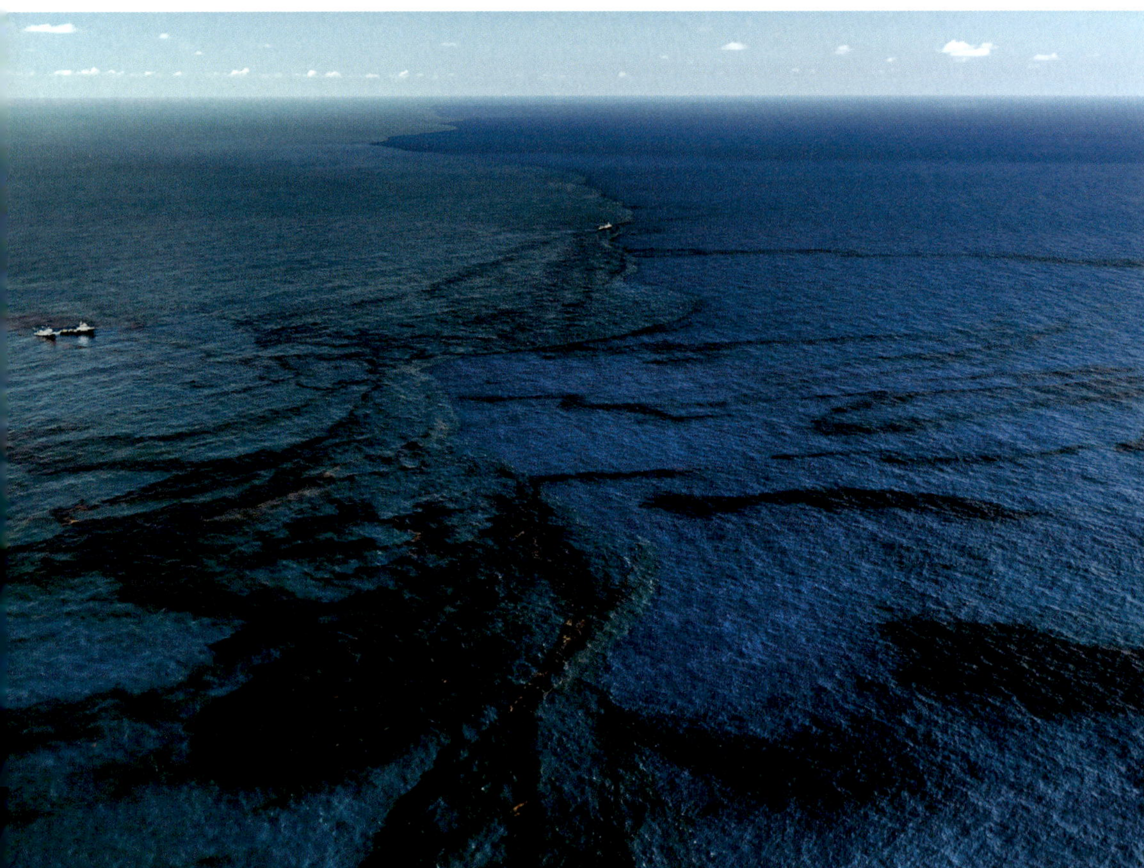

Edward Burtynsky, *Oil Spill #9*, Oil Slick at Rip Tide, Gulf of Mexico, 2010

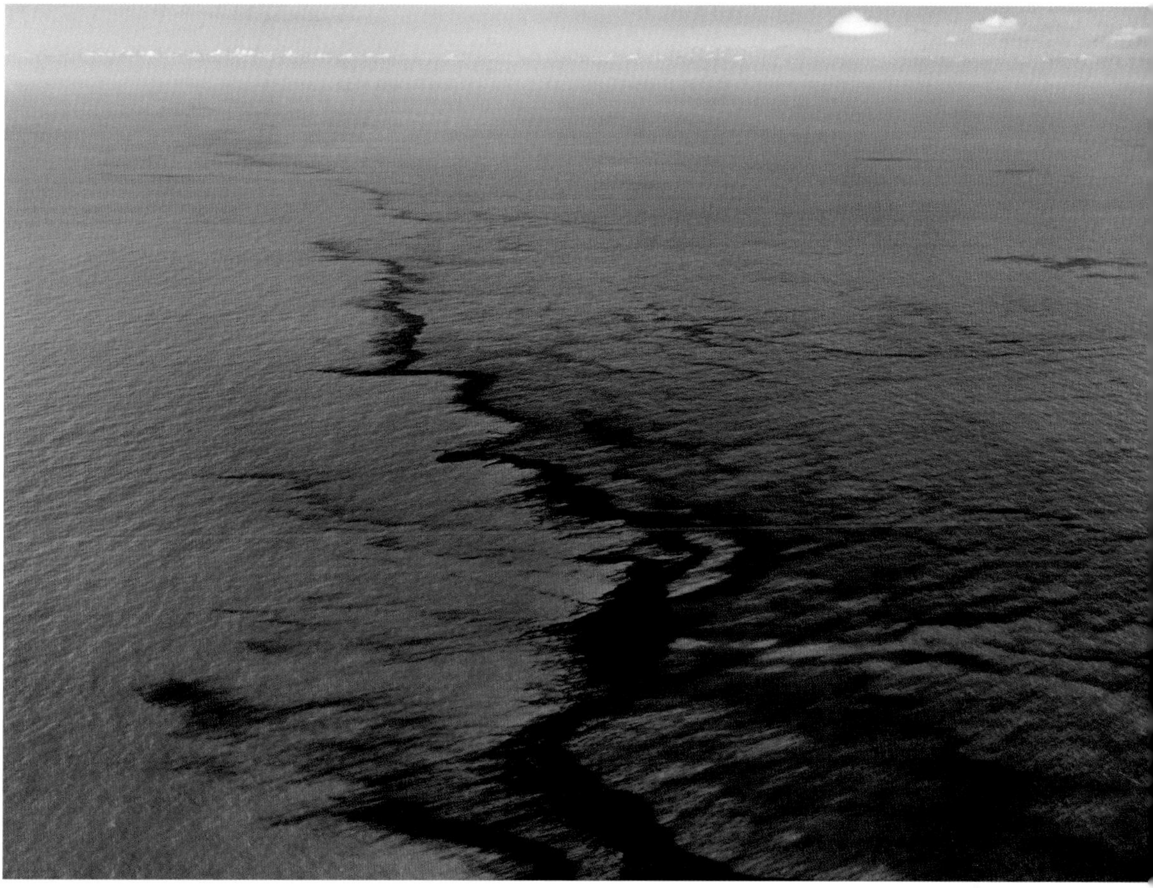

Edward Burtynsky, *Oil Spill #10,* Oil Slick, Gulf of Mexico, 2010

at the bottom of the image. The gesture in *Oil Spill #10* is contained in the thick black line that runs between the green water.

The Colorado River Delta images are an eerie mixture of representation and abstraction. The tree-like forms dominant in some of these images are the obvious result of the Delta being deprived of water. Their foliage is not something alive–it is dying. The metaphoric tree-like formations also resemble broken blood vessels. In *Colorado River Delta #20*, the surface of the "trees" looks impressed upon the ground beneath it; the different textures are so finely realized that they have a three-dimensional or sculptural feel to them. The contrast between the green water at the top of *Colorado River*

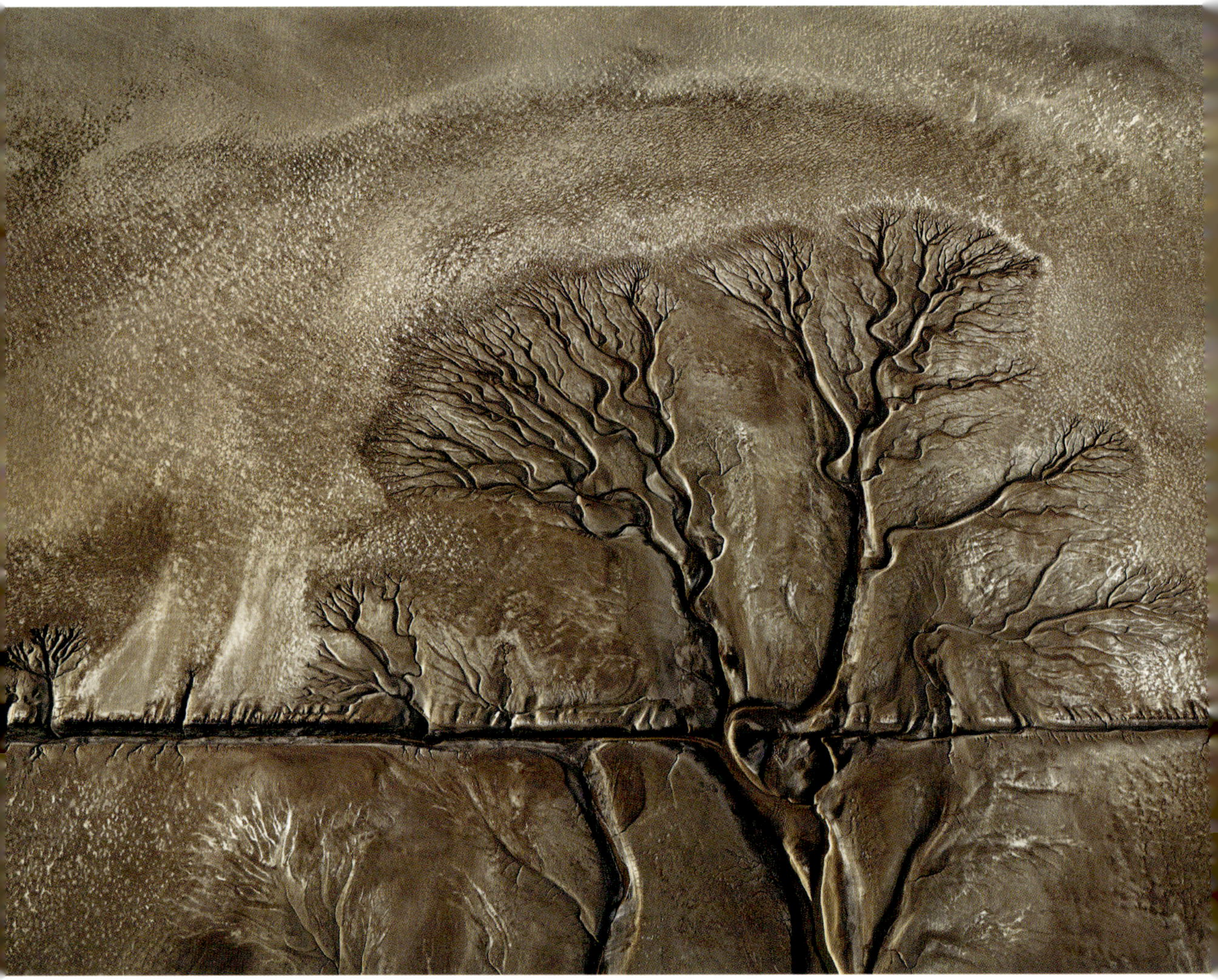

Edward Burtynsky, *Colorado River Delta #20*, Sonora, Mexico, 2012

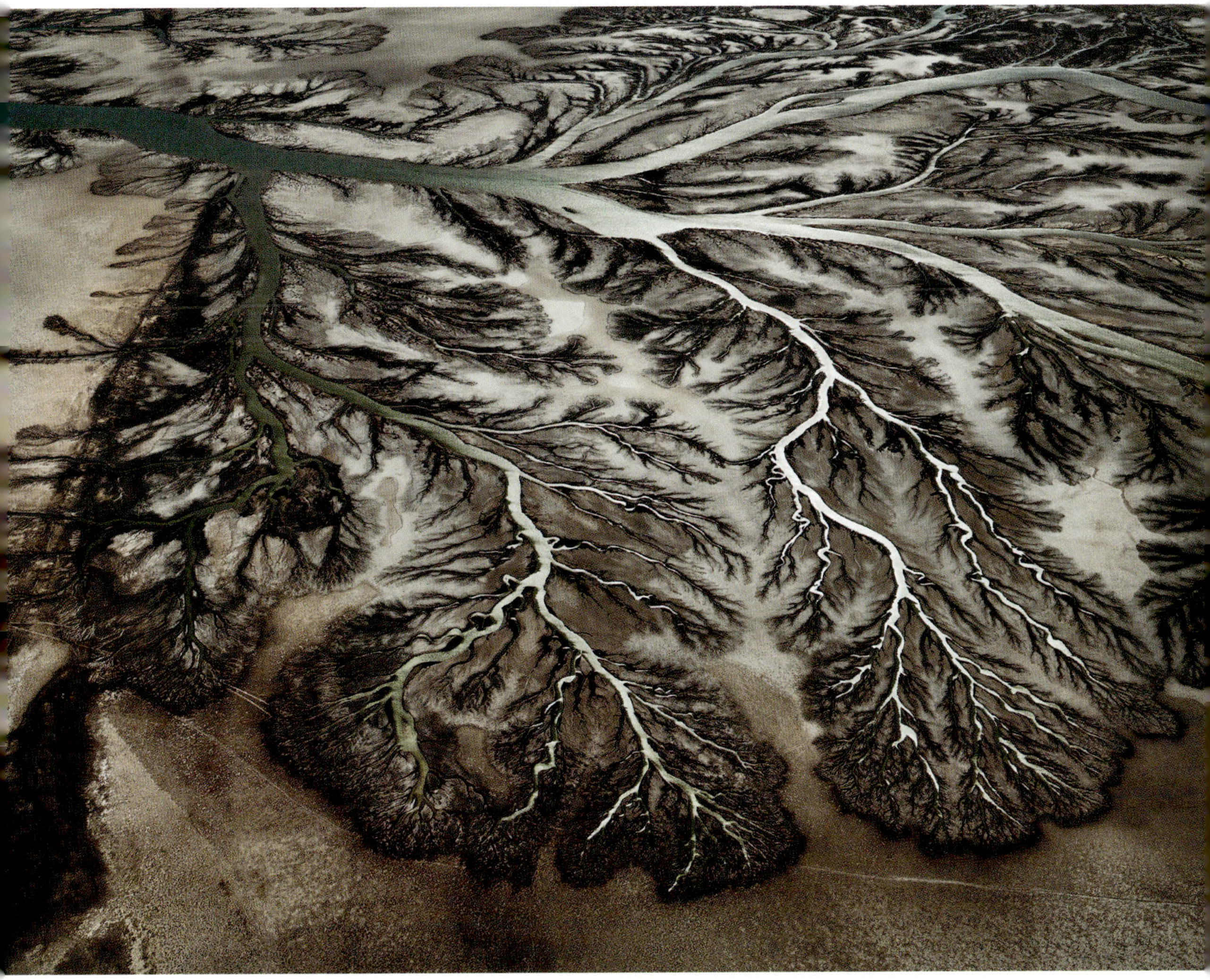

Edward Burtynsky, *Colorado River Delta #1*, near San Felipe, Baja, Mexico, 2012

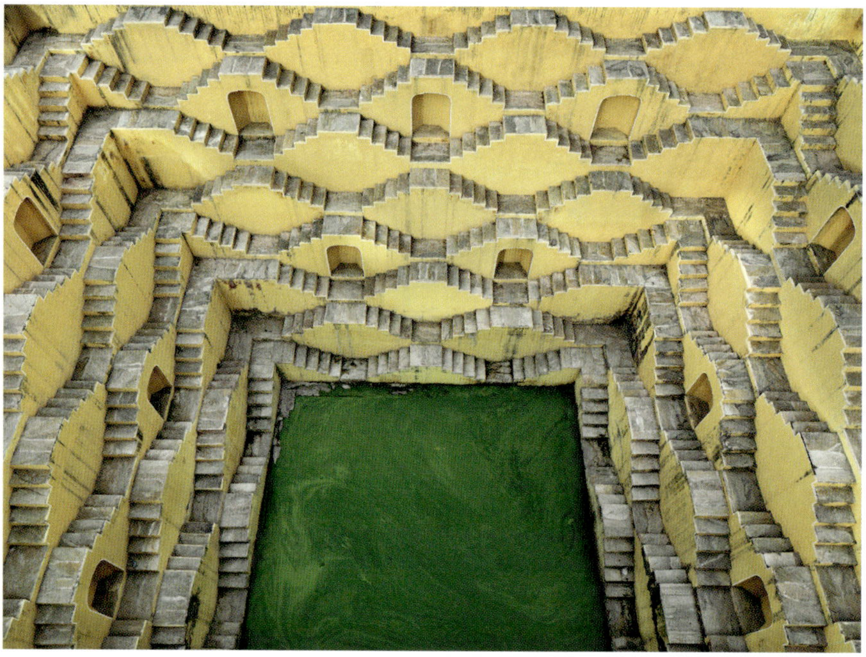

Edward Burtynsky, *Stepwell #2*, Panna Meena, Amber, Rajasthan, India, 2010

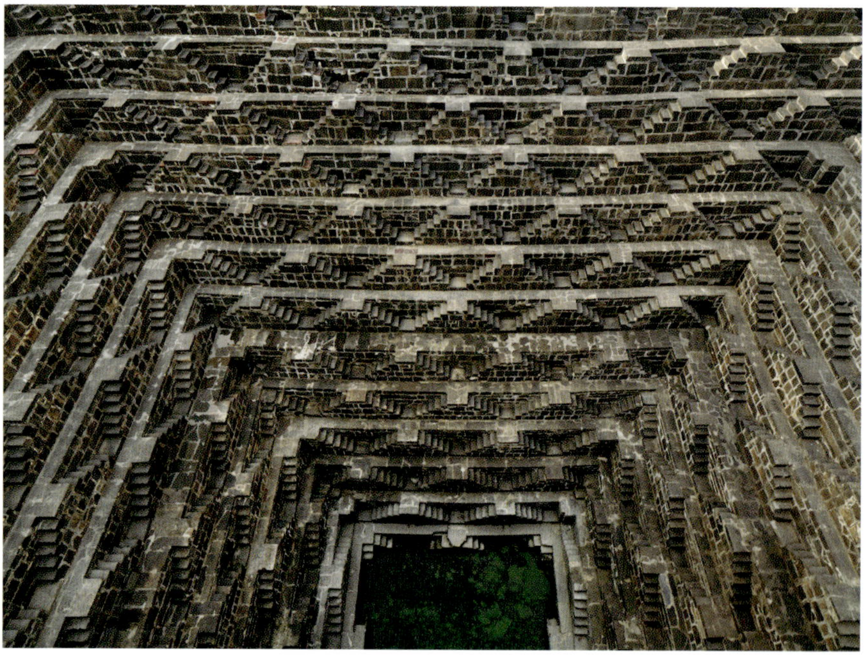

Edward Burtynsky, *Stepwell #3*, Chand Baori, Abhaneri, Rajasthan, 2010

Delta #1 and the "vegetation" emanating from it gives the image a sinister edge. This wasteland, so parched, appears beyond restoration.

In India, stepwells are inverted pyramids dug into the earth to ensure water is available year-round. Their walls are lined with stone blocks that fit together without mortar and with stairs leading down to the water, and some of them are embellished with elaborate, often geometrical details. During the summer months, the galleries surrounding these structures provided relief from the heat.

For Burtynsky, these wells were another form of inverted skyscraper tunnelling into the earth's surface. He was also attracted to the patterns painted on or sculpted into their walls. These wells may also be thought of as ruins because drilling below the water table has rendered them useless. In *Stepwell #2* and *Stepwell #3*, Burtynsky created elaborate views looking down these wells; the repeating patterns along the steps create M. C. Escher-like abstractions.

In the *Pivot Irrigations* photographs, Burtynsky fashioned huge, bold circular compositions from the tracts of land irrigated from the dry earth bordering them. Bright circles were a specialty of Robert Delaunay but

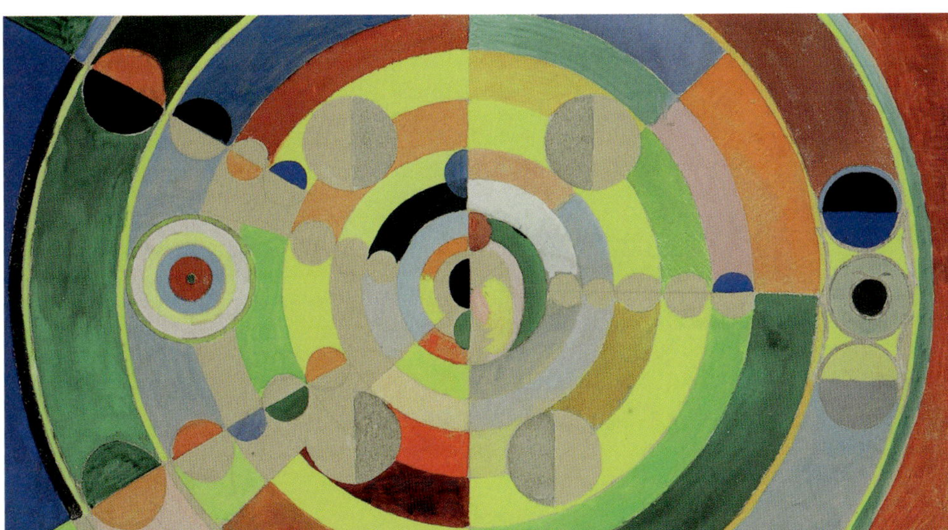

Robert Delaunay, *Relief-disques*, gouache and sand over pencil on board, 1936. Private collection

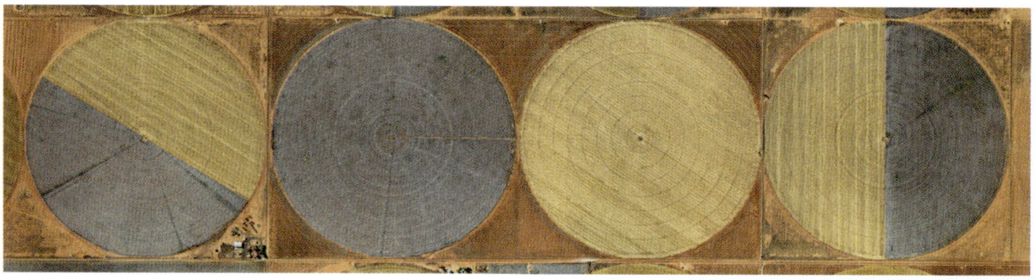

Edward Burtynsky, *Pivot Irrigation #13*, High Plains, Texas Panhandle, 2011

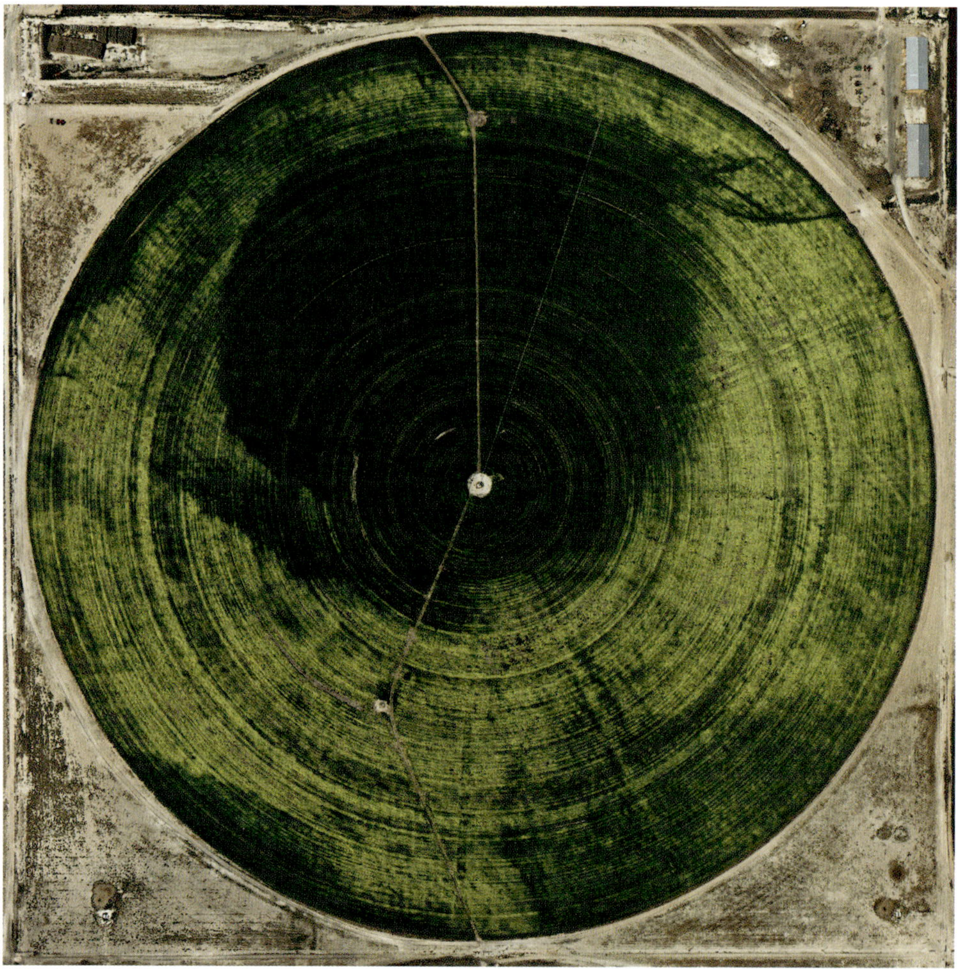

Edward Burtynsky, *Pivot Irrigation #39*, High Plains, Texas Panhandle, 2012

can be seen in the art of David Shapiro, Jasper Johns, Wassily Kandinsky, and others. Burtynsky's take on circular composition was often more staid than theirs because he was confined to browns and a limited number of greens. He deliberately chose not to photograph too many green irrigation circles, concentrating more on the end-of-season and post-harvest colours and on traces of moisture, which sometimes appear like radar-screen ghostings. His compositions also differ from his predecessors because the monumental size of the resulting photographs gives them an epic quality.

The contrast between the earth that is being replenished and that which is not may be striking, but such remarkable abstractions are only possible if water from the aquifer is available, which is rapidly disappearing.

One of the major themes of Burtynsky's entire project is enshrined here: like oil, there is a limited amount of inland fresh water in existence. Water moves from bodies of water (oceans, rivers, lakes) into the atmosphere and becomes rain. As Burtynsky has observed, "there is a kind of self-cleansing and healing aspect of water. It's just we're using it faster than nature can replace it."[15]

In northeastern Spain, the Aragonese farmlands at Monegros are carved out of gypsum hills. To make this semi-desert land arable, farmers have banded together to conserve and share what little rainfall there is. Olive groves persist, but the main crops are wheat, oats, and barley. The rice terraces at Yunnan are, just as in Spain, the result of careful, communal planning in water management. During the rainy season, mollusks, snails, shrimp, and frogs are cultivated. During the dry season, the water in paddies dry, rice matures and can be harvested at season's end.[16]

The overhead shots of Monegros are monochromatic arrangements of black, brown, and white passages sliding in and out of each other, reminiscent of Jean Dubuffet (see p. 246). Burtynsky remarked on the process: "Colour variation between adjacent fields is a result of varying moisture and mineral content, crop stubble and 'dryland coating,' materials left on the field surface to produce erosion."[17] His shots of Yunnan add

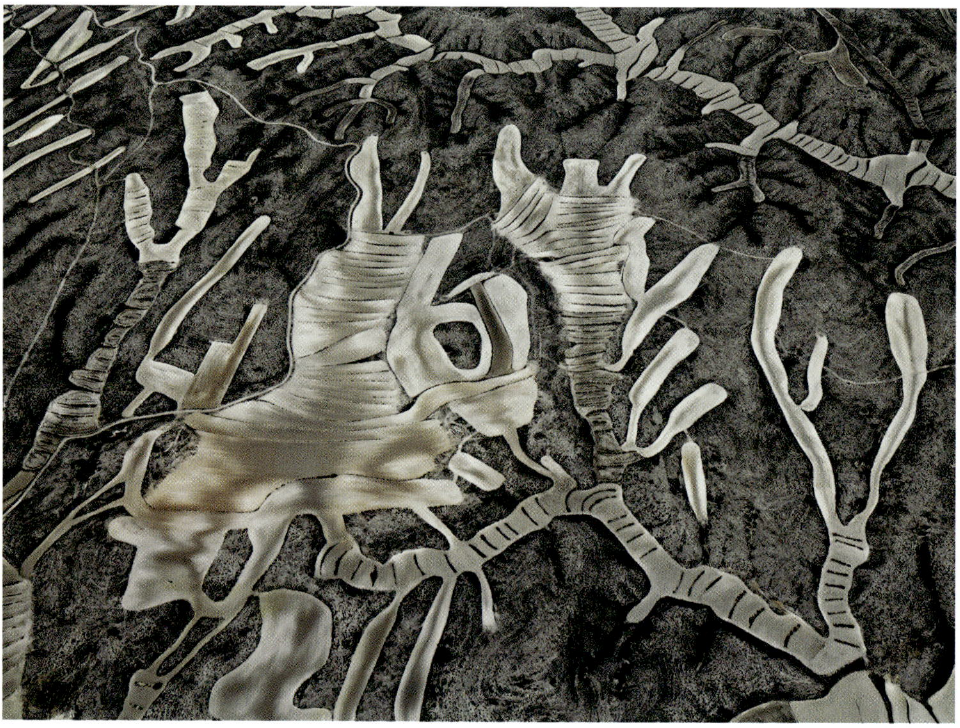

Edward Burtynsky, *Dryland Farming #1*, Monegros County, Aragon, Spain, 2010

another colour: green. Here, the carefully arranged divisions between the various plots of land create a wave-like effect of emerald shades.

"Photographing in the Thjorsá River Delta [in Iceland] proved a challenge," Burtynsky recalled: "I kept trying to find the right spatial distance to capture what I knew would make a great picture. Normally I shoot aerial subjects from between 600-800 feet, but in this case, I kept saying to the pilot, 'I'm much too close, take me up.' By the time I started shooting I had given him at least five cues to go higher. Ultimately, we climbed to 2,000 feet before the compositions started yielding those beautiful voluminous spaces and the gestural painterly imagery I was after. The glacial meltwater runs offer a fantastic colour palette. These mineralized formations are so visually exciting they appear as if wrought by the hand of an abstract impressionist."[18] The blue colours of the meltwater may be beautiful, but they exist because of sediments (known as "glacial flour") suspended in the water.

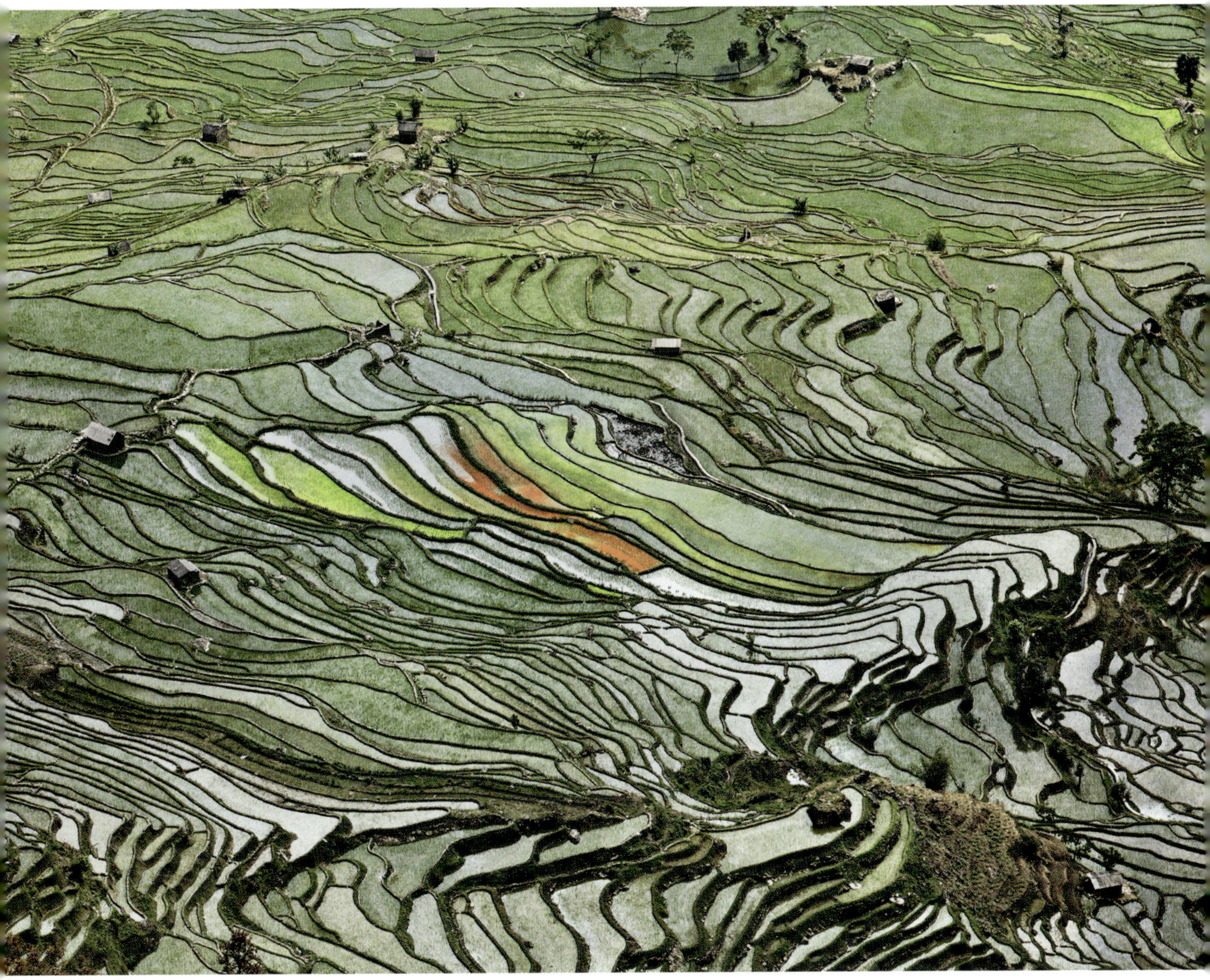

Edward Burtynsky, *Rice Terraces #2*, Western Yunnan Province, China, 2012

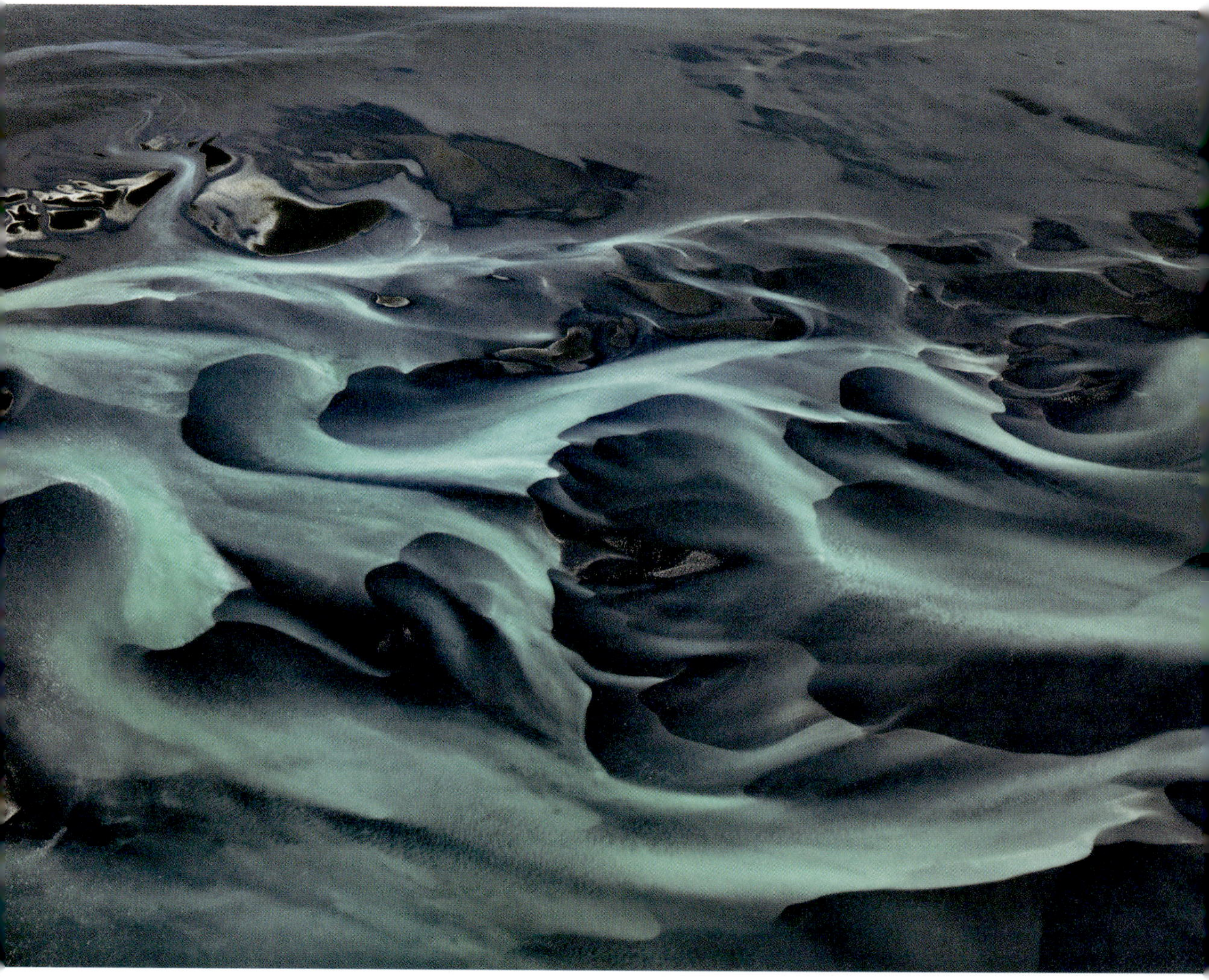

Edward Burtynsky, *Ölfusá River #1*, Southern Region, Iceland, 2012

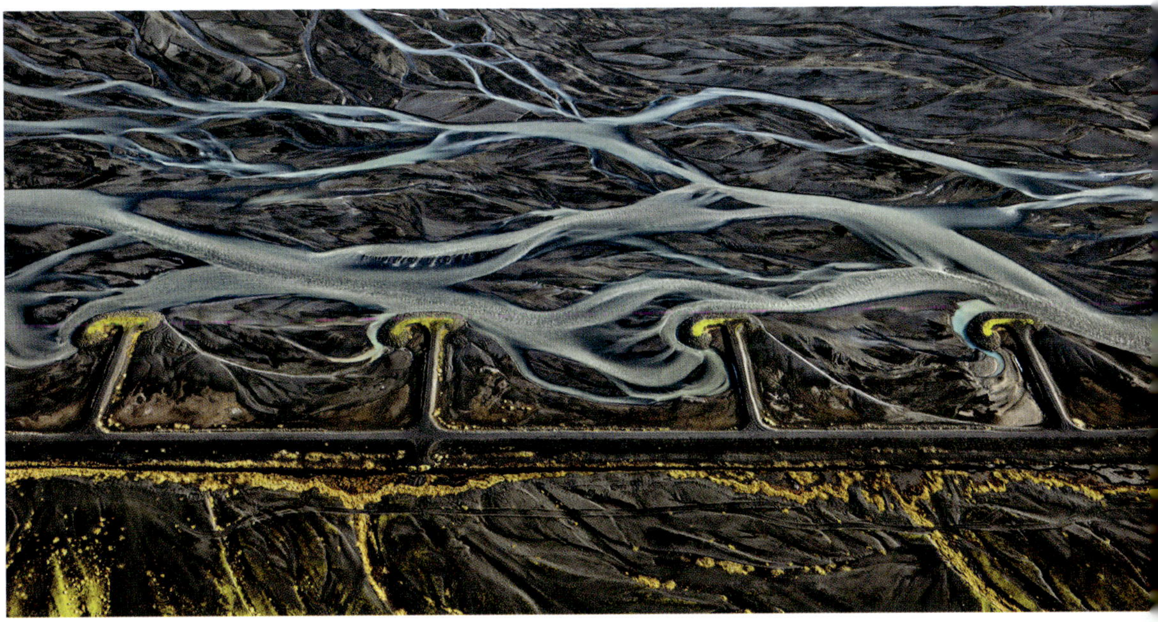

Edward Burtynsky, *Markarfljót River #3*, Erosion Control, Southern Region, Iceland, 2012

Water contains other gripping images. The mighty eruption unleashed at Xiaolangdi during the annual silt release demonstrates the potency of water. The turbulent, swirling convergence in *Xiaolangdi Dam #2* is in the manner of Turner (see p. 31). The rigid class separation illustrated by the parched land belonging to the Indigenous in Arizona and the manicured lawns of the suburb adjoining their lands is perfectly encapsulated in *Salt River Prima-Maricopa Indian Reservation/Suburb Scottsdale.* Water as a gateway for spiritual rejuvenation is captured in *Kumbh Mela #1*.

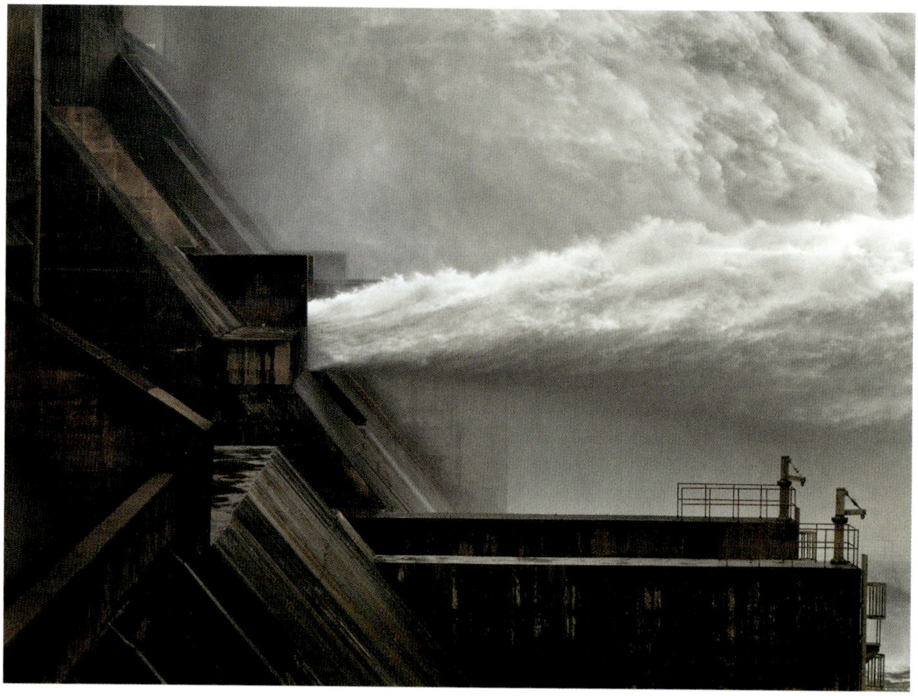

Edward Burtynsky, *Xiaolangdi Dam #1*, Yellow River, Henan Province, China, 2011

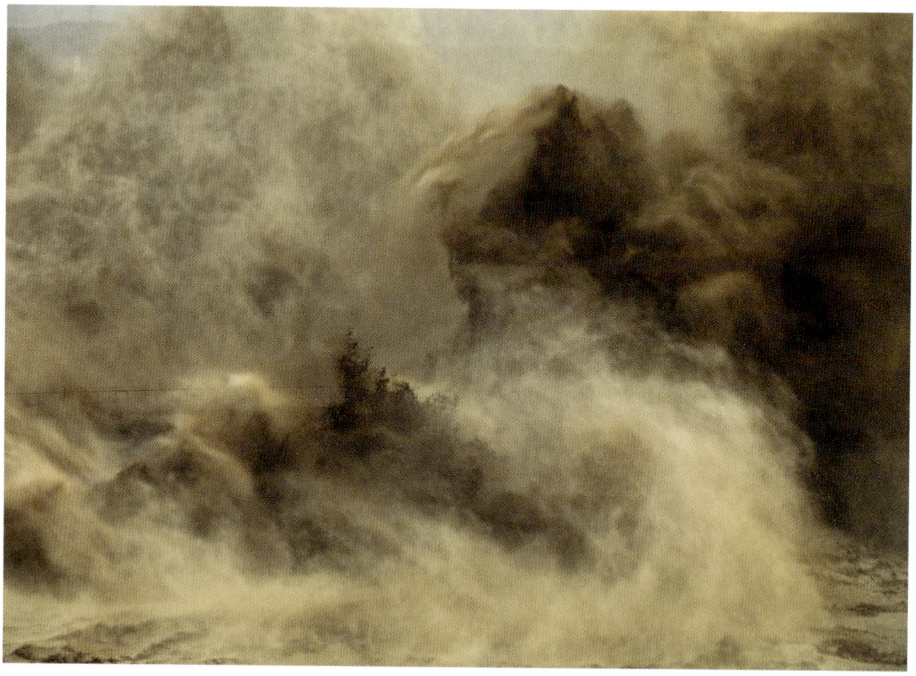

Edward Burtynsky, *Xiaolangdi Dam #2*, Yellow River, Henan Province, China, 2011

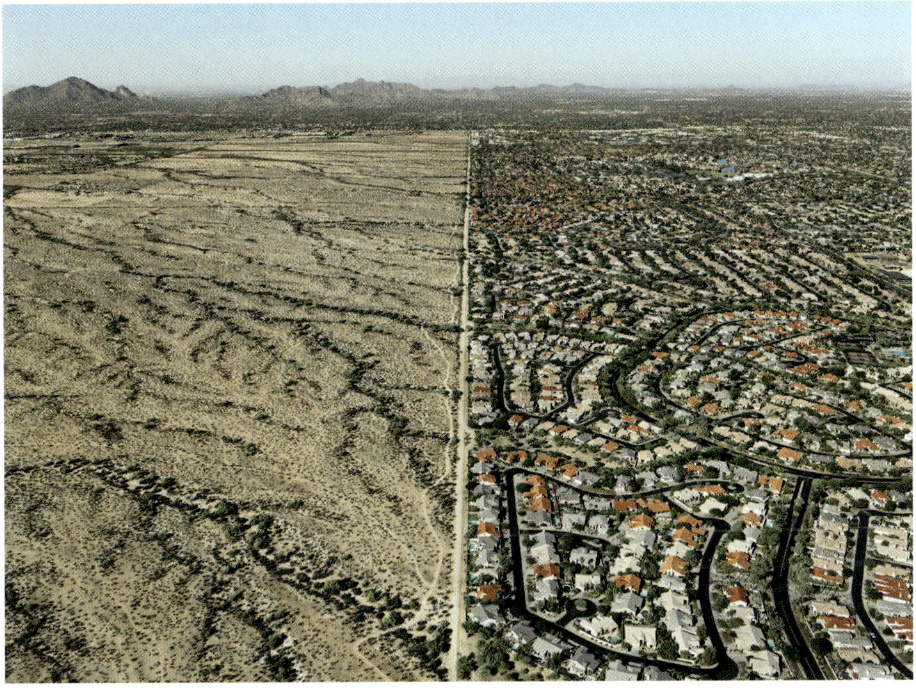

Edward Burtynsky, *Salt River Pima and Maricopa Indian Community Suburb*, Scottsdale, Arizona, 2011

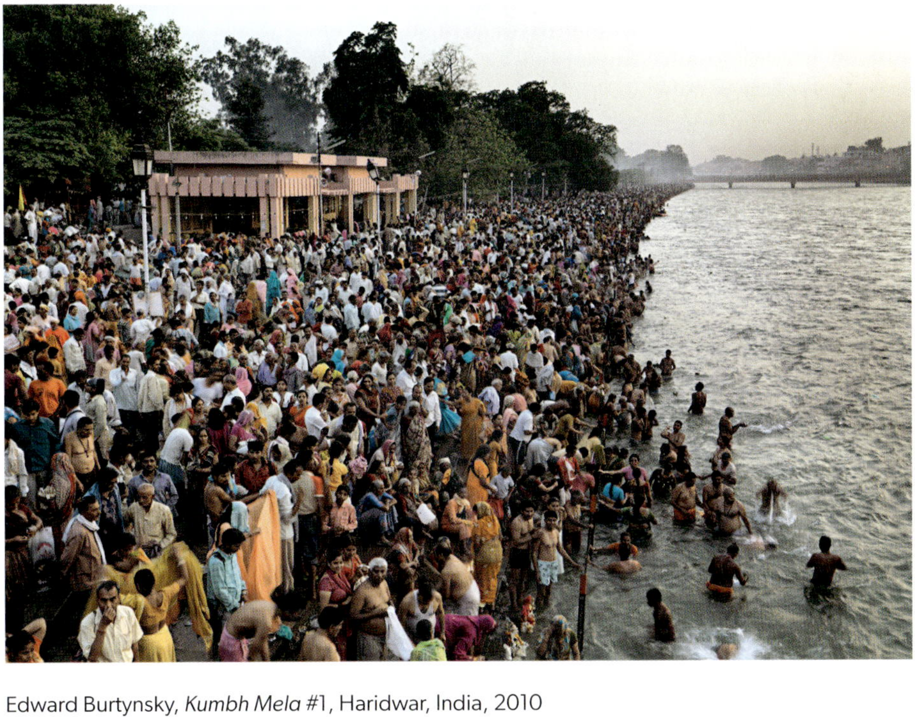

Edward Burtynsky, *Kumbh Mela #1*, Haridwar, India, 2010

Burtynsky is often, mistakenly, perceived as an artist who restricts himself to images of toxic waste and man's incursions into nature. Many of the images in *Water* in fact move in the opposite direction, especially in their highlighting of the creative use of water at Yunnan and Monegros and of water as a vehicle for psychic restoration in India.

In a lengthy, sensitive review of *Water* in *Photomonitor*, Paul Carey-Lent saw the enormous range of Burtynsky's accomplishment:

> At least half of the photographs look decidedly painterly–and certainly not like the digitally unmanipulated photographs which Burtynsky assured me they are. The obvious comparisons are with abstract painting, but images of silt in spray look like Turneresque clouds; agricultural studies of fields are so unnaturally demarcated that they seem diagrammatic; and pivot irrigation in Arizona, which imposes giant circles on the landscape, calls minimalism to mind. Burtynsky himself says he was pleased to see images emerging which referenced some of his favourite painters, citing Friedrich, Dubuffet, Shapiro and Diebenkorn . . .
>
> Burtynsky says he's interested in the questions "how does water shape us and how do we shape water?" As with previous projects, the images themselves have great intrinsic power . . . Burtynsky credits Google Earth as a transformative selection aid, and it's the choice of location linked to the tilted aerial perspectives–and consequent lack of a horizon–which allows that strikingly painterly quality to be achieved.[19]

From the outset of his practice, Burtynsky has, when composing his images, caught glimpses of the work of artists he admires. He has never intentionally mimicked other artists, but he has never been averse to allowing them to inform his art. A canvas by Richard Diebenkorn such as *Berkeley #32* (1955), which displays an overhead, map-like view of its subject, is an approach favored by Burtynsky. The interlocking grids in a canvas such as Jean Dubuffet's *Dispositif aux vaisselles* (1955) are reflected in the Monegros

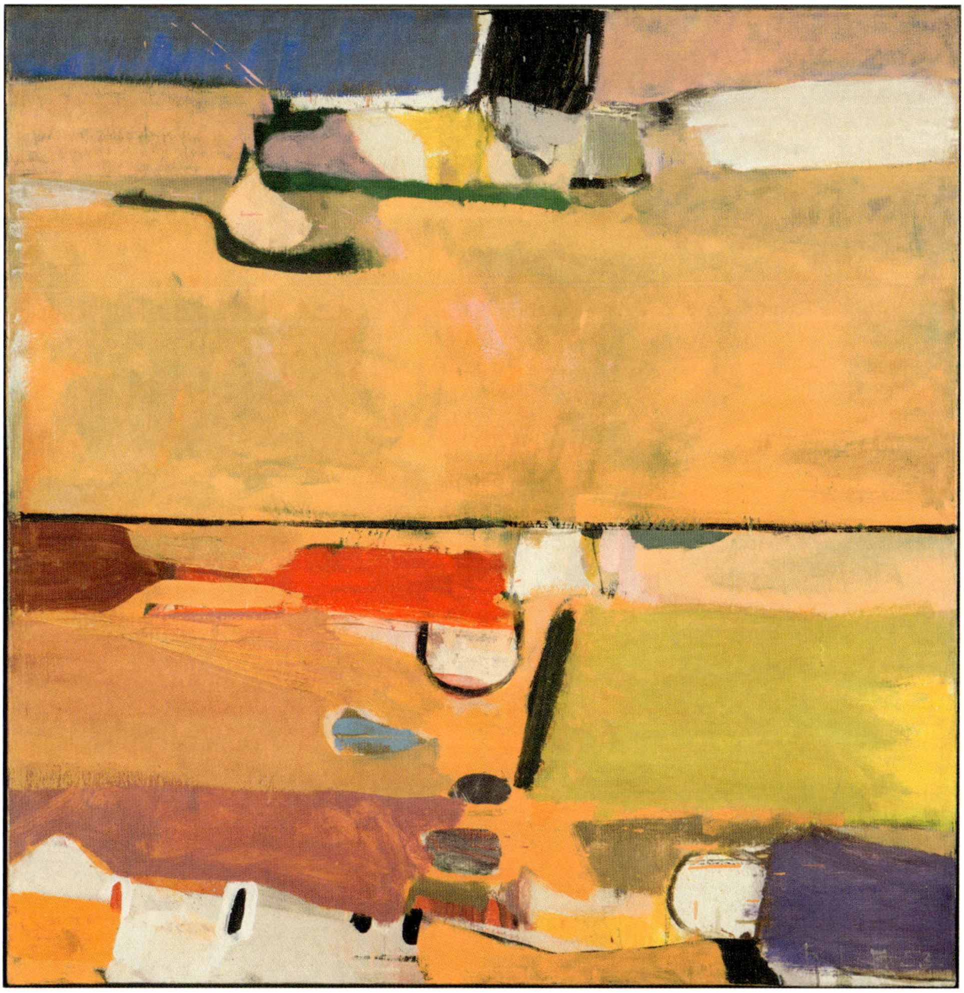

Richard Diebenkorn, *A Day at the Race*, oil on canvas, 1953. Carnegie Museum

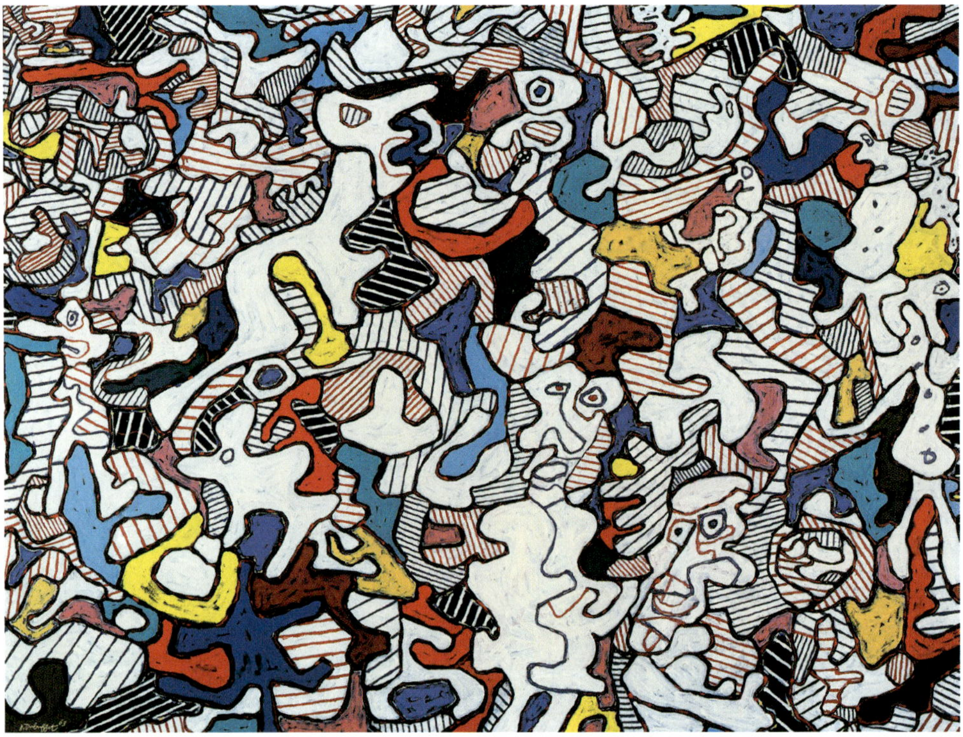

Jean Dubuffet, *La Vie de Famille*, oil on canvas, 1963. Musée Des Arts Décoratifs, Paris

David Shapiro, *Origin and Return 08*, lithograph relief, 2004. Nicholas Metivier Gallery

images. David Shapiro's propensity to place circular images in opposition to squares and triangles is mirrored in the *Pivot Irrigation* series. *Xiluodu Dam #4* plays with the minimalist fascination with seriality that can also be seen in Shapiro. The lonely sublimity of Friedrich can be witnessed in the images of Mount Edziza, B.C.

At the conclusion of the *Water* project and despite the polemical statements he made in *Watermark*, Burtynsky still maintained that he was averse to pushing a political agenda. As he told an interviewer in 2013, "The minute you say, 'This is right, and this is wrong,' you've probably shut out half of the people who are getting the message and already disagree." As the interviewer observed, "He'd rather keep doing what he's doing. 'Artists don't really have the power to affect policy,' he adds, 'but they can certainly bring awareness and raise the questions about where all of this is heading.'"[20]

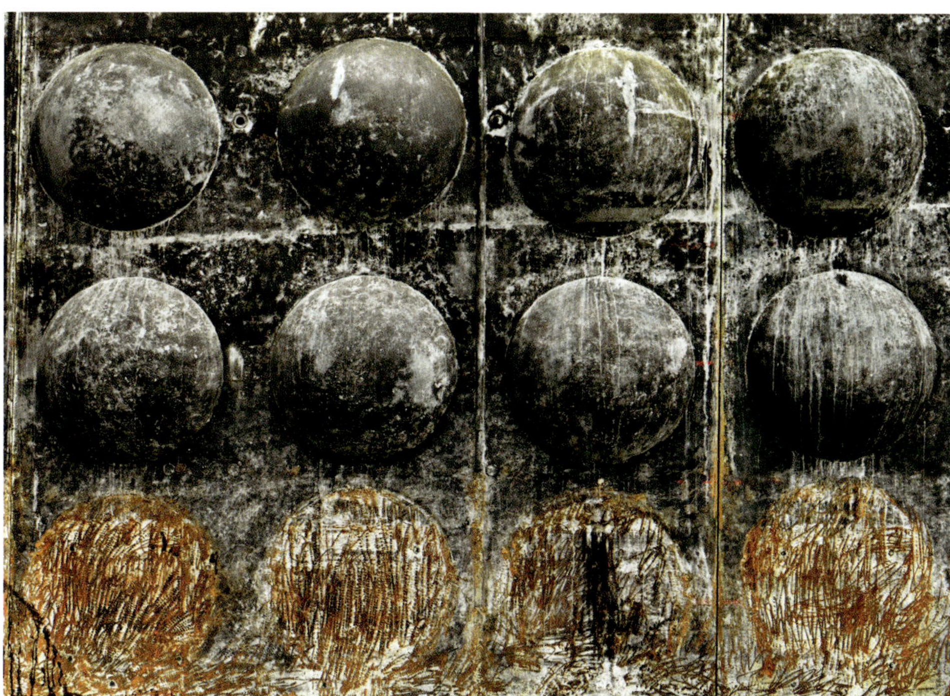

Edward Burtynsky, *Xiluodu Dam #4*, Yangtze River, Yunnan Province, China, 2012

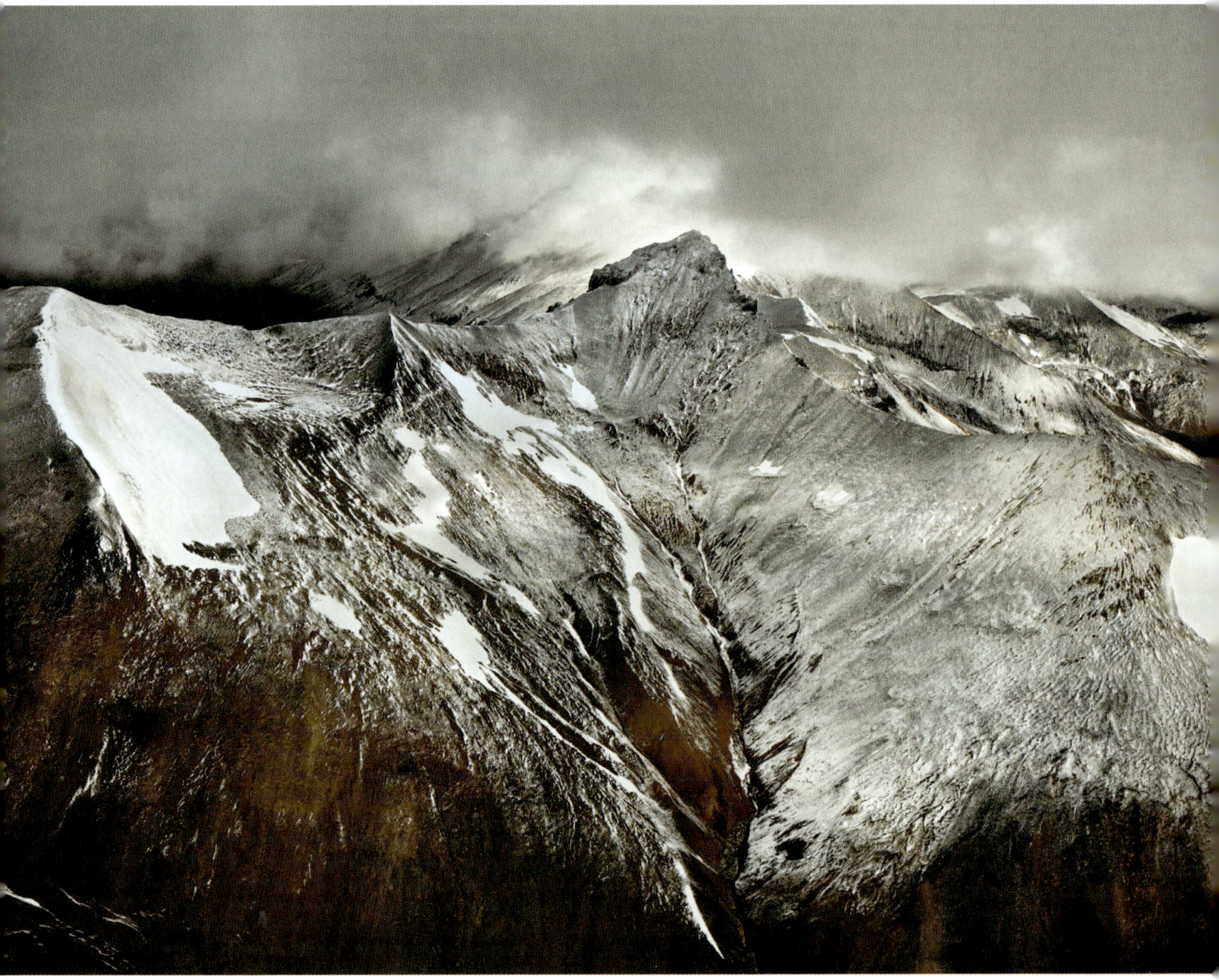

Edward Burtynsky, *Mount Edziza Provincial Park #1*, Northern British Columbia, 2012

"MUTED AND PAINTERLY"

Three years after the publication of *Water*, in 2016, Burtynsky embarked upon another water-related project: the salt pans in the Little Rann of Kutch in Gujarat, India, on the Arabian Sea. A decade before, he had visited Sambhar Salt Lake in Rajasthan but focused then on interiors. In this new set of images, he concentrated instead on aerial views. As he arrived at the Little Rann, he remembered, the "land below our helicopter was harsh and barren. The salt pans appeared as multi-coloured rectangles of white, beige, and pastel pink, as well as various hues of blues and rusty brown. . . . Dropping to 300 feet we could see the parched, cracked surface of the earth."

Salt is the main industry in this region. Every year for eight months, more than one hundred thousand salt workers, known as Agariyas, fan out over the delta and toil in the brutal sun for paltry wages.[21] Evaporation pulls the salt up from underground deposits of saline water. Burtynsky took no photographs of the salt pans at ground level or of the workers. Rather, he provided a dazzling assortment of shots of both from the air that push toward complete abstraction.

Gazing at these new images, Loring Knoblauch saw how they differed from Burtynsky's previous series:

> Burtynsky offers a more muted and painterly approach to his signature ecologically-minded monumental landscapes, introducing a tighter theme and variation dedication to a single subject than we have typically seen in his work. His subject here is the salt pans of Gujarat, India, where rectangular drying pools are carved out of a harsh wasteland of dusty grey earth. This is industry taking place at the very edge of inhospitality, where workers are subject to extremes of isolation that appear almost dystopian or other worldly, at least from the safety of the air. Valuable raw materials are being harvested from this barren desert, carving the desolate land into an ugly tangle.

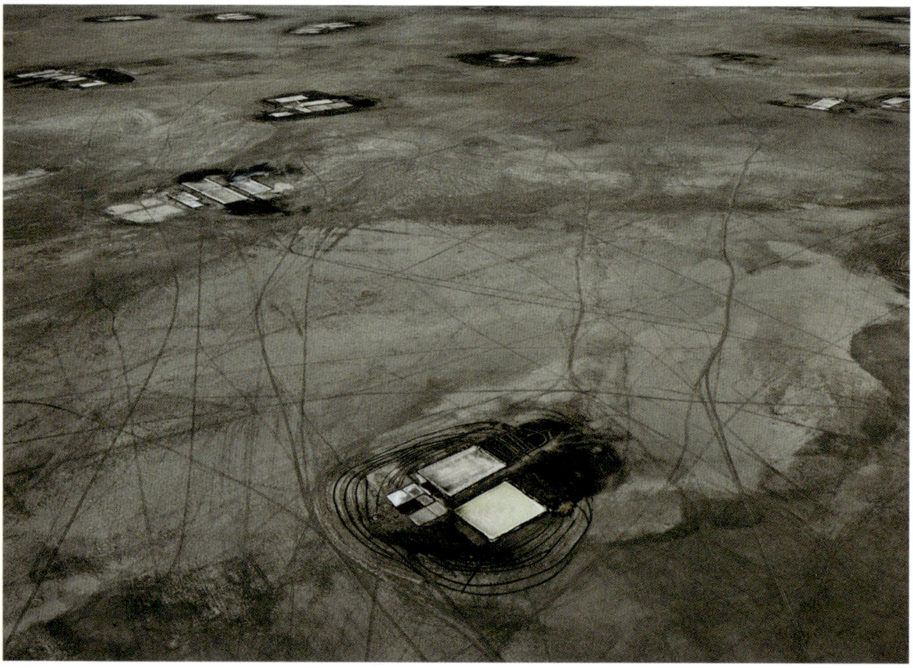

Edward Burtynsky, *Salt Pan #1*, Little Rann of Kutch, Gujarat, India, 2016

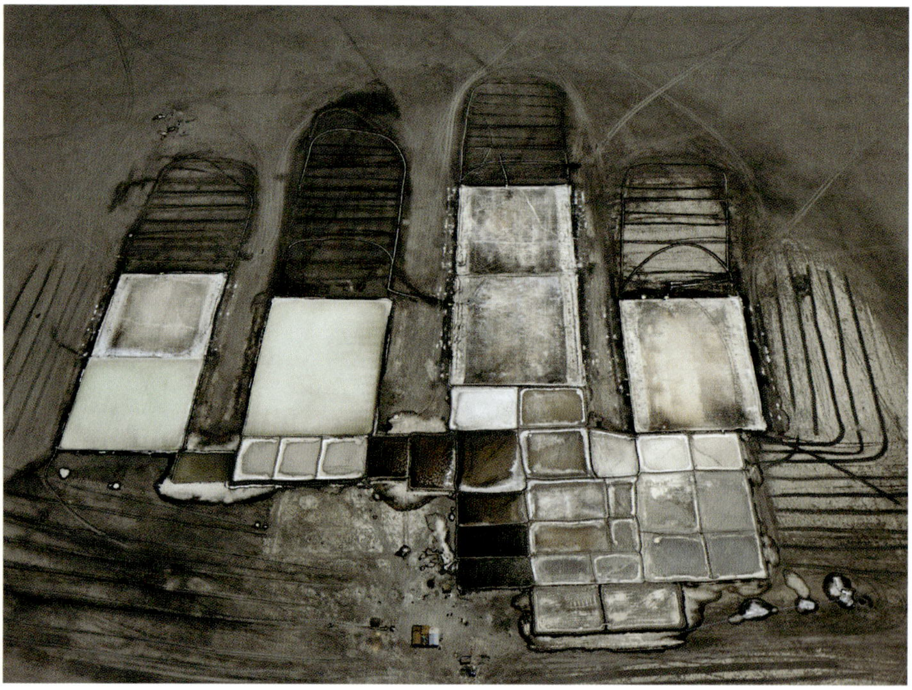

Edward Burtynsky, *Salt Pan #23,* Little Rann of Kutch, Gujarat, India, 2016

As discouraging as this setting is, Burtynsky has largely made its realities into abstractions. Silvery polygons and rectangles float on a muddy grey ground, seeming to shift and shimmer like the layered browns of Cubist painters Braque and Picasso. Radiating from these central forms are various trenches and troughs, that from afar are reduced to the simplicity of etched lines, with repetitions creating stripes, mazes, and messy squiggles . . . Burtynsky has drawn out painterly gesture, turning incisions, scars, and leaking earthly wounds into works built on pared down formal grace.

When seen in the context of the arc of Burtynsky's artistic career, there is an understated subtlety to these compositions that we have never seen before. These pictures are neither bombastic in their sweeps of view nor eye popping in their patterns and repetitions–instead, they are almost humble in their reductive thinking. Having nearly reached the tipping point where majesty turns into caricature, he has smartly pivoted to a more intimate and delicate set of aesthetic ideas. While these pictures will perhaps mystify those who have preferred his most awe-inspiring visual shoots, their hushed quality offers a dose of restrained nuance that has its own richness and depth.[22]

The grey trenches radiating out from the rectangles look like scratch marks and add even more texture to these minimalist compositions. With their frugal colour values and their concentration on the juxtaposition of shapes, this sequence contains the most concentrated, demanding, and purest abstracts Burtynsky has created.

(2014–2015)

13 LIFE!

In 2014 Burtynsky was commissioned to make images of "the current landscapes of 'sacred' sites of the Holocaust." The theme of the project was "Legacy" and incorporated eight sub-themes: Inclusion/ Exclusion, Isolation, Identity, Fear, Survival/Resilience, Loss, Legacy, and Resistance. Burtynsky took over 250 photographs and reproduced 51 as a portfolio in the book *Chai* ("Life").[1] Six of those photographs, depicting Treblinka, Auschwitz, Berlin, Mauthausen, and Theresienstadt, were destined to become large-scale images for the National Holocaust Monument in Ottawa.

At first glance, these photographs do not seem to fit into Burtynsky's usual purview. But, by displaying the ravaged landscapes and buildings at those sites, he provided further evidence of man's capacity to create devastation. Unlike his usual practice, some of the images in *Chai* are in black and white (eighteen) to commemorate the solemnity of these now sacred places, some of which are ruins; they also create a sense of distance from the horror of those places.

Burtynsky's trip, covering more than four thousand kilometres across Europe, began in Germany and then went through the Czech Republic, Austria, Hungary, Poland, and Lithuania, before ending back in Germany. The sequencing of the photographs in the book does not strictly adhere to the journey but, in order to stick to the identified themes, Burtynsky emphasized railway lines, open and closed doors, and interior recesses.

The railway lines lead nowhere; doors are both open and closed to emphasize inclusion and exclusion; recesses that should allow for reflection become scenes of terror. Another key image is of a quarry–reminiscent of ones in the *Rock of Ages* series–that was "used to mine granite used in Hitler's huge building projects." From there, prisoners were forced to carry large blocks of granite up the 186 "stairs of death."

Images 1 to 4 are of exteriors before moving inside buildings (images 5 to 10); the wall in the Pinkas Synagogue in Prague (11), where the names of 78,000 Jews killed in Bohemia and Moravia are inscribed, is shown. Images 12 to 32 are exterior shots of various kinds, followed by an aerial view (image 33); the images then return to interior shots for images 34 through 41. Two photographs (images 42 and 43) of Antoni Domanski, an Auschwitz survivor, follow; images 44 to 51 are a combination of exterior and interior images.

The images are arranged in a cinematic manner. They begin outdoors, move indoors, return outdoors, and then go indoors again before focusing on Domanski; the final images are a mixture of exterior and interior views. This arrangement forces the reader's perspective to move outside and inside, creating a sense of displacement. These shifts are accentuated by a mixture of colour and of black-and-white images. Black and white forces the reader back into the past, while the colour is a glaring reminder of what has been left: buildings and landscapes tinged with horror.

The experience created by this arrangement is visceral. One of the most unsettling images in *Chai* is a calm, elegant landscape in black and white that appears detached from the tragic remnants seen in most of the images. Its name betrays its significance: *Death March Site, near Sankt Florian, Austria.*

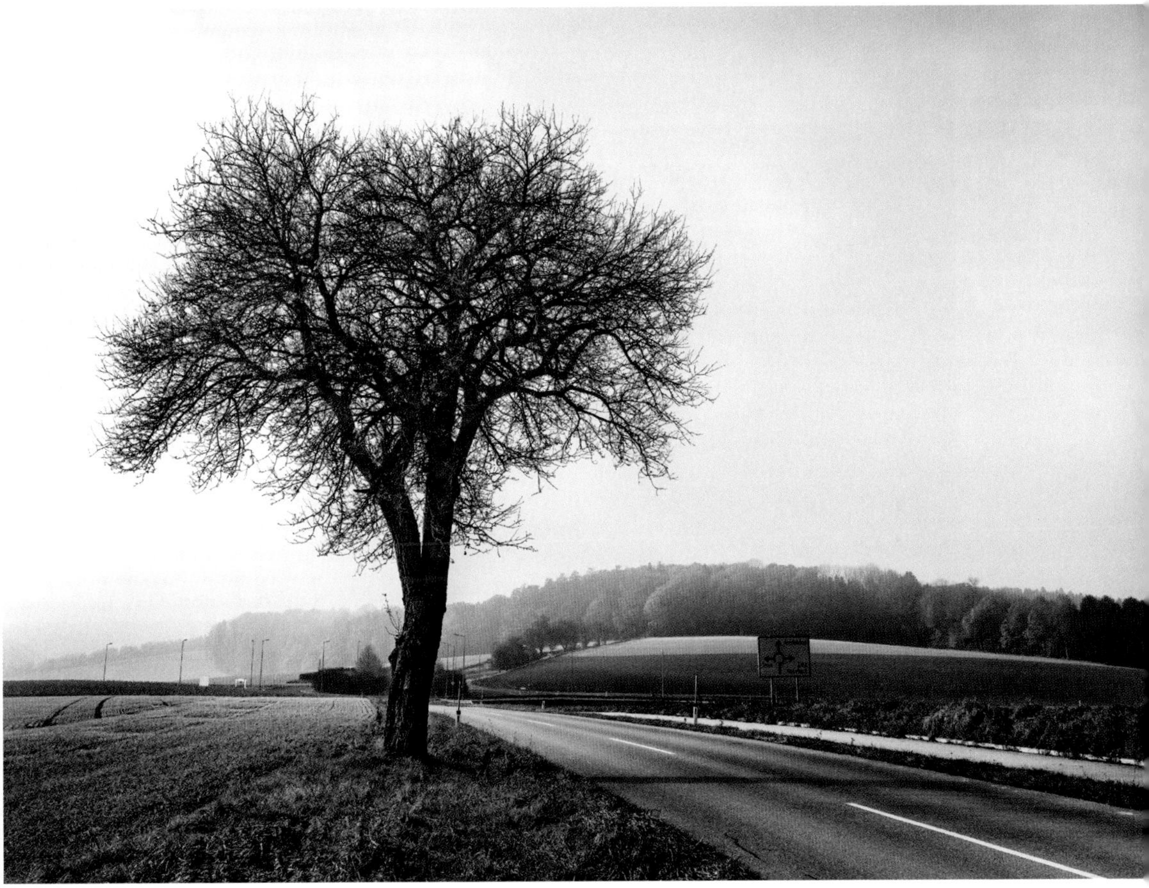

Edward Burtynsky, *Death March Site*, near Sankt Florian, Austria, 2014

Although there are no pictures of people, with one exception, Doris L. Bergen has observed that "Yet people are present in these landscapes, still lifes, and interiors. I don't just mean their ghosts, though these seem almost visible."

The first image in the book is a grand suburban villa in Berlin. The accompanying text reads: "At a January 1942 meeting of government and Party officials held on a lake in Wannsee, a Berlin suburb [where] . . . the SS streamlined the transportation and killing of Jews." On the far right of the photograph, electric lights are left on because it was in those rooms that the "Final Solution" was adopted.

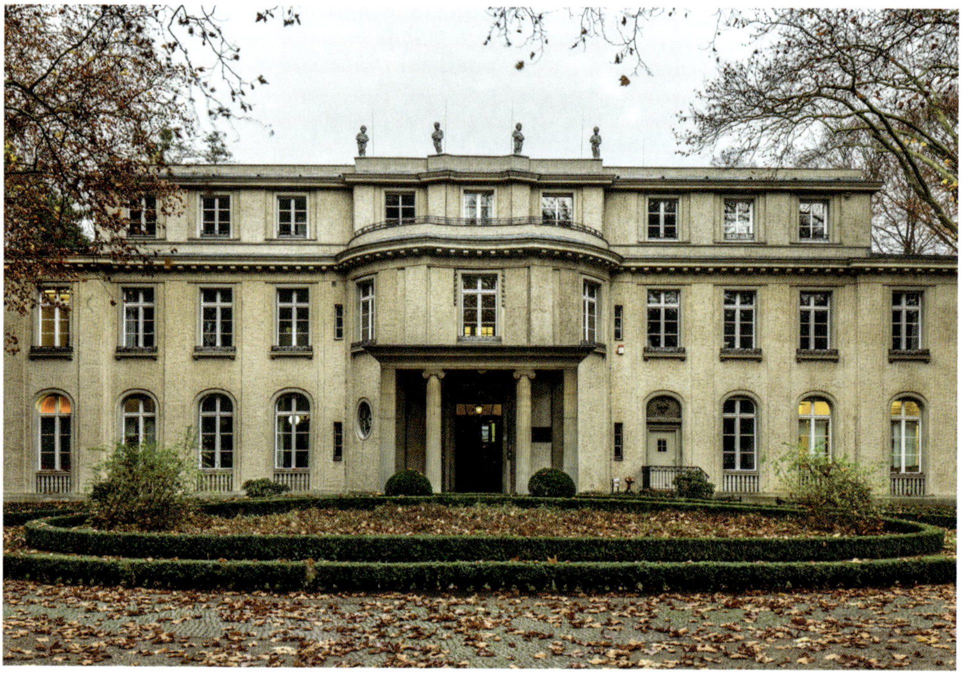

Edward Burtynsky, *Villa, Berlin*, Germany, 2014

There are images shot at the village of Chelmno, Poland, which was a "major killing site." There is a colour photograph of the church that was a "holding pen" for Jews when they arrived; it is followed by a remote shot in black and white of the grounds of the mansion (with the church behind it) where gas vans were located; then by a tranquil colour shot of the nearby Ner River, where the bones and ashes of some of the slain were thrown. The colour images are of tranquil everyday scenes in the present, but *Mansion Remains* shows the actual killing site as it stands today, with the rubble on which the vans stood. In this arrangement, the viewer is pulled back from the everyday present to the devastating past and then back to the present.

The effect of the black-and-white photograph showing one of the basement cells in Block 11 in Auschwitz I, where the SS first experimented with the insecticide Zyklon B as a killing agent, is claustrophobic. The lines descending from the window, and the extraordinary texture captured in this image, reinforce the notion of this place as one of no exits.

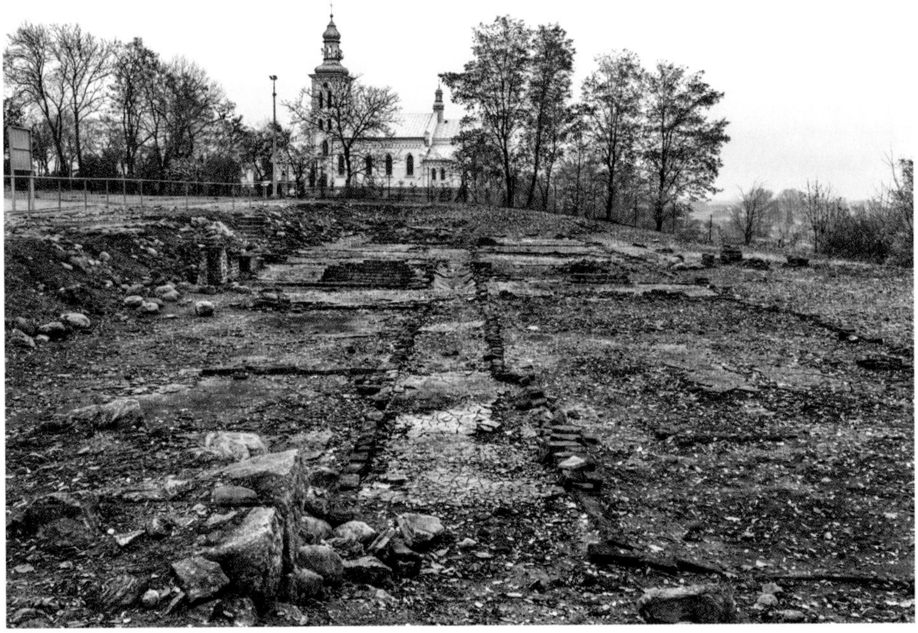

Edward Burtynsky, *Mansion Remains*, Chelmno, Poland, 2015

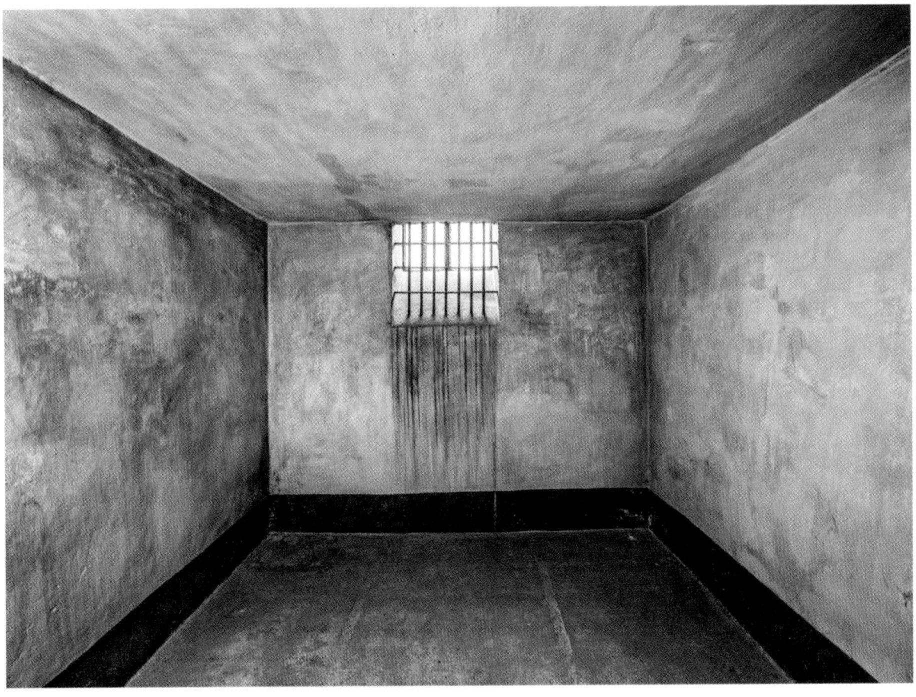

Edward Burtynsky, *Basement Cell, Zyklon B Test Site*, Auschwitz, Poland, 2014

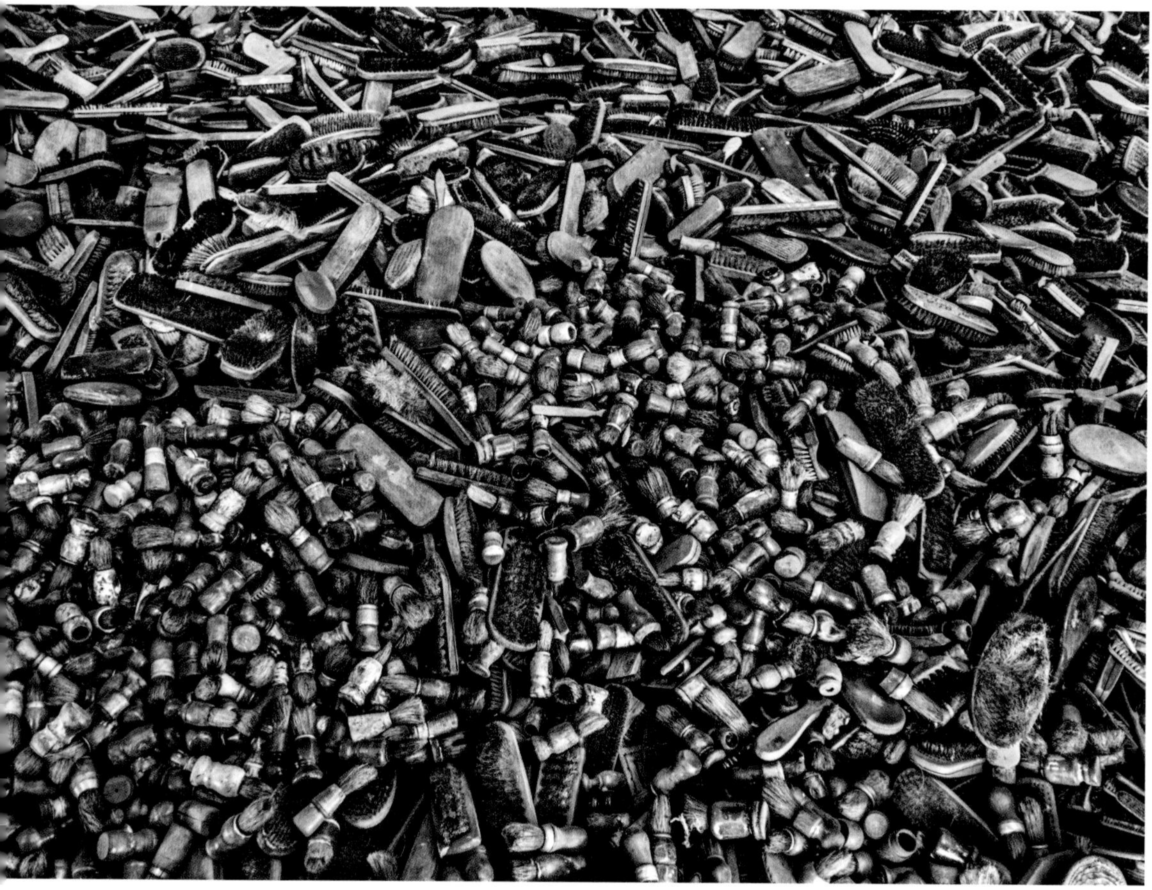

Edward Burtynsky, *Hair and Shaving Brushes*, Auschwitz-Birkenau State Museum, Poland, 2014

The brushes for hair and shaving on exhibition at the Auschwitz-Birkenau State Museum are photographed with the precision and texture Burtynsky had previously used to shoot scrap yards. In the only sequences with colour in Steven Spielberg's *Schindler's List* (1993), a young girl is shown in a red coat–one of the many whose blood was shed during the Holocaust. When Burtynsky photographed the sixty pairs of iron shoes along the east bank of the Danube in Budapest, commemorating the Jews shot there, he placed two tiny shards of red, wilted carnations on the shoes in the foreground in an otherwise monochromatic colour image.

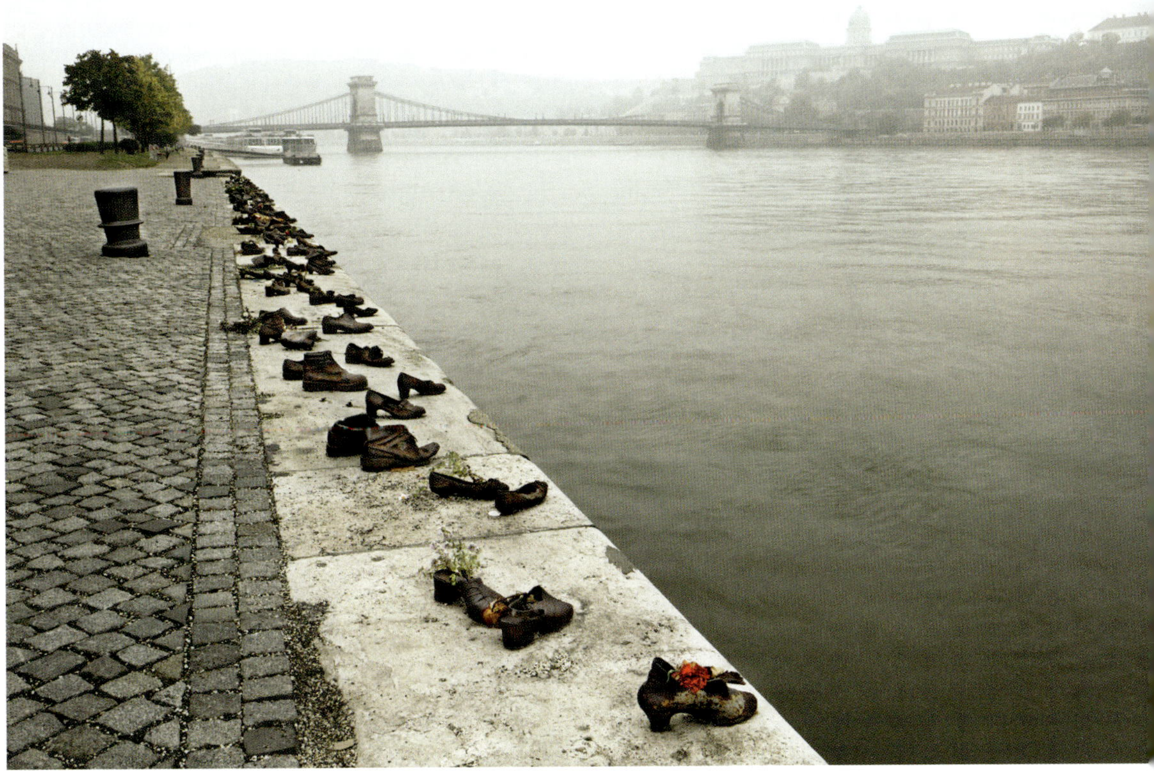

Edward Burtynsky, *Iron Shoe Memorial*, Budapest, Hungary, 2014

In preparing to photograph the *Sacred Sites* series, Burtynsky watched Claude Lanzmann's epic nine-and-a-half-hour documentary, *Shoah* (1985), which tells the story of the Holocaust through interviews with witnesses. He also saw *Schindler's List* (1993), but his project shares many affinities with Alain Resnais's thirty-minute documentary from 1956, *Nuit et brouillard* (*Night and Fog*), where colour footage of present-day Auschwitz is juxtaposed with black-and-white footage and photographs from the 1940s (many taken by the SS). At that film's conclusion, the narrator states: "With our sincere gaze we survey these ruins, as if the old monster lay crushed forever beneath the rubble. We pretend to take up hope again as the image recedes into the past, as if we were cured once and for all of the scourge of the camps. We pretend it happened all at once, at a given time and place. We turn a blind eye to what surrounds us and a deaf ear to humanity's never-ending cry."

Burtynsky's images capture "these ruins" at the same time he exhibits "the old monster." The image of the Old Jewish Cemetery in Prague, bathed in sunshine, is one of the few images that offers a glimmer of hope.

"It was not until I visited the actual sites: the camps, monuments, and killing fields–in order to generate imagery for the architecture of the monument–that the full impact of what those places must have been like and what they still represent, hit me," Burtynsky recalled. "Not only were there victims at these terrible places, but there were also survivors. The project has become as much a testament to the indomitable human spirit as it is a memorial to those who perished." He added: "For the sake of future generations we must continue to acknowledge those critical moments in

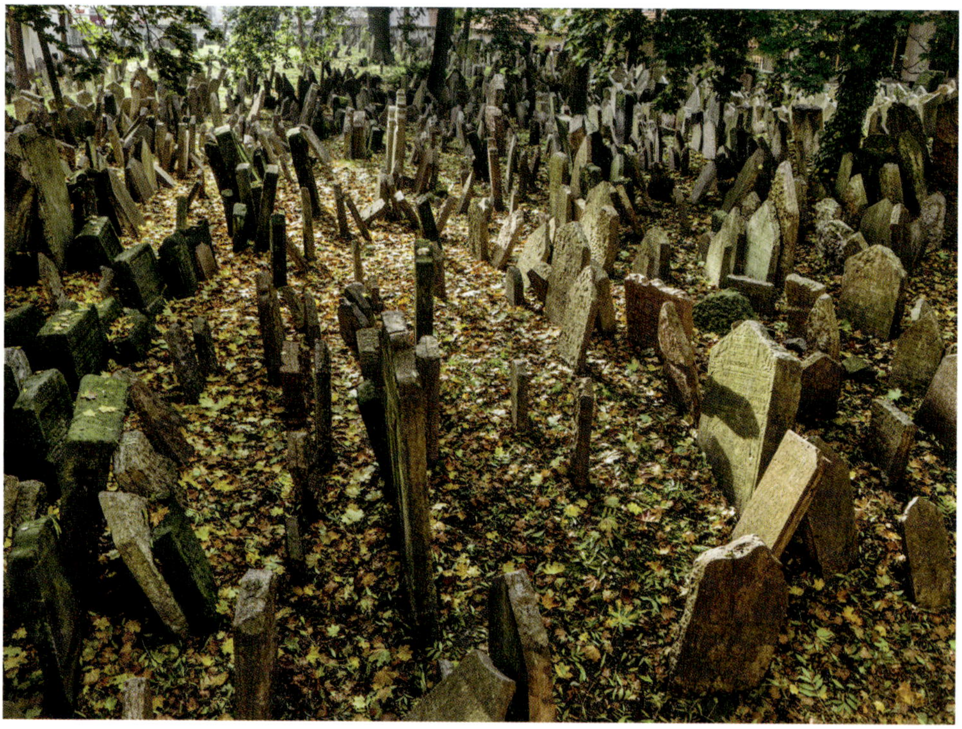

Edward Burtynsky, *Old Jewish Cemetery*, Prague, Czech Republic, 2014

history that stand as examples of turbulent, questionable political affairs and their devastating effect on human lives."[2] In making these reflections, Burtynsky would have been mindful of his mother's experiences in the Holodomor, her servitude in Germany, and her incarceration in a post-war detention camp.

When he was commissioned to design the National Holocaust monument in Ottawa, the Polish-American architect, Daniel Libeskind, wanted to create a space that would not be monolithic in shape. Instead, he depicted the six points of the star of David in concrete in triangular, cast-in-place planes, which, he stated, "remains the visual symbol of the Holocaust–a symbol that millions of Jews were forced to wear by the Nazis to identify themselves as Jews, exclude them from humanity and mark them for extermination." The triangular spaces also represent the other groups that experienced genocide: gays, lesbians, Jehovah's Witnesses, socialists, and trade unionists. "Two different ground planes, create two paths, one ascending and one descending. The descending path leads visitors to the monument's interior spaces, and the other symbolically 'points to the future,' the architect said in a press release."[3] The interior contains three individual contemplation areas, a large gathering and orientation space, and a thirty-foot-tall structure that encloses the visitor in a cathedral-like space and frames the sky from above.

Fittingly, Burtynsky's images on six wall spaces of the monument are black-and-white murals applied using specially formulated paint to withstand exposure to sunlight and other weather conditions. They will remain survivors. For Doris L. Bergen, "Burtynsky's artist eye finds beauty in the midst of destruction. That beauty makes it easier for us to look and perhaps to see. The Holocaust did not happen in some distant planet; it was here."[4]

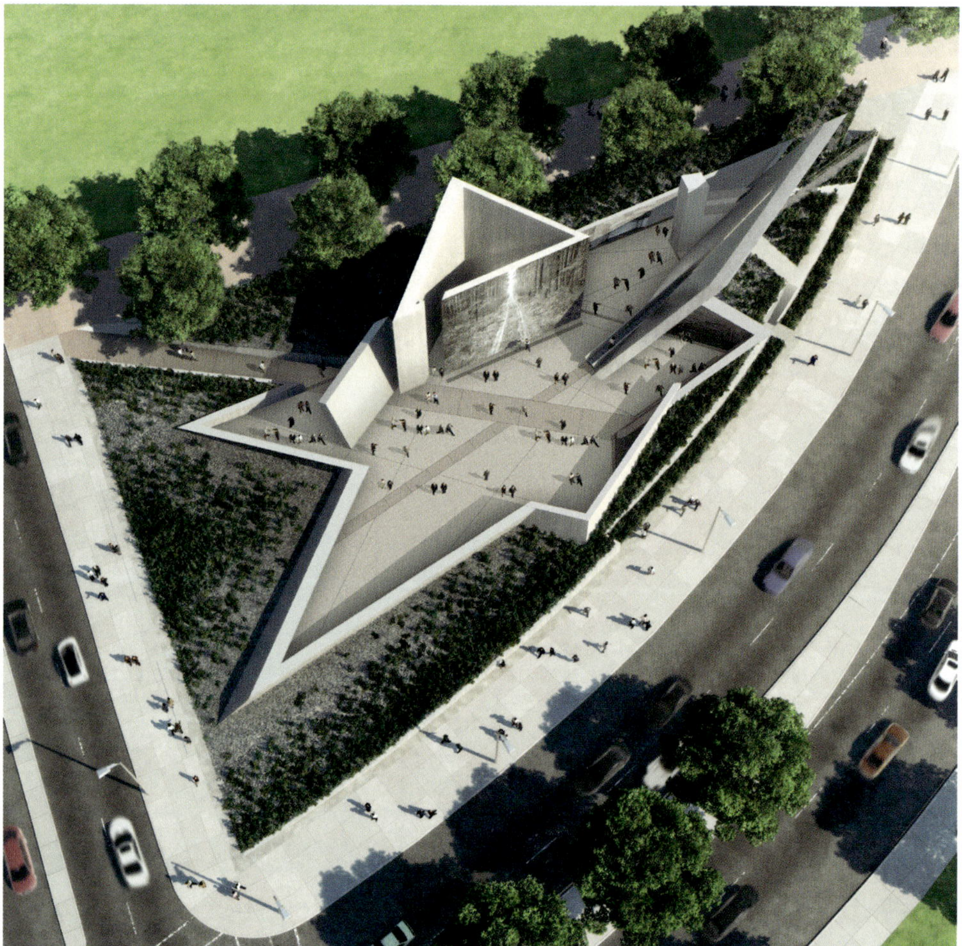

Aerial view, National Holocaust Monument, Ottawa

14 FROM HOLOCENE TO ANTHROPOCENE

The possibility of a third collaboration between Baichwal and Burtynsky was broached when the two were in Washington, D.C., in 2014 to screen *Watermark*. She turned to him and asked, "What if we could make 'Anthropocene' a household word?"

That controversial term was created in 2000 by the biologist Eugene Stormer and the Dutch Nobel laureate chemist Paul Crutzen. Burtynsky, Baichwal, and de Pencier had long been convinced that mankind's incursions into nature were threatening human existence and in this new term they found evidence for such an obvious truth.

The International Union of Geological Sciences still maintains that the world remains in the Holocene, a period that began 11,700 years ago after the last major ice age. Those who argue for Anthropocene insist that a new era began with one of several events: the Industrial Revolution in the 1800s, the bombing of Hiroshima and Nagasaki in 1945 that released radioactive particles, or in 1950 when the "Great Acceleration" began–a simultaneous surge in a wide-ranging series of activities that have altered the planet.

During his career, Burtynsky had witnessed a slew of changes that indicated that mankind was heading down an increasingly perilous path. "In the past," he reflected in 2018:

> . . . I wanted my work . . . to make us connect and to understand that we're creating wastelands, and that the scale at which we're taking these things that we need is mind-boggling. Now we've growing evidence that we're totally reshaping climate and we have the potential of tipping it into a state that will be very inhospitable for life. Fifteen, twenty years ago, I was in my grief stage. Now I've just kind of accepted that there's a big problem. . . . I feel like I got the best part: no war, mostly growth, and the excitement of technology, and watching it change the world in a dramatic way. I've experienced all of those things and now I'm sitting back and looking at it, and it's painful.[1]

Burtynsky had never sat back, but he became infused with a new conviction. Through his leadership role in the *Anthropocene* project, he commented vocally on the destruction of the Earth's frail ecosystem. Previously, he had claimed, his images just "showed what was happening"–and insisted his material did not contain editorial commentary. Now, he reframed that point of view. He remained convinced that his images spoke for themselves, but he no longer detached himself from offering his opinions on pressing ecological issues.

UNCOMFORTABLE TRUTHS

In *Watermark*, Burtynsky, Baichwal, and de Pencier had displayed a wide assortment of ways in which water was used and misused. That film had been decried by some critics who said that its point of view was not firmly established and that the footage and photographs were spectacularly beautiful in capturing what was, in essence, devastation.

In their new film, which came to be titled *Anthropocene: The Human Epoch*, the trio saw no need to resort to new kinds of imagery–after all, they were capturing the truth. They also stuck to their previous decision to show a wide variety of "truths," but took steps to make their intentions crystal clear. After the footage of the film *Anthropocene* had been edited, the celebrated Swedish actor Alicia Vikander was engaged to read a voice-over commentary. Moreover, the catalogue and photobook versions of *Anthropocene* contain substantial educational guidance. In this arrangement, the books and the film are separate but intertwined projects. *Watermark* had been directed by Baichwal and Burtynsky, with de Pencier as principal cinematographer; *Anthropocene* was directed by all three.

This new collaboration allowed the photographer and the filmmakers to follow separate paths. The three travelled to some locales together, but the filmmakers visited places Burtynsky did not, and he travelled to spots that do not appear in the film.

Baichwal and de Pencier concentrated on sequences that could be shown vividly on film (e.g., the interior of a GM lithium factory in Michigan, the Gothard Base Tunnel, farming in underground tunnels in London, flooding in Venice, endangered animals at London Zoo, and the Great Barrier Reef). In turn, Burtynsky visited sites where he felt he could make evocative photographs such as Nigeria, Borneo, and Indonesia. Their paths crossed in Zumaia in Spain, Norilsk and Berezniki in Russia, Carrara, the Hambach mine in Germany, the Dandora landfill site in Nairobi, China, Hong Kong, phosphate mines in Florida,[2] and Wyoming.[3] The diving expedition footage in Indonesia was shot by Jim Hellemn, and his son, Brian Burtynsky, drove down about thirty feet to direct the still photography.

The new project had a complex schedule. The three travelled to Germany in December 2015, then to Kenya in late April 2016, and later that year to Italy. The following year they went to Russia and British Columbia. Jim Panou was a member of those five expeditions and travelled with Burtynsky to Nigeria and India in April 2016, to Indonesia in July 2016, to Chile in May 2017, and to Kenya and Ghana in October 2017.

The intent remained investigative in the documentary's seven parts (Extraction, Terraforming, Technofossils, Anthroturbation, Boundary Limits, Climate Change, Extinction), each one of which concentrates on a single issue and supplies examples.

As with *Manufactured Landscapes* and *Watermark*, the film opens with a startling prologue–a ferocious, angry fire consuming elephant tusks. Then, the footage momentarily switches to the beach at Zumaia, Spain. The film returns to the tusk burning, where a former park keeper provides some gruelling statistics: on that day, 105 tonnes of tusks recovered from poachers (with a street value of $150 million–and representing the killing of ten thousand elephants) were being destroyed.

Extraction begins in Norilsk, Siberia, a closed city three hundred kilometres north of the Arctic Circle that was founded as a slave labour camp but which is now a centre for nickel mining and ore processing. Access to the city is difficult to obtain because of its strategic importance in the production of that mineral. It is also one of the most polluted areas in the world. This sequence visits factories, sites of extraction, and a group of women who have "adjusted" to working there. A joyful celebration of the summer holiday follows; the workers, the film implies, wish to remain oblivious of the consequences of living in such a dangerous place.

The film then moves its attention to Carrara and a workshop of artisans creating sculptures (several of which are replicas of Michelangelo's *David*).

The focus then turns to the Atacama Desert in Chile, where lithium is being extracted, followed by a GM lithium assembly plant in Michigan.

The Hambach mine, the largest open-pit mine in Germany, is in the process of eating up the surrounding farmlands and villages. Its enormous extractors swallow the countryside and "terraform" it into wave-like piles of earth. On Vancouver Island, in British Columbia, old-growth forests are being destroyed by logging that redesigns the landscape. Logging in Lagos has become a major industry, and the resulting prosperity has led in part to the building of the Redeemed Christian Church of God, which seats one million people.

This megachurch is a part of the massive urban sprawl that is reshaping Lagos into a megacity, and Burtynsky, Panou, and Reid went to an overnight church service there. No good still image resulted, as Jim Panou recalled: "Mike, with his camera on a gimbal [steadying device], just wandered through the crowds shooting. There was no planned effort to shoot for the film. Mike did not shoot any audio . . . The church however filmed the entire event and posted the full 8 to 10-hour proceedings on YouTube. My contact within the church pointed me to the YouTube material, which was great, and we got their permission to use both audio and video from it. The entire sequence is made up of a mix of Mike's footage and the church's material."[4]

The Technofossils section deals with the search for plastics. The demand is so intense that the enormous Dandora landfill in Nairobi, Kenya, has streets that can be navigated by the "jobbers"–waste pickers who live in nearby shacks and scavenge the site. Although supposedly shuttered in 2012, this site still accepts 2,000 tonnes of garbage daily.

In Anthroturbation, human tunnelling is examined by documenting the Gothard Base Tunnel in Switzerland. Organic farming, as practised in some shafts that are no longer in use shafts and were once part of London's Underground, is also shown. The Boundary Limits segment (the Berezniki potash mine in Russia, phosphate mines in Florida, and oil refineries in Houston) focuses on the grim fact that man has imposed no barriers in exploiting the earth to search for materials that suit nefarious purposes.

The climate change segment documents the elaborate Gudong seawall at Dongying, which was built to protect the Shengli Oil Field in Shandong province; the flooding in Venice has been catastrophic to the well-being of the city; at Batu Bolong Reef off the island of Komodo in Indonesia, the coral is glowingly healthy, whereas bleaching is destroying Australia's Great Barrier Reef. In Extinction, a number of species at the London Zoo, including the Sumatran tiger, are on the verge of disappearing entirely. Meanwhile, at Prestige Crafts in Hong Kong, an ivory dealer proudly displays his wares; however, for the sake of survival and political correctness, he is switching to mammoth tusks. Then the film circles back to the tusk burning in Nigeria. One journalist who watched the documentary observed that "[the bonfires of ivory act like a blazing barricade against an unacceptable future, and simultaneously as beacons of distress, signaling a break with the past and the over-exploitation of nature that has been going on since our stone-age beginnings."[5]

Anders Dunker pointed out that a viewer of *Anthropocene: The Human Epoch*, although exposed to myriad events, is not subjected to a "monotonous panorama of destruction. The segments are real visual stories, and there is a strong sense of place, of locality, and of humanity. Sudden, interjected segments show real humans–not mankind the monster, the destroyer of worlds–but people like you and me. Even in the inhuman landscapes and industrial smelting plants in Siberia, we meet workers who laughingly acknowledge the grimness of their surroundings, but who still feel *at home,* who chat over lunch–before returning to their ominous machines."

In his appreciative notice, Dunker also observed:

> The trio writing and directing the film do not fully take on the task of explaining what the Anthropocene is, but rather deploys the concept of "the human epoch" as a frame, within which we can see ourselves as what we really are: consumers. Not so much of products, but of that which our products are essentially made of–the Earth itself.

> Consuming basically means digging, cutting, drilling, and killing. Not always pleasant. Something that is done with a sense of ambivalence, as when altering a landscape forever. Something witnessed with a passing sorrow, as the felling of a majestic tree. Sometimes it may even be revolting, as in huge chemical processes, smelting and churning, which can be vaguely nauseating, like rivers of lava from a volcano. It is precisely in this sensually disquieting way that humanity's new status as an "overwhelming power of nature" is presented in the film.[6]

The reviewer writing for *Point of View*, in September 2018, offered some helpful distinctions between the three films: "While *Watermark* benefited from its clear focus on the lakes, rivers, and other bodies quenching the earth, there isn't much to immediately distinguish *Anthropocene: The Human Epoch* from *Manufactured Landscapes* aside from the discernible advances in camera technology. That's not necessarily a bad thing–*Landscapes* is one of the best documentaries ever made–and the similarity between the films highlights the superior craftsmanship that allows the trio to capture the scale of human activity with sweeping grandeur."[7]

TRANSFORMATIVE MOMENTS

Still images have a different aesthetic from moving images. The photobook, just titled *Anthropocene*, is restricted to moments. As a result, the images are more contemplative and require a different arrangement from the documentary. The book is divided into nine sections: Deep Time, Technofossils, Urbanization, Agriculture, Deforestation, Extraction, Energy, Biodiversity, and Extinction.

Since Burtynsky had been exploring the Anthropocene well before the term came into existence, he had a backlog of images that fit under that umbrella. He inserted some of those into the photobook, which contains 102 images, most made from 2015 to 2017.[8]

The photobook is more intricate in its arrangement than the earlier books by Burtynsky that he published with Steidl. Its emphasis is on Extraction–almost half the images are placed in this category–and that section, located in the centre of the book, contains some of the strongest images Burtynsky had ever created. The book also comprises two essays, reflections by the three collaborators, and verses by Margaret Atwood commenting poignantly on her reactions to the photographs.

The prologue of the documentary includes some fleeting moments at Zumaia. In contrast, the photobook begins with a section titled Deep Time, in this small town in the Basque region of Spain, where thirteen kilometres of beach are embellished with rock layers, over 100 million years old, known as flysch. These layers are chains of shale interbedded with thin, hard sandstone, which were formed during a continental collision when a subducting plate pushed on the plate above it, causing the top plate to

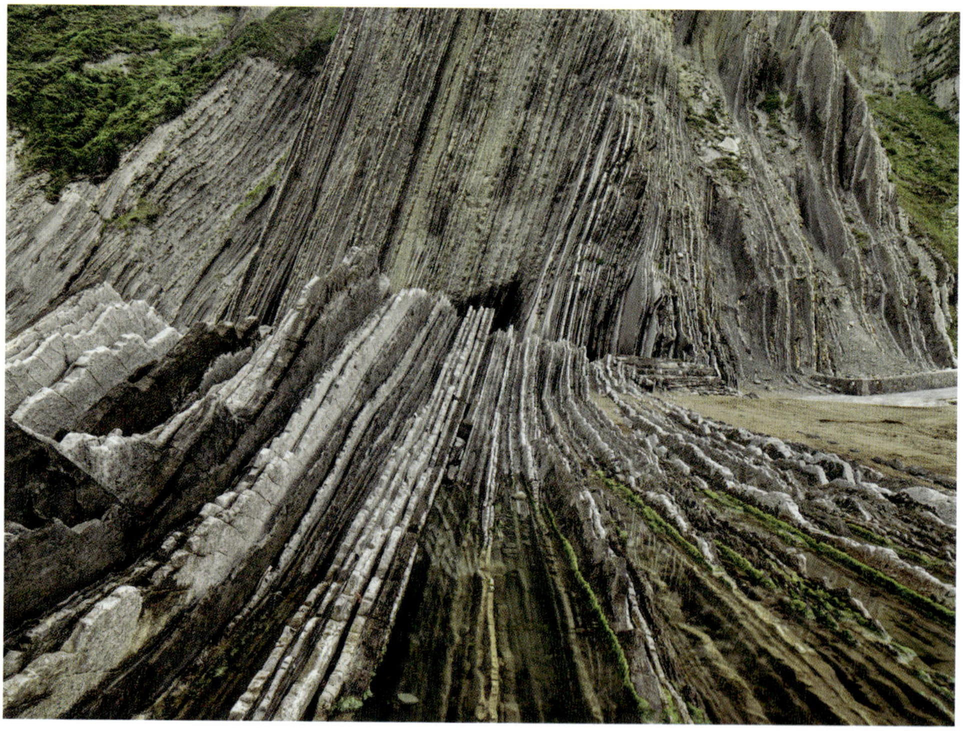

Edward Burtynsky, *Basque Coast #1*, UNESCO Geopark, Zumaia, Spain, 2015

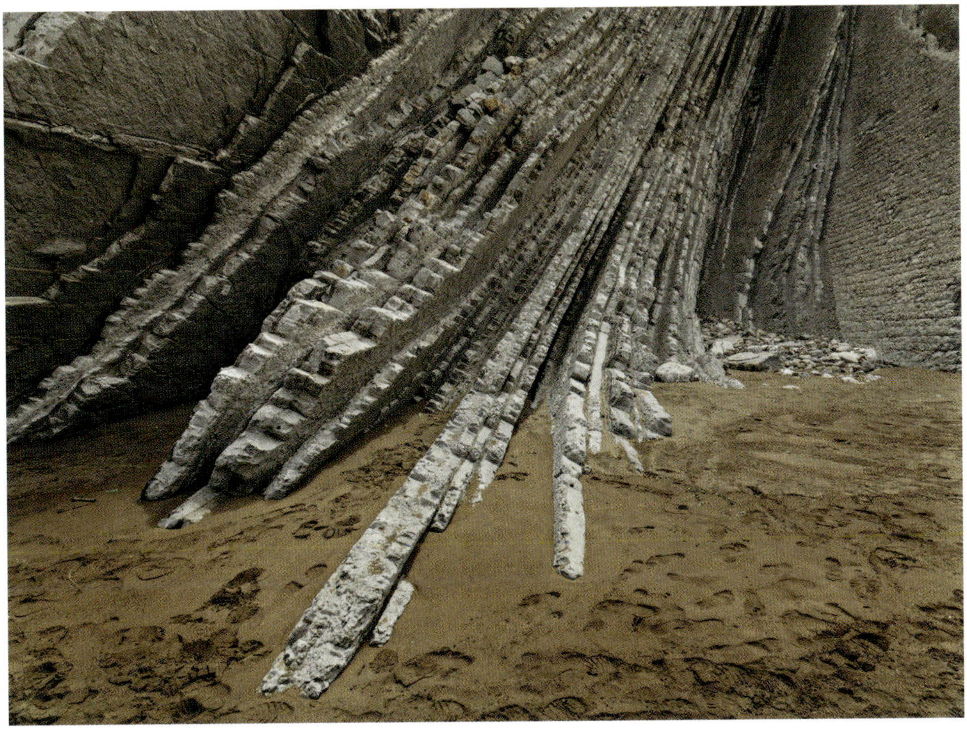

Edward Burtynsky, *Basque Coast #2*, UNESCO Geopark, Zumaia, Spain, 2015

fold. More specifically, sediment was built up on "sea-sea floors adjacent to evolving mountain chains. When the sea floor was pushed up into land through tectonic forces, this jagged layering occurred."[9]

In *Basque Coast #2*, the lower portion of the flysch reaches up to its counterpart, rising steeply above it. The green that subtly embroiders both surfaces imparts a sense of life to this geologic confrontation, whereas the contrast between the grey tones of the flysch and the dark brown sand in *Zumaia #2* emphasizes a clash between the dead flysch and the footprints on the beach. The power of both images is underscored by monochromatic colour values.

The Technofossils section begins with images of the Gudong sea wall at Dongying but move to *Cankun Aluminum, Xiamen City* (2005). Although the bright colours flickering on the compacted boxes reference earlier *Urban Mines* images, (see pp. 115 and 171), this particular image paves the way

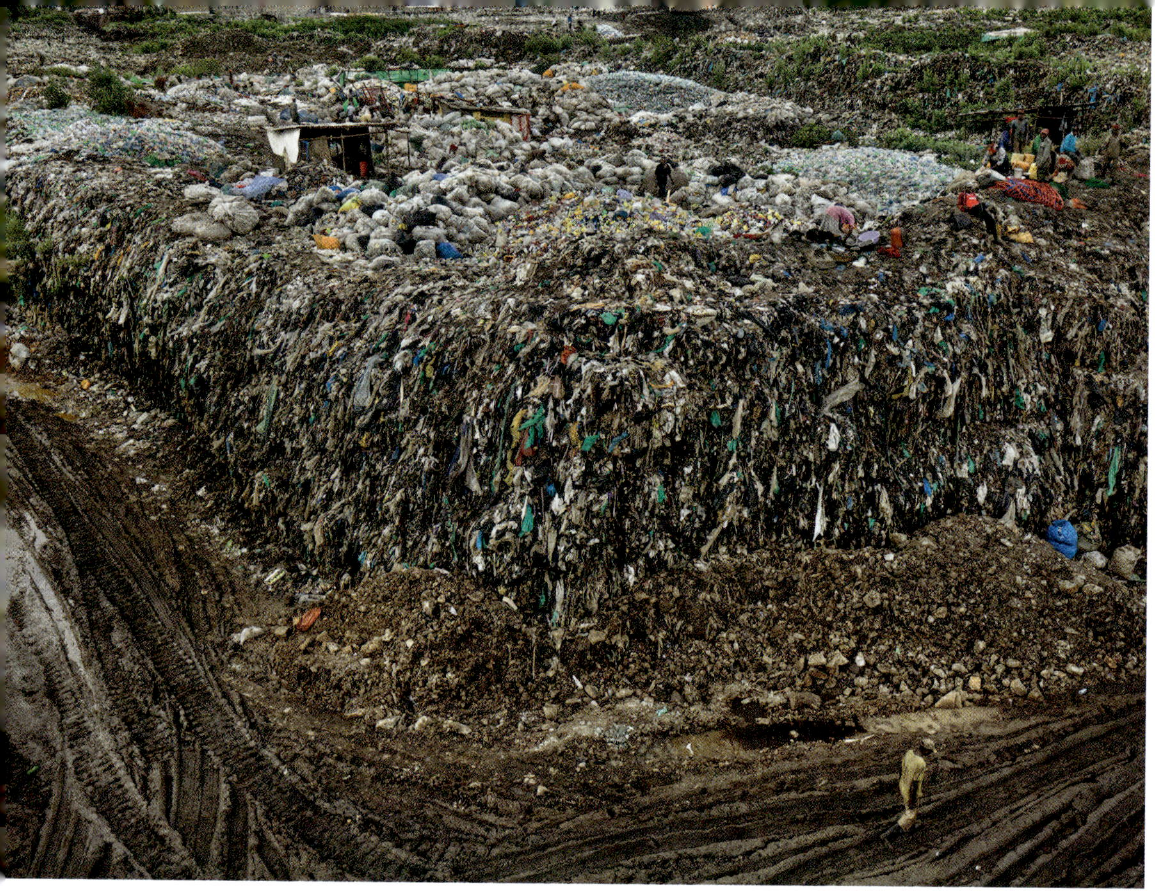

Edward Burtynsky, *Dandora Landfill #1*, Nairobi, Kenya, 2016

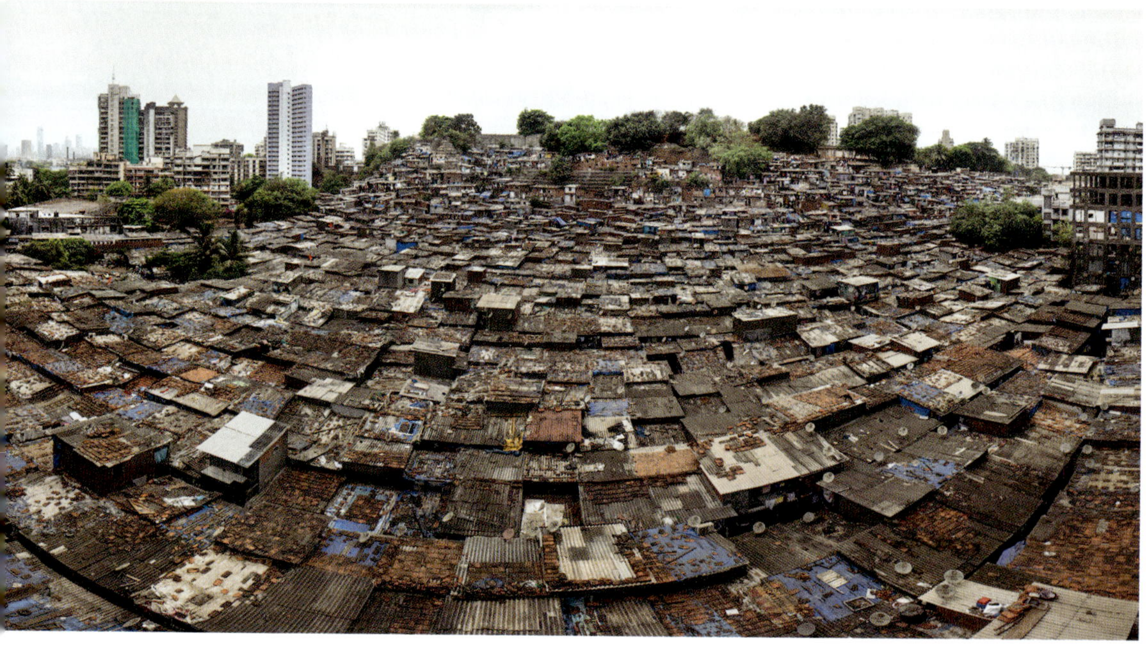

Edward Burtynsky, *Sidarth Nagar*, Worli, Mumbai, India, 2016

for one of the enormous Dandora landfill in Nairobi–in many ways, the culmination in its tragic grandeur of all the earlier images of such sites. Aerial views of gigantic urban sprawl in Lagos; Los Angeles; Baytown, Texas; Irwindale, California; and Mumbai comprise *Urbanization*.

Except for two images taken in Borneo and Saudi Arabia, the entries in the Agriculture section (Spain; the Imperial Valley, Holtville, California) were made well before the beginning of the *Anthropocene* project. The satellite capture in Saudi Arabia is reminiscent of the *Pivot Irrigation* images; this image shows a massive assortment of attempts to obtain water using the same method as in the U.S. Midwest, and the inevitable exhaustion of the aquifer as evidenced by the disappearing faint circles that have been abandoned. In Borneo, plantations devoted to the production of palm oil–an endeavour requiring huge amounts of nitrogen and potash–have continued to thrive. Aerial views of this toxic way of farming may faintly

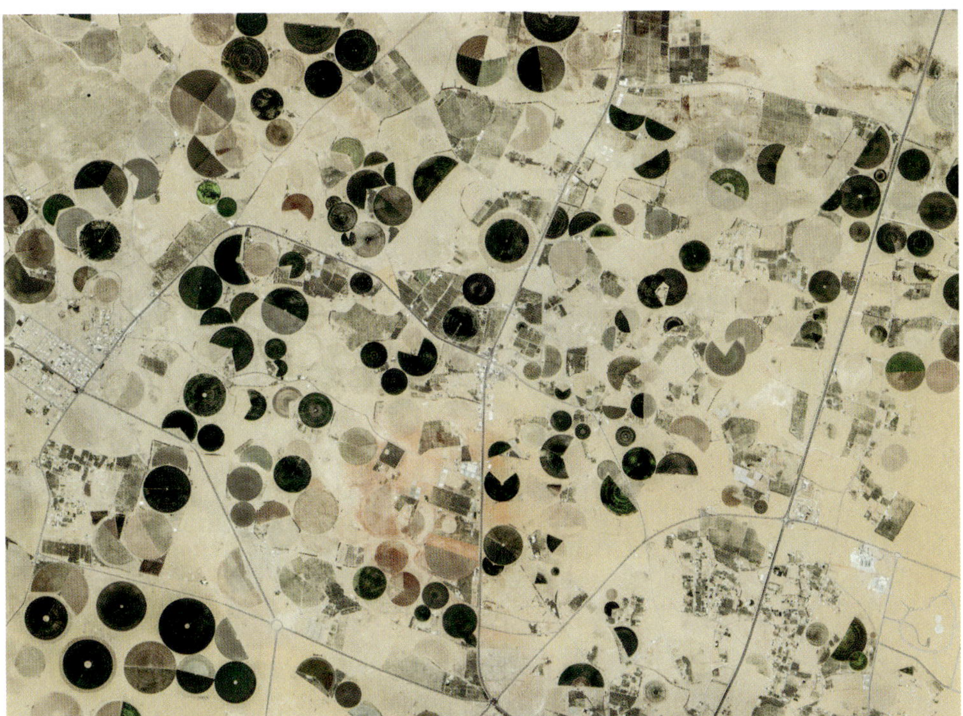

Edward Burtynsky, *Satellite Capture*, near Buraydah, Saudi Arabia, 2018

resemble the dry farming in Monegros, but the land depicted in *Saw Mills #3* has been stripped bare in this process–not replenished.

The results of the decimation of ancient forests in Lagos are shown in three images in the Deforestation section and bear a strong resemblance to the activities of the logging industry on Vancouver Island.

The lithium mines in Chile's Atacama Desert, photographed in 2017, not surprisingly resemble the salt pans in Gujarat of the year before.

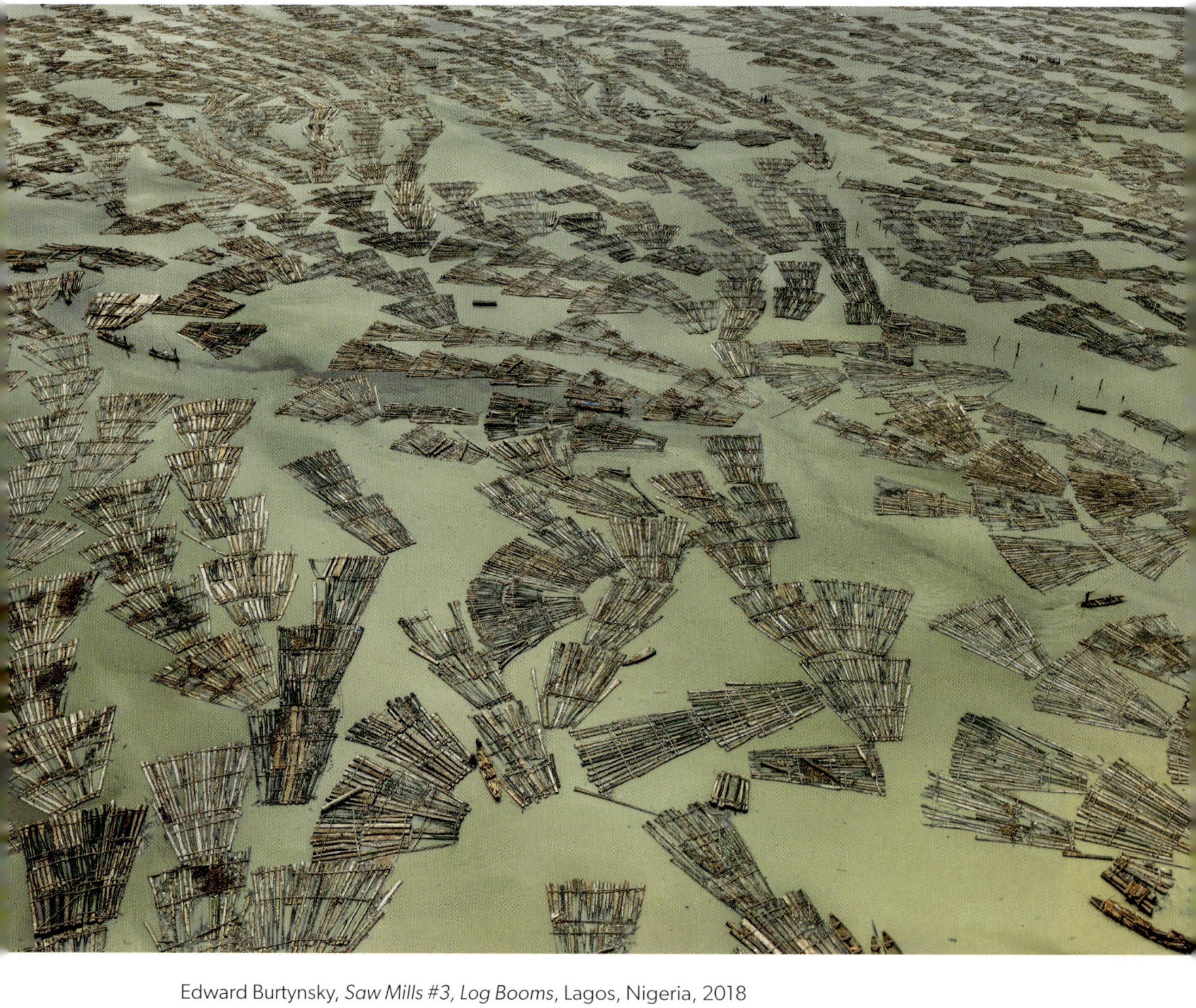

Edward Burtynsky, *Saw Mills #3, Log Booms*, Lagos, Nigeria, 2018

Lithium Mines #1 shows the various colour stages the water goes through in the acquisition of lithium. When he revisited Carrara in 2016 to take images for the Extraction section, Burtynsky took a very different approach from twenty-three years before. Now, his wide-angle shots emphasize the architecture of the entire site and, in the process, make it look like an abandoned ancient city. The image of fracking in Wyoming from 2015 reveals a completely desolate, snow-swept landscape, with only a sliver

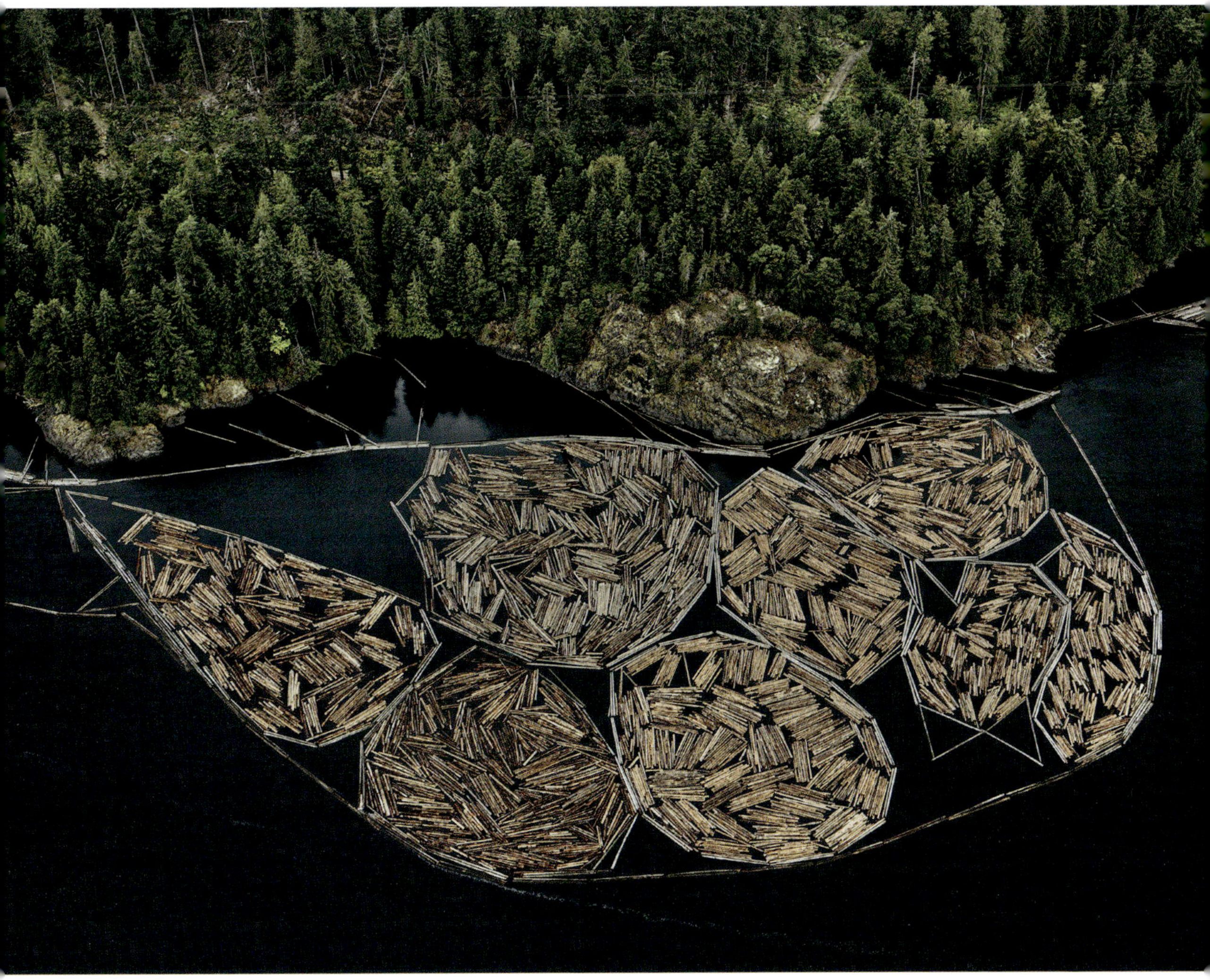

Edward Burtynsky, *Log Booms #1*, Vancouver Island, British Columbia, Canada, 2016

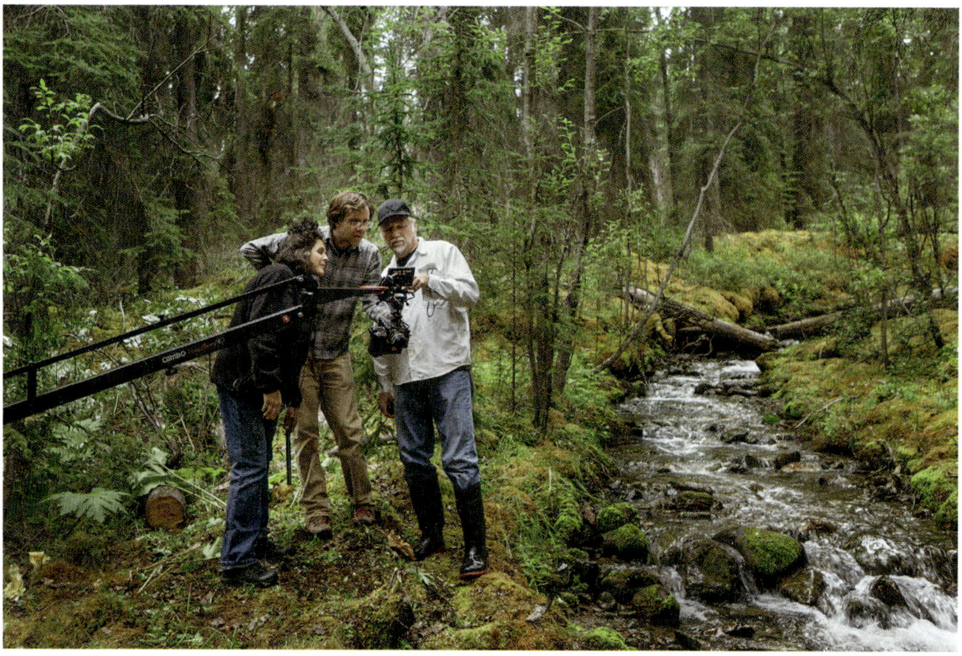

Jennifer Baichwal, Nick de Pencier, and Edward Burtynsky on location on Vancouver Island, British Columbia, 2016. Photograph by Alex Buri

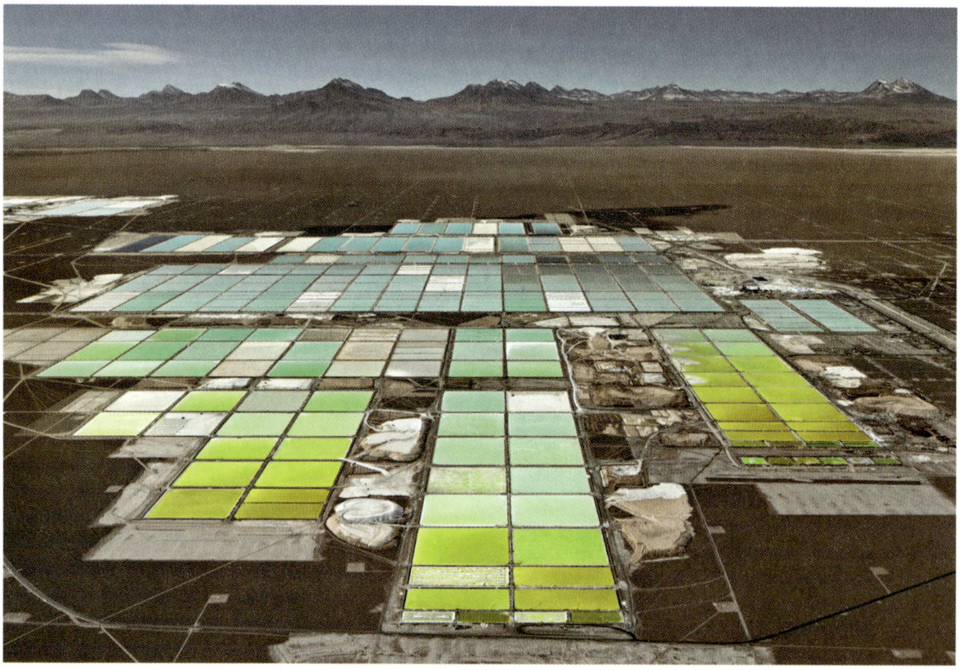

Edward Burtynsky, *Lithium Mines #1*, Salt Flats, Atacama Desert, Chile, 2017

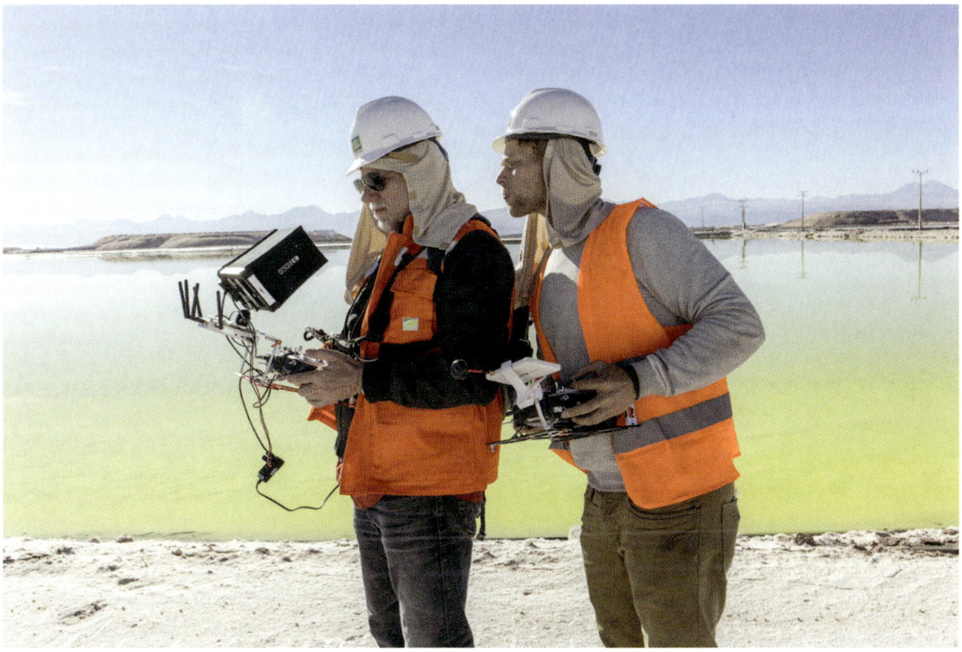

Edward Burtynsky with Mike Reid in the Atacama Desert, Chile, 2012. Photograph by Alex Buri

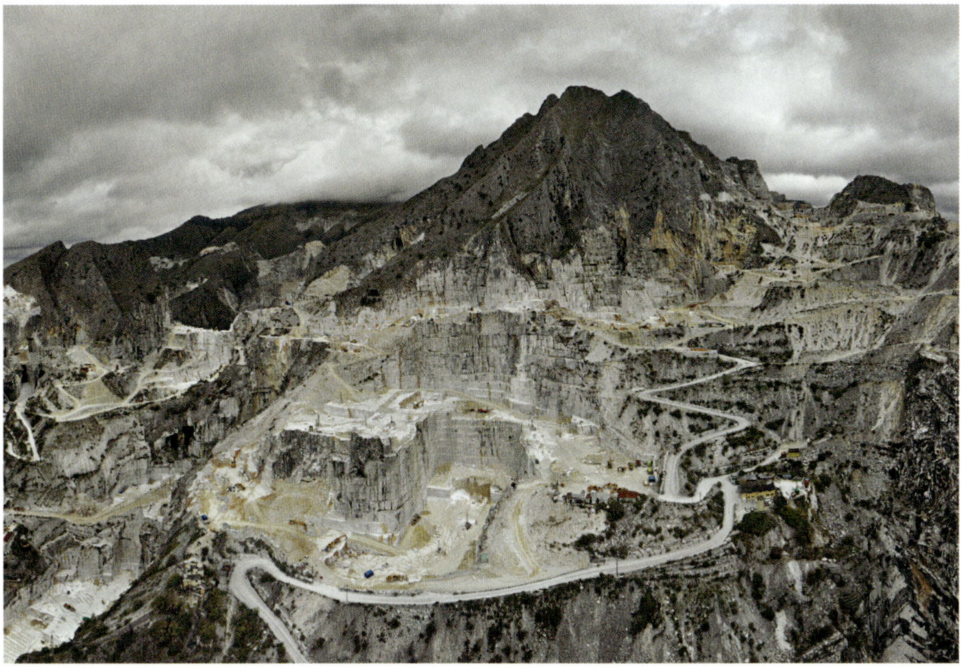

Edward Burtynsky, *Carrara Marble Quarries, Carbonera Quarry #1*, Carrara, Italy, 2016

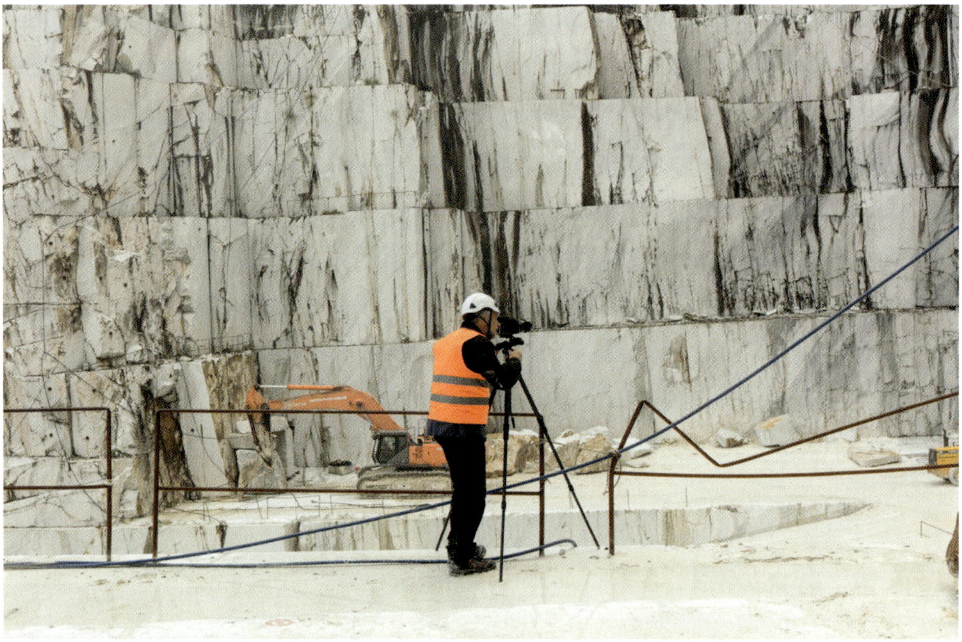

Edward Burtynsky on location at Carrara, 2016. Photograph by Jim Panou

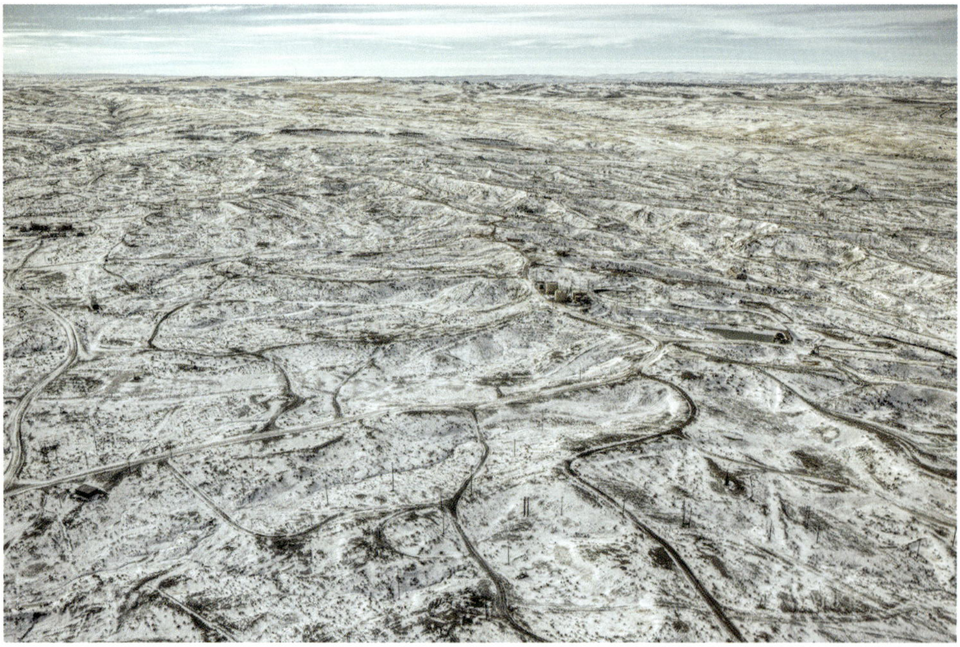

Edward Burtynsky, *Fracking*, near Gillette, Wyoming, 2015

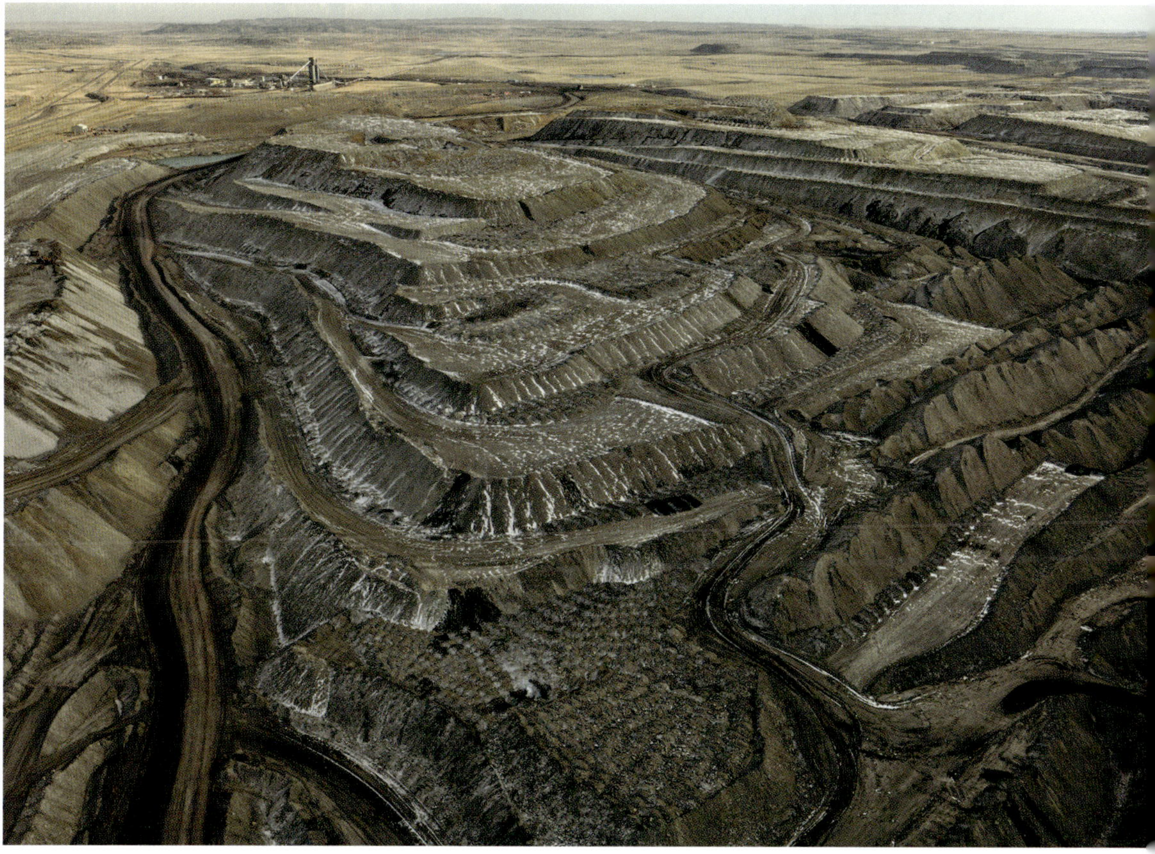

Edward Burtynsky, *Coal Mining*, near Gillette, Wyoming, 2015

of blue horizon allowed at the top of this monochromatic colour image. It is followed by a stunning assembly of images depicting coal mining in Wyoming (2015); copper mining in Calama, Chile (2017); the Chino mine near Santa Rita in New Mexico (2012); the Tyrone mine in nearby Silver City, New Mexico (2012); the Morenci mine in Arizona (2012); and mining in Highland Valley in British Columbia.

As a group, these are among the most accomplished mining images in Burtynsky's career and display considerable differences in exploring the same subject matter. The complex, interwoven lines of brown, beige, and russet leading to the bottom of *Chino #5* in New Mexico are precisely delineated; similar restricted lines of colour can be seen in *Tyrone Mountain #3*, but zig-zag across the top of the image.

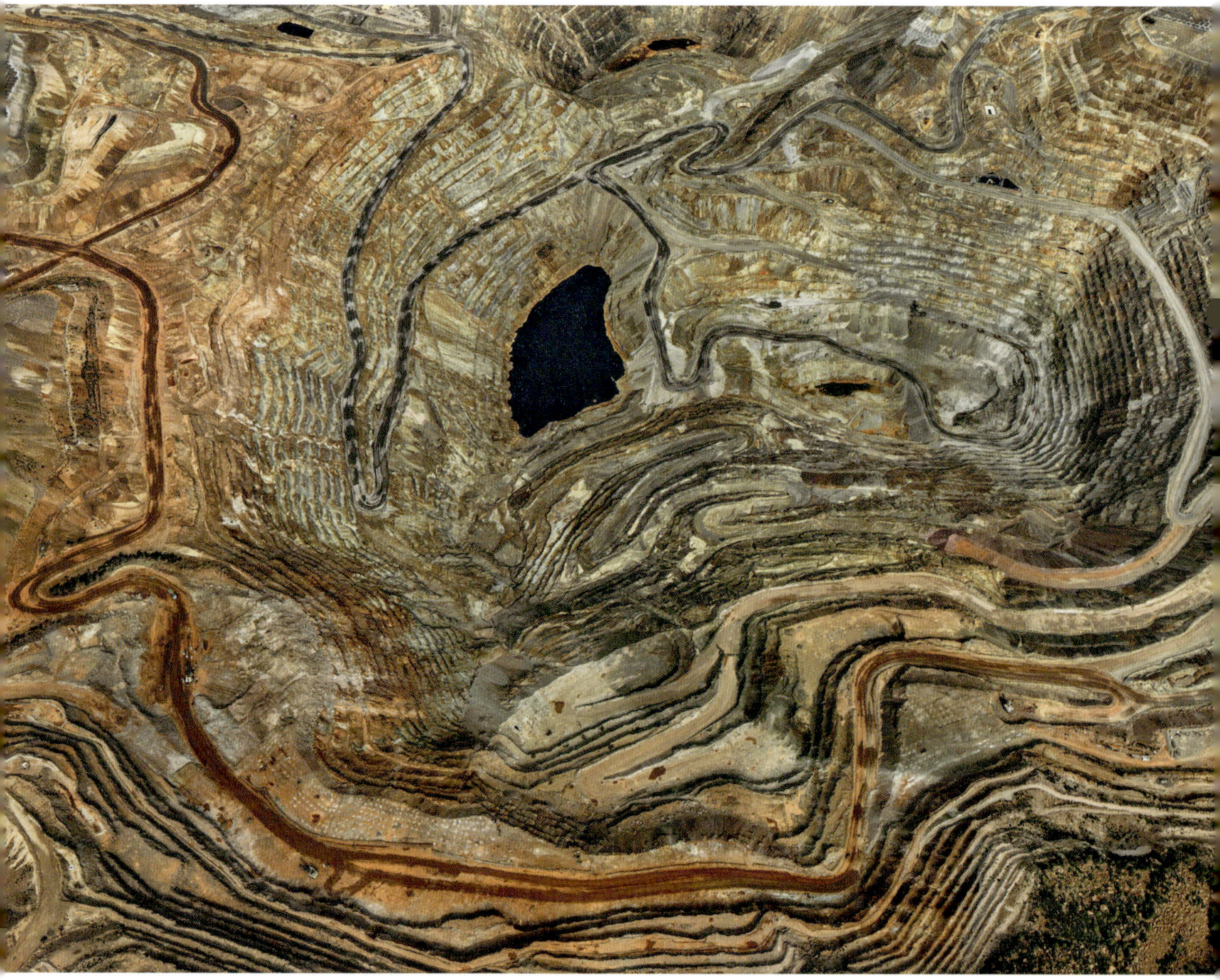

Edward Burtynsky, *Chino Mine #5*, Silver City, New Mexico, 2012

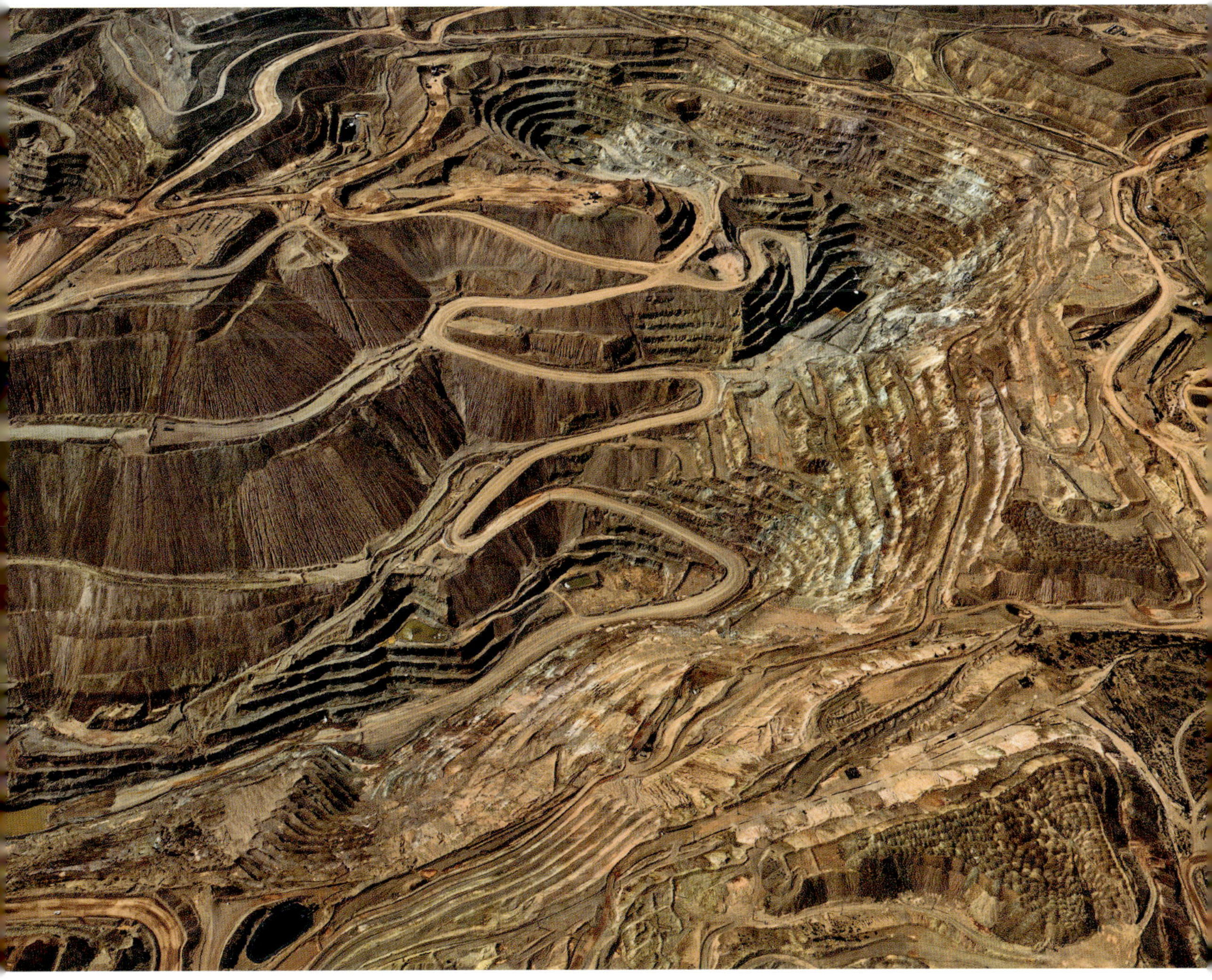

Edward Burtynsky, *Tyrone Mine #3*, Silver City, New Mexico, 2012

In the Introduction to *Anthropocene*, Suzanne Boettger adroitly compares *Morenci Mine #1* to a Clyfford Still abstract.[10] The long oblong panels in *Morenci Mine #2* are reminiscent of the ceilings of Baroque churches–or, as Marc Mayer has suggested, illuminated manuscripts.[11]

The giant excavators at the German Hambach mine remove enormous chunks of overburden (also called waste or spoil) and sculpt them into an assortment of different shapes, almost as if the drivers of these machines are creating earth art. *Coal Mines #1, #2, and #3* display three samples of this astounding accidental artistry.

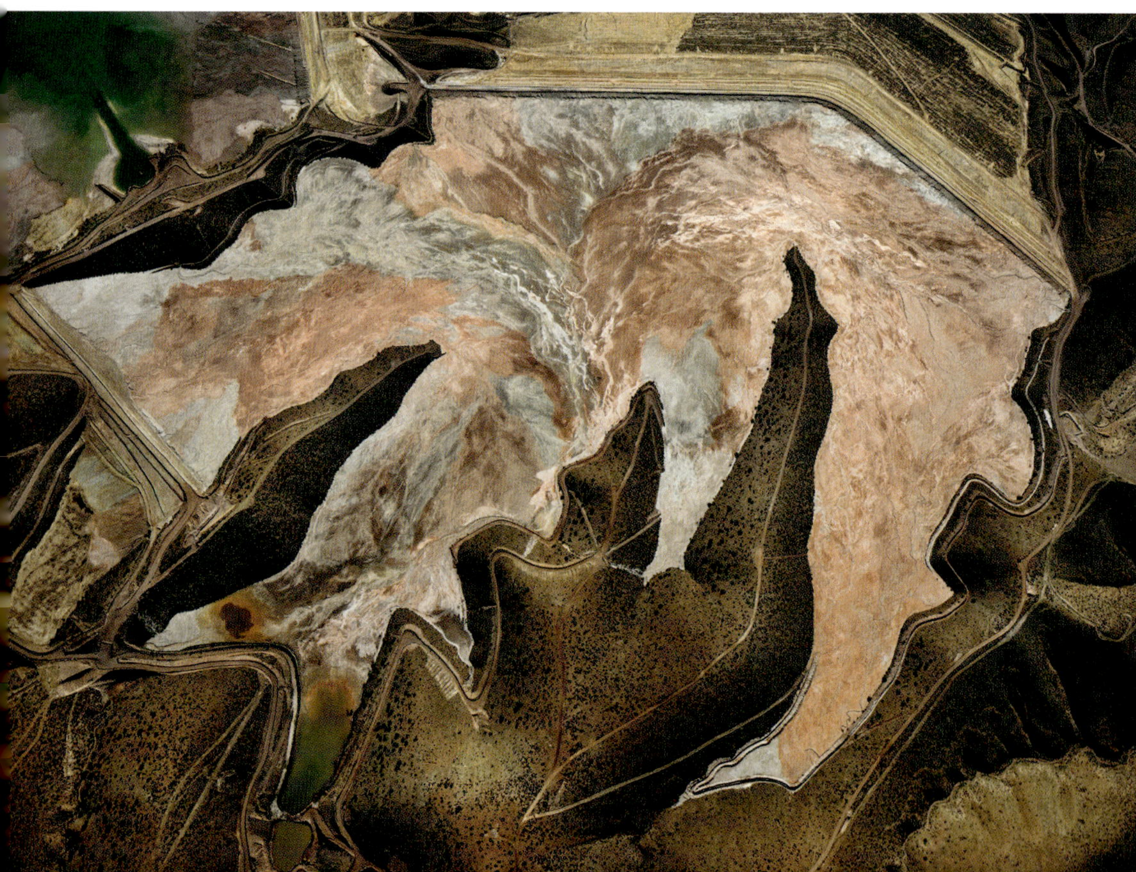

Edward Burtynsky, *Morenci Mine #1*, Clifton, Arizona, 2012

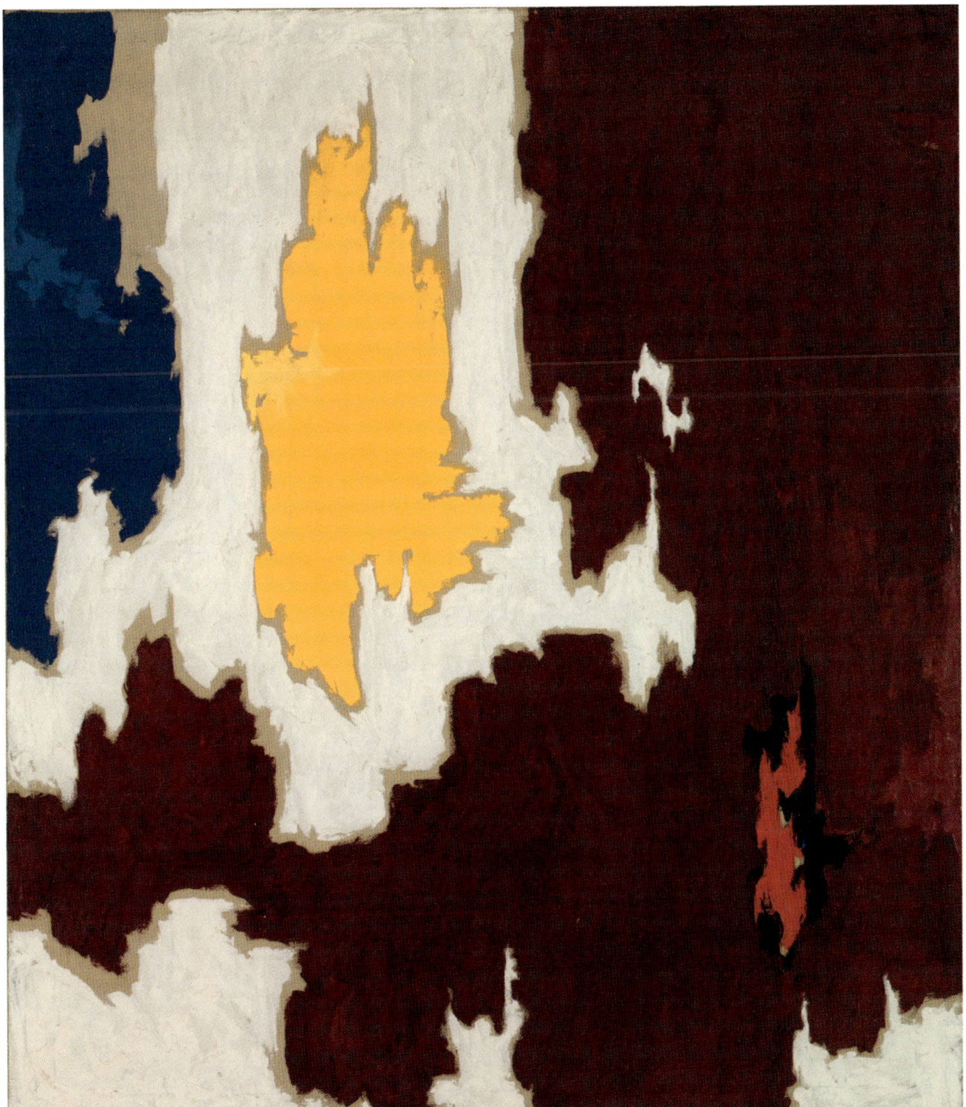

Clyfford Still, *October 1950*, oil on canvas, 1950. Buffalo AKG Museum

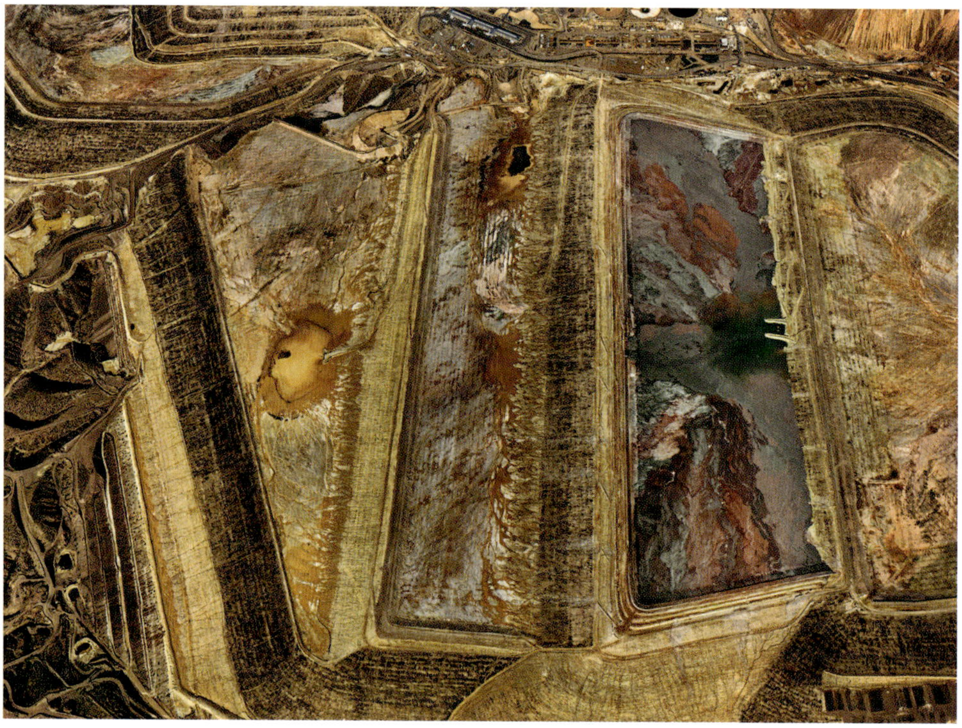

Edward Burtynsky, *Morenci Mine #2*, Clifton, Arizona, 2012

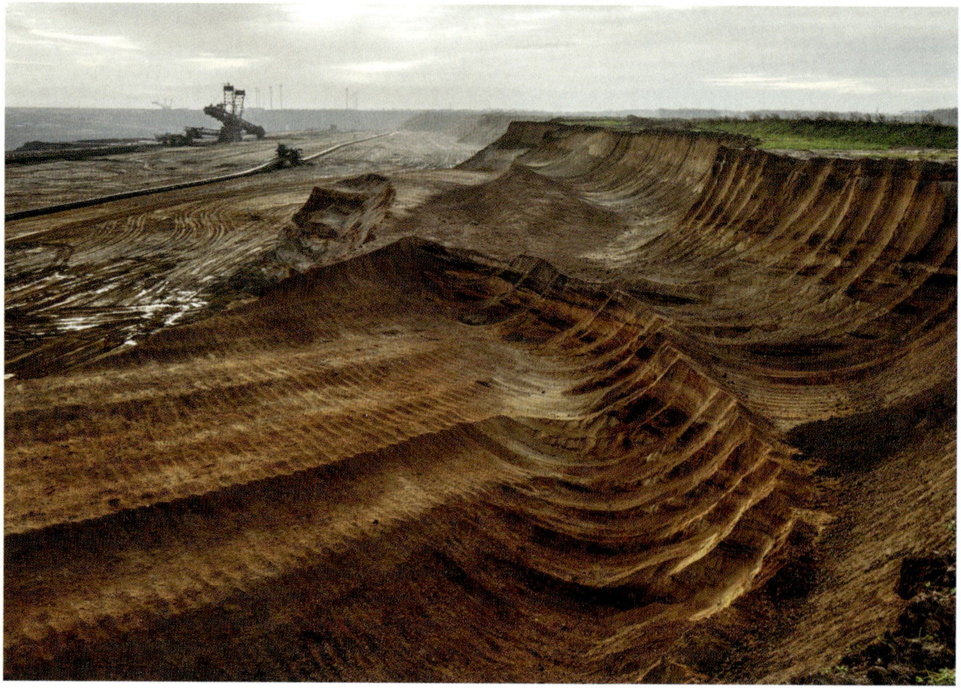

Edward Burtynsky, *Coal Mine #1*, North Rhine, Westphalia, Germany, 2015

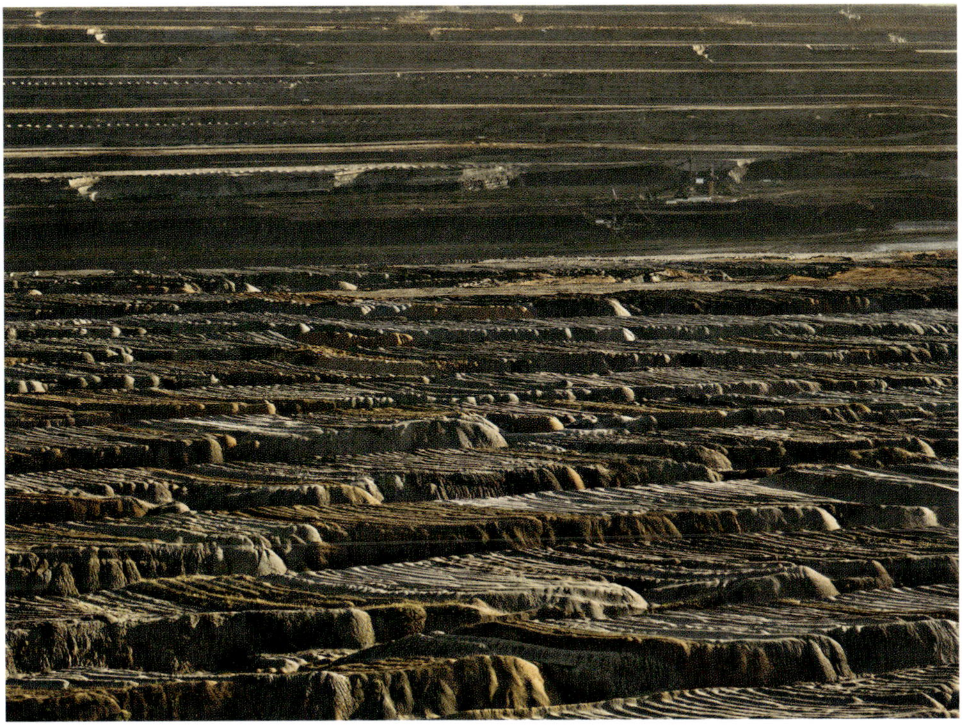

Edward Burtynsky, *Coal Mine #2,* North Rhine, Westphalia, Germany, 2015

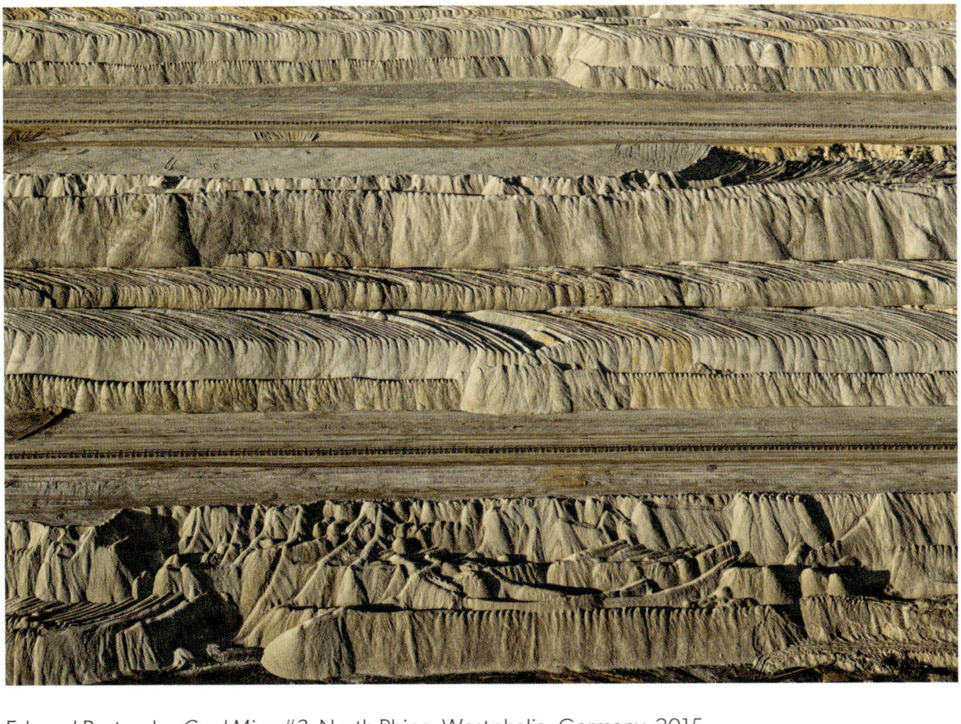

Edward Burtynsky, *Coal Mine #3,* North Rhine, Westphalia, Germany, 2015

Six images are devoted to oil bunkering, the pirating of crude oil from pipelines by impoverished communities in Nigeria. When these pipelines break, they leak considerable amounts of crude oil and toxic by-products into the nearby mangrove forests and waterways.[12] By design, this sequence has no redeeming features, but it did lead to a "transformative moment," as Burtynsky recalled:

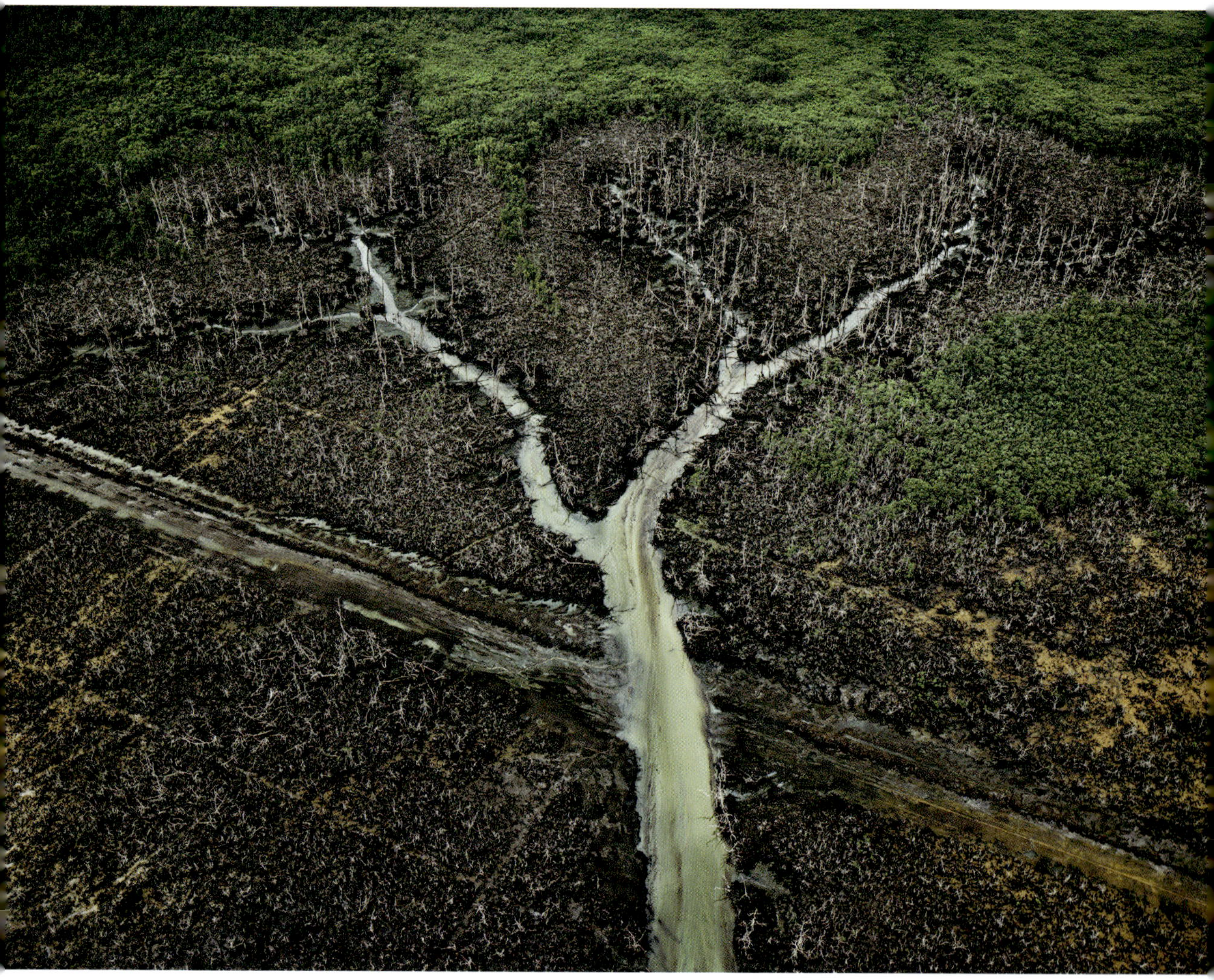

Edward Burtynsky, *Oil Bunkering #9*, Niger Delta, Nigeria, 2016

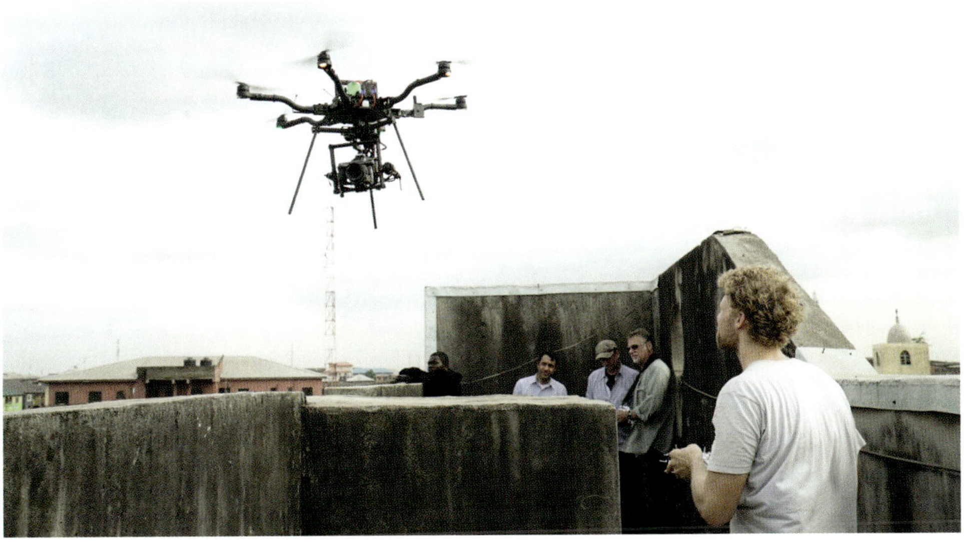

Mike Reid flying a drone, with (left to right) unidentified person, Raffi Khatchadourian, Jim Panou, and Edward Burtynsky, Lagos, 2016. Photograph by Dan Prior

This was where my decades-long investigation about the subject of oil had finally led me–to a remote landscape akin to Hell on Earth. The stark result of corporate profiteering, poverty, ingenuity, and ruthless piracy; even more primal than the derelict oil-drenched sands and pools of Baku, or the tragically operatic scenes of the shipbreakers in Bangladesh, this heart of darkness in the Niger Delta easily ranks among the most profoundly disturbing, devastated landscapes ever created by humankind. This was a location where several ongoing themes from the arc of my career coalesced: extraction, water, oil, and deforestation. It's impossible to describe the visceral experience of witnessing the evidence of such rapacious ecological destruction. Coming to grips with the experience of that landscape was a major turning point in my understanding about the degree to which we as a species are capable of defiling our planet. These landscapes completely elude popular awareness, and by finding and showing them, I have been able to fulfill one of my longstanding preoccupations: to send a potent message about how poorly we are treating our precious, finite planet.[13]

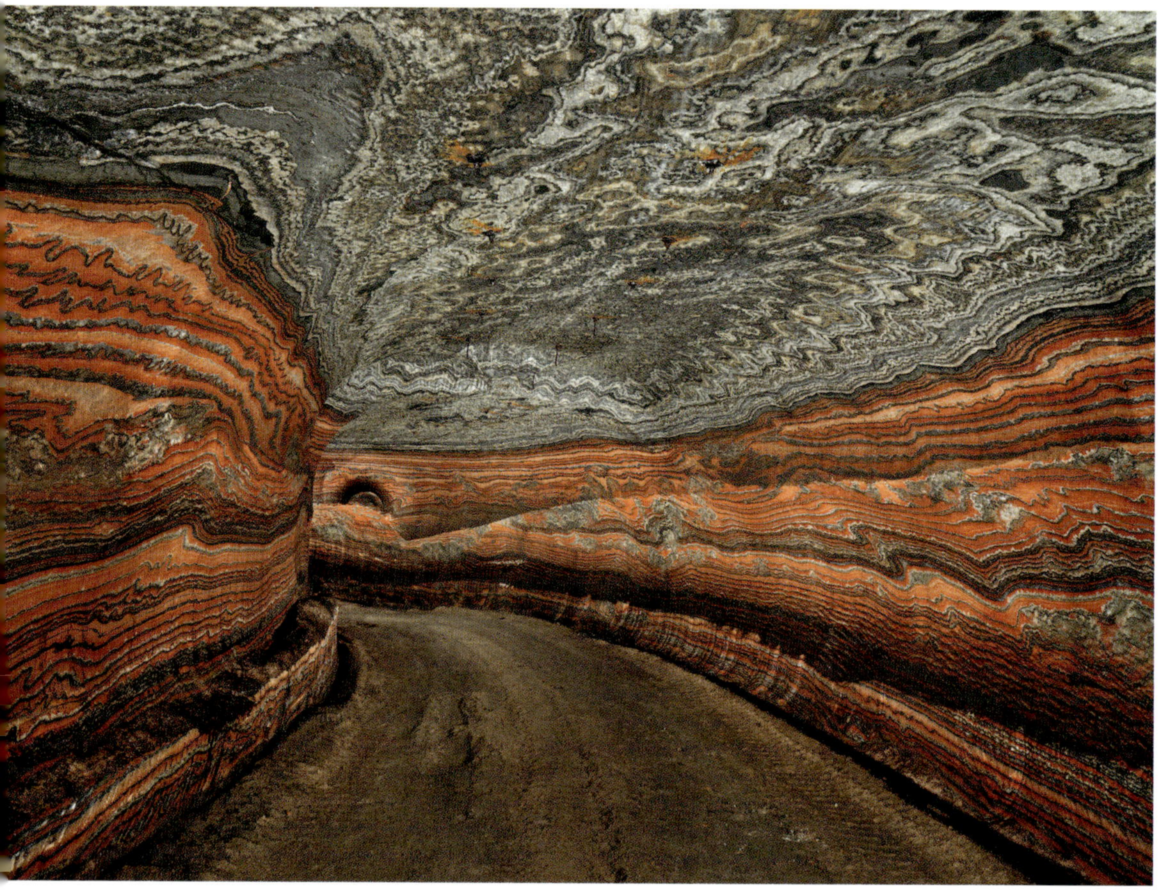

Edward Burtynsky, *Uralkali Potash Mine #2*, Berezniki, Russia, 2017

Like the oil bunkering images, many of the terrains Burtynsky photographed had earth tones and lacked vivid colour contrasts. The Uralkali potash mine in Berezniki was an exception. There are five mines in Berezniki, with a total of 10,000 kilometres of tunnel that exist in total darkness. They can only be navigated with the use of heavy banks of lighting–and, for this reason, they are difficult to photograph. When the tunnels are exposed to light, however, their colours glow, revealing the startling red and grey colours left behind on an ancient sea floor. This lighting gave Burtynsky licence to use highly saturated hues–and he took full advantage of this opportunity photographing a landscape 350 metres underground.

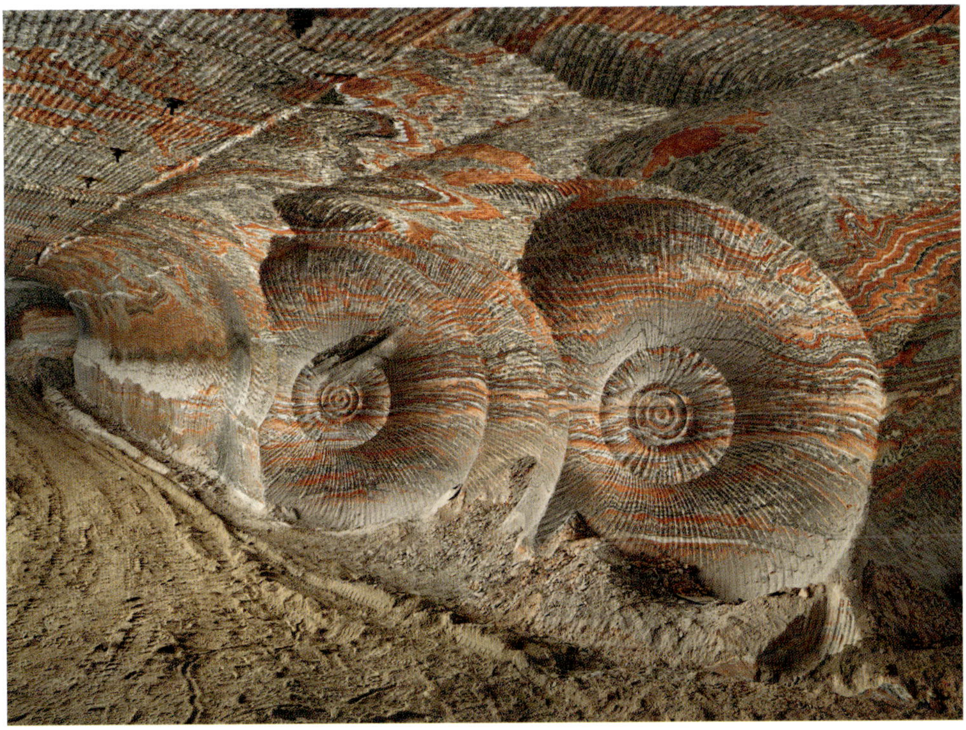

Edward Burtynsky, *Uralkali Potash Mine #4,* Berezniki, Russia, 2017

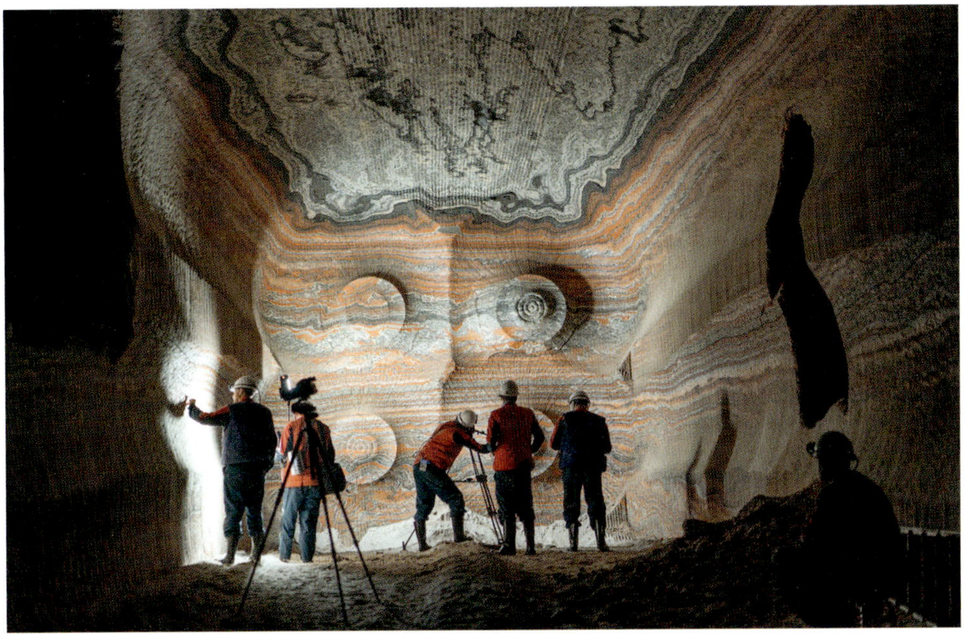

Burtynsky (centre) photographing at Uralkali Potash Mine, 2017. Photograph by Darya Kuznetsova

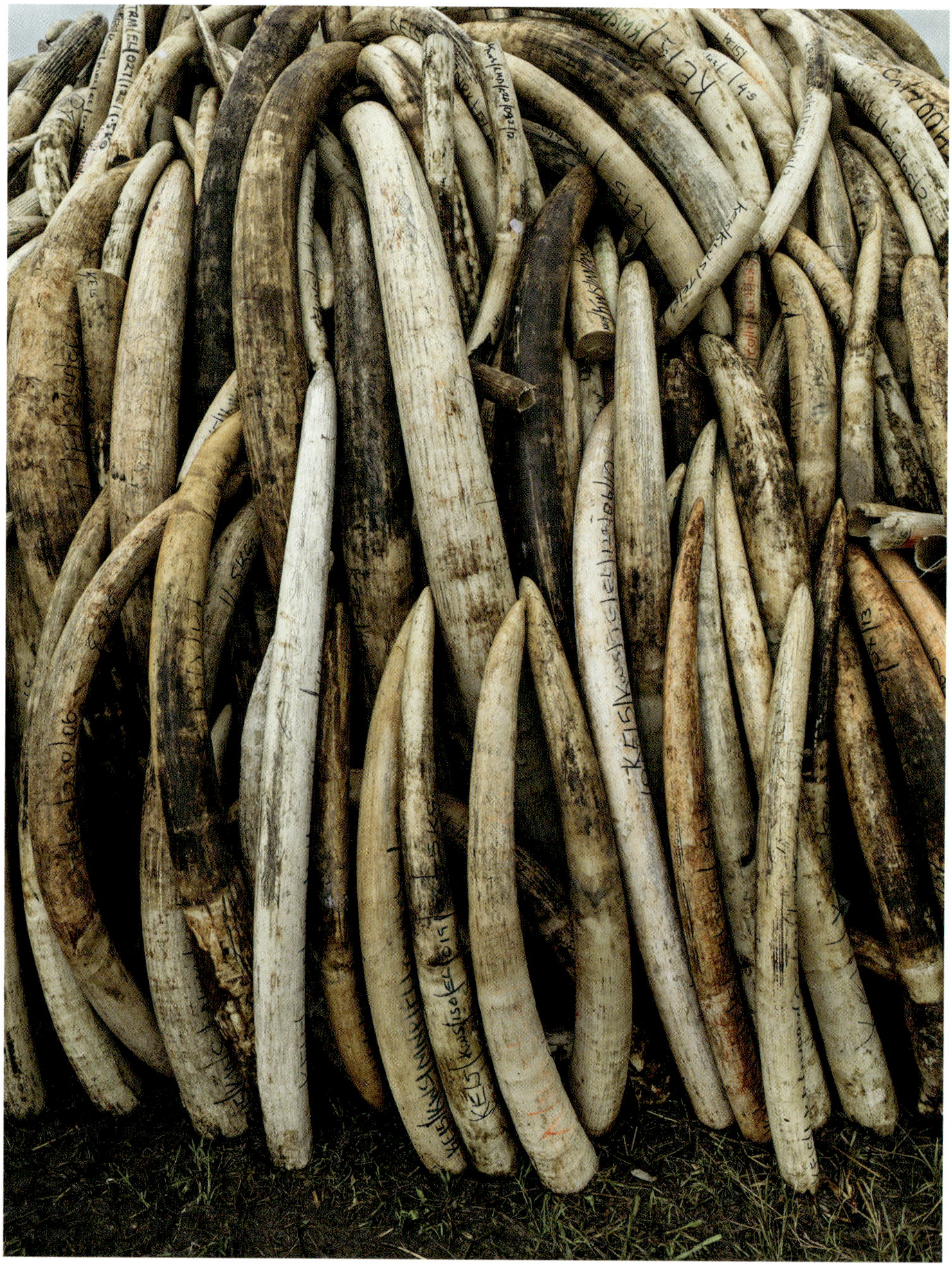

Edward Burtynsky, *Ivory Tusks*, Nairobi, Kenya, April 25, 2018

Except for the *Cerro Dominador Solar Project* in the Atacama Desert, most of the entries in Energy are older images from sites Burtynsky visited between 2007 and 2010. Their presence suggests that even more ways of collecting solar energy are needed if the dominance of fossil fuel is to be overcome.

The vibrant life of the coral in Komodo National Park in Indonesia (see pp. 342-3), contrasted with the threatened rainforests in British Columbia, is the focus of the Biodiversity section. These two places were important to Burtynsky because they brought "into sharper focus some of the wondrous ecosystems that are endangered, the beauty and biodiversity that we are at risk of losing."[14]

Extinction bears witness to the burning of the elephant tusks that begins and ends the documentary. The photograph *Ivory Tusks* shows another side of Burtynsky's skills in a still life that captures all the tonalities in colour and texture of his subject.

The final portion of the book is devoted to Augmented Reality as a potentially useful device for making the experience of the Anthropocene more vivid, especially in museum installations.

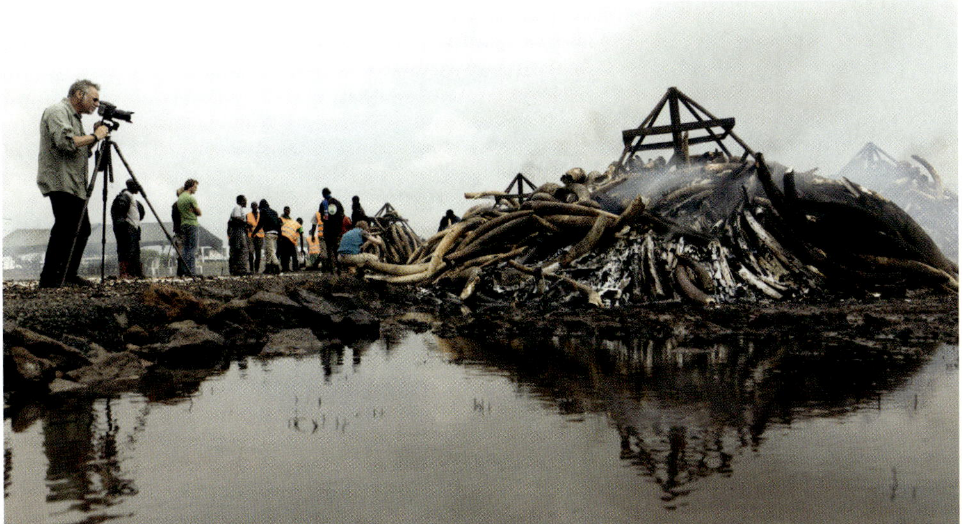

Edward Burtynsky at the Tusk Burning, 2016. Photograph by Jim Panou

The photobook contains a wide array of Burtynsky's best work, whereas the catalogue that goes with the documentary is in large part restricted to images taken between 2015 and 2017. What this catalogue does is bring the film and photobook together by inserting still images taken by Baichwal and de Pencier into the narrative, emphasizing the differences between the photographer and the filmmakers. The photographer searches for the perfect single instant, whereas a filmmaker concentrates on moments where image, movement, and montage are in accord.

In his essay for the photobook and catalogue, de Pencier commented on the centrality of the two media in contemporary society when he observed: "Cameras are a natural evolution of our ability to abstract from reality . . . This unique human capacity for recording abstractions is ultimately the reason the Anthropocene can exist at all."[15] Film and photography, more than other forms of art, *seem* to capture reality and, as a result, they can extract meaning from what they display–they allow their audiences to "abstract" meaning from what is shown.

Baichwal made this point differently: "Burtynsky's photographs take people to places they are connected to or responsible for but would never normally see, and he finds the wide view that communicates them in one frame. Having been with him in these landscapes, I know that isn't easy. Our films . . . try to explain and extend the narratives of place by deepening understanding of context and detail, then reflecting this back to ourselves."[16] As for Burtynsky, he hoped that this project would "bring our audience to an awareness of the normally unseen result of civilization's cumulative impact on the planet."[17]

Yet the tasks of the photographer and the filmmakers can be psychologically disorientating, as de Pencier reflected: "It's hard not to marvel at the engineering ingenuity of the massive industrial sites we filmed, and equally hard to ignore the devastation they represent. . . . The Anthropocene is rife with staggering human folly. Many of the environments we visited were so toxic they elicited a disorientating revulsion and palpable relief when we left."

DETAINED

Many of Burtynsky's trips to various destinations are rigorously planned by his field producer Jim Panou, who uses Google Earth to scout for locations that might interest his boss. Once he has some destinations in mind, Panou meets with Schubert and Burtynsky to review, discuss, and create a short list. Then Panou does further work on how they might gain access to selected sites: what organizations might be welcoming, which might be persuaded through lobbying, and which will do everything in their power to deny them entry.

Once the hurdle of gaining access is cleared, Panou puts the infrastructure for the trip in place: consular services in the places they are to visit; fixers in a chosen area that can assist them if any problems arise; hotel bookings; air bookings; and the often-difficult task of renting planes, helicopters, and, if needed, extra drones. Burtynsky has said of Panou, "He's like an extension of my consciousness."[18]

Despite the considerable abilities of Jim Panou, things did not always go to plan during the filming of *Anthropocene*. On arriving at Norilsk, for example, the Burtynsky group was presented with a bill for $2,500 for "overweight luggage." A further difficulty on the trip was that the sun did not set in Norilsk at that time of year. The good news was that filming went well, but the bad was that Burtynsky could not obtain images that satisfied him. On this particular trip, Burtynsky was sharing the direction of the film with Baichwal and de Pencier; this caused him some anxiety. As he wrote in one of his notebooks, "By and large I have run my own shoots for decades–this [trip] does take some pulling back & sharing how the shoot will flow."[19] He also lamented: "Looking back at the shoot, Norilsk looks like a bust."[20]

Baichwal recalled that at Norilsk she and her crew "were detained and fingerprinted by the Federal Security Bureau for being 'journalists who came into the city under false pretenses' because they approached three women to ask about their lives."[21] Then, 1,800 kilometres south of Norilsk at Berezniki, de Pencier, Panou, assistant Mike Reid, and Burtynsky himself were escorted from the mine, questioned at their hotel, and accused of carrying false passports. The interrogators spoke English but at first pretended not to do so. Eventually, after hours of interrogation, the group was allowed to return to the site for filming.

The visit to the island of Komodo went smoothly, however, and Burtynsky reflected that "[t]he idea is that in the Anthropocene we need to preserve habitat and diversity and to me nothing expresses this better than the beauty of the coral reefs there."[22]

Most impediments were foreseen. Some were not. And, sometimes, there was overkill. When Burtynsky and Panou arrived at Lagos's Murtala Muhammed International Airport, two SUVs were waiting for them. A *New Yorker* article later described the scene: "Each vehicle came with an off-duty police officer (who remained at all times uniformed and armed), and, for assignments of potentially heightened danger, Panou had brought in a team from the State Security Service–a domestic intelligence agency with a portfolio that includes guarding the President. Amused, Burtynsky called the men 'my army.'"[23]

In the Niger River Delta, there was the considerable risk that men on the ground might fire at a helicopter 450 feet above them. Nonplussed, Panou told his boss: "On the water there's much more sheen than the other days. Pay attention to that aspect in your shooting."

Later on the same trip while filming at Makoko, a shantytown propped up on stilts, a group of residents climbed aboard Burtynsky's catamaran. It was Burtynsky, rather than Panou, who took matters in hand "by inviting one of the *baales* [leaders] to look at his work on a laptop. Scrolling through images, he explained, 'I am a painter, but I use a camera–and I don't speak badly [of others].' The *baale* watched, unmoved. Speaking badly was not the point, it turned out. The issue was primarily one of respect, a Yoruba-speaking member of Burtynsky's crew explained. With further discussion (and some cash), respect was communicated, the deck cleared, and shooting commenced."[24]

ESSENTIAL ELEMENTS

In 2016, during the midst of the *Anthropocene* project, the book *Edward Burtynsky: Essential Elements*, by William A. Ewing, was published. It contains a sensitive, expository essay, "A Conflict of Its Elements," about Burtynsky's career up to 2013:

> For several decades the photographer has been providing a constant stream of compelling proof: from vast piles of abandoned tyres to blasted rock faces that strip the vegetation off entire mountains, to tracts of land denuded of flora and fauna and criss-crossed by rivers of waste, Burtynsky has been demonstrating just how profoundly we are altering the face and body of our planet. That he manages to delight the eye, while simultaneously planting seeds of doubt, is a sign of his consummate skill as an artist.[25]

Out of 175 photographs in the book, 140 photographs display the photographer's career from 2000; the other 35 cover the years from 1985 to 1999. The plates are divided into five sections and are arranged to highlight effective contrasts and comparisons. Ewing "constructed the pairings with care, highlighting intriguing similarities and differences, and raising what I consider significant questions. What is shared by his mines and museums, his oil fields and rice terraces . . . The cliché has it that oil and water don't mix, but in Burtynsky's universe they decidedly do."[26]

There are four sections of passages that contain excerpts from writings by Burtynsky and commentators such as Michael Mitchell, Marc Mayer, and Mark Kingwell. In the afterword, "Unearthing Photography," Joshua Schuster writes about the "enigmatic quality" of Burtynsky's images: "With every Burtynsky photograph, the viewer is caught between a desire to fix and a desire to look. The dilemma can be frustrating because, on being presented with devastation, we want to be told how to change it all. Yet stirring our imagination and provoking our creative capacities is more important than offering moral directives."[27] In his next project, Burtynsky determined to provoke his audience's creative capacities by altering the deep-seated, often incorrect ways the West pictured Africa.

(2015–2019)

15 OUT OF AFRICA

"My interest in Africa," Burtynsky observed,

> owes its genesis to an earlier body of work that I produced about China back in 2004. For that project, and while researching several topics including the Three Gorges Dam, urban renewal, and recycling, I learned how the new Chinese factories were being created. At the time, heavy machinery was literally being unbolted from concrete floors in Europe and North America, then shipped and refastened to the floors of gigantic facilities in China. This represented a paradigm shift [in] industry, and it seemed obvious that China was rapidly becoming a leading manufacturer for the world. I realized even then that the African continent was poised to become the next, perhaps even the last, territory for major industrial expansion.[1]

On April 14, 2019, he confided to his journal, "I have been searching for visual moments showing China and its involvement in Africa by looking at projects they are doing in various countries." He added: "I have also been looking at the splendor of the landscape when it presents itself."[2]

African Studies is, as Burtynsky emphasized, a sequel to *China*, especially in its examination of China's attempt to impose economic enslavement on nations that had previously been exploited by Western countries. This collection of photographs goes well beyond that topic, however, to demonstrate how Africans themselves have polluted and destroyed their own environment. In looking at Africa, Burtynsky also established clear parallels between that continent and many of the issues he had treated elsewhere: for instance, greenhouses, salt pans, highways, tailings, coal mines, and dams. To that list, he added a new subject: refugee camps. Refocusing on topics he had explored elsewhere also further unleashed the photographer's fascination with abstraction–and to discover new ways to frame his images.

He found drone photography essential to this new venture: "Most of the subjects photographed for this project were taken from fixed-wing aircraft, helicopters, and drones. As such there is a continuity from where the *Anthropocene* project left off. Seeing the landscape from lofty perspectives reveals the design, structure, and scale of the marks we inscribe on the surface of the earth–the extraordinary vistas not visible from ground level. Making use of drones to position my camera in the middle distance, at altitudes where conventional aircraft are forbidden, allows me to situate the viewpoint so as to optimize the rendering of very fine detail in the scene below."[3] Drones, he emphasized, added "real value to my practice. Mike Reid flies the drone and I bark out my corrections from the side–it works."[4]

Using this approach, Burtynsky portrayed Africa in a way that was very different from the Western perspective that had previously dominated its representation. As Nigerian art curator Azu Nwagbogu has argued, "Burtynsky's photographs illustrate a corrective mode of the visual depiction of Africa and Africans in Western imagery. In contrast to the overt and primary exploitation of human beings as the exotic 'other' and stereotyped images of flora and fauna, which have been the staples of Africa in the Western canon, Burtynsky's slant challenges the traditional Western-centric approach. By way of images showing industrial landscapes in which humans and flora and fauna take a back seat, Burtynsky's work highlights the changing representation of Africa as expressed through photographic books and exhibitions."[5]

This new project required extensive travel. Burtynsky and Panou journeyed to Ethiopia in April 2018, South Africa in August 2018, Namibia in December 2019, Senegal and Botswana in April 2019, and Madagascar and Ethiopia in October 2019. The photographs for *African Studies* were taken during those trips but earlier images of bunkering and logging in Nigeria and of the Dandora site in Kenya–part of the *Anthropocene* project–were also included.

By shunning the condescending approach inherent in the treatment of Africa and Africans as the exotic "other," Burtynsky offered a clear-headed view of the perils facing the sub-Sahara while emphasizing the inherent beauty of its terrains. He wrote:

> Flying over Kenya in 2015 afforded me an aerial view of the Rift Valley landscapes, and there I was struck by the extraordinary range of colour palette and glowing, sumptuous tones. Seeing that primordial landscape early into the project inspired another thread of exploration–a series about Africa's untouched landscapes.

In such places he was able to get "a handful of magical images that remind me of looking up into the night sky and pondering the cosmos." This adds to my natural landscapes of Africa series, which is really becoming the largest chapter of the project.[6]

Those landscapes, which open the book, include the Tsaus Mountains and the Skeleton Coast in Namibia. For Burtynsky, they were "a visual feast."[7] The Tsaus mountain range, located in a desert area within the Diamond Restricted Area (a diamond mining zone), extends over 121 square kilometres and reaches a height of over 1,100 metres.

In *Tsaus Mountains #3*, the camera captured the mountains' horizontally layered structures in a wide variety of browns, rising to a final layer lighter in colour. The formations revealed in the rapidly moving sand call to mind the bleached whale bones and shipwrecks that give the Skeleton Coast its name.

The discharge from saline hot springs in *Lake Logipi #2* in Kenya's Rift Valley resembles that of *Xiaolangdi Dam #3* from six years before, although the colours here are more saturated.

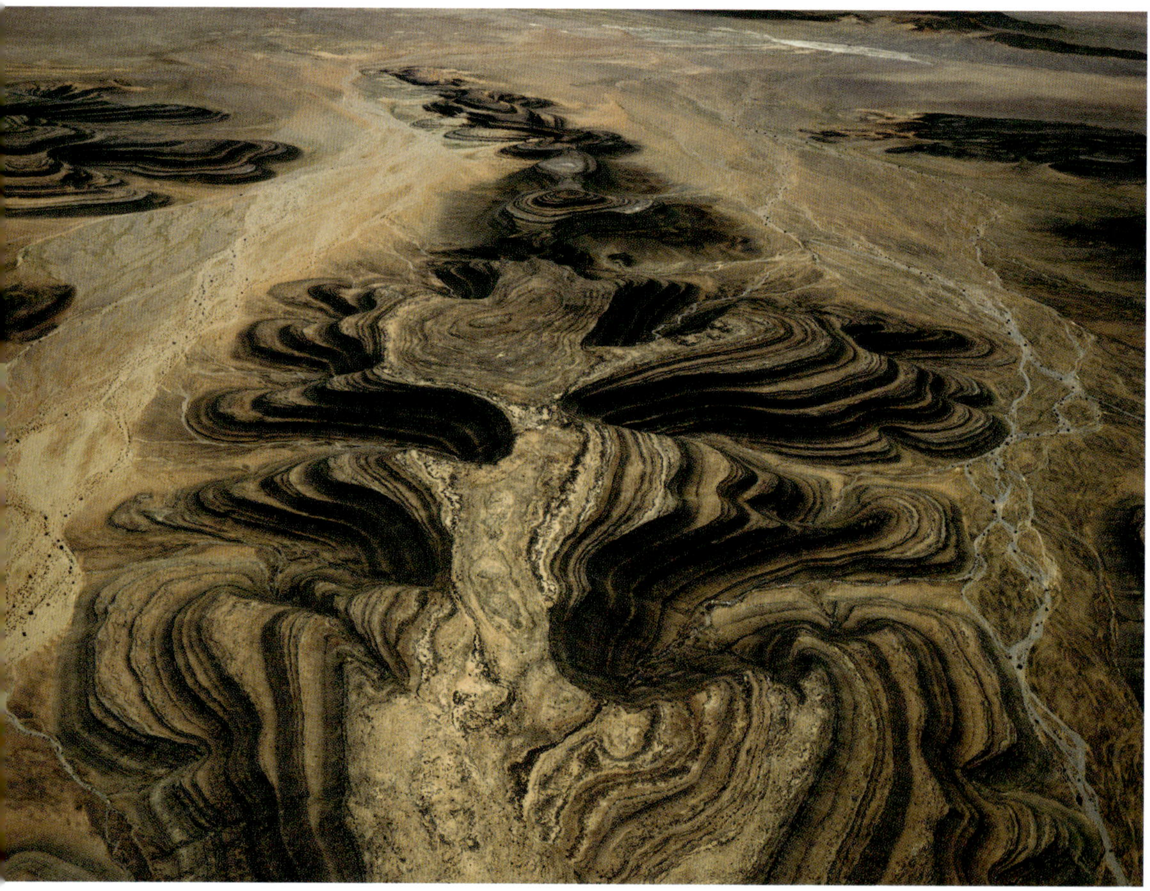

Edward Burtynsky, *Tsaus Mountains #3*, Sperrgebiet, Namibia, 2018

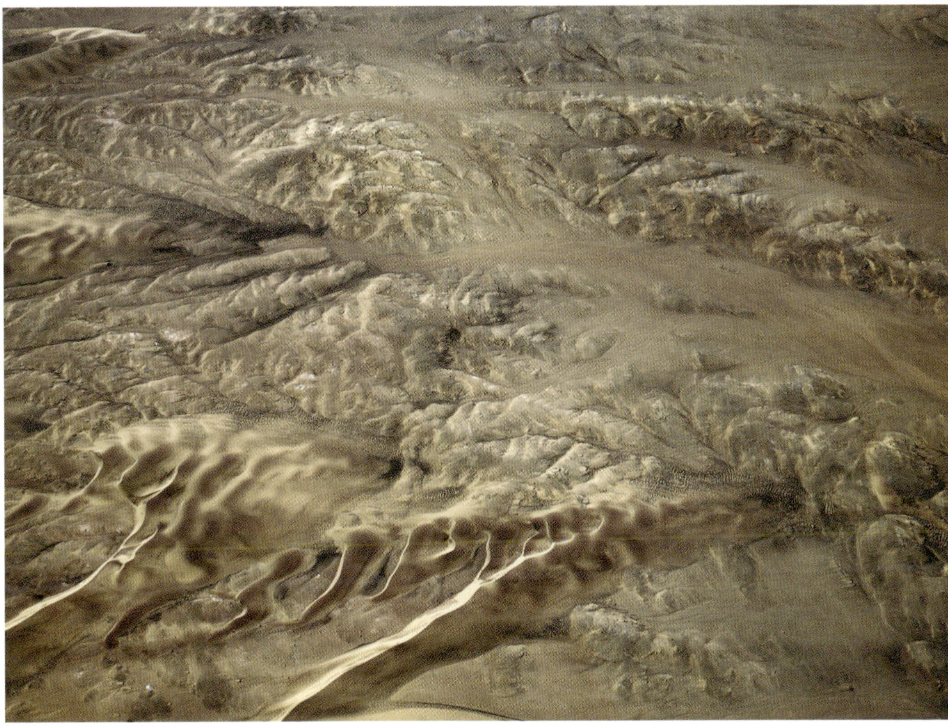

Edward Burtynsky, *Sand Dunes #2*, Skeleton Coast, Namibia, 2018

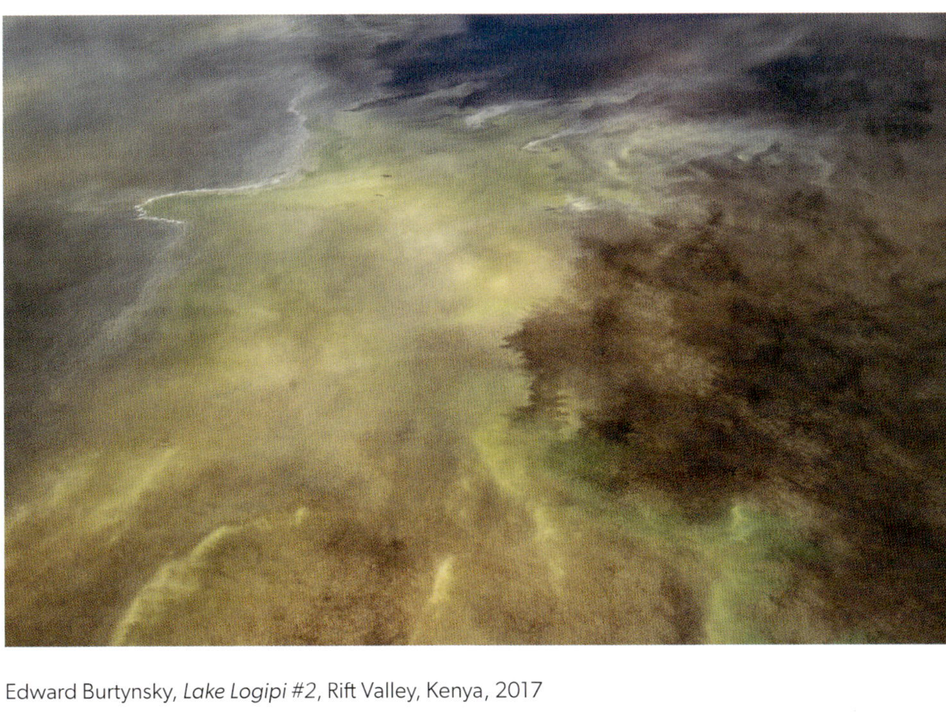

Edward Burtynsky, *Lake Logipi #2*, Rift Valley, Kenya, 2017

As Burtynsky recalled, the Danakil Depression in Ethiopia–an area 200 × 50 kilometres in size–was a huge challenge, as can be seen in *Sulfur Springs #2*: "All our drone equipment wasn't working because we were 400 feet below sea level. So, the drone GPS was saying: 'You're not supposed to be here. You're at the bottom of the ocean.' The heat was unbearable." In addition, "getting to [the sulfur springs at Daillol] required that we carry our heavy equipment while climbing rocks for about 1.5 km."[8]

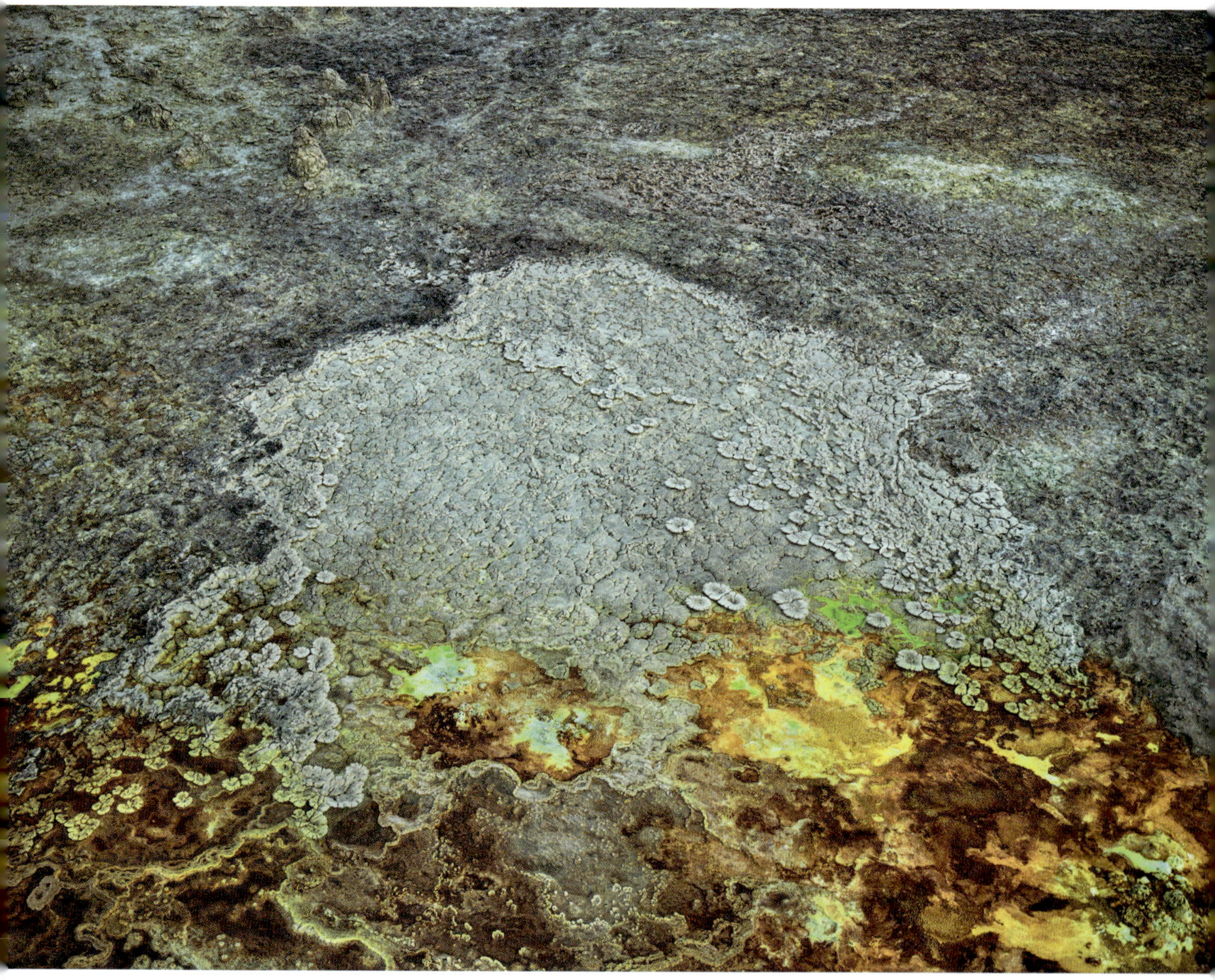

Edward Burtynsky, *Sulfur Springs #2*, Dallol, Danakil Depression, Ethiopia, 2018

Of the new book's Extraction images, *Salt Pans #32,* taken in Namibia, resembles the same subject in Gujarat, which had led to the most concentrated series of abstract images in the photographer's career (see p. 250). However, in the photographs at the *Salt Ponds #4* near Fatick in Senegal, Burtynsky uncovered a different type of abstraction in the area's white, grey, yellow, and brown rectangular shapes. The colour variations he found are created when salt water evaporates and the different

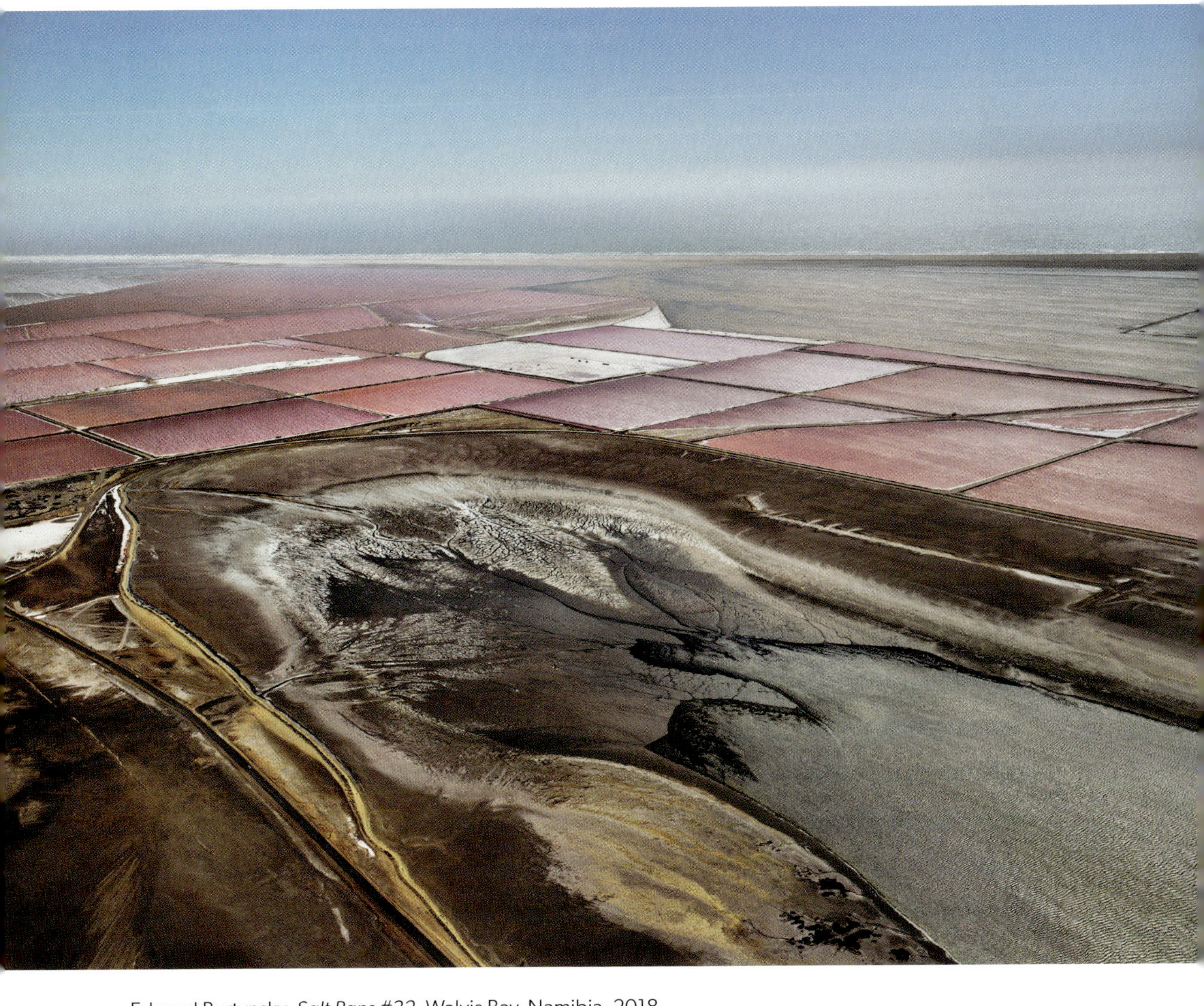

Edward Burtynsky, *Salt Pans #32*, Walvis Bay, Namibia, 2018

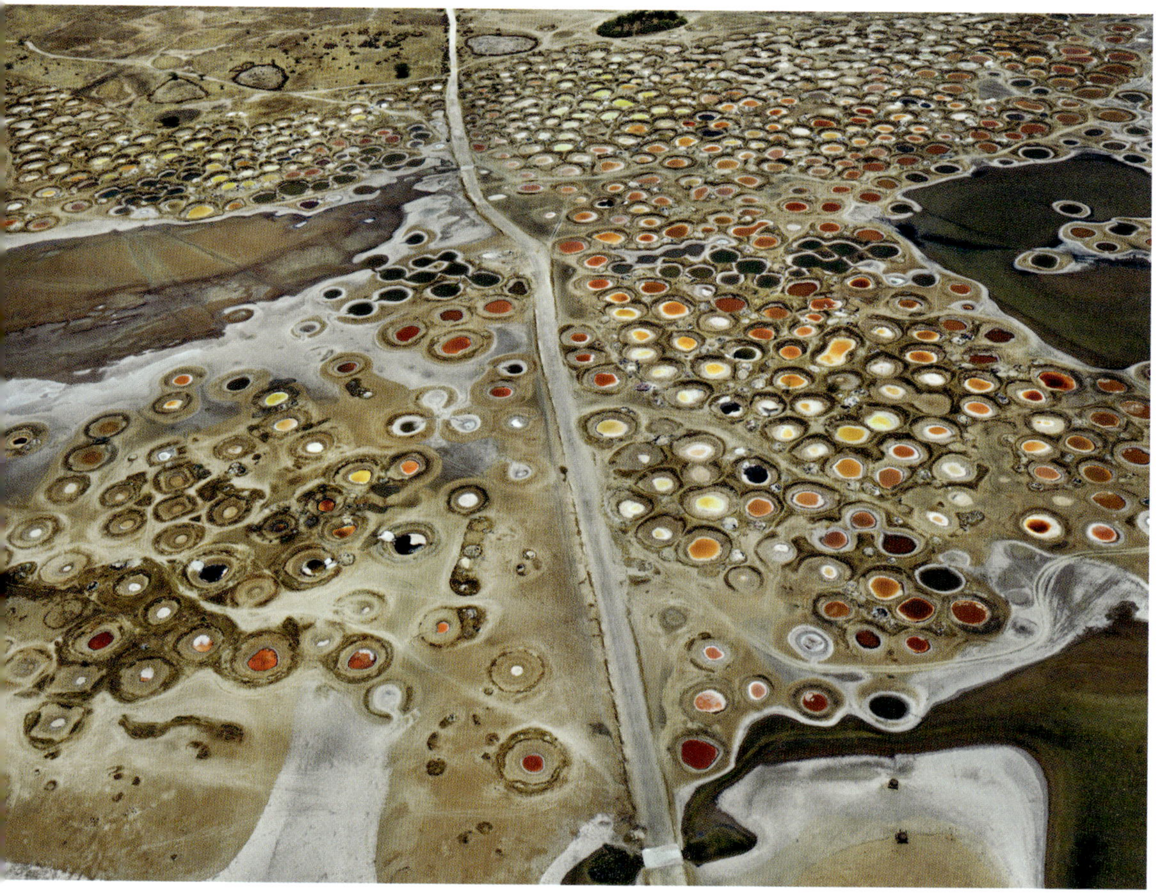

Edward Burtynsky, *Salt Ponds #4*, near Naglou Sam Sam, Senegal, 2019

kinds of microorganisms inhabiting the man-made depressions reveal themselves.

Burtynsky recalled, "Near Fatick, small-scale harvesters dig shallow depressions by hand which are then filled with salt water from nearby canals. Once the water has evaporated and the remaining salt is cleared away or piled up by workers, minerals, pigments, and various algae combine with reflections of the sky to create a spectacle for the eye. Seeing these landscapes from a bird's-eye view is breathtaking–their intricate, organic structures become almost hypnotic."[9]

The Magadi Soda Company has been in operation at Lake Magadi, a shallow soda lake in Kenya, since 1924, but its expansion had been bitterly

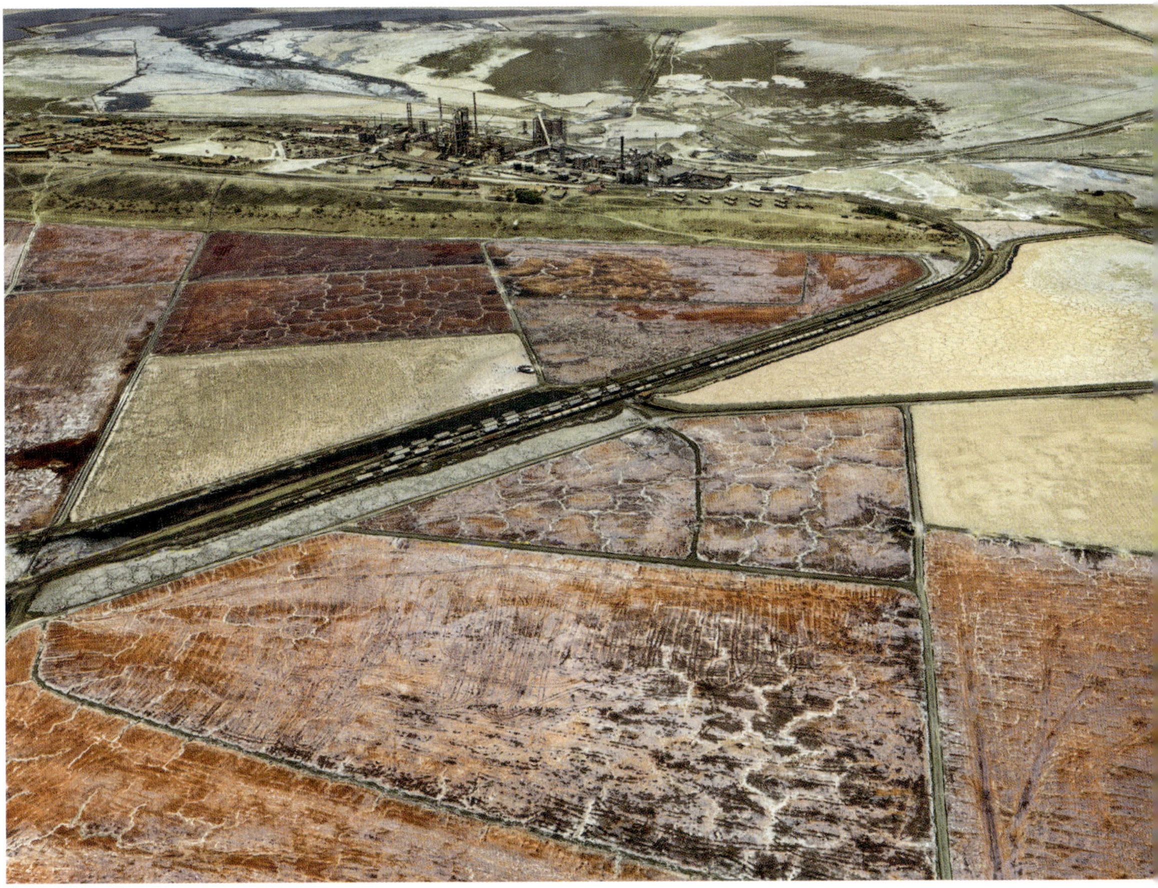

Edward Burtynsky, *Magadi Soda Company #1*, Lake Magadi, Kenya, 2007

opposed by the Maasai whose land was being taken over. Also, the workers there had been at loggerheads over the harsh working conditions. The pink and brown salt pans in *Magadi Soda Company #1* occupy most of the picture area while the factory–the centre of oppression–sits menacingly at the top.

Tailings ponds had long been a Burtynsky specialty, but he found even more compelling ways of capturing this subject in *Tailings Pond #3* at the Orapa Mine in Botswana and *Tailings Pond #1* at the Wesselton Diamond Mine in South Africa. In both images, the conveyor belts carrying tailings to the waste ponds look like stems, and the ponds are transformed into sinister, flower-like compositions. The evenly placed *Blasting Holes #1*

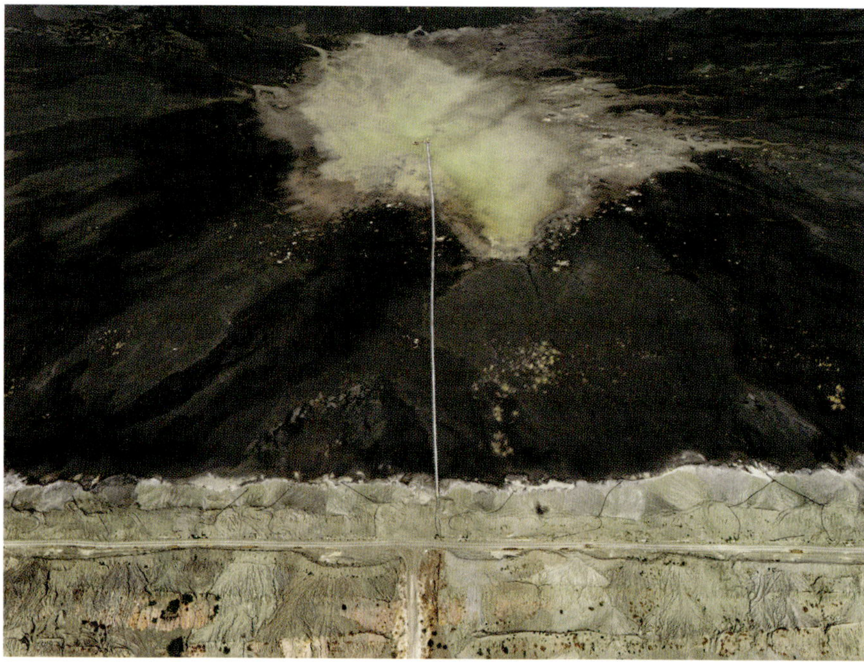

Edward Burtynsky, *Tailings Pond #3*, Orapa Diamond Mine, Botswana, 2019

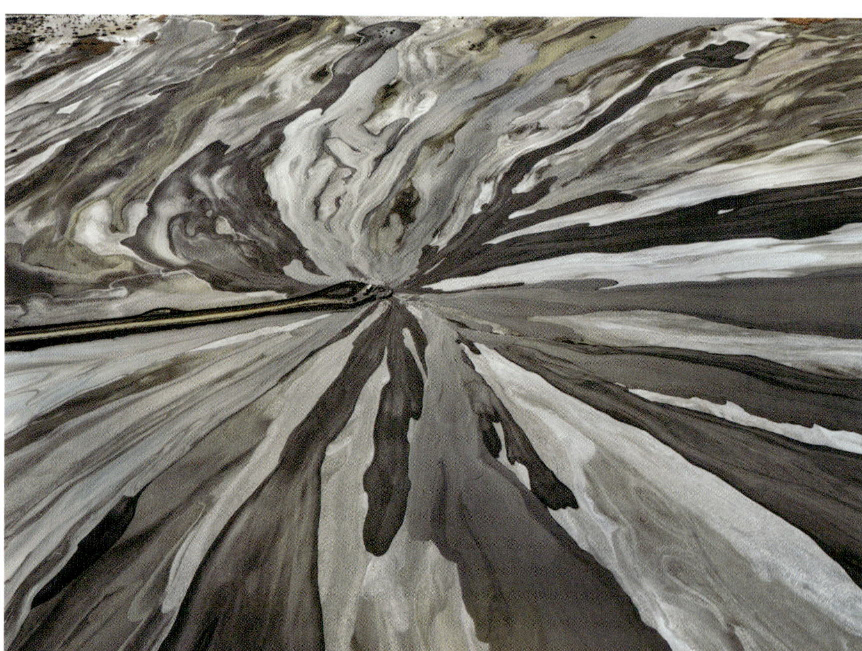

Edward Burtynsky, *Tailings Pond #1*, Wesselton Diamond Mine, Kimberley, Northern Cape, South Africa, 2018

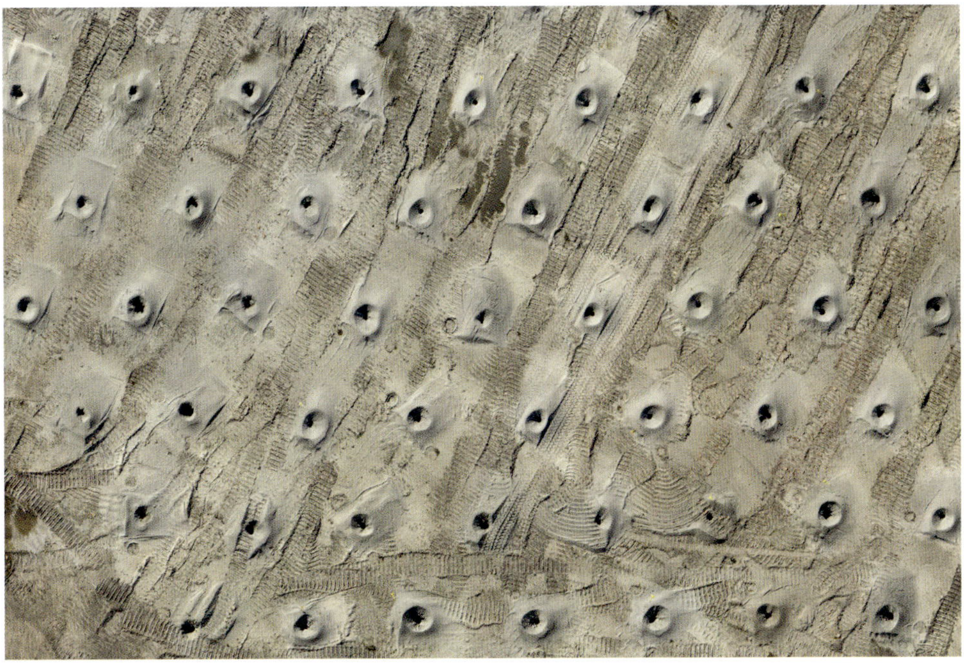

Edward Burtynsky, *Blasting Holes #1*, Orapa Diamond Mine, Botswana, 2019

at the Orapa Diamond Mine, about to be filled with dynamite, create an abstract composition in various shades of grey.

Ten oil bunkering images from 2016 are in the section of the book devoted to extraction, and are placed just before four images taken at the Sishen Iron Ore Mine in Kathu, South Africa. *Uranium Tailings #13*, shot in Namibia, surpasses in intensity Burtynsky's much earlier images of the same subject taken at Elliot Lake (see p. 113).

Futility is the subtext of the next set of photographs, which document artisanal sapphire mining near the town of Sakaraha in southeastern Madagascar, the source of about half of the high-quality specimens of this gem worldwide. The drought and starvation in this area have driven farmers to settle there. The arduous work of mining sapphires, involving hand-digging in deep pits, is usually unrewarded because most of the gems exist under the water table and the would-be miners do not have access to pumps strong enough to search there. Despite these odds, the men band together to overcome obstacles and eventually unearth the precious jewels.

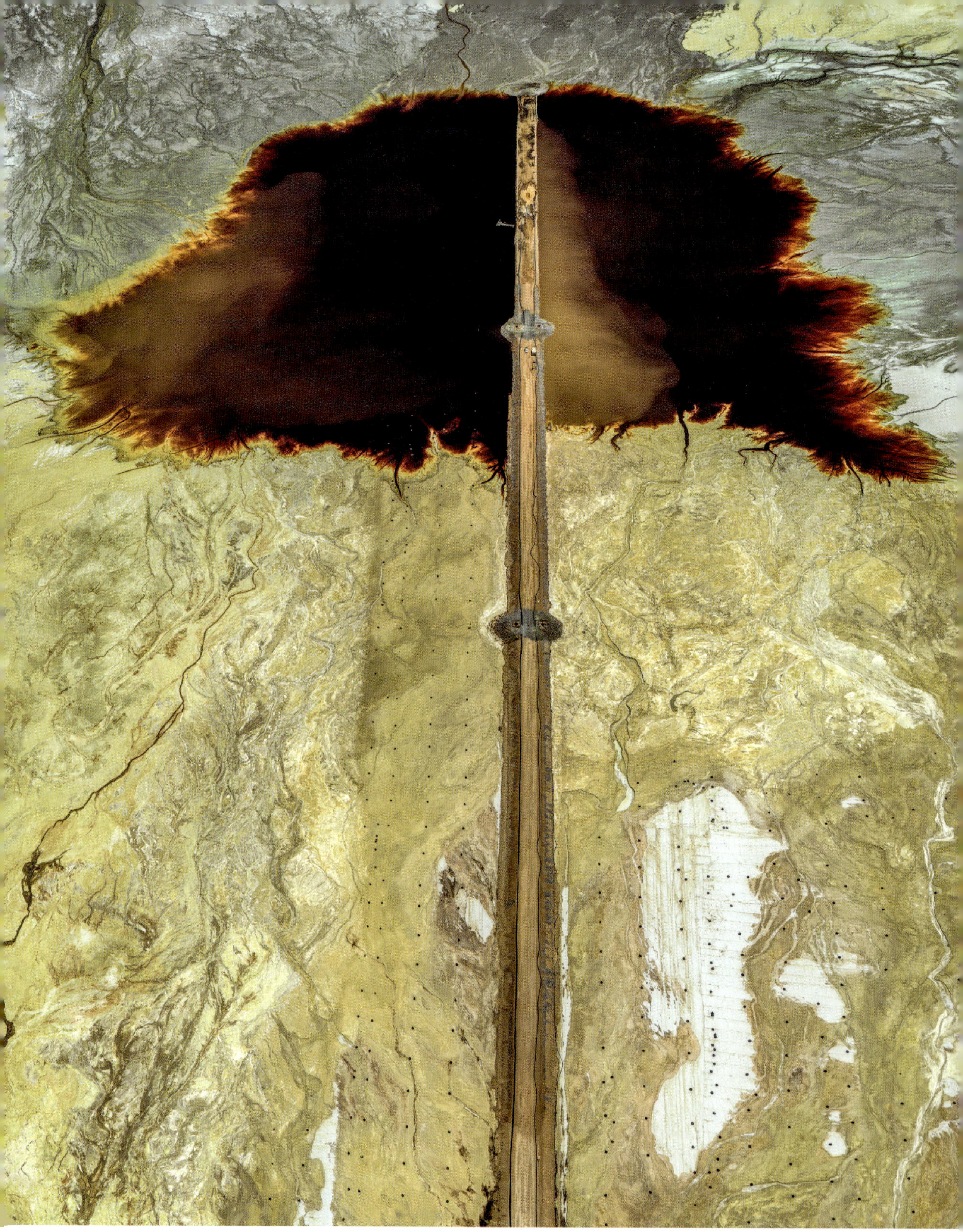

Edward Burtynsky, *Uranium Tailings #13*, Husab Uranium Mine, Namibia, 2018

Since excavators are not available, the workers have to form conveyor belts themselves to carry their finds from the pits to dry land. In *Sapphire Mining Settlement #1*, Burtynsky added a new element to his work when he showed–in astounding detail–how various members of this community work the unprotected pits.

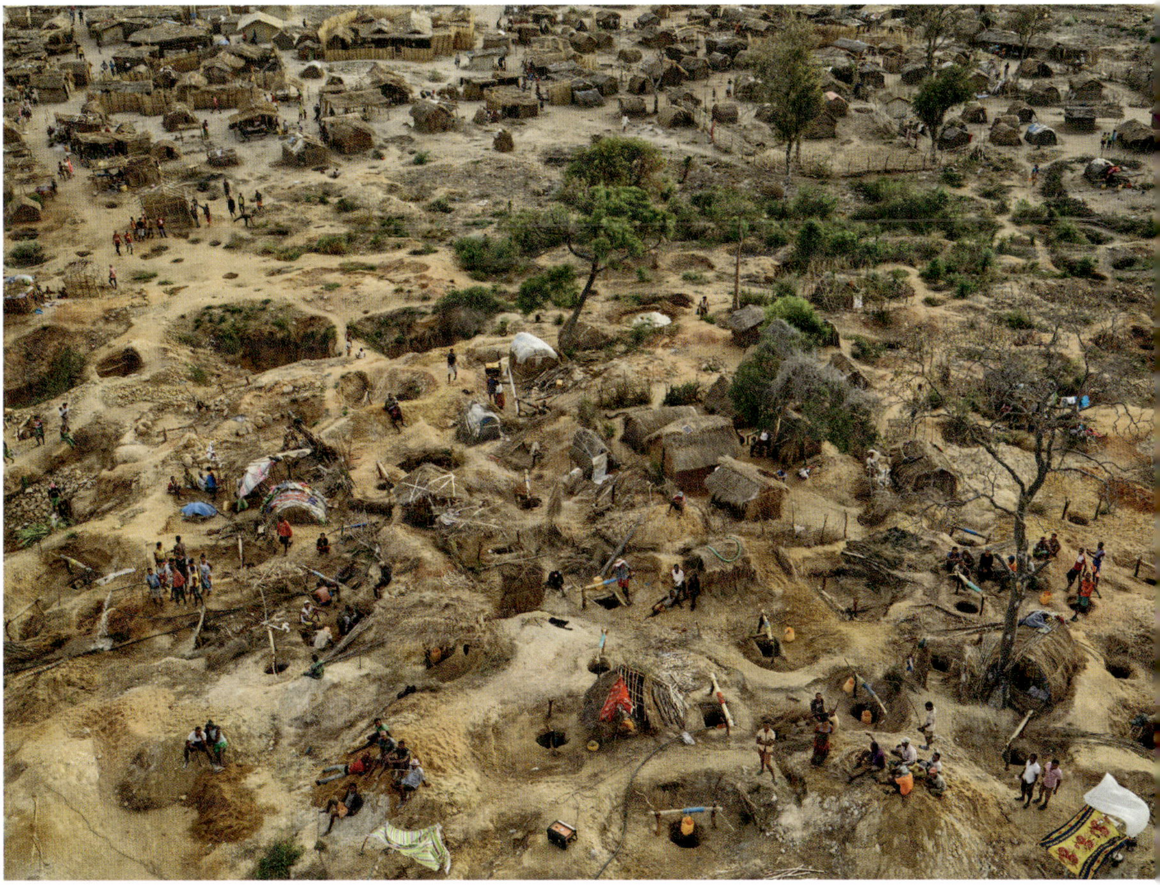

Edward Burtynsky, *Sapphire Mining Settlement #2*, Sakaraha, Madagascar, 2019

Pivot irrigation images, as employed in South Africa, are grouped under the heading of Agriculture. Under the same heading are the mysterious-looking desert spirals at Verneukpan in the Northern Cape region of South Africa, which allowed Burtynsky to create startling images of uncanny incursions into the earth. These patterns are actually a way of reclaiming the desert: as a friend once described to Jim Panou, "some farmers in arid areas sometimes use a plow to dig spirals to trap rainwater. It is not a common practice, hence the apparent mystery. The spirals encourage the water to sit in the furrows instead of running off or evaporating quickly. This way, the water is trapped and more likely to seep into the earth, feeding the water table and

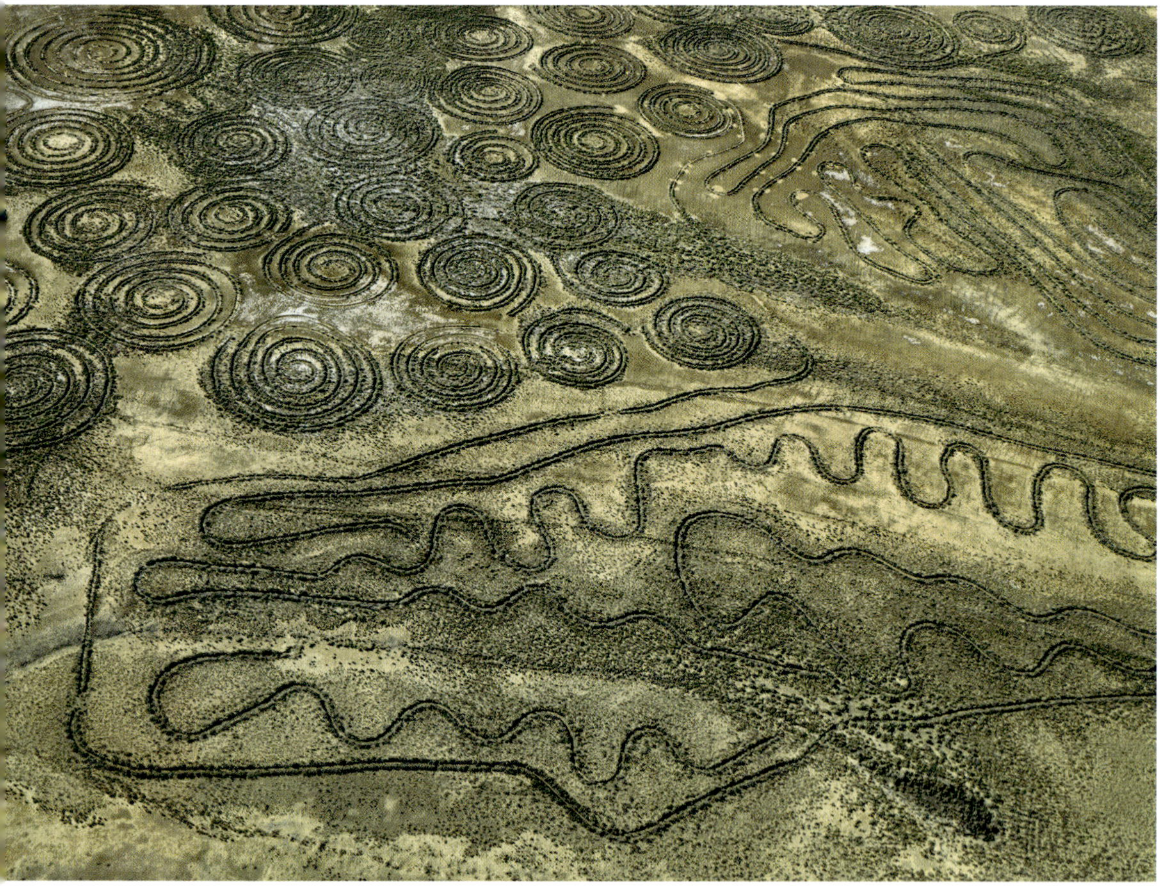

Edward Burtynsky, *Desert Spirals #4*, Verneukpan, Northern Cape, South Africa, 2018

encouraging the growth of plants for grazing. The tractors used to drag the plows that cut the furrows don't leave any major impression, making the furrows appear to have been created by some other mysterious force or power."[10] From an aerial perspective, however, they resemble the work of primeval artists–and appear even more uncanny.

The images in the sections Settlements and Urbanization depict the burden of overcrowding, and return to the sawmills at Lagos and the Dandora landfill site in Kenya as seen in *Anthropocene*. An image such as *Refugee Camp #1*, however, is overpowering and chillingly illustrates the idea that the world is overcrowded and that many people simply have nowhere to go.

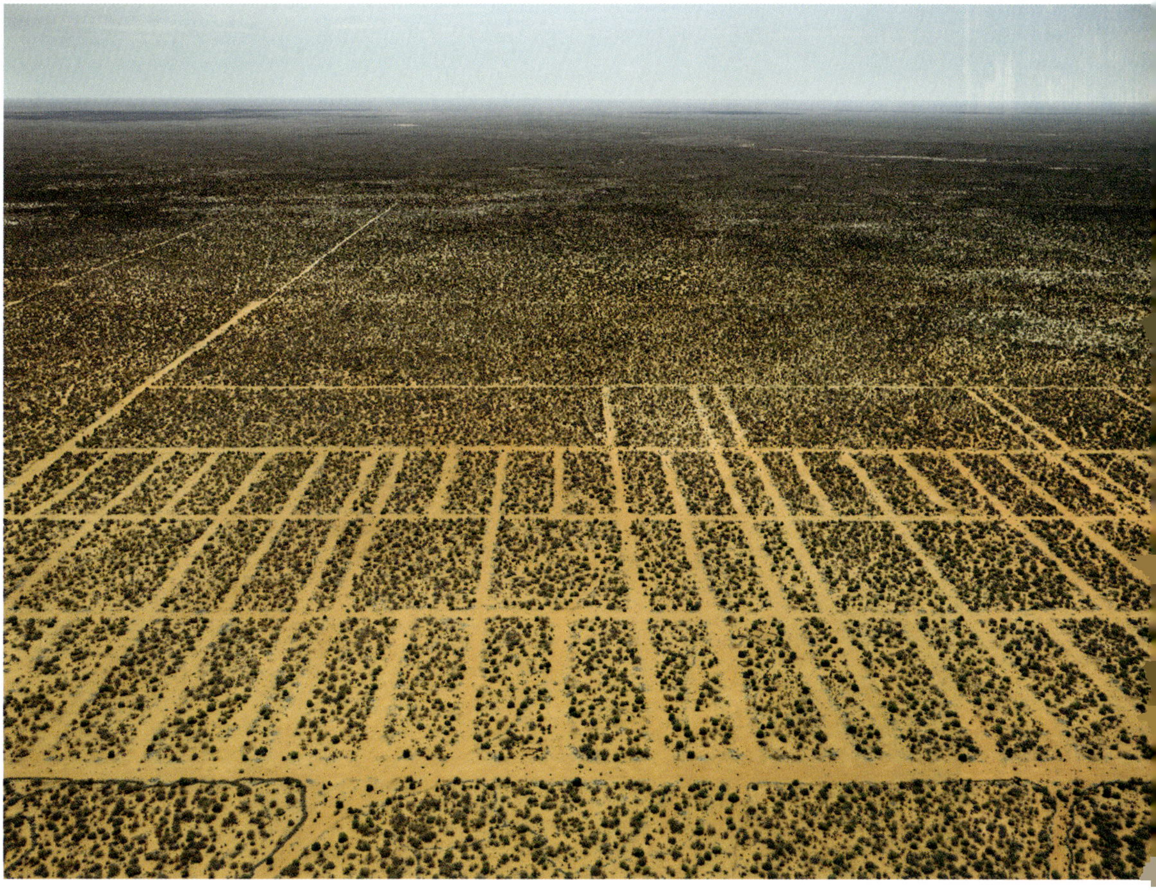

Edward Burtynsky, *Refugee Camp #1*, Hagadera, North Eastern Province, Kenya, 2017

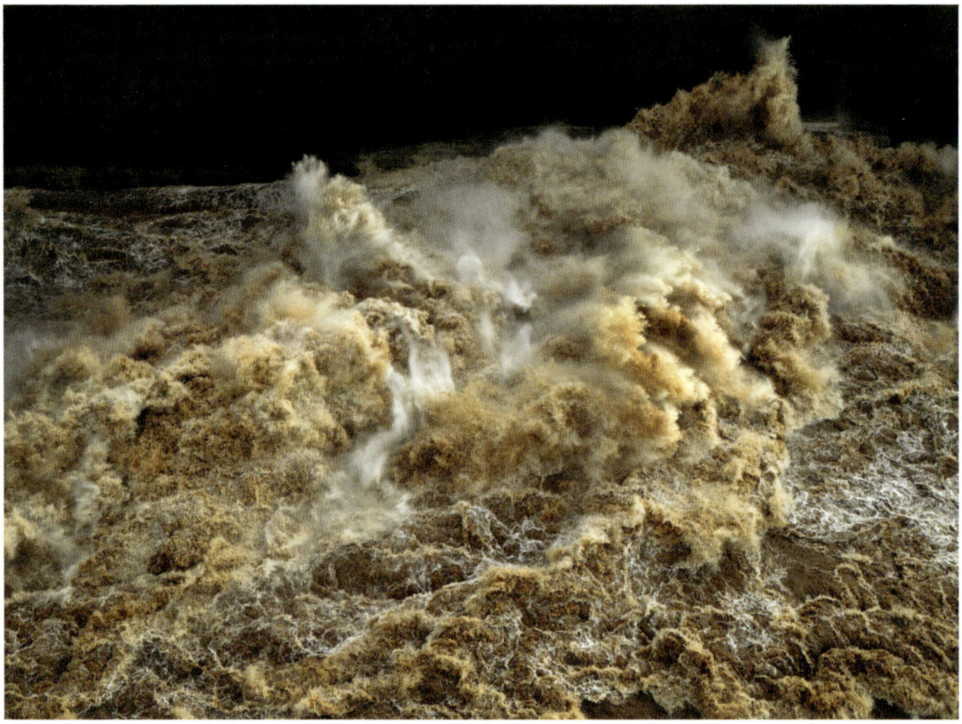

Edward Burtynsky, *GERD #7*, Benishangul-Gumuz Region, Ethiopia, 2019

Photographs of the Grand Ethiopian Renaissance Dam (GERD) come next. An image such as *GERD #7* is reminiscent of *Xiaolangdi Dam #2* (see p. 242) and segues into the section titled "China in Africa," where manufacturing factories in Senegal and Ethiopia are shown to be eerily like those seen in the *China* project.

China offers Africa huge trade-offs. As Burtynsky sees it, China will build infrastructure "in exchange for access to resources whether it's farmland for food security, whether it's oil . . . It's like economic colonialism. I don't think they want full control of these countries. They want an economic advantage, they want the resources, and they want the opportunity those resources provide."[11]

The factory photographs in *African Studies* look like reenactments of the same subjects in China. The sad truth is that they are the new reality. Some of the new manufacturing images, Burtynsky recalled, "were taken in Hawassa, which is a 350-acre Special Economic Zone, like Shenzhen in China. The Chinese built what they call sheds, which are more like warehouses . . . So, you can look at that picture–with the roadways, with the lighting, with the plumbing, with everything. All done, start to finish . . . all the structures were brought in by ship and then by rail into Ethiopia and erected like a Meccano set. And when I was there, they were filling these sheds with sewing machines and textile makers. All built in one year!"

Burtynsky also reflected on the reasons for the creation of these factories in Ethiopia. "China is heavily polluted–especially its water. The labour force is rebelling against low wages. The answer is to train young girls in Africa to do work no longer tenable in China. That's their goal. And they're training these young 16, 17-year-olds, taking them away from their families and then putting them right into the sewing-machine sweatshop."[12]

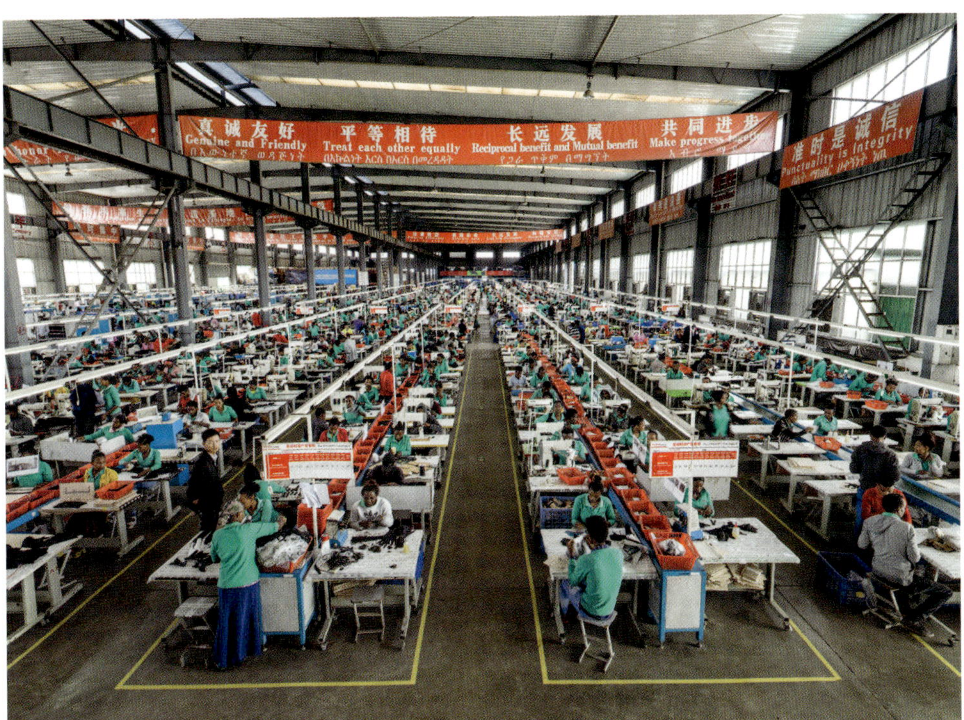

Edward Burtynsky, *Huajian Shoe Factory #1*, Dukem, Ethiopia, 2018

Although Burtynsky tellingly illustrates China's intrusion into Africa, his attraction to the vibrancy of the continent is this portfolio's greatest strength. In *Collector Daily*, Loring Knoblauch was drawn to the photographer's skillful use of colour gradation throughout:

> Deep greens cover the tea plantations of Kenya, while softer reds and pinks emerge from the iron mines of South Africa and the salt flats of Botswana. In other works, warm sun-baked orange dominates his scenes of deserts in Namibia, and there's even some shiny gold to be found, on the edges of a platform amid an image of a tailings pond in South Africa. And when the colours are somewhat less vibrant, settling into ranges of earthy yellows, beiges, and browns, Burtynsky then pulls bolder pattern forward, in the bars and spots of salt ponds in Senegal, the gestural curves of roadways at iron ore mines in South Africa, and the swirls of dune tops in Namibia.[13]

The landscapes in Burtynsky's new book in particular appealed to the writer and photo editor Ellyn Kail: "Looking at [the] abstract landforms and rich, glowing colours is not unlike stepping back in time and witnessing the world as it might have been before we intervened. It's a stunning and haunting reminder of what the continent stands to lose."[14]

For Burtynsky, his new portfolio ultimately became about "this juxtaposition between [the] wild landscape and these very synthetic landscapes that humans have created."[15] Of course, even more man-made landscapes, he is suggesting, are in the process of being fashioned with the discovery of oil in Tanzania and northern Kenya.

China was a narrative of a country in the process of achieving superstar status–and the often-unsavoury means it had taken to do so. *African Studies* is the gruesome story of a continent trampled on in the past by European nations and now in the process of being desecrated by China.

In this grim story, many beautiful landscapes remain–perhaps ripe for exploitation.

In Conrad's *Heart of Darkness*, greed is shown to be at the heart of the colonial enterprise. The same truth holds today. The last image in *African Studies* is of a desolate road winding its way through a dry landscape.

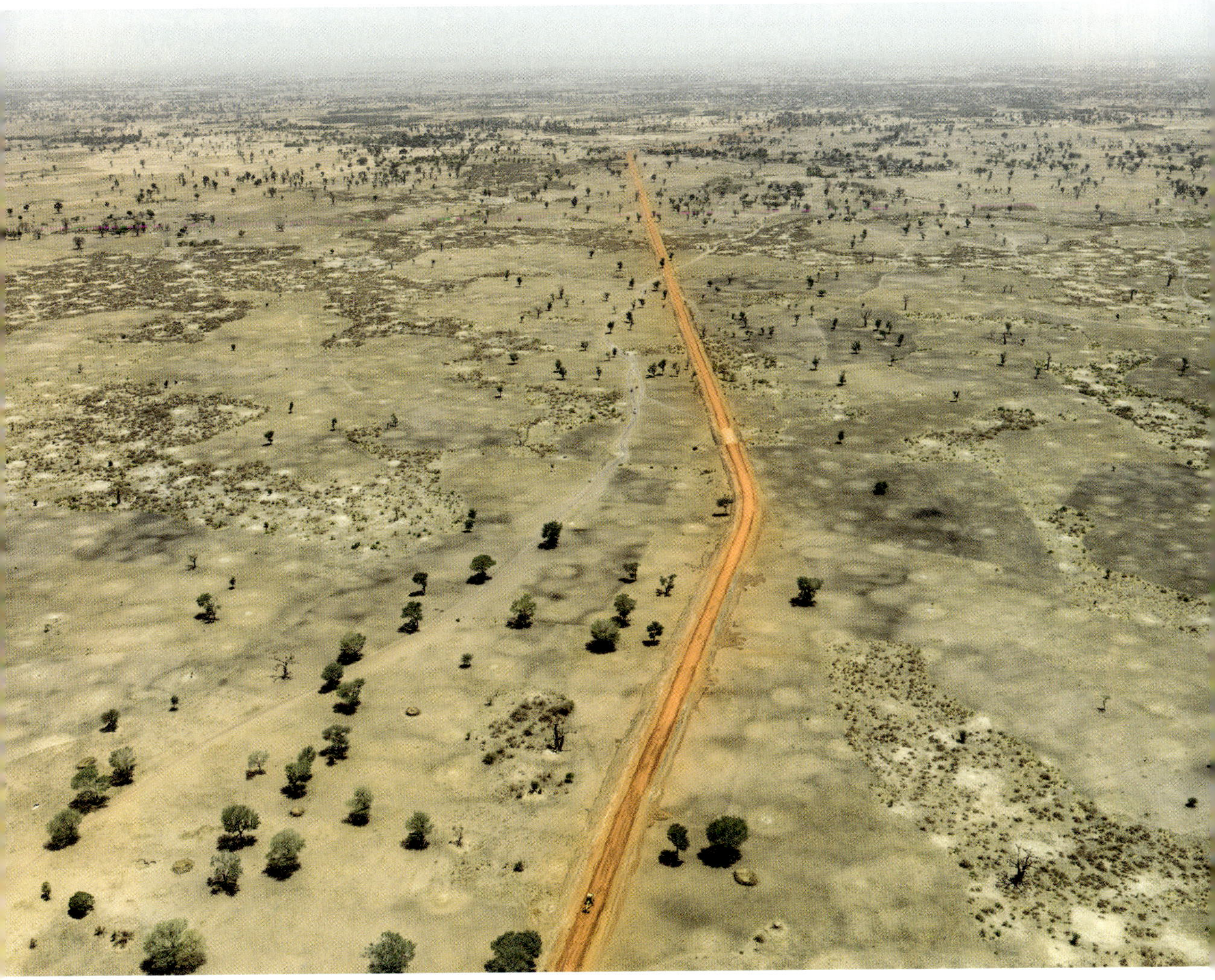

Edward Burtynsky, *Nguénièene to Tiadiay Road #1*, Senegal, 2019

16 DOES THE NATURAL ORDER STILL EXIST?

LIFE SUSPENDED

At the beginning of 2020, Burtynsky was about to embark on a new project–*In the Wake of Progress.* Two years earlier, Naomi Campbell, the artistic director of the Luminato Festival in Toronto, had approached him with a concept that had caught her off-guard. She had been at Yonge-Dundas Square [now Sankofa Square], Toronto's version of Manhattan's Times Square and an area filled with twenty-two huge media screens advertising a wide range of goods. Standing there, she had felt overwhelmed by the grimness: "It's concrete and consumerism. It's just all ads." At that point, Burtynsky recalled, "She had the idea to invite an artist to take over all the media screens." When Campbell encouraged him to be that person, he thought, "Wouldn't it be great as a feedback loop to show the origins of these towers of concrete, glass, steel and copper, and manufacturing? I thought it would be great to take all those screens and showcase the other part of the world that allows us the possibility for the urban lives we lead."[1] This assignment would also serve as a form of retrospective because it would include images from his entire career to date.

Planning for this project came to an abrupt halt with the onset of the COVID-19 pandemic in the spring of 2020. Offices in Toronto closed, including Image Works and the Studio. Meetings could only be conducted on Zoom, and so work on *In the Wake of Progress* was put on hold.

Starting in 1982, Burtynsky remembered, "entranced by the beauty and vistas of the Beaver Valley area on my way to the Bruce Peninsula," he and Jeannie spent the "following three years searching for a piece of land or cottage to buy."[2] In 1985, they purchased fifteen acres with no building on it. Seven years later, they completed work on a house.

Thirty-five years later, on April 27, 2020, Burtynsky, his wife Julia Johnston, and their dog Barkley were at that house during their seventh week of isolation. He told his diary, "It seems the decade is off to a bad start as we are holed up here due to a pandemic called Covid 19 [sic] that got its start in Wuhan, China–my first stop in China in 2002."[3]

In retreat, Burtynsky remembered that forty years before he had looked at the "landscape around this area during spring and late fall with leaves down and colours & tone displaying almost in black and white." He specifically recalled the Easter weekend in April 1981 when he took *Grasses* and *Landscape #4* (see pp. 46 and 48).

Long afterward, in 2020, he began taking pictures every day "for pivoting off" *Landscape #4*. With a new camera, the Phase One IQ4, "I wanted to go back to my early beginnings of me, my camera, my feet and my car as the only tools necessary to make work."

> I am also trying to find some new ways to consider this landscape. With the new camera there is feature called focus stacking. This involves finding a still subject (no wind) and then taking a series of images at different focus distances making sure that sharpness overlaps between frames and then using photoshop to stitch the sharpest parts of each stack spot to give you depth-of-field unattainable in a single image. This has given me a whole new way to consider what images I can make. I am also trying to break my normal sense of composition in order to find some things I had never considered in previous work. This has made the engagement with the subject fun and informative to keep my mind in the present while working. I have also been microdosing with small amounts of THC that comes in liquid form and taken by putting small amounts under your tongue. [If I do this] I can stop thinking of all the craziness going on in the world and be present in the moment.[4]

He had a specific agenda in mind: "So far, I've gone out at least 10 times and have captured around 100 images. I'm hoping that the best of the images to date speak to my emotional state of mind . . . most of our thoughts and emotions are unstructured and chaotic, and it is a very small percentage of what goes through our minds [that] is ordered and rational."[5]

In a Thoreau-like exploration of his surroundings, he reflected on how significant this terrain had been at the outset of his career:

> As I continue to make these images something occurred to me. The original 1980s work was created by me driving through areas looking for moments from the side of the road. In this [new] work I tried to do work inside the forest while on foot. It is very hard to find a frame on these walks that contains the complexity and energy that I am looking

> for. When I went back to driving on roads and reacting to things I see from the truck window, the more interesting images started happening.[6]
>
> As in the early '80s work, I am not necessarily looking at pristine, unspoiled nature. I'm looking at the front line of nature as it pushes against the elevated road I am standing on. This is how there is often waste at the foot of the image. (It's the ditch) and it's also how there is a wall of texture as the road clears a space between me and the scene. In fact, grasses, the progenitor of all my landscape works, is green shoots pushing through compressed grasses from the winter snow. It's actually a ditch alongside a country road in the Bruce Peninsula shot at this time of year. These are, in fact, human influenced landscapes. I'll keep walking the forest with [my] camera to see if I can break that code into something interesting and worthy as an image.[7]

At a critical time in human history, he thought, "bringing images of trees, vines and shrubs that live in a wild, shared accommodation with each other seems like the right thing to do." He was happy to be taking things slowly: "It's been a very, very long time since I've slowed my pace and thinking to this level. [It] feels good."[8] He reflected on why he had become a photographer, his days at Ryerson, and especially his trip to the Bruce Peninsula in 1981 and recalled that the "success of the Bruce Peninsula shoot reinvigorated my interest to keep working with large format colour."[9]

The Bruce Peninsula was also the place where "I have always come back to find my center. Having seen what humans are capable of and at what scale, this place would [always] bring me back to first principles. These images felt right to make during this time. They are an affirmation of the complexity and wonder of the natural colour of things."[10] He also wrote in his diary: "I am unabashedly making beautiful images of nature. I want to bring beauty into the world as only nature can deliver."[11]

SHOOTING. VISUALLY. METAPHORICALLY. NOSTALIGICALLY. CALMLY. TECHNOLOGICALLY.

The landscape images from 2020, Burtynsky has stated, "are all from a place, Grey County, Ontario. They are also from a place in my mind that aspires to wrest order out of chaos, to act as a salve in these uncertain times." He also wrote that he was "Shooting. Visually. Metaphorically. Nostalgically, Calmly. Technologically. I'm learning about this new camera and software daily and I'm loving it. This is the first time the digital camera is feeling as good as my old film days with 4 × 5 and 8 × 10." For him, "most of the magic was happening" once again.[12]

Many of the images in *Natural Order* are, at first glance, akin to *Grasses* and *Landscape #4*.[13] Since they were taken at similar locations, this is to be expected, but the images from 2020 are unlike those from 1981. The digital technology of his new camera allowed the photographer to capture the trees and grasses in a much more focus than before. In particular, the depth of field he could attain let him create incredible detail and texture.

All landscape photography depicts something the unaided eye cannot see. The photograph frames what it sees, places it in a rectangle or square, and, through that process, removes it from its physical existence. The more advanced digital features of the IQ4–and the stacking process–provides detail and texture that are profoundly different from what was previously attainable by a camera. The detail is more than the unassisted eye can take in.

This new technology resulted in a portrait of the natural world that is profoundly dissimilar to what came before. This may have happened in part because Burtynsky was perceiving this landscape with an altered sensibility. In *Landscape Study #3* (1981), the viewer looks into the land and grasses whereas, in *Natural Order #19* (2020), the viewer is barred from scrutinizing the landscape because the trees and grasses act as a blockade to what is behind them. In composition, *Natural Order #14* resembles

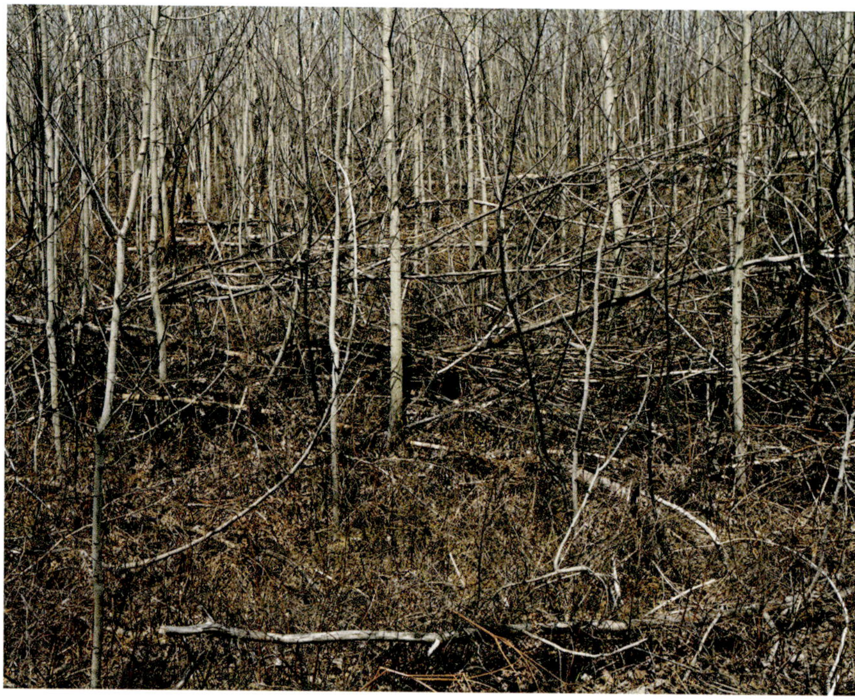

Edward Burtynsky, *Landscape Study #3*, near Sudbury, Ontario, 1981

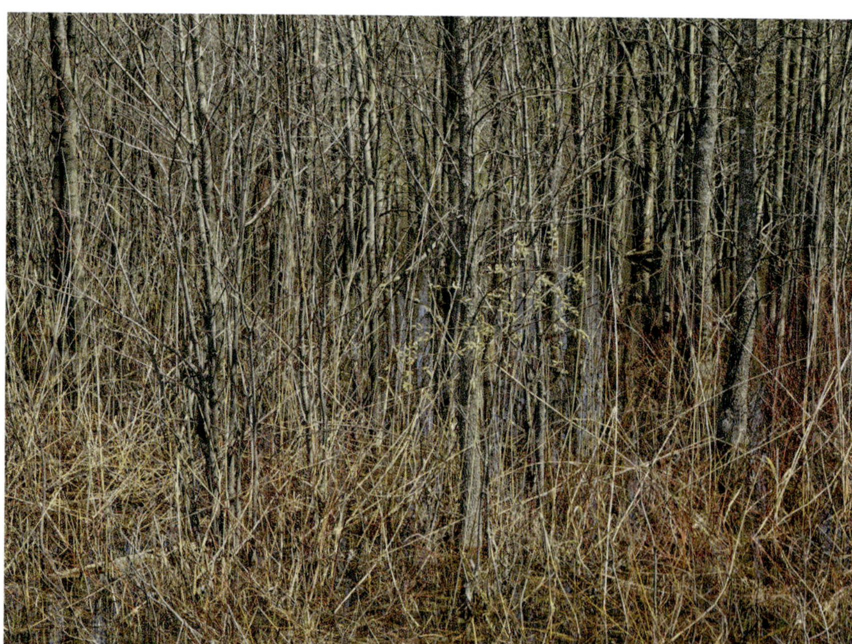

Edward Burtynsky, *Natural Order #19*, Grey County, Ontario, Spring 2020

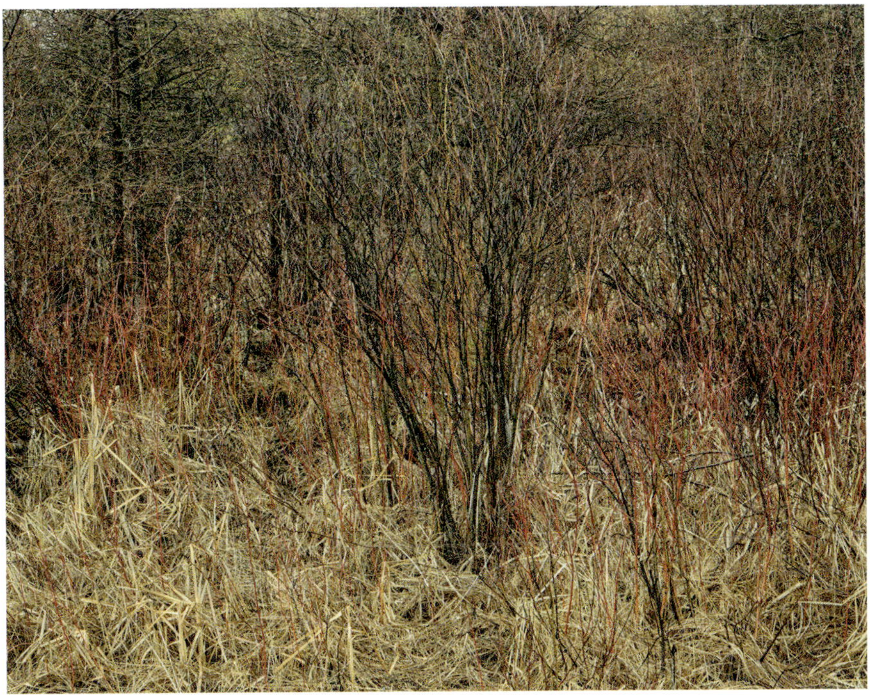

Edward Burtynsky, *Natural Order #14*, Grey County, Ontario, Spring 2020

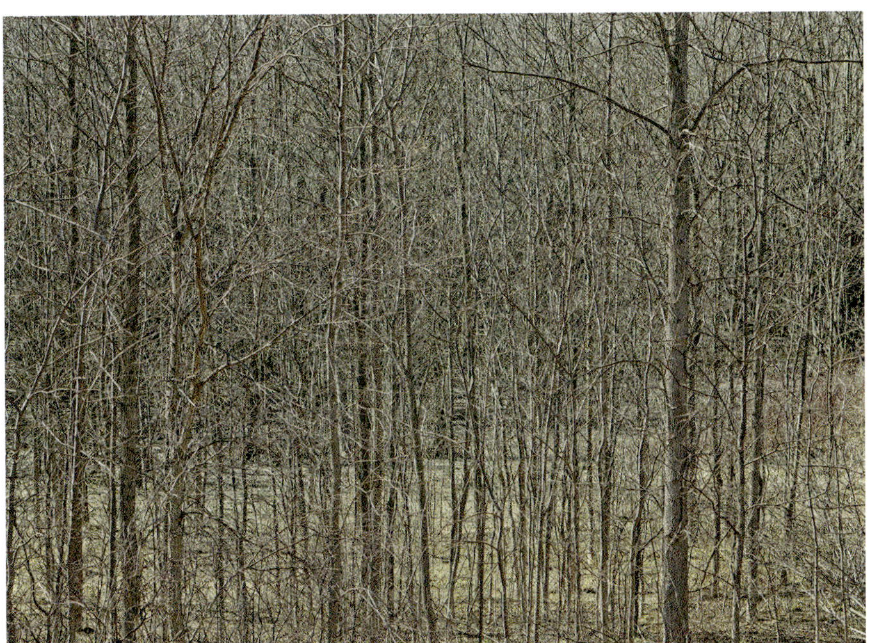

Edward Burtynsky, *Natural Order #4*, Grey County, Ontario, Spring 2020

Grasses, but the grasses and trees present in 2020 also form a barrier. Even in *Natural Order #14*, which allows a view into the forest, the arrangement and density of the trees are not inviting.

Nature in Bruce County had not changed significantly in forty years, but Burtynsky had. In making these new images, moreover, he was deliberately trying to "break," he said, his "normal sense of composition in order to find some things I had never considered before."[14] The extraordinary depth of field in the new landscapes may be attributable in large part to new equipment, but this "natural world" also derives, in part, from his altered perspective. He had "never considered before" how this beautiful landscape had, for him, changed irrevocably. During his career, he had witnessed all kinds of man-made intrusions into the natural world and his respect for nature had grown exponentially. In these new landscapes, nature is separated from man. The artist has become the intruder.

17 A SUBLIME SENSE OF WONDER

"WE'RE ALL INCRIMINATED"

Confined to his country home with trips to Toronto, Burtynsky, in addition to photographing *Natural Order*, worked on the postponed *In the Wake of Progress* (ITWP) by storyboarding "the chronology of his work, mapping out more than 230 images and close to ten minutes of video footage to tell a visual story."[1] But he was "mapping out" his narrative in a way that was very different to what he was familiar with. All his previous work had been in still photography and in documentary film making. Since *Wake* was conceived as an outdoor multimedia product, it required a different approach.

At this point in her husband's career, Julia had provided crucial assistance in setting up and making the *Anthropocene* project a reality–the film, the book, and the exhibition at the Art Gallery of Ontario. At this point, in the midst of COVID, she worked assiduously with her husband to overcome the setbacks the pandemic had put in their path. In particular, she used her considerable skills as an entrepreneurial lawyer to provide the networking necessary to make this new turn in his career work.

After he had assembled the images he wanted to include, Burtynsky added an industrial-sounding score in the style of Brian Eno. When that did not work to his satisfaction, he hired the composer and sound designer Phil Strong to create the soundtrack. Wordless vocals by the Cree-Métis musician wasekwan iskwē were then commissioned, which Burtynsky found "haunting. At the very beginning, I saw her opening voice as the land

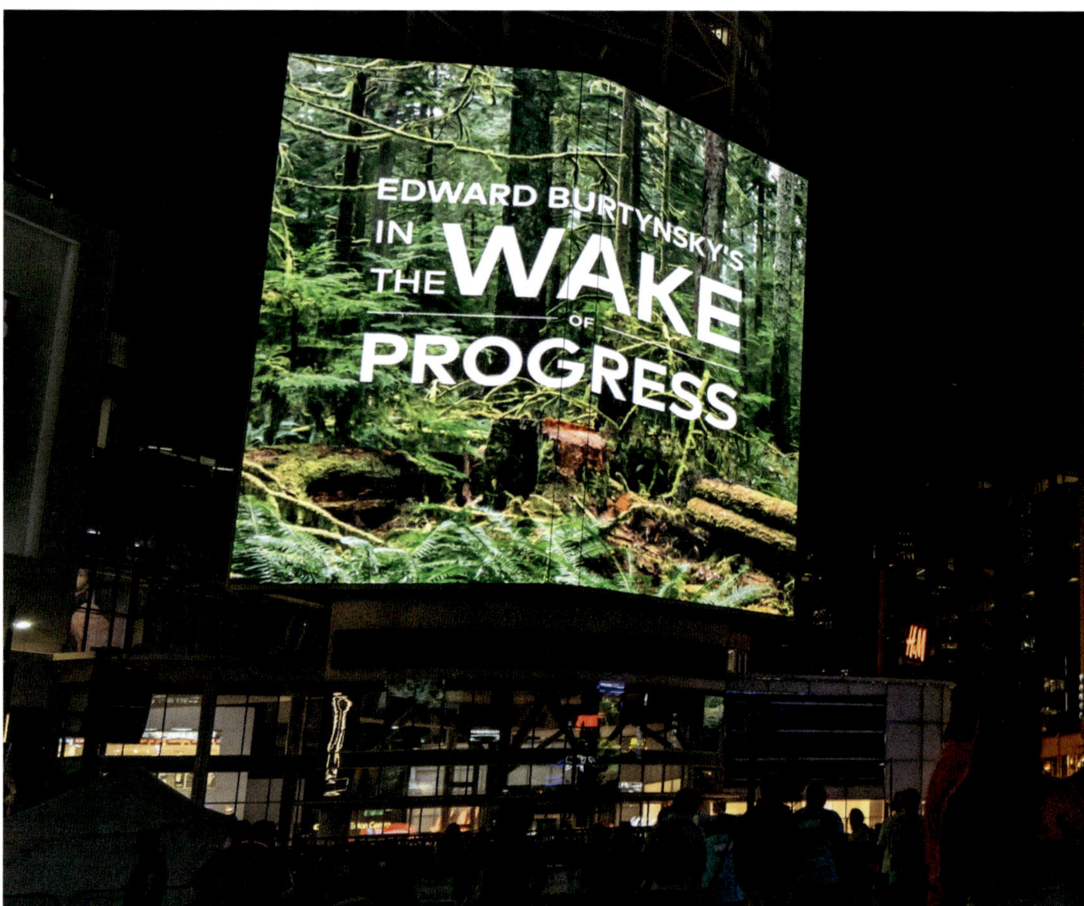

In the Wake of Progress on display at Bay and Dundas, Toronto (2022). Photograph by Jim Panou

acknowledgement."[2] Her vocals captured the feelings she experienced in watching the film: chaos, fear, anxiety, and dread. The violinist Byungchan Lee, and other musicians from the Glenn Gould School under the direction of Claudio Vena, provided additional stirring accompaniment.

"With pictures you don't need words," Burtynsky pointed out. "And because there are zero words, [the film] can then go around the world. It's speaking universally and it doesn't need a translation anywhere."[3] At the film's climax, there is a dramatic crescendo when a pot of molten metal bubbles and flames out. "It's like being in Hell," Strong felt, and he composed music appropriate to that feeling. Meanwhile, much of the material was being harnessed together by the producer Bob Ezrin.

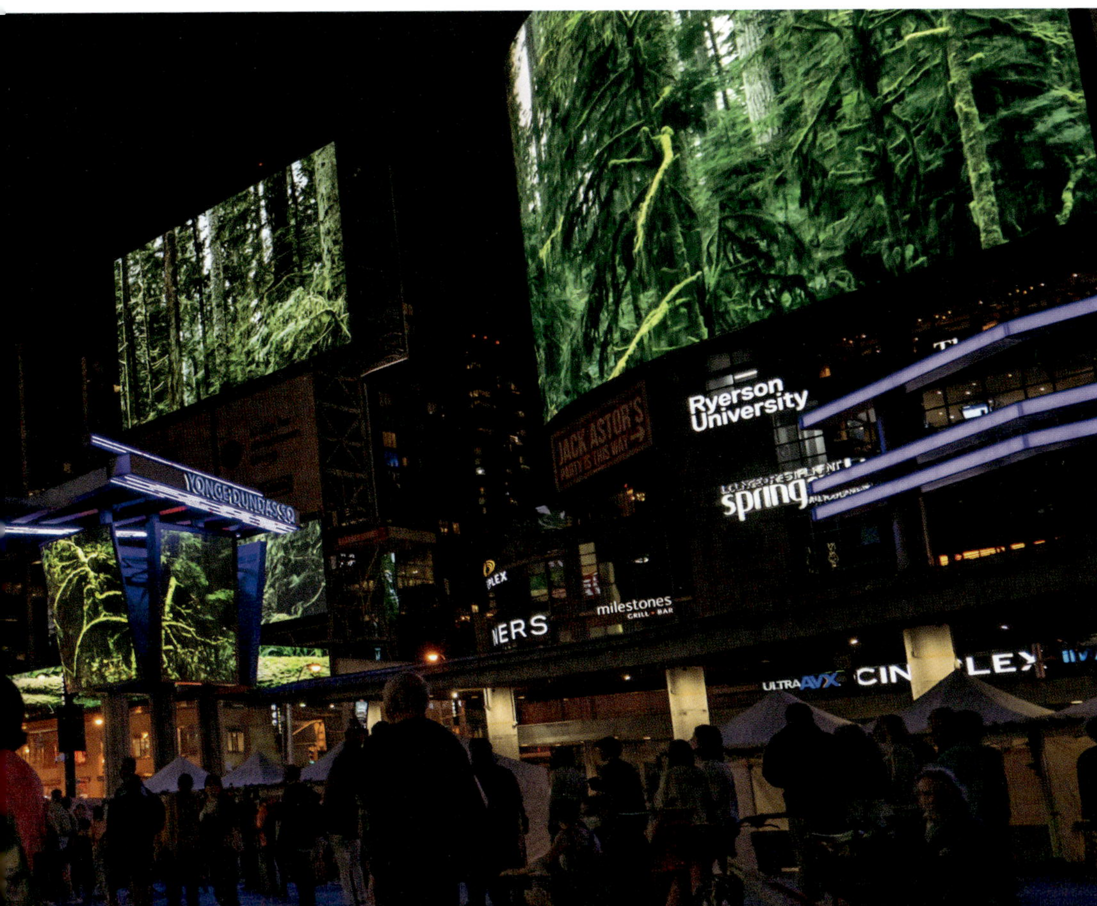

The twenty-two-minute multimedia project *In the Wake of Progress* premiered, as originally planned, at Sankofa Square (formerly Yonge-Dundas Square) on June 11, 2022; it was the first time that all twenty-two outdoor screens performed in unison. The experiment went better than Burtynsky expected, although the soundtrack struggled against the competing street noise and the low-resolution screens did not refresh quickly enough, he felt, for viewers to take in the full experience.

Wake is, as Burtynsky observed, a lament for nature wherein the word "progress" is used ironically; as such, it stands in marked contrast to the outdoor metropolitan square in which it was first shown. "That's why the piece is buttressed at the beginning and at the end with the natural world–to show that we live in it." Nothing, he felt, could be further from the natural world than the intersection of Yonge and Dundas, where the audience was shown throughout the presentation how the natural world has been ravaged to manufacture the products advertised on the screens. "I'm a big believer that if you can reach out and hit somebody in the heart and gut, then there's a better chance that they'll digest it and intellectualize it in a different way, and possibly it will even motivate them to make a difference in their own lives." Earlier, in a rehearsal late at night at Yonge and Dundas, Burtynsky was aghast when his mossy forest shots were replaced one by one by the fashion ads usually on display: "It went from the poetic to the profane. All these models and runaways. It was grotesque." Burtynsky pinpointed why Yonge and Dundas was the ideal local for this piece. It reminded consumers that "[w]e're all incriminated. Nobody is outside of this."[4]

One observer described how the multimedia piece "moves from one devastating image to another, interspersed with reminders of natural landscapes. In one moment we get an Orwellian view of a textile factory in China where a sea of workers sew in synchrony, and in the next, we're taken to an apocalyptic graveyard for rusting freighter ships on the coast of Bangladesh. Then, swirling water in Lake Superior."[5] The back and forward thrust of contrasting images reminds the viewer of the sublimity of nature while simultaneously displaying how it is being threatened. It is significant,

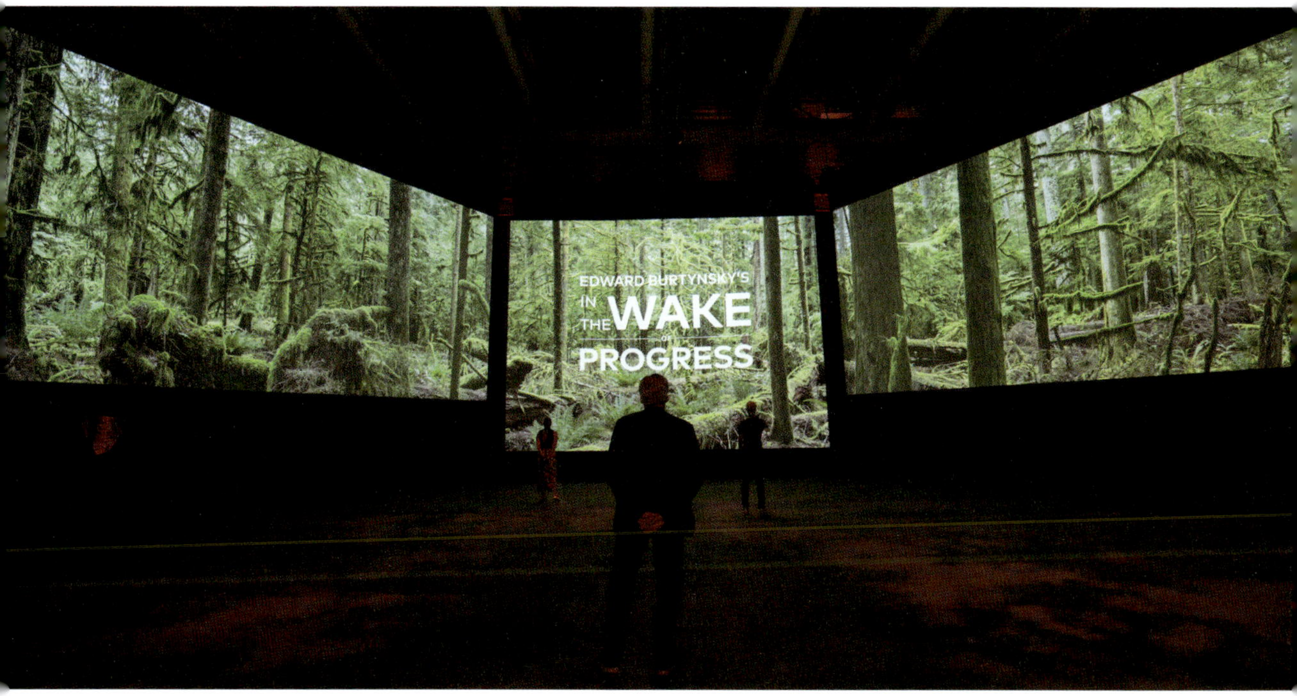

In the Wake of Progress, Canadian Opera Company Theatre, 2022. Photograph by Jim Panou

then, that the film opens and closes with images of uncontaminated nature.

After it was shown at Yonge and Dundas, the multimedia project moved on June 25 to the Canadian Opera Company Theatre for a three-week run, where it was exhibited on three nine-metre screens.

The book version of *In the Wake of Progress* recaptured the experience of being immersed in the film by illustrating screenshots at the opening of each of its divisions–Ancient Forests, Deforestation, Railcuts, Homesteads, Agriculture, Urbanization, various depictions of Extraction, Oil, Recycling and Water, Container Ports, Shipyards, Manufacturing, Nature-Source, and Natural Order–and thus recreating in part how the film was shown on three screens at The Canadian Opera Company Theatre.

Since the contents of the film and printed versions of *Wake* were chosen to demonstrate the full range of the photographer's accomplishments up to 2020, *Wake* also became a retrospective glance at Burtynsky's career.

GUT FEELINGS

Wake may have been an excellent showcase for Burtynsky's work, as intended, but it did not do justice to his accomplishments because none of his actual photographs were on display. As such, this project could not reveal the intricacies of the prints themselves and, in a sense, deprived viewers of experiencing how haptic they are, of admiring their intricate details and of entering them in a fully visceral way. Aware of this predicament, Burtynsky began to consider a large-scale survey that would demonstrate the scale of the photographs.

While pondering this dilemma, Burtynsky wanted to expand his portfolio. He obviously did not wish to be confined, as he had been during COVID. He needed the freedom to explore new opportunities–to make even more dramatic images of the increasingly fragile natural order. As before, he trusted his gut instincts to lead him in the right directions.

In 2021, he accepted a commission from the Italian non-profit Fondazione Sylva, in Puglia, to document the deteriorating state of olive groves in the region. Early in his career, he had documented greenhouses–environments in which plants were protected. This new project would demonstrate how nature was vulnerable when it lacked a protective shield. *Xylella fastidiosa* is a vector-transmitted bacterial pathogen that causes significant disease in a wide variety of plant life, and numerous species of xylem sap-sucking insects are the vectors of the bacterium. The existence of *X. fastidiosa* had been detected in Puglia in October 2013; two years later, the disease had infected almost a million trees.

The task that the Fondazione Sylva set itself was to make the public aware of this devastation and to insist that such devastated landscapes had to be reforested and, thus, reborn. Burtynsky's assignment was to show the devastation accurately, dramatically, and poignantly. In this way, his photographs would capture the reality of a grim situation and, at the same time, suggest that it should be rectified.

Before starting any assignment, Burtynsky researches it thoroughly.

He did the same before setting out for Puglia, but the situation he faced on arrival was not what he had anticipated. He had been planning to photograph the brown tones of the grasses, but, two weeks before his arrival, there had been a massive rainfall. What was supposed to be brown was green. "I started driving around thinking that I have to reframe this whole thing. I had to rethink everything. And then I started working with the colour palette that's there, and I started figuring it out." He was, as he put it, "slammed right into reality." He had to take his skills and experiences and "muster" them; and, as usual, his "gut feelings" came into play.[6]

The resulting photographs position the browns of the infected, rotting olive trees in opposition to the lush landscape in which they stand. These images showcase the blighted trees as monumental pieces of sculpture dying within nature's radiant greenery. Aerial shots emphasize the differences between blighted and unblighted groves.

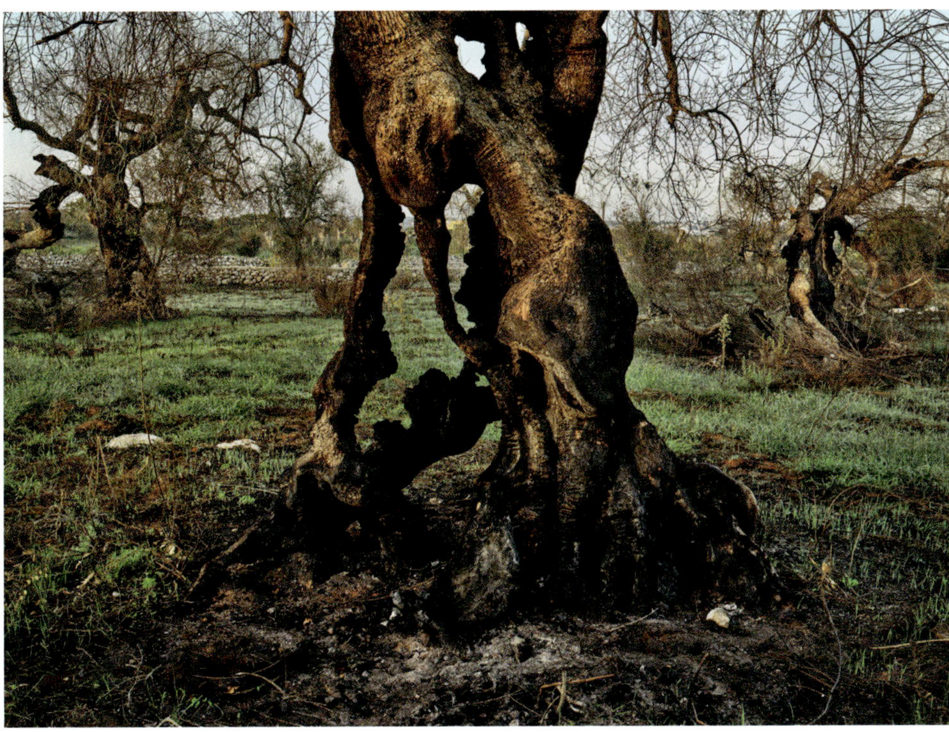

Edward Burtynsky, *Xylella Studies #9*, Lecce, Puglia, Italy, 2021

He kept busy with other projects as well. In 2022, he was commissioned by Borusan Contemporary Art in Istanbul to photograph erosion in Türkiye; he also undertook a series in Australia's Hunter Valley, New South Wales, at the Ravensworth Mine and the Kooragang Coal Terminal–open cut mines producing coal for export. The following year, he travelled to the Coastal Mountains of British Columbia to demonstrate how significantly their

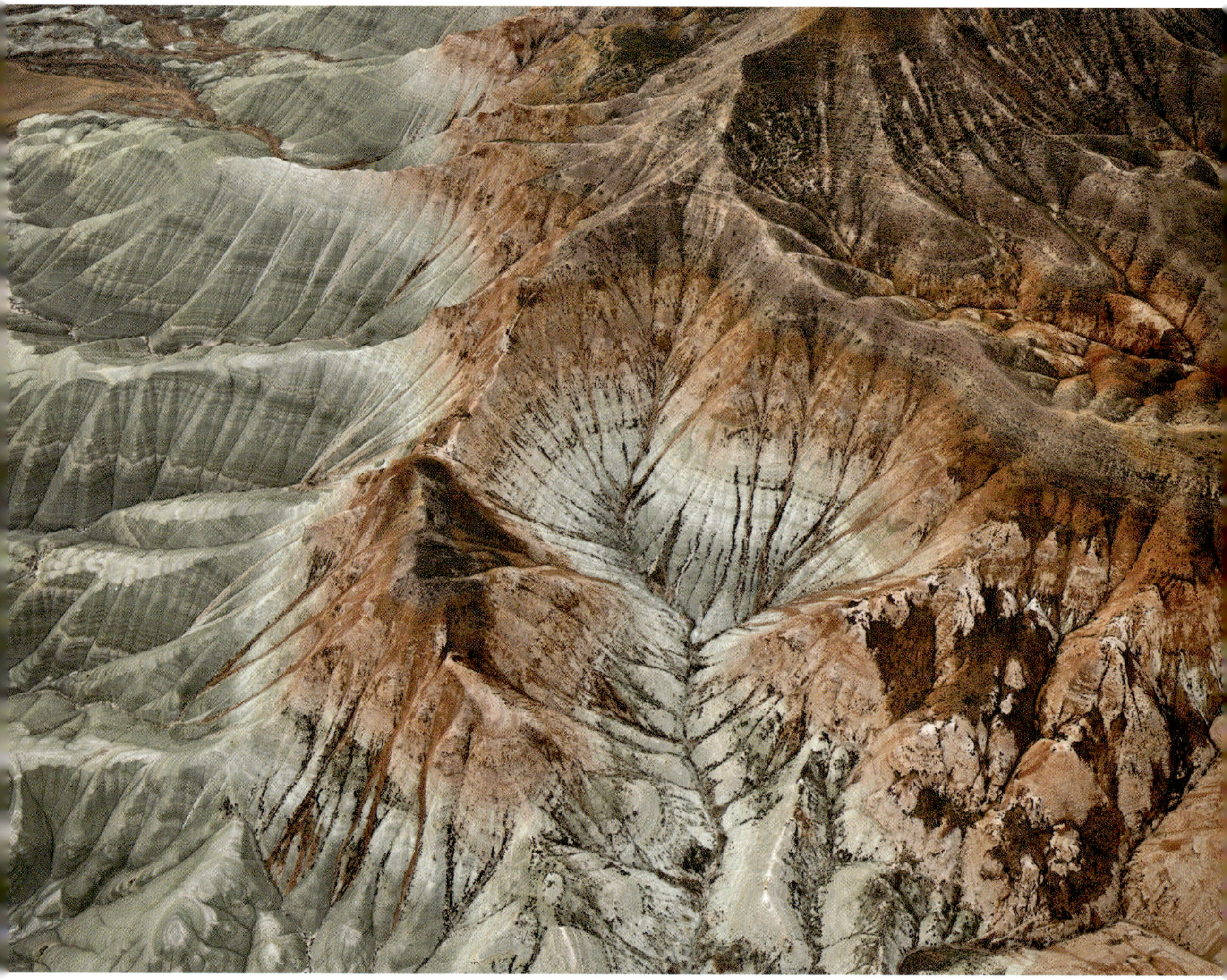

Edward Burtynsky, *Erosion #3*, Nallıhan, Ankara, Türkiye, 2022

glaciers–which are as much as 150,000 years old–have receded in the past twenty years. (The earlier *Mount Edziza Provincial Park #1* [see p. 248] from 2021 can be compared to the British Columbia images from 2023; in both, the solemn majesty of the mountains is enshrined, but the ones from 2023 display glacial disintegration.)

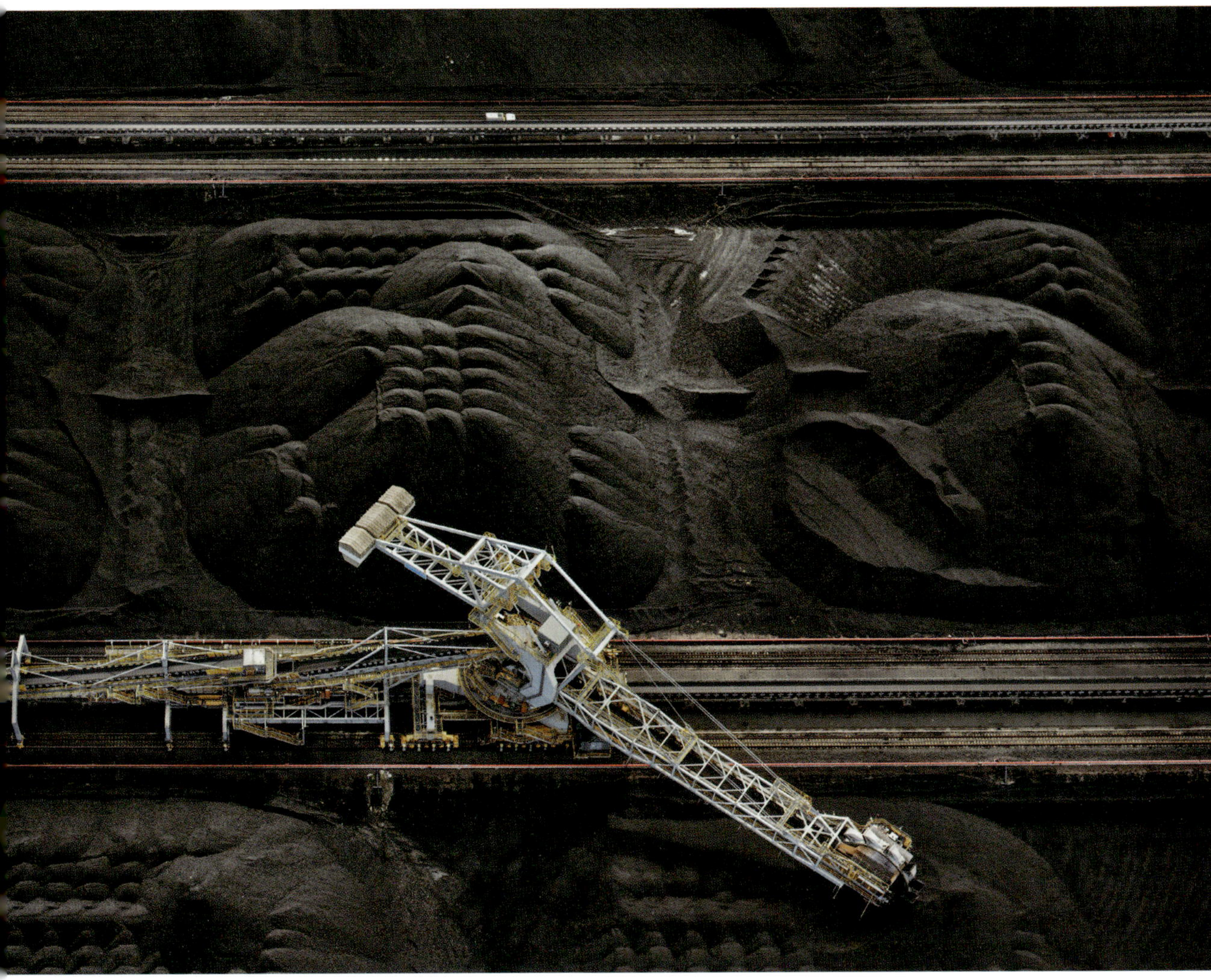

Edward Burtynsky, *Coal Terminal #1*, Kooragang Coal Terminal, Newcastle, New South Wales, Australia, 2022

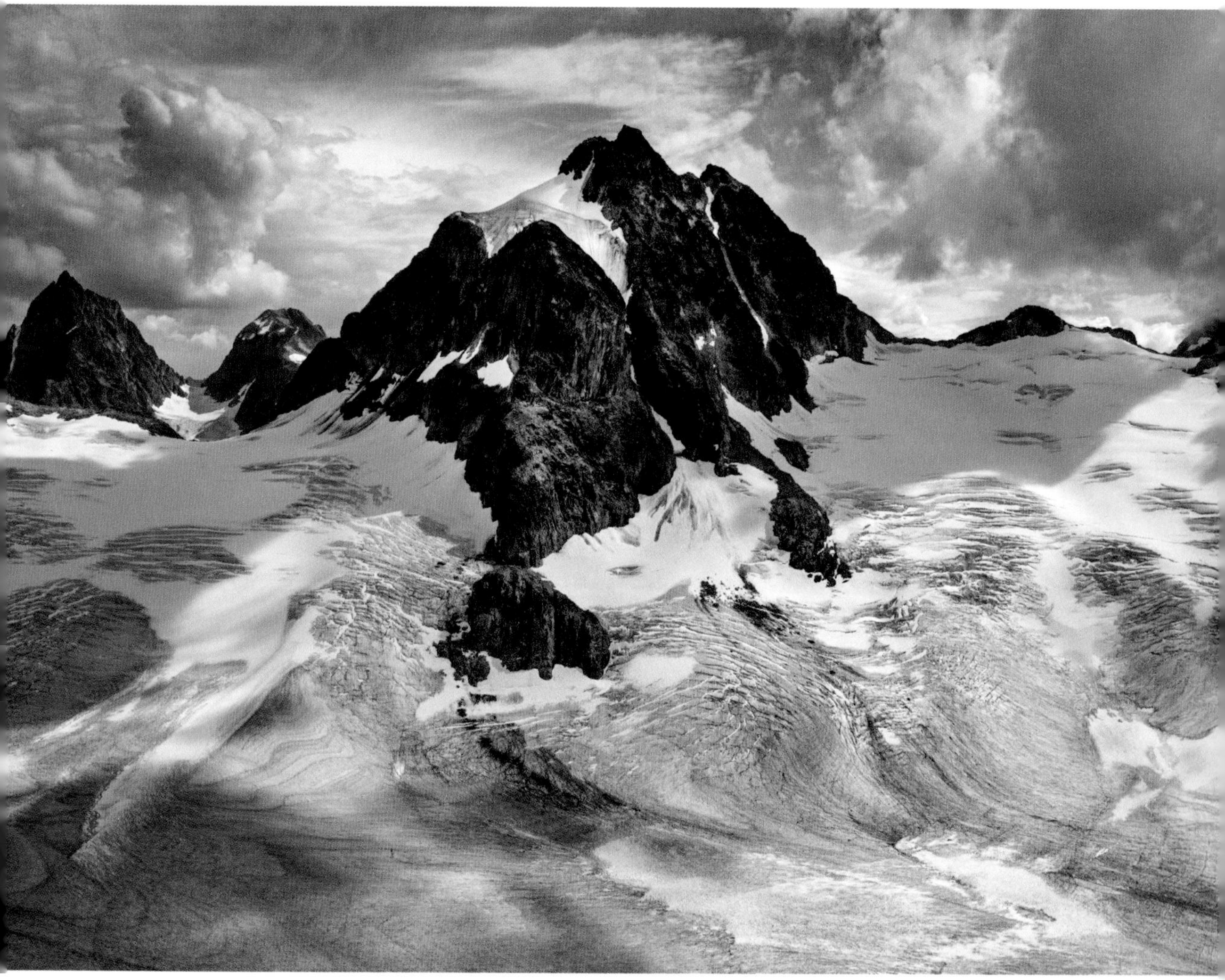

Edward Burtynsky, *Coast Mountains #16*, British Columbia, 2023

IMMERSION

Slowly, Burtynsky and his team began to ponder the next steps forward in making the photographs themselves available in a large exhibition that would display their unique qualities and, at the same time, publicize the reality behind them: humankind has become like the passengers on the *Titanic* dancing the night away before the collision with the iceberg.

The exhibition at the Saatchi Gallery in London, curated by Marc Mayer, was also formulated to demarcate Burtynsky's work from that of all other contemporary photographers specializing in the environment: it was to draw a line in the sand between Burtynsky and his competitors by emphasizing his forty-year commitment to showing, in a variety of ways, the impact of humanity on the planet. Although it was the largest exhibition ever staged of Burtynsky's work, with eight galleries of art, it was a survey, not a retrospective, and it foregrounded images from 2011 to 2012 and from 2016 to 2019.[7]

What immediately made Burtynsky's work in this exhibition stand out from that of his peers was his astounding attention to detail, especially in the ways his large photographs resemble paintings. Their textures have incredible depth; details pop out; the surfaces in some passages resemble brush strokes. The viewer is invited to enter and become immersed. Many locales are ones visitors are unfamiliar with and could not visit. Moreover, these places are represented from vantage points and perspectives that are closed off from most eyes. Viewers soon realize that seeing reproductions of Burtynsky's work in books, magazines, and on the internet could never do justice to experiencing the immediacy of the photographs on display.

By concentrating on works from 2011 to 2019, the exhibition focused on works that demonstrated Burtynsky's artistic and technical maturity. The emphasis on Africa in the overall selection of photographs was determined by two factors: Burtynsky considered them some of the most accomplished images he had made throughout his career and those images had been overlooked because they were released during COVID.

The exhibition was divided into two parts: Abstraction is emphasized in the first three galleries and the remaining five concentrate on various forms of Extraction (Agriculture, Manufacturing, Infrastructure, and Waste), although many of those images show the artist's penchant for abstraction. Although a significant number of the photographs in *Edward Burtynsky: Abstraction/Extraction* are taken from an aerial perspective, many other viewpoints are present.

Adjacent to the galleries was a small room containing *The Process Archive* (curated by Schubert and Panou), which was an exhibition both of the tools Burtynsky used in his trade and photographs of him on-site in a wide variety of locations. Both the selection of photographs and equipment move

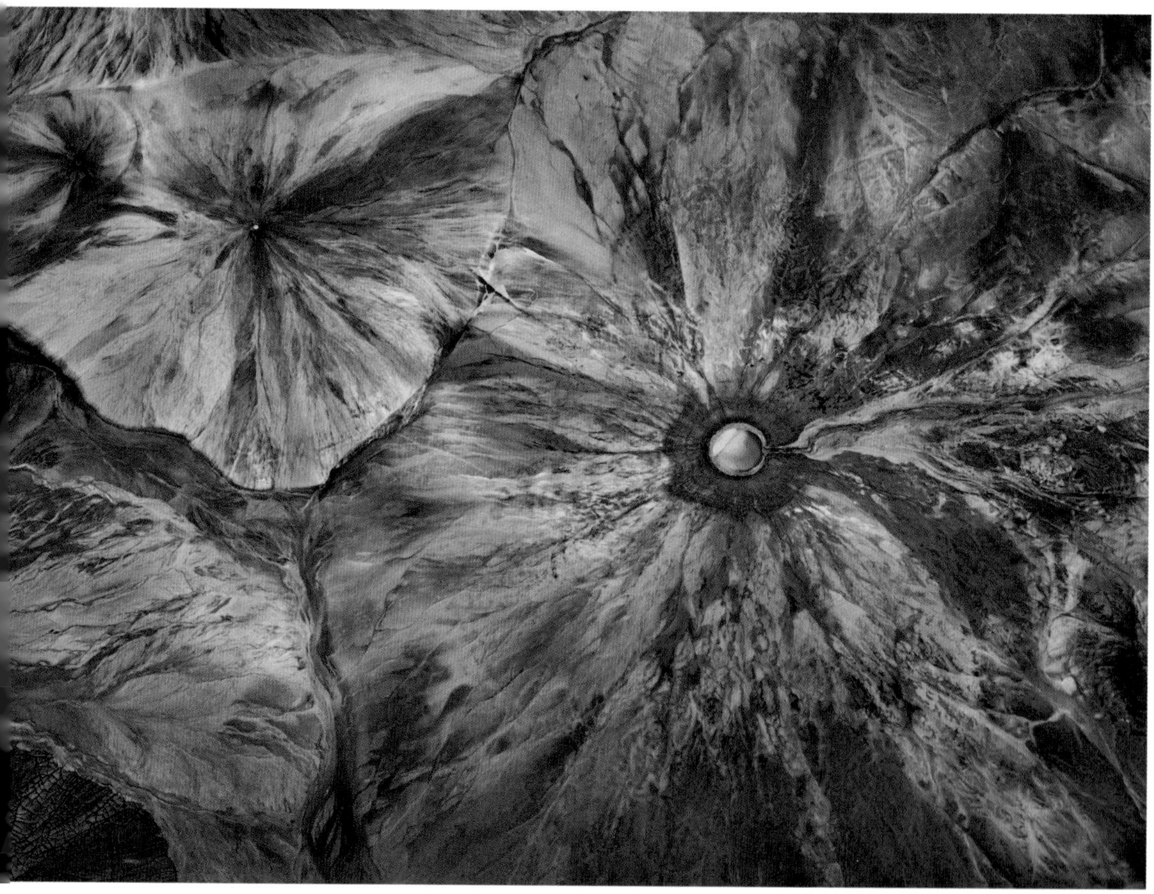

Edward Burtynsky, *Ravensworth Coal Tailing #1*, Hunter Valley, New South Wales, Australia, 2022

chronologically from analog to digital photography and show the many adaptations Burtynsky has made in taking photographs over the years.

One pleasure of the exhibition was seeing the connection between images such as the sinister, petal-like structures in *Tailing Ponds #1* (2018) and *Coal Tailing #1* (2022), which were taken four years apart. Another was perceiving how intimate all the entries were in demonstrating new methods of looking at the earth, eliciting momentary gasps as viewers saw the world in an entirely new way.

Walking through the galleries, visitors also realized that the varied landscapes and the diversity of approaches resonate with the artistry of a single eye. They are uniform in their precise craftsmanship, in their use of a limited palette (browns, greys, blues, and greens with a few strokes of fiery orange and bright red) redolent of earth, and in attention to the abstraction that underlines the natural world. Representation and abstraction are conjoined. That single eye searches for truths underlying our existences and forces us to reimagine the world we live in. Two images from 2022 underscore this: *Farming #4*, taken in Türkiye, and *Coal Mining Complex #3*, taken in Australia. The ploughed field in the centre of *Farming #4* appears like a large abstract canvas floating over the landscape, whereas the horizontal striations in the top half of the monochromatic *Coal Mining Complex #3* look like a series of enormous charcoal drawings weaving across the ground in direct contrast to the three rectangle-like vertical shapes in the lower half.

In the Wake of Progress was shown at Saatchi and a shorter, ten-minute version at Outernet, the large entertainment complex on Charing Cross Road. Since the film includes many of the photographer's early, iconic work, the photos in the gallery and the works shown in the film complement each other. The visitors to Saatchi witnessed examples of Burtynsky's entire career.

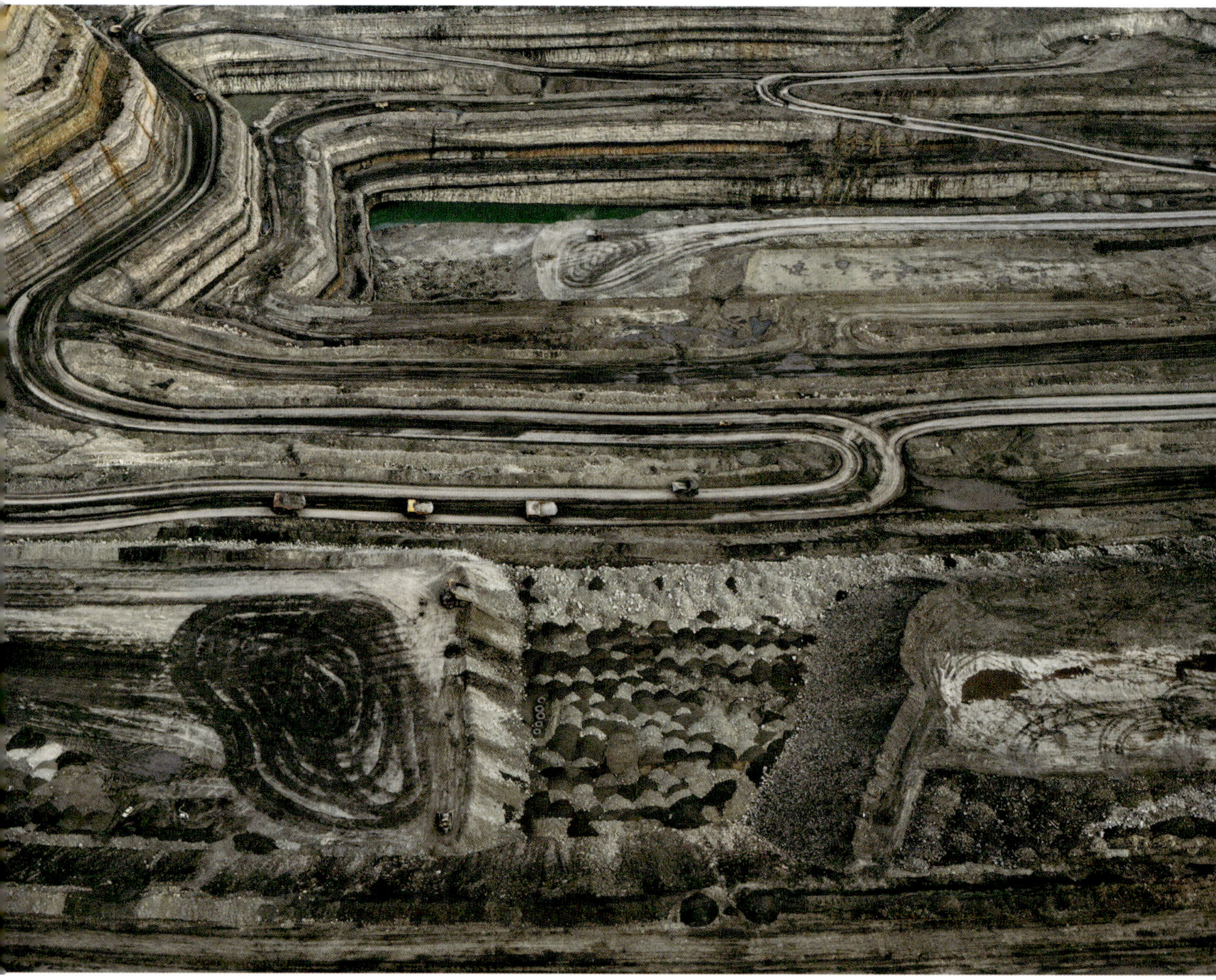

Edward Burtynsky, *Coal Mining Complex #3*, Ravensworth Mine, Hunter Valley, New South Wales, Australia, 2022

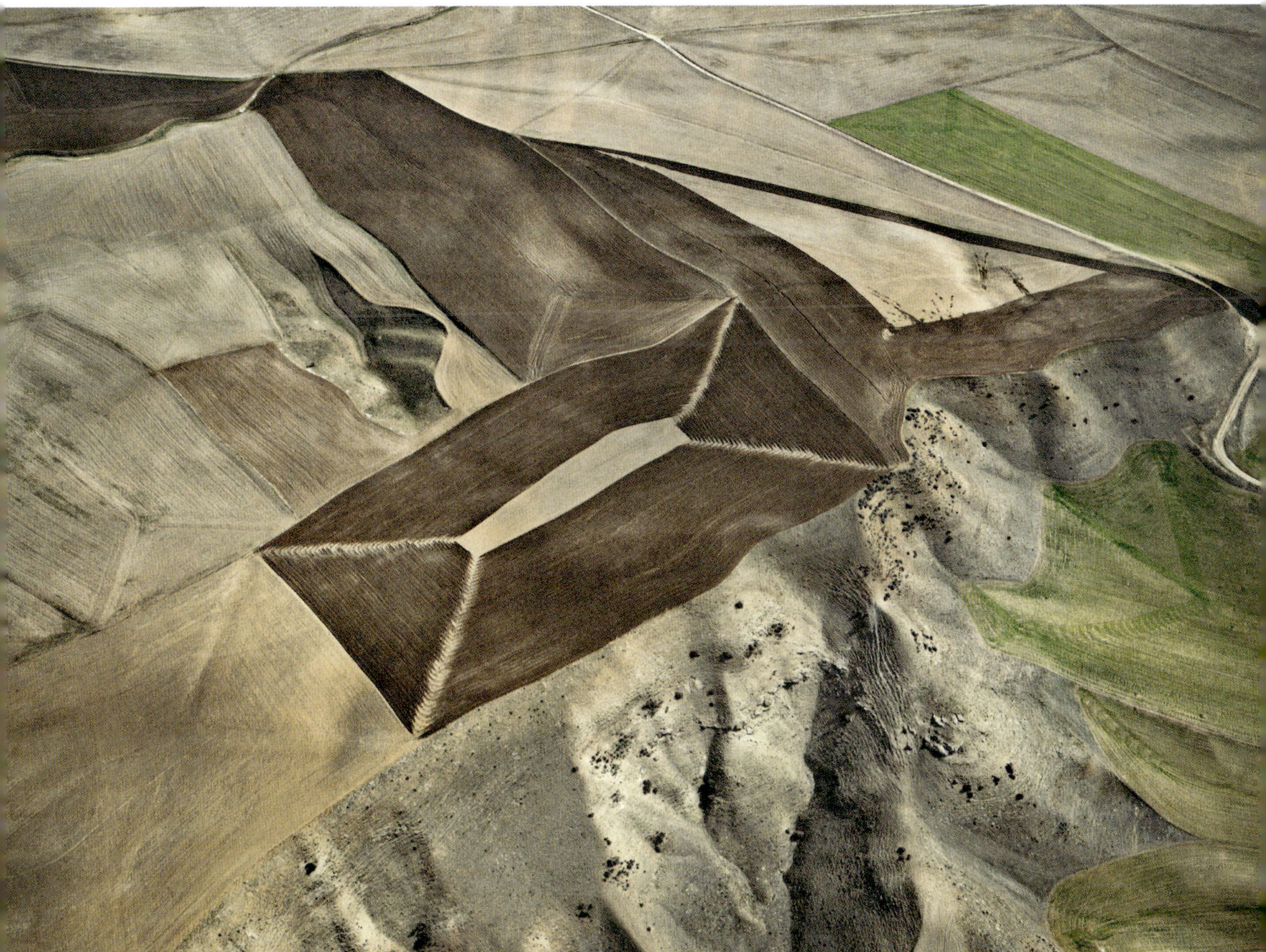

Edward Burtynsky, *Farming, #4*, Cingil, Ankara Province, Türkiye, 2022

When Rachel Haliburton of the *Financial Times* visited the exhibition, she warned her readers, "What you're most likely to feel is a sense of wonder as you enter the first room." She was also taken by the vastness of what she saw: "Edward Burtynsky's disturbingly beautiful photography brings a giant's eye view to our ravaged planet, rendering mining sites as glimmering jewel boxes, desertscapes as geometric puzzles and dumping grounds as Jackson Pollock-like eruptions of chaos and colour. This fascinating exhibition covers his journey of more than 40 years–hanging out of Cessna planes, elevated by cranes, and latterly deploying drones–to document the way large-scale industry and agriculture have impacted on the natural world." She emphasized that "Burtynsky's distinctive aesthetic has spawned several imitators, but none who match the scale or impact of his uncompromising vision." This is a crucial point because the Saatchi exhibition was intended to separate Burtynsky from the copycats who ape his approach, especially in aerial photography.

Haliburton was also moved by *In the Wake of Progress* (2022) and how it moved "across three screens, contemplating a pristine forest from British Columbia, then suddenly whirling through landscapes blighted by logging, over-farming, oil spillage, snaking road systems, or industrial chemicals that blotch the feet of child-workers. It would be easy to be overwhelmed, but the curator has paced the exhibition judiciously, allowing for a slow build in intensity and creating a subtle balance between amazement and concern. What's most striking, though, is a sense of one man's determination to discover everything he can about some of the most inaccessible environments on our planet and reveal them as places in which we are all invested. Burtynsky discovers beauty where we least expect it–some of the most ravishing pictures are from the mollusc-like patterns left behind by an extractor machine in a Siberian potash mine."[8] All in all, "There's no prettification here–Burtynsky simply observes and presents what he finds, inviting us to contemplate the paradoxes of a world in which beauty often walks hand in hand with destruction."

One of "the most ambitious and labour-intensive photographs" Burtynsky has ever made caught the eye of Ravi Ghosh of the *British Journal of Photography* when he toured the exhibition with the photographer:

> It is a blanket of golf-ball sized orbs and growths in pink, orange, green and brown, unfurling across an entire wall in London's Saatchi Gallery. *Pengah Wall #1 from* 2017 is an underwater photograph–or rather, a digital image composed of around 200 individual shots–made off the coast of Komodo Island in Indonesia in 2017. Burtynsky stands back slightly and admires the coral, its fleshy, sprouting texture lending a sense of alien vitality. He mentions the work of painter Jackson Pollock; the idea was to emulate the motion and energy of his canvases in the image. "Abstract Expressionism was one of the things I loved in 20th-century art," the Canadian photographer says. "That there is no singular central point in the images, and their alloverness, texture and modulation–the whole surface has been considered." In terms of production cost, the reef image dwarfs anything else that Burtynsky has made. Three photographers and six professional divers ventured to a depth of 60 feet to divide the coral into a grid; they then moved slowly up and down making photographs of the shifting seawall, returning intermittently to a boat with a 30-strong crew to examine their pictures on screen. The swirling currents presented a challenge, as did needing to illuminate the reef manually. A Photoshop expert then worked for three months to stitch the final image together, meticulously selecting when to splice and blend each tendril to create a smooth, almost one-to-one scale composition.[9]

Although sufficient emphasis is often begrudgingly given to Burtynsky's obsession with the beauty of the nature, this mural speaks to the wonder he has always beheld in an imperilled world.

The Saatchi exhibition is a record of a career still very much in progress. Burtynsky has recently been commissioned by MP Materials to explore the world of rare earth elements.[10] In the future, he plans to show even more of the world in its magnificent diversity. To do so, he wants to stay ahead of the curve.

Edward Burtynsky's images demonstrate his commitment to examining various forms of extraction, but they are similar stylistically because his

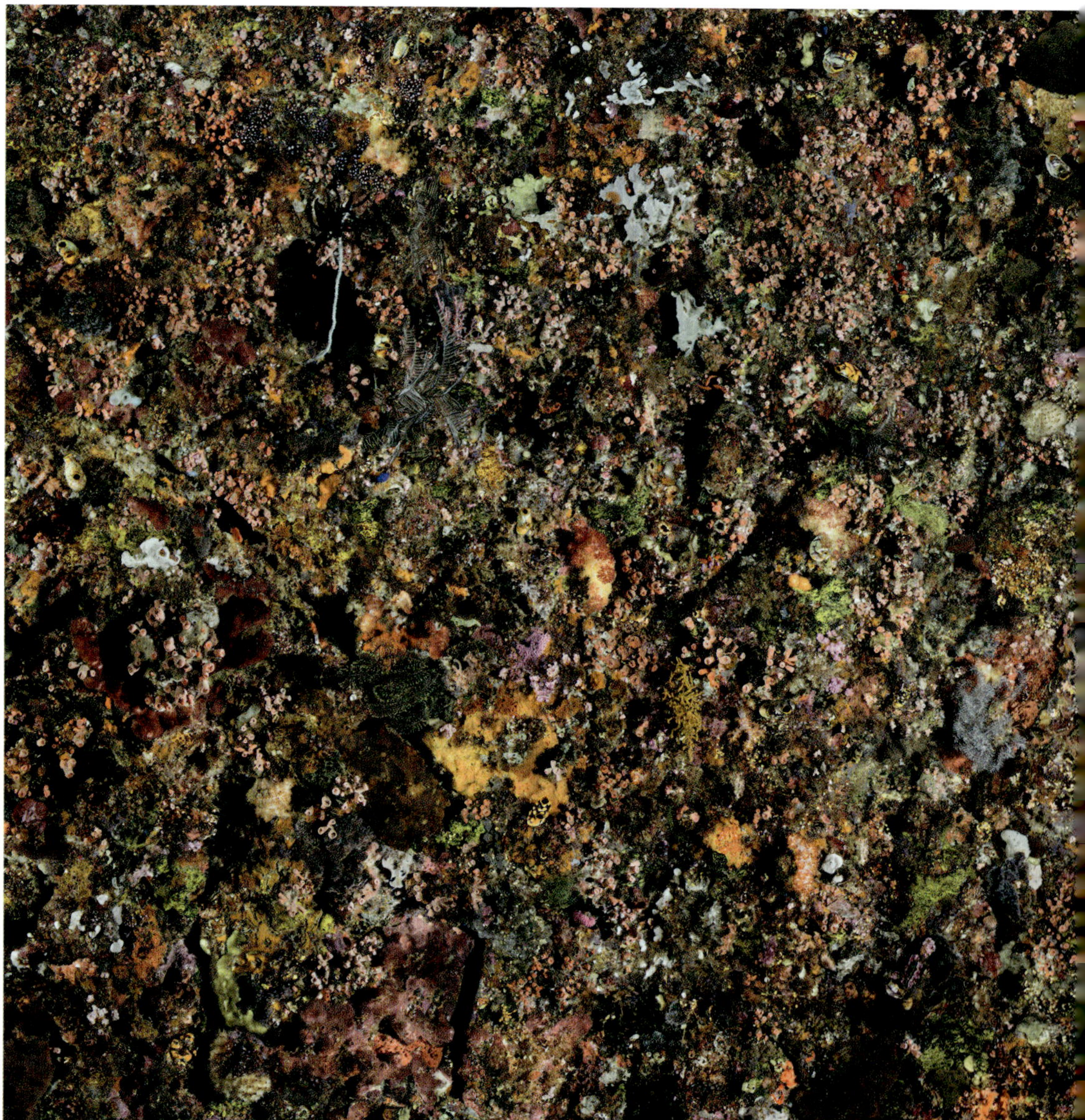

Edward Burtynsky, *Pengah Wall #1*, Komodo National Park, Indonesia, 2017

eye penetrates the inner world of landscapes–especially their beauty under threat. Ultimately, his emphasis on abstraction transports his audience from the world of representation to an alternate universe of sublimity. Such is the power of his art.

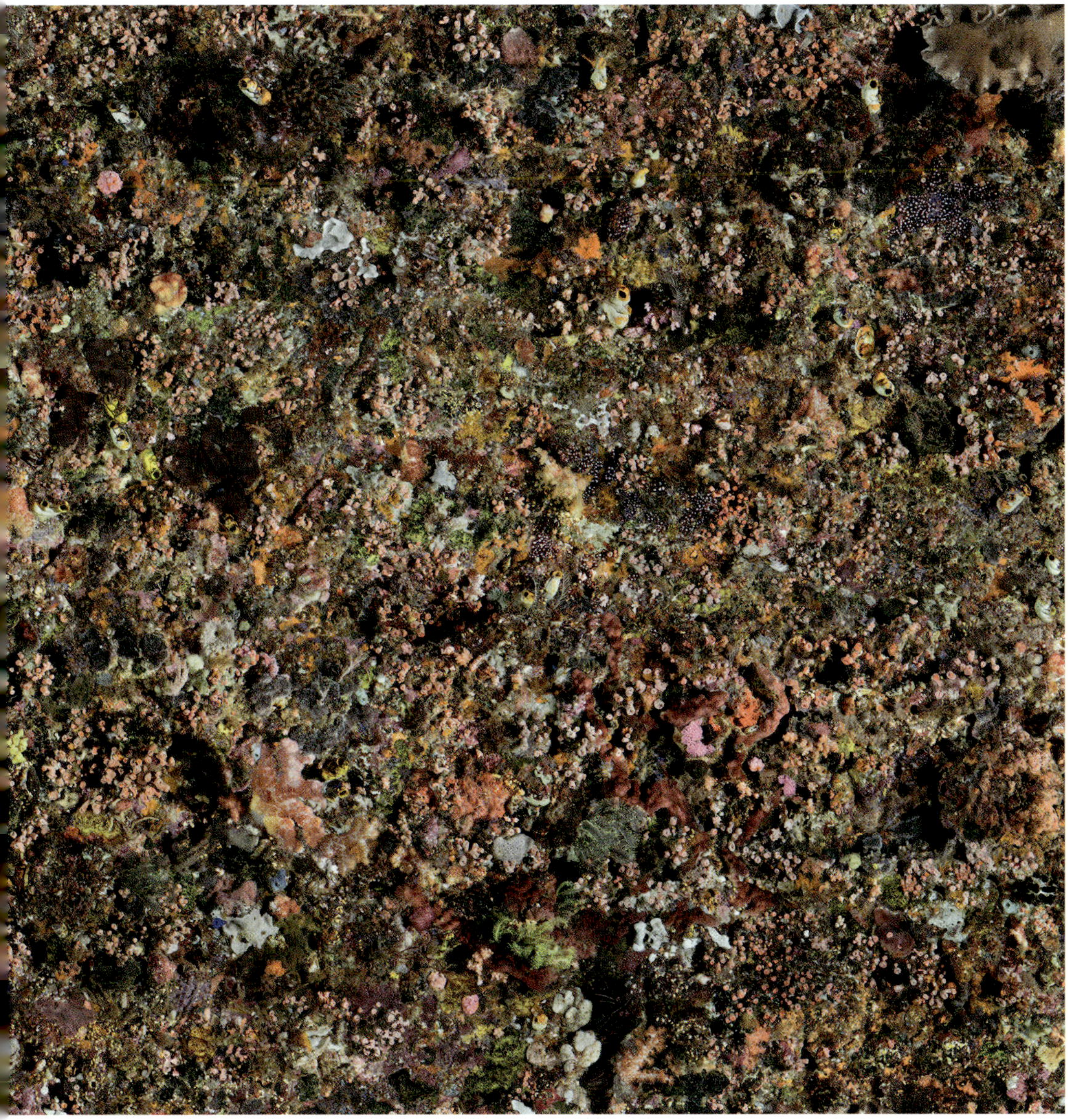

ACKNOWLEDGEMENTS

This book has been immeasurably enriched by the voices of many people. I learned a great deal from conversations with Daniel Beltrá, Stephen Bulger, Claudio Cambon, Joseph Hartman, Archie Hood, Nicholas Metivier, Michael Torosian, and Mike Weir. Jennifer Baichwal and Nicholas de Pencier spoke movingly of their collaborations with Ed, while his sisters, Ollie and Krys, shared with candour the memories of their childhood. To all of them, I am deeply grateful for their openness and trust. I also want to thank Michael Levine, my agent, for his steadfast belief in this project.

At the Burtynsky Studio, I was received with unfailing warmth. Karen Machtinger guided me through the image archives; Paul Sergeant unearthed essential materials; Julia Johnston, Ed's wife, offered constant support; Jim Panou described in detail the complexities of staging photo shoots across the globe; and Marcus Schubert became my reliable point of contact in confronting obstacles large and small.

My greatest thanks go to Ed. With calm generosity, he endured the endless questions of his biographer and shared with him his unpublished diaries. Those conversations and notebooks are the backbone of this book.

Mary Buratynsky, indomitable in spirit, told me her life story in unforgettable detail: her youth in Ukraine during the Holodomor, her imprisonment during the Second World War, her subsequent existence in an internment camp, her immigration to Canada, and her enduring closeness with her son. Her resilience and devotion inspired me throughout the writing of this book. This book is dedicated to her.

SHORT TITLES AND ABBREVIATIONS

EB Edward Burtynsky

EB-JK Citations are from James King's interviews, phone calls, and emails with Edward Burtynsky

MANUSCRIPTS

EB's Notebooks (all in EB's personal archive)

Blue Notebook

Entries are from 1979-1980

Grey Notebook

Entries are from 1979-1982

Ryerson Notebook

Grey-covered notebook with entries from c. 1978–1983

Random Happening Notebook

Five Subject notebook labelled "Random Happenings" by EB; entries are from 1982 and 1985

Travel Notebook

Grey-covered notebook labelled "The Nothing Book" by the manufacturer. Entries are from 1985–1987

Orange Notebook

Orange Rhodia notebook; entries are from 2017–2019

Covid Notebook

Leather-covered notebook with entries from 2020

PRINTED SOURCES

Anthropocene

Edward Burtynsky, Jennifer Baichwal, and Nicholas de Pencier, *Anthropocene* (Toronto and Ottawa: The Art Gallery of Ontario in collaboration with The National Gallery of Canada, 2018).

Essential Elements

Edward Burtynsky, *Essential Elements*, ed. William A. Ewing (London: Thames and Hudson, 2016).

Manufactured Landscapes

Manufactured Landscapes: The Photographs of Edward Burtynsky (New Haven and London: Yale University Press, 2003).

New Yorker

Raffi Khatchadourian, "The Long View: Edward Burtynsky's quest to photograph a changing planet," *The New Yorker*, December 11, 2016.

Photo-wisdom

Lewis Blackwell, *Photo-wisdom* (San Francisco: Chronicle Books, 2009).

Residual Landscapes

Edward Burtynsky, *Residual Landscapes: Studies of Industrial Transfiguration* (Toronto: Lumiere Press, 2001). Contains an interview with EB by Michael Torosian.

Noah Richler, "Residual Landscapes: Photographer Ed Burtynsky Finds Natural Beauty in the Things We Leave Behind," *Saturday Night*, May 19, 2001, 25–29.

Wake

Edward Burtynsky, *In the Wake of Progress* (Toronto: Burtynsky Studio, 2021).

Weekly Reflections

Weekly Reflections by EB posted on Instagram.

NOTES

Introduction

1 Noah Richler, "Residual Landscapes: Photographer Ed Burtynsky Finds Natural Beauty in the Things We Leave Behind," *Saturday Night,* May 19, 2001.

2 John K. Grande, "An Interview with Edward Burtynsky," *Grand Tour–Perspecta* 41 (June 2008), 153–58.

3 Covid Notebook. Entry for April 29, 2020.

4 Ibid.

5 Edward Burtynsky, *Residual Landscapes: Studies of Industrial Transfiguration* (Toronto: Lumiere Press, 2001), 49.

6 Geoff Manaugh and Nicola Twilley, interview with Edward Burtynsky, *Venue*, June 2012. https://v-e-n-u-e.com/Primary-Landscapes-An-Interview-with-Edward-Burtynsky.

7 EB interview with Mark DeWitte, *PhotoEd*, Spring 2003.

8 Edward Burtynsky, *Essential Elements*, ed. William A. Ewing (London: Thames and Hudson, 2016), 105. Burtynsky also pointed out: "History is full of examples of beautiful things depicting problematic situations, such as Shakespeare wrapping beautifully crafted works around human tragedies and deception, Bosch making beautiful paintings depicting hell."

Chapter 1

1 *Residual Landscapes*, 39.
2 *Residual Landscapes*, 41.
3 Random Happening Notebook.
4 EB in conversation with his mother, August 2015.
5 Ibid.
6 Ibid.
7 During the day I spent with her, Mary Buratynsky told me in vivid detail about her early life.
8 Richler.
9 JK interview with Ollie.
10 *Residual Landscapes*, 42.
11 Richler.
12 John Davies, "Edward Burtynsky: The Photographer Who's Out to Save the World from Itself," *Art World*, Feb/March 2008, 126–28.
13 EB-JK.
14 Edward Burtynsky, *Burtynsky–Water* (Göttingen, Germany: Steidl, 2013), 9.
15 Jared Bland, "Why We Love the Art We Love: Edward Burtynsky on the Beauty of Photography," *Globe and Mail*, June 15, 2015.
16 *Residual Landscapes*, 38.
17 Edward Burtynsky, *In the Wake of Progress* (Toronto: Burtynsky Studio, 2021), 158.
18 Random Happening Notebook.
19 *Residual Landscapes*, 40.
20 Jared Bland, *op. cit.*
21 Ibid.
22 Ibid.
23 Raffi Khatchadourian, "The Long View: Edward Burtynsky's Quest to Photograph a Changing Planet," *The New Yorker*, December 11, 2016.
24 EB-JK.
25 EB-JK.
26 EB-JK.
27 EB-JK.
28 Blue Notebook. Entry for December 7, 1979.
29 *Residual Landscapes*, 39.
30 Blue Notebook. Entry for December 7, 1979
31 Covid Notebook. Entry for May 2, 2020.
32 *Residual Landscapes*, 40.
33 EB-JK.
34 *New Yorker*.
35 *Residual Landscapes*, 8.
36 *Residual Landscapes*, 40.

Chapter 2

1 EB-JK.

2 Blue Notebook. Entry for December 7, 1979.

3 John Davies, "Edward Burtynsky: The photographer who's out to save the world from itself," *Art World*, Feb/March 2008, 26–28.

4 JK interview with Archie Hood.

5 *Residual Landscapes*, 40.

6 *New Yorker*.

7 Peter Higdon, "In Pursuit of Meaning," in *Phil Bergerson: A Retrospective* (Toronto: Daylight Books, 2020), 14.

8 Higdon, 31.

9 Cited by Anne Cibola in her online Art Canada Institute biography of Maggs.

10 EB-JK.

11 *Residual Landscapes*, 43.

12 CBC *Sunday Morning*, September 17, 2023.

13 *Residual Landscapes,* 40–41.

14 *Residual Landscapes,* 40–41.

15 Higdon, 18.

16 *Residual Landscapes,* 42.

17 *Sunday Morning* interview (CBC Radio), September 17, 2023.

18 Grey Notebook. Entry for April 17, 1981.

19 Comment on dustjacket of *Phil Bergerson: A Retrospective.*

20 John K. Grande, "Manufactured Landscapes": an interview with Ed Burtynsky," *Etc,* September-November 2006.

21 EB-JK.

22 JK interview with Marcus Schubert.

23 Grey Notebook.

24 Laura Cameron, "The List: 10 Things Celebrated Photographer Edward Burtynsky Can't Live Without," *Toronto Life,* May 5, 2001.

25 *Residual Landscapes*, 41.

26 *Residual Landscapes,* 45.

27 Edward Burtynsky, *Monegros* (Portland: Nazraeli Press, 2012), 3.

28 Ibid.

29 Random Happening Notebook.

30 Ryerson Notebook.

31 Ibid.

32 In an undated memorandum about "Aims," "Method," and "Evaluation," Heath summarized his pedagogical aims. Under "Aims," he stated: "To differentiate between work (metaphoric and symbolic expression) and ego (self-expression) so as to place one's creativity in [an] appropriate social context. . . . To develop in the student a comprehension of the need for

challenge, confrontation, self-inquiry and the expression of community impulse which, taken in their inter-relatedness, can be said to be the measure of the creatively free mind." His "Method" was to "seek through dialogic encounter and critique to draw out, engage and test the student for ideas rather than merely encouraging self-expression." Under "Evaluation," he maintained that in assigning grades, "evaluation is basically subjective but not without perspective grounded on the factuality of the student's work. For my part it is firmly based on my ability to perceive whether a student has distinguished for him/her self the difference between being given a problem for an answer and finding (self-generating) a problem for solution."

33 EB-JK.

34 David DeKok, *Unseen Danger: A Tragedy of People, Government, and the Centralia Mine Fire* (Philadelphia: University of Pennsylvania Press, 1986), 17.

35 EB-JK.

36 Ibid.

37 Diane Smith, "Planet," *British Journal of Photography*, August 15, 2007.

38 *New Yorker*.

39 Kirsten Hoving, "Digging Deep: Edward Burtynsky's Vermont Quarry Photographs," in *Nature Transformed: Edward Burtynsky's Vermont Quarry Photographs in Context*, ed. Juliette Bianco and Peter Broucke (Hanover: Hood Museum of Art, 2012), 10.

40 Alexander Herman, Paul Matthews, and Andrew Feindel, *Kickstart: How Successful Canadians Got Started* (Toronto: Dundurn, 2008), 152.

41 *Residual Landscapes*, 37.

42 Weekly Reflection, October 19, 2020.

43 Covid Notebook. Entry for May 4, 2020.

44 Ibid.

45 Ryerson Notebook.

46 Ryerson Notebook. Entry for March 3, 1982.

47 Burtynsky was also inspired by the sculptor and land artist Robert Smithson, whose beliefs reinforced his own. Smithson's concept of entropy was based, in part, on his argument that the finest places for land art had been destroyed by industry, urban spread, and the disregard of nature.

48 Ryerson Notebook. Entry for March 3, 1982.

Chapter 3

1 EB-JK.

2 Edward Burtynsky, *Oil* (Göttingen: Steidl, 2009), 9.

3 Travel Notebook. Entry for April 15, 1985.

4 Ryerson Notebook. Entry for October 3, 1983.

5 Ibid.

6 Orange Notebook.

7 Martha Langford, *Breaking Ground* catalogue.

8 Ryerson Notebook. Entry for October 3, 1983.

9 Michael Mitchell, "Evidence and Entropy," in Edward Burtynsky, *Australian Minescapes* (Welshpool: Western Australian Museum, 2009), 11.

10 Grey Notebook. Entry for August 18, 1982.

11 When Burtynsky thought of returning to photograph contemporary animal husbandry in the early 2000s, he also tried to do a project on animal husbandry, mass poultry farming, pig farming: "they didn't want me going anywhere near! It does say something about the world we are creating. Once you could see where your chicken came from, but now the whole process is behind closed doors, nobody is allowed to see it." *Photo-wisdom*, 60.

12 The title is derived from Henry David Thoreau's *Walking* (1862).

13 Travel Notebook. Entry for May 5, 1985.

14 Weekly Reflection #3, July 15, 2020.

15 Lori Paul interview with Burtynsky, November 2000. *Manufactured Landscapes*, 18.

16 Weekly Reflection #2, July 8, 2020:

> Kennecott is a copper mine that, in the brochure, claimed it was 3 miles across and 1 mile deep, but if one was to drive along the ridges from top to bottom, they'd be driving for 500 miles. At that time, workers at the mine were moving 480,000 tonnes of material on a daily basis. It was a peculiarly boastful way of advertising this incredible hole in the ground.
>
> One of the things that this image represented for me was an inversion of the notion of the sublime. If we look back to earlier romantic notions of the sublime, it was always Nature as the ultimate force that humans were dwarfed by–see J.M.W. Turner's ships cast about by the sea, or Herman Melville's *Moby Dick*. There was a time when humans were awed in the presence of the natural world.
>
> But now, in the technological sublime, we are dwarfed in the theatre of our own making. If you observe this photograph at full scale you can see a school bus transporting workers; it's a stark realization of the sense of scale, and how we are dwarfed by these massive landscapes.
>
> It is an image that demands standing in front of it to perceive these minute details. It's also where the large format camera became a powerful instrument in the creation of this project.

17 Travel Notebook. Entry for April 22, 1985.

18 *Manufactured Landscapes*, 17.

19 Weekly Reflection #5, July 2020.

20 Travel Notebook. Entry for October 3, 1985.

21 Ryerson Notebook.

22 Travel Notebook. Entry for May 12, 1985.

23 Ryerson Notebook.

24 Ryerson Notebook. Entry for May 4, 1984.
25 Travel Notebook. Entry for May 1,1985.

Chapter 4

1 This was the original title for *Landscape Study #12*, 1981, which is reproduced in Chapter 2.
2 From about 1982 to 1992 Burtynsky recorded his sales in a Blue Book. I have compiled my statistics from that manuscript.
3 EB-JK.
4 Jeannie Baxter. Video interview with Nick de Pencier.
5 Campos Photography Center opened in 1979 and is still in operation.
6 From various sources, he raised $250,000.
7 Alexander Herman, Paul Matthews, and Andrew Feindel, *Kickstart: How Successful Canadians Got Started* (Toronto: Dundurn, 2008), 154.
8 Morden Yolles. Video interview with Nick de Pencier.
9 Business Plan manuscript. EB personal archive.
10 Jeannie Baxter.
11 Jeannie Baxter.
12 EB-JK.
13 EB-JK.
14 EB-JK.
15 Raphael Bernstein. Video interview with Nick de Pencier.
16 EB-JK.
17 Raphael Bernstein.
18 EB interview with JK. Some of images in *Money Matters* are similar to the photographs of cityscapes and buildings that Nicholas Nixon contributed to *New Topographics*.
19 EB-JK.
20 Raphael Bernstein.
21 Raphael Bernstein.
22 *Chicago Tribune*. April 5, 1991.
23 EB-JK.
24 EB-JK.
25 *Money Matters: A Critical Look at Bank Architecture* (New York: McGraw-Hill, 1990), 288, 292.
26 Raphael Bernstein.
27 Raphael Bernstein.

Chapter 5

1 This show was also at Gallery TPW, June 11-30, 1988.

2 JK interview with Nicholas Metivier.
3 EB-JK.
4 Doug Clark, *Sweet Immortality* (Toronto: Art Gallery of Ontario, 2005), 9.
5 EB-JK.
6 EB-JK.
7 EB-JK.
8 EB-JK.
9 Edward Burtynsky, "Artist Statement," in *Quarries* (Göttingen: Steidl, 2007), 9.
10 Juliette Bianco, "An Interview with Edward Burtynsky," in *Nature Transformed: Edward Burtynsky's Vermont Quarry Photographs in Context*, ed. Juliette Bianco and Peter Broucke (Hanover: Hood Museum of Art, 2012), 61.
11 EB-JK.
12 A quarryman in Ontario also told Burtynsky that he should look at quarries in Vermont. *Nature Transformed*, 1.
13 EB-JK.
14 EB-JK.
15 Juliet Bianco, *Nature Transformed*, 3.
16 Covid Notebook. Entry for April 29, 2020.
17 EB-JK, May 2023.
18 Robert Stacey, *Canadian Art*, 10, no. 1 (Spring 1993), Number 1.
19 EB-JK.
20 EB-JK.
21 EB-JK.
22 EB-JK.
23 Jonathan Bordo, "The Wasteland–An Essay on Manufactured Landscapes," *Material Culture Review*, 63 (Spring 2006).
24 Christopher Hume, *Toronto Star.*
25 Interview with Geoff Manaugh in *Venue*, June 2012.
26 EB-JK.
27 *Etc*, 2006.
28 "Edward Burtynsky: Quarries," *Dwell*, 2008.

Chapter 6

1 *Residual Landscapes*, 43.
2 *Wake*, 66.
3 *Wake*, 69. Kenneth Hayes has lamented that Burtynsky avoided showing headframes in his Sudbury images, as such shots would have indicated the miners' presence. Moreover, when Burtynsky returned to Sudbury in 1995, he infused the tailing ponds "with the gruesome appeal of an apocalyptic scene." Hayes also pointed out that the photographer's low point of view

makes “the stream appear larger, and in the other tailings pond pictures, he often centred his camera above the source of the effluent.” See Hayes, “Sudbury’s Image,” *Prefix Photo* 12 (2012).

4 Richard Rhodes, “Tailings,” *Canadian Art*, Fall 1996.

5 Kenneth Hayes, in “Sudbury’s Image,” describes the contrasting ways Louie Palu, Allan Sekula, and Burtynsky have photographed the mine and landscape there: “These Sudbury works are distinguished from the efforts of earlier generations of documentary photographers in that they were conceived as photographic; indeed, the focus on industry identifies this work as explicitly modern art.” Hayes explains that Palu’s work is modelled after that of Dorothea Lange. “The long duration of Palu’s project and his deep identification with hardrock mining towns won him unprecedented access to intimate moments in the lives of the miners and their families . . . He understood and presented Sudbury as part of a broader culture of mining . . .” Sekula, for Hayes, “is mining photography’s most astute critic to date. His extensive theoretical work is the indispensable basis for any future critical history of mining photography.” In comparison to Palu and Sekula, Burtynsky “began his photographic career with some notion of documentary practice, but rather than being content with depicting sites as they are (which is to say, categorically, by type), he actively sought confirmation of scenes that existed a priori, in his imagination.” This is not what Burtynsky claimed: “I ask myself does the subject have the capacity to transport me to a place outside my experience, and the viewer’s experience.”

In his article, Hayes distinguishes among three different approaches, but he prefers those of Palu and Sekula; he does not take into account that Burtynsky is working from a completely different aesthetic from the other two.

6 *Wake*, 66.

7 *Wake*, 55.

8 *Wake*, 62.

9 Andy Pedersen, “Disfigured Landscapes,” *Daily News* (Halifax), November 1, 1997.

10 Dan Falk, “Mining Modern Industry for Art Gems,” *Globe and Mail*, May 5, 1998.

11 *Wake*, 134.

12 Mannin Young suggests another possible source: “The images of tire graveyards and metal scrap-piles from the late 1990s evoke more than anything the pictorial abstraction of twentieth-century avant-garde painting. *Densified Oil Filters #1*, for instance, could have been dreamt up by Jean-Paul Riopelle, Canada’s great Abstract Expressionist painter.” See Young, “Manufactured Landscapes: The Photographs of Edward Burtynsky,” *Afterimage* 30, no. 6 (2003).

13 *Wake*, 100.

14 Hood Gallery website.

15 John McPhee, “A Reporter at Large: Duty of Care,” *The New Yorker*, June 28, 1993, 72.

16 *Recordnet.com*, September 26, 1999.

17 Weekly Refection #10. September 2, 2020.

18 Press Release, Canadian Centre for Architecture Press, Montreal, February 28, 2000.

19 Michael Torosian website.

Chapter 7

1 William Langewiesche, "The Shipbreakers," *The Atlantic Monthly*, August 2002.
2 He did not reference the stunning picture that graced the cover of *The Atlantic Monthly* that was taken by Sebastião Salgado at Chittagong.
3 EB–JK.
4 Michael Mitchell in Edward Burtynsky, *Oil* (Göttingen: Steidl, 2009), 193.
5 *The Atlantic Monthly,* February 22, 2002.
6 Jim Panou interview with JK.
7 Sean Callahan, "Viewpoints: Photographer Edward Burtynsky's Politically Charged Industrial Landscapes Are Carefully Crafted to Elicit Different Interpretations," *Smithsonian*, April 2002, 94.
8 Edward Burtynsky, *Pentimento* (Toronto: Burtynsky Studio, 2011), 2.
9 Kenneth Baker, "Form Versus Portent: Edward Burtynsky's Endangered Landscapes," *Manufactured Landscapes*, 41: "The towering hull fragments . . . will seem familiar to anyone who has seen Serra's giant installations of heavy sheet steel arcs stood on edge. Serra, who worked in shipyards during his student years, positions precisely shaped masses of steel to make possible subtle proprioceptive experiences."
10 Richler.
11 Callahan, 94.
12 Ibid.
13 Richler.
14 Richler. His use of the word "Victorian" introduces an issue raised by Kenneth Baker. For him, perhaps unfairly, Burtynsky's "pictures make startling visual parallels to the expeditionary images of ancient monuments in exotic lands by nineteenth-century photographers . . . The Shipbreaking pictures faint echo of a discredited colonialist, 'Orientalist' vision complicates our admiration for them." Kenneth Baker, "Form Versus Portent," *Manufactured Landscapes*, 41.
15 *National Post,* April 25, 2001.
16 Margaret Loke, "Art in Review: Edward Burtynsky," *The New York Times*, February 22, 2002.
17 JK interview with Metivier.
18 Edward Burtynsky, *Pentimento,* 2.
19 Ibid.
20 Nicholas Metivier suggested that the collection should be so named.

Chapter 8

1 *Wake*, 90.
2 Clint Roenisch, "Dust Postponed: The Machinations of Man in the Work of Edward Burtynsky," in *Edward Burtynsky: Works from Two Decades* (Kitchener, ON: The Waterloo-Kitchener Gallery, 2002), 18.

3 "The grid patterns of squares recall . . . the chance-ordered grids of colour in abstract paintings of Ellsworth Kelly and Gerhard Richter." Kenneth Baker, *Manufactured Landscapes*, 43.
4 Roenisch, 28.
5 *Manufactured Landscapes*, 33.
6 *Manufactured Landscapes*, 40.
7 *Manufactured Landscapes*, 45.
8 *Manufactured Landscapes*, 34.
9 *St. Catharines Standard*, February 27, 2004.

Chapter 9

1 "I had a scout [Noah Weinzweig] on the ground for a period of three years. He would go into dozens of factories and send me digital files back. And so I would be getting posts every few days of what he'd found and I'd say, "oh this looks interesting, find out if we can shout it.'"
2 Lucas Lackner, "Before the Flood," in *Edward Burtynsky, Before the Flood* (Toronto: Burtynsky Studio, 2003), 27-28.
3 EB-JK.
4 Weekly Reflection #17, November 26, 2020.
5 Jennifer Baichwal interview with JK.
6 Weekly Reflection #20, January 2021.
7 Keith Axline, "Endless Assembly Plants and Giant Cafeterias; Inside China's Vast Plants," *Wired*, June 2007.
8 Edward Burtynsky, *China: The Photographs of Edward Burtynsky* (Göttingen: Steidl, 2005), 9.
9 Weekly Reflection #19, January 2021.
10 Axline.
11 David Segal, "Beauty in the Beast," *The Washington Post*, October 31, 2005.
12 EB-JK.
13 Bruno Giussani, *The Huffington Post*, July 29, 2007.
14 *Flash*, 2007.
15 *Wake*, 134.
16 EB-JK.
17 *Wake*, 75.
18 *Africa*, 199.
19 Mark A, Cheetham, "Natural Anxieties: Why Go to a Museum to See the Sun?" *The Walrus*, April 2006.
20 All the Steidl books are produced in the Burtynsky Studio but printed at Steidl. Marcus Schubert has been the initial designer and managing editor for all the Steidl books.
21 *Photo-wisdom*, 60.

Chapter 10

1 *Manufacturing Landscapes* film.
2 Edward Burtynsky, *Oil* (Göttingen: Steidl, 2009), 190.
3 At Cold Lake, the ancient seabed containing bitumen is about 800 feet down. Steam is used in the extraction process and, as a result, the bitumen becomes very hot and is then pumped up to the surface.
4 Mary-Beth Laviolette, "Man Made Space: The Oil Sands Seen Through the Lens of Edward Burtynsky," *Swerve*, February 2009.
5 "Edward Burtynsky's Best Shot," *The Guardian*, August 8, 2008.
6 *Photo-wisdom*, 60.
7 Edward Burtynsky, *Water* (Göttingen: Steidl), 3.
8 Weekly Reflection #18, December 2020.
9 *Water*, 3.
10 Burtynsky now uses drones as much as possible, as they are less expensive than helicopters and highly controllable. They also have a much lower flight path allowance.
11 *Oil*, 9.
12 *Photo-wisdom*, 58-60.
13 *Oil*, 190.
14 Ibid.
15 *National Post*, December 17, 2009.
16 *The Globe and Mail*, October 10, 2009.
17 *Niagara This Week.com*, May 17, 2012.
18 *The Art Daily*, December 7, 2009.
19 Amy Cavanaugh, "Refined Close-Up on Crude," *Washington Post Express*, September 2009.

Chapter 11

1 He has subsequently received many other distinctions: among them, the Kraszna-Krausz Book Award (2010) for *Oil*; six honorary degrees from Mount Allison University (2011), the University of British Columbia (2013), Middlebury College (2013), the University of Toronto (2017), Brock University (2018), and McGill University (2024); the Governor General's Award in the Visual and Media Arts (2016); the Gold Medal of the Royal Canadian Geographical Society (2019); an Outstanding Contribution to Photography, Sony World Photography Awards (2022); and Induction into the International Photography Hall of Fame (2022).
2 EB-JK.
3 Edward Burtynsky, *Quarries* (Göttingen: Steidl, 2009), 25.
4 Edward Burtynsky, "Artist's Statement and Portfolio," *Frank Gehry in Toronto: Transforming the Art Gallery of Ontario* (Toronto: AGO, 2009), 31.

5 Ibid.
6 *Quarries*, 9.
7 Among other commissions are Integral House, Toronto in 2006; Royal Alexandra Theatre, Toronto in 2007, Koerner Hall, Toronto in 2011, and TAS, Urban Toronto, in 2022.
8 *Frank Gehry*, 31.
9 Edward Burtynsky, *Australian Minescapes* (Welshpool: Western Australian Museum, 2009), 9.
10 JK interview with Joseph Hartman.
11 *Wake*, 58.
12 Ibid.
13 *The Australian*, Victoria Laurie, April 7, 2008.
14 *The New Critic*, September 2008.
15 *Australian Minescapes*, 13.
16 *Australian Minescapes*, 7.
17 Sophie Hackett, "Far and Near: New Views of the Anthropocene," in *Anthropocene* (Toronto: AGO, 2019), 16.
18 EB–JK.
19 Michael Fried, *Why Photography Matters as Never Before (*London and New Haven: Yale University Press, 2008), 37.
20 Photographs by the Bechers were included in *New Topographics* in 1975.
21 As quoted by Richler.
22 *Photo-wisdom,* 58.

Chapter 12

1 Edward Burtynsky, *Water* (Göttingen: Steidl, 2013), 3.
2 In 2006, Panou travelled to AMARC in Tucson, Arizona, to assist Burtynsky who had not done a digital aerial shoot at that time. At Panou's insistence, a gyro was used. In 2009, he travelled to California for the *National Geographic* shoot. In 2010, he was with Burtynsky in India for the stepwells shoot and the first shoot at Kumbh Mela. That year he accompanied Burtynsky twice to the Gulf of Mexico: the first was to make still shots and the second with de Pencier and a Cineplex cameraman. In 2011, he was with Burtynsky in California, Arizona, and Texas; in 2012 at the Colorado River delta, Iceland, Florida, New Mexico, and Arizona. In 2013, they were together for the second shoot at Kumbh Mela and the following year for the Holocaust shoot in Europe.
3 JK interview with Marcus Schubert.
4 JK interview with Jim Panou.
5 *New York Times* blog, October 29, 2013. Burtynsky was aware that Ansel Adams had photographed there, especially *Winter Sunrise, Sierra Nevada from Lone Pine* (1944).
6 *American Photo*, September 2013.

7 Lizzy Hill, "A Terrible Beauty: Edward Burtynsky's Water," *National Gallery of Canada Magazine*, November 19, 2013.
8 Marc Glassman interview with Jennifer Baichwal and Nicholas de Pencier, *Point of View Magazine*, September 4, 2013.
9 Ibid.
10 *Georgia Straight*, October 19, 2013.
11 April 3, 2004.
12 *Slant,* March 31, 2014.
13 *Water*, 3.
14 Glassman interview.
15 EB-JK.
16 The Monegros images were first published by Nazraeli Press in 2012.
17 *Wake*, 33.
18 Studio Reflections, 2021.
19 Paul Carey-Lent, *Photomonitor*, November 7, 2013.
20 *Reader's Digest*, September 13, 2013.
21 The Koli Agaryias as a group were listed as a Criminal Tribe under the colonial Criminal Tribes Act of 1871 because of their resistance to British rule in India.
22 *Collector Daily*, December 12, 2016.

Chapter 13

1 Edward Burtynsky, *Chai* (Toronto: Burtynsky Studio, 2012). Since the book does not have page numbers, I do not provide them when quoting the text.
2 "Six Questions About Canada's New National Holocaust Monument," *Canadian Art,* 2017.
3 Ayida Ayoubi, *ARCHITECT: The Journal of the American Institute of Architects*, 2017.
4 *Chai,* unpaginated.

Chapter 14

1 Jessica Wei, "Edward Burtynsky's *Anthropocene* premieres at TIFF," *National Post,* September 5, 2018.
2 "Originally it was Ed and I on that shoot. When video footage was wanted, I co-ordinated a shoot for Nick, a helicopter and cameraman to shoot the same locations we had done previously. One thing new that was included was the site of a collapsed tailings pond that had been destroyed a little while previously." Email from Jim Panou to JK, October 12, 2023.
3 "I put together a flight plan on a Cessna for Ed and Nick. They shot the coal trains footage together." Email from Jim Panou to JK, October 12, 2023.
4 Email from Jim Panou to JK, October 12, 2023.

5 Anders Dunker, "Into the Flames," *Modern Times Review*, October 11, 2019.
6 Ibid.
7 *Point of View*, September 13, 2018.
8 Twenty-one are from 2005-2018: one from 2005, 2 from 2007, one from 2008, one from 2009, five from 2010, eight from 2011, two from 2013, and one from 2018. (The AGO catalogue reproduced mainly images from 2015-2017).
9 *Anthropocene*, 60.
10 See "The Mirror of Our Nature: Edward Burtynsky's Images of the Anthropocene," in Edward Burtynsky, *Anthropocene* (Göttingen: Steidl, 2018).
11 Edward Burtynsky, *Extraction/Abstraction* (Göttingen: Steidl, 2024), 72.
12 Akintunde Akinleye photographed the devastation caused by a major petroleum leak on the outskirts of Lagos on December 26, 2006.
13 Edward Burtynsky, *African Studies* (Göttingen: Steidl, 2022), 6.
14 *Anthropocene*, 192.
15 Ibid, 206.
16 Ibid, 198.
17 Ibid, 194.
18 *New Yorker.*
19 Orange Notebook. Entry for June 25, 2017.
20 Ibid.
21 *Anthropocene*, 200.
22 Ibid.
23 *New Yorker.*
24 *New Yorker.*
25 *Essential Elements*, 7.
26 *Essential Elements*, 13.
27 *Essential Elements*, 182.

Chapter 15

1 Edward Burtynsky, *African Studies* (Göttingen: Steidl, 2022), 5.
2 Orange Notebook. Entry for April 14, 2019.
3 *African Studies*, 6.
4 Orange Notebook. Entry for April 14, 2019.
5 *African Studies*, 198.
6 Orange Notebook. Entry for April 27, 2019.
7 Ibid.
8 "Edward Burtynsky's Photos Show the Scars of Human-Altered Landscapes," *BBC Culture*, May 9, 2023. Burtynsky interview with Gaia Vince.
9 Jim Panou interview with JK.

10 Jim Panou interview with JK.
11 EB interview with Gaia Vince.
12 Ibid.
13 April 20, 2023.
14 *Feature Shoot*, July 18, 2023.
15 EB interview with Gaia Vince.

Chapter 16

1 *Canadian Geographic*, June 23, 2022.
2 Covid Notebook. Entry for May 9, 2020.
3 Covid Notebook. Entry for April 27, 2020. Burtynsky had flown to Yichang, which is located in western Hubei province. Wuhan is in Yiling, the same province and administrative district as Yichang.
4 Covid Notebook. Entry for April 29, 2020.
5 Covid Notebook. Entry for April 29, 2020.
6 Covid Notebook. Entry for May 1, 2020.
7 Ibid.
8 Covid Notebook. Entry for May 2, 2020.
9 Covid Notebook. Entry for May 9, 2020.
10 Undated reflection at end of Covid Notebook.
11 Covid Notebook. Entry for May 1, 2020.
12 Covid Notebook. Entry for May 4, 2020.
13 Edward Burtynsky, *Natural Order* (Göttingen: Steidl, 2021).
14 Covid Notebook. Entry for April 29, 2020.

Chapter 17

1 Sue Carter, "Edward Burtynsky's 'In the Wake of Progress' Lets Visitors Get Up Close to Nature's Destruction," *The Toronto Star*, June 30, 2022.
2 Ibid.
3 Ibid.
4 Irene Galea, "'We're All Incriminated,'" *The Globe and Mail*, June 25, 2022.
5 Michela Rosano, "Edward Burtynsky Discusses New Installation," *Canadian Geographic*, June 25, 2022.
6 EB-JK.
7 Among the ninety-four images and thirteen murals, only twenty-seven images from 1982 to 2010 were displayed; the seventeen images from 2011 to 2012 included photographs from the Netherlands, China, Iceland, the Texas Panhandle, Arizona, and Florida and the six from

2016 show Gujarat, Indonesia, and Kenya. The exhibition contained forty-six entries from 2017 to 2019: those from 2017 included ten images from Atacama, Berezniki, Kenya, Saudi Arabia, Malaysia, and California; from 2018 on, twelve from South Africa, Namibia, Senegal, and Ethiopia; and from 2019 on, twenty-four from Senegal, Botswana, Madagascar, Nigeria, and Ethiopia. There were seven entries from 2022, and two from 2023. (The Flowers Gallery showed some of the British Columbia coastal images from 2023.) The exhibition ended with three early photographs from Elliot Lake (1995), Bangladesh (2000), and Sudbury (1996)–as if to remind the view of the photographer's early work.

8 February 28, 2024.

9 February 23, 2024.

10 The mural *MP Materials #6* and the photograph *MP Materials #8,* both taken at Mountain Pass Mine, Mountain Pass, California, were shown at the Saatchi. Burtynsky also produced and directed a short video piece entitled *Rare Earth: Mining the Future*.

IMAGE CREDITS

With the exception of the sources listed below, all images are copyright of the Edward Burtynsky Studio and have been supplied by them.

The Art Institute of Chicago, page 116.

Boston Museum of Fine Art, page 32.

Buffalo AKG Museum, page 283.

Carnegie Museum, page 245.

Courtesy of Claudio Cambon, page 126.

Courtesy of Emmet Gowin, pages 73, 217, 218.

Courtesy of Sebastião Salgado, page 127.

Paul Getty Museum Los Angeles, page 43.

Guggenheim Museum, New York, pages 117, 133.

Guggenheim Museum, Bilbao, page 136.

Hamburg Kunsthalle, page 30.

Los Angeles County Museum of Art, page 36.

Metropolitan Museum of Art, New York, pages 45, 70, 172.

Moderna Museum, Stockholm, page 57.

Musée Des Arts Décoratifs, Paris, page 246.

Museum of Modern Art, New York, pages 35, 60.

National Holocaust Museum, Ottawa, page 262.

Nicholas Metivier Gallery, Toronto, page 246.

Private collection, page 235.

Sheldon Museum of Art, page 69.

Tate Gallery, London, pages 31, 194.

INDEX

Page numbers in **bold** indicate the reproduction of a work of art.

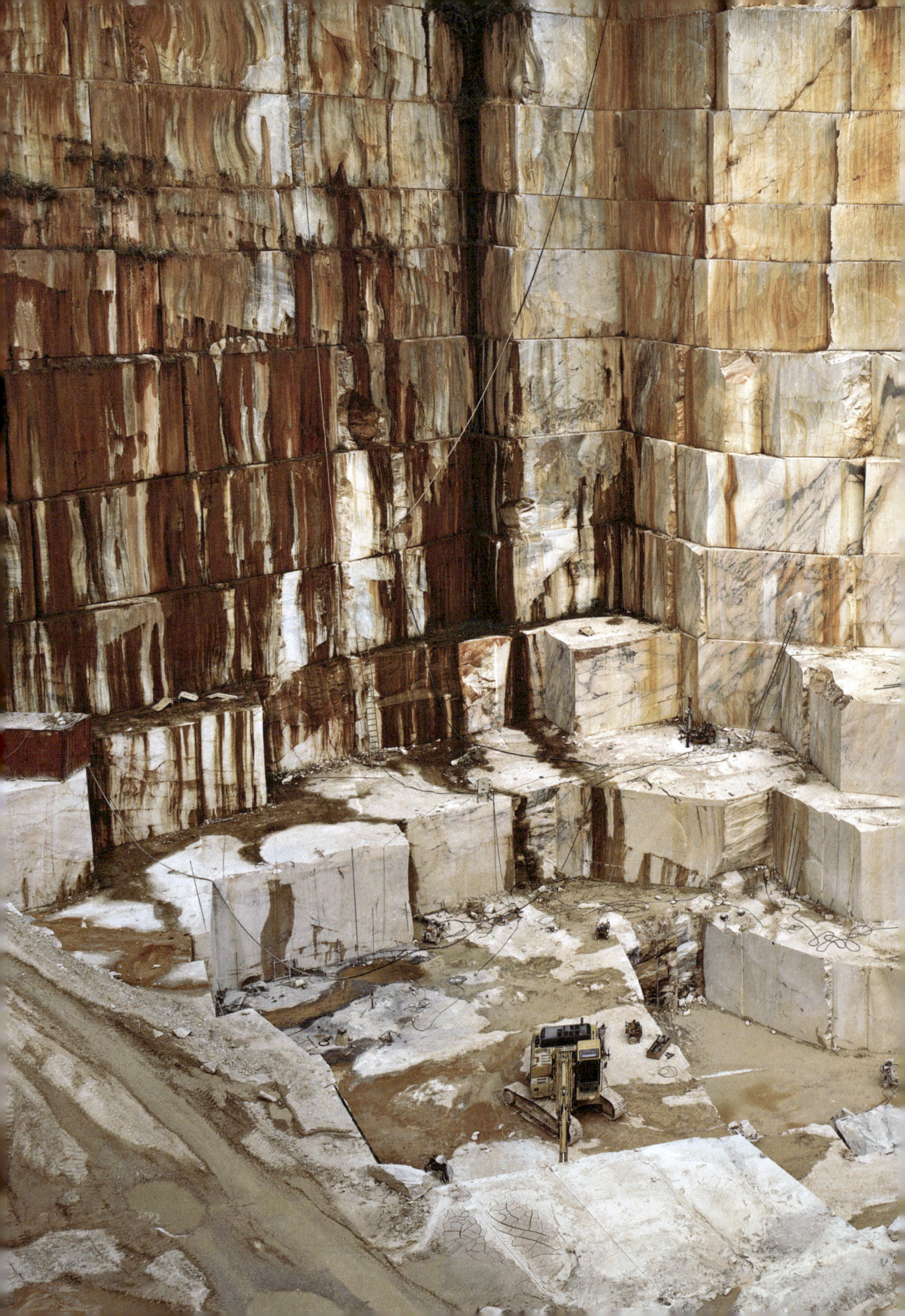